DICTIONARY OF

TWENTIETH CENTURY CULTURE

Hispanic Culture of South America

DICTIONARY OF

TWENTIETH CENTURY CULTURE

Hispanic Culture of South America

Edited by
Peter Standish

Associate Editors

Ninotchka D. Bennahum   Ricardo Gutiérrez Mouat   Jan Michael Hanvik

Stephen M. Hart   Florencia Bazzano Nelson   Robert L. Smith

A MANLY, INC. BOOK

Gale Research Inc.

An International Thomson Publishing Company

I(T)P
Changing the Way the World Learns

NEW YORK • LONDON • BONN • BOSTON • DETROIT • MADRID
MELBOURNE • MEXICO CITY • PARIS • SINGAPORE • TOKYO
TORONTO • WASHINGTON • ALBANY NY • BELMONT CA • CINCINNATI OH

Printed in the United States of America

Published simultaneously in the United Kingdom
by Gale Research International Limited
(An affiliated company of Gale Research Inc.)

The paper used in this publication meets the minimum requirements of American National Standard for
Information Sciences–Permanence Paper for Printed Library Materials, ANSI Z39.48-1984. ∞™

Library of Congress Catalog Card Number 95–20002

ISBN 0–8103–8483–3

The trademark I⊤P™ is under license.

10 9 8 7 6 5 4 3 2 1

TABLE OF CONTENTS

TOPICAL TABLE OF CONTENTS

EDITORIAL PLAN

Culture is a broad term that has different meanings for different people. It is a word that is used variously to describe how we are alike, how we are different, and what we should aspire to know and appreciate. Thus the title of this work was the subject of careful deliberation by the advisory board at the initial planning meeting in 1990. At issue were basic definitions that determined the fundamental elements of the editorial rationale.

The consensus was that the *Dictionary of Twentieth-Century Culture (TCC)* should undertake to provide a ready reference for the vocabulary of culture, which the board defined as the broad language drawing on shared knowledge used by people of similar backgrounds to communicate with one another. A standard dictionary of language records the definitions of words used in verbal discourse; the advisory board agreed that such dictionaries are inadequate to define more complicated structures of meaning that *TCC* addresses. Communication is frequently extraverbal, drawing on shared experiences, common concepts, communal notions about celebrities, and universally construed messages conveyed by certain images. Culture embraces all aspects of life, from the mundane to the sublime, from the knowledge of grocery-item brand names and the images they connote to a familiarity with classic works of literature, music, and art.

Culture broadly construed is an unmanageable topic for a dictionary-type reference work. Comprehensive coverage would fill a large library. For practical reasons, it was necessary to narrow the scope of *TCC*. The advisory board elected to restrict the series to entries on people, places, terms, art forms, and organizations associated with creative expression in the humanities, those forms of creativity that seek to describe and interpret the human condition. Certainly physicists, chemists, physicians, mathematicians, jurists, and legislators are as creative in their own ways as writers, artists, actors, dancers, and musicians. But as specialists, they view the world from different, though no less important, perspectives than creative artists in the humanities do. Because we cannot do justice to all these worldviews in a single series, we have limited ourselves to the rich world of art, music, literature, drama, radio and television performance, movies, and dance. The advisory board elected not to include entries on individual works because works are described in entries devoted to their creators. Both high and low art that meet the qualification of having made a lasting impression on society will be covered. Endurance is a matter of editorial judgment, and it will be left to volume editors and the editorial board to make the necessary decisions about inclusion.

Obviously it is a distortion to suggest that creative expression occurs in isolation. Most art is not about art but about people from all walks of life and the ways they act, individually and in the company of others. The people, events, and ideas outside the arena of creative expression that stimulated artistic responses have a special significance in culture, and entries are provided to describe certain specific social and historical forces and the creative responses they prompted.

The purpose of *TCC* is not to prescribe what people should know about modern culture; rather, *TCC* attempts to describe and define what people have collectively thought was significant. The purpose of *TCC* entries is definition rather than analysis. Entries are concise, in some cases as brief as a few sentences. In rare cases does an entry exceed one thousand words.

The decision to organize *TCC* volumes geographically was a difficult one, determined by practical considerations and by assumptions about the readership for the series. In fact, of course, there are several distinct cultural groups in most countries, defined sometimes by religion, sometimes by ethnicity, sometimes by socio-economics. Careful attention is due separate cultural groups around the world, but that responsibility must be left to another work. *TCC* is devoted to cultural commonality, not cultural diversity.

Related to the decision to take the broad view of distinct cultures is the advisory board's perception of the audience for *TCC:* American high-school and college students and the patrons of American public libraries. The board has assumed a certain ethnocentrism among the audience, and thus *TCC* will be disproportionately American in character. Other volumes will, in most cases, concentrate on the dominant cultures of a country. Unarguably, comprehensive coverage of the topic is the work of lifetimes.

Certainly many significant entries could be added to those included here. Almost as certainly, entries that should have been included are inadvertently omitted. Significance is a subjective judgment, determined in large part by the cultural background to which the editors themselves are bound. There is some comfort in the anticipation that *TCC* will be a living project that continues its evolution after publication of this volume.

Richard Layman
Columbia, South Carolina
18 April 1994

DICTIONARY OF TWENTIETH-CENTURY CULTURE PUBLISHING PLAN

American Culture After World War II
American Culture Before World War II
Russian Culture After World War II
Russian Culture Before World War II
German Culture
African-American Culture
Arab Culture in the Middle East
Arab Culture in Northern Africa
French Culture
Hispanic Culture of South America

Hispanic Culture of Mexico, Central America, and the Spanish Caribbean
Italian Culture
British Culture After World War II
British Culture Before World War II
Native American Culture
Japanese Culture
Chinese Culture
African Culture South of the Sahara
Eastern European Culture
South East Asian Culture

ACKNOWLEDGMENTS

This book was produced by Manly, Inc. Karen L. Rood is senior editor. Ann González was the in-house editor. She was assisted by associate editor Julie E. Frick.

Production coordinator is James W. Hipp. Photography editor is Bruce Andrew Bowlin. Photographic copy work was performed by Joseph M. Bruccoli. Layout and graphics supervisor is Penney L. Haughton. Copyediting supervisor is Laurel M. Gladden. Typesetting supervisor is Kathleen M. Flanagan. Systems manager is George F. Dodge. The production staff includes George Anderson, Phyllis A. Avant, Ann M. Cheschi, Patricia Coate, Joyce Fowler, Stephanie C. Hatchell, Erica Hennig, Margaret B. Meriwether, Kathy Lawler Merlette, Jeff Miller, Pamela D. Norton, Laura S. Pleicones, Emily R. Sharpe, William L. Thomas Jr., and Jonathan B. Watterson.

Walter W. Ross and Robert S. McConnell did library research. They were assisted by the following librarians at the Thomas Cooper Library of the University of South Carolina: Linda Holderfield and the inter-library-loan staff; reference-department head Virginia Weathers; reference librarians Marilee Birchfield, Stefanie Buck, Cathy Eckman, Rebecca Feind, Jill Holman, Karen Joseph, Jean Rhyne, Kwamine Washington, and Connie Widney; circulation-department head Caroline Taylor; and acquisitions-searching supervisor David Haggard.

The editor wishes to thank Daniel Nelson, Charles Reinhart, Amy Leigh, Jody Nimerichter, Irene Hasseler, Kathleen Foster, Tony Lammoglia, and Andrea Seidel.

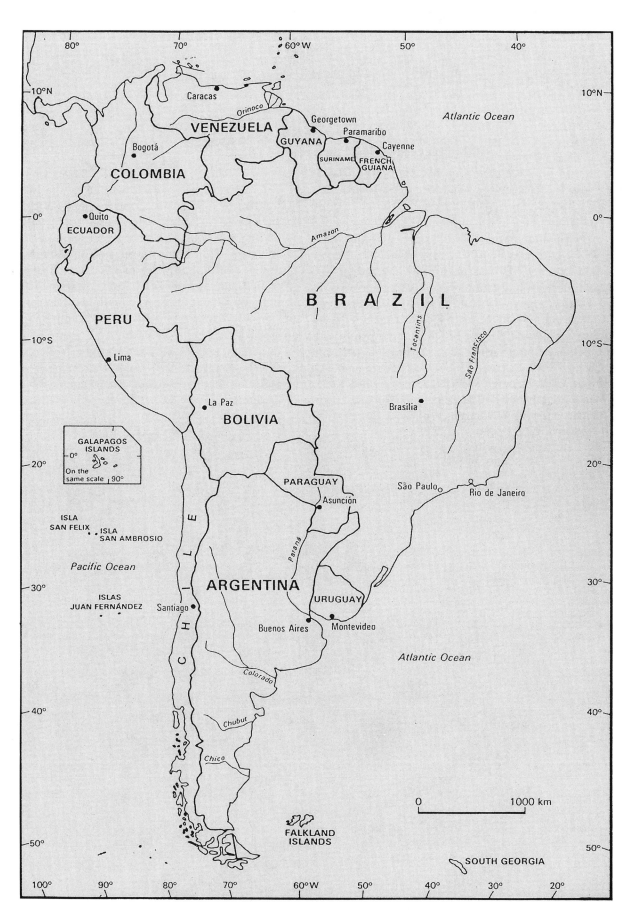

FOREWORD

This volume of the *Dictionary of Twentieth-Century Culture* is the first of two devoted to the culture of the countries of the Americas where Spanish is the predominant language. The present volume deals with South America — that is, with territories from Colombia to Tierra del Fuego at the southern tip of the continent; the second deals with Mexico, Central America, and the Hispanic Caribbean. Spanish American countries share much in common in view of their colonial past, but they differ culturally from each other, resulting from the fact that they have been subject to varying outside influences and more especially because some of them enjoy the added richness of having a significant indigenous heritage. For example, Argentina is primarily the product of Spanish, Italian, and other European immigration; Bolivia is largely the product of the superimposition of Spanish culture on indigenous practices; Colombia has a significant African-based cultural input, especially along its Caribbean coast. Overall, the area encompassed in these volumes — all of Spanish America except Hispanic elements in the United States — is vast, and coverage necessarily has had to be selective.

While the Spanish language is a convenient rallying point, and political boundaries a tempting means of classification, the fact is that cultural activities sometimes "speak" through gestures or visual means that are not language-bound and not always inclined to respect national frontiers. Much of what is covered in the entries in this volume can therefore be described as Latin American (involving French-speaking and Portuguese-speaking countries, as well as Spanish). Painters, dancers, musicians, and filmmakers collaborate, exhibit, and perform in ways that often frustrate the wishes of nationalists (and compilers of reference works). Even literature, in which regional vocabulary or a concentration on local settings and themes has often been used in an attempt to forge distinct national traditions, has become internationalized: the Colombian writes in expectation that the Argentinean (or Spaniard) can read his work. As the twentieth century closes, Spanish ranks fourth among the world's most widely spoken languages, after Chinese, English, and Russian, and the number of Spanish speakers is growing.

In 1992, five hundred years after Columbus first landed in the Bahamas, there was considerable controversy surrounding the term *New World,* a designation which many critics felt reflected the arrogance of the European conquerors who had in fact encountered, and largely destroyed, some highly developed civilizations that were in some ways more advanced than those of the "Old World." The writer Augusto Monterroso tells a story that illustrates the point: a Catholic friar, captured by Indian warriors and about to be sacrificed on the local pyramid, confident in his knowledge that an eclipse is due, boasts to the Indians that if they do not release him, he will cause the sun to be covered; they kill him anyway as they recite from their calendar all the dates on which eclipses are predicted. Just as some indigenous peoples had a sophisticated knowledge of astronomy, others had advanced social organizations. Whether deliberately or inadvertently, the arrival of the Spaniards, rather than preserving what was valuable, brought disease and destruction. Indeed, it is remarkable that so much of the indigenous cultures has survived into our day; for example, in music and dance forms or practices survive relatively intact or by fusion (syncretism) with imported cultural manifestations.

Just as the Spaniards brought new diseases to America, so they took others, such as syphilis, back with them. More positively, the "Encounter" (to use a more fashionable term than "Discovery") between different cultures brought the previously unknown horse to America and the potato (an Inca staple) to Europe. A process of cross-fertilization was under way, including the mixing of races.

In an effort to preserve the indigenous heritage, there have been conscious movements, sometimes confused with political motives, to extol the indigenous in art and literature, especially in the late nineteenth and early twentieth centuries. In our own day there are increased signs of respect for indigenous cultures in the form of official bodies charged with their protection. The defense of Indian interests may be said to have its beginnings with Fray Bartolomé de las Casas, who in 1542 wrote *Brevísima relación de la destruyción de las Indias* (1552; Brief Account of the Destruction of the Indies), dedicated to Philip of Spain and denouncing the treatment of the Indians by Spaniards. When Indian labor was insufficient, African slaves were imported, and thus, unintentionally, the cultural mix was further complicated.

From the point of view of the Europeans, a "New World" it most certainly was (rather as nowadays we might talk of discovering a "new planet"), for they had previously lived in ignorance of America's existence; the "Indians" were so called precisely because Columbus thought he must have been in the Far East. It is important to realize that what motivated Spain was not greed alone. Like others before and since, the Spaniards were driven by a more insidious combination of greed and an absolute belief that they had their God on their side. Spain itself had suffered its own invasion by other crusaders, the "Moors," who had occupied much of the Iberian Peninsula since 711. By the late fifteenth century, its various kingdoms were coming together. The "Catholic Monarchs," Ferdinand and Isabella, had expelled not only the Moors but also the Jews, and it was logical to continue the Catholic crusade in combination with economic and political expansion. Spain profited handsomely from the New World in wealth, prestige, and power. From a religious standpoint, the Indians had to be "saved"; thus, the part that religion has played in shaping Spanish American culture is not to be underestimated. Yet somehow indigenous beliefs and practices have survived, often by assimilation to Catholic ones. In the twentieth century indigenous groups have been subjected to Protestant missionary pressures as well.

During the colonial period there was little interest in preserving the cultures of indigenous peoples such as the Incas; on the contrary, the aim was to convert them to European ways, and the main responsibility for achieving their conversion lay with the Church. In the eighteenth century, however, the powers of the Church in the colonies were somewhat compromised when the Jesuits, important educators and missionaries, were expelled from the Americas because Charles III of Spain found them too active in politics. The Jesuits therefore turned their energies against Spain. The Inquisition retaliated with more effective repression in the rebellious colonies. Then, against the background of the Napoleonic War in Europe, the new republics of Spanish America began to emerge. By the third decade of the nineteenth century the greater part of Spanish America had been liberated from Spain. There followed a new era of emigration from various countries, one which reached massive proportions in certain areas, particularly in the Río de la Plata region in the early decades of the new century; it was a flow later revitalized by the two world wars. Thus, it is no surprise that nowadays one finds Argentineans called Benedetti and Pizarnik, Chileans called Edwards and O'Higgins, Peruvians called Fujimori and Westphalen. All have served to enrich the culture of Spanish America, while the Spanish language remains the vital link among so many diverse peoples.

The result of these influences on the modern culture of South America is a rich diversity that is primarily the product of indigenous, African, and European contributions. As the new republics took shape during the latter half of the nineteenth century, they became anxious to define their separate identities. In consequence art, music, and literature often markedly emphasized peculiar characteristics — such as the flora and fauna and the indigenous elements — that were not to be found in the Old World. Yet the artists, writers, and musicians who devoted their energies to such ends often employed European forms of expression. Creolism in literature, Indigenism in literature and art, and nationalism in music all relate to this need to affirm an independent identity. Eventually, less nationalistic, more mature and sensitive artistic attempts to capture the complexities of the New World evolved to portray the worldview of the indigenous peoples and to explore the contradictions of a continent unified to a great degree by language, yet composed of countries proud of their own distinctiveness, and equivocal in their attitude toward the United States (the new colonial power) and toward Europe (the colonial power of the past and the continent that still exerts considerable influence on Latin American intellectuals).

The political course of the twentieth century has not been easy for many of these countries, victims of economic hardship, dictatorial regimes at home, and interference from their powerful neighbor to the north. In many instances, the repression that characterized most of the colonial period has only been replaced by new forms of intolerance and censorship, with the result that large numbers of creative artists have sought exile, whether by choice or necessity, in Europe or the United States. Ironically, repression has in fact been the driving force behind much creative activity. The result has often been works of impressive quality, deeply felt indictments of injustice realized in artistic forms that show no signs of aesthetic compromise. The place of politics in art has also been a polemical issue among intellectuals, some of whom regard as traitors those artists whose creative works are not overtly committed to social and political reform or are cosmopolitan rather than rooted in the day-to-day realities of Latin American life.

Yet cosmopolitanism and exile are two factors that have contributed to a new awareness of Spanish American culture outside Latin America. Even those artists whose work is focused on Latin American and regional issues aim at an international audience. In the twentieth century, Latin American artistic activity has come into its own, grown beyond imitative styles and provincial themes, and has come to be regarded with respect by the cultural powers that once dominated.

So many different countries functioning in the Latin American cultural context cannot fully be accounted for in volumes such as these. This series does attempt, however, to cover the major writers, artists, and performers, the most significant background events, personalities, cultural phenomena, and organizations that have led to the most lasting manifestations of twentieth-century culture, both elevated and popular.

The state of knowledge itself regarding different cultural activities varies a great deal; at one extreme, literature, documentary by nature, is also highly documented and has attracted wide critical attention during the second half of the twentieth century; at the other extreme, dance is a subject about which little documentation currently exists. Thus, the literature entries are the result of ruthless sifting and selection, involving many omissions of writers whose reputations may well last beyond the century, whereas the dance entries are often the first attempts to map out that particular area of cultural activity. Other broad subject areas fall between these two extremes: art is well studied; music, cinema, and the media less so. For this reason, certain films have been given entries of their own because they are milestones in an industry that remains small, especially by comparison with the power and scale of Hollywood: in 1993, for example, only about thirty feature-length movies were produced in the whole of Latin America. There are a few long entries designed to provide an overview of subject areas, sometimes with essential historical background; examples are those entitled Art, Newspapers and Magazines, Fiction, Theater, and Music. Within entries, a word or group of words in **bold** indicates that an entry on that topic exists in this volume.

Finally, those readers who are unfamiliar with the structure of Spanish names should note the following: two surnames (family names) are normal, the first being inherited from one's father and the second from one's mother. These surnames are most often used both together, but sometimes only the first is used: thus Roberto Matta may also be referred to as Roberto Matta Echaurren; either way, Matta, the first family name, is the key word. Some confusion has been generated through the misuse of Spanish names by English speakers: for example, Gabriel García Márquez, the Nobel Prize winner, is often referred to as Márquez in the English-speaking world, but in the Spanish world he is always García Márquez.

—P.S.

TIMELINE: SELECTED WORKS AND EVENTS

1900s

Literature
Modernismo is in vogue.

1900

Historical and Political Events
A mid-August earthquake in Ecuador and Peru kills thousands.

Literature
José Enrique Rodó, *Ariel*

Photography
Chile's weekly *Sucesos* introduces a section on photography.

1901

Historical and Political Events
Leonidas Plaza is elected president of Ecuador. The American Smelting and Refining Co. (ASARCO), controlled by American Meyer Guggenheim and his sons, begins to extend its operations into copper and nitrate mining in Chile and tin mining in Bolivia.

1902

Historical and Political Events
In December, when Venezuela does not meet its debt obligations to several Western powers, Great Britain and Germany seize the Venezuelan navy, and Italy joins in blockading Venezuelan ports until the issue is resolved the following February.

Art
Martín Malharro introduces Impressionism in Argentina.

Photography
A Foto Club is founded in Valparaíso, Chile.

1903

Historical and Political Events
The senate of Colombia turns down a proposal to lease a six-mile strip of the Isthmus of Panama to the United States for the construction of the Panama Canal; the United States sends a cruiser to Panamanian waters, and Panama, backed by U.S. government and business interests, declares its independence. José Batlle Ordóñez, who becomes known as the maker of modern Uruguay, is elected to his first term as president.

Art
Joaquín Torres-García begins to work with Antoni Gaudí in Barcelona, Spain.

1904

Historical and Political Events
Colombian president José Manuel Marroquin is succeeded by Rafael Reyes, who assumes dictatorial powers. Liberal Party exiles invade Paraguay, overthrowing the Colorado Party, which has controlled the government since 1878; the Liberals dominate Paraguayan politics until 1936. *The Christ of the Andes,* a twenty-six-foot-high statue by Mateo Alonzo, is dedicated at Uspallato Pass on the Argentinean-Chilean border to commemorate the peaceful settlement of disputes between the two countries that date back to their declarations of independence from Spain in 1816 and 1817.

Photography
A Foto Club is founded in Santiago, Chile.

1905

Historical and Political Events
Bolivian store clerk Simon Ituri Patiño of Cochabamba is given a seemingly worthless tin mine, which becomes the basis for his Consolidated Tin Smelters Ltd, earning him $200 million and making Bolivia one of the major worldwide sources for tin.

Art
Fernando Fader exhibits Impressionist paintings in Argentina.

1906

Historical and Political Events
Eloy Alfaro is elected president of Ecuador.

1907

Art
Impressionist Andrés de Santa María shifts toward Postimpressionism with his painting *En la Playa de Macuto: María Mancini a Caballo* (On Macuto Beach: María Mancini on Horseback).

The Impressionist group Nexus forms in Buenos Aires, Argentina.

1908

Historical and Political Events
Juan Vicente Gómez begins twenty-seven years of nearly uninterrupted rule in Venezuela.

Dance, Music, and Theater
Teatro Colón opens in Buenos Aires, Argentina.

1909

Historical and Political Events
President Rafael Reyes of Colombia resigns because of domestic discontent over his negotiation with the United States of a treaty recognizing the independence of Panama; the Conservative Party controls the government for the next two decades.

Literature
Leopoldo Lugones, *Lunario sentimental* (Sentimental Lunar Poems)

1910

Historical and Political Events
Reformist politician Roque Sáenz Peña takes office as president of Argentina. The extremely productive Chuquicamata copper mine in Chile is acquired by the U.S. company ASARCO; a trans-Andean railroad linking Argentina and Chile is completed.

Art
Joaquín Torres-García decorates the Uruguayan Pavillion in the Brussels International Exhibition.

1911

Historical and Political Events
President Eloy Alfaro of Ecuador is forced into exile, and Emilio Estrada, who dies after four months in office, becomes president; when Alfaro returns to Ecuador and attempts to regain power, he dies at the hands of a lynch mob in early 1912. U.S. explorer Hiram Bingham discovers the ruins of the ancient Inca city of Machu Picchu.

Art
Pedro Figari, *El arte, la estética, y el ideal* (Art, Aesthetics, and the Ideal)
Grupo de Barracas (later known as the Boedo group) is formed in Buenos Aires, Argentina.
Joaquín Torres-García begins to work on murals at the Palace of the Generalitat in Barcelona, Spain.

1912

Historical and Political Events
President Roque Sáenz Peña of Argentina secures passage of a law establishing universal, secret, compulsory suffrage for all males over the age of eighteen. Leonidas Plaza is elected to a second term as president of Ecuador.

1913

Art
Joaquín Torres-García publishes his first book on art.

1914

Historical and Political Events
World War I begins in Europe, just as the Panama Canal opens; in December a British squadron sinks four German ships in the Battle of the Malvinas (Falkland Islands), off the coast of Argentina.

Art
Salón de Recusados (Salon of the Rejected) is created in Argentina.

1916

Historical and Political Events
Radical Party candidate Hipólito Irigoyen is elected president of Argentina; he steps aside in favor of fellow Radical Marcelo Torcuato de Alvear in 1922 but runs for the presidency again in 1928 and is elected. Alfredo Baquerizo Moreno becomes president of Ecuador, but Leonidas Plaza retains control of the military until 1925.

Art
Rafael Barradas and Joaquín Torres-García produce Vibrationist works in Barcelona, Spain.

1917

Historical and Political Events
Colombia and Ecuador settle their long-running border disputes.

Art
Asociación Nacional de Artistas is formed in Argentina.
José Sabogal has his first exhibition in Lima, Peru.

Dance
The dance company of famed Russian ballerina Anna Pavlova

1918

Historical and Political Events
World War I ends. Under the leadership of José Batlle Ordóñez (president 1903–1907, 1911–1915), Uruguay adopts a system of government in which the president shares power with a nine-member National Council of Administration.

Art
Salón de Artistas Independientes (Independent Artists Salon) is established in Buenos Aires, Argentina.

1919

Historical and Political Events
Augusto Leguía, who served as elected president of Peru in 1908–1912, becomes military dictator of the nation.

Art
The Escuela de Bellas Artes is founded in Lima, Peru.

1920s

Art and Literature
Avant-garde movements experience their heyday in Latin America.

1920

Historical and Political Events
José Luis Tamayo becomes president of Ecuador. Twenty years of Liberal Party rule in Bolivia ends with the election of Bautista Saavedra to the presidency. Reformist candidate Arturo Alessandri becomes president of Chile under a governmental system that places most of the power in the hands of the legislative branch.

1921

Literature
Jorge Luis Borges's Ultraísta manifesto is published in *Nosotros,* the most widely read magazine in Buenos Aires, Argentina.

1922

Historical and Political Events
At Lake Maracaibo in Venezuela an oil well owned by Royal Dutch–Shell spills nearly one million barrels of oil into the lake before it is capped; Gulf Oil and Standard Oil of Indiana have leased the oil rights to land nearby.

Literature
Vicente Huidobro explains the theory of *creacionismo.*

tours South America for the first time.

Dance and Music
Argentinean guitarist and vocalist Carlos Gardel's "Mi noche triste" marks the heyday of the early tango.

Photography
Martín Chambi exhibits his work for the first time and publishes the first picture postcard in Peru.

Literature
Horacio Quiroga, *Cuentos de la selva* (translated as *South American Jungle Tales*)

Music
At the Teatro Colón, Felipe Boero premieres his first opera, *Tucumán,* following the predominant musical trend of nationalism.

Photography
F. M. Steadman publishes a manual of photography in Venezuela.

Literature
Alcides Arguedas, *Raza de bronce* (Bronze Race), Indigenist novel

The Boedo and Florida groups are active.

Art
Norah Borges publishes woodcuts and Rafael Barradas contributes illustrations in Ultraist magazines in Madrid, Spain.
Pedro Figari joins the avant-garde Florida group.

Photography
Martín Chambi opens a commercial photography studio in Cuzco, Peru.

Art
Camilo Alejandro Egas, *Ritual,* symbolist painting

Cinema
A movie version of *María,* the nineteenth-century Romantic novel by Jorge Isaacs, is released in Colombia.

Literature
César Vallejo, *Trilce*

1923

Historical and Political Events
The Anaconda Co. buys the Chuquicamata copper mine in Chile for $70 million from the U.S. company ASARCO, after its owners, the Guggenheim family, leaves the copper business.

Art
Xul Solar, *Nana-Watzin,* avant-garde watercolor

1924

Historical and Political Events
Gonzalo S. Córdova becomes president of Ecuador. Argentinean physiologist Bernardo Alberto Houssay proves that the pituitary gland, as well as the pancreas, is involved in breaking down sugar in the human body.

Art
Emilio Pettoruti and Xul Solar join the avant-garde Florida group.

Emilio Pettoruti exhibits his work at the Galería Witcomb in Buenos Aires, Argentina.

Literature
The Argentinean avant-garde journal *Martín Fierro* is founded.
Pablo Neruda, *Veinte poemas de amor y una canción desesperada* (translated as *Twenty Love Poems and a Song of Despair*)
José Eustacio Rivera, *La vorágine* (translated as *The Vortex*), regionalist novel

1925

Historical and Political Events
President Gonzalo S. Córdova of Ecuador is overthrown in a military coup that begins fifteen years of upheaval in that nation. President Arturo Alessandri of Chile succeeds in putting in place a new constitution that strengthens the presidency.

Cinema
Bajo el cielo antioqueño (Beneath the Sky in Antioquía), directed by Arturo Acevedo

Corazón aymara (Aymara Heart), directed by Pedro Sambarino, the first Bolivian feature film

Literature
Oliverio Girondo, *Veinte poemas para ser leídos en el tranvía* (Twenty Poems to Be Read in the Streetcar)

Photography
Martín Chambi produces his series of photographs of Machu Picchu.

1926

Historical and Political Events
Hernando Siles is elected president of Bolivia.

Art
Adolfo Bellocq, a founding member of the Boedo group, produces his series *Proverbios* (Proverbs).
Joaquín Torres-García shares a studio in Paris with Jean Helion.

Literature
Amauta begins publication.
Ricardo Güiraldes, *Don Segundo Sombra* (translated), the classic gaucho novel
Corín Tellado, the most prolific author of the novela rosa, is born in Spain.

1927

Historical and Political Events
Backed by the military, Carlos Ibáñez establishes a quasi-dictatorship in Chile. Peruvian pilot Toribio Mexta Xesspe discovers huge drawings of birds, reptiles, and other animals – made by the pre–Inca Nazca civilization and visible only from the air – on the plains of southern Peru.

Art
Camilo Alejandro Egas establishes the Centro de Arte Egas, a meeting place for artists and intellectuals who reject the dominant academic style.
Emilio Pettoruti, *Quintet,* Cubist painting

1928

Architecture
Sergio Larraín begins work on his design for the Edificio Oberpaur in Chile.

Art
Minister of Public Instruction Pablo Ramírez gives selected Chilean artists – who come to be known as the Montparnasse Group – grants to study in Paris.

Literature
Rómulo Gallegos, *Doña Bárbara* (translated)
José Carlos Mariátegui, *Siete ensayos de interpretación de la realidad peruana* (translated as *Seven Interpretative Essays on Peruvian Reality*)

Popular Culture
Raúl Roux initiates the adventure comic strip in Argentina with *El tigre de los llanos* (The Tiger of the Plains).

1929

Architecture
Le Corbusier visits Buenos Aires, Argentina.

Art
Jorge Vinatea Reinoso, *Balseros del Titicaca* (Titicaca Rafters), Indigenist painting

Literature
Roberto Arlt, *Los siete locos* (translated as *The Seven Madmen*)

1930

Historical and Political Events
Liberal-coalition candidate Enrique Olaya Herrera is elected president of Colombia. President Augusto Leguía of Peru resigns and flees the country in August, after a military revolt led by Col. Luis Sánchez Cerro, who is elected president in 1931. In September a military coup, supported by big landholders and major business interests and led by Gen. José Félix Uriburu, ousts President Hipólito Irigoyen of Argentina after fourteen years of social reform government. President Hernando Siles of Bolivia is overthrown. Pan American Airways begins flights to South America. The first subway line in South America opens in Buenos Aires, Argentina. Uruguay wins the first World Cup soccer competition by beating Argentina 4–2.

Art
Antonio Berni returns to Argentina from Europe.
Escuela Nacional de Bellas Artes of the Universidad de Chile is founded.
Joaquín Torres-García cofounds the Cercle et Carré group.

Literature
Arturo Uslar Pietri, *Las lanzas coloradas* (translated as *The Red Lances*)

1931

Historical and Political Events
The resignation of President Carlos Ibáñez of Chile is followed by months of political chaos. *Christ the Redeemer*, a 125-foot monument by French sculptor Paul Maximilian Landowski, is dedicated on Corcovado (Hunchback Mountain) in Buenos Aires; its outstretched arms have a span of ninety-two feet.

Architecture
Carlos Raúl Villanueva designs the Plaza de Toros (Bull Ring) in Maracay, Venezuela.

Art
Antonio Berni, *El Botón y el Tornillo* (The Button and the Screw), Surrealist painting

Literature
Sur magazine is founded in Argentina by Victoria Ocampo.

1932

Historical and Political Events
The Chaco War, a border dispute between Bolivia and Paraguay, begins. Arturo Alessandri is reelected president of Chile. Gen. Agustín P. Justo is elected president of Argentina.

Art
Camilo Alejandro Egas paints the mural *Festival* at the New School for Social Research in New York City.

Cinema and Music
Carlos Gardel's first starring role is in *Melodía de arrabal* (Suburban Melody).

Literature
Oliverio Girondo "markets" *Espantapájaros* (Scarecrow) by driving a scarecrow in a hearse through Buenos Aires streets and sells all five thousand copies of his book in a month.

1933

Historical and Political Events
President Luis Sánchez Cerro of Peru is assassinated in April and is succeeded by Oscar Benevides, who serves until 1939. President Gabriel Terra of Uruguay abolishes the National Council of Administration.

Art
Mexican Muralist David Alfaro Siqueiros visits Buenos Aires, Argentina, and collaborates with Antonio Berni, Lino Spilimbergo, and Juan Carlos Castagnino on an experimental mural.

Photography
Guillermo Facio Hebequer, a founding member of the Boedo group, releases his portfolio of prints, *Tu historia, compañero* (Your History, Comrade).

1934

Historical and Political Events
Liberal candidate Alfonso López is elected president of Colombia. The League of Nations rules in favor of Colombia in a border dispute with Peru. María Velasco Ibarra becomes president of Ecuador and is overthrown by the military less than a year later.

Architecture
Gregorio Sánchez, Julio Lagos, and José María de la Torre begin work on the design of the Kavanagh building, a modern high-rise apartment building in Buenos Aires, Argentina.

Art
Antonio Berni, *Desocupados, o Desocupación* (Unemployed, or Unemployment)

Cinema
Norte y sur (North and South), directed by Jorge Delano, the first Chilean talkie

Cinema and Music
Carlos Gardel stars in *Cuesta abajo* (Downward Slope).

1935

Historical and Political Events
Bolivia and Paraguay agree to end their war over the Chaco territory but do not work out a peace treaty until 1938. After a dictatorship of twenty-six years, President Juan Vicente Gómez of Venezuela dies, and Gen. Eleazar López Contreras becomes head of a provisional government.

Art
Joaquín Torres-García founds Asociación de Arte Con-

1936

Historical and Political Events
The Febristas, led by social activist Col. Rafael Franco, take power in Paraguay. Eleazar López Contreras become president of Venezuela. After a period of unrest in Bolivia related to the nation's defeat in the Chaco War, a military coup installs Col. David Toro as president; he is overthrown in a coup led by Col. Germán Busch in 1937.

Art
Asociación de Arte Constructivo begins publication of the

1937

Historical and Political Events
A military coup in Paraguay places popular Marshal José Félix Estigarriba in the presidency.

Architecture
Alberto Horacio Prebisch designs the Grand Rex movie theater in Buenos Aires, Argentina.

1938

Historical and Political Events
Roberto M. Ortiz becomes president of Argentina. Eduardo Santos becomes president of Colombia. Popular Front candidate Pedro Aguirre Cerda is elected president of Chile, beginning a domination of left-wing parties that continues until the 1960s. In December twenty-one American nations meeting in Peru adopt the Declaration of Lima, agreeing to consult each other if the "peace, security, or territorial integrity" of any of their countries is threatened.

1939

Historical and Political Events
World War II begins in Europe. In December British ships heavily damage the German battleship *Graf Spee* in the harbor of Montevideo, and Hitler has the ship scuttled to keep the British from taking it. Manuel Prado becomes president of Peru. An earthquake in Chile kills thousands.

1940s

Literature
Pablo Neruda writes his *Canto general* (1950; translated as *General Song*), an epic poem in fifteen cantos that chronicles the

1940

Historical and Political Events
President José Félix Estigarribia of Paraguay dies in an air-

Literature
Jorge Icaza, *Huasipungo* (translated), Indigenist novel

structivo in Montevideo, Uruguay, and publishes his book *Estructura* (Structure).
Mario Urteaga exhibits his Indigenist paintings in Lima, Peru.

Cinema and Music
Carlos Gardel stars in *El día que me quieras* (The Day You Love Me). In June he dies in an airplane crash in Medellín, Colombia.

periodical *Círculo y Cuadrado*.
Raquel Forner begins her allegorical series of paintings about the horrors of war.

Photography
A Foto Club is founded in Buenos Aires, Argentina.
Grete Stern and Horacio Coppola settle in Buenos Aires, open a studio, and participate in an exhibition sponsored by the magazine *Sur*.

Art
Juan Miguel Luis Batlle Planas, *Radiografías Paranoicas* (Paranoic X Rays) series
Marina Núñez del Prado, *Danza de Cholas* (Cholas Dancing), Indigenist sculpture

Art
French poet André Breton invites Roberto Matta to join the Surrealist movement.
Joaquín Torres-García, *Monumento cosmico* (Cosmic Monument), granite sculpture in Parque Rodó, Montevideo, Uruguay

Cinema
Infierno verde (Green Hell), directed by Luis Bazoberry, documentary on the Chaco War between Bolivia and Paraguay

Dance
The Teatro Colón becomes the home of the Municipal Ballet of Buenos Aires.

Art
Members of the Surrealist Grupo Orión exhibit together in Buenos Aires, Argentina.

Newspapers and Magazines
The Uruguayan weekly *Marcha* is founded.

history and geography of Latin America from creation to the present

plane crash; he is succeeded by Higinio Morínigo, who assumes dictatorial powers, governing until 1948. Vice President Ramón S. Castillo becomes acting president of Argentina owing to the illness of President Roberto M. Ortiz and succeeds to the presidency on Ortiz's death in 1942. Shipping wheat and other foodstuffs to war-torn Europe, Argentina becomes the richest country in South America over the next five years. Carlos Alberto Árroyo del Río becomes president of Ecuador through election fraud. Gen. Enrique Peñaranda is elected president of Bolivia.

Art
Asociación de Arte Constructivo of Montevideo, Uruguay, dissolves.
Eduardo Kingman founds the Galería Caspicara in Quito, Ecuador.

1941

Historical and Political Events
Isaías Medina Angarita becomes president of Venezuela. Peru invades Ecuador in a border dispute that is resolved in Peru's favor at the Inter-American Conference of 1942.

Architecture
Carlos Raúl Villanueva designs low-cost housing in Caracas, Venezuela.

Art
Juan Miguel Luis Batlle Planas, *La mecánica* (Mechanics)
Mexican Muralist David Alfaro Siqueiros visits Chile and paints several murals in Chillán.

1942

Historical and Political Events
Alfonso López is elected to another term as president of Colombia. At an Inter-American Conference in Rio de Janeiro twenty-one Western Hemisphere nations agree to coordinate defenses against invasion and adopt a unanimous resolution to break diplomatic ties with the Axis powers.

Art
Roberto Matta exhibits his work in New York City.

1943

Historical and Political Events
President Ramon S. Castillo is overthrown by the Argentinean military. Gen. Enrique Peñaranda of Bolivia is overthrown by Maj. Gualberto Villarroel; his overthrow in 1946 is followed by six years of conservative governments.

Architecture
The construction of the Casa del Puente (Bridge House), designed by Amancio Williams, is begun in Mar del Plata, Argentina.

1944

Historical and Political Events
Amid public indignation over the resolution of the border dispute with Peru, President Alberto Arroyo del Rio of Ecuador is overthrown, and José María Velasco Ibarra resumes the presidency, which he holds until 1972, with interruptions in 1948–1952 for the presidency of Galo Plaza and in 1956–1960 for that of Camilo Ponce. World War II ends in Europe (8 May) and the Pacific (14 August).

Architecture
Carlos Raúl Villanueva begins his design of Ciudad Universitaria in Caracas, Venezuela.

Cinema
Mexican comedian Cantinflas achieves international success when he stars in *Ahí está el detalle* (There Is the Detail), his first full-length feature.

Dance
Both the Ballets Kurt Jooss and the Ballets Russes tour South America.

Literature
Adolfo Bioy Casares, *La invención de Morel* (translated in *The Invention of Morel and Other Stories*)

The Surrealist magazine *La mandrágora* sponsors an exhibition in Chile.

Cinema
Cantinflas stars in *Ni sangre ni arena* (Neither Blood nor Sand).
Flores de Valle (Flowers of the Valley), directed by Máximo Calvothe, the first Colombian talkie

Literature
Ciro Alegría, *El mundo es ancho y ajeno* (1940; translated as *Broad and Alien Is the World*), Indigenist novel

Dance
Ballet Nacional Chileno is founded.
De Basil Original Ballets Russes of Monte Carlo tours Chile.

Literature
Adolfo Bioy Casares collaborates with Jorge Luis Borges to write *Seis problemas para don Isidro Parodi* (translated as *Six Problems for Don Isidro Parodi*), published under the pseudonym H. Bustos Domecq.

Art
Grupo de los Cinco is founded in Chile.
The Taller Torres-García is founded in Montevideo, Uruguay, by Joaquín Torres-García.

Dance
The Ballet de Lima is founded in Peru.

Art
The abstract art group Arturo is formed in Buenos Aires, Argentina.
Gyula Kosice, *Röyi*, abstract articulated wood sculpture
Roberto Matta, *Le vertige d'Eros* (The Vertigo of Eros), Surrealist painting
The Taller Torres-García begins publication of the magazine *Removedor* (until 1951) and produces Constructive Art murals for Hospital Colonia Saint Bois.
Joaquín Torres-García publishes his book *Universalismo constructivo* (Constructive Universalism).

Cinema
Antonia Santos, directed by Gabriel Martínez

Literature
Jorge Luis Borges, *Ficciones* (revised, 1956; translated as *Fictions* and as *Labyrinths*)

1945

Historical and Political Events
On the eve of the presidential election the Acción Democrática party of Venezuela, led by Rómulo Betancourt, collaborates in the military overthrow of President Isaías Medina Angarita. Popular Front candidate José Luis Bustamante becomes president of Peru.

Art
Asociación de Arte Concreto-Invención is formed.

Ricardo Grau is appointed director of the Escuela Nacional de Bellas Artes (National School of Fine Arts) in Lima and begins progressive reforms in Peru.

Literature
Gabriela Mistral is the first Latin American to be awarded the Nobel Prize for literature.

1946

Historical and Political Events
Juan Domingo Perón is elected to his first term as president of Argentina. Conservative Mariano Ospina Pérez becomes president of Colombia.

Art
Antonio Berni produces murals on the ceiling of the Galerías Pacífico building in Buenos Aires, Argentina.
Lucio Fontana, *Manifiesto Blanco* (White Manifesto)
The Madí group is formed in Buenos Aires, Argentina.

1947

Historical and Political Events and Art
Norah Borges is jailed in Argentina by the Peronist administration.

1948

Historical and Political Events
Rómulo Gallegos becomes the first democratically elected president of Venezuela, but he is overthrown later this year, and his government is replaced by a military dictatorship. Liberal politician Jorge Eliécer Gaitán is assassinated in Colombia on 9 April, precipitating violent rioting in Bogotá while the city is hosting the Ninth Pan-American Conference, at which the Organization of American States (OAS) is founded on 30 April. The rioting begins La Violencia (The Violence), a period of civil disorder in Colombia that continues until 1958. After a civil war in Paraguay President Higinio Morínigo steps down and is succeeded by J. Natalicio González.

Art
Marco Ospina shows his earliest works of abstract art in Bogotá, Colombia.

Alejandro Otero exhibits his *Cafeteras* (Coffeepots) series in Caracas, Venezuela.

Cinema
Dios se lo pague (God Bless You), directed by Luis César Amadori

Literature
Alejo Carpentier, "De lo real maravilloso americano" ("On the Marvelous Real in America"), seminal essay on magical realism
Leopoldo Marechal, *Adán Buenosayres*
Ernesto Sábato, *El túnel* (translated as *The Tunnel*)

Photography
Grete Stern begins to publish her photomontages in the magazine *Idilio*.

1949

Literature
Jorge Enrique Adoum begins writing poems that are compiled in *No son todos los que están* (1979; Not All Are Here That Are).

Jorge Luis Borges, *El Aleph* (revised, 1952; translated as *The Aleph and Other Stories*)

1950

Historical and Political Events
Conservative Laureano Gómez is elected president of Colombia; he steps aside because of illness in 1951, and Roberto Urdaneta Arbeláez becomes acting president. Uruguay wins the fourth World Cup soccer championship, the first to be held since 1938, beating Brazil 5–4.

Art
Jesús Rafael Soto participates in the Réalités Nouvelles exhibition in Paris.

Literature
Juan Carlos Onetti, *La vida breve* (translated as *A Brief Life*)

1951

Historical and Political Events
Uruguay once again creates a plural presidency, the National Council, which remains in place until 1966. Western Hemisphere athletes compete in the first Pan-American Games, held in Buenos Aires.

Art
Oswaldo Guayasamín, *El camino de lágrimas* (The Road of Tears), series of Indigenist paintings
Alejandro Otero joins the group "los disidentes" (the dissidents) in Paris.
Fernando de Szyszlo exhibits Informal Abstract paintings in Peru.

Literature
Julio Cortázar, *Bestiario* (translated as *Bestiary*)

1952

Historical and Political Events
Marcos Pérez Jiménez becomes president of Venezuela. Víctor Paz Estenssoro becomes president of Bolivia. Eva Perón, Argentinean idol and wife of the dictator Juan Domingo Perón, dies.

1953

Historical and Political Events
The Gómez government of Colombia is deposed in a military coup led by Gen. Gustavo Rojas Pinilla.

Art
Nemesio Antúnez founds Taller 99 in Santiago, Chile.
Ocho Contemporáneos (Eight Contemporaries) avant-garde group exhibits in La Paz, Bolivia.

1954

Historical and Political Events
Gen. Alfredo Stroessner becomes president of Paraguay.

Art
Enrique Tábara and Araceli Gilbert exhibit their abstract artworks in Ecuador.

1955

Historical and Political Events
In September a military junta in Argentina overthrows President Juan Domingo Perón; Eduardo Lonardi becomes president but is overthrown in November, when Gen. Pedro Aramburu is made provisional president.

Art
Abstract artists found the Rectángulo group in Chile.
Fernando Botero's work is poorly received in Bogotá, Colombia.

1956

Historical and Political Events
Manuel Prado regains the presidency of Peru. Ecuador begins an emphasis on banana production that will make it the world's major exporter of the fruit in less than ten years.

1957

Historical and Political Events
President Gustavo Rojas Pinilla of Colombia turns over power to a military junta.

Art
Raquel Forner begins her neofigurative *Serie del espacio* (Series of Space).
Carlos Cruz-Diez founds Estudio de Artes Visuales in Caracas, Venezuela.

Cinema
La casa del ángel (The House of the Angel), directed by Leopoldo Torre Nilsson

Radio and Television
Argentina begins television broadcasting.

Architecture
Carlos Raúl Villanueva completes the Aula Magna (Olympic Stadium) in Caracas, Venezuela.

Radio and Television
Venezuela begins television broadcasting.

Cinema
Vuelve Sebastiana (Sebastiana, Come Home), directed by Jorge Ruiz

Photography
Grete Stern's series of photographs are published in the book *Buenos Aires.*

Literature
Nicanor Parra, *Poemas y antipoemas* (translated as *Poems and Antipoems*), Surrealist narrative monologues

Radio and Television
Chile begins television broadcasting.

Edgar Negret begins his *Aparatos Mágicos* (Magic Apparatuses) abstract sculpture series.
Alejandro Otero begins his abstract series *Colorritmos* (Color-Rhythms).

Cinema
Colombia linda (Beautiful Colombia), directed by Camilo Correa
Graciela, directed by Leopoldo Torre Nilsson

Cinema
La vertiente (Watershed), directed by Jorge Ruiz

Radio and Television
Uruguay begins television broadcasting.

Dance
The Ballet del Sur is founded in Bahía Blanca, Argentina.

Literature
The Premio Biblioteca Breve de Novela is instituted.
Rodolfo Walsh, *Operación masacre* (translated as *Operation Massacre*)

Theater
Osvaldo Dragún, *Historias para ser contadas* (Stories To Be Told), a trilogy of one-act plays

1958

Historical and Political Events
The two major political parties of Colombia bring an end to La Violencia by creating the National Front coalition and agreeing to alternate presidential nominations between their two parties; their candidate, Lleras Camargo, becomes president of Colombia. Peronist Arturo Frondizi is elected president of Argentina. Facing corruption charges, President Marcos Pérez Jiménez flees Venezuela.

Art
Antonio Berni produces his first works focusing on Juanito Laguna, a poor child from the slums.
Marina Núñez del Prado, *Venus Negra* (Black Venus), sculpture

Jesús Rafael Soto begins his *Vibración* (Vibration) series of Op Art sculptures.

Cinema
El jefe (The Boss), directed by Fernando Ayala

Literature
José María Arguedas, *Los ríos profundos* (translated as *Deep Rivers*)
H. A. Murena, *El pecado original de América* ([Latin] America's Original Sin)

Radio and Television
Peru begins television broadcasting.

1959

Historical and Political Events
Cuban dictator Fulgencio Batista resigns on 1 January and flees the country as rebel troops led by Fidel Castro advance on Havana; Castro officially assumes the office of premier on 16 February. *Pasajes de la guerra revolucionaria* (translated as *Reminiscences of the Cuban Revolutionary War*), an account of the Cuban Revolution written by Castro's adviser Ernesto "Che" Guevara, is published this year. Rómulo Betancourt becomes president of Venezuela.

Art
Fernando Botero, *Mona Lisa a los doce* (Mona Lisa, Age Twelve)
Informal Abstraction works are exhibited for the first time in Argentina.
Eduardo Mac Entyre, Miguel Angel Vidal, and Ignacio Pirovano found the Arte Generativo group.
Manuel Rendón exhibits semiabstract work in Ecuador.

Cinema
El candidato (The Candidate), directed by Fernando Ayala
La caída (The Fall), directed by Leopoldo Torre Nilsson
Un vintén p'al Judas (A Dime for the Judas), directed by Ugo Ulive

Dance
The Ballet de Santiago is founded in Chile.

Literature
Mario Benedetti, *Montevideanos,* stories about the inhabitants of the Uruguayan capital
The annual Casa de las Américas Prize for Latin American literature is instituted in Cuba.

1960s

Literature
The major novels of the Boom are published.

Music
The Nueva Canción movement grows in Chile.

1960

Historical and Political Events
A major earthquake near Concepción, Chile, creates seismic waves that wreak heavy damage as far away as Japan; the death toll is estimated at one thousand. Buenos Aires, with a population of 4.5 million, and São Paulo, with 4 million, are on the list of 141 world cities with more than 1 million inhabitants.

Architecture
The building of Banco de Londres y América del Sur, designed by Clorindo Testa with Estudio SEPRA, begins in Buenos Aires, Argentina.

Art
Carlos Cruz-Diez begins work on his *Fisicromías* (Physichromies) series, blending aspects of painting and sculpture.

Kenneth Kemble organizes the Arte Destructivo exhibition in Argentina.
Julio Le Parc joins the Groupe de Recherche d'Art Visuel in Argentina.
Alejandro Otero works with Informal Abstraction in Paris.

Cinema
Cantinflas stars in *Pepe.*
Como el Uruguay no hay (There's Nowhere like Uruguay), directed by Ugo Ulive
Tire dié (Throw Me a Dime), directed by Fernando Birri

Photography
Sara Facio and Alicia D'Amico open a commercial studio in Buenos Aires, Argentina.

1961

Historical and Political Events
Latin American nations form a free-trade association.

Art
Luis Felipe Noé, *Convocación a la barbarie* (Call to Barbarism), neofigurative artwork
The Otra Figuración group exhibits for the first time in Buenos Aires, Argentina.

César Paternosto joins Grupo Si, an Informal Abstract group in Argentina.

Literature
Carlos Germán Belli, *¡Oh Hada Cibernética!* (Oh Cybernetic Sprite!)
Juan Carlos Onetti, *El astillero* (translated as *The Shipyard*)
Ernesto Sábato, *Sobre héroes y tumbas* (translated as *On Heroes and Tombs*)

1962

Historical and Political Events
National Front candidate Guillermo Léon Valencia becomes president of Colombia.

Art
Gonzalo Fonseca, *Orphic Paraphernalia,* sculpture
"Forma y Espacio" (Form and Space) international exhibition

is organized by the Rectángulo group in Chile.
Taller Torres-García closes.

Cinema
Los inundados (Flooded Out), directed by Fernando Birri

1963

Historical and Political Events
Arturo Illia becomes president of Argentina. Belaúnde Terry is elected president of Peru.

Art
Antonio Berni introduces his character Ramona Montiel, a courtesan, that he uses in a series of works.
Jorge de la Vega, *El espejo al final de la escalera* (The Mirror at the End of the Stairs), collage

Cinema
La pampa gringa, directed by Fernando Birri
Paula la cautiva (Captive Paula), directed by Fernando Ayala

Literature
Julio Cortázar, *Rayuela* (translated as *Hopscotch*)
Mario Vargas Llosa, *La ciudad y los perros* (translated as *The Time of the Hero*)

Theater
Egon Wolff, *Los invasores* (The Invaders)

1964

Historical and Political Events
Raúl Leoni becomes president of Venezuela. President Víctor Paz Estenssoro of Bolivia is overthrown in a military coup; over the next seven year the country is ruled by the military regimes of Generals René Barrientos, Alfredo Ovando Candia, and Juan José Torres. Christian Democrat Eduardo Frei becomes president of Chile.

Art
Jacobo Borges, *Ha comenzado el espectáculo* (The Show Has Begun)
Jesús Rafael Soto, *Cinco varillas grandes* (Five Large Rods), early kinetic sculpture

Cinema
Revolución (Revolution), directed by Jorge Sanjinés

1965

Art
Luis Camnitzer and Liliana Porter cofound the New York Graphic Workshop.
Marisol Escobar's installation *The Party* is exhibited in New York City.
Marta Minujín, *El batacazo* (The Long Shot), installation
Luis Felipe Noé, *Así es la vida, señorita* (That's Life, Miss), three-dimensional assemblage
César Paternosto begins to work with hard-edge abstraction.
Jorge de la Vega, *Vida cotidiana* (Everyday Life), satirical artwork

Ramón Vergara Grez's Chilean avant-garde group takes the name Forma y Espacio.

Cinema
¡Aysa! (Landslide!), directed by Jorge Sanjinés
Carlos: Cine-retrato de un caminante (Carlos: Film-Portrait of a Tramp), directed by Mario Handler
Hotel alojamiento (Hotel Lodging), directed by Fernando Ayala

Radio and Television
Paraguay begins television broadcasting.

1966

Historical and Political Events
President Arturo Illia of Argentina is deposed and succeeded by Gen. Juan Carlos Onganía. National Front candidate Carlos Lleras Restrepo is elected president of Colombia.

Architecture
Emilio Duhart designs the United Nations regional headquarters, the Comisión Económica Para América Latina (Economic Commission for Latin America), or CEPAL, building in Vitacura, Chile.

Art
Antonio Antúnez produces his series *Stadiums* in New York City.
Jacobo Borges begins work on his multimedia event *Imágenes de Caracas* (Images of Caracas).

Groupe de Recherche d'Art Visuel stages the happening *Day in the Street* in Paris.
Julio Le Parc wins Grand Prize for Painting at the Venice Biennial.
Marta Minujín, *Simultaneity on Simultaneity,* happening

Cinema
Elecciones (Elections), directed by Mario Handler and Ugo Ulive
La hora de los hornos (The Hour of the Furnaces), directed by Fernando Solanas and Octavio Getino of Cine Liberación
Jarawi, directed by Eulogio Nishiyama, Luis Figueroa, and César Villanueva of the Cuzco School
Ukumau (That's the Way It Is), directed by Jorge Sanjinés

Literature
Mario Vargas Llosa, *La casa verde* (translated as *The Green House*)

1967

Historical and Political Events
Ernesto "Che" Guevara is executed by government troops in Bolivia, where he has been leading revolutionary guerrillas. Oscar D. Gestido becomes president of Uruguay; he dies in December and is succeeded by Vice President Jorge Pacheco Areco. The 2,336-foot Angostura Bridge opens at Ciudad Bolívar, Venezuela.

Art
Fernando Botero, *La familia presidencial* (The Presidential Family)
Grupo VAN is formed in Ecuador in opposition to Indigenism.
Marta Minujín, *Minúfono,* conceptual installation

Cinema
Erase un niño, un guerrillero y un caballo (There Once was a Child, a Guerrilla, and a Horse), directed by Helvio Soto

The Viña del Mar Film Festival is organized in Chile by Aldo Francia.

Literature
Macedonio Fernández, *Museo de la novela de la Eterna* (Museum of the Novel of the Eternal Woman), published posthumously
Gabriel García Márquez, *Cien años de soledad* (translated as *One Hundred Years of Solitude*)
The first Premio Rómulo Gallegos de Novela is awarded to Peruvian Mario Vargas Llosa's *La casa verde* (translated as *The Green House*).

Photography
Grete Stern, *Los patios,* photography book

1968

Historical and Political Events
Union of Cuban Artists and Writers (UNEAC) awards Heberto Padilla a poetry prize but identifies him as a counterrevolutionary; in 1971 Padilla is arrested and forced to make a public confession of his politically incorrect views. The military government of Juan Velasco Alvarado takes control in Peru.

Architecture
Eladio Dieste's design is used in the construction of the Iglesia de San Pedro church in Durazno, Uruguay, which had been partially destroyed by fire.
Rogelio Salmona designs the Torres del Parque (Park Towers) buildings in Bogotá, Colombia.

Art
Casa de la Cultura de Quito organizes the First Quito Biennial and is opposed by Grupo VAN's Antibiennial in Ecuador.
Alberto Pérez's installation series *Barricada* shocks the Chilean public.
Roberto Plate's installation *El baño* (The Bathroom), at In-stituto Di Tella in Buenos Aires, Argentina, is censored by the police.
Fernando de Szyszlo, *Inkarri,* informal abstract painting

Cinema
A film festival is held in Mérida, Venezuela, following the success of the Viña del Mar Film Festival.
Me gustan los estudiantes (I Like Students), directed by Mario Handler
Tres tristes tigres (Three Trapped Tigers), directed by Raúl Ruiz
Valparaíso mi amor (Valparaíso My Love), directed by Aldo Francia

Literature
Leandro Katz, *Es una ola* (It's a Wave)

Photography
Sara Facio and Alicia D'Amico publish *Buenos Aires, Buenos Aires.*

1969

Historical and Political Events
Rafael Caldera becomes president of Venezuela.

Art
César Paternosto, *Oblique Vision* multicanvas series
Jesús Rafael Soto produces his first kinetic environment in his *Penetrable* series.

Cinema
Caliche sangriento (Blood Stained Mineral), directed by Helvio Soto

Don Segundo Sombra, directed by Manuel Antín
Yawar malku (Blood of the Condor), directed by Jorge Sanjinés

Dance
Danza L.U.Z. is founded in Maracaibo, Venezuela.

Literature
Manuel Puig, *Boquitas pintadas* (translated as *Heartbreak Tango*), subtitled folletín (serial)

1970s

Historical and Political Events
Many people in Chile and Argentina "disappear."

Literature
The dictatorship novel experiences its heyday.

1970

Historical and Political Events
La Guerra Sucia (The Dirty War) begins in Argentina and lasts until 1982. National Front candidate Misael Pastrana Borrero is elected president of Colombia. In May the most destructive earthquake in Western Hemisphere takes place in Peru, killing seventy thousand and injuring another fifty thousand. In November Salvador Allende takes office as president of Chile. The population of Latin America reaches 283.3 million.

Art
Luis Camnitzer, *Leftovers,* conceptual installation

Cinema
El chacal de Nahueltoro (The Jackal of Nahueltoro), directed by Miguel Littín

La colonia penal (The Penal Colony), directed by Raúl Ruiz

Liber Arce, liberarse (Liber Arce, Liberation), directed by Mario Handler
Los caminos de la muerte (Roads to Death) is begun by the Ukumau Group but is left unfinished.
La muralla verde (The Green Wall), directed by Armando Robles

Literature

1971

Historical and Political Events
Gen. Juan José Torres of Bolivia is overthrown by Col. Hugo Banzer Suárez.

Art
Víctor Grippo, *Analogía I* (Analogy I), conceptual installation
Alejandro Otero produces abstract "spatial sculptures" at Massachusetts Institute of Technology (MIT).

Cinema
El coraje del pueblo, (also released as *The Courage of the People* and *The Night of San Juan*), directed by Jorge Sanjinés with the Ukumau Group
Nadie dijo nada (Nobody Said Anything), directed by Raúl Ruiz
¿Qué es la democracia? (What is Democracy?), directed by Carlos Álvarez

1972

Historical and Political Events
President José María Velasco Ibarra of Ecuador is overthrown in a military coup led by Gen. Guillermo Rodríguez Lara. Juan María Bordaberry is elected president of Uruguay.

Art
Eduardo Ramírez Villamizar, *16 Torres* (16 Towers), monumental sculpture in Parque Nacional, Bogotá, Colombia

1973

Historical and Political Events
Héctor J. Cámpora becomes president of Argentina but steps aside in July so that Juan Domingo Perón can run for the office; Perón is elected in September. President Salvador Allende of Chile dies in a bloody September coup that brings to power Gen. Augusto Pinochet. A military junta takes power in Uruguay.

Art
Libero Badii, *Conocimientos siniestros* (Sinister Knowledge), sculpture series
Jacobo Borges, *Reunión con círculo rojo* (Meeting with Red Circle), painting
Fernando Botero begins to produce sculptures.

Cinema
El enemigo principal (The Principal Enemy), directed by Jorge Sanjinés
The Equipo Tercer Año group operates in Chile from February through September.

1974

Historical and Political Events
President Juan Domingo Perón of Argentina dies in July and is succeeded by his wife, Vice President Isabel Martínez de Perón. Liberal Party candidate Alfonso López Michelsen is elected president of Colombia. Carlos Andrés Pérez becomes president of Venezuela.

Art
Alejandro Otero's monumental sculpture *Ala Solar* (Solar

José Donoso, *El obsceno pájaro de la noche* (translated as *The Obscene Bird of Night*)
Testimonial narrative receives formal recognition as a genre.

Theater
Jorge Díaz founds the Teatro del Nuevo Mundo (New World Theater).

Literature
Alfredo Bryce Echenique's *Un mundo para Julius* (translated as *A World For Julius*) wins the 1972 National Prize for Literature in Peru.
Ariel Dorfman, *Para leer al Pato Donald* (translated as *How To Read Donald Duck*)
Eduardo Galeano, *Las venas abiertas de América Latina* (translated as *The Open Veins of Latin America*)
Pablo Neruda wins the Nobel Prize for literature.

Music
Mario Davidovsky wins the Pulitzer Prize for *Synchronism No. Six.*

Photography
Grete Stern, *Los aborígenes del Gran Chaco Argentino*

Cinema
La expropiación (The Expropriation), directed by Raúl Ruiz
El realismo socialista (Social Realism), directed by Raúl Ruiz

Literature
José Donoso, *Historia personal del "boom"* (translated as *The Spanish American "Boom": A Personal History*)

Metamorfosis del jefe de la policía política (Metamorphosis of the Political Police Chief), directed by Helvio Soto
Plantas: testimonio de un etnocidio (Plantas: Testimony about an Ethnocide), directed by Jorge Silva and Marta Rodríguez
Un sueño como de colores (Color-tinted Dreams), directed by Valeria Sarmiento

Dance
Contradanza is created by Hercilia López.

Literature
Julio Cortázar, *Libro de Manuel* (translated as *A Manual for Manuel*)
Jorge Edwards, *Persona Non Grata* (translated), criticism and exposé of Fidel Castro's suppressive government in Cuba

Photography
La Azotea Photographic Publishers is founded in Argentina by Sara Facio, Alicia D'Amico, and María Cristina Orive.

Wing) is installed in Bogotá, Colombia.
Marta Minujín begins her series of ephemeral monumental projects.
María Luisa Pacheco, *Catavi,* informal abstract painting

Cinema
Pueblo chico (Small Town), directed by Antonio Eguino
La tierra prometida (The Promised Land), directed by Miguel Littín

Dance
The Taller de Danza de Caracas is founded in Venezuela.

Literature
Augusto Roa Bastos, *Yo el Supremo* (translated as *I, the Supreme*), dictatorship novel
Rodrigo Rojas, *Jamás de rodillas* (Never on My Knees), testimonial narrative
Hernán Valdés, *Tejas Verdes: Diario de un campo de concentración*

1975

Art
Leandro Katz publishes the artist's book *Self-Hypnosis.*
Liliana Porter begins her *Magritte Series.*

Cinema
Actas de Marusia (Letters from Marusia), directed by Miguel Littín
Dos años en Finlandia (Two Years in Finland), directed by Angelina Vásquez
Los hijos del subdesarrollo (The Children of Underdevelopment), directed by Carlos Alvarez
Part I of *La batalla de Chile* (The Battle of Chile), a three-part

(translated as *Tejas Verdes: Diary of a Concentration Camp*), documentary narrative

Photography
Sara Facio publishes her series of photographs titled *Funerales.*

documentary directed by Patricio Guzmán with Equipo Tercer Año, is released.

Dance
Alejandro Cervera begins choreography.

Literature
Julio Cortázar, *Fantomas contra los vampiros multinacionales* (Fantomas against the Multinational Vampires)
Gabriel García Márquez, *El otoño del patriarca* (translated as *The Autumn of the Patriarch*), dictatorship novel
The Premio Miguel de Cervantes de Literatura for Spanish-language writers is instituted in Spain.

1976

Historical and Political Events
President Isabel Martínez de Perón of Argentina is overthrown in a military coup, and the generals who have been waging the Guerra Sucia (Dirty War) against leftist guerrillas since 1970 assume government of the country, continuing their systematic violation of human rights until 1982. Aparicio Mendez becomes president of Uruguay. Orlando Letelier, Chilean ambassador to the United States during the presidency of Salvador Allende and an outspoken critic of the government of Augusto Pinochet, is killed by a car bomb in Washington, D.C.

Cinema
Fuera de aquí (Get Out of Here), directed by Jorge Sanjinés
Los perros hambrientos (The Hungry Dogs), directed by Luis Figueroa

Dance
Compañía Nacional de Danza is founded in Quito, Ecuador.

Literature
Manuel Puig, *El beso de la mujer araña* (translated as *Kiss of the Spider Woman*)

1977

Art
Catalina Parra exhibits *Imbunches* in Chile.

Cinema
Muerte al amanecer (Death at Dawn), directed by Francisco Lombardi
El recurso del método (Reasons of State), directed by Miguel Littín

Dance
Ballet Contemporáneo del Teatro San Martín is founded in Buenos Aires, Argentina.

Literature
Rolando Carrasco, *Prigué* (translated as *Chile's Prisoners of War*), testimonial narrative
Aníbal Quijada Cerda, *Cerco de púas* (Barbed Wire), testimonial narrative
Mario Vargas Llosa, *La tía Julia y el escribidor* (translated as *Aunt Julia and the Scriptwriter*)

1978

Historical and Political Events
Julio César Turbay Ayala becomes president of Colombia. Hugo Banzer Suárez is force out of office by the military in Bolivia.

Art
Liliana Porter begins to produce silk-screened still lifes.

Cinema
Splits, directed by Leandro Katz
Org, directed by Fernando Birri

Dance
Estudio de Danza Contemporánea Melo Tomsich is opened in Cochabamba, Bolivia.

1979

Historical and Political Events
Luis Herrera Campins takes office as president of Venezuela. Jaime Roldós Aguilera becomes president of Ecuador.

Cinema
¡Basta ya! (That's Enough!), directed by Jorge Sanjinés

The Cuban Film Institute in Havana begins hosting the festival of the New Latin American Cinema.
Los hijos de Fierro (The Sons of Fierro), directed by Fernando Solanas
Julio comienza en julio (Julio begins in July), directed by Silvio Caiozzi

People from Everywhere, People from Nowhere, directed by Valeria Sarmiento
La viuda de Montiel (Montiel's Widow), directed by Miguel Littín

Photography

1980

Historical and Political Events
Fernando Belaúnde Terry is reelected as president of Peru after twelve years of military rule.

Art
Colectivo de Acciones de Arte is active in Chile.
César Paternosto, *Trilce II,* abstract geometric painting

Cinema
Muerte de un magnate (Death of a Magnate), directed by Francisco Lombardi

1981

Historical and Political Events
Celso Torrelio Villa becomes president of Bolivia. Osvaldo Hurtado Larrea becomes president of Ecuador. Gregorio Alvarez takes office as president of Uruguay.

Architecture
Rogelio Salmona's design is followed for the building of the Casa de Huéspedes Ilustres (Inn for Distinguished Guests) in Cartagena, Colombia.

Cinema
Nuestra voz de tierra, memoria, y futuro (Our Voice of Earth, Memory and Future), directed by Jorge Silva

1982

Historical and Political Events
Refusing to recognize British claims to the Malvinas (Falkland Islands), Argentina invades the disputed territory in April; Argentinean forces are defeated by the British and surrender in June. Belisario Betancur Cuartas becomes president of Colombia. Hernán Siles Zuazo becomes president of Bolivia.

Cinema
El hombre, cuando es hombre (Man, When He is A Man), directed by Valeria Sarmiento
Metropotamia, experimental film directed by Leandro Katz

1983

Historical and Political Events
After eight years of military rule, Argentineans elect Raúl Alfonsín president in December.

Art
Eugenio Dittborn begins his *Pinturas aeropostales* (Airmail Paintings) conceptual series.
Leandro Katz begins his *Orpheus Beheaded* multimedia installation.

Cinema
Camila, directed by María Luisa Bemberg

1984

Historical and Political Events
Jaime Lusinchi becomes president of Venezuela. León Febres Cordero becomes president of Ecuador.

The Asociación Argentina de Fotógrafos is founded in Buenos Aires, Argentina.

Radio and Television
Bolivia begins television broadcasting.

Yawar Fiesta, directed by Luis Figueroa

Dance
Ballet de la Fundación Teresa Carreño, which becomes Ballet Nacional de Caracas, is founded in Venezuela.
Ballet Metropolitano de Caracas is founded in Venezuela.
Danzahoy is founded in Caracas, Venezuela.

Literature
Ricardo Piglia, *Respiración artificial* (Artificial Respiration)

Dance
The Ballet Metropolitano de Caracas stages *The Nutcracker* in December.
Ballet Nuevo Mundo is founded in Caracas, Venezuela.

Photography
The Asociación de Fotógrafos Independientes is founded in Chile.
Paz Errázuriz begins her photographic project on psychiatric hospitals.

Presencia lejana (Distant Presence), directed by Angelina Vásquez

Dance
Ivan Nagy takes over as director of Ballet de Santiago.

Literature
Isabel Allende, *La casa de los espíritus* (translated as *The House of the Spirits*)
Mario Benedetti, *Primavera con una esquina rota* (Spring with a Broken Corner)

No habrá más penas ni olvido (A Funny, Dirty Little War), directed by Héctor Olivera

Dance
Coreoarte is founded in Venezuela.

Literature
Luisa Valenzuela, *Cola de lagartija* (translated as *The Lizard's Tail*)

Music
Alberto Ginastera dies.

Art
Luis Camnitzer, *From the Uruguayan Torture,* conceptual photoetchings

Cinema

Amargo mar (Bitter Sea), directed by Antonio Eguino
Cómo aman los chilenos (How Chileans Love), directed by A. Alvarez
Notre mariage (Our Marriage), directed by Valeria Sarmiento
Pasajeros de una pesadilla (Passengers in a Nightmare), directed by Fernando Ayala
Les trois Couronnes du marin (*The Three Crowns of the Sailor*), directed by Raúl Ruiz

Dance

Danza Teatro Abelardo Gameche is founded in Venezuela.

Literature

Colección Archivos, the editorial project to establish, document, and promote knowledge of major works of twentieth-century Latin American literature, is instituted.

1985

Historical and Political Events

The commission headed by Ernesto Sábato makes public a report, *Nunca más* (translated as *Never Again*), that holds Argentinean military forces responsible for thousands of "disappearances" of presumed political enemies during the Guerra Sucia (Dirty War). The Bolivian Congress elects Víctor Paz Estenssoro president after neither he nor the person winning the most votes, Hugo Banzer Suárez, wins a majority of the popular vote in the presidential election. Julio María Sanguinetti is inaugurated president of Uruguay after twelve years of military rule. In Peru Alan García Pérez is elected president. Eruption of a volcano in Colombia leaves twenty-five thousand dead or missing in November.

Cinema

Los hijos de la guerra fría (Children of the Cold War), directed by G. Lustiniano
Nueva Fundación de Cine Latinoamericano (New Latin Amer-

ican Film Foundation) is established in Havana, Cuba, by Gabriel García Márquez.
Otra historia de amor (Another Love Story), directed by Américo Ortiz Zárate

Cinema and Music

Tangos, el exilio de Gardel (Tangos, the Exile of Gardel), directed by Fernando Solanas

Dance

Acción Colectiva is founded in Caracas, Venezuela.
Karin Schmidt begins her activity in Bolivia and founds Draga Danza.

Literature

Antonio Skármeta, *Ardiente paciencia* (translated as *Burning Patience*)

1986

Historical and Political Events

Virgilio Barco Vargas becomes president of Colombia.

Art

Alfredo Jaar, *Oro en la mañana* (Gold in the Morning), conceptual installation
Liliana Porter, *Triptych,* mixed media work

Cinema

Gerónima, directed by Raúl A. Tosso
La historia oficial (The Official Story), directed by Luis Puenzo
Hombre mirando al sudeste (*Man Facing Southeast*), directed by Eliseo Subiela

Perros de la noche (The Dogs of Night), directed by Teo Kofman

Dance

Danza Contemporánea de Maracaibo is founded in Venezuela.
Danzahoy begins its residency in Teatro Teresa Carreño in Caracas, Venezuela.

Literature

Jorge Luis Borges dies.
Alvaro Mutis, *La nieve del Almirante* (translated as *The Snow of the Admiral*)

1987

Art

Eugenio Dittborn, *Historia de la física* (History of Physics), Video Art work
Alfredo Jaar's *A Logo for America* is broadcast in Times Square, New York City.
Guillermo Kuitca, *El mar dulce,* painting

Dance

Asociación Amigos del Ballet del Sur is established in Bahía Blanca, Argentina.

Literature

Amnesty International awards the Golden Flame prize to Mario Benedetti's *Primavera con una esquina rota* (1982; Spring with a Broken Corner).
Mario Vargas Llosa, *El hablador* (1987; translated as *The Storyteller*)

1988

Historical and Political Events

Rodrigo Borja Cevallos becomes president of Ecuador. Luis Alberto Lacalle takes office as president of Uruguay.

Cinema

La boca del lobo (The Mouth of the Wolf), directed by

FranciscoLombardi
Juliana, feature film by the Grupo Chaski
Sur (Southside), directed by Fernando Solanas
Técnicas de duelo (A Matter of Honor), directed by Sergio Cabrera

1989

Historical and Political Events

Paraguay dictator Alfredo Stroessner is overthrown in Febru-

ary, after thirty-five years in office; he is replaced by Gen. Andrés Rodríguez. In May Argentineans elect Peronist Carlos Saúl Menem president. Colombian presidential candidate

Luis Carlos Galán is assassinated in August, as President Virgilio Barco Vargas vows to crack down on the drug cartels that have murdered scores of government officials and newspaper editors. In December Patricio Aylwin is elected president of Chile, to succeed Gen. Augusto Pinochet, who remains as military chief of staff. Carlos Andrés Pérez becomes president of Venezuela.

Art
César Paternosto publishes a book on Inca sculpture, *Piedra*

1990

Historical and Political Events
César Gavira Trujillo becomes president of Colombia. Alberto Fujimori becomes president of Peru, after defeating novelist Mario Vargas Llosa. Patricio Aylwin is inaugurated as president of Chile.

Cinema
Amelia López O'Neill, directed by Valeria Sarmiento

1991

Art
Liliana Porter, *The Simulacrum*

1992

Historical and Political Events
President Alberto Fujimori of Peru suspends the constitution and assumes dictatorial powers in April, as he struggles against the powerful Sendero Luminoso (Shining Path) revolutionaries; in September Lima police capture Sendero Luminoso leader Abimael Guzmán Reynoso. Sixto Durán Ballén becomes president of Ecuador.

Dance
Casa de la Danza opens in Quito, Ecuador.

1993

Historical and Political Events
Gonzalo Sánchez de Lazada takes office as president of Bolivia. Juan Carlos Wasmosy becomes president of Paraguay.

Cinema
La estrategia del caracol (1993; The Snail's Strategy), directed by Sergio Cabrera, wins a Colón de Oro prize at the Huelva Film Festival in Spain.

1994

Historical and Political Events
Ernesto Samper Pizano becomes president of Colombia.

abstracta, la escultura Inca: Una vision contemporánea (Abstract Stone).

Cinema
Old Gringo, directed by Luis Puenzo
Tiempo de morir (A Time to Die), directed by Jorge Alí Triana

Literature
Antonio Skármeta returns to Chile from exile.

Sandino, directed by Miguel Littín

Photography
Paz Errázuriz, *Chile From Within, 1973–1988*
Paz Errázuriz publishes photographs of marginal people in *La manzana de Adán* (Adam's Apple).

Music
When Claudio Arrau dies, the Chilean government declares a day of national mourning.

Literature
Gonzalo Rojas is awarded the first Spanish Reina Sofía Prize for poetry.

Music
Astor Piazzola dies.

Dance
The Americas Center division of the World Dance Alliance holds its first biennial meeting in New York City.

Music
Atahualpa Yupanqui dies.

Eduardo Frei Ruíz Tagle takes office as president of Chile.

DICTIONARY OF

TWENTIETH CENTURY CULTURE

Hispanic Culture of South America

A

ACCIÓN COLECTIVA

This contemporary dance company based in Caracas, Venezuela, was founded in 1985 by Venezuelan dancer-choreographer Carlos Orta, choreographer Diane Noya, and British-born dancer-choreographer Julie Barnsley. The company's artistic adviser is Venezuelan painter Alirio Palacios. As many as ten dancers form the corps, whose artistic statement describes the spiritual dimension as its highest priority, technical virtuosity being only one of the elements called upon to express that spirituality. Acción Colectiva follows the broad lines of expressionism and dance theater. The artistic mission states that dancers in the company will dance like "thinking beings," not "marionettes," and that their use of "tragic humor" will reject beauty and the smoothness of the formalism of classical dance in favor of the "honest expression of daily human life." Choreographers featured in the repertoire include Barnsley, Noya, Lisa Bleyer, and Celeste Hastings.

— J.M.H. & N.D.B.

WALTER ACHUGAR

A Uruguayan film distributor and producer, Walter Achugar (1938–) has been closely involved with the **New Latin American Cinema.** He, along with Argentinean Eduardo Pallero, was a managing producer of a series of films entitled *Latin America Seen by Its Filmmakers,* funded in the early 1970s by RAI-TV, the Italian state-run broadcasting system. Because of political and budgetary problems, only one of the intended six films made it to the big screen: *El coraje del pueblo* (1971; also released as *The Courage of the People* and *The Night of San Juan*), by **Jorge Sanjinés** and the **Ukumau** group of Bolivia. The promotion and distribu-

tion of Latin American cinema have kept Achugar on the move throughout the Americas, Europe, and beyond. Since the early 1960s, political and economic vicissitudes have compelled him to shift his home base from Uruguay to Argentina, then to Venezuela, and later to Spain, where he lived for nearly a decade before a more hospitable political climate permitted him to move back to Montevideo, Uruguay, in 1985.

REFERENCE:

Julianne Burton, ed., *Cinema and Social Change in Latin America: Conversations with Latin American Filmmakers* (Austin: University of Texas Press, 1986).

— S.M.H.

MARTÍN ADÁN

Martín Adán is the pen name of Rafael de la Fuente Benavides (1908–1984), one of the founders of modern Peruvian poetry and author of the avant-garde poetic sketch *Casa de cartón* (1928; Cardboard House). The sonnets of *Travesía de extramares* (1950; Overseas Crossing) best exemplify Adán's baroque and hermetic style. His long poem *La mano desasida* (1964; The Unclasped Hand) is a tribute to the Peruvian monument Machu Picchu, the Inca fortress discovered by American archaeologist Hiram Bingham in 1911 and exalted by **Pablo Neruda** in the second section of his *Canto general* (1950).

REFERENCES:

James Higgins, *The Poet in Peru* (Liverpool: Francis Cairns, 1982);

Mirko Lauer, *Los exilios interiores: una introducción a Martín Adán* (Lima: Hueso Húmero, 1983).

— R.G.M.

3

Jorge Enrique Adoum

Jorge Enrique Adoum (1926–), born of Lebanese immigrants in the small town of Ambato, is Ecuador's major living writer, having distinguished himself in the fields of poetry, narrative, and drama. In the 1940s Adoum belonged to the Madrugada (Dawn) poetic group in Ecuador and served briefly as **Pablo Neruda**'s private secretary. In fact, it is as a poet that Adoum is best known to his compatriots. His first major poetic work was the four-volume *Cuadernos de la tierra* (Earth Notebooks). The first two titles appeared in 1952 and were later disowned by the author on account of their rhetorical (mostly Nerudian) ballast. The third notebook, *Dios trajo la sombra* (God Brought Shadow), won the prestigious Cuban **Casa de las Américas** Prize in 1960. The theme of the book is the historical encounter between the Spanish conquistador and the Andean Indian, represented in an antiepic, demystified manner, with anthropological undertones. The final volume of the *Cuadernos* — Eldorado y las ocupaciones nocturnas (El Dorado and Nocturnal Occupations) — appeared in 1968 and prolongs the historical vein of the author's poetry. With *Informe personal de la situación* (1973; Personal Report on the Situation) Adoum's poetry becomes experimental.

In 1979 a compilation of Adoum's poems dating back to 1949 appeared in Spain as *No son todos los que están* (Not All Are Here That Are). In 1992 Adoum brought out a comprehensive anthology of modern Ecuadoran poetry, *Poesía ecuatoriana: siglo XX*. Adoum's latest collection of poetry is *Del amor desenterrado y otros poemas* (1993; Of Love Unearthed and Other Poems). The title refers to the "lovers of Sumpa," a couple who died in remote times locked in an embrace and whose skeletal remains were recently exhumed by archaeologists.

Adoum's best-known novel is *Entre Marx y una mujer desnuda* (1976; Between Marx and a Naked Woman), a work that pokes fun at the concerns of the New Left in the late 1960s. The author currently lives in Quito after decades of residence in Paris, where he worked for UNESCO.

REFERENCES:

Antonio Sacoto, *Novelas claves de la literatura ecuatoriana* (Cuenca, Ecuador: Universidad de Cuenca, 1990);

Saúl Yurkievich, "De lo lúcido y lo lúdico," in his *La confabulación por la palabra* (Madrid: Taurus, 1978).

— R.G.M.

Demetrio Aguilera Malta

Ecuadoran novelist, playwright, and painter Demetrio Aguilera Malta (1909–1981) is best known for *Siete lunas y siete serpientes* (1970; translated as *Seven Serpents and Seven Moons*), a standard example of **magical realism.** This novel is set in a rural community dominated by a lustful cacique and is told through myth and legend. Its undertone of social protest connects the novel with the author's earlier works, *Don Goyo* (1933) — set in the coastal region of Ecuador — and *Canal Zone* (1935), an anti-imperialist tract motivated by the control of the Panama Canal Zone by the United States. Aguilera Malta has also written historical novels, two of which are *Manuela la caballeresa del sol* (1964; Manuela the Lady of the Sun) — dealing with Simón Bolívar's lover Manuela Sáenz — and *Un nuevo mar para el rey* (1965; A New Sea for the King), based on the exploits of Vasco Núñez de Balboa, the discoverer of the Pacific Ocean. *El secuestro del general* (1973; translated as *Babelandia*) is the author's **dictatorship novel.**

REFERENCE:

Antonio Fama, *Realismo mágico en la narrativa de Aguilera-Malta* (Madrid: Playor, 1977).

— R.G.M.

Aguinaldo

The aguinaldo is a religious folk song prominent in much of Latin America. A descendant of the Spanish **villancico,** which could express either sacred or secular texts, the aguinaldo is closely associated with the Christmas season, and in some countries the term *aguinaldo* refers to a Christmas gift that may vary from a seasonal delicacy to a salary bonus. As a folk genre, the aguinaldo presents a rather straightforward melody, not adventurous in terms of chromaticisms but reflecting the vital rhythms of other Latin American music. Its formal structure is based on the alternation of an *estribillo* (choral refrain) and *coplas* (verses).

REFERENCE:

Gerard Béhague, "Latin American Folk Music," in *Folk and Traditional Music of the Western Continents* by Bruno Nettl, third edition, revised and edited by Valerie Woodring Goertzen (Englewood Cliffs, N.J.: Prentice-Hall, 1990).

— R.L.S.

Delmira Agustini

Uruguayan poet Delmira Agustini (1886–1914) wrote during the period immediately following the heyday of **Modernismo** and was noted as much for her poetry as for her tragically brief life, prematurely brought to an

Delmira Agustini

REFERENCE:

Sidonia C. Rosenbaum, *Modern Women Poets of Spanish America* (New York: Hispanic Institute in the United States, 1945).
— R.G.M.

ALFAR

Alfar was an avant-garde monthly founded in September 1923 in La Coruña, Spain, by the Uruguayan consul J. J. Casal. After a hiatus in publication (October 1927–February 1929) the magazine was relocated to Montevideo. *Alfar* appeared without interruption until 1955, but the review lost its avant-garde identity and literary importance in its Atlantic crossing.
— R.G.M.

ISABEL ALLENDE

Chilean author Isabel Allende (1943–) is well known for her best-selling novels, such as *La casa de los espíritus* (1982; translated as *The House of the Spirits*), *De amor y de sombra* (1984; translated as *Of Love and Shadows*), *Eva Luna* (1988), *Cuentos de Eva Luna* (1989; translated as *Stories of Eva Luna*), and *El plan infinito* (1991; translated as *The Infinite Plan*). Her characteristic style is an uncritical strain of **magical realism,** especially prevalent in the first of her novels (which is closely and self-consciously related to **Gabriel García Márquez**'s *One Hundred Years of Solitude*) and in the Eva Luna cycle. In *De amor y de sombra* Allende tries her hand at a more documentary style of narration in order to explore human relationships in the context of a repressive dictatorship. *El plan infinito* is the author's first novel set in the United States, where she has lived since the mid 1980s. All of Allende's works are unified by the presence of a female storyteller, a kind of authorial persona who manifests herself even when the narrative is in the third person. In *De amor y de sombra,* for example, the impersonal narrative is preceded by a short note portraying the (implicit) author as the confidante of people who tell her their stories in the hope of preserving them from oblivion. *Eva Luna* is explicitly modeled after Scheherazade, the archetypal female storyteller.

Isabel Allende was born in Peru but in early childhood moved to Chile. Her father was Tomás Allende, first cousin to President **Salvador Allende** and a diplomat attached to the Chilean embassy in Lima. Her stepfather, Ramón Huidobro, is a veteran diplomat and was one of Salvador Allende's foreign policy advisers in the years of the Popular Unity gov-

end by her estranged husband who then killed himself. Agustini was brought up in a well-to-do family and educated at home. She was quick to learn the role she would play into her twenties, that of spoiled child of the bourgeoisie whose eccentricities sometimes alarmed relatives and friends. Her poetry is decidedly sensual and sometimes more explicit than social morality allowed. The seemingly spontaneous passion of Agustini's poetry — embodied in dreams, yearnings, and visions and intensified by the frequent use of direct address — more than makes up for its formal deficiencies. Agustini lived long enough to publish three books: *El libro blanco* (1907; The White Book), *Cantos de la mañana* (1910; Morning Songs), and *Los cálices vacíos* (1913; The Empty Chalices). Other poems were published posthumously in 1924 in the two volumes of her complete works, *El rosario de Eros* (The Rosary of Eros) and *Los astros del abismo* (The Stars of the Abyss).

Isabel Allende

ernment (1970–1973). Isabel Allende lived and practiced journalism in Chile until the mid 1970s, a period of severe military repression that forced thousands of Chileans into exile as many others were imprisoned, tortured, and "disappeared." Allende moved to Caracas, Venezuela, and later took up residence in San Rafael, California. In 1994 she won the recently instituted Gabriela Mistral Prize in Chile in recognition of her literary prominence throughout the world. Also in 1994 Allende published *Paula* (translated), an autobiographical account motivated by the death of her daughter from a rare disease.

REFERENCE:

Patricia Hart, *Narrative Magic in the Fiction of Isabel Allende* (Rutherford, N.J.: Fairleigh Dickinson University Press, 1989).

— R.G.M.

SALVADOR ALLENDE

Chilean physician and politician Salvador Allende (1908–1975) was elected president of the nation in 1970 after running unsuccessfully in three previous elections. He was the only Marxist candidate in Latin America to be elected to the highest national office through democratic constitutional procedures. Allende helped found the Chilean Socialist Party (1933) and occupied various political and governmental positions before 1970, when he won the three-way election with 36.3 percent of the vote. Ominously, his government coalition of left-of-center parties (Popular Unity) never obtained more than 49.7 percent of the popular vote in local or regional elections, a fact that conspired against the successful implementation of Allende's policies.

Allende's platform of radical change by legal means (including nationalization of the copper, coal, and steel industries; expropriation of foreign firms such as ITT and

Ford; land reform; and state control of banking) met with the skepticism of the militant wing of Popular Unity and with the downright hostility of traditional party elements, the military, and the U.S. government, which repeatedly tried to sabotage Allende's programs, either by overt actions (withholding loans from international banks and discouraging private investment) or covert ones involving the CIA. By mid 1973 the economic and political situation of the country had irreparably deteriorated. Inflation was rampant, the opposition was more and more intransigent, and massive street demonstrations had become routine. On 11 September 1973 the Chilean air force bombed and nearly demolished the presidential palace. Allende died either by his own hand or at the hands of military officers. The brutal coup that put Gen. **Augusto Pinochet** in power took the lives of thousands and dealt a mortal blow to Chile's long democratic tradition that until then had been upheld by a highly professional army.

REFERENCE:

James R. Whelan, *Allende: Death of a Marxist Dream* (Westport, Conn.: Arlington House, 1981).

— R.G.M.

Julio Alpuy

JULIO ALPUY

Uruguayan artist Julio Alpuy (1919–) was a member of the **Taller Torres-García** (TTG). He studied with **Joaquín Torres-García** and participated in all the TTG's activities, including the project for the Saint Bois Hospital, to which he contributed two murals. After Torres-García's death in 1949, Alpuy left Uruguay and traveled throughout Europe and the Near East. He returned to Uruguay in 1953, where he taught at the TTG and produced a series of mural paintings for the Liceo Larrañaga and the Asociación Cristiana de Jóvenes. During these years he worked within the parameters of **Constructive Art,** applying the combination of orthogonal structures and geometric archetypes typical of the TTG to diverse media, such as mosaics, furniture design, and pottery.

Alpuy left Uruguay once again in 1957. He lived in Colombia from 1957 to 1959, and in Caracas for a year, until he received a scholarship to work at the New School for Social Research of New York. Eventually he settled in New York, where he still lives. During the 1960s Alpuy abandoned the style of the TTG and began to produce paintings such as *La edad primaria* (1963; The Primal Age) and wood reliefs such as *Génesis I* (1964), which depict people living in natural states in primordial landscapes. His figurative style retains the geometric simplification of Constructive Art but also emphasizes the curvilinear patterns of natural forms.

REFERENCE:

Mari Carmen Ramírez, ed., *The Taller Torres-García: The School of the South and Its Legacy* (Austin: University of Texas Press, 1992).

— F.B.N.

CARLOS ALVAREZ

Carlos Alvarez (1938?–) was one of the most outspoken documentary filmmakers of the late 1960s in Colombia, openly supporting the militant radical tendencies in Latin American cinema such as are found in the work of Uruguayan **Mario Handler** and the Argentinean **Cine Liberación.** His most widely disseminated film was *¿Qué es la democracia?* (1971; What is Democracy?), which analyzed the Colombian elections of 1970. This documentary pointed to the widespread abstention in voting, the fact that many presidents had been previous ambassadors in Washington, and the domination of national political life by a few families. Soon after the film was released, Alvarez was arrested together with his wife, the filmmaker Julia Alvarez, on suspicion of being members of the guerrilla organization, the Ejército de Liberación Nacional (Army of National Liberation), or ELN. He was in prison from July 1972 to January 1974, when he was pardoned. Shortly after his release from prison, Alvarez made a documentary, *Los hijos del subdesarrollo* (1975; The Children of Underdevelopment), which examines the conditions causing thousands of Colombian children to die of malnutrition. He actively supported what he called an "imperfect" and "third" cinema, by which he meant a type of film technique which rejects the formal perfection of Hollywood-style movies, and instead espouses a more earthy focus better suited to the everyday reality of Third World Latin America.

REFERENCE:

John King, *Magical Reels: A History of Cinema in Latin America* (London & New York: Verso, 1990).

— S.M.H.

AMAUTA

Amauta was a Peruvian monthly (1926–1930) founded by **José Carlos Mariátegui** and committed to the diffusion of new ideas in the social sciences and the arts that would help realize the socialist transformation of Peru. *Amauta,* whose title means "priest" or "sage" in Quechua, was tremendously influential throughout Latin America. One of its themes was the vindication of indigenous cultures and the recuperation of autochthonous social and political values. Another was the importance given to avant-garde literature, which Mariátegui interpreted as the demise of the bourgeoisie and the harbinger of a new social order. Surrealism in particular was identified as a transcendental revolution of the spirit, whose aim was the creation of a society free from oppression.

REFERENCE:

Alberto Tauro, *'Amauta' y su influencia* (Lima: Amauta, 1971).
— R.G.M.

ALBALUCÍA ANGEL

Colombian novelist Albalucía Angel (1939–) is best known for *Estaba la pájara pinta sentada en el verde limón* (1975; The Speckled Bird Was Perched on the Lemon Tree), a kind of revolutionary bildungsroman (or novel of education) that narrates the heroine's rejection of the social order to which the hero of the traditional bildungsroman aspires to integrate himself. The title of the novel is from a children's ditty, and its epigraph (from Dylan Thomas) indicates the disloca-

tions to which the temporal sequence of narrated events is subjected in the novel: "The memories of childhood have no order and no end." The novel, which is presented in the form of a collage of voices, spans over a quarter of a century of the protagonist's life, which is interspersed with events from contemporary Colombian history, sometimes quoted from news reports and other documentary sources. Some of the key experiences that shape the protagonist's life are her discovery of sexual gratification, her rejection of the social pretensions of her class and family, and her political engagement against the forces of repression.

Other works by Angel are *Misiá Señora* (1982; Madame Lady) and *Las andariegas* (1984; The Rovers).

REFERENCE:

María Mercedes Jaramillo, Angela Inés Robledo, and Flor María Rodríguez-Arenas, *¿Y las mujeres? Ensayos sobre literatura colombiana* (Medellín, Colombia: Editorial Universidad de Antioquía, 1991).
— R.G.M.

ANGEL MALO

Angel Malo (Bad Angel) was the most popular soap opera ever made in Chile. Originally a Brazilian soap, it was Chileanized by Jorge Díaz, who did such a good job that its foreign roots are hardly discernible. During a four-month television run of about one hundred hours in the first half of 1986, *Angel Malo* averaged more than a 60 percent share of the national audience in the ratings and attracted nearly a 90 percent share of viewers for certain episodes. Remarkably enough, it was made for and shown on channel 13, which is owned and operated by the Catholic Church. The director of dramatic productions on channel 13, Ricardo Miranda, had decided to produce "telenovela" (soap opera) series in the mid 1970s, since Mexican soaps were too violent and the Brazilian variety too "tropical" for Chilean tastes. *Angel Malo* tells the story of an ambitious, ruthless nanny who sets out to marry her employer; in order to make her dream come true, she is prepared to lie to, manipulate, and even destroy anyone who gets in her way. The subplots reinforce the main plot: brothers who steal each other's fiancées and then discard them; a father-in-law who ruins the economic future of his son-in-law; the stealing of documents through greed; and a nanny who implicates her brother as an accomplice in her marriage schemes. A secret of the soap's success was its ability to delve into provocative themes not normally treated on Chilean television; especially provocative was its treatment of the relationship between social classes in contemporary Chile. Thus, when the protagonist, Nice, is asked why she wants to marry her employer, Roberto, she answers: "I want luxury, money, marriage. . . . I want to stop being a nanny and have others serve me." Perhaps even more revolutionary was her later comment to her brother Luis: "The rich are easy to control because they are self-absorbed and underestimate us [the poor]. They forget that we see, we hear, we think." Nice's scheme eventually comes to fruition; she marries Roberto after tricking him into thinking that his girlfriend has another lover. But Nice, a Chilean Scarlet O'Hara, is eventually discomfited; she becomes pregnant, her husband falls out of love with her, and, in the penultimate episode, she dies in childbirth.

REFERENCE:
Gertrude Yeager, "*Angel Malo* [Bad Angel], A Chilean Telenovela," *Studies in Latin American Popular Culture,* 9 (1990): 249–262.
                                                                                        — S.M.H.

Nemesio Antúnez

The Chilean Nemesio Antúnez (1918–) is an important figurative artist who has also directed several Chilean art institutions. Antúnez studied architecture in Santiago and in New York, where he turned to painting and began working at the Stanley W. Hyter graphic workshop. After his return to Santiago in 1953 he founded and directed Taller 99, which soon became part of the Universidad Católica. During this period Antúnez produced his series of paintings called *Bicycles* and *Tablecloths,* featuring spoons and knifes floating over undulating tablecloth patterns, which reflected his interest in Op Art and **Geometric Abstraction.** The fluid treatment of space and the odd combination of objects also connect his work with **Surrealism.** In the early 1960s, Antúnez also produced a series of lyrical landscapes. In 1961 he was appointed director of the Museo de Arte Contemporáneo of the Universidad de Chile, but he resigned in 1964 to become the Cultural Attaché of the Chilean Embassy in New York, where he painted the mural landscape *The Heart of the Andes* (1966) for the United Nations building.

In New York, Antúnez produced a series called *Stadiums,* including *New York, New York, 10008* (1967), which continued his tendency to combine a geometric treatment of space with a surrealist juxtaposition of images. In his compositions Antúnez created vertical and horizontal translucent planes with thin lines, suggesting the divisions of football fields. A multitude of minute beings stand crowded, trapped between the planes as in a prison yard, anonymous individuals dwarfed by New York's gigantic scale as observed by Antúnez from a high-rise building in Manhattan.

After Antúnez returned to Santiago in 1969, he became the director of the Museo de Bellas Artes, turning it into an active cultural center, but he resigned in 1973 and left for Europe, living in Catalonia, London, and Rome. His continuing series of *Stadiums* acquired a tragic dimension: *Estadio negro* (1977; Black Stadium) stands as a powerful metaphor for the assassination of political prisoners in a Santiago stadium during the 1973 military coup. Other important series during the 1970s and 1980s featured landscapes, tango dancers, beds, and love rituals. In 1983 Antúnez returned once more to Santiago and organized a new Taller 99.

REFERENCE:
Lowery S. Sims, "New York Dada and New World Surrealism," in *The Latin American Spirit: Art and Artists in the United States, 1920–1970,* by Luis R. Cancel and others (New York: Bronx Museum of the Arts / Abrams, 1988).
                                                                                        — F.B.N.

Architecture

At the beginning of the twentieth century the dominant architectural styles in Spanish America were of European origin. After independence from Spain, Spanish baroque architecture was rejected in favor of French neoclassicism, which became associated with the ideas of the French Revolution. French beaux arts architecture remained popular until the first decades of the twentieth century, when it was replaced by a variety of historical revival styles, which prescribed neo-Gothic architecture for churches, neo-Greek for educational institutions, and neo-Roman for courts and banks. During these years Art Nouveau and Spanish neocolonial revival also had a brief period of popularity in several countries. In Latin America the interest in modern architecture, also called rational or functional architecture, began in the 1920s with Gregorio Warchavchik's functionalist manifesto (1929) in Brazil, Jose Villagrán García's work in Mexico, the Alberto Horacio Prebisch and Ernesto Vautier utopian projects in Argentina, and the work of Sergio Larraín in Chile. Although noted French architect Le Corbusier visited Latin America in 1929, modern architecture did not become viable until the following decade and then only as one more style in the general eclecticism.

In the 1930s economic pressures pushed large sections of the rural population to migrate to the main urban areas, which, together with the influx of European immigrants, resulted in marginal poor neighborhoods in a vernacular style of architecture, constructed by using traditional local techniques and materials but

Amancio Williams's Casa del Puente (1943–1945; Bridge House) in Mar del Plata, Argentina

without professional advice. By contrast, most middle-income families lived in nicer suburbs, in housing usually constructed by Italian builders who followed Mediterranean models and used Italian neoclassic ornamentation. The accelerated urban growth encouraged important urban architectural projects which, during the 1940s and 1950s, established modern architecture as the dominant style. In Argentina, among the first notable modern buildings were Prebisch's movie theater Grand Rex (1937) and Gregorio Sánchez, Julio Lagos, and José María de la Torres's Kavanagh building (1934–1936), an imposing high-rise apartment building. During the same period, modern architecture was introduced into Uruguay by architects interested in renewing the earlier beaux arts style, such as Julio Vilamanjó, who designed the Facultad de Ingeniería (College of Engineering) of the Universidad de Montevideo (1930), an austere but innovative building featuring Le Corbusier's pilotis (thin columns). **Joaquín Torres-García,** the influential Uruguayan artist, sought to integrate **Constructive Art** and architecture; among the few real results are the **Taller Torres-García**'s murals in the Saint Bois Hospital and other works by this

group incorporated into homes designed by the architect Mario Payssé Reyes. In Chile the reaction against neoclassical architecture began in the late 1920s with Sergio Larraín's efforts as professor of architecture in the Universidad Católica and through works of his such as the Edificio Oberpaur (1928–1929). In Venezuela the discovery of oil in 1917 gave rise to a period of rapid growth in Caracas, with numerous poor neighborhoods springing up around the city; later on, detailed city-planning projects were launched to replace them with large housing developments designed according to the principles of rational functionalism by architects often trained in the United States.

After returning from Europe in 1928, **Carlos Villanueva** began his brilliant carreer in Caracas. His first important commission was the Plaza. de Toros (Bullring) in Maracay, in which he combined traditional design with modern construction methods such as the use of concrete. His ambitious design for the Ciudad Universitaria (University Campus) of the Universidad Central de Caracas was begun in 1944. It is an example of large-scale urbanism comparable to two other important projects that took place later during the 1960s: the Ciudad Universitaria in Mexico City and the construction of Brasilia. Villanueva organized the campus into activity zones, such as the central covered plaza connected to the rest of the buildings by covered walks, which provide protection from the tropical sun. The Aula Magna, a remarkable feat of engineering, features a plaster ceiling animated by dramatic acoustical clouds designed by Alexander Calder, while the Olympic Stadium also makes daring use of reinforced concrete for the cantilevered roof, which seems to float over the grandstand.

During the 1940s and 1950s Villanueva, like many other Latin American architects, began to question the adaptability of modern international architecture to the Latin American context, in which technological capabilities were lower and topographical, climatic, and economic needs more varied. For this reason these architects attempted to combine the construction methods and materials of traditional vernacular architecture, which were economically more efficient, with the abstract treatment of form that characterized rational architecture; it was a process that culminated two decades later with the works of **Eladio Dieste** and **Rogelio Salmona.** After the mid 1940s, construction increased enormously, in part because of the massive housing developments funded by populist governments. In Argentina the administration of **Juan Domingo Perón** sponsored large residential projects but did not include the participation of any of the skilled architectural studios (such as those of José Aslan and Héctor T. Ezcurra and the Estudio SEPRA) which became very successful during this period. Official architecture turned grandiloquent, as can be seen in the massive building for the **Eva Perón** Foundation in Buenos Aires (now the university's College of Engineering), while the state's numerous housing developments favored standardized chalet styles of mediocre design quality. Some of the most innovative work during this period was left to independent architects such as **Amancio Williams,** whose Casa del Puente (1943–1945; Bridge House) was supported by a concrete bridge extended over a stream bed, effectively merging the house with nature. The most serious challenge to rationalist architecture, however, was the building of the Banco de Londres y América del Sur (1960–1966), designed by the artist and architect Clorindo Testa together with the Estudio SEPRA. The building is enveloped by sculptural shapes of molded concrete, in a style related to **Geometric Abstraction** in which it is difficult to distinguish between decoration and support.

In Uruguay there were also several housing projects carried out during the military dictatorship of the 1970s, but the state paid little attention to the quality of

Uruguayan architecture: parks fell into decay, and historic sites were demolished and replaced by mediocre buildings. On the other hand, alternative cooperative organizations, which sought the advice of capable professionals, funded numerous lower- and middle-class neighborhoods, such as Ayuda Mutua Mesa 1 (1971–1975). Many of these highly successful residential complexes emphasized privacy as well as communal space, while combining a modern understanding of form with the use of local traditional materials, such as brick. A similar hybrid approach was followed by the engineer Eladio Dieste, whose work marked an important break with rational architecture. His Church of San Pedro in Durazno (1967–1971) features a brick, self-sustaining vault which seems to float over the natural light that enters the central space through the clerestory. The austerity of the forms is balanced by the rich texture of the brick walls and the remarkable treatment of natural light.

In Chile since the 1950s many housing developments have been built through the action of the Corporación de la Vivienda (Housing Corporation or CORVI), such as the Unidad Vecindad Portales (Portales Neighborhood). They consist mainly of standardized bungalows surrounded by gardens, faithfully continuing the principles of rational architecture. These neighborhoods extended Santiago's area by 150 percent while decreasing its density to the point where further construction became economically questionable. Rational architecture reached its zenith with **Emilio Duhart**'s building for the Comisión Económica Para América Latina of the United Nations (1966; Economic Commission for Latin America or CEPAL). In recent years many Chilean architects, such as Cristián Fernández Cox, Francisco Vergara, and Aldo Bravo, have emphasized local characteristics in their architectural designs, employing sturdy construction (developed earlier to withstand earthquakes), formal simplicity, and traditional urban patterns with homes built next to each other around communal areas.

In Colombia the questioning of rational architecture began in the 1950s with the emergence of topological or organic architecture. Rational architecture, supported by the government and most studios, favored technology over lower costs and efficiency over aesthetics. Topological architecture advocated traditional building techniques and materials, which were more economical and better integrated into the urban context. By the 1960s these two tendencies came together in the works of important architects such as Rogelio Salmona, who adapted modern architecture to the specific climatic and urban needs of the site. The main example of this change is Salmona's Torres del Parque (1968–1973; Park Towers) in Bogotá, three high-rise buildings for middle-income families which follow a

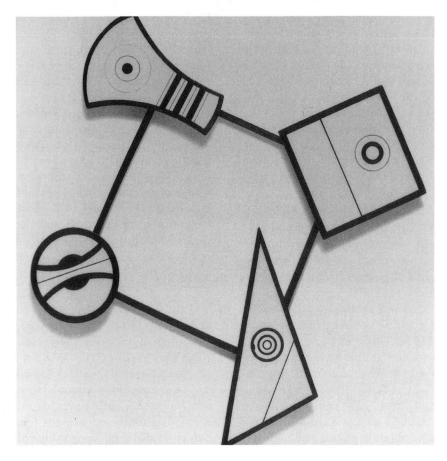

Coplanal (1945), by Carmelo Arden Quin (Collection of M. von Bartha, Basel)

stepped circular motion that blends the towers' profiles with the surrounding mountains, while the use of brick surfaces efficiently makes the building merge with its urban context. The emphasis on local building traditions increased during the 1970s and 1980s, with brick becoming an important building material for several housing developments, such as Alfonso García Galvís's Conjunto de Vivienda (1981; Housing Complex) in Bogotá. The exploration of local craftsmanship and historical contextualization reached its culmination with Simón Velez's rural home in Melgar, Tolima (1977), built in a traditional way out of wood, and Salmona's Casa de Huéspedes Ilustres (1981; House for Distinguished Guests) in Cartagena, built next to the Fuerte de Manzanillo, a fort restored by Germán Tellez. Salmona designed this inn to blend easily with the fort: he used stone surfaces and simple volumes reminiscent of early military architecture.

The architecture of Latin America in recent years has continued to see the value of traditional methods and to emphasize the smooth integration of new buildings into their surrounding contexts.

REFERENCES:

Leopoldo Castedo, *Historia del arte iberoamericano, 2: Siglo XIX. Siglo XX* (Madrid: Editorial Andrés Bello, Alianza Editorial, 1988);

Roberto Segre, ed., *América Latina en su arquitectura* (Mexico City: Siglo XXI Editores, 1975);

Antonio Toca, ed., *Nueva arquitectura en América Latina: Presente y futuro* (Mexico City: Ediciones G. Gilli, 1990).

— F.B.N.

CARMELO ARDEN QUIN

Carmelo Arden Quin (1913–) cofounded the Concrete Art movements Arturo and **Madí** and helped organize several avant-garde groups that advocated abstract geometric art. Born in Uruguay and educated in Brazil and Argentina, Arden Quin was interested in both Marxism and art, and in the early 1940s he developed an aesthetic approach based on dialectical materialism. In the 1930s he met **Joaquín Torres-García,** who showed him his series of modular toys, encouraging Arden Quin and other artists to explore the concept of articulated sculpture. In 1938 Arden Quin attempted, without success, to publish the interdisciplinary magazine *Arturo* in Buenos Aires. After meeting a new group of abstract artists who shared his interest in concrete art and articulated sculpture, he revived *Arturo* and published a single issue in 1944. With part of this group, Arden Quin cofounded the Movimiento de Arte Concreto-Invención in 1945, which became the **Madí** group in 1946, which was in turn organized by **Gyula Kosice** and Arden Quin in 1946. (See also **Asociación de Arte Concreto-Invención.**)

During these years, Arden Quin produced a series of mobile pieces whose forms range from an organic and curvilinear approach to geometry, such as the wood mobile sculpture *Astral Buenos Aires* (1946), articulated with ligatures, to the calculated playfulness of the painting-relief *Coplanal* (1945), made up of four two-dimensional geometric shapes attached to the corners of a thin rectangular armature. Arden Quin soon broke with Kosice and abandoned Madí, settling in Paris, where he created the Centre de Recherches et d'Etudes Madistes and directed, with Kosice and Rothfuss, the Salon des Réalités Nouvelles. In 1953, after lecturing on Madí in Paris and São Paulo, he returned to Buenos Aires and participated with other abstract artists in the Asociación de Arte Nuevo. In 1956 he returned to Paris, where he still lives.

REFERENCE:

Aracy Amaral, "Abstract Constructivist Trends in Argentina, Brazil, Venezuela, and Colombia," in *Latin American Artists of the Twentieth Century,* edited by Waldo Rasmussen, Fatima Bercht, and Elizabeth Ferrer (New York: Museum of Modern Art, 1993).

— F.B.N.

José María Arguedas

The greatest of the indigenist writers (see **Indigenism in Literature**) and one of the very few to write about the subject from within the Indian culture and language, José María Arguedas (1911–1969) (not related to the Bolivian writer Alcides Arguedas) was born in the Andean province of Andahuaylas, Peru. Spanish was spoken at home, but Quechua, the language of the former Inca empire, prevailed in the fields. Arguedas spent his earliest years among the Indian laborers of his stepmother's hacienda. To the end of his life Arguedas's literary Spanish (which was structured by Quechua syntax and included many Quechua expressions) was influenced by this early bilingualism and biculturalism.

José María Arguedas, circa 1962

It was only at the age of twenty that the future writer moved to Lima, the Peruvian capital, after spending much of his adolescence traveling with his father — an itinerant judge — throughout the Andean provinces of Peru. At that time middle- and upper-class city dwellers were disdainful if not ignorant of the country's indigenous heritage, though about half the Peruvian population was of unmixed Indian stock. (Only in 1975 was Quechua officially recognized as the country's second language). This cultural breach between the two worlds that Arguedas was to inhabit had a determining influence on the writer's work and life, and its contradictions eventually drove him to commit suicide in 1969.

In Lima, Arguedas entered the University of San Marcos and earned a marginal living working for the post office. He became a schoolteacher and in 1944 suffered a nervous breakdown that kept him from writing for several years. In 1946 he enrolled in the newly created Institute of Ethnology at the University of San Marcos, and in 1957 he obtained the equivalent of a master's degree with a thesis on the evolution of the Indian communities of Huancayo, a province in the central Andes. His doctoral dissertation, defended in 1963, focused on the Spanish origin of Indian communities. The following year Arguedas was named director of the National Museum of History, one of several official honors he received in his lifetime. In 1966 he completed the translation of a newly found sixteenth century manuscript detailing the myths and legends of the Huarochirí valley. Later that year he attempted suicide for the first time. The following year he was appointed to the social sciences faculty of the Universidad Agraria de la Molina, where in November 1969 he shot himself in the head.

Arguedas's most accomplished novel is *Los ríos profundos* (1958; translated as *Deep Rivers*), a bildungsroman in which the author evokes the itinerant years of his childhood and adolescence, the time passed in his stepmother's hacienda, and his experience at a boarding school. The narrator is a fourteen-year-old criollo boy (see **Peoples and Races**) who experiences a painful shock in passing from his childhood years (spent in a communal Indian village) to the world of the Andean haciendas, where the Indians are serfs tied to the owner's land. The nostalgia of childhood evocation becomes outrage when the protagonist confronts the servile state of the Indians and the violence at large in the Catholic school in which he is a boarder. The climax of the novel is a triple rebellion against authority that despite the author's strong feelings on the subject is devoid of pamphleteerism and ideological baggage: the narrator's schoolmates rebel against the older boys and overturn their code of violence; the "chicheras" (the women who run the local pubs where "chicha" is served) in the city rebel against the lack of salt, whose distribution has been halted by government orders; and the Indian serfs in the hacienda rebel to protest the lack of magical assistance in the face of a typhus epidemic. The connections and transitions among these events are flexible and sustain the lyrical rhythm with which nature is described in the narrative. At the same time, however, many ethnological or "costumbrista" (see **Costumbrismo**) passages which are not fully incorporated in the narrative structure detract from the novel's effectiveness as a literary artifact. Arguedas belongs to the prehistory of the Latin American modern novel (the latter so well exemplified by his compatriot and younger admirer **Mario Vargas Llosa**); that is, to a historical phase and a cultural context in which the novel was not yet a clearly differentiated discursive object and tended to legitimate itself

in terms of some other discipline (like ethnology) or in terms of some extraliterary aim such as social reform.

Arguedas's subsequent novels were *El Sexto* (1961; the title alludes to the name of the prison where the author was confined for a year in 1937 for political reasons) and *Todas las sangres* (1964; All Bloods). The latter is a vast mural attesting to the conflict between social classes within a dependent economy. The novel's setting ranges from the Andean haciendas to the mining centers, and from the slums of the city to Lima's upscale neighborhood of Monterrico. Despite its obvious Marxist inspiration *Todas las sangres* is not programmatic but ultimately poetic in that hope for the future is proclaimed to rest with the untarnished Indian communities. An unfinished but impressive novel — *El zorro de arriba y el zorro de abajo* (The Fox from Above and the Fox from Below) — was published posthumously in 1971. One of the strands of the narrative is the author's diary, where in a matter-of-fact tone Arguedas discusses his first attempt at suicide, the possibility that the writing of this novel will save him, and his irrevocable decision to try suicide again should this possibility fail. The novel's ambitious design is to project a total image of Peru in the late 1960s showing the nation's contradictions and its chaotic entrance into the world of industrial capitalism. The title alludes to one of the main conflicts in Peru dating back to the days of the Spanish conquest, the disparity between the highlands (the domain of the Fox from Above) and the coast (where the Fox from Below holds sway). The most recent incarnation of this contradiction in Peruvian history is the terrorist war waged against the government in the 1980s and early 1990s by **Sendero Luminoso,** a guerrilla army of Andean extraction whose aim is to smash the national government centered in the coastal city of Lima.

Arguedas's self-appointed mission as writer and ethnologist was to mediate between the two nations that comprise modern-day Peru, the indigenous world of Arguedas's childhood and the Hispanic world of the writer's adult years, to a degree associated respectively with the highlands and the coast. An important element of Arguedas's enterprise was the socialist ideology of fellow Peruvian **José Carlos Mariátegui** in which the author of *Deep Rivers* found a convincing explanation of the country's problems and a vision of its future. Arguedas's socialist sympathies, however, are tinged with a magical outlook inimical to ideological rigor.

REFERENCES:

Sara Castro-Klarén, *El mundo mágico de José María Arguedas* (Lima: Instituto de Estudios Peruanos, 1973);

Antonio Cornejo Polar, *Los universos narrativos de José María Arguedas* (Buenos Aires: Losada, 1973).

— R.G.M.

ROBERTO ARLT

Roberto Arlt (1900–1942), a writer associated with the **Boedo** group, is the paramount interpreter of the Argentinean urban middle classes at the very moment when these groups, mostly made up of recent European immigrants, had achieved political power only to lose it in the military coup of 1930. Arlt, the son of German immigrants, was born in Buenos Aires. He was expelled from school at the age of ten and soon found himself adrift in the big city, where he mingled with derelicts and outcasts of all kinds. In his mid twenties he was a police reporter for the sensationalist daily *Crónica* and later joined the staff of *El Mundo,* where he published many of his "Aguafuertes porteñas," penetrating sketches of everyday life in Buenos Aires and of the social types that gave the city its character.

Despite the popular success of these sketches, Arlt had higher literary ambitions. He wrote novels, stories, and plays that got a mixed reception among the critics, many of whom complained about the author's lack of literary culture, the improvised structure of his works, his bad taste, and even his poor command of Spanish. Arlt's chief novels, still read and admired today, are *Los siete locos* (1929; translated as *The Seven Madmen*) and its sequel *Los lanzallamas* (1931; The Flamethrowers). A book of short stories, *El jorobadito* (The Little Hunchback), came out in 1933 at a time when Arlt was almost wholly given over to the theater.

Critics have noted that Arlt's themes are readily identifiable with the author's lower-middle-class status. The recurring theme in Arlt's writings is money, or, rather, the lack of money and the need to obtain it, either by acting on improbable fantasies (such as scientific inventions to generate a quick profit) or by assimilation into the workaday world. The two poles of this thematic universe can be discerned in Arlt's next-to-last play, *La isla desierta* (1938; The Desert Island), set in a blank office space overlooking the broad Rio de la Plata where steamships and luxury liners sail back and forth carrying the promise of deliverance from the impersonal routine of the bureaucratic world. When the clerks fall into a collective reverie of escape to a desert island, their boss appears to fire them all.

REFERENCE:

Gerardo Mario Goloboff, *Genio y figura de Roberto Arlt* (Buenos Aires: Editorial Universitaria de Buenos Aires, 1988).

— R.G.M.

CLAUDIO ARRAU

Chilean virtuoso pianist Claudio Arrau (1903–1991) was celebrated for his performances of traditional Eu-

Claudio Arrau

ropean music (Franz Liszt, Frédéric Chopin, Johannes Brahms, Claude Debussy, Robert Schumann, Johann Sebastian Bach, Wolfgang Amadeus Mozart, and especially Ludwig van Beethoven). An exceptional keyboard technique and a scholarly approach to piano literature enabled Arrau to produce several distinctive series of recitals, such as those dedicated to the complete piano or keyboard works of individual composers.

Two years after his debut at the age of five, Arrau was sent to study in Berlin. Following his first recital in Germany at the age of eleven, he toured Europe, South America, and the United States. He combined concert tours with teaching at his alma mater, the Stern Conservatory, from 1924 to 1940, when he fled Berlin for the United States. After World War II he continued to give concerts in Europe and the Far East but refused to play in Chile from 1967 to 1984 to protest government policies.

Arrau's legacy of numerous recordings reveals his inimitable sensitivity to minute detail. For a period following his wife's death (1989) he concentrated on recording, shunning the concert stage. Upon his death, the Chilean government declared a day of national mourning.

— R.L.S.

ART

During the twentieth century a wide variety of artistic expression developed in Latin America as a consequence of the contextual differences determined by diverse national, cultural, and racial heritages as well as by political and social circumstances. Since colonial times, many blends of Indo-American, African, and European cultural heritages have emerged. After the period of independence, as nations consolidated and defined their own cultural identities, other cultural exchanges occurred with the arrival of new waves of European immigrants, who often reinforced the cultural links between Latin America and Europe.

Until the 1960s most Latin American artists and architects received part of their formal training in Europe, where modernism was the dominant artistic trend; returning home, they disseminated this international trend and others. These imported trends were subsequently synthesized with the arts of the various nations and transformed at the local level into new artistic expressions that reflected local cultural features in innovative ways. Although the most important artistic movements in twentieth-century Latin America developed in the general context of modernism, the chronology of art trends in Europe, and later in the United States, did not determine the development of art in Latin America, since other local and regional cultural pressures were at work. Movements such as **Impressionism, Surrealism,** or **Conceptual Art** must be understood in terms of the Latin American context, where chronological developments and cultural assumptions have been very different.

The first modern trends to appear in Spanish America at the turn of the century were **Impressionism and Post Impressionism.** The main exponents were **Fernando Fader, Pedro Figari, Armando Reverón,** and **Andrés de Santa María.** Their rebellious rejection of the outdated but dominant late-academic schools and of the Spanish so-called modernist style popularized by Ignacio Zuloaga and Joaquín Sorolla paved the way for the more radical **avant-garde art of the 1920s.** Most significant among the many avant-garde groups which arose in the early part of the century were **Florida, Boedo,** and **Montparnasse.** Also influential were the Brazilian Pau-Brasil and Antropofagia movements and Mexican Muralism. The effect of Mexican Muralism in particular continued into the 1930s and often inspired the work of **indigenists** and **social realists,** especially in the Andean countries. Yet by the time Muralism's influence reached the Southern Cone, it was already suffering the effects of the worldwide economic depression, and lack of government funding conspired against the development of a mural movement in that region.

Surrealism was introduced into Spanish America in the 1930s by a series of isolated groups and artists who either used dreamlike images in their work in order to construct invented realities (artists such as **Juan Batlle Planas**), or followed the more characteristically Surrealist exploration of the unconscious through dream imagery or automatist techniques (such as **Roberto Matta**). At the end of the 1930s several artists joined forces to organize Surrealist exhibitions in their various countries: in Argentina the members of the Surrealist Grupo Orión exhibited together in 1939, and in Chile the Surrealist magazine *La mandrágora* (1938–1943) sponsored an exhibition of Surrealist art in 1941. Many South American artists have worked in Surrealist modes at different times of their careers, but the principal representative of this movement in this region is Matta, whose art has achieved international recognition.

Also in the 1930s, another artistic trend of lasting consequence began to develop in South America, a variation of European Constructivism defined by the Uruguayan artist **Joaquín Torres-García.** Torres-García blended the innovative aspects of Cubism, Surrealism, and Neoplasticism with pre-Columbian art in a synthesis he called **Constructive Art** or Constructive Universalism. His aim was to express his American roots in modern and universal terms. After his return to Montevideo in 1934 he disseminated his ideas by founding two art schools, the Asociación de Arte Constructivo (1935–1940) and the **Taller Torres-García** (1943–1962). Torres-García and the members of his workshop had a lasting impact on the arts of Uruguay and well beyond that country's borders; his encouragement of artistic experimentation facilitated the beginnings of **Geometric Abstraction** in Argentina, Brazil, and Venezuela, and his Americanist ideals inspired several generations of Latin American artists who followed.

Geometric Abstraction, which emerged after the 1940s, includes a variety of hard-edge styles often called Concrete Art, Constructivism, Generative Art, or **Kinetic Art,** and the soft-edge abstraction known as Geometría Sensible. Geometric Abstraction became important especially during the periods of economic optimism and utopian desire for modernization that followed World War II and was perceived as a universal language with the power to connect the personal projects of its practitioners to a wider international exploration of abstract art. In Argentina the concrete artists of the **Asociación de Arte Concreto-Invención** and **Madí** groups advocated a pure abstract art based on concrete plastic elements such as lines, planes, and colors. This tendency toward geometry continued later on with the Artistas Modernos de la Argentina and

Figura bajo un uvero (1920; Figure under an Uvero Tree), by Armando Reverón (Collection of Dr. and Mrs. David Brillembourg)

Arte Generativo groups. In Chile the Rectángulo and Forma y Espacio groups formed during the 1950s advocated a rational geometric art based on flatness and orthogonal compositions. The interest in geometry-based styles in Venezuela began in the 1940s and was further encouraged by architect **Carlos Villanueva** and his 1950s design for the Ciudad Universitaria of the Universidad Central in Caracas. Kinetic Art, which explores the effects of optical and real movement in abstract geometric sculptures, eventually became Venezuela's dominant style. In Colombia, Geometric Abstraction did not emerge until the 1950s and early 1960s through the art of Marco Ospina, Omar Rayo, Carlos Rojas, and Fanny Sanin, as well as the sculptures of **Eduardo Ramírez Villamizar** and **Edgar Negret.** Geometric Abstraction continues to be a strong tendency in the art of Latin America.

During the 1950s Latin American artists began to reject the emphasis on rationality of Geometric Abstraction in favor of more personal and culturally based solutions. **Informal Abstraction,** also called Informalism, advocated a variety of nongeometric abstract styles based on more-spontaneous creative processes. Although Informal Abstraction has ante-

cedents in European Informalism and North American Abstract Expressionism, it often differs from these trends, especially in the Andean countries, in its affirmation through colors and textures of cultural meanings native to South America. In the Andean region the beginning of Informal Abstraction and the demise of Indigenism happened simultaneously. In Peru, Informal Abstraction provoked a hostile reaction when it was introduced by **Fernando de Szyszlo.** Critics labeled it un-Peruvian, in spite of the fact that de Szyszlo had successfully incorporated the native myths and traditions of Peru into his abstract work. **María Luisa Pacheco** played a similar role in renovating the art of her native Bolivia: she produced a type of Informal Abstraction which had the power to evoke her homeland, and her international success encouraged other Bolivian artists to work with abstraction. In Ecuador the first artists to turn toward abstraction included Manuel Rendón, Estuardo Maldonado, **Enrique Tábara,** Aníbal Villacís, and Oswaldo Viteri. During the 1960s these and other artists formed the Grupo VAN, which exhibited at the Galería Siglo XX and issued a manifesto opposing institutionalized Indigenism.

Ha comenzado el espectáculo (1964; The Show Has Begun), by Jacobo Borges (Fundación Galería de Arte Nacional, Caracas)

Informal Abstraction was introduced in Uruguay later than in the Andean region due to the strong influence of the Taller Torres-García. In Argentina, Colombia, and Venezuela, Informal Abstraction also emerged as a reaction against geometry-based styles prevalent during the previous years. In Buenos Aires, Informal Abstraction spread quickly during the late 1950s and 1960s through the activities of **Kenneth Kemble** and Alberto Greco. Their use of unorthodox materials paved the way for several radical movements, such as Arte Destructivo, **Otra Figuración** and **Pop Art, Assemblages, and Happenings.** In Colombia, Guillermo Wiedemann, Antonio Roda, Armando Villegas, and Judith Márquez worked with Informal Abstraction during the 1960s, but later, with the exception of Wiedemann, they turned to figuration. **Alejandro Obregón,** one of the most important Colombian artists, blended the abstract treatment of plastic elements with figuration, producing a semiabstract mode that is hard to categorize. Although Informal Abstraction was represented by numerous artists in Venezuela, it never achieved the same importance there as did Geometric Abstraction.

After the long emphasis on abstract modes that characterized the international art scene during the midcentury, a generalized trend toward figuration emerged in Europe, the United States, and Latin America during the 1950s. **Neofiguration** or New Figuration (a term coined in 1962 in Paris by Michel Ragon) blended the textural surfaces of Informal Abstraction with expressionist figuration and the use of unorthodox materials in hybrid collages, an approach which resulted in monsterlike images of alienated beings. Neofiguration first became an important trend in Mexico, with the work of José Luis Cuevas and the Nueva Presencia group; soon thereafter it emerged in Argentina, where it was developed in the early 1960s by **Antonio Berni** and the members of the Otra Figuración group. In Venezuela Neofiguration can be found in the work of **Jacobo Borges.**

Although Pop Art in the United States often represented neutral images disseminated by the mass media, in Latin America Pop Art, Assemblages, and Happenings (closely associated art forms that emerged during the 1960s and 1970s) employed unorthodox materials and popular images for ideological purposes. Among the most spectacular examples of this radical art were a series of Happenings by **Marta Minujín,** which involved the massive participation of the public. The Groupe de Recherche d'Art Visuel, an experimental group active in Paris during the 1960s under the leadership of **Julio Le Parc,** also explored the active participation of the spectator in the artistic experience. During the 1960s Chilean Pop Art took the form of politicized collages and assemblages produced by artists such as Francisco Brugnoli, Hugo Marín, Alberto Pérez, Juan Pablo Langlis, Guillermo Núñez, and Valentina Cruz. Although the uncompromising poverty of this art shocked the public, its emphasis on radical protest continued in spite of the strict censorship established by the military dictatorship after 1973. This use of poor materials and ephemeral structures in Pop Art also characterized **Conceptual Art,** making it difficult to differentiate between the two.

In Colombia, Pop Art had many supporters; as in Argentina and Chile, their purpose was often political and social comment. An example is the work of the world-renowned **Fernando Botero,** whose whimsical, inflated figures offered memorable caricatures of Colombian society. In Venezuela in the 1960s Jacobo Borges participated in the production of *Imágenes de Caracas* (Images of Caracas), a multimedia installation/happening in which the audience was immersed and confronted with audiovisual effects created by props, lights, and fragmented film projections. The Venezuelan **Marisol,** who has lived in New York since 1950, also works with social content in assemblages featuring portraits of social stereotypes which she constructs with wood and found objects.

Among the most important movements to emerge in Latin America in recent times is Conceptual Art, a radical artistic expression that defines the work of art as an idea or a concept, relegating the material aspect of the artistic object, which could be in any kind of media, to the secondary role of simply documenting or presenting the essential information. During the 1960s and 1970s the military dictatorships that took power in countries such as Argentina, Chile, and Brazil strictly censored museums, art galleries, and art magazines; many artists resorted to the radical strategies of Conceptual Art effectively to circumvent these art institutions. As a result, their actions and unorthodox methods were perceived by the state as marginal and unimportant, and they were treated with indifference, allowing conceptual artists to deal with political issues in a way that both subverted and drew attention to the repressive powers of the state. In Argentina the Centro de Arte y Comunicación (CAYC) group supported technologically oriented conceptual artists such as Víctor Grippo, but there were other independent groups that produced more politically oriented art. In

Chile political issues were of paramount importance for the conceptual Avanzada movement, which supported many "art actions," organized events intended as political protests; the most notable were produced by members of Colectivo de Acciones de Arte (CADA). In Colombia conceptual artists have often articulated political commentaries with a sense of humor. **Beatriz González** paints or prints images of political significance on household objects such as draperies and wallpaper. **Bernardo Salcedo,** who began as a pop artist, has transformed old photographs by partially covering them with small objects and giving them witty and intriguing titles. Although many leading Spanish American conceptual artists have moved to New York, they have continued to produce art that deals primarily with Latin America. For instance, **Luis Camnitzer** often works with the theme of state-sponsored terrorism and torture. Conceptual Art continues to be one of the most creative and meaningful art movements in Latin America.

After the emergence of the Neofiguration movement during the 1960s, figuration continued to be a strong expressive mode in Latin America, often developing side by side with Geometric Abstraction and Conceptual Art. In fact, several artists have worked with both trends, combining them to the point of blurring their limits. **Figuration since the 1970s** in Spanish America has become remarkably diverse, ranging from the realism of the Uruguayans **José Gamarra** and Horacio Torres to the expressive distortions of the Colombians González and Fernando Botero, from the conceptual-like approach of the Argentinean **Liliana Porter** to the Surrealist images of the Chilean Nemesio Antúnez. One of the major features characterizing their work is the frequent quotation of earlier European art, an attempt to define the place of the Latin American artist in the broader tradition of Western art. Other important features include references to the artists' political, social, and cultural circumstances (humorously, as in the case of Botero and González, or through the more conceptual approach of Porter and Antúnez); religious and mythical allusions; and the treatment of sexual and psychological issues. In recent years figuration in Latin America has been given renewed impetus by the work of artists using neo-expressionist modes.

REFERENCES:

Dawn Ades, with Guy Brett, Stanton Loomis Catlin, and Rosemary O'Neill, *Art in Latin America: The Modern Era, 1820–1980* (New Haven: Yale University Press, 1989);

Gilbert Chase, *Contemporary Art in Latin America: Painting, Graphic Art, Sculpture, Architecture* (New York: Free Press, 1970);

Waldo Rasmussen, Fatima Bercht, and Elizabeth Ferrer, eds., *Latin American Artists of the Twentieth Century* (New York: Museum of Modern Art, 1993).

— F.B.N.

Asociación de Arte Concreto-Invención

The Asociación de Arte Concreto-Invención (AACI) and **Madí,** groups of concrete artists active in Buenos Aires during the 1940s, included the Uruguayans **Carmelo Arden Quin** and Roth Rothfuss and the Argentineans Martín Blaszko, Manuel Espinosa, **Alfredo Hlito,** Enio Iommi, **Gyula Kosice,** Rafael Lozza, Raúl Lozza, **Tomás Maldonado,** and Lidy Prati, among others. The antecedents for the AACI and Madí are varied, including the abstract European avant-garde movements known as De Stijl, Bauhaus, Cercle et Carré, and Abstraction-Création, the artistic breakthroughs of the Uruguayan **Joaquín Torres-García,** and the abstract work of more-established Argentinean artists, such as **Emilio Pettoruti, Lucio Fontana,** and Juan del Prete, the latter having participated personally in the activities of the French Abstraction-Création movement. The artists of the AACI, like their European counterparts, developed a completely abstract geometric art called concrete because it is based on plastic elements, such as planes, colors, and lines, which are considered concrete objects rather than tools to create the illusion of reality. Its emphasis on rationality was perhaps a way to balance the sense of chaos created by the Spanish Civil War and World War II and, more immediately, the unstable political reality of the military coup of 1943 and **Juan Domingo Perón**'s administration of 1946, which denounced the art of the AACI as "degenerate."

The activities of these concrete artists began in 1944 with the formation of the interdisciplinary group called Arturo, which included Arden Quin, Kosice, Prati, Maldonado, Rothfuss, and the poet Edgar Bayley, and the publication that year of the only issue of the magazine *Arturo.* The artists' objective was to produce abstract works, redefine the relationship between the surface and frame of paintings through "cut out" or "shaped" frames, and explore the possibility of making articulated sculptures, such as Kosice's *Röyi.* In 1945 Arturo separated into two groups, the Movimiento de Arte Concreto-Invención — founded by Arden Quin and including Kosice, Blaszko, Rothfuss, and **Grete Stern** — and the **Asociación de Arte Concreto-Invención** — formed by Espinosa, Hlito, Iommi, Maldonado, Prati, and the two Lozzas (the Lozza brothers later founded the Perceptismo movement). Arden Quin and Kosice's group,

which in 1946 adopted the name **Madí,** had three exhibitions in 1945, but the members of the AACI, led by Maldonado, did not exhibit until 1946, when they participated in the Salón Peuser. That year they published two issues of a bulletin, the second including their "Inventionist Manifesto." This text explained their materialist aesthetics, which favored a scientific approach to art and the elimination of emotional and fictional elements. Like the Bauhaus, the AACI had a utopian aim of making society better by improving the environment: they believed that when the illusion of fiction is eliminated from art and design and individuals are finally placed in the real world of concrete objects, their will to act will increase, and likewise their freedom. The AACI continued to experiment with cut out frames and radical new materials, such as aluminum, plexiglass, and cut out sheet metal. The AACI ended in 1948, when Maldonado left for Europe.

REFERENCES:

Aracy Amaral, "Abstract Constructivist Trends in Argentina, Brazil, Venezuela, and Colombia," in *Latin American Artists of the Twentieth Century,* edited by Waldo Rasmussen, Fatima Bercht, and Elizabeth Ferrer (New York: Museum of Modern Art, 1993);

Nelly Perazzo, *El Arte Concreto en la Argentina* (Buenos Aires: Gaglianone, 1983).

— F.B.N.

Atahualpa Yupanqui

Perhaps the world's best known interpreter of the Argentinean **milonga,** Atahualpa Yupanqui (1908–1993) traveled extensively in concert tours and made many recordings for the world market. His real name is Héctor Chavero. He took his stage name in homage to an Inca leader. An excellent folk guitarist, composer, and master of metaphor, his voice expressed with unique melancholy the realities of lives far poorer than his own. Atahualpa's repertoire included the most notable folk genres of his time, such as the **baguala,** the **zamba,** the **vidala,** and the *Chacarera.* His compositional career began with *Camino del indio* (1934; Path of the Indian) which became a classic of Argentinean folk music. In this work and subsequent ones he demonstrates a unique ability to translate into verse and song the profound sentiments of a nation-building people. Born in 1908, he eventually took residence in Paris where he performed frequently until his death in 1993. In 1986 the French government decorated Atahualpa Yupanqui with the title of Knight of the Order of Arts and Letters.

REFERENCE:

Vicente Gesualdo, *La música en la Argentina* (Buenos Aires: Editorial Stella, 1988).

— R.L.S.

AVANT-GARDE ART OF THE 1920S

During the first two decades of the twentieth century, several avant-garde movements developed in Latin America, often grouping together artists and writers: Muralismo and Estridentismo in Mexico, Pau-Brasil and Antropofagia in Brazil, the **Florida** group (also called **Martín Fierro**) and the **Boedo** group, both in Argentina. Many of the artists who participated in them — Diego Rivera, David Alfaro Siqueiros, and Jean Charlot (Mexico); Lasar Segall, Anita Malfatti, and Tarsila do Amaral (Brazil); as well as **Norah Borges, Emilio Pettoruti,** and **Xul Solar** (Argentina) — spent their formative years in Europe, actively working within the avant-garde movements they encountered there.

Most of these artists — like their fellow vanguardist writers — adopted classic avant-garde attitudes which led them to reject the artistic production of earlier generations they considered too bourgeois, to appropriate the art of non-European cultures as a strategy for formal renewal, and to hail technology as a means of social progress. Into their work they also incorporated characteristics of Cubism, Futurism, Spanish Ultraism, Russian Constructivism, and German Expressionism, selectively choosing formal strategies which might prove useful for their personal objectives.

When these artists and writers returned to Latin America, they opposed the tired late-academic and **impressionist** styles still predominant in their various countries. Instead, they advocated new modern artistic languages, better able to convey the changes brought about by rapid urban and industrial growth in cities like Buenos Aires and São Paulo, and by the new political landscape of postrevolutionary Mexico. In order to defend and disseminate their ideas, the first modernists in Latin America used typical vanguardist tactics: they formed cohesive groups that often included artists, writers, and in some cases musicians and architects; they published aggressive manifestos and magazines attacking both the status quo and other vanguard groups with opposing ideologies; and they held exhibitions as well as regular meetings where new strategies were planned. Women also played leading roles within these movements. Although artists and writers like **Borges** and Norah Lange in Argentina, Tina Modotti in Mexico, and Malfatti and Amaral in Brazil strove alongside male artists to introduce modernity, attitudes about their gender often had a limiting effect on their work. Their fellow male vanguardists held their meetings mostly at times and in places off-limits to respectable women. Furthermore, the use of radical styles and the direct treatment of sexual issues so characteristic of the avant-garde often produced scandalous results: their families, usually the first to view their works, often felt them to be inappropriate, and the women often censored themselves.

An intense process of synthesis characterized the initial period of modern art in Latin America. While admiration for European avant-garde models was widespread, in most cases artists and writers followed them selectively, adopting and reinterpreting only those formal and conceptual strategies capable of expressing their own personal and cultural concerns. For instance, Figari, Rivera, and Amaral transformed the empty modernist appropriation of non-European cultures into a recuperation of the native and popular traditions of their own countries, which engendered a renewed sense of national identity. Similarly, Norah Borges, Pettoruti, and Xul Solar were attracted to styles like Cubism, Futurism, and Expressionism because they emphasized the experience of city life and were more suitable for evoking the conflicting cultural identities present in Buenos Aires during the 1920s.

The polarization of the Mexican avant-garde into ideologically opposed groups of modernists, muralists, and stridentists was paralleled in Argentina by the opposition of the Florida and Boedo groups. Florida — associated with the magazine **Martín Fierro,** whose offices were on the affluent Florida Street — emphasized the need for an aesthetic revolution. On the other hand, Boedo — whose members were linked with **Claridad,** located in the working-class neighborhood of Boedo — considered art and literature to be vehicles for describing the plight of the poor and for inspiring social change.

Most of the Latin American avant-garde movements that began in the 1920s dissolved at the end of the decade, with the exception of Muralism, whose influence was felt throughout the Americas during the 1930s and 1940s.

REFERENCES:

Jorge Schwartz, ed., *Las vanguardias latinoamericanas: Textos programáticos y críticos* (Madrid: Ediciones Cátedra, 1991);

Edward J. Sullivan, "Notes on the Birth of Modernity in Latin American Art," *Latin American Artists of the Twentieth Century,* edited by Waldo Rasmussen, Fatima Bercht, and Elizabeth Ferrer (New York: Museum of Modern Art, 1993), pp. 18–37.

                                                    — F.B.N.

FERNANDO AYALA

The Argentinean director Fernando Ayala (1928?–), like **Torre Nilsson,** made a significant impact on Argentinean cinema in the late 1950s, in particular with *El jefe* (1958; The Boss). He formed his own production company, Aries Cinematográfico, with Héctor

Olivera; the company has continued successfully down to the present day. *El jefe* is based on a short story by **David Viñas,** writer and critic, about young men who follow a charismatic but corrupt leader. The leader, a clear reference to **Juan Domingo Perón,** eventually falls, but a new man is ready to take his place who might be equally successful in tricking the next generation. Ayala continued his political satire in his next feature, *El candidato* (1959; The Candidate), which was less successful, and *Paula la cautiva* (1963; Captive Paula) which, despite its quality, was largely ignored.

A far better money-spinner for him was the enormously popular sex comedy *Hotel alojamiento* (1965; Hotel Lodging). His more recent movie, *Pasajeros de una pesadilla* (1984; Passengers in a Nightmare), was also very successful.

REFERENCE:

John King, *Magical Reels: A History of Cinema in Latin America* (London: Verso, 1990).

— S.M.H.

B

LIBERO BADII

With his bronze and polychrome sculptures, Libero Badii (1916–) expressed his personal theories about the cosmos and his idea of a "sinister art" that reflects Latin American reality. Originally from Italy, Badii moved to Argentina as a child. He studied art at the Escuela Superior de Bellas Artes in the 1940s and traveled throughout South America and Europe. During the 1950s and 1960s Badii's sculptures reflected three different stages in his theory of space. In early works, such as *La fecunda* (1953; Fertile Woman), space is contained within the form of the sculpture. In later pieces, such as *Espacio* (1967; Space), the central figure has tubelike protrusions reaching out toward the stars, thus connecting the work with the cosmos. Inspired by the use of color in pre-Columbian sculptures, Badii began to construct polychromed pieces with juxtaposed planes of brightly painted wood, such as the series *Los muñecos* (1967; The Dolls). These are produced somewhat in the manner of **Neofiguration:** semifigurative, totemlike figures are connected with ropes to each other and to points on the wall, symbolizing interpersonal and cosmic communication and marking the third stage of Badii's spatial theory. During the 1970s he worked on *Conocimientos siniestros* (Sinister Knowledge), a series of seven sculptures based on the notion that because reality in the Americas is "sinister" — a term which, according to him, suggested elusiveness and mystery — art should be sinister as well. In recent years he has continued to produce polychrome sculptures and work in other areas, such as painting and printmaking.

REFERENCE:
César Magrini, "Libero Badii: La creación como juego, el juego como creación," in *Arte argentino contemporáneo,* edited by Gabriel Levinas (Madrid: Ameris, 1979), pp. 72–74.

— F.B.N.

BAGUALA

The baguala is an Andean folk song of indigenous derivation especially prominent in the northwestern sector of Argentina. There are several types that vary according to geographical region and the nature of the text interpreted. Generally, however, the baguala tends to serve dramatic purposes with vestiges of ritual usage. Of limited melodic range, the baguala usually features a triadic melody that emphasizes the three notes of a chord. Its basic rhythmic pattern consists of a quarter note and two eighth notes that are reiterated by an accompanying drum (**bombo**).

REFERENCE:
Isabel Aretz, *El folklore musical argentino* (Buenos Aires: Ricordi Americana S.A.E.C., 1952).

— R.L.S.

BAILECITO

Probably of Peruvian origin, the bailecito is also prominent in Bolivia and Argentina. It is sometimes referred to as "bailecito boliviano" and sometimes simply as "boliviana." A folk song/dance, the bailecito rhythm is characterized by the syncopation derived from combining 6/8 and 3/4 meters simultaneously. The form normally consists of two sections in contrasting tempi: the first lively, the second more somber, followed by repetition of the first section. When sung, the first section, the verse, consists of hexasyllabic couplets followed by a communal refrain. The final section may be sung to nonsense syllables. The bailecito may be played as an instrumental accompaniment to the dance by typical Andean instruments (**charango,** guitar, and Andean drum).

REFERENCE:

Isabel Aretz, *El folklore musical argentino* (Buenos Aires: Ricordi Americana S.A.E.C., 1952).

— R.L.S.

BALLET CONTEMPORÁNEO DEL TEATRO SAN MARTÍN

Ballet Contemporáneo del Teatro San Martín, the resident contemporary dance company of the General San Martín Municipal Theater of Buenos Aires, Argentina, was created in 1977 by Kive Staiff. The company was originally formed by the corps de ballet and the Taller de Danza (Workshop of Dance) of the Teatro San Martín, and by members of the dance group directed by the internationally renown Argentinean choreographer Oscar Araiz. The company was directed by **Ana María Stekelman** until 1981, and again starting in 1988, until her replacement as artistic director by Araiz. The more than thirty different works performed by the company are generally nonabstract, but centered around a musical, pictorial, or literary image. In addition to Stekelman and Araiz, choreographers such as Alejandro Cervera, Ana Itelman, Julio López, Mauricio Wainrot, Roberto Trinchero, Susana Tambutti, Inés Vernengo, Lisu Brodsky, Luís Arrietta, Lía Fernández, Flavio Fernández, Miguel Angel Elías, and Mónica Fracchia have created works for the company. The company has toured the Soviet Union, Spain, Brazil, Puerto Rico, Mexico, and the United States.

— J.M.H. & N.D.B.

BALLET DE LIMA

Formerly the Asociación de Artistas Aficionados Ballet (Association of Ballet-Loving Artists), the Ballet de Lima was founded in 1943 by choreographer–artistic director Dimitri Rostoff. Beginning in 1948 it has been directed by Roger Fenonjois of Paris, who brought with him the training methods of French ballet master Gustave Ricaux. Performance sponsorship has been secured from such sources as the International Bank of Peru, International Petroleum Company, and Pacific Insurance Company.

— J.M.H. & N.D.B.

BALLET DE SANTIAGO

The Chilean company Ballet de Santiago, originally called the Ballet de Arte Moderno (Modern Art Ballet), was founded by Octavio Cintolesi, a former member of the **Ballet Nacional Chileno,** in 1959. In 1982 Ivan Nagy, former principal dancer with the American Ballet Theater, became artistic director. On the celebration of its twenty-fifth anniversary in 1983, the company changed its name to Ballet de Santiago. Composed of fifty dancers of twelve nationalities, the majority of them Chileans and Latin Americans, the company performs six different programs repeated four times each season, as well as holding many lecture-demonstrations for students and touring throughout Chile and various Latin American countries.

— J.M.H. & N.D.B.

BALLET DEL SUR

Ballet del Sur, created in 1957, is a contemporary dance company based at the Teatro Municipal in Bahía Blanca, Argentina. Composed of approximately forty dancers, it has been directed since 1992 by noted Argentinean dancer and choreographer Alejandro Cervera. The Asociación Amigos del Ballet del Sur de Bahía Blanca (Friends of the Ballet del Sur) was created in 1987 to provide moral and economic support for the company. The Asociación finances the hiring of guest performers and guest choreographers, as well as some members of the permanent teaching staff. In its repertoire the company includes such works as *The Nutcracker, Carmina Burana, Don Quixote, Peer Gynt, Afro Roots for Them,* and works by Artistic Director Cervera, such as *Tango Vitrola, Satie-Satie,* and *Bolero.*

— J.M.H. & N.D.B.

BALLET METROPOLITANO DE CARACAS

The Ballet Metropolitano de Caracas, founded by Keyla Ermecheo in 1980, has presented *The Nutcracker* annually in December at the Teatro Municipal. The first classical ballet production mounted entirely within Venezuela, *The Nutcracker* was performed by a cast of 120 with choreography by the Argentinean Héctor Zaraspe. The company's repertory also includes *The Bluebird* and *Carnival in Venice* by Marius Petipa, as well as works by Ermecheo and guest choreographers with music by Venezuelan and European composers. The Ballet Metropolitano, composed of

Scene from a production by the Ballet Nacional Chileno (photograph by
Jack Ceitelis)

twenty dancers, is supported by the Fundación Ballet
Metropolitano.

— J.M.H. & N.D.B.

BALLET NACIONAL CHILENO

The Ballet Nacional Chileno, based at the University
of Chile, has been called the most highly respected
dance company in South America. Created in 1942, it
was the first professional dance company in the country. Previously, only foreign dance companies — M.
Poncot's in 1850, the Roussets in 1856, **Anna Pavlova**'s
company in 1917–1918, and De Basil's Original Ballets
Russes of Monte Carlo and the **Ballets Kurt Jooss** in
the 1940s — had been presented in Chile. The founders
of the Ballet Nacional Chileno were former Jooss
dancer-choreographer Ernst Uthoff, his wife, Lola
Botka, and Rudolf Pescht, contracted by the govern-

ment to create a school and company after a tour to
Chile by the Ballets Jooss. Uthoff and Botka, together
with Andreé Haas and Rudolf Pescht, also formed the
first dance school of the University of Chile. The Russian-
trained Elena Poliakova, a classmate of Tamara
Karsavina and Lydia Kyasht, became ballet mistress in
1952. The founding of the company also stimulated the
development of related artistic activities: music, costume, set, lighting design, and the visual arts. *The
Green Table,* the best-known dance of the Kurt Jooss
legacy and German dance expressionism, is in the
company's repertoire, as are works by Delibes
(*Coppélia,* the first work performed by the company),
Uthoff, Kurt Jooss, John Butler, Pauline Koner, Birgit
Cullberg, and many Chilean choreographers, including
Michael Uthoff, son of the founders. The dancers, who
enter at the age of fourteen or fifteen, receive the
equivalent of a junior-college degree, studying music
appreciation, dance history, Labanotation, Dalcroze,
modern dance, and ballet. The company is wholly sub-

sidized by the government. Funds for the institute have come from a special tax on movie tickets, and members of the company are salaried government employees. As an indication of the level of activity, in 1959 the company gave 110 performances and toured Peru, Argentina, and Uruguay, as well as Chile. Later tours took the company to the United States, Canada, Puerto Rico, and Bolivia. In 1986 Maritza Parada Allende assumed the direction of the company.

— J.M.H. & N.D.B.

BALLET NACIONAL DE CARACAS

Since 1984 Venezuelan choreographer Vicente Nebrada, a founding member of the Harkness Ballet of New York, has been artistic director of this company, whose full title is Ballet Nacional de Caracas "Teresa Carreño." Founded in 1980 as the Ballet de la Fundación Teresa Carreño, after the theater in which it is based, the company performs many works by Nebrada and by other current Latin American choreographers, as well as works by Russian-born choreographer George Balanchine, artistic director of the New York City Ballet. Works by Nebrada include those based on the lives of George Sand and Vincent van Gogh, as well as the classical repertory, including *Romeo and Juliet, Swan Lake, Don Quixote,* and *Coppélia.* The company, composed of approximately forty dancers whose average age is less than twenty-one, has toured Colombia, Peru, France, and the United States. Such internationally known artists as Rudolf Nureyev, Alexander Godunov, Patrick Bissell, and Fernando Bujones have appeared as guest performers.

— J.M.H. & N.D.B.

BALLET NUEVO MUNDO

The New World Ballet of Caracas, Venezuela, whose artistic director is the prima ballerina Zhandra Rodríguez, was founded in 1981. As one way of securing its financial stability, the Ballet Nuevo Mundo created a relationship with the Cleveland–San Jose Ballet and with the Venezuelan company Rajatabladanza. Choreographers represented in the repertoire include Americans Ulysses Dove, Alvin Ailey, and Elisa Monte; Dutch choreographer Hans Van Manen; and director of the Taller de Danza Contemporánea of Venezuela (Venezuelan Contemporary Dance Workshop) José Ledezma, as well as Rodríguez and Carlos Carvajal. The company of twenty dancers, 80 percent of whom are Venezuelan, is supported by the govern-

ment of Venezuela, which considers Ballet Nuevo Mundo cultural ambassadors of Venezuela when sending the company on international tours. Agencies of the government which support the company include the Congress, the presidency, the Ministry of Foreign Relations, the Ministry of Education, the government of the Federal District, Petróleos de Venezuela, and the Centro Simón Bolívar. The company has visited Russia, Italy, the United States, Argentina, Uruguay, Brazil, and the Far East.

— J.M.H. & N.D.B.

BALLET PERUANO

The Ballet Peruano is directed by American dancer Kaye Mackinnon. The repertory combines classical works with others based on Peruvian folk and legendary Indian themes. Among others, it has presented works by U.S. choreographer Grace de Aviles, including *Atahualpa* (based on the story of the last Inca leader and his resistance to the Spanish conquerors) and *Malabrigo.* Company members receive salaries as physical education teachers in the high schools of Lima. The company is supported by the government of Peru.

— J.M.H. & N.D.B.

BALLETS KURT JOOSS

The Ballets Kurt Jooss, a dance company established by the German choreographer Kurt Jooss, left Germany in 1934, after the rise of Nazism the previous year, and was based thereafter in England. In April 1940 it found itself stranded in Cuba owing to the impossibility in wartime of receiving funds from England to finance its return home. The company therefore created a pioneering cooperative venture to tour all of South America until the crisis was over. When it arrived in Montevideo in May 1940, it was the first foreign dance company to have visited South America since **Anna Pavlova**'s company toured in 1918. In a full year of continuous performing, the Ballets Jooss was seen in every South American country except Paraguay and Bolivia and appeared in nearly every city of any size on both coasts. In many of these places it was the first nonlocal theatrical group ever to perform. In all, the Ballets Jooss presented 310 performances in South America, from a repertoire consisting of *The Green Table, Chronica, The Prodigal Son, The Seven Heroes, The Big City, Pavane, A Ball in Old Vienna, Ballade,* and *A Spring Tale.* The longest single engagement of the company in South America was in Buenos Aires, where it played for a total of ten weeks over a five-month period, presenting ten performances a week to completely sold-out houses. These ten weeks established the reputation of the company throughout the continent and assured its success for the balance of the tour. The company played for a full month in Santiago, Chile, the population of which was only 700,000 at the time; yet there was only one performance for which the theater was not filled, and that was owing to an earthquake. This tour led to the creation of the **Ballet Nacional Chileno** under the direction of former Jooss dancers.

—N.D.B. & J.M.H.

José Balza

Winner of the 1991 National Prize for Literature and a psychologist by profession, José Balza (1939–) is an experimental Venezuelan writer who refers to his work as "narrative exercises." In Balza's "exercises" conventional plot and character development are replaced by a stream of consciousness dwelling on the evanescence of memory and identity. The complexity of Balza's prose is enhanced by the author's frequent reliance on dreams, hallucinations, and metafiction (that is, texts within the text), an approach that generates ambiguity through the deliberate confusion of fiction and reality. Balza has published *D: Ejercicio narrativo* (1977; D: A Narrative Exercise), *Medianoche en video — 1/5* (1988; Midnight on Video — 1/5), *El vencedor: Ejercicios narrativos* (1989; The Victor: Narrative Exercises), and *Tres ejercicios narrativos* (1992; Three Narrative Exercises). He is also the author of a book on narrative technique: *Este mar narrativo: Ensayos sobre el cuerpo novelesco* (1987; This Sea of Stories: Essays on the Novelistic Corpus).

REFERENCE:
Julio Ortega, *Venezuela: Fin de siglo* (Caracas: Casa de Bello, 1993).

—R.G.M.

Bambuco

The bambuco is a traditional song/dance from Colombia that embodies a vibrant and revealing combination of elements from the indigenous, European, and African musical cultures originating in the region west of the Andes. With alternating 6/8 and 3/4 meters in a moderately quick tempo, performance of the bambuco is subject to variations of style and interpretation in different regions of Colombia. In the district of Cauca,

the bambuco is typically accompanied by an ensemble known as *Chirimia,* consisting of one to four reed flutes, a single-membrane drum, a double-membrane drum, maracas, and a scraper instrument. In more-urban areas the accompaniment may consist of strings, clarinets, transverse flutes, and double bass. The widespread regional popularity of the bambuco contributes to its reputation as one of the most representative genres of Colombian folk music.

REFERENCE:
Octavio Marulanda, *El folclor de Colombia: Práctica de la identidad cultural* (Bogotá: Artestudio Editores, 1984).

—R.L.S.

Bandola

A small **chordophone** of the lute family, the bandola is closely associated with Colombian folk music of the Andean and eastern plains regions. Its development appears to have been related to the Spanish bandurria and, perhaps, the Neapolitan mandolin. Early versions of the bandola might have had four or five courses of double strings. In the twentieth century the number and organization of the strings extended to four triple courses and two doubles, thereby considerably expanding the resources of the instrument. The bandola is typical of the folk ensembles that perform the instrumental **bambuco** and **pasillo** of the Andean region of Colombia and the **joropo** of the eastern plains region.

REFERENCE:
Octavio Marulanda, *El folclor de Colombia: Práctica de la identidad cultural* (Bogotá: Artestudio Editores, 1984).

—R.L.S.

Bandoneón

The origin of the bandoneón is attributed to Alexander Band in Germany, and its early name, "bandolium," was in homage to its originator. Appearing in Europe in the 1830s, the instrument became known in South America around the turn of the twentieth century. The bandoneón's early use in Argentina is attributed to Sebastián Ramos Mejía, a former slave, to another black musician named Santa Cruz, and to his son, **Domingo Santa Cruz,** who also composed early **tangos.**

The bandoneón has buttons for both bass and treble notes rather than the traditional keyboard for the treble. A typical instrument has eight bass buttons and twenty-one treble buttons. Notes may be played individually or in chords. Larger instruments with as

Daniel Berenboim, age nine, playing the piano, with Bruno Bandini and the Radio Orchestra, Argentina, 1951

many as seventy-one buttons were used with the tango ensembles.

The bandoneón is also played throughout Argentina to accompany folk dances such as the **zamba.** In folk ensembles it often substitutes for the violin. In the northeastern region of Argentina it is normally accompanied by the **bombo,** while on the Atlantic littoral the guitar is preferred.

In the early years of the twentieth century several *orquestas típicas* (typical creole bands) incorporated the bandoneón; one of the first was Vicente Greco's *Orquesta Típica,* in which Greco played the bandoneón. Another outstanding player in what is now called the *Guardia Vieja* (the Old Guard) was Tano Genaro Espósito, who early on played with the Pizzaro Orchestra and later led his own ensemble. Augusto Berto and Francisco Canaro, both *bandoneonistas* (players of the instrument), were also orchestra leaders of the first generation of *orquestas típicas.*

In the second decade of the twentieth century the *Guardia Nueva* (New Guard) introduced a new sophistication to the tango, **milonga,** and other popular genres. Although the trio format of violin, bandoneón, and guitar continued to be popular, the sextet, consisting of two violins, two bandoneóns, piano, and contra-

bass, became the preferred ensemble of a more-affluent audience. In this context the bandoneón exercised a more prominent and varied role as played by Pedro Maffia, Pedro Laurenz, Roberto Goyeneche, Osvaldo Fresedo, and Julio Vivas, who performed with **Carlos Gardel.**

The decline of the tango during the 1930s has been attributed to various causes, one of which was competition from foreign music. Jazz and North American popular music diverted consumer interest away from the tango and the bandoneón. A fervent revival of the tango and the bandoneón in the 1940s was led by bandoneón players Domingo Federico and Aníbal Troilo.

By midcentury many of the great tango salons of Buenos Aires had disappeared, and the tango's signal instrument, the bandoneón, was relegated to a nostalgic role in folk music and as guardian of the vestiges of the tango. Ensembles came together more for recording sessions than for live performances. But a new star on the scene revived interest once again: **Astor Piazzola,** the undisputed leader of the revolutionary vanguard of the tango in the second half of the century, was a virtuoso player of the bandoneón who practically abandoned his career as a classical composer and conductor to dedicate his talent and skill to the *Nuevo Tango* (New Tango) and to the instrument he referred to as his "second wife."

REFERENCES:

Isabel Aretz, *El folklore musical argentino* (Buenos Aires: Ricordi Americana S.A.E.C., 1952);

Gerard Béhague, "Latin American Folk Music," in *Folk and Traditional Music of the Western Continents,* by Bruno Nettl, third edition, revised and edited by Valerie Woodring Goertzen (Englewood Cliffs, N.J.: Prentice-Hall, 1990);

Argentino Manrique Carriego, ed., *No habrá más penas ni olvido: Carlos Gardel 50 Años, 1935–1985* (Medellín, Colombia: Editorial Percepción, 1985);

Peter Manuel, *Popular Musics of the Non-Western World* (Oxford: Oxford University Press, 1988).

— R.L.S.

Rafael Barradas in Barcelona, circa 1916–1917

DANIEL BARENBOIM

A child prodigy, Daniel Barenboim (1942–   ) began his piano studies with his parents and made his Buenos Aires debut at the age of seven. Two years later the family left Argentina for Europe, eventually settling in Israel. Young Daniel pursued an active regimen combining concerts with studies in Salzburg, Rome, and Paris, where he studied composition with master teacher and harpsichordist Nadia Boulanger. Before the age of fifteen he played major concerts in Salzburg, London, and New York. He later performed as accompanist or conductor with his cellist wife, Jacqueline Dupré, whom he married in June 1967. By the age of twenty he had made his debut as a conductor in Israel and Australia, beginning a career with the baton that was to place him as guest conductor before some of the best orchestras in the world: the London and Chicago Symphony Orchestras, the Berlin and New York Philharmonic Orchestras, as well as other leading ensembles. The Orchestre de Paris appointed him conductor in 1975; his time in that position, however, was fraught with problems, and in 1993 he took over from George Solti as principal conductor of the Chicago Symphony Orchestra.

Not content to work exclusively with orchestras, Barenboim has been active as an operatic conductor, a chamber-music pianist, and an accompanist for outstanding singers and instrumentalists. He has made approximately one hundred sound and video recordings as conductor and performing artist. His musical preference appears to focus on major works from the traditional European repertoire, of which he is acknowledged by experts as a leading interpreter.

— R.L.S.

RAFAEL BARRADAS

Rafael Pérez Barradas (1890–1929) was one of the first avant-garde Uruguayan artists. Born in Montevideo to a family of Spanish immigrants, he learned art from his father, a painter. During his adolescence he published his drawings of city life in local periodicals and had his first exhibition in 1910. He traveled to Italy in 1913, where he met Filippo Marinetti and became interested in Futurism. During World War I he sought refuge in Spain, settling in Barcelona around 1916, where he befriended **Joaquín Torres-García,** a fellow Uruguayan artist. Barradas worked in a style he called **Vibrationism,** one which synthesized aspects of Futurism and Cubism and celebrated the "vibrant" dynamism of city life. In paintings such as *Verbena de Atocha* (1919; Atocha Festival), Barradas adopted the Futurists' use of fragmentation and repetition of highly simplified forms to suggest the feverish activity of a busy street. He exhibited his Vibrationist paintings in 1917 at the avant-garde Dalmau gallery.

In 1918 Barradas moved to Madrid, where he created set and costume designs for the Teatro Eslava;

these designs were later exhibited at the 1925 Exposition Internationale des Arts Décoratifs et Industriels Modernes in Paris. Barradas also associated with the Ultraists, including **Norah Borges** and **Jorge Luis Borges,** and contributed illustrations to avant-garde magazines, such as *Reflector* and *Revista de Occidente.* He returned to Catalonia in 1926 after contracting tuberculosis. In his last period he painted views of the Catalonian town of Hospitalet de Llobregat, mystical religious images, such as *The Adoration of the Kings and Shepherds* (1928), and the series of *Estampones* (Large Prints), such as *Gaucho* (1927), which evoke the Montevideo of his childhood. Barradas died in 1929, soon after his return to Montevideo in 1928.

REFERENCE:

Edward J. Sullivan, "Notes on the Birth of Modernity in Latin American Art," in *Latin American Artists of the Twentieth Century,* edited by Waldo Rasmussen, Fatima Bercht, and Elizabeth Ferrer (New York: Museum of Modern Art, 1993), pp. 18–37.

— F.B.N.

BARRANQUILLA GROUP

Named after Colombia's main Caribbean port, the Barranquilla Group, a small coterie of friends whose literary aspirations were fueled by their discovery of modern authors such as William Faulkner, Ernest Hemingway, Franz Kafka, Marcel Proust, and Virginia Woolf, introduced modern fiction to Colombian literature. Their geographical location facilitated their acquaintance with "imported" writers fairly unknown in the early 1950s in more traditional cultural centers like Bogotá, isolated in the Andean highlands. The most famous member of the group is **Gabriel García Márquez,** then a young and unknown journalist working for the local newspaper *El Heraldo.* The eventual Nobel laureate incorporated the other members of the group as characters in *Cien años de soledad* (1967; translated as *One Hundred Years of Solitude*), including the Catalan bookseller Ramón Vinyes, who provided the literary novelties and who appears in García Márquez's novel as the "Catalonian wise man." The Barranquilla group also included literary critic Germán Vargas, journalist Alfonso Fuenmayor (son of a novelist), and Alvaro Cepeda Samudio, author of *La casa grande* (1962; translated), a novel influenced by Faulkner and similar in subject matter and tone to García Márquez's masterpiece.

— R.G.M.

LA BATALLA DE CHILE

La batalla de Chile (1975–1979; The Battle of Chile) is a three-part documentary directed by **Patrico Guzmán** and aided by the Equipo Tercer Año team. Often considered to be Guzmán's masterpiece, this film conveys in great detail the nature and consequences of political events in Chile during the last year of the government of **Salvador Allende** (1972–1973). The film has three parts. Part 1, "The Insurrection of the Bourgeoisie," concentrates on the mass uprising of the middle and upper sectors and the repressive measures taken by the government and the Left. Part 2, "The Coup d'Etat," continues with the struggle between Right and Left and focuses on dissension within the Left. Part 3, "Popular Power," is a sympathetic evocation of mass organizations during the Popular Unity government, particularly in its last year.

REFERENCE:

Julianne Burton, ed., *Cinema and Social Change in Latin America: Conversations with Latin American Filmmakers* (Austin: University of Texas Press, 1986).

— S.M.H.

JUAN MIGUEL LUIS BATLLE PLANAS

Juan Miguel Luis Batlle Planas (1911–1965) was one of the first Argentinean **Surrealists.** Originally from Catalonia, he was raised in Buenos Aires, where he studied art with his uncle Juan Planas Casas and the printmaker Pompeyo Audivert. During the 1930s Batlle Planas became interested in Zen Buddhism, psychoanalytic theory, and automatic drawing techniques and began producing Surrealist works. In 1937 he exhibited his *Radiografías Paranoicas* (Paranoic X Rays) series, combining Surrealist automatic techniques and semiabstract biomorphic shapes reminiscent of noted Catalan painter Joan Miró. From 1939 to 1943 he radically simplified his figurative style and depicted occult themes in small works executed with great attention to detail, a precise manner he had learned while studying printmaking. Paintings such as *El mensaje* (1941; The Message) and *La mecánica* (1941; Mechanics), feature angelic messengers communicating through supernatural senses and occult powers.

Batlle Planas's style became more realistic by the mid 1940s. He produced two important series, *Las Noicas,* a title he explained as referring to fairies of life and destiny, and *Mecanismo del número* (Mechanism of the Number), which included references to chance, destiny, and astrology. In 1948 his art became influenced by Wilhelm Reich's writings about cosmic energy. Batlle Planas believed that form is a materialization of the energy an artist transfers to the artwork in the process of creation. This concept is reflected in his later abtract works, such as *Cabeza* (1964; Head), which combines geometric shapes and some of the letters that spell the name of the artist's first wife, Elena Salgueiro. During the last years of his life Batlle Planas produced a series of boxes and polychromed sculptures, which he exhibited in 1960.

REFERENCE:

Susana Sulic, "Batlle Planas," in *Pintores argentinos del siglo XX*, no. 24 (Buenos Aires: Centro Editor de América Latina, 1980).

— F.B.N.

Carlos Germán Belli

One of the key figures of contemporary Latin American poetry, Carlos Germán Belli (1927–) was born in Trujillo, Peru, and published his first collection of poems in 1958. His subsequent books have been published in various Hispanic countries and translated into English and Italian. His poetry is immediately striking for his original reworking of Spanish renaissance and baroque tropes as well as a rare mixture of traditional and elevated poetic language with the language of colloquial and modern technical speech. The appeal to traditional tropes and styles is for Belli a rhetorical way to organize or appropriate language by avoiding the onrush of language in its wild, unbound state; as such, the poet's gesture toward tradition complements the strictures of grammar, which have the same ordering function. Belli, easily labeled a neobaroque poet, is not, however, a decorative poet. He descends from the Symbolists and Surrealists of an earlier age, who venerated poetry for its visionary and divining powers. For Belli poetry is a passage into the unknown, a glimpse of what lies beyond the mask of everyday experience.

In *¡Oh Hada Cibernetica!* (Oh Cybernetic Sprite!), first published in Lima in 1961 and republished in an expanded edition the following year, Belli predicates the orphic power of poetry on carnal and spiritual love as he implores the peculiar ladylove of the title — a modernized avatar of the traditional fairy godmother — for release from earthly suffering and travail. (*¡Oh Hada Cibernetica!* is also the title of a collection of Belli's poems published in Caracas, Venezuela, in 1969.) In this book Belli's preoccupation with the lot of the poor and with the baroque theme of *desengaño* (disillusion) is evident.

In *En alabanza del bolo alimenticio* (1979; In Praise of the Alimentary Bolus) the poet descends into the interior of his bodily self and raises the alimentary

bolus to a symbol of physical matter, displacing love and erotic desire in the process. Belli also scrutinizes the poetic act in its most irreducible physical dimensions — such as the weight and size of the letters on the blank sheet of paper or the contours of the graphic sign — in the poem "The Wedding of the Pen and the Letter." Although the poet represents himself as a "pesaletras" (letter weigher) or a "feliz calígrafo" (happy calligrapher), in this extraordinary comic work Belli does not abandon preoccupation with transcendental questions.

Later books by Belli are *Más que señora humana* (1987; A Lady More than Human), which was republished as *Bajo el sol de la media noche rojo* (1990; Under the Red Sun of Midnight), and *Acción de gracias* (1992; Thanksgiving).

REFERENCE:

W. Nick Hill, *Tradición y modernidad en la poesía de Carlos Germán Belli* (Madrid: Editorial Pliegos, 1985).

— R.G.M.

Mario Benedetti

Mario Benedetti (1920–) is a prolific and versatile Uruguayan author and journalist who was one of the first writers in his country to deal with the themes of the modern city. In the 1950s Benedetti wrote stories, poems, essays, and a novel on the office worker (government bureaucrat or clerical employee) as a national stereotype, a social type that seemed to summarize the aspirations of the nation known as "the Switzerland of South America." *Montevideanos* (1959), stories about the inhabitants of the Uruguayan capital; *Poemas de la oficina* (1956; Office Poems); *El país de la cola de paja* (1960; The Country with the Straw Tail), essays of moral criticism targeting national lethargy; and the novel *La tregua* (1960; The Truce) belong to this period of his production, during which Benedetti became Uruguay's most widely read writer. However, it is striking that neither then nor afterward did he depart from a realist mode of writing, a fact which sets him apart from writers of the **Boom** of the 1960s.

Benedetti cemented his solidarity with the **Cuban Revolution** and Fidel Castro's regime after first visiting Cuba in 1966. His political awakening coincided with a moment of institutional crisis in Uruguay that was to have its most dire repercussions in the early 1970s. In 1971 Benedetti published *El cumpleaños de Juan Angel* (Juan Angel's Birthday), a novel in verse detailing the conversion of the middle-class protagonist into a revolutionary. That same year the author became the

Desocupados, o Desocupación (1934; Unemployed, or Unemployment), by Antonio Berni (Collection of
Elena Berni)

leader of a leftist political front opposed to the government.

After the military takeover of 1973 Benedetti's books were banned in Uruguay, and the author went into exile and lived for long periods in Cuba and Spain. In Spain he published numerous articles in *El País,* the country's leading daily. Many of Benedetti's later works reflect the political situation of Uruguay under the military regime and in particular the poignant predicament of the thousands of exiles scattered around the world. The novel *Primavera con una esquina rota* (1982; Spring with a Broken Corner) is about a political prisoner who serves years in prison and cannot resume his personal relationships when he is freed. In 1987 it received the Golden Flame award from Amnesty International. The stories of *Geografías* (1984; Geographies) center on the psychological effects of exile, and the play *Pedro y el capitán* (Pedro and the Captain), staged in 1979 in Mexico by an exiled Uruguayan troupe, deals with the theme of political torture. Benedetti's journalism — much of it of a political character — is collected in

El desexilio y otras conjeturas (1984; The End of Exile and Other Conjectures). The author's most recent books are a collection of poems, *Las soledades de Babel* (1991; The Solitudes of Babel), and the novel *La borra del café* (1992; The Dregs of Coffee), a bildungsroman about a boy growing up in the Rió de la Plata region.

REFERENCE:

Hugo Alfaro, *Mario Benedetti* (Montevideo: Ediciones Trilce, 1986).

— R.G.M. & P.S.

ANTONIO BERNI

Although the Argentinean artist Antonio Berni (1905–1981) worked in different styles, ranging from **Surrealism** and **social realism** to **Neofiguration,** his interest in the social and political issues of his time remained paramount in his art. From 1927 to 1930 Berni studied in Paris, where he admired the art of Giorgio De

Chirico and was introduced into Surrealist and Marxist circles by the poet Louis Aragon. His paintings of this period show surreal juxtapositions of unrelated objects, such as *El Botón y el Tornillo* (1931; The Button and the Screw). When Berni returned to Argentina in 1930, his concern for the social problems caused by the Great Depression led him to become a social activist. He cofounded the Nuevo Realismo group and produced monumental canvases on social and political themes, such as *Manifestación* (1934; Demonstration) and *Desocupados, o Desocupación* (1934; Unemployed, or Unemployment), done in a realistic style that retained a subtle surreal quality. His works were often based on photographs he took to record the life of the poor in different areas of Argentina.

When David Alfaro Siqueiros visited Argentina in 1933, Berni collaborated with him in an experimental mural, but they were unable to develop a muralist movement. Berni continued his social activism by directing a group of artists who worked for unions and political organizations. From 1937 to 1945 he taught at the Escuela de Bellas Artes of Buenos Aires and in 1941 traveled along the west coast of South America with a state grant to study colonial and pre-Columbian art, which resulted in series of paintings inspired by Indian cultures, such as *Mercado indígena* (1942; Indigenous Market). Berni also produced several murals — for instance, the ceiling of the Galerías Pacífico building in Buenos Aires in 1946, on which he worked as a member of the Taller de Arte Mural.

In 1958 and 1963 respectively Berni introduced two memorable characters, Juanito Laguna, a poor child from the slums, and Ramona Montiel, a courtesan, both of whom became the protagonists of several works based on their lives (produced serially). By then Berni's style had radically changed; although he continued working on a large scale, he made collages often considered antecedents of Neofiguration for their expressionistic quality. He used urban trash and found objects, compounding the social message of his works through his choice of materials.

REFERENCE:

Marta Nanni, *Antonio Berni: Obra pictórica, 1922–1981* (Buenos Aires: Museo Nacional de Bellas Artes, 1984).

— F.B.N.

Biarritz Festival

The Festival International de Biarritz, subtitled "Cinémas et Cultures de l'Amérique Latine" and held in southwest France since the late 1970s, has developed into a major showcase in Europe for Latin American culture in general and films in particular. Each year there is an open film competition and a retrospective series of movies from a featured Latin American country. Literature, music, and the plastic arts occupy a smaller part of the program but have been important enough to attract many luminaries such as **Fernando Botero** and **Mario Vargas Llosa.** Three prizes are awarded in the film competition; winners have included Ricardo Larraín (Chile) for *La frontera* (The Border), Eliseo Subiela (Argentina) for *El lado oscuro del corazón* (The Dark Side of the Heart), Carlos Azpurúa (Venezuela) for *Disparen a matar* (Shoot to Kill), Sergio Cabrera (Colombia) for *La estrategia del caracol* (The Snail's Stratagem), José Ramón Novoa (Venezuela) for *Sicario,* and Luis Argueta for *El silencio de neto* (Neto's Silence), the first feature film ever made in Guatemala.

— P.S.

Biblioteca Ayacucho

Named after the battle that sealed the independence of Spanish America from Spain in 1824, the Biblioteca Ayacucho (Ayacucho Library) is an ambitious collection of over 150 classics of Latin American letters established by presidential decree in Venezuela in 1976. The dream of Simón Bolívar, "the Liberator," was the unification of Spanish America, a project that the Biblioteca Ayacucho undertakes on the cultural level. The collection includes a variety of authors from all parts of Latin America, including Brazil, and a variety of genres, such as poetry, fiction, and political and sociological essays. The initial volume comprises the political writings of Simón Bolívar. A few of the individual volumes are anthologies on subjects such as indigenous literatures, Cuban **costumbrismo,** gauchesque poetry, and Uruguayan and Argentinean popular theater. Each volume includes a substantial prologue, a bibliography, and a far-ranging chronology of the author's period. After 1987 the last section was deleted from individual volumes, and a comprehensive chronology from 900 B.C. to 1985 A.D. was published separately. Some of the modern poets and novelists represented in the collection thus far are **Pablo Neruda, Gabriel García Márquez, Julio Cortázar, José Donoso, Vicente Huidobro, César Vallejo,** Carlos Fuentes, Juan Rulfo, and Alejo Carpentier.

REFERENCE:

Angel Rama, "La Biblioteca Ayacucho como instrumento de integración cultural latinoamericana," *Latino América,* 14 (1981): 325–339.

— R.G.M.

Adolfo Bioy Casares and Jorge Luis Borges

ADOLFO BIOY CASARES

An Argentinean novelist and short-story writer known to many as the collaborator of **Jorge Luis Borges** in various narrative ventures, Adolfo Bioy Casares (1914–) is a major literary figure in his own right.

Bioy Casares, born in Buenos Aires, published his first (though admittedly forgettable) book at the age of fifteen; by that time he had already traveled to Europe and New York with his parents, who were wealthy and cultured landowners. Later Bioy became a frequent visitor of the Ocampo household and an occasional contributor to *Sur.* At **Victoria Ocampo**'s house Bioy met Borges in 1932. The first of their joint efforts was the *Antología de la literatura fantástica* (1940; translated as *The Book of Fantasy*), published the same year that Bioy Casares married **Silvina Ocampo,** the third compiler of the book. The anthology includes uncanny and supernatural stories culled from the vast repertoire of world literature, and it helped consolidate the fantastic genre in the Río de la Plata region. It is also an indirect manifesto of the kind of stories that appealed to both Bioy and Borges, stories

that combined a penchant for the bizarre with a rigorous formal construction.

Other books in collaboration followed: *Seis problemas para don Isidro Parodi* (1942; translated as *Six Problems for Don Isidro Parodi*), a parody of G. K. Chesterton's Father Brown stories published under the pseudonym H. Bustos Domecq; *Un modelo para la muerte* (1946; A Model for Death), published under another pseudonym, B. Suárez Lynch; and *Dos fantasías memorables* (1946; Two Memorable Fantasies), published once again with the Bustos Domecq pen name. In 1955 Bioy and Borges co-authored two film scripts, *Los orilleros* (the title designates the inhabitants of the outskirts of Buenos Aires in the early years of the twentieth century) and *El paraíso de los creyentes* (The Believers' Paradise). Two more volumes of Bustos Domecq stories followed (1967, 1977), complemented by another joint film script, *Invasión* (1969). It should be added that many of Bioy's stories and novels have been made into films.

Bioy established his considerable reputation early and on his own with the short novel *La invención de Morel* (1940; translated in *The Invention of Morel and Other Stories*), which in 1941 won the first Municipal Prize for Literature awarded by the city of Buenos Aires. The novel's genre is a mixture of science fiction, the adventure story, and the fantastic, but its theme is love, a theme that recurs in Bioy's fiction in a variety of guises. The title of the novel (recalling H. G. Wells's *The Island of Dr. Moreau*) refers to a holographic device abandoned on a deserted island in which a fugitive seeks refuge. The machine has recorded the comings and goings of a small party assembled on the island by Morel — the gadget's inventor — and projects the stored images according to the rhythm of the tides. The story is told by the befuddled fugitive in the form of a diary. Long before the narrator realizes the illusory nature of the characters playing out their dance for all eternity, the narrator falls in love with the female lead, a certain Faustine, whose name alludes to the Faustian theme of the compact with the devil, in this case Morel's technology. The narrator gradually learns the workings of the machine and memorizes the movements and dialogue of the characters, enabling him to insert himself into the fiction at the appropriate moments in a pathetic effort to be with Faustine. The real-life actors of Morel's play are all dead by the time the fugitive arrives on the island, consumed by radiation disease. The narrator accepts the price of death in exchange for the nearness of his phantom beloved. The denouement is made all the more pathetic by the portrayal of the narrator as a bungling fellow whose powers of observation and deduction are inferior to those of the reader.

La invención de Morel originally appeared with an important prologue by Borges in which the merits of the adventure novel (fiction that emphasizes plot over characterization) are affirmed against those of the prevalent realist or psychological genres. Borges characterizes Bioy's novel as perfectly plotted, as building a mystery that seems impenetrable (except in terms of dream or symbol) and deciphering it with a single stroke that is fantastic but not supernatural.

The projection of images, and by extension the imagination's ability to effect external reality, is the theme of the inaugural story of *La trama celeste* (1948; The Celestial Plot), the book that Bioy dates as the legitimate beginning of his efforts to be a short-story writer. His earlier attempts, according to Bioy, merely constitute the stages of a learning process at the expense of the reader. The volume contains six stories belonging to the fantastic and detective genres. "En memoria de Paulina" (In Memory of Pauline) belongs to the former. The narrator, bookish and absorbed by literature like many of Bioy's characters, establishes a quasi-spiritual relation with a girl in childhood and assumes that when the time comes he and Paulina will be married. But a despicable rival with literary pretensions intervenes, seduces Paulina, and marries her, but then kills her in a fit of jealousy. Her image, however, appears in the narrator's mirror when he returns from studying abroad and learns of the fate of his beloved. It is Paulina's soul materializing, but not as projected by the narrator; instead, the vision of Paulina is projected and contaminated by the despicable rival; her apparition translates what the narrator suspects she is doing and saying in the rival's apartment. "El perjurio de la nieve" (The Perjury of the Snow) has significant affinities with the detective story. The protagonist writes a report detailing an official trip to Patagonia and mentions a wake that he and an occasional acquaintance attended in a secluded homestead. Later the friend is killed by the father of the girl whose wake he had attended, in the mistaken belief that he had previously seduced her. A third friend who "publishes" the report reads between the lines and speculates that the girl — held as a virtual prisoner by her father — was indeed seduced but by the author of the report, not by the friend hunted down and shot. The story is an exercise in interpretation making the roles of reader and detective coincide. To this extent it recalls Borges's "Death and the Compass."

In 1972 Bioy Casares published his revised and selected stories in two volumes: *Historias de amor* (Love Stories) and *Historias fantásticas* (Fantastic Stories). His latest collections are *Historias desaforadas* (1987; Off the Wall Stories) and *Una muñeca rusa* (1991; A Russian Doll and Other Stories). Unlike Borges, who never wrote one, Bioy authored several novels after *La invención de Morel*. For example, *Plan de evasión* (1945; translated as *A Plan for Escape*) is a multilayered and ambiguous epistolary novel set on Devil's Island. *Diario de la guerra del cerdo* (1969; translated as *Diary of the War of the Pig*) is set in the future and imagines a social war between roving gangs of youth and the old. *La aventura de un fotógrafo en La Plata* (1985; translated as *The Adventure of a Photographer in La Plata*) is a deliberately banal story in which the reader's expectations that something momentous is about to happen are kept up throughout but are ultimately deflated, as are the expectations of the two characters who have fallen in love but who end up separated for a commonplace reason. One of the author's latest novels is *Un campeón desparejo* (1993; Uneven Champion). Adolfo Bioy Casares received the **Premio Miguel de Cervantes** in 1990.

REFERENCE:

Suzanne Jill Levine, *Guía de Bioy Casares* (Madrid: Fundamentos, 1982).

— R.G.M.

FERNANDO BIRRI

Founder of the Documentary Film School at the National University of the Littoral in Santa Fe, Argentina, Fernando Birri (circa 1920–) is recognized as a precursor of the social documentary and a pioneer of what has become the **New Latin American Cinema** movement. He stated that the aim of documentary was "to confront reality with a camera and to document it" and to use documentary as a tool in "the awakening of consciousness of reality." Though political developments interrupted his work in Latin America, even in his absence his example bore fruit in countries across the hemisphere. His most important films are *Tire dié* (1960; Throw Me a Dime), which features children from a shanty community in the Santa Fe area in Argentina who daily risk their lives begging for money from passengers on passing trains; *La pampa gringa* (1963), a historical film commemorating the role played by European immigrants in opening up the Argentinean pampa; the neorealist feature *Los inundados* (1962; Flooded Out); and the experimental *Org* (1978), which is aimed less at the conscious mind than at the subconscious, as Birri himself has stated. Birri moved to Rome in 1964, has made frequent and prolonged visits to Cuba and Mexico, and has lived in Venezuela since 1979. In 1986 Birri was named director of the Escuela de Cine y Televisión (School of Film and Television), constructed in San Antonio de los Baños, Cuba.

REFERENCES:

Julianne Burton, ed., *Cinema and Social Change in Latin America: Conversations with Latin American Filmmakers* (Austin: University of Texas Press, 1986);

Zuzana M. Pick, *The New Latin American Cinema* (Austin: University of Texas Press, 1993).

— S.M.H.

BOEDO

Boedo is a main street in a lower-middle-class Buenos Aires neighborhood that in the 1920s and 1930s stood as a symbol of a group of writers and artists who professed the aesthetic and ideological tenets of social realism. In contrast, **Florida** was the upscale street downtown where the latest European fashions were displayed and the wealthy *porteños* (inhabitants of Buenos Aires) took their strolls. Because of its cosmopolitan connotations, Florida Street was associated with the avant-garde writers whose center of gravity was the journal *Martín Fierro* and, later, *Sur.* Some of the individual writers aligned with the Boedo group were **Roberto Arlt,** Leónidas Barletta, Roberto Mariani, and Raúl González Tuñón. The Florida group was composed of **Jorge Luis Borges, Xul Solar, Eduardo Mallea, Oliverio Girondo,** and **Victoria Ocampo,** among others.

The artists of the Boedo group were also called the Group of Barracas, Group of Five, and Artists of the People (the name they themselves favored). Their activities began in 1912, when Guillermo Facio Hebequer joined José Arato, Adolfo Bellocq, Abraham Vigo, and Agustín Riganelli in an association loosely called the Group of Barracas because they lived and worked in the Barracas neighborhood, near the docks and slaughterhouses of Buenos Aires. Many of the recently arrived European immigrants who lived in the area brought with them an awareness of anarchist and socialist ideas that contributed to the mood of social unrest prevalent in Buenos Aires during the first decades of the century. The Group of Barracas joined the social dissenters and associated with anarchist and leftist periodicals.

Soon the artists adopted the name Group of Five and began to attack official academies and other art institutions under the control of the Nexus Group, which advocated a nationalistic **impressionism** infused with reactionary values. The Group of Five wanted to professionalize art and literature through the development of alternative artistic and literary channels. In 1914 they supported the creation of the Primer Salón de Recusados (First Salon of the Rejected), and in 1917 they helped found the unionlike Sociedad de Pintores y Escultores (Society of Painters and Sculptors), which in 1918 established the Salón de Artistas Independientes (Independent Artists Salon), the first in Argentina with no juries or prizes.

During the 1920s the Group of Five adopted the name Artists of the People, loosely associated themselves with the writers of Boedo, and so came to be known by this name as well. Both artists and writers shared several traits with the European avant-gardes, in their rejection of middle-class values, their identification with the working class, and their belief in political ideologies that advocated radical change in society and in the contents of art and literature. While the artists of Florida defended Europeanized vanguard models, the Boedistas privileged social concerns over aesthetic change and saw recent avant-garde developments as unsuitable for expressing their political ideas, preferring to work with styles closer to nineteenth-century realism.

The Artists of the People also admired the writings on art of the sociologist Juan María Guyau and Russian novelist Leo Tolstoy. Guyau considered art as a means of communication between individuals at an emotional level, capable of engendering a sense of well-being and community among people. These artists adopted Tolstoy's notion that art transmits emotions and thoughts when viewers associate images presented by the artist with internal ones, evoking compatible feelings and thoughts. However, for artists like Bellocq, the purpose of art was not happiness but truth. Their point of departure was reality and the belief that an artist could prove the validity of truth through realistic representation.

The truth the Artists of the People wanted to represent was the poverty of workers and immigrants living in crowded tenement houses and their struggle to improve social conditions. For this reason, the group preferred the techniques of drawing and engraving, such as Bellocq's series *Proverbios* (1926; Proverbs) and Facio Hebequer's portfolio *Tu historia compañero* (1933; Your History Comrade), which were inexpensive and affordable to a broader public. Similarly, they also produced works for popular magazines and books, such as Arato's illustrations for Leónidas Barletta's *Los pobres* (1925; The Poor). In spite of their radical program, these artists quickly achieved critical acceptance during the 1920s, winning first prizes in official salons and obtaining positions in important art schools. Their association dissolved in the 1930s, after the deaths of Arato in 1929 and Facio Hebequer in 1935.

María Luisa Bombal

REFERENCES:

Marcelo E. Pacheco, *Reflexiones sobre la obra grabada de Adolfo Bellocq 1899–1972: Una aproximación a la acción del Grupo de Barracas* (Buenos Aires: Facultad de Filosofía y Letras, Universidad de Buenos Aires, 1988);

Adolfo Prieto, ed., *Antología de Boedo y Florida* (Córdoba: Universidad Nacional de Córdoba, 1964);

Diana Weschler and Miguel Angel Muñoz, *Los Artistas del Pueblo* (Buenos Aires: Galería Forma / Sociedad Argentina de Artistas Plásticos, 1989).

— F.B.N. & R.G.M.

Stubborn Cat), and *Crepúsculo pampeano* (1930–1940; Pampas Twilight).

REFERENCES:

Rodolfo Arizaga and Pompeyo Camps, *Historia de la música en la Argentina* (Buenos Aires: Ricordi Americana S.A.E.C., 1990);

Gerard Béhague, *Music in Latin America: An Introduction* (Englewood Cliffs, N.J.: Prentice-Hall, 1979).

— R.L.S.

FELIPE BOERO

One of several early–twentieth century Argentinean composers whose nationalistic tendencies found their greatest expression in opera, Felipe Boero (1884–1954), a graduate of the National Conservatory, set folk legends and popular Argentinean themes in the Italian lyric style. His five operas premiered at the Teatro Colón: *Tucumán* (1918), *Raquela* (1923), *El matrero* (1929; The Vagabond), *Siripo* (1937), and *Zincalí* (1954). Boero also composed songs, works for piano, an oratorio, and orchestral works, including *Suite de danzas Argentinas* (1920–1930; Suite of Argentinean Dances), *El gato porfiado* (1940–1950; The

MARÍA LUISA BOMBAL

The reputation of Chilean writer María Luisa Bombal (1910–1980) is based on two short novels published in the 1930s and on a handful of short stories. Bombal graduated from the Sorbonne in 1931 and returned to Santiago, where an unhappy love affair resulted in her attempted suicide. She left for Buenos Aires and made the acquaintance of **Victoria Ocampo,** who had recently founded the review *Sur.* Both of her novels were published in the Argentinean capital: *La última niebla* (1935; translated as *House of Mist*) and *La amortajada* (1938; translated as *The Shrouded Woman*). Bombal's stories were originally published in *Sur:* "Las islas nuevas" (1939; The New Islands), "El árbol" (1939; The Tree), and "Historia de María Griselda" (1946; The

Story of Maria Griselda). The author lived in New York for many years and resettled in Chile in 1973.

Bombal's works are notable for their poetic quality and for their rejection of the dominant literary strain of their time, **criollismo.** Their constant theme is the exploration of woman's condition in a patriarchal society. Bombal's female characters, drawn from the middle and the upper-middle classes, have no effective options at their disposal to escape their conditions of confinement. They are reflections of masculine desire, and what they themselves desire is only a perfected image of their oppressive world — for example, the secret lover as opposed to the indifferent husband. Dreams, death, and a mythical identification with nature are the means of escape favored by Bombal's heroines, but none of her female characters manages a definitive break with the prevailing social mores.

REFERENCE:

Marjorie Agosín, Elena Gascón-Vera, and Joy Renjilian-Burgy, eds., *María Luisa Bombal: Apreciaciones críticas* (Tempe, Ariz.: Bilingual Press, 1987).

— R.G.M.

BOMBO

A large cylindrical bass drum typically made from a hollowed tree trunk to which is added two animal-skin heads, the bombo is common to much Latin American music, especially of the Andean and surrounding areas, where it is often the only percussion instrument in an ensemble. The skin heads are made from the hides of llamas, sheep, goats, or other animals common to the zone. In some cases the hair is shaved off; in others it is left on the hide. The bombo is played in a variety of ways that vary with the genre and the culture: with both hands; with a drumstick that has a tightly wrapped bulb of wool or other soft material on one end; or with an unwrapped stick that plays a rhythmic counterpoint on the rim of the drum between the strokes of the wrapped drumstick.

REFERENCE:

Thomas Turino, "Music in Latin America," in *Excursions in World Music,* by Bruno Nettl, Charles Capwell, and others (Englewood Cliffs, N.J.: Prentice-Hall, 1992).

— R.L.S.

MARCELO BONEVARDI

The Argentinean Marcelo Bonevardi (1929–) has developed a unique synthesis of painting and sculpture. Raised in the city of Córdoba, he studied architecture

there until the early 1950s, when he went to Italy to study art privately. In 1956 he was appointed professor of art at the Universidad Nacional de Córdoba's Facultad de Arquitectura (School of Architecture), but he resigned and moved to New York when he received two consecutive Guggenheim Fellowships in 1959 and 1960. In New York Bonevardi rejected the dominant Abstract Expressionist style and developed a type of painting-construction that drew on a variety of sources: the boxlike compositions of Joseph Cornell, the metaphysical and universalist concerns of his friends **Julio Alpuy** and **Gonzalo Fonseca** (who taught him about the **Taller Torres-García**), and the emphasis on **Geometric Abstraction** prevalent in Argentina during the 1950s.

In works such as *Cámara Privada* (1966; Private Chamber), *Paisaje I: Altar de la Luna* (1964; Landscape I: Moon Altar), and *Angel I* (1975), Bonevardi created dramatic effects of light and shadow by activating the surfaces of his canvases through protrusions and niches, often holding mysterious sculptural figures, fetishistic objects, and mechanical artifacts which he carved himself. He softened the bold geometry of his pieces through the use of earthy textures and colors, which evoke ancient sites and cosmic rituals. In later works Bonevardi has emphasized the architectural quality of his pieces by including subtle friezelike patterns, molded fragments, and illusionistic references to three-dimensional spaces. Since the 1970s Bonevardi has also worked on paper. His drawings address some of the same concerns as his painting-constructions, but they depict more-threatening images, such as hooks, ropes, and mechanical devices of uncertain use, in a dramatic light reminiscent of the style of Italian architect and engraver Giambattista Piranesi. Although Bonevardi lives and works in New York, he often spends long periods in Argentina.

REFERENCE:

Mari Carmen Ramírez, ed., *El Taller Torres-García: The School of the South and its Legacy* (Austin: University of Texas Press, 1992).

— F.B.N.

BONGOS

Small double drums played by the hands, bongos are more closely associated with Afro-Caribbean than with South American music. The drum barrels are firmly attached, allowing the player to hold them between the legs. Typically tuned a fourth apart, the bongo heads were traditionally made by folk musicians from male and female goat skins. Currently, heads made of synthetic materials are easily available from various manufacturers. Unlike the conga drums and the **timbales** that often accompany them in percussion sections, the bongos are not restricted to repetitive rhythmic patterns and often provide a rhythmic counterpoint to the main rhythm.

—R.L.S.

BOOM

The term *Boom* refers to the internationalization of Latin American fiction in the 1960s, a decade in which a handful of Latin American novels broke the language barrier and became fashionable in Europe and the United States, mostly among the literary intelligentsia but occasionally among the general public as well. Much has been said about the commercial aspect of the Boom. Its legitimacy as an organic cultural phenomenon has also been questioned by nationalists and left-wing critics. It is true that practically all of the Boom's novelists wrote their great works abroad and that many of them were published in Spain by Seix Barral. But this outward turn in itself does not represent a break with hallowed Latin American tradition (except for unrepentant nationalists). One of the great Argentinean works of the nineteenth century — *Facundo* — was written and published in Chile, where its author was living in exile, and most of the poetry written in the 1920s and 1930s by the Peruvian poet **César Vallejo** was written and originally published in either France or Spain.

More important, the Boom marked a crucial turning point for Latin American fiction because the novels published in the 1960s (and many published earlier that were later assimilated into the Boom) consciously broke with the outmoded **regionalist** and **indigenist** traditions that had dominated narrative production in the continent in the previous decades. The Boom became the Latin American version of European and American modernism. William Faulkner, Ernest Hemingway, Henry James, Virginia Woolf, Thomas Mann, John Dos Passos, Marcel Proust, and other modern novelists were critical in determining the course of the new novel in Latin America, although overall the most influential writer on the Boom was Argentinean **Jorge Luis Borges.**

The 1960s novel, furthermore, also meant the rise of the middle classes in Latin America and the widening of the reading public brought about by a more efficient and democratic educational establishment. The **Cuban Revolution** (1959) provided the political "glue" that for a while held together the various novelists of the period.

The authors universally designated as the core of the Boom are **Mario Vargas Llosa, Julio Cortázar,** Carlos Fuentes, and **Gabriel García Márquez,** and the novels that constitute the essential reading list of this literary phenomenon are *La ciudad y los perros* (1963; translated as *The Time of the Hero*), *La casa verde* (1966; translated as *The Green House*), and *Conversación en la catedral* (1969; translated as *Conversation in The Cathedral*) — all by Vargas Llosa; *Rayuela* (1963; translated as *Hopscotch*), by Cortázar; *La muerte de Artemio Cruz* (1962; translated as *The Death of Artemio Cruz*), by Fuentes; and *Cien años de soledad* (1967; translated as *One Hundred Years of Solitude*), by García Márquez. One should also include the Cuban Guillermo Cabrera Infante's *Tres tristes tigres* (1967; translated as *Three Trapped Tigers*) and **José Donoso**'s *El obsceno pájaro de la noche* (1970; translated as *The Obscene Bird of Night*). The absence of female writers from the previous catalogue helps explain the interest in Latin American women's fiction in the 1970s and 1980s.

The signature style of the Boom was **magical realism,** whose intention was to convey an original vision of Latin American reality by circumventing previous representations of the continent steeped in European positivism or rationalism. In writers of the Boom, particularly those working with indigenous materials, *magical realism* simply meant the incorporation of the Indian perspective in the representation of national reality. In general the Boom novel is characterized by the postulation of formal or aesthetic systems of meaning (myth, allegory, symbolism) to account for personal, cultural, or national identity.

REFERENCES:

José Donoso, *The Spanish American 'Boom': A Personal History* (New York: Columbia University Press, 1977);

Angel Rama, "El boom en perspectiva," in his *La crítica de la cultura en América Latina* (Caracas: Ayacucho, 1985).

—R.G.M.

JACOBO BORGES

Venezuelan artist Jacobo Borges (1931–) has explored political, social, and psychological issues in his **Neofigurative** art. Borges studied in Caracas and lived in Paris during the 1950s. After returning to Venezuela he associated with the Caracas artistic and literary groups Tabla Redonda (Round Table) and **El Techo de la Ballena.** By then he had abandoned his earlier post-Cubist style and, like other neofiguratist, worked in an expressionistic mode which combined figuration with the techniques of **Informal Abstraction.** During the 1960s Borges used his art to question the authority of repressive governments and the role played by the media in legitimizing state power and perpetuating social stereotypes. In *Ha comenzado el espectáculo* (1964; The Show Has Begun) Borges symbolizes the sinister spectacle of the state: monsterlike representatives of the lower and upper classes, the church, and the military look on while a female nude is embraced by a soldier.

In 1965 Borges stopped painting and participated for several years in the production of *Imágenes de Caracas* (Images of Caracas), a multimedia event not unlike a Happening, and one critical of the Venezuelan government and mass media. Borges's interest in stereotypical images continued after he returned to painting. In *Reunión con círculo rojo* (1973; Meeting with Red Circle), Borges subverts the objectivity and authority of an official photograph, while in *La comunión* (1981; The Communion), he explores deeper psychological aspects of family images. Borges's most recent works often deal with the theme of perception of time, such as the series of drawings *La montaña y su tiempo* (1977; The Mountain and Its Time), in which he contrasts the permanent presence of Avila Mountain with the ever-changing appearance of nearby Caracas, where he lives.

REFERENCES:

Dore Ashton, *Jacobo Borges* (Caracas: Armitano, 1982);

Carter Ratcliff, "On the Paintings of Jacobo Borges," in *60 obras de Jacobo Borges: De la pesca al Espejo de aguas* (Monterrey: Museo de Monterrey, 1987).

— F.B.N.

JORGE LUIS BORGES

Jorge Luis Borges (1899–1986) was born in Buenos Aires, Argentina, spent his adolescent years in Europe (1914–1921), and returned to his native city with a firsthand experience of the avant-garde movements that were then flourishing in the various European capitals. Borges's first contribution to Argentinean literature was the dissemination of avant-garde ideas and of **ultraísmo,** a style in which the poems of Borges's first book, *Fervor de Buenos Aires* (1923; Buenos Aires Fervor), are cast. At that time Borges was committed to the search for novelty in language and to the abolition of the older Romantic and Symbolist idioms. He reduced the discourse of poetry to its "primordial" constituent, metaphors, and endorsed in particular images that would synthesize two or more metaphors in one. Years later Borges rejected the avant-garde search for original and shocking images, declaring valid only those metaphors sanctioned by tradition and invented, as it were, by everyone and no one. Borges's best-known poems are in this neoclassical style.

Yet Borges's immense reputation does not rest on these poems but on the short stories written between 1939 and 1956 and published in *Ficciones* (1944; revised, 1956; translated as *Fictions* and as *Labyrinths*) and in *El Aleph* (1949; revised, 1952; translated as *The Aleph and Other Stories*). Borges's stories are such remarkable literary artifacts that they may be said to constitute a special genre of the short story. Their raw material is literary, linguistic, philosophical, and theological speculation, and their form is a deceptive hybrid of narrative and essay mixed with nonliterary genres such as book reviews and even necrological notes. Their language is elegant, incisive, often mordant, but just as often gleaming with poetic insight. They are prodigiously concise and at the same time impossibly ambitious in their scope. Thick layers of erudition — some of it fabricated — line the approach to a story's structural and thematic center, where the reader is more likely to find a void or a displaced meaning than a substantial ending satisfying the expectations mobilized by the story but thwarted by narrative detours, dead ends, and gaps. Borges constructs his stories like a labyrinth in order to keep the reader at bay and to prevent him from having recourse to facile interpretive strategies. At the root of this ironic attitude toward the reader lies Borges's profound distrust of language and his disdain for realist and psychological novels and for the uncritical reading habits they foster. Borges's *ficciones,* by contrast, belong to the genre of the fantastic and show strong affinities with the adventure novel and with other popular forms such as the detective story and the spy thriller, all of them forms that require persistent vigilance over details of plot and structure. (Some of Borges's most notable influences are G. K. Chesterton, Thomas Carlyle, Edgar Allan Poe, Robert Louis Stevenson, Rudyard Kipling, and H. G. Wells.)

Finally, Borges's stories are theoretical artifacts, narratives that propose literary theories and dispose of them in various ways. For this reason they became widely influential not only among practicing writers of different nationalities (John Barth, Italo Calvino, Umberto Eco, Claude Ollier) but also among the literary theorists usually associated with structuralism and poststructuralism, whose work is foreshadowed in Borges's stories and essays. Borges's literary theory is structuralist in that it reaffirms the notion of narrative as an autonomous system of interrelated meanings, and poststructuralist in its denial of originality and of the writer's authority over the text. For Borges, texts are "intertexts" or palimpsests in which it is impossible to separate the author's "original" contributions to the story from the borrowings and unintended quotations that make up the stuff of literature. The writer is first

Jorge Luis Borges and Ernesto Sábato in a Buenos Aires café

a reader, and his stories or poems or ideas, as Borges says, are half-forgotten memories of his readings.

Paradoxically, Borges was well on his way to becoming an international pop icon before his countrymen deigned to acknowledge him as a modern master of Argentinean literature. In the 1950s Borges's stories were known to a select minority of readers but were resisted by nationalist intellectuals as too foreign to be representative of Argentinean culture. Borges responded to his nationalist critics in a lecture titled "The Argentinean Writer and Tradition," in which he cleverly dismantles the various nationalist paradigms and claims for the Argentinean writer the same eccentric relationship to Western culture as the one historically displayed by Jewish and Irish authors. Thus, according to Borges, the Argentinean writer is not only entitled to European literature but is in an outstanding position to transform and renew it, since he owes no allegiance to any one cultural tradition and can operate inside any of them.

As Borges's stories and essays seeped through the literary culture of Latin America, the Argentinean master became the fountainhead of the new Latin American novel and was quickly recognized as such by critics and novelists in equal measure. His inventions are patently influential on works such as *Cien años de soledad* (1967; translated as *One Hundred Years of Solitude*) by the Colombian **Gabriel García Márquez** and *Terra Nostra* (1975; translated) by Mexican novelist Carlos Fuentes.

After *Ficciones* Borges did not publish a new story collection until 1970, a delay partially due to his progressive blindness and to the extensive traveling demanded by his newfound fame. The stories of this new collection, *El informe de Brodie* (translated as *Doctor Brodie's Report*), mark a turning point in Borges's prose comparable to the change reflected in his poetry after the avant-garde years. Borges was done by then with the baroque style of his earlier fiction and was ready to engage in direct narration; he no longer tries to amaze the reader with smoke and mirrors but attempts instead to move or distract him; he gives up the shock of unexpected endings for the sake of an ending prepared well in advance. Borges's last volume of short stories, *El libro de arena* (translated as *The Book of Sand*), was published in 1975.

Although Borges has been the Latin American writer most easily assimilated by the literary institutions of Europe and the United States, it would be shortsighted not to see him as an essentially Argentinean writer. A significant portion of Borges's work actually deals with Argentinean themes, but also the cosmopolitan nature of the work as a whole bears the stamp of a city — Buenos Aires — that at the turn of the century became a crossroads of European humanity.

REFERENCES:

Gene Bell-Villada, *Borges and His Fiction: A Guide to His Mind and Art* (Chapel Hill: University of North Carolina Press, 1981);

John Sturrock, *Paper Tigers: The Ideal Fictions of Jorge Luis Borges* (Oxford: Clarendon Press, 1977);

Guillermo Sucre, *Borges, el poeta* (Mexico: Universidad Nacional Autónoma de Mexico, 1967).

— R.G.M.

NORAH BORGES

Norah Borges (1901–1991) was the first Argentinean to introduce modern art to Buenos Aires. Until recently her role in the Argentinean **avant-gardes of the 1920s** was obscured by critics who only considered the contributions of her male counterparts to the history of this period. Borges went to Europe with her family and studied art in Geneva and Madrid. In Europe she admired the art of the German expressionists and also saw the works of Irène Lagut, Marie Laurencin, Henri Matisse, Pablo Picasso, and Henri Rousseau, all of which had a significant impact on her art. Norah Borges and her brother **Jorge Luis Borges** participated in Spanish and Argentinean **Ultraism.** She published her woodcuts in Ultraist publications such as *Grecia* and *Ultra* in Madrid and after her return to Buenos Aires in 1921 in *Prisma* and *Proa*. In 1924 the Borgeses joined the **Florida** group, and during the 1920s she exhibited her works with other Florida artists, including **Pedro Figari, Emilio Pettoruti,** and **Xul Solar.** She also illustrated books by her brother, by Norah Lange, and by **Eduardo Mallea,** among others. After marrying the Spanish Ultraist writer Guillermo de Torre in 1928, Borges lived alternately in Spain and Argentina. In 1947 she was jailed for a month under false charges of political disturbance brought by the government of **Juan Perón** with the intention of harassing her family.

Borges's woodcuts simultaneously show radical Cubist-like fragmentations and nostalgic evocations of childhood memories. In her illustration for *Prisma: Revista Mural* the fragmented image produced by a prism reveals glimpses of neighborhood houses, crowning balustrades, and the checkerboard patios of old Buenos Aires. The recurrent themes of her paintings were idealized images of children, young adults, and angels — inhabitants of a joyful and well-ordered world, one which, in her words, was "invented to uplift the artist and viewers." In her undated painting *Las Moradas* (The Homes) Borges subtly balances the emphasis on geometry with soft harmonious tones, in a style reminiscent of Rousseau in the otherworldliness of the space and of Picasso's classical period in the solidity of the volumes.

REFERENCE:

Patricia Artundo, *Norah Borges: Obra Gráfica, 1920–1930* (Buenos Aires: Secretaria de Cultura, Fondo Nacional de las Artes, 1993).

— F.B.N.

FERNANDO BOTERO

The Colombian Fernando Botero (1932–) is one of the best-known Latin American artists. He began his artistic career as an illustrator for the Medellín newspaper *El Colombiano*. During the early 1950s he went to Europe and studied at the Real Academia de Bellas Artes de San Fernando in Madrid and the Accademia San Marco in Florence. In Europe he admired the work of the Italian Renaissance artists and of Diego Velázquez and Francisco Goya, who would later become important influences on his art. Botero returned to Bogotá in 1955, but his work was not well received. He then left for Mexico in 1956 and met the artists Rufino Tamayo and José Luis Cuevas. His work at that time was in the post-Cubist style of the School of Paris, but toward the end of the decade it became increasingly expressionistic and closer to **Neofiguration.**

After returning to Bogotá in 1958, Botero taught at the National University's Escuela de Bellas Artes and had several successful exhibitions in the United States, a fact that encouraged him to settle in New York in 1960. During this period he met Franz Kline, Mark Rothko, and other Abstract Expressionists, and in works such as *Mona Lisa a los doce* (1959; Mona Lisa, Age Twelve) he explored the spontaneous treatment of painting favored by these artists. However, Botero soon rejected their approach and developed a distinctive figurative style closer in technique to the old European masters he admired. In paintings such as *La familia presidencial* (1967; The Presidential Family) Botero creates an inflated, balloonlike version of reality. His rotund figures — everyday objects, people, an-

Fernando Botero with a self-portrait

imals, and even nature — fill up the space of the canvas and would create a sense of heaviness were it not for the humor of his ironical renderings.

In much of his art Botero satirizes different aspects of his native Colombia, especially the power of the military and the church, perpetuated by a middle class trapped by its own conventions. His selection of themes varies, ranging from marginal figures, such as prostitutes and transvestites, to humorous images of religious figures, including bishops, nuns, and saints, and in recent years images of bullfighting and related scenes. Botero also pays homage to old masters such as Caravaggio, Velázquez, and Edouard Manet by often reproducing their works in his own style, as for instance in his painting *Los Arnolfini (según Van Eyck)* (1978; The Arnolfinis [after Van Eyck]). In 1973 Botero settled in Paris and began working with sculpture, producing three-dimensional versions of his inflated figures in marble, bronze, and cast resin. Although Botero's work was ignored by art critics, he

won public recognition in the United States during the late 1960s, when Pop Art brought about the reemergence of figuration; in the context of Latin America he has become one of the most significant examples of **Figuration** since the 1970s.

REFERENCE:

Carter Ratcliff, *Botero* (New York: Abbeville Press, 1980).
— F.B.N.

ALFREDO BRYCE ECHENIQUE

A contemporary Peruvian author of novels and short stories, Alfredo Bryce Echenique (1939–   ) came into his own at the very close of the decade of the **Boom.** Among Peruvian writers he is second in prominence only to **Mario Vargas Llosa**. Bryce was born and grew up in Lima. His father (of Scottish descent) was a banker; his mother could recite passages from Marcel Proust by heart. He attended English schools as a boy and later enrolled in the University of San Marcos, where he obtained his master's degree in literature in 1962. He then won a grant and left to write his dissertation in Paris in 1963. Bryce stayed in France for twenty-one years.

In Paris, Bryce emulated Ernest Hemingway and found an apartment near the Place de la Contrescape. He supported himself by teaching Spanish and wrote his first short stories in his spare time. These were published in Havana in 1968 as *Huerto cerrado* (Secret Garden, or Hortus Conclusus to give it the title of the Latin topic it consciously evokes) and received an honorable mention in the **Casa de las Américas** contest.

The following year Bryce taught at the University of Nanterre as he worked on his first novel, *Un mundo para Julius* (1971; translated as *A World For Julius*), one of two finalists for the 1970 **Biblioteca Breve** prize, which ultimately was not awarded due to a rift in the sponsoring organization. In 1972, however, it won the National Prize for Literature in Peru, and it was translated into French the following year. *Un mundo para Julius* is a semi-autobiographical account of growing up in the privileged and sheltered world of the Peruvian upper classes. The protagonist, Julius, is an impressionable child endowed with a somewhat extravagant sensibility.

In 1974 Bryce published his second collection of short stories, *La felicidad, ja, ja* (Happiness, Ha! Ha!), with a title borrowed from the lyrics of a popular song. In 1980 he began teaching Latin American literature at the University of Montpellier, and the following year he published another successful and remarkable novel, *La vida exagerada de Martín Romaña* (The Exagger-

Alfredo Bryce Echenique in Paris, circa 1977

ated Life of Martín Romaña), in which Bryce narrates the adventures of his alter ego in the Paris of the 1968 student riots. Martín is married to a political radical who demands from him a "committed" novel about the Peruvian fishing industry, about which he knows next to nothing. A novel dealing with a similar theme had been written by **José María Arguedas** and published posthumously in 1971 with the title *El zorro de arriba y el zorro de abajo* (The Fox from Above and the Fox from Below). But Martín is no Arguedas, and he opts in the end for creative freedom. The novel also por-

trays a kind of "lost generation" of Latin American students and artists struggling to make ends meet in Paris. Bryce's tone is ironic without being judgmental.

The sequel to this novel appeared in 1985 as *El hombre que hablaba de Octavia de Cádiz* (The Man Who Talked about Octavia de Cádiz). Martín Romaña is now thirty-three years old and is teaching at the University of Nanterre, where one of his students, Octavia, falls in love with him. The novel details Martín's erotic and erratic life as the protagonist wanders through Europe.

Bryce's next book, a volume of short stories, *Magdalena peruana* (1986; Peruvian Madeleine), deliberately echoes Proust. The protagonist of Bryce's 1988 novel, *La última mudanza de Felipe Carrillo* (1988; Felipe Carrillo's Last Move), is less bohemian than Martín Romaña, but equally extravagant things happen to him, particularly his involvement with a Spanish journalist whose Oedipal son interferes with the relationship. In an attempt to dissolve the mother-son bond and consolidate his unchallenged position as lover, Felipe takes them both on an improbable vacation to Colán, a remote resort on the Peruvian coast where they are hit by the natural phenomenon known as El Niño (an atmospheric disturbance resulting from temperature changes in the ocean currents) and the unnatural love that erupts between Felipe and a local servant. Much of the novel centers on the protagonist's cultural and personal identity, a level of meaning structured in terms of the culture/nature opposition. Clearly the facile association between culture and Europe, on the one hand, and nature and Latin America, on the other, is disturbed in the novel by the existence of the Oedipal relationship, which impedes the crystallization of culture by prolonging the natural affinity between mother and son.

Bryce Echenique has most recently published his memoirs, *Permiso para vivir: Antimemorias* (1993; Permission to Live: Antimemoirs).

REFERENCES:

Fernando R. Lafuente, ed., *Alfredo Bryce Echenique* (Madrid: Ediciones de Cultura Hispánica, 1991);

Julio Ortega, *Al hilo del habla: La narrativa de Alfredo Bryce Echenique* (Guadalajara: Universidad de Guadalajara, 1994).
　　　　　　　　　　　　　　　　　— R.G.M.

C

CABALLO VERDE PARA LA POESÍA

Caballo Verde para la Poesía (Green Horse for Poetry) was a poetry magazine (1935–1936) directed by **Pablo Neruda** in Madrid. Four issues were published, containing mostly Surrealist poems. Each issue was preceded by a Neruda editorial, one of which, "Hacia una poesía sin pureza" (Toward an Impure Poetry), is Neruda's poetic manifesto directed against the notions of pure poetry then held by the influential Spanish poet Juan Ramón Jiménez and by Neruda's compatriot and antagonist **Vicente Huidobro.**

— R.G.M

CAMILA

Camila (1983), produced by Lila Stantic (for GEA Cinematográfica S.R.L.), is one of the most famous Spanish American films of the 1980s. It is based on the true story of Camila O'Gorman, a woman from the Argentinean aristocracy who eloped with a priest during the dictatorship of Juan Manuel de Rosas in the mid–nineteenth century and was executed with her lover for sexual immorality and blasphemy. Directed by Argentinean María Luisa Bemberg, it has captured the imagination of audiences all over the world. Shooting began the day after the surprise election victory in December 1983 of Raúl Alfonsín, the leader of the Radical Party. In December 1986 the Church in Argentina tried to prevent state television from showing *Camila* over the Christmas period since, the Church argued, it would undermine traditional worship. The film, in its depiction of a brutal dictatorship, also referred in a transparent manner to contemporary events in Argentina, and in particular to the **Guerra Sucia** (Dirty War) of 1976–1983, in which the military hunted down and exterminated "subversives." A clear contrast is set up in the film between the traditional patriarchal family and the utopian family established by the lovers, between state power and love, and between traditional and progressive Catholicism. In particular, a discursive configuration of love-womanhood-literature is set against one of violence-manhood-repression. When released in 1983, so soon after the horrors of the Dirty War, the movie allowed Argentinean audiences to engage in a form of collective catharsis, enabling them to experience in public the emotions that had had to remain private during the years of the dictatorship. Two million people wept at the story of Camila O'Gorman, which they saw as their own story; for many months the film outgrossed the main Hollywood features of the moment, *E.T. The Extra-Terrestrial* and *Porky's*.

REFERENCES:

David William Foster, *Contemporary Argentine Cinema* (Columbia & London: University of Missouri Press, 1992);

Zuzana M. Pick, *The New Latin American Cinema* (Austin: University of Texas Press, 1993).

— S.M.H.

LUIS CAMNITZER

Luis Camnitzer (1937–) is one of the leading figures in Latin American **Conceptual Art.** Born in Germany to a Jewish family, he and his parents relocated to Uruguay in 1939 after they were forced to flee Nazi Germany. Camnitzer studied art and architecture in Montevideo at the University of Uruguay's Escuela de Bellas Artes and in Munich at the Akademie der Bildenden Künste. In 1962 he received a Guggenheim Fellowship to study printmaking in New York, where he eventually settled in 1964. The following year he cofounded the New York Graphic Workshop with the

Torture (1986–1987), an installation by Luis Camnitzer at the 1988 Venice Biennale

Argentinean **Liliana Porter** (his wife at the time) and the Venezuelan Julio Castillo. The workshop, which disbanded in 1970, was an experimental printmaking studio whose most radical formulation was the FANDSO, the Free Assemblage, Nonfunctional, Disposable, Serial Object. The FANDSO utilized the strategies of **Pop Art** and conceptual art, movements which opposed the definition of the work of art as a unique luxury item, commodified through the museum and art gallery system.

During the 1960s Camnitzer abandoned his earlier expressionist style and adopted conceptualist strategies to explore the relationship between art and language. His work *Adhesive Labels* (1966–1968) consisted of stickers printed with tautological texts such as "This is a mirror. You are a written sentence." Camnitzer mailed the labels to different people and also affixed them to elevators and bathrooms, a tactic which simultaneously undermined their commercial value and made them accessible to a wider public. Toward the end of the decade he became increasingly concerned with political repression in Latin America and the possibility of suggesting multiple levels of interpretation in his works. In the etching *Che* (1968), which shows only the three letters of the title on a white background, the use of **Che Guevara**'s name implies, among other possible meanings, the idea of revolution and political strife in Latin America. In his large installation *Leftovers* (1970), a FANDSO consisting of two hundred boxes (later reduced to eighty)

individually wrapped in gauze soiled with blood-colored stains and stenciled with the word *leftover,* Camnitzer designs suggestive elements that place the viewers in the role of producers of meaning. The disquieting visual clues provided by the artist eventually force the observers to arrive at somber conclusions about political repression in Latin America.

During the 1970s Camnitzer switched his focus away from politics to the general relationship between images, objects, and words. In conceptual wall installations such as *Arbitrary Objects and Their Titles* (1979) the artist places small objects over titles evocative enough to tempt the viewers into connecting them into a narrative, in spite of the randomness of their association. In the 1980s Camnitzer returned to political subjects in his art, especially the issues of torture and state terrorism. In his remarkable series *From the Uruguayan Torture* (1984) he combines photoetchings of banal objects with understated captions that obliquely allude to specific incidents of torture documented by human-rights groups. In recent years he has concentrated on recovering suppressed historical information through his series on the Mexican *San Patricio Batalion,* formed by American deserters during the war between Mexico and the United States in 1846–1848. Although Camnitzer has lived in the New York area since the 1960s, he has made Latin America the focus of his art and of his numerous critical and art-historical publications.

REFERENCE:

Luis Camnitzer, Mari Carmen Ramírez, and Gerardo Mosquera, *Luis Camnitzer: Retrospective Exhibition, 1966–1990* (New York: Lehman College Art Gallery, 1991).

                                                                    — F.B.N.

CANTINFLAS

During the 1940s and 1950s the Mexican comedian Cantinflas (1911–1993) was the most popular movie star in the Spanish-speaking world. Born Mario Moreno, he started his acting career in the tent shows held in Jalapa, moved on to the music-hall circuit in the big cities, and then graduated to the movies. His characteristic role was the *peladito,* a picaresque "wise guy" from the slums of Mexico. He made his film debut in Miguel Contreras Torres's *No te engañes, Corazón* (1936; Don't Deceive Yourself, Heart) and later appeared in *Siempre listo en las tinieblas* (1939; Always Ready in the Darkness) and *Jengibre contra dinamita* (1939; Ginger Versus Dynamite). In 1940 Cantinflas scored an international success with his performance in *Ahí está el detalle* (There Is the Detail), his first full-length feature. The film's high point, which created a following for Cantinflas throughout Spanish America, is the final courtroom scene in which he flouts social and legalistic convention and succeeds in completely confusing both the judge and the attorneys. His second full-length feature, *Ni sangre ni arena* (1941; Neither Blood nor Sand), a parody of Vicente Blasco Ibáñez's bullfighter novel *Sangre y arena* (1909; translated as *Blood and Sand*), which had recently been filmed in Hollywood, was vastly popular and a box-office record. In the same year *El gendarme desconocido* (The Unknown Policeman) was also hugely successful. As a result of these two films, Cantinflas established himself as the most well-known Spanish-speaking actor in South America. North American moviegoers are more likely to know his two Hollywood films, the moderately successful *Around the World in 80 Days* (1956), and *Pepe* (1960), which flopped.

REFERENCES:

Charles Ramírez Berg, *Cinema of Solitude: A Critical Study of Mexican Film, 1967–1983* (Austin: University of Texas Press, 1992);

Carl J. Mora, *Mexican Cinema: Reflections of a Society 1896–1980* (Berkeley, Los Angeles & London: University of California Press, 1982).

                                                                    — S.M.H.

CARNAVALITO

Also sometimes called simply "carnaval," the carnavalito is an animated dance-song of the Indians of the Andean altiplano, one that has not only survived but prospered since early colonial times. Performance of the carnaval or carnavalito is not restricted to any particular season of the year and is appropriate for both religious and secular celebrations.

Rhythmically set in duple meter, the melodic content is generally pentatonic. It is usually accompanied by instruments common to the region, including **quenas** (flutes), **sikus** (panpipes), **charango** (small guitar), and **bombo** (drum). The text consists of couplets and may be sung by a soloist or group in Spanish, Quechua, or bilingual mixtures. Performances may include dancing by men, women, and children grouped in circles or in facing lines.

REFERENCES:

Isabel Aretz, *El folklore musical argentino* (Buenos Aires: Ricordi Americana S.A.E.C., 1958);

Gerard Béhague, "Latin American Folk Music," in *Folk and Traditional Music of the Western Continents,* by Bruno Nettl, third edition, revised and edited by Valerie Woodring Goertzen (Englewood Cliffs, N.J.: Prentice-Hall, 1990);

Thomas Turino, "Music in Latin America," in *Excursions in World Music,* by Bruno Nettl, Charles Capwell, and others (Englewood Cliffs, N.J.: Prentice-Hall, 1992).

                                                                    — R.L.S.

CASA DE LAS AMÉRICAS

Casa de las Américas is a publishing enterprise established in Cuba only a few months after Fidel Castro and his revolutionary forces wrested control of the island from Fulgencio Batista in 1959. Through its journal and annual literary prize, Casa de las Américas has become a focal point in Latin American letters. Almost all the major Latin American authors have published works or had their books reviewed in *Casa de las Américas.* The Casa de las Américas Prize was instituted to stimulate and publicize Latin American literature and, in a less explicit way, to place the **Cuban Revolution** at the center of Latin American cultural endeavors. Most of the great names of Latin American literature have either received one of the annual prizes or have been members of the awards jury. In the thirty-four years since the first prizes were awarded in 1959, 16,034 book manuscripts have been entered in the competition, 440 authors have received awards, and 920 writers have been members of the jury. In 1994 Casa de las Américas prizes were awarded for entries in the categories of fiction, poetry, children's literature, sociohistorical essays, women's studies, Brazilian literature, Caribbean literature in English or Creole, and literature in three Amerindian languages (Mapuche, Aymara, and Mayasense). In the late 1960s the category of **testimonial narrative** was introduced into the competition, a move that endorsed this significant genre of Latin American cultural discourse and stimulated its production in the following decade. In the early 1990s the Casa de las Américas prize was worth three thousand dollars, paid in the national currency of the individual winners.

REFERENCE:

Judith A. Weiss, *Casa de las Américas: An Intellectual Review in the Cuban Revolution* (Chapel Hill, N.C. & Madrid: Editorial Castalia, 1977).

— R.G.M.

CASA DE LA DANZA

Founded in 1992, the Casa de la Danza, located in Quito, was the first modern dance school in Ecuador. Its purpose is to contribute toward the development of the Ecuadoran modern dance movement, as well as to foster cooperation among the arts and with the community at large. The building contains five dance studios, a theater with a capacity of two hundred, dressing rooms, a conference room, a projection room, a music and recording studio, a video and book library, administrative offices, and a café. More than ninety performances of dance, theater, and music have been presented since its opening. A dance photography exhibition, lectures, dance video shows, open rehearsals, and acting workshops have also been organized. The student body numbers approximately one hundred. The director of the Casa, choreographer and dancer Susana Reyes, is responsible for creating a link with the American Dance Festival, a modern dance teaching and performance festival, founded in 1933 at Connecticut College and currently based at Duke University in Durham, North Carolina, under the direction of Charles and Stephanie Reinhart. This festival hosts choreographers and modern dance companies from all over Latin America in its International Choreographers Residency program, established in 1983. It also has brought teachers from the United States to conduct teaching workshops and organize performances in Ecuador and other Latin American countries.

— N.D.B. & J.M.H.

CASAS DE CULTURA

Casas de Cultura, or cultural centers, are found in many villages, towns, and cities throughout Latin America. Entirely government funded, they often house libraries, museums (of music, handicrafts, archaeology, or paintings), and schools of visual art, music, and dance where students study at government expense or for nominal fees. These Casas de Cultura often serve as springboards for the creation of ballet, modern dance, and folk dance companies which later spin off as independent entities or remain affiliated with the Casas de Cultura. The Casas de Cultura preserve and promote both contemporary manifestations of traditional arts, and imported and contemporary forms.

— N.D.B. & J.M.H.

CENSORSHIP

The history of censorship in Spanish America is complex and has taken different forms at different times, from the control of information exerted by the Spaniards and the Catholic church during colonial times, through the birth of the newspaper in Spanish America — which coincided with independence — to the present century and the manipulation of the media to influence public opinion.

From the 1820s to the 1940s traditional Latin American caudillos, or strongman presidents, often silenced the press so as to minimize political opposition. Later, however, dictators used the mass media to "reeducate" the masses through the "subsidy" system. Thus, a government would gain sympathetic coverage in return for subsidizing the price of importing or manufacturing newsprint, printing presses, or broadcasting station equipment.

A similar pattern of censorship is evident in several South American republics. In Peru, for example, before the 1930s censorship of the media took the form of silencing the press during the dictatorship of Augusto B. Leguía from 1919 to 1930. President Manuel Prado subsequently lifted all censorship in 1945, but press censorship was reinstated when Gen. Manuel Odría took over the government in 1948. In 1956 freedom of the press returned to Peru but was later curtailed during the military regime of Gen. Velasco Alvarado (1968–1975); newspapers such as *Expreso* and *Extra* and magazines such as *Caretas* were closed down. A degree of freedom of the press returned during the 1980s, but it was reduced again as a result of Alberto Fujimori's "autogolpe" (his coup d'état of his own government) in 1992.

Venezuela is among the handful of Latin American nations with a free press and genuinely free and independent media (since 1958). The most influential magazine in Venezuelan national life, *Resumen,* enjoys international prestige. Colombia, like Venezuela, has also enjoyed for many years now a genuine freedom of press although television news does have a degree of governmental guidance. The 1948 riots, or "bogotazo" (see **La Violencia**), which shook Bogotá for three days in April of that year, despite their destabilizing impact on national life, were widely covered in the national press; *El Tiempo* and *El Espectador* of Bogotá and *El Colombiano* of Medellín were free to express opinions about the events without government interference. This freedom was curtailed, however, when Rojas Pinilla became president following a coup in 1953. At various junctures during Rojas Pinilla's term of office (1953–1958), the press was muzzled; *El Tiempo, El Siglo, El Colombiano, El Liberal,* and *La República* were all closed down. After Rojas Pinilla's demise in 1958, constitutional democracy returned to Colombia and with it freedom of the press.

Uruguay and Chile offer interesting cases of the influence of media censorship during a period of dictatorship. During the military dictatorship in Uruguay between 1973 and 1984, all types of media were severely censored. Twenty-four newspapers and magazines were closed down in the first two years of military rule. The songs of many Uruguayan composers were banned; in 1973 Daniel Viglietti, a well-known Uruguayan composer and singer, was arrested and forced into exile. Well-known Argentinean and Spanish entertainers were denied entry to the country. In December 1976 the police chief of Montevideo informed radio stations that they could not play seven tangos by **Carlos Gardel** (dead for forty years) because the tangos represented a "state of mind" that had been "totally conquered." Six radio stations were closed down. Perhaps worst of all, the public was denied access to newspaper editions of entire years of the country's history, stored in the national library.

A similar pattern of censorship took place in Chile. Not surprisingly, throughout the seventeen years of **Augusto Pinochet**'s dictatorship in Chile (1973–1991), the Left was negatively portrayed in government media. Some oppositional media functioned, but Chile was basically an ideologically monopolized media environment. As a result of a paper-and-pencil survey conducted in Santiago in November 1989, it emerged that censorship of the press during Pinochet's regime had produced a situation whereby the dependence of leftists on progovernment mass-media sources for political information had pushed them not more to the left (as might initially have been expected) but more to the right. The censorship had been effective.

Argentina arguably presents the most interesting case of state censorship of the mass media. **Juan Domingo Perón**, after coming to power in 1943, influ-

enced the mass media explicitly, banning certain motion pictures, radio programs, and musical recordings; he even went so far as to have a popular comedian, Luis Sandrini, fired when he told an anti-Perón joke on Radio Belgrano. Perón's understanding of the power of the media dates back to his advice to the military government of which he was part in 1943: "We are being attacked on all sides. I suggest we try advertising. Propaganda is a powerful arm, especially when one has control of the media. It is time to think how we are going to advertise." During his political campaign of 1946, he monopolized popular broadcasts, radio time, and theater newsreels; even the bus and trolley transfers in Buenos Aires carried his name and slogan. Perón also used the beauty of his wife, Evita, enhanced by mass-media glamorization, for political ends. He closed down sixty dailies, including the prestigious *La Prensa,* for so-called anti-Argentinean activities. From 1955, when Juan Domingo Perón was ousted from office, until 1966, when the military leaders took power, Argentina enjoyed freedom of the press, but tactics similar to those used by Perón against hostile media sources were used by the military generals after 1966. Newspapers were closed down, editors were intimidated, and imported political textbooks such as works by Karl Marx and Friedrich Engels were ordered burned by the post office. Freedom of the press again returned to the national scene in the constitutional democracy of 1973–1976, but when Gen. Jorge Videla came to power in 1976, his newly formed Ministry of Press and Broadcasting issued a document, *Principles and Procedures,* which encouraged the press to regulate itself and which included instructions to journalists not to "investigate fields which are not for public debate" and to "eliminate publicizing among the masses the opinion of persons not qualified or without specific authority to give opinions on subjects of public issue." For failing to follow instructions a prestigious daily, *La Opinión,* was closed down. Press restrictions grew even tighter as the **Guerra Sucia** (Dirty War) followed its ever more gruesome course. The junta drew up blacklists of journalists, artists, and entertainers and prohibited many foreign and national films, books, and magazines. During its regime seventy-two journalists disappeared and were probably murdered, hundreds were jailed, and many fled into exile. Censorship in Argentina, as the prominent intellectual Héctor Olivera said in 1980, had become "the most arbitrary, reactionary, incoherent and castrating in the Western world." After the **Malvinas** (Falklands) War and President Leopoldo Galtieri's demise in 1983, constitutional democracy returned to Argentina, and with it came much greater freedom of the press. Gradually and often painfully, stories that were taboo under the military have appeared in the newspapers, politicians have returned to

Scene from *El chacal de Nahueltoro* (1969; The Jackal of Nahueltoro)

the television screens, and new voices speak on the radio. (See **Dictatorship Novels.**)

REFERENCES:

Marvin Alisky, *Latin American Media: Guidance and Censorship* (Ames: Iowa State University Press, 1981);

Elizabeth Fox, ed., *Media and Politics in Latin America: The Struggle for Democracy* (London: Sage, 1988);

Pablo Halpern, *Media Dependency and Political Perceptions in an Authoritarian Political System: The Case of Chile's Left* (Washington, D.C.: Woodrow Wilson Center, 1993);

David E. Hojman, "YES or NO to Pinochet: Television in the 1988 Chilean Plebiscite," *Studies in Latin American Popular Culture*, 11 (1992): 171–194;

Steve Wiley-Crofts, "Social Semiosis and Authoritarian Legitimacy: Television in Pinochet's Chile," *Studies in Latin American Popular Culture*, 10 (1991): 239–255.

— S.M.H. & P.S.

CENTRO DE DOCUMENTACIÓN E INVESTIGACIÓN DE LA DANZA

The Centro de Documentación e Investigatión de la Danza (Center for Dance Documentation and Investigation) of Caracas, Venezuela, directed by Teresa Alvarenga, aims to rescue and preserve the dance history and traditions of Venezuela and to put these resources

within the reach of present and future generations of Venezuelans. The center, among its many documentation and research functions, publishes articles on Venezuelan dance history, maintains archives on international as well as national dance history, and has established a dance video and publications library.

— N.D.B. & J.M.H.

EL CHACAL DE NAHUELTORO

El chacal de Nahueltoro (1969; The Jackal of Nahueltoro), directed by **Miguel Littín,** is one of the trailblazers of Latin American documentary cinema and the **New Latin American Cinema;** the lead was convincingly played by **Nelson Villagra.** The movie focuses on a true story of a man who murders a homeless woman and her five children in an act of violence and drunkenness. He is arrested, put in prison, and executed. In 1960 the sensationalist press painted the man as a "jackal," but Littín was at pains to show how social conditions act as breeding grounds for drunkenness, violence, and despair. The film was released a year before the Popular Unity government under **Salvador Allende** came to power, and suggested that the policies of the outgoing Christian Democrats were rhetoric rather than reality. The story was filmed with

Martín Chambi at an exhibit of his photographs, circa 1930

documentary devices: press cuttings, legal depositions. The first half of the film treats the murder and trial; the second half deals with the protagonist's time in prison on death row where, ironically, he finds some of the sense of community which was so lacking in his life. The prisoner's suffering is likened to Christ's through a series of juxtaposed images; the ultimate message of the film is that the true blame for the "jackal's" crime lies with society rather than the individual.

REFERENCES:

Julianne Burton, ed., *Cinema and Social Change in Latin America: Conversations with Latin American Filmmakers* (Austin: University of Texas Press, 1986);

Michael Chanan, ed., *Chilean Cinema* (London: BFI, 1976).

— S.M.H.

MARTÍN CHAMBI

The Peruvian photographer Martín Chambi (1891–1973) recorded the landscape, architecture, and local traditions of his native Cuzco. His oeuvre is one of the finest examples of South American **photography.**

Chambi was born to a family of farmers descended from the Incas. His father later worked for an English gold mining company, and Chambi became the assistant of the company's photographer. Chambi left for Arequipa in 1908, where he was an apprentice for nine years in Max T. Vargas's studio. He exhibited his work for the first time in 1917, the year he published the first picture postcard in Peru.

In 1920 Chambi opened his own commercial studio in Cuzco, which had been the center of the Inca empire and still functioned as an important market for the region's farmers and artisans. His patrons included Cuzco's well-to-do families, government officials, intellectuals, and artists. He portrayed them using natural light, which gave his remarkable photographs a personal style. Chambi was also interested in documenting the traditional lifestyles of the people of Cuzco. From 1920 to the 1950s he traveled through the Cuzco region on muleback, sometimes for months at a time, recording everything from local costumes to people's lives and the native architecture, and producing his well-known series of photographs of Machu Picchu (1925). By then he had switched to a view camera because he preferred to make direct-contact prints from large glass negatives rather than having to enlarge his images later.

Chambi was the first photographer of Inca ancestry, a fact which gave him greater insight into his subjects while completely avoiding interpretations which emphasize the exotic and anthropological. His photographs reveal not only the great respect he felt for the people he portrayed, but also the inherent dignity of his subjects. His work is linked to **Indigenism** and its leading exponents in art, such as J. Uriel García, **José Sabogal,** Luis A. Pardo, and Luis Valcárcel. Chambi actively participated in their efforts to revaluate the indigenous cultures of Peru. Chambi was also a founding member of the Instituto Americano de Arte del Cuzco, whose objective was to develop the art, literature, and historical research of Peru, as well as to promote the importance of Inca culture and heritage.

Chambi published his photographs in newspapers in Peru and in Argentina and exhibited his work on numerous occasions until 1950, when Cuzco experienced a terrible earthquake that left thirty-five thousand people dead. At great emotional cost Chambi recorded the suffering of the local population. At that time he stopped traveling and participating in national exhibitions, just as his earlier photographs were acquiring an even more poignant value as the only records of the buildings destroyed in the earthquake. Chambi's work became internationally known and appreciated through the efforts of his family and of the photographer Edward Ranney, who in 1977 was instrumental in the process of cleaning and cataloguing more than sixteen thousand glass plates and negatives from Chambi's studio to preserve one of the largest oeuvres by a Latin American photographer.

REFERENCE:
Roderic Ai Camp, "Pioneer Photographer of Peru," *Américas,* 30 (March 1978): 5–10.

— F.B.N.

CHARANGO

The charango is a small **chordophone** typical of the Andean region and modeled on a type of Spanish guitar that had five double strings. The charango has five pairs of strings, each pair tuned in unison, except for the middle pair that are tuned an octave apart. Normally strummed, providing a harmonic/rhythmic accompaniment, it may also be played in a plucked style, fulfilling a melodic role. Traditionally, the body of the instrument was made from the shell of an animal such as the armadillo, but more-recent models are constructed from wood. The presence of the charango in

any ensemble immediately adds an Andean flavor to music, but it is almost essential to the **bailecito, yaravi, huaiño, carnavalito,** and other genres native to the mountainous regions of Bolivia, Peru, Ecuador, and Argentina.

REFERENCES:
Isabel Aretz, *El folklore musical argentino* (Buenos Aires: Ricordi Americana S.A.E.C., 1952);
Gerard Béhague, "Latin American Folk Music," in *Folk and Traditional Music of the Western Continents,* by Bruno Nettl, third edition, revised and edited by Valerie Woodring Goertzen (Englewood Cliffs, N.J.: Prentice-Hall, 1990).

— R.L.S.

CHORDOPHONES

Chordophones are instruments that produce sound from the vibrations of strings. Vibrations are initiated by strumming the string or by drawing a bow across it. When European colonists and missionaries brought violins, harps, and guitars to the New World, indigenes not only learned to play them, they created new versions of them from accessible materials. Homemade violins, harps, and numerous adaptations of guitar- and lute-type instruments proliferated throughout Latin America. Among those modeled after guitars and lutes are **charango, tiple, bandola,** and **cuatro venezolano.**

REFERENCE:
Isabel Aretz, *El folklore musical argentino* (Buenos Aires: (Ricordi Americana S.A.E.C., 1952).

— R.L.S.

CINE LIBERACIÓN

In Argentina during the 1960s a group of political filmmakers set up an independent cooperative called Cine Liberación, whose principal organizer was **Fernando Solanas** and whose major work was *La hora de los hornos* (1966–1969; The Hour of the Furnaces), codirected with Octavio Getino. In preparation for this documentary, which focuses on working-class struggles in Argentina, Cine Liberación interviewed 150 workers, intellectuals, and union leaders and traveled and filmed in some of the most isolated regions of Argentina. The result was a huge documentary (nearly four and a half hours long) in three separate parts: "Neo-Colonialism and Violence," "An Act for Liberation," and "Violence and Liberation." The first part presents a historical, geographical, economic, and social analysis of Argentina. The content of the second and third parts was developed out of points raised during audience discussion following the necessarily clandestine screenings of the first. Because of the time at which it appeared, its ambitious scope, its formal eclecticism, and the circumstances surrounding its production and distribution, *The Hour of the Furnaces* has been regarded as the single most influential documentary to have emerged from the entire **New Latin American Cinema** movement. With the resumption of military rule in Argentina shortly after the release of *The Hour of the Furnaces*, the Cine Liberación group could no longer show its films in Argentina, even clandestinely, because of the severe penalties attached to any activities critical of the government, nor was it possible to smuggle them abroad.

REFERENCE:

Zuzana M. Pick, *The New Latin American Cinema* (Austin: University of Texas Press, 1993).

— S.M.H.

CINEMA IN ARGENTINA

After the first cinema theater was opened in Argentina in 1900, the national film industry became very active between 1915 and 1921 and produced around one hundred films. During the 1920s there was a sharp decline until the arrival of sound helped to popularize local production. Argentinean talkies, with simple melodramatic plots punctuated by song, particularly the **tango,** became extremely popular in the 1930s. Hollywood was well aware of the success of this formula and made several "Argentinean" films starring the legendary **Carlos Gardel** specifically for a Latin American audience. This growth was halted, however, with the advent of World War II; commercial sanctions imposed because of Argentina's neutral policy during the war led to a shortage of raw film stock and a critical situation for the national industry. In 1944, in an effort to counter the invasion of foreign, mainly United States, films, a government decree established several protectionist norms, subsidizing the local film industry and compelling theaters to exhibit national productions. From the 1950s onward, however, with the progressive opening-up of the economy, national film production was less able to compete with foreign material. The number of Argentinean films released decreased from fifty-six in 1950 to thirty-five in 1952. An attempt to regulate the flow of foreign films was made in 1962; the National Film Institute proposed that six foreign films be allowed in Argentina in proportion to each local film released.

In 1976 the production cost of a modest film was approximately forty million Argentinean pesos

($163,000). The average income per ticket after tax deductions was 180 pesos, of which a maximum of 25 percent went to the producer. Thus, to pay for a locally produced film, some 887,000 spectators were required (a rather high figure for a country with an annual cinema attendance estimated at only 63 million).

Despite economic adversity and the pervasive influence of Hollywood, however, Argentina has managed to produce some impressive native talent, such as the acclaimed **Leopoldo Torre Nilsson.** In the 1960s a group of political filmmakers set up an independent cooperative called **Cine Liberación.** An influential film director since the 1980s has been **María Luisa Bemberg,** whose works have achieved international acclaim. Other important Argentinean movies of the 1980s include *Gerónima* (1986), directed by Raul A. Tosso; *La historia oficial* (1986; The Official Story), directed by Luis Puenzo; *Hombre mirando al sudeste* (1986; *Man Facing Southeast*), directed by Eliseo Subielo; *No habrá más penas ni olvido* (1983; A Funny, Dirty Little War), directed by Héctor Olivera; *Otra historia de amor* (1985; Another Love Story), directed by Américo Ortiz Zárate; *Pasajeros de una pesadilla* (1984; Passengers in a Nightmare), directed by **Fernando Ayala**; and *Perros de la noche* (1986; The Dogs of Night), directed by Teo Kofman.

REFERENCES:

Julianne Burton, ed., *Cinema and Social Change in Latin America: Conversations with Latin American Filmmakers* (Austin: University of Texas Press, 1986);

David William Foster, *Contemporary Argentine Cinema* (Columbia & London: University of Missouri Press, 1992);

Jorge A. Schnitman, *Film Industries in Latin America* (Norwood, N.J.: ABLEX, 1984).

— S.M.H.

CINEMA IN BOLIVIA

Study of the cinema in Bolivia shows that film production in a small-market developing country can attain a cultural importance that at first glance seems surprising, given the country's economic infrastructure. During the presound era (1896–1929) Bolivia produced *Corazón aymara* (1925; Aymara Heart), directed by the Italian immigrant Pedro Sambarino and usually regarded as the first Bolivian feature film; *Wara-Wara* (1930), a romantic story set near the end of the Inca empire; and *Hacia la gloria* (1931; Toward Glory). Film production was disrupted in Bolivia in the 1930s by the Chaco War (1932–1935), waged against Paraguay, and the only feature-length film released during this period was *Infierno verde* (1938; Green Hell), a documentary on the war, directed by Luis Bazoberry. The only filming activity during the 1940s was the work of two amateurs, Jorge Ruiz and Augusto Roca. The two most ambitious films of the 1950s were directed by Ruiz: *Vuelve Sebastiana* (1953; Sebastiana, Come Back!), a semidocumentary on the Chipaya Indians, which was awarded the first prize for ethnographic films in the 1953 Montevideo international festival, and *La vertiente* (1958; The Waterfall), the first Bolivian feature film with sound, a semidocumentary combining a love story with a background plot about a community struggle to secure a source of safe drinking water. In 1956 Ruiz became the technical director of the Bolivian Film Institute. Despite the political instability which has characterized the modern period in Bolivia (a succession of military coups and dictatorships since the nationalist government of Victor Paz Estenssoro was overthrown in 1964), some high-quality films have been produced. **Jorge Sanjinés** and his collaborators in the production group called **Ukumau** films have produced several features, the best known of which is *Yawar Malku* (1969; *Blood of the Condor*). In addition, some commercial films, more right-wing than those of the Ukumau group, were produced in the 1970s, notably *La chaskanawi* (1976; Starry-Eyed Indian Girl), directed by the Cuellar brothers, a folkloric and romanticized version of the 1940s Bolivian novel of the same name by Carlos Medinacelli, and *El embrujo de mi tierra* (1977; Bewitching Land), directed by Jorge Guerra.

REFERENCE:

Jorge A. Schnitman, *Film Industries in Latin America* (Norwood, N.J.: ABLEX, 1984).

— S.M.H.

CINEMA IN CHILE

During the presound era of motion pictures (1896–1929) Chile was unable to establish a film industry to compare with those of other Latin American countries such as Argentina, Brazil, and Mexico. When attempts were finally made to organize a film industry after the advent of sound, they met with competition from three sources: Hollywood movies, European (mainly French and British) movies, and (for those who preferred to see films with a Spanish-speaking cast) Mexican, Argentinean, and Spanish movies. For a country like Chile, as well as Colombia, Peru, and Venezuela, the odds against a stable national film industry were high. Some notable films were produced, however. The first Chilean talkie, *Norte y sur* (1934; North and South), directed by

Jorge Delano, included generous doses of folkloric music and dance, a feature which characterized Chilean cinema for the next two decades. In 1941 Chile Films, a national film company, was founded, but given that its productions failed to penetrate the Spanish American market (some of their movies flopped in Mexico in the 1940s), it was in effect defunct by the end of the decade. The Chilean film industry languished in the 1950s, but, due to new cultural premises such as the growth of low-budget independent productions via universities, television, and political parties, it began to gain new momentum in the early 1960s. The University of Chile established a "cineclub" (film society) and created a Department of Experimental Cinema as well as a "Cinemateca" (film archive). Perhaps most important, the **Viña del Mar Film Festival** provided a forum for Chilean and foreign film directors. In 1967 the festival organized the first meeting of new Latin American filmmakers, an event which heralded the baptism of the **New Latin American Cinema.** National film production grew during the 1960s, up from four in 1966 to ten in 1968. Some of these new films, for example those directed by **Helvio Soto,** were controversial and subsequently banned by the Censorship Board because of their ideological content. At the time that **Salvador Allende** came to the presidency (1970) the distribution of about 80 percent of the films shown in Chile was in the hands of the large United States–based companies, and 95 percent of the films shown on television were from the United States. In order to balance this North American bias, Allende injected Chile Films with new funds, thereby encouraging a national film industry. Chilean cinema was nationalized and began producing a program of newsreels and documentaries following the Cuban model. The most widely distributed of these movies was *El primer año* (1971; The First Year), made by Patricio Guzmán, whose later *La batalla de Chile* (1975–1979; The Battle of Chile) is even better known. Founded as a cooperative, Cinematografía Tercer Mundo (1968–1973) produced its best-known film *El chacal de Nahueltoro* (The Jackal of Nahueltoro) in 1969, directed by **Miguel Littín;** Littín was later appointed head of Chile Films. After the military coup of 1973 which brought **Augusto Pinochet** to power at Allende's expense, many Chilean film directors were forced into exile; Littín, for example, left Chile and resumed work in Mexico. Under Pinochet's military dictatorship the communications and filmmaking schools were closed. During this period only three full-length commercial feature films were produced by the independent sector: *Julio comienza en julio* (1979; Julio begins in July) by Silvio Caiozzi, *Cómo aman los chile-*

Stills from the final sequence of *La batalla de Chile,* part 1 (1975; The Battle of Chile), in which a cameraman films his own execution

nos (1984; How Chileans Love) by A. Alvarez, and *Los hijos de la guerra fría* (1985; Children of the Cold War) by G. Lustiniano. Only the first, presented at the Cannes Film Festival, met with any success.

REFERENCES:

Michael Chanan, ed., *Chilean Cinema* (London: BFI, 1976);

María de la Luz Hurtado, "Repression and Innovation Under Authoritarianism," in *Media and Politics in Latin America: The Struggle for Democracy,* edited by Elizabeth Fox (London: Sage, 1988), 103–115;

Jorge A. Schnitman, *Film Industries in Latin America* (Norwood, N.J.: ABLEX, 1984).

— S.M.H.

CINEMA IN COLOMBIA

Though there were some earlier sporadic showings, cinema arrived in Colombia in 1909. In the Salón del Bosque, where the National Library in Bogotá now stands, the Italian Di Doménico brothers (Francisco and Vicente) showed three short films, "Lámpara de la abuelita" (Grandmother's Lamp), "Polidor se cortó un dedo" (Polidor Cut His Finger), and "Max Linder de Levita." The first important movie filmed in Colombia was *El drama del 15 de octubre* (The Drama of 15 October), about the death and burial of General Uribe, filmed in 1915 by the Di Doménico brothers. A film version of *María,* the nineteenth-century Romantic novel by Colombian novelist Jorge Isaacs, was released in Buga in 1922 and was apparently well received in Colombia and abroad, although no negative or copy of the film now exists. The most important film of the 1920s was *Bajo el cielo antioqueño* (1925; Beneath the Sky in Antioquía), a rather intricate love story directed by Arturo Acevedo. The Di Doménico brothers were an important presence in the early days of Colombian cinema until their company was bought out by Cine Colombia in 1928. The Colombian movie industry came under increasing competition from United States movies and distributors, and, as elsewhere in Spanish America, the arrival of the talkies in 1929 was the prelude to a fallow period. The first Colombian talkie was *Flores del valle* (1941; Flowers of the Valley), directed by Máximo Calvo. The most significant film of the decade was *Antonia Santos* (1944), directed by Gabriel Martínez, which dealt with the eponymous heroine's role in the Colombian independence movement; the lead was played by Lily Alvarez, a popular actress of the 1940s. The period 1947–1960 was one of great change. The movie industry was affected by several new social movements, which included the growth of commercialism and tourism and a growing interest in folklore and social critique. In addition, a more methodical film criticism was established, foreign distribution was stabilized, and more joint ventures with foreign film companies were initiated. Furthermore, the new era of television led to greater competitiveness in the movie industry. *Colombia linda* (1955; Beautiful Colombia), a poor-quality but well-known film directed by Camilo Correa, focused on Colombian songs and reflected the folkloric bias popular at the time. Decree 879, passed on 22 May 1971, had a decisive effect on the movie industry over the next two decades; the decree supported a policy of "colombianidad" (Colombian-ness). Companies were now obliged to have shares bought with at least 80 percent national capital, employ a minimum of 85 percent Colombian personnel, and agree to produce and show at least three hundred meters per month of films with a national focus.

In the 1960s and 1970s Colombian cinema reached maturity. Some of the best-known directors of this period are Carlos and Julia Alvarez, famous for their documentaries such as ¿Qué es la democracia? (1971; What is Democracy?); José María Arzuaga, Pasado el meridiano (1965–1967; Once the Meridian Is Passed); José Angel Carbonell, El cráter (1964; The Crater); Alberto Giraldo C., Una tarde ... un lunes (1969; One Afternoon ... One Monday), and Al día siguiente (1971; The Following Day), examples of surrealist cinema; Julio Luzardo, one of the most important directors of the 1960s, whose tripartite sequel, Tiempo de sequía (1961; The Time of the Drought), La Sarda (1962), and El río de las tumbas (1964; The River of Tombs), is an atmospheric, existentialist piece centering on the eruption of violence in a small fishing community; Francisco Norden, whose films, including Balcones de Cartagena (1966; The Balconies of Cartagena), La ruta de los libertadores (1969; The Path of the Liberators), about Simón Bolívar (a leading figure in the liberation of South America from Spanish rule during the nineteenth century), and Se llamaría Colombia (1970; Colombia Would Be Its Name) are known for their formal perfection. More-recent works, such as Muletazos al vacío (The Struggles of a Matador) directed by Alberto Giraldo, La patria boba (The Stupid Mother Country) directed by Luis Alberto Sánchez, Corralejas (Rodeo) directed by Ciro Durán and Mario Mitrotti, and Favor correrse atrás (Please Run Behind) directed by Lisandro Duque, are normally classed under the umbrella term "atmosphere cinema." The directors who have made the greatest impact in Colombia and abroad are **Marta Rodríguez** and **Jorge Silva.**

In recent years there has been something of a revival of Colombian cinema in the form of coproductions, mainly with the El Instituto Cubano del Arte e Industria Cinematográficas (Cuban Film Institute), or ICAIC. This connection has largely emerged as a result of the ICAIC's director, Gabriel García Márquez, the Nobel Prize–winning Colombian novelist, who has always had an interest in the movie industry since his film column in the Colombian daily *El Espectador* in 1954–1955. Film versions of many of García Márquez's novels and short stories have been produced. *Mary My*

Dearest (1983), jointly written by García Márquez and Jaime Humberto Hermosillo and directed by the latter, is based on *María de mi corazón. Chronicle of a Death Foretold* (1987), a Franco-Colombian venture directed by Francesco Rosi, is based on *Crónica de una muerte anunciada. Letters from the Park* (1988), directed by Cuban Tomás Gutiérrez Alea, is based on *El amor en los tiempos del cólera;* and *A Time to Die* (1989), a joint Colombian-Cuban venture (Focine and ICAIC) directed by Jorge Alí Triana, is based on *Tiempo de morir.*

REFERENCE:

Hernando Martínez Pardo, *Historia del cine colombiano* (Bogotá: América Latina, 1978).

— S.M.H.

ANTONIO CISNEROS

Peruvian poet Antonio Cisneros (1942–) emerged in the 1960s as one of the most original voices in Latin American poetry, with his books *Comentarios Reales* (1964; Royal Commentaries) and *Canto ceremonial a un oso hormiguero* (1968; Ceremonial Song for an Anteater). The title of the former is an ironic allusion to one of the greatest works of Peruvian literature, the *Royal Commentaries of the Incas,* written by Inca Garcilaso de la Vega in the early seventeenth century. This monumental work, authored by the son of a Spanish conquistador and an Inca princess and published in Europe, vindicated Peruvian culture and history less than a century after Spain had overrun the Incan empire. In contrast, Cisneros's approach to Peruvian history is disillusioned and often cynical. The poet's meditations on the glories of the nation's pre-Columbian and colonial past and on the nineteenth-century wars of independence against Spain are presented from the point of view of history's victims and are therefore devoid of any heroic or grandiloquent rhetoric. The tone of the poems is colloquial, informal, at times sarcastic, not unlike that of the American Beat poets. Cisneros's poems, however, also evince a formal design closer to the poetry of Robert Lowell. (Cisneros's interest in English-language poetry is well attested; he lived for some time in England and in 1972 published a translation of contemporary British poetry.)

Canto ceremonial a un oso hormiguero continues the poet's search for a contemporary and original idiom — for an "unceremonious" poetic language — based on the spoken word. The book debunks some national myths, but the historical strand is qualified by existential concerns. Overall, Cisneros's style is a mixture of high poetry and popular and mass genres.

Other important works by this Peruvian poet are *El libro de Dios y de los húngaros* (1978; The Book of God and the Hungarians), *Crónica del Niño Jesús de Chilca* (1982; Chronicle of Baby Jesus of Chilca), and *Monólogo de la casta Susana y otros poemas* (1986; Monologue of Chaste Susana and Other Poems). The first of these books chronicles the poet's experiences in Hungary (where Cisneros lived between 1974–1975) and his apparently unrelated conversion to a revolutionary kind of Christianity associated with **Liberation Theology.** *Crónica del Niño Jesús de Chilca* is the story of a Peruvian coastal community told in the voices of the fishermen who see their way of life threatened by the encroachment of modern industry. The combination of social concerns and New Testament motifs relates Cisneros's poetry to that of Nicaraguan poet Ernesto Cardenal, an ordained priest and militant revolutionary who in the 1980s was minister of education in the left-wing Sandinista government.

Cisneros's collected poetry was published in Mexico with the title *Por la noche los gatos* (1989; Cats at Night).

REFERENCE:

James Higgins, *The Poet in Peru: Alienation and the Quest for a Super-Reality* (Liverpool: Cairns, 1982).

— R.G.M.

CLARIDAD

Claridad was an Argentinean left-wing journal (1926–1941) with close links to the **Boedo** group, a group of lower-middle-class writers and intellectuals who opposed the aristocratic orientation of their rival **Florida** faction. The prototype for *Claridad* was the French *Clarté,* edited by Henri Barbusse. *Claridad* replicated itself in other Latin American countries.

— R.G.M.

JULIA CODESIDO

Julia Codesido (1892–), a Peruvian painter and print-maker, was a member of the **indigenist** movement. Like her contemporary **Jorge Vinatea Reinoso,** she belonged to the first generation of students who attended the Escuela de Bellas Artes (School of Fine Arts), founded in Lima in 1919. Although this school emphasized the conservative taste of its director, the **impressionist** painter Daniel Hernández, Codesido was more influenced by the work of one of her professors, the indigenist painter **José Sabogal.** During the 1920s her art was closer to Sabogal's, but after a visit to Mexico in 1935, where she saw the art of the muralists, she adopted some of the stylistic characteristics of David Alfaro Siqueiros. Although Codesido worked with typical indigenist themes, affirming the native traditions of Peru, her art had a significant avant-garde quality. In paintings such as *Tapadas Limeñas* (Veiled Women from Lima), she transforms this Peruvian theme into a bold semiabstract composition based on strong diagonal and vertical lines, radically simplified shapes, and an expressive treatment of the surface.

REFERENCE:

Teodoro Núñez Ureta, *Pintura contemporánea: Segunda parte* (Lima: Banco de Crédito del Perú, 1976).

— F.B.N.

COFRADÍAS

Preservation of local dance traditions, an amalgam of European and indigenous themes and styles, has become the primary function of the cofradía, an association of adults affiliated with a local church. Originally the cofradía, which takes its name and patron saint from its affiliated church, was a mutual-aid society for its members, and its functions were more diverse. Today, however, its visibility derives from its organization of dance pageants on the annual saint's day and other religious holidays.

— N.D.B. & J.M.H.

COLECCIÓN ARCHIVOS

The Colección Archivos, an ambitious editorial project instituted in 1984, has four explicit aims: a) to establish through rigorous philological analysis the definitive text and its variants for the major works of twentieth-century Latin American literature; b) to gather an exhaustive dossier on the selected authors and works; c) to compile textual and contextual critical analyses of the works selected; and d) to contribute to the knowledge of these works in the context of North-South relations. In consonance with the last of these aims the University of Pittsburgh Press announced in 1991 that it would undertake the translation and distribution of selected titles from the collection. The Archivos collection is directed by Professor Amos Segala of the University of Paris and sponsored by UNESCO, with the participation of official entities from eight European and Latin American governments. The first published titles include works in Spanish and Portuguese by Miguel Angel Asturias, Clarice Lispector, Jorge Icaza,

A *Cuy* comic strip by Juan Acevedo. The title rodent and a mongrel dog vow to work together to overcome societal marginalization.

Teresa de la Parra, José María Arguedas, César Vallejo, José Lezama Lima, and Julio Cortázar.

— R.G.M.

COMIC STRIPS AND BOOKS

Comic strips began to appear in Spanish America after the turn of the twentieth century. Between 1900 and 1929 the development of Spanish American comic strips roughly followed United States trends, in large part because the first strips were translations of American originals. Their growth was primarily centered in Mexico and Argentina. As early as 1902 American strips appeared in Mexico, and within a year the first Mexican strip, the humorous *Don Lupito* by Andrés Audiffred, was published. By about 1910 reprints of U.S. strips first appeared in Argentinean newspapers, and 1912 saw the publication of the first Argentinean strip, the humorous *Sarrasqueta*, by Manuel Redondo.

From the 1920s through the 1940s adventure strips surpassed in popularity even the popular humorous strip; the comic book was born in the mid 1930s. The period from the late 1930s through the 1940s is referred to as Mexico's "Golden Age"; in 1936 Germán Oliver Butze first published the humorous *Los Supersabios* (The Superbrains), and the following year Gabriel Vargas brought out *La familia burrón* (The Donkeyson Family), which achieved wide distribution in the South. The 1928–1949 period was also one of tremendous growth in Argentina; Raúl Roux in 1928 initiated the adventure strip with *El tigre de los llanos* (The Tiger of the Plains). Ever since 1950 throughout Spanish America political satire, underground, and Marvel superhero comics have flourished. In Mexico the most important innovation was Manuel de Landa's creation of "mini" comic books, pocket-size comics

that sold at bargain-basement prices, the best known of which is Guillermo de la Parra and Yoland Vargas's Editorial Argumentos, which publishes Mexico's best-selling romance comic *Lágrimas, risas y amor* (Tears, Laughter, and Love). The contemporary period in Argentina is marked by a wealth of outstanding talents and works. Perhaps best known throughout Spanish America and Spain is *Mafalda,* begun in 1965 by Joaquín Salvador Lavado (Quino). Other important comic strips are Peruvian Juan Acevedo's consciousness-raising *Cuy* (an indigenous rodent), Colombian Ernesto Franco's humorous *Copetín* (Half-pint), and Cuban Hernán H.'s *Gugulandia,* which occupied the back page of the magazine *Dedeté* (DDT) in the 1960s and 1970s.

REFERENCE:

Harold E. Hinds Jr., "Comics," in *Handbook of Latin American Popular Culture,* edited by Hinds and Charles M. Tatum (Westport, Conn.: Greenwood Press, 1985), pp. 81–110.

— S.M.H.

COMPAÑÍA NACIONAL DE DANZA

Founded in Quito, Ecuador, in 1976, the Compañía Nacional de Danza is directed by one of its founding members, Arturo Garrido. The annex school of the company was initially staffed by classical ballet teachers from Romania, Cuba, and the former Soviet Union and by contemporary dance teachers. The company of seventeen dancers is supported by the Ministry of Culture, the Casa de la Cultura, Diners' Club, and the Ministries of Information and Tourism. Repertory by Arturo Garrido includes *The Rite of Spring,* to music by Igor Stravinsky, and *Scent of Gardenias*, set to the poem "Men of the Dawn" by the Mexican poet Efraín

Huerta, and dealing with such themes as love and hatred against a depressed urban backround peopled by prostitutes and homosexuals.

— N.D.B. & J.M.H.

CONCEPTUAL ART

Conceptual Art, also called Idea Art, emerged in Latin America during the 1960s and continues to be of paramount importance. This radical artistic expression defines the work of art as an idea or a concept rather than in terms of its material qualities, which may prove to be temporary or disposable. In order to convey such concepts, artists rely on a variety of media and visual elements, such as texts, photographs, everyday objects, electronic media, and multimedia installations. Conceptual Art has several antecedents, which include the radical innovations introduced by Marcel Duchamp and the experiments with common objects, unorthodox materials, and artist/public participation that characterized **Pop Art, Assemblages, and Happenings.**

In Latin America, Conceptual Art did not emphasize the self-referential or tautological, as did this type of art in Europe and the United States, but instead developed a markedly ideological bent. During the 1960s and 1970s countries such as Argentina, Brazil, Uruguay, and Chile were under military dictatorships which strictly censored most popular cultural expressions. In Conceptual Art many artists found useful strategies for circumventing traditional artistic circuits (the art market, museums, and art galleries), and as a result most governments regarded their actions as marginal and unimportant; thus, artists were free to use their art to make public political statements that both subverted and highlighted the repressive power of the state. Another important difference of Conceptual Art in Latin America is its greater emphasis on the appearance of the work of art, whose formal attributes and visual appeal are as carefully considered as in other more traditional approaches.

In Argentina the members of the Centro de Arte y Comunicación (CAYC) group, such as Víctor Grippo and Luis Benedit, supported a type of Conceptual Art that often involved technological and scientific processes. For example, Grippo's series *Analogías* (Analogies) of the 1970s often included gauges that measured the electricity produced in the fermentation of potatoes, a metaphor for the unused energy stored in Latin America. Furthermore, conceptual groups expressed their political views through installations made with perishable materials, such as *Tucumán arde* (1968; Tucumán Burns), as well as "art actions," activities which involved the artists and the public. In Chile Con-

ceptual Art took the name of the Avanzada movement, which supported numerous art actions of a political nature, especially those produced by the members of CADA (Colectivo de Acciones de Arte), a group of writers and visual artists that included Juan Castillo, **Diamela Eltit,** Raúl Zurita, and Lotty Rosenfield. CADA's art action *Para no morirse de hambre en el arte* (1980; Not To Die Of Hunger In Art) denounced poverty and hunger in Chile through a series of events which included the distribution of milk among poor families and a parade of milk trucks in front of the Museo de Bellas Artes. Other members of the Avanzada movement, such as **Gonzalo Díaz, Eugenio Dittborn, Alfredo Jaar,** and **Catalina Parra,** have produced complex installations to express their views. Díaz's *Marco/Banco de Pruebas* (1988; Frame/Testing Bench) uses a variety of objects such as wood balustrades, iron boxes, and printed images to suggest, in a deliberately oblique way, the power of the state to control public perceptions.

In Colombia Conceptual Art was also related to Pop Art and emerged at the end of the 1960s and in the 1970s with the work of Alicia Barney, Adolfo Bernal, Antonio Caro, Ramiro Gómez, **Beatriz González, Bernardo Salcedo,** and Juan Camilo Uribe. Beatriz González combined common household objects with mass-media images of heroic or official figures. In *Decoración de interiores* (1981; Interior Decoration) she silk-screened onto a two-hundred-yard-long living-room drapery an image showing a former Colombian president hosting a party, while in her forty-foot frieze *Parrots* (1986) she painted military men whose faces are repeated as in wallpaper. Salcedo, who had earlier worked with Pop Art, began producing conceptual pieces after the 1970s. In his series *Señales particulares* (1980s; Personal Signs) Salcedo presents framed photographs partially covered by ordinary objects, always accompanied by the witty titles that make his art intriguing and show his interest in language and puns. Uribe and Caro have also used humor as a critical tool, especially when working with popular images in collages and installations. In Uribe's collage *Declaración de amor a Venezuela* (1976; Declaration of Love for Venezuela) he repeats the images of a well-known Venezuelan saint and the head of Christ in order to form the shape of a heart, while in Caro's painting *Colombia* (1976) he simply presents the name of that country written in the characteristic type of the Coca-Cola logo, a reference to the economic and political interference of the United States in Colombia. Ramiro Gómez has produced a series of installations with natural and discarded objects, such as *Verano* (1980; Summer), made up of dried leaves, branches, and wood. He was a member of El Sindicato, a group of concep-

A *Logo for America* (1987), by Alfredo Jaar, installed on the Spectacolor lightboard in Times Square, New York City

tual artists in Barranquilla who often exhibited together. In 1978 they presented the installation *Alacena con zapatos* (Pantry with Shoes), which scandalized the more traditional elements of the Colombian public.

Many Latin American conceptual artists have relocated to the United States, such as the Uruguayan **Luis Camnitzer,** the Chileans **Alfredo Jaar** and **Catalina Parra,** the Brazilians Regina Vater and Josely Carvalho, and the Argentinean **Leandro Katz,** all of whom, in spite of living abroad, have continued to produce an art that deals primarily with Latin America. In fact, they have been considered to be among the leading conceptual artists in Latin America; to their names should be added those of three artists who live in their native Brazil: Waltercio Caldas, Cildo Meireles, and Jac Lerner. Camnitzer, who lives in the New York area, has worked in a variety of media, including graphics and installations. In many of his pieces the artist alludes to the theme of state-sponsored terrorism and torture, such as in his photoetching series *From the Uruguayan Torture* (1984) and his installation at the Venice Biennial (1988). Jaar, who moved to New York in the 1980s, designed his *A Logo for America* (1987) for the Spectacolor lightboard in Times Square in New York City. This conceptual piece presented a series of images denouncing the appropriation by the United States of the name America, which belongs to the whole continent, a point symbolic of larger geopolitical issues.

REFERENCES:

Mari Carmen Ramírez, "Blueprint Circuits: Conceptual Art and Politics in Latin America," in *Latin American Artists of the Twentieth Century,* edited by Waldo Rasmussen, Fatima Bercht, and Elizabeth Ferrer (New York: Museum of Modern Art, 1993);

Ramírez and Beverly Adams, *Encounters/Displacements: Luis Camnitzer, Alfredo Jaar, Cildo Meireles,* with essays by Jacqueline Barnitz and Paulo Herkenhoff (Austin: Archer M. Huntington Art Gallery, University of Texas at Austin, 1992).

— F.B.N.

CONSEJO NACIONAL DE DANZA DE PERÚ

Among its principal activities, the Consejo Nacional de Danza de Perú (National Dance Council of Peru) organizes the Dance Festival of Lima in collaboration with the Peruvian–North American Cultural Institute. The council is government sponsored but relies heavily on private support. Participating companies and individuals have included Do Ut Des Grupo de Danza and Sociedad de Arte Rossana Peñaloza (Peru); Nelson Díaz (Ecuador); Danza Lima; Danza Viva (Lima); the Mary Street Dance Theatre of Miami; the Mimi Garrard Dance Theatre of New York; Artilugio Magnético of Uruguay; the Ballet Nacional of Peru; and the Ballet Municipal of Lima. Support for the festival has come from J. Walter Thompson, the United States Information Service, the Gran Hotel Bolívar, Peruvisión Tours, and Miriam Sano.

— N.D.B. & J.M.H.

CONSTRUCTIVE ART

Defined by the art and theories of the Uruguayan artist **Joaquín Torres-García,** Constructive Art, also called Constructive Universalism, is a variation of European Constructivism. In Constructive Art, Torres-García synthesized innovative aspects of different avant-garde movements, such as Cubism, **Surrealism,** and Neoplasticism, with pre-Columbian art. In his sculptural reliefs and paintings he transformed images of everyday objects into symbols by reducing them, in the manner characteristic of Cubism, to schematic geometric shapes. The symbols he depicted are also archetypes because they reach the viewer at an intuitive and emotional level, thus reflecting the painter's interest in Surrealism's exploration of the collective unconscious. Taking his inspiration from the orthogonal grid used by neoplasticists such as Piet Mondrian, Torres-García placed these archetypes within a "structure" or grid determined by the Golden Section, a traditional system of proportion that for him had a deep cosmic significance since it was able to transform the painting into a cosmic microcosm. In many of his works Torres-García also included archetypes found in the art of pre-Inca cultures and Native American groups such as the Hopi, in order to root his Constructive Art in the ancient heritage of the Americas and thus establish a new kind of modern art.

The visual and theoretical proposals of Constructive Art were disseminated in Uruguay and Latin America through the activities of two institutions founded by Torres-García, the Asociación de Arte Constructivo (1935–1940) and the **Taller Torres-García** (1943–1962), which held several art exhibitions in Montevideo, Buenos Aires, São Paulo, and Rio de Janeiro, and also through the publications of the periodicals *Círculo y cuadrado* (1936–1943) and *Removedor* (1944–1951), as well as Torres-García's books *Estructura* (1935; Structure) and *Universalismo constructivo* (1944; Constructive Universalism). Constructive Art had a lasting impact on the arts of Uruguay and became the dominant style for many years. It was also influential in Buenos Aires during the 1940s, where it encouraged radical artistic experimentation, facilitating the beginnings of the concrete-art movements called **Asociación de Arte Concreto-Invención** and **Madí.** Torres-García's artistic and theoretical legacy inspired the development of concrete and abstract geometric movements in Brazil and Venezuela during the 1950s and 1960s. In addition, the Americanist project of Constructive Art has influenced several generations of Latin American artists, whose members include the Peruvian **Fernando de Szyszlo,** the Ecuadoran **Estuardo Maldonado,** and the Argentineans **César Paternosto** and Elizabeth Aro, all of whom are interested in developing abstract styles that go beyond formal considerations to connote a sense of cultural identity.

REFERENCES:

Valerie Fletcher, ed., *Crosscurrents of Modernism: Four Latin American Pioneers: Diego Rivera, Joaquín Torres-García, Wifredo Lam, Matta* (Washington, D.C.: Hirshhorn Museum and Sculpture Garden, 1992);

Mari Carmen Ramírez, ed., *The Taller Torres-García: The School of the South and Its Legacy* (Austin: University of Texas Press, 1992).

— F.B.N.

CONTRADANZA

Venezuelan choreographer Hercilia López, trained in classical ballet, created Contradanza in 1973 as a reaction to the claustrophobia she experienced in traditional ballet. She has established a school and teaching method for contemporary dance which draws on her knowledge of anthropology as well as of music and theater. Works by López in the repertoire include *¡Qué bonitos ojos tienes!* (What Beautiful Eyes You Have), *Amapola* (Poppy), and *Sonido de Amor Sobre Mi Cuerpo* (Sound of Love over My Body). Her style attempts to move away from convention to express the universality of womanhood, characterized by solitude, honesty, and eroticism.

— N.D.B. & J.M.H.

COREOARTE

Carlos Orta and Noris Ugueto created Aka Ballet Coreoarte as a foundation, a dance company, and a dance training center in 1983. Orta was a principal dancer with the José Limón Dance Company in New York concurrently with his duties as director of Coreoarte. One aim of the school and company is to form integrated dancers, dancers capable of expressing, in an original style, a Latin American language which preserves Latin American values. Thus, the dancers train in known dance techniques while at the same time investigating their own, and Venezuela's, ethnic heritage. The young dancers comprising the company represent a wide diversity of sociocultural backgrounds. The repertory includes works by Orta, Joachim Schlomer, and Arnaldo Alvarez, with original music as well as music by Hector Villa-Lobos, Willie Colón, and Aurelio de la Vega.

– N.D.B. & J.M.H.

JULIO CORTÁZAR

An Argentinean writer born in Brussels, Julio Cortázar (1914–1984) achieved a worldwide reputation with the publication of *Rayuela* (1963; translated as *Hopscotch*) and of several stories that preceded and followed the author's great "antinovel." No other modern Argentinean writer, with the exception of **Jorge Luis Borges,** has had such a lasting and profound influence as Cortázar on Latin American and world literature.

At the end of World War I Cortázar's parents returned to Argentina, and the future writer began to study literature. Cortázar taught high school in small provincial towns until 1944, when he became a profes-

Julio Cortázar

sor of French literature at the University of Cuyo in Mendoza. A year later he resigned his position in protest against the incoming government of **Juan Domingo Perón** and moved to the capital city of Buenos Aires, where he started to publish his extraordinary stories. The first one, "Casa tomada" ("House Taken Over"), appeared in 1946 in a literary magazine directed by Borges, followed in the next two years by "Bestiario" ("Bestiary") and "Lejana" ("The Distances"), stories later included in *Bestiario* (1951; translated as *Bestiary*), which was Cortázar's first collection of stories and the only one really to have an organic design linking all eight stories. The book generates a labyrinthine space in which secret passageways connect one story to another; echoes are heard from story to story, and the theme of the expulsion of the monster from the depths of the self resonates in several of the plots, reminiscent of a 1949 dramatic poem Cortázar published based on the myth of the Minotaur and the labyrinth. The book's title alludes to medieval bestiaries where real species

coexist with imaginary ones. In like manner Cortázar's stories are populated by both real and imaginary beasts, with the distinction between them a matter of irreducible ambiguity.

In 1951 Cortázar immigrated to Europe, where he earned a living as a translator for a United Nations agency in Vienna and continued writing in Paris. Later on, he settled in Provence, in southern France, and did not return to Argentina except for a brief visit shortly before his death. The dialectic between the author's Argentinean and European identities is one of the main themes of his most famous novel, *Rayuela*. In the 1950s Cortázar published two more books of short stories: *Final del juego* (1956, revised, 1964; translated as *End of the Game*) and *Las armas secretas* (1959; Secret Weapons). Most of these stories belong to the realm of the fantastic, and they emphasize not the laws of reality but their exceptions (to paraphrase Cortázar's Surrealist precursor Alfred Jarry). Cortázar's early stories from his first three collections are available in English as *End of the Game and Other Stories* and *Blow Up and Other Stories.*

For Cortázar the fantastic is the moment of "extrañamiento" ("estranging" or "strangeness") that supervenes when the metaphysical and ontological assurances of everyday reality collapse under the pressure of the unknown, opening a new perspective through which a secret reality is glimpsed behind or under the facade of the routine habits that compose our personal world. One of the structural devices used by Cortázar to project the perturbing vision of the fantastic is analogy, reminiscent of the correspondences of French poet Charles Baudelaire. In Cortázar's stories the analogy often takes the form of the doppelgänger (double) or of a counterpoint between different times and places that are shown to be identical or to have secret affinities. It is not difficult to detect the presence of French Surrealism and Symbolism in Cortázar's theory of the fantastic; one of the key influences on Cortázar was Edgar Allan Poe, also a favorite of Baudelaire and the initiator of the modern short story. Unlike Poe, however, who instead set his weird tales in unreal settings, Cortázar deliberately avoided the Gothic paraphernalia of his American precursor (whose prose works he translated) and instead set his stories in the here and now of daily life. Cortázar's language, in consequence, is free from the trappings of "literary" style and is often colloquial and humorous. His stories affirm that the fantastic may appear in a bus taken to some banal destination (as in "A Yellow Flower") or in a concert casually attended (as in "The Band") or in the Jardin des Plantes as one gazes on that strange salamander called the axolotl.

If Cortázar is a consummate storyteller, he is also one of the major Latin American novelists of the twentieth century. His first published novel, *Los premios* (1960; translated as *The Winners*), employs the "ship of fools" motif to combine realistic detail with social criticism, allegory, and metaphysical and literary speculation. In an earlier novel, published posthumously, *El examen* (1986; The Exam), Cortázar had used the metaphor of the plague to describe the coming of Peronism; in *Los premios* another plague shuts off half the ship in which the winners of a lottery are due to sail on a cruise. The action of the novel hinges on the mystery of the forbidden space and on the meaning of the plague. The unknown region of the ship may be interpreted as the unconscious or as the domain of the Other in a more general way. Cortázar relates the characters' need to know what is in the forbidden space to their past experience and their mental life, thus creating social portraits tinged with existentialist anguish and inauthenticity. Literally above the passengers, on the ship's deck, hovers the mysterious Persio, whose soliloquies interrupt the action of the novel at regular intervals. Persio is a reflection of the author and his quest for the "figura" (the symbolic configuration) whose form will unify and explain the disparate strands of the plot.

Three years after *Los premios* Cortázar published *Rayuela,* a novel that has altered the landscape of narrative fiction in Latin America and elsewhere. *Rayuela* is a quest novel at the thematic and formal levels. The protagonist, Oliveira, embarks on a radical search for what the surrealists called the absolute, that is, the point or perspective from which all contraries cease to be such and are integrated into a superreality. Oliveira's quest seeks to integrate pairs of opposites such as intellectual analysis/intuitive response, Buenos Aires/Paris, and reason/madness. Much of the protagonist's quest involves symbolic passages between doubles. Bridges are ubiquitous symbols in the novel; they are present in Oliveira's meanderings through Paris and also define the role of one of the characters, Talita, who in one of the most brilliant chapters of the novel crawls across a plank joining Oliveira and his double as the two of them watch the life-and-death spectacle from their windows. Other "chanced-upon" objects (a kaleidoscope, the upper hole of a circus tent) act as symbols of the transcendental perspective sought by Oliveira, while the geometric representation of the game of hopscotch (one more "figura") is like a mandala, a symbolic itinerary describing the way to the "center." The hopscotch figure, however, also has a formal dimension in that it symbolizes the structure of the book and the process of reading. *Rayuela* is divided into three parts: "Over There" (set in Paris), "Over Here" (set in Buenos Aires), and "Elsewhere" (composed of "dispensable" chapters interspersed through the main narrative according to the directions printed at the beginning of the novel). The reader has the option of skipping among chapters instead of following the usual linear order joining chapter 1 to chapter 56, the last one of the second part. The latter itinerary is presented as an alternative for the "passive" reader, but the text invokes an "active" reader (the author's accomplice) to accompany the author and the protagonist in their search for meaning. The metafictional aspect of the novel, whose theme is the search for form, is well developed in the third part through the presence of Morelli, a nebulous character who functions as the author's alter ego and who speculates on the conditions of narrative discourse. The minimum condition of productivity espoused by Morelli is the rejection of the "literary," which can only distort and falsify a narrative project. Accordingly, the language of *Rayuela* may be rarefied and pedantic, but even the worst intellectual excesses of the novel are mitigated by humor (often self-deprecating humor) and by the refreshing colloquiality, even slang, that characterizes its style. The imperative of authenticity also explains the antinovelistic form of *Rayuela*.

Chapter 62 of *Rayuela* generated Cortázar's next novelistic project, aptly titled *62: Modelo para armar* (1968; translated as *62: A Model Kit*). This often amusing novel further explores the notion of the "figura" as a constellation of heterogeneous elements which together have a meaning denied them by themselves. The transpersonal character of these obscure configurations is best expressed by one of the novel's statements to the effect that one is not the sum of one's actions but of the actions of others.

In the 1960s Cortázar underwent a political transformation as a result of the **Cuban Revolution** and of the solidarity that it nurtured among Latin American intellectuals and writers. He became an ardent supporter of both the Cuban and the Nicaraguan revolutions and an eloquent critic of the Southern Cone dictatorships of the 1970s. Yet Cortázar never sacrificed the autonomy of the literary enterprise to the urgent demands of politics. In fact, his last novel, *Libro de Manuel* (1973; translated as *A Manual for Manuel*), is an attempt to work out the contradictions between autonomous literature and the politically engaged writer. One of the questions raised by the novel is the question of language itself: with a new reading public having been made available by the revolutionary process, is it legitimate to use the language of high culture when telling a story? Or is it better to secure an intelligible communication with the public even at the risk of simplifying literary language? The novel also attempts to integrate political with erotic liberation and to take the literary work out of the study and into the street. To achieve the latter purpose Cortázar incorporates newspaper clippings (about political events such as the Vietnam War and the torture of political prisoners) into the novel for the characters to read and discuss. The novel is envisioned as an album or collage put together for the future Latin American reader, symbolized by the infant Manuel.

Other notable works by Cortázar are the story collections *Todos los fuegos el fuego* (1966; translated as *All the Fires the Fire*), *Octaedro* (1974; some of whose stories are included in *Change of Light and Other Stories*), *Alguien que anda por ahí* (1977; some of whose stories are also in *Change of Light and Other Stories*), *Queremos tanto a Glenda* (1980; translated as *We Love Glenda So Much*), and *Deshoras* (1983; translated as *Afterhours*), as well as the collage books *La vuelta al día en ochenta mundos* (1967; translated as *Around the Day in Eighty Worlds*) and *Ultimo round*

(1969; translated as *Last Round*). Julio Cortázar died in Paris in February 1984.

REFERENCES:

Steven Boldy, *The Novels of Julio Cortázar* (Cambridge & New York: Cambridge University Press, 1980);

Fernando Burgos, ed. *Los ochenta mundos de Julio Cortázar* (Madrid: Edi-6, 1987);

Terry J. Peavler, *Julio Cortázar* (Boston: Twayne, 1990).

— R.G.M.

COSTUMBRISMO

Costumbrismo refers to a literary and journalistic genre that flourished around the middle of the nineteenth century in Latin America. Cultivators of the genre were inspired by emergent nationalism and by the folk leanings of Romanticism to describe local human types and regional customs ("costumbres," in Spanish; thence the designation *costumbrismo*). If the intention was not moral, then it was to celebrate whatever was typical of a given nationality. Spanish costumbristas Mariano José de Larra and Mesonero Romanos heavily influenced their Latin American counterparts. Some of the more noted American practitioners of the genre were Mexican Guillermo Prieto, Chilean Jotabeche, Peruvian Ricardo Palma, and Argentinean Juan María Gutiérrez. (See also **Criollismo**.)

REFERENCE:

Susana Zanetti, ed., *Costumbristas de América Latina* (Buenos Aires: Centro Editor de Américana Latina, 1973).

— R.G.M.

CREACIONISMO

Creacionismo is a poetic theory propounded in 1916 by Chilean avant-garde poet **Vicente Huidobro** in a lecture at the Ateneo Hispano of Buenos Aires. The theory focuses on the autonomy of the poetic object and highlights the image as the fundamental poetic device. For Huidobro a poem was a new fact added to the facts of nature, a created object that did not resemble the natural world but incorporated the generative principle of nature for its own ends. In one of the manifestos in which he developed his poetic theory, Huidobro states that the creacionista poem can only exist in the poet's head; a poem, he says, is not beautiful because it evokes something beautiful we have seen nor because it anticipates a vision that we may yet have; it is beautiful in itself. The created poem does not admit any terms of comparison and does not exist outside the book. It is its own end and it creates its own sense of the marvelous through the skillful use of images.

The title of one of Huidobro's books (originally published in French, like most of his manifestos) illustrates the poet's conception of the image and of the creacionista poem. *Horizon Carré* (1917) means "squared horizon," an image that does not exist in reality (or in language) and one that betrays an intellectual and calculated effect alien, for example, to Surrealist poetry (of which Huidobro disapproved for its neglect of poetic consciousness in favor of unconscious anarchy). The topographical reference of Huidobro's title is also significant. It is echoed by the titles of two of his collections in Spanish that best exemplify the practice of creacionismo: *Poemas árticos* (1918; translated as *Arctic Poems*) and *Ecuatorial* (1918). The line of the horizon marks a vanishing boundary that the experimental poet must cross in search of new poetic territories; the Arctic metaphor makes possible a comparison between the poet and the explorer, who both conquer virgin regions. The Arctic, in addition, is of the same color as the blank page. The terrestrial equator, the circle that divides the earth's surface into the northern and southern hemispheres, can be read in conjunction with the main structural device of the long poem that composes the book: a string or thread (sometimes materialized in the poem in the form of a telegraph wire) that holds the images together as pearls are held together in a necklace. For Huidobro the creacionista poem had to be a new creation as a whole and in its every component part.

Creacionismo has significant affinities with Cubist theory and in particular with the poetry of Pierre Reverdy, the poet with whom Huidobro co-founded the *Nord-Sud* review in Paris in 1917. Huidobro heatedly argued his paternity of the "Nord-Sud" style against the claims of the French poet, one of the reasons why poetic manifestos written in French by Huidobro proliferated at the time. The vertiginous succession of avant-garde movements, however, and the advent of Surrealism in the mid 1920s made this debate and the whole theory of creacionismo obsolete. Huidobro's main poetic work, *Altazor* (1931), deals in part with the contradictions inherent in the poetics of autonomous art.

REFERENCE:

Cecil Wood, *The Creacionismo of Vicente Huidobro* (Fredericton, N.B.: York Press, 1978).

— R.G.M.

CRIOLLISMO

Criollismo denotes a current of realism in the Latin American novel of the first three decades of the twentieth century, one concerned with the portrayal of typical landscapes, speech patterns, and characters. In colonial Spanish America the word *criollo* designated the Spaniard born in America and was sometimes generalized to cover anyone born in the New World regardless of race. *Criollismo* thus signifies the awareness of one's native environment and always implies an affirmation of local traditions and values. In spite of its dependence on regional turns of speech, human types, and landscapes, criollismo is not at odds with nationalism but on the contrary provides its foundation. Criollista authors believed that in describing their corner of the world they were revealing the national essence of their country and, perhaps, the American essence of their continent. With notable exceptions, such as Joaquín Edwards Bello's *El roto* (1920) —whose title (the "tattered" or "ragged" one) refers to the typical representative of the Chilean proletariat — criollista novels are usually set in the countryside. Because these novels rely on the description of folk customs and other "typical" traits of regional or national character, criollismo has some affinities with **costumbrismo,** a nineteenth-century genre that exulted in local color and that usually circulated in the form of sketches known as "cuadros de costumbres" (sketches of manners). These sketches would be integrated with greater or lesser skill into the plot of romantic or realist novels, as happens with *Cecilia Valdés,* by the Cuban Cirilo Villaverde, and with *María,* by the Colombian Jorge Isaacs, two of the most important romantic novels in Latin America. Though it is not always easy to distinguish between costumbrismo and criollismo, it may be said that the former had a satirical or moral intention or no intention at all beyond picturesque display; whereas an explicit concern with national essence underlay the latter. Some outstanding criollista writers were the Colombian Tomás Carrasquilla, the Chilean Mariano Latorre, the Argentinean Benito Lynch, and the Uruguayan Enrique Amorim. (See also **Regionalist Novel.**)

REFERENCE:

Ricardo Latcham, Ernesto Montenegro, and Manuel Vega, *El criollismo* (Santiago, Chile: Editorial Universitaria, 1956).

— R.G.M.

CARLOS CRUZ-DIEZ

In his **geometric abstract** artworks, the Venezuelan Carlos Cruz-Diez (1923–) explores subtle visual effects produced through color interactions, a type of optical dynamism that connects his work with Op Art and **Kinetic Art.** Cruz-Diez and his classmates **Jesús Rafael Soto** and **Alejandro Otero** studied at the Escuela de Artes Plásticas y Aplicadas in Caracas dur-

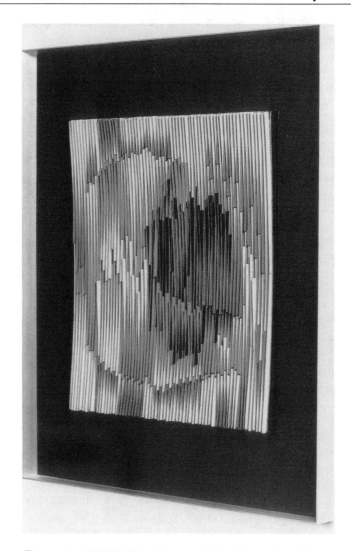

Fisicromía, 48 (1961; Physichromy, 48) by Carlos Cruz-Diez

ing the early 1940s. From 1946 to 1955 he worked in Caracas as a graphic designer for the Creole Petroleum Corporation and as art director for the MacCann-Erickson Advertising Agency. In 1955 Cruz-Diez traveled to Europe, where he became interested in the dynamic qualities of color interactions after seeing Soto's kinetic sculptures in Paris. After his return to Caracas in 1957, he founded the Estudio de Artes Visuales, a graphic art and industrial design studio. From 1958 to 1960 he became assistant director of the Escuela de Bellas Artes, where he taught layout and design in the Facultad de Periodismo (School of Journalism) at the Universidad Central de Venezuela.

After Cruz-Diez settled in Paris in 1960, he produced his best-known series of *Fisicromías* (Physichromies), blending aspects of painting and sculpture. The series consists of parallel narrow strips with little space between them attached at a right angle to a flat support. The strips protrude slightly from the backboard and are painted with different colors on their three sides, triggering a series of color interactions when the viewer changes position in front of the work, an approach reminiscent of works by Israeli artist Yaacov Agam. In *Fisicromía, 48* (1961) cardboard strips of different heights form uneven shapes that produce an expressive pattern in bold colors, while in *Fisicromía, 506* (1970) narrow, evenly cut wood and Plexiglas strips modulate into subtle translucent planes as the viewer moves about. Since the 1970s Cruz-Diez has produced *Fisicromías* for public sites, such as the Simón Bolívar International Airport in Caracas (1974–1979) and the Place du Venezuela in Paris (1975–1978).

REFERENCE:

Aracy Amaral, "Abstract Constructivist Trends in Argentina, Brazil, Venezuela, and Colombia," in *Latin American Artists of the Twentieth Century*, edited by Waldo Rasmussen, Fatima Bercht, and Elizabeth Ferrer (New York: Museum of Modern Art, 1993).

—F.B.N.

CUATRO

The Venezuelan cuatro is a small instrument of the guitar family, similar in form to the ukulele. Both were probably descended from the Portuguese *machete*. The cuatro is prominently used in the western plains region of Venezuela and the eastern plains of Colombia. A popular folk instrument, the cuatro fulfills a harmonic/rhythmic role in genres such as the **joropo, aguinaldo, vals,** and Spanish Christmas carols (*villancicos*). With four single strings, the Venezuelan cuatro should not be confused with the Puerto Rican cuatro, which has five double courses.

REFERENCES:

Gerard Béhague, "Latin American Folk Music," in *Folk and Traditional Music of the Western Continents,* by Bruno Nettl, third edition, revised and edited by Valerie Woodring Goertzen (Englewood Cliffs, N.J.: Prentice-Hall, 1990);

Octavio Marulanda, *El folklore de Colombia: Práctica de la identidad cultural* (Bogotá: Artestudio Editores, 1984);

Thomas Turino, "Music in Latin America," in *Excursions in World Music,* by Bruno Nettl, Charles Capwell, and others (Englewood Cliffs, N.J.: Prentice-Hall, 1992).

—R.L.S.

THE CUBAN REVOLUTION AND CULTURAL POLITICS

The Cuban Revolution of 1959 had a major impact on the politics and culture of South America. From the start the Cuban Revolution sought to have an international appeal grounded on the moral idealism of its two chief leaders, Fidel Castro and **Ernesto "Che" Guevara.** The early 1960s were the years of Guevara's "New Man" and of Castro's "Bread Without Fear" slogan. The political and the moral revolution marched hand in hand. Guevara led futile expeditions to the Congo and to Bolivia in an effort to propagate the revolutionary faith. Cuban radio stations beamed their revolutionary message to other parts of Latin America. Young revolutionaries came to Cuba to be trained in guerrilla warfare, and Cuban-style guerrillas opened fronts in Peru, Venezuela, and Mexico.

Culture, too, was envisioned as having a role to play in the international projection of the Cuban Revolution. In a June 1961 speech to artists and intellectuals meeting to form the UNEAC (Union of Cuban Artists and Writers), Castro proclaimed, "Within the revolution, everything; outside the revolution, nothing"; the line dividing the inside from the outside was not precisely demarcated. Created shortly after Castro took power, the **Casa de las Américas** publishing enterprise became central to Latin American letters. Without the Cuban Revolution and its international dimension, the **Boom** of the Latin American novel would have been less explosive and more fragmented. The Instituto Cubano del Arte e Industria Cinematográficas (Cuban Film Institute), or ICAIC, was also founded in 1959 and contributed not only to a blossoming of the Cuban film industry in the 1960s but also to the increasing prominence of **New Latin American Cinema,** in large part through sponsorship of an annual Latin American film festival (1979–1991).

In 1968 there began a chain of events that led many writers and intellectuals who had been fervent advocates of the Cuban Revolution to withdraw their support. The poet Heberto Padilla was awarded a poetry prize by UNEAC but with a disclaimer identifying him as a counterrevolutionary. In 1971 Padilla was arrested and forced to make a public confession of his politically incorrect views. The Padilla case marked the change from the relatively autonomous status of culture in the 1960s to its stringent control (at least in theory) by the Communist Party. European and Latin American intellectuals (including Jean-Paul Sartre, Simone de Beauvoir, Italo Calvino, Octavio Paz, Carlos Fuentes, and **Julio Cortázar**) signed a letter entreating Castro to review the situation created by the Padilla affair and defending the intellectual's right to critical dissent. Castro counterattacked and broke ranks with his former admirers. In an address to the First Congress of the Communist Party four years later, Castro reaffirmed his conviction that writers and artists would no longer be the conscience of society but would instead base their legitimacy on a pledge of allegiance to the principles of Marxism-Leninism. The ministry of culture was then created to direct and supervise artistic activities.

The early 1970s saw a decline in artistic creativity and an especially harsh crackdown on theatrical companies for allegedly harboring an inordinate number of sexual deviants. The Padilla case showed that in times of crisis Castro was willing to resort to repressive tactics that in better times he chose not to implement. It also served notice that artistic freedom in Cuba was conditional at all times. Yet Cuba's role as an international purveyor of culture continues. In 1985 **Gabriel García Márquez** established his **Nueva Fundación del Cine Latinoamericano** (New Latin American Film

Foundation) in Havana. The project has helped to sponsor several successful films, shot by Latin American and Spanish directors.

REFERENCE:

Edmundo Desnoes, ed., *Los dispositivos en la flor* (Hanover: Ediciones del Norte, 1981).

— R.G.M.

Currulao

Following its appearance in the Colombian and Ecuadoran Pacific coastal regions in the seventeenth century, the currulao was known as *baile de esclavos* (slave dance), a label that endured for many years. It is currently better described as a black secular ritual in which symbolic or social alliances between men and women may be realigned. The music of the currulao has a complex rhythmic structure presented by a **marimba** with two players, by two **bombos,** one male conical drum (*cununo macho*), one female conical drum (*cununo hembra*), **maracas,** and various *guasás* (bamboo shakers). Male and female voices provide a communal response to the solo calls of a male singer.

REFERENCES:

Bruno Nettl and Gerard Béhague, "Afro-American Folk Music in North and Latin America," in *Folk and Traditional Music of the Western Continents,* by Nettl, third edition, revised and edited by Valerie Woodring Goertzen (Englewood Cliffs, N.J.: Prentice-Hall, 1990);

Octavio Marulanda, *El folclor de Colombia: Práctica de la identidad cultural* (Bogotá: Artestudio Editores, 1984);

Thomas Turino, "Music in Latin America," in *Excursions in World Music,* by Bruno Nettl, Charles Capwell, and others (Englewood Cliffs, N.J.: Prentice-Hall, 1992).

— R.L.S.

D

DANCE

Dance culture in Spanish America, like musical culture, is the result of a complex syncretic process involving pre-Columbian dance forms and a variety of foreign imports, particularly from Spain. It must also be understood in the context of performance spaces, whether urban or rural, since they encourage such different forms of activity. The effect of Spanish domination during the colonial period has often been to influence or alter the dances seen today at an Indian village feast, a wedding ceremony, a birth initiation, or a funeral event. For example, a Spanish dance form may be absorbed and modified by native tradition as a part of male initiation ceremonies common among the tribes for centuries. The teaching of the French minuet and galliard and the Spanish pavane and zarabanda to tribes exemplifies the importation of western European dance culture and its superimposition upon South American indigenous traditions. Thematically, too, indigenous dances show the effect of colonization. The Yanomami tribes of Venezuela and Brazil, for example, evoke the brutal contact between Indians and their Spanish conquerors in the form of ritual duels, some of the dancers clothed as Spanish conquistadors and others as Indian slaves.

Indigenous dance in any form that can be described as authentic or pure is rarely found, owing to the many political and cultural pressures to which such dances have been subject. Those few cases where indigenous traditions have survived unscathed, usually because geographical isolation has kept out foreign influences, offer a rare window into the past, which allows a perspective on change.

Foreign influence on South America's dance culture has extended well beyond the colonial period and involved not only Spain. There were, for example, massive waves of immigration from other countries into the Southern Cone of South America, particularly in the late nineteenth and early twentieth centuries. In urban contexts, fashion dictated the pursuit of particular forms, and touring dance companies were hosted in the cities.

African slaves who came to South American and Caribbean coastal regions account for another dimension of dance: some of the many transformations of rhythm (particularly involving the use of drums) and costume, as well as the incorporation of legendary elements into traditional dances, are traceable to African influence. The zamba or zambacueca seen today in Chile provides a good example of a dance which combines African, Spanish, and indigenous elements.

Among dances that came to South America from Spain or other European countries, particularly to Argentina and Brazil, are the fandango, the malagueña, the pasillo, the **vals** (waltz), and the **tango.** The individual footwork, the complex changes of direction, and dancing with partners distinguish these dances from indigenous ones which remain collective, danced as processionals or performed in circles. Another important Spanish contribution comes from **flamenco.** Complex footwork akin to the flamenco, **zapateo** is to be found in the Quechua and Aymara dances of the Indians of Peru and Bolivia. *Taconeo* (heelwork) and *pitos* (shouting) are widespread. The use of a wooden prop, such as a stick, to create a rhythmic pulse to accompany and lead dancers is frequent in indigenous dance, resembling a gypsy flamenco custom of using a cane to keep the beat of a danced measure. Quite possibly flamenco performers and musicians accompanying sailors to the New World had contact with the peoples of the coastal regions. Certainly in the twentieth century flamenco stars La Argentina, La Argentinita, Carmen

Dancers performing the cueca, the national dance of Chile

Amaya, and Vicente Escudero have given rise to a lasting interest in the flamenco technique.

The twentieth century also brought Russian ballet to South America through the tours of **Anna Pavlova** and Serge Diaghilev's Ballets Russes in the second and third decades, as well as Americans Isadora Duncan and touring teachers and choreographers from Martha Graham's company, bearing witness to the vast foreign influence on dance in this region. The managerial support of Otto Kahn, A. Meckel, and Sol Hurok was instrumental in bringing huge touring companies of ballet, modern, and flamenco dance to the continent between the two world wars. Major touring companies, which came to highly populated urban areas, affected dance there but had little influence on rural culture.

Today there are major ballet companies in every South American capital city; the ballet companies of Lima, Caracas, and Santiago all have a strong Russian technical base and a mixture of folkloric (Spanish) and indigenous dance in their choreography. Contemporary modern and ballet choreographers such as **Ana María Stekelman, Melo Tomsich,** and **Karin Schmidt** are combining Russian ballet technique, American modern expressionist dance, Spanish classical technique, flamenco dances, South American folk dance,

African samba, and remnants of indigenous dances to create new forms of dance that speak to entire populations.

—N.D.B. & P.S.

DANCES OF CHILE

The national dance of Chile is the cueca, a handkerchief dance symbolizing courtship, in which the couple dancing represent a hen and a cock. Possibly derived from the Moorish zambra, an outdoor festival that included both music and dance, the origin of the cueca might equally as well be African, since so many Africans originally destined by the slave trade for Peru, Bolivia, and northern Argentina were left in Chile, unable to acclimatize to the intense cold of those regions.

The cueca is closely related to the zamba, the national dance of Argentina. Similar in form, both feature a characteristic rhythmic structure that combines 6/8 and 3/4 meters. While the cueca is typically sung, the zamba is essentially instrumental but may occasionally include sung verses. The similarities are probably the result of a common ancestry with the older Peruvian zamacueca, or zambacueca. The cueca is typically accompanied by the guitar, with hand-clapping accents provided by the singers; in the Andean region a **charango,** a guitarlike instrument, is often added to the ensemble.

The floor design of the cueca is set, but the steps are not. The woman, restricting both her steps and her gestures, and with her eyes down, brushes the floor with her foot. By contrast, the "huaso" (the man) stamps about as noisily as possible, marking time with the sound of his spurs. Using the handkerchief, the woman either beckons or fends off the man. The stylized use of the handkerchief is always delicate, complicated, and meant to function aesthetically. The "huasa" (woman) is dressed as a country girl with her hair in two braids. Her companion wears spurred boots, a soft hat, and a poncho. In southern Chile the cueca takes the name of sajuriana. The handkerchief is present, but the floor design is different, the dance more refined, and footwork more apparent.

On the island of Chiloé, an ancient dance called el costillar is still performed. It is a solo dance in which two rows of bottles are placed on the floor and the performer must dance around and between them without knocking any over. Since the dance is frequently performed as a kind of party game, during which local corn alcohol is consumed, precision and accuracy are frequently sacrificed.

Many Chilean folk dances are preserved by Bafochi, a Chilean folkloric dance ensemble. The twenty-eight dancers of the company present dances from the hula of Easter Island (Rapa Nui) to the **tango, gaucho,** and Andean dance forms.

REFERENCES:

Gerard Béhague, "Latin American Folk Music," in *Folk and Traditional Music of the Western Continents,* by Bruno Nettl, third edition, revised and edited by Valerie Woodring Goertzen (Englewood Cliffs, N.J.: Prentice-Hall, 1990);

Jorge Cardoso, *Musical Rhythms and Forms of South America,* translated by Pilar Alvarez (San Francisco: Guitar Solo Publications, 1986).

                                                    — N.D.B., J.M.H. & R.L.S.

DANCES OF COLOMBIA

Typical Colombian dances include the pasillo, a shortened waltz movement of Spanish origin (no longer performed in Spain), and the bambuco and the torbellino, both derived from the pasillo. Of all Colombia's native dances, the fandango, which is also known as the cumbia and is danced in the coastal regions, is the most characteristic. This dance is of almost pure African origin, devoid of **zapateo.** The name *cumbia* appears to come from an African term meaning "dance of Negroes." The cumbia's characteristic steps are confined to the shuffling of either bare or sandaled feet. It is a group dance in which the women, each bearing a lighted candle in her right hand, move in a circle around the musicians. The men form a circle outside the women and move in the opposite direction. The dancers, frequently in ones or twos, quit the group occasionally to find something to drink. As dawn arrives, the dancers fall into sleep, the women with their right arms covered in candle wax. In another version the woman holds a package of lighted candles above her head and revolves stiffly, while the man dances animatedly and flirtatiously around her.

The music of the cumbia is very rhythmic and depends in large part on various types and sizes of drums and **maracas.** Melodic roles are performed on millet cane flutes and instruments of the reed family (**gaitas**). In urban settings the accordion often replaces the melodic roles of the cane flutes and reeds; electric guitars and basses may also be used. Melodic content is characterized by repetition of short phrases. Traditionally cumbia music was an instrumental accompaniment to the cumbia dance, but popular versions often feature a singer. The cumbia is most prominent in the Atlantic coastal region of Colombia, but its popularity extends north through Panama and Central America and south to Chile.

REFERENCES:

Gerard Béhague, "Latin American Folk Music," in *Folk and Traditional Music of the Western Continents,* by Bruno Nettl, third edition, revised and edited by Valerie Woodring Goertzen (Englewood Cliffs, N.J.: Prentice-Hall, 1990);

Octavio Marulanda, *El folklore de Colombia: Práctica de la identidad cultural* (Bogotá: Artestudio Editores, 1984);

Thomas Turino, "Music in Latin America," in *Excursions in World Music,* by Bruno Nettl, Charles Capwell, and others (Englewood Cliffs, N.J.: Prentice-Hall, 1992).

                                                    — N.D.B., J.M.H. & R.L.S.

DANCES OF PARAGUAY

The characteristic folk dances of Paraguay originated with the Guaraní Indians of the region but borrow their present names — the polka, the galop, the malagueña — from Spain and France. Although there is little difference in the steps of these dances — each being a sort of two-step with frequent pauses — they do have distinguishing features. The malagueña is punctuated by sudden, sharp, and extremely strong beating of the bare feet against the ground or floor. The polka is danced by a couple in waltz position. The galop is a woman's solo danced to petition the Virgin Mary for a special favor.

The most unusual of the Paraguayan traditional dances is the Santa Fé, a competition among women. All the dancers — the number of them not fixed — walk into the dancing space, which might be a patio or open dirt-floored area, balancing bottles of wine or beer on their heads. Clutching the hems of their full skirts, they move about with free-swinging, improvised steps, embellished with wide sweeping movements of the upheld skirts. The woman who dances the longest without dropping her bottle is the winner. There are many other pure indigenous dances, not affected by syncretism, but they differ from each other only in the name given to each of them and the reason given for their performance. The only step is a somewhat stiff hopping from one foot to the other.

— J.M.H. & N.D.B.

DANCES OF THE AMAZON REGION

Dance in the interior of South America, the vast Amazonian region comprising areas of Colombia, Bolivia, Venezuela, Peru, Paraguay, and Brazil, is generally practiced by widely dispersed indigenous groups and consequently is poorly documented. There has been little European or other modern influence on the dance culture of the region, although such influences are increasing.

Indigenous musical instruments and rhythms have long been incorporated into the popular and classical music of the urban areas adjacent to the region. Due to the relative nontransportability of dance, which requires groups and large open areas for its performance, the region's dance has been slow to influence contemporary choreographers in urban regions of bordering countries. Such choreographers and companies are increasingly turning to ethnographic films, trips to the interior, and contacts with semiurbanized indigenous peoples to enrich their own dance vocabulary as well as to foment appreciation of the region's Indians by incorporating their myths, dance steps, body painting, and other performance traits into contemporary performances.

It is difficult to extrapolate from extant indigenous dance what the purest aboriginal dances in their earliest forms looked like. Since most of the world's indigenous populations and their physical environments have been corrupted, changed, or driven to the point of extinction, there are few living laboratories where dance in its earliest forms can still be observed. The remoteness of some parts of the interior of South America, however, still affords this rare opportunity.

For example, the Yanomami Indians, comprising approximately twenty thousand individuals in the border regions of Venezuela and Brazil, still perform ritual duels as a way of settling differences or working off aggression. They may take the form of boxing matches, with the fighters aiming at their opponents' pelvic area or chest. A duel with huge wooden clubs is more violent and may finish with broken heads and bones; the fighters take turns aiming blows at their opponents' skulls, and if one collapses after the first blow, the other can reciprocate, ending the duel.

Since the first purpose of dance was often functional, the ritual of the duel gives an important illustration of a stylized activity beginning to take on the first aspects of dance. Dance in this context refers to a series of steps created and repeated as a means of ritual expression, as opposed to performing the ritual itself. Elaborate body-painting rituals involving as many as eighty different designs are also evidence of predance activity; although such designs may be worn every day, some are reserved for special events or celebrations.

Another clear-cut example of early dance among the Yanomami is performed by shamans after inhaling the drug ebena. The shaman dances back and forth with arms raised, while singing and invoking spirits to come and enter his body; other shamans kneel on the ground and imitate the mythical beasts they believe they are becoming. In another ritual, known as "Asking for Presents," several pairs of men stand facing each other at the center of the village and discuss the items they hope to barter. The discussion takes the form of antiphonal song, accompanied by rhythmic motions suggesting barter or exchange.

Carved ancient petroglyphs on stones found in the Tukano Indian territory, on the border of present-day Colombia, Brazil, and Venezuela, depict sacred flutes and trumpets which represent both the vagina and women's domination over men. The Tukano Indians of today still hold major celebrations several times a year in which these instruments are kept concealed from the eyes of the women. In another important predance ritual of the Tukano, the shaman asks permission of the Master of Animals to hunt and kill game. Charms as well as rites are equally important components. Among the Tukano bark-cloth and resin masks play an important role in celebrations held when certain fruits and crops are harvested. A masked dancer with an oversized attached phallus made of wood is meant to stimulate the fertility of the flora and fauna. Fish, bird, and jaguar spirits are represented in these rituals. Masks are also used to ward off evil spirits, including parrot demons, during funeral ceremonies characterized by stylized wailing and moaning. The masks, stuck in the ground, are burned to conclude the ceremony. Wooden sticks or staffs used exclusively in dancing ceremonies are treasures of the Tukano.

Several other Tukano ceremonies may also be considered dances. Participants play particular roles, among them dance masters, healers, and shamans. The dance masters have the specific responsibility of defining a dance path which is followed by the dancers within the house where the dance is performed. This dance path, known as the "basá ma," is always defined as the zone between the inner and outer circles of the traditional circular communal hut. The master also determines the sequence of the steps, as well as the rhythms to which they are danced. Some dances are pantomimic, for example the "Dance of the Anaconda," in which the men line up behind each other with their hands on the shoulders of the man in front, the lead man representing the anaconda's head. Their rhythmic movements imitate the snake, with the dancers symbolizing the individual, or community subgroups. Special feather bands and crowns are worn for these dances, and the use of hallucinogenics and chanting of mythical texts are additional components.

The disappearance of traditional, open-style communal housing throughout the region and the adoption of smaller single-family dwellings go hand in hand with the passing of the dance culture of the indigenous peoples, since the new huts are no longer big enough to hold the traditional dances.

—J.M.H. & N.D.B.

DANCES OF THE ANDEAN REGION

Having survived conquests by Incas and Spaniards, the culture of Bolivia, in particular, displays a remarkable richness of dance. The **indigenous cultures** of Bolivia (mostly Quechua, but with a substantial Aymara minority) and their distinctive dances are divided into three regions: the Altiplano, or high, cold, dry plains region; the lower, more fertile valley; and the tropical region which forms part of the Amazon basin. Due to social changes beginning in the early 1980s, the manifestations of folkloric dances typical of each region have been increasing. By initiative of the indigenous peoples themselves, more traditional dance and music festivals are being created. The fact that Bolivian music, fiestas, and customs in the three regions have always been maintained, combined with social changes permitting more political and social freedoms to indigenous peoples, has created conditions appropriate for the creation of more fiestas. These serve as a meeting ground for sharing and reinforcing folkloric dance traditions. The Museo de Etnografía y Folklor in La Paz,

like other, similarly named museums throughout Latin America, has sought to preserve whatever remains of the national dance culture. The Centro Pedagógico y Cultural de Portales, a cultural archive, research, and documentation center located in Cochabamba, is the single most important repository of historical dance and music information on Pan-Andean, largely Bolivian, music and dance in the country.

El bailecito (the little dance) is a criollo dance performed in pairs with handkerchiefs to a 3/4 rhythm much like the cueca of Chile but with a more melancholic spirit. The chaluya, which is characterized by a sudden change of tempo from very slow to very fast, is of Inca origin. A Catholic dance now performed by groups of men on religious feast days, the chaluya still preserves elements of its indigenous origins. The **huaiño** is also of Inca origin but has been distorted by European influence. Danced by a couple, it is a competition of **zapateo.**

The portability of musical instruments during the long period when indigenous cultures in the Andes were suppressed by the Spanish conquerors assured greater potential for survival of Andean music than of Andean dance. In fact, the essence of some of the traditional or folkloric dances of the Andes, the key which allows them to be passed along, lies in their accompanying music. The many types of flutes and other wind instruments were easily carried about or hidden and could be played unobtrusively, and the music could be performed solo, none of which applies to dance. Stories told in song provide important indicators of the specific movements and gestures which were essential to each dance. La despedida (the farewell) reflects the influence of the African slaves brought to work in the mines. The theme of the dance called jacku is the return to one's roots. Antepasados (ancestors) is an homage to the ancestors. Todos santos (all saints) is an homage to the dead. Huellas de mi llamita (my llama's tracks) is inspired by the graceful movements of the llama. Desde La Paz, doctorcitos (little doctors from La Paz) mocks and pantomimes the arrogance of the Spanish colonizers. (The diminutive -ito is the element which mocks the self-importance of the educated urbanite, represented by the term *doctor.*)

The reconstruction of forgotten or half-forgotten dances is made feasible by appealing to the memories of elders; to associated religious, societal, or seasonal clues; and, particularly, to the accompanying music. Above all, the rich diversity of the flute in Andean culture ensures the preservation of Andean dance. In Aymara culture, music and poetry, not dance, were the predominant artistic expressions. The little extant dance of Aymara culture derives from a need to make offerings in appeasement of their deities. As a product

An Aymara dancer in Bolivia

of what in Aymara culture is termed the *aka pacha* (the earth plane intermediate between the plane of entities corresponding to the Christian God and saints) and *mancha pacha* (the plane of the night watchman or the devil), the musical instrument represents the offering, the intermediary, the safe ground. Dancers honor musicians, and not the reverse. It is postulated that music, rather than dance, predominated, because of the vegetable nature of the musical instruments themselves.

Inca dance is inextricably linked to Inca music. This music, built like much Asian music on the pentatonic scale, is extremely varied in theme. The instruments which accompanied the ancient dances were the **quena** (a flute originally made from the shinbone of a man), rattles of gourds, drums made from available simple natural elements such as animal skins, gourds, and wood, and sometimes, brass trumpets. The dances sprang from sources related either to religion or sexuality, both of which were strictly controlled in the Inca empire by legislation. They were performed at regularly occurring feasts, most often by men. Of ancient

dances still extant, two are particularly noteworthy. The arrow dance is one of the few employing pantomime and carrying a story. The solo dancer wears a skirt of palm fiber and feathers, a headdress of feathers and ornaments of seeds or beads, and even brightly colored birds suspended by their beaks, and carries a bow and arrows. To a tempo of 2/4 and a melody of four bars, repeated twice, one after the other, the soloist's opening steps are strong and defiant, with heavy marked beating by sandaled feet on the dirt floor. Soon he sees Inca enemies approaching. As he tries to escape from his encircling enemies, the music, not otherwise changing, doubles in speed. The chorus of dancers, who represent the conquering Inca, all dressed in short, vicuña-wool tunics, now appears with bows and spears. An Inca draws his bow and, to a loud drumbeat, mimes piercing the solo dancer's breast; under the latter's shirt red paint is released from a thin-skinned bag, the scene representing the violent nature of the conquest of the Aymara people by the Incas. Now realistically bloodied, with the music changed to a funeral tempo, the soloist "dies" within the circle of Inca spears.

The sling dance, played and danced with writhing movements of the body to a more lively tempo, represents a display of skill with a sling, a tool critical to Inca hunters. The costume is a wool tunic falling to just above the knees and belted at the waist. Over the tunic are sewn stylized leaves cut from thin sheets of brass. At the height of the Inca empire these leaves were probably made of gold. A wool fringe encircles the legs below the knee, representing the rays of the sun. In a similar vein, the forehead is covered by a beaten brass miniature of the sun.

Among other Inca dances are the spring dance, performed by young women carrying garlands and wreaths of flowers, and the dance of libation, performed by a group around a huge pot of tshitsha (beer made of maize, called *chicha* in Spanish); the dancers carry large drinking cups which they fill from the pot and empty over their shoulders as an offering to Inti, the Inca sun god. For three days beginning 6 January, another slow dance celebrating the Pascua de Reyes, or Feast of the Magi, is performed. This Christian demonstration is directly related to a similar dance worshiping Inti, although its precise origin remains unknown. The steps of the dance are slow and stiff, a characteristic necessitated by the long, tight costume, heavily trimmed in beaten brass. The headdress, whose heavy crest is composed of hundreds of flowers, both real and paper, rises high into the air. The marriage dance takes place when a marriage is announced. A group of friends, meeting the groom on the street, make a circle around him. The best girl dancer steps into the center, and a competitive dance, a sort of jig, takes place and continues until the man has managed to outdo his challenger. The shepherd dance takes place at the time of year when the sheep are earmarked, denoting their ownership. The smallest girl among the dancers, decorated with a necklace of bread and bananas, begins to dance on a blanket. As the adults drink tshitsha their spirits rise, and they join in until all the shepherds and their families become performers.

In some places that were once part of the Inca empire, particularly in Peru, the family hires professional dancers to follow the body to the burial ground. During the ceremony they dance in a circle around the grave. After burial they beat down the soil above by dancing on the grave. Returning home, the same dancers put on an energetic performance to cheer the bereaved. In certain periods and groups, funeral dirges are played on instruments made out of pottery, the music continuing for several days after the burial without pause. Legends are told of listeners so overcome

by the melancholic nature of this funereal music that they died of sorrow. The playing of these dirges has been prohibited during certain periods in post-conquest Inca history, including the twentieth century.

Other dances still performed in the Andean region in the twentieth century are often poorly documented. Among them are the Colombian areitos, a generic name for festivals involving dance, and the Inca or Pan Andean azucena, whose Spanish name (meaning *lily*) has been used since the colonial period for what survives of an Inca dance having three performers. Also Inca are baile de rueda, a military dance performed in a wheel formation; quicuchicoy, a girls' puberty ritual; itu, performed whenever special help of the gods was needed; yahuayra, a dance performed with a gold or woolen chain; yapakis, a festival performed during the month of August, involving many sacrifices; kamay (or camay), to mark the beginning of summer in the month of January; situa (or citua), a festival dance for the month of September, performed in hopes of good fortune; taqui, a generic name for dance and songs; waracilcoy, a boys' puberty ritual; way-yaya, a traditional dance of the Inca royal family; tinya, a tambourine dance; qhapaq raymi, danced during a festival for the month of December, in which boys' maturity rites were performed; huari (or guari, or warri), a dance usually performed during a festival celebrating male puberty; coya raymi, performed during the month of September in order to prevent sickness or bad fortune, and also known as situa; raymi, a generic name for dances at calendrical festivals; recorrido, a Spanish name for a walking dance; rutuchicoy, for a weaning and hair-cutting ceremony; cachachuaena, a warriors' dance performed in pairs; cachamba (or kachamba), a warriors' dance symbolizing entering armies; chahuac huarquiz, an agricultural celebration; and cachua, a victory dance. Some dances are found in culturally mixed groups surrounding former government centers of the Inca empire: calcheo, a dance based on stripping ears from corn; wayara, a processional dance performed in the four cardinal directions, in the fields; guaconi, one of the most common dances, performed only by men; guay ayt urilla, a dance performed by men and women in a line, with a leader at the head; hayli (or haylli), a farmers' dance performed on many occasions; caracolito, a dance with movements which simulate battle (the Spanish name — *snail* — indicating the circular paths of the dance); and cayo, a fast dance performed as a part of the Inti Raymi Festival of the Sun. The Moguex-Paez linguistic grouping accounts for these: bel covi coo, a dance for great festivities; ech covi coo, a dance of the phantom's — or gatekeeper's, or devil's — flutes; gueyo coo, a dance to ask for money; imegnuei coo, a dance of the sparrowhawk; onza coo, a dance of rats; itsako, a dance celebrating female puberty; quimb coo, a dance of the drum; vito coo, a dance of the rod or stick; and xsita coo, a dance of seashells or of the armadillo. Aymara dances are kusillu, dance of the monkey; quena, a warriors' dance with a jaguar motif; sicuris, a dance of the condor; tinya pallao, a generic name for dances of a totemistic nature; uka uku, a dance of the bear; ccara, a jaguar dance; chaco, a dance based on actions of small animals, particularly the guinea pig, and of men; chuno, the name referring to a small dried potato which was and is the staple food item of the Andean diet, and the dance thus marking a potato festival; and coquela, a dance based on the actions of the hunt but performed on the occasion of a successful harvest. The name *kawin* (coming from the Mapuche-Huillicha linguistic group) refers to a ceremonial complex which includes dancing, singing, and drinking.

Whether Spanish or Indian origins predominate in the masked processions of the Quechua peoples cannot be determined. Whatever the case, processions involving dance provide indigenous groups with an opportunity to express themselves and to reflect their social, economic, and political conditions. Various styles of masks represent the Iberian conquerors, priests, local authorities, and, especially in the latter part of the twentieth century, foreigners, such as United States representatives of mining companies.

— J.M.H. & N.D.B.

DANCES OF THE RÍO DE LA PLATA REGION

The paucity of indigenous cultures in Argentina and Uruguay, as compared with the significant indigenous populations and technological accomplishments of the Mayan cultures of Mesoamerica and the Inca culture of the Andes, accounts for a weak tradition of indigenous dance in most of the Southern Cone, the area covered by Argentina, Uruguay, and Chile. Extant indigenous populations in Argentina are largely confined to Amazonian remnants in the northwest. In addition, the countries of the Southern Cone consciously preferred to imitate the cultures of Europe. The early merchant and governing classes of the Southern Cone imported their culture — wives, clothing, furniture, educators, dance, painting, and music — from Europe.

A form of "indigenous" culture which arose in the colonial era, after the period of dispersion or extermination of true indigenous peoples, was the **gaucho** culture, which reflected a synthesis between the landowners and their employees, the gauchos, on the gigantic pampa ranches that formed the backbone of the Argentinean and Uruguayan economy. Entertainment was rough-hewn, and dances built upon Spanish, Indian, and African influences developed among the gaucho or "cowboy" culture. The landowners' preference for European-style entertainments and the rough realities of the gaucho's lifestyle were not irreconcilable and resulted in new dance forms. One of these is the zamba (sometimes, rather confusingly, referred to as the samba). The national dance of Argentina, the zamba is a simple, circular grapevine, step pattern dance with a kerchief symbolically used to lasso the woman in what is clearly a representation of courtship. Both the zamba and the Chilean **cueca** originated from the zamacueca or zambacueca, which evolved naturally from European of colonial Peru. The zamba's classic musical structure consists of four, two-measure phrases with the third and fourth phrases always repeated. Typically, an eight-measure introduction precedes the dance section. Recent zambas feature more flexibility in the numbers and types of phrases. The characteristic rhythmic structure actually combines the feeling of two rhythms: 6/8 in the melodic parts and 3/4 in the percussion parts, resulting in conflicting accentuation. Essentially an instrumental genre, the zamba may occasionally be sung. The basic instrumentation includes violin (melody in 6/8), **bombo** (basic rhythm in 3/4), and guitar (harmonic accompaniment). The capability of the diatonic harp to play melodic, rhythmic, and harmonic parts allows occasional solo performances of the zamba. In more remote areas, the violin and guitar may be replaced by an accordion.

El malambo is a competition between two gauchos, dancing alternately to the rhythms of guitar or of clapping hands, expressed in **zapateo**. Singing while they dance, the men engage in competitive displays of noisy footwork that suggest virtuosity, strength, and improvisational ability. Nowadays the dance has practically disappeared. The gato ("cat"), a quick dance, is also accompanied by guitar, the men singing while they dance; but it also has nearly disappeared.

El cuando is a hybrid of the minuet and the gato. It reflects a new world in which the European idea of ethereal feminine nature is juxtaposed with the uninhibited spirit of the indigenous country woman. The steps of el sombrerito circle a hat on the floor. The movements of el llanto evoke the sadness suggested by its title (weeping), while the dancers utter appropriate cries, with or without a handkerchief. El triunfo (the triumph) comes to gaucho culture from Peru and is a version of the Inca Inti Raymi feast dance. El escondido, el conejo (the rabbit), and el palapala mimic animals with their steps. The first mimes the cat, the second the rabbit, and the third mimes eight distinct animals. Danced by one couple and composed entirely of animal mimicry, the poncho serving as the "wings" of the eagle, the palapala is the most Indian of all the gaucho dances. In its lyrics Quechua and Spanish words mix indiscriminately.

Among other nongaucho dances of the region whose steps and floor patterns probably originated in Uruguay is the pericón, a group dance that is the chief national dance of Argentina. The pericón is usually accompanied by a guitar and the singing of the dancers, as happens with the **milonga,** a version danced by the lower classes with an accordion added to the accompaniment.

The fourteen traditional dances of Uruguay, some borrowed from neighboring countries, include the **tango,** the zamba, the gato, the cielito, and the ranchera. If one looks for finer distinctions, traditional Uruguayan dances can be said to number forty-two, but the differences are so subtle that only the most devoted practitioner or aficionado can distinguish them. The names of nearly all the dances are derived from the *coplas,* or short poetic phrases, sung as their accompaniment, a trait of European, not indigenous, origin. Most are couple dances and employ zapateo, and many feature the use of handkerchief and castanets. The origins are predominantly Spanish, with some African and minor indigenous influences. El gato is a dance for one couple (or for a group of couples dancing only with their partners), danced sometimes with castanets, but more often with the snapping of fingers. With a waltz step, the man and woman make a wide circle completely around each other. Arriving at their original position, they execute a smaller circle in place. Then the woman marks an understated rhythm with her feet while the man begins an explosive display of zapateo and taconeo (heelwork); once again they execute a small circle after which there is another exhibition of zapateo by the man; a half circle is formed to change places; the music stops and the caller cries "¡Segunda!" (meaning "second time"), and the dancers repeat all the same figures. The characteristic looseness of foot and ankle inside a heavy boot gives the effect of rubberiness or lack of control on the part of the dancer. The arms hang loose. The face of the woman can be bored, while that of the man can be ferocious.

REFERENCES:

Isabel Aretz, *El folklore musical argentino* (Buenos Aires: Ricordi Americana S.A.E.C., 1952);

Gerard Behágue, "Latin American Folk Music," in *Folk and Traditional Music of the Western Continents,* by Bruno Nettl, third edition, revised and edited by Valerie Woodring Goertzen (Englewood Cliffs, N.J.: Prentice-Hall, 1990);

Jorge Cardoso, *Musical Rhythms and Forms of South America,* translated by Pilar Alvarez (San Francisco: Guitar Solo Publications, 1986).

—N.D.B., J.M.H. & R.L.S.

Danza Contemporánea de Maracaibo

In 1986 Yasmín Villavicencio and Marlon Barrios created Danza Contemporánea de Maracaibo, which resides in the Centro Bellas Artes (Fine Arts Center) of Maracaibo, Venezuela. Villavicencio's choreography forms the core of the company's repertory. Accompanying musical selections are by Johann Sebastian Bach, Andreas Vollenweider, Charles Gounod, and Meredith Monk. One concern of the company has been the destruction of the habitat and lifestyles of the Yanomami Indians of the Amazonian region of Venezuela. Stylized interpretations of Yanomami body painting, rituals, and myths are incorporated into a signature work of the company.

—N.D.B. & J.M.H.

Danza L.U.Z.

Danza L.U.Z. is a contemporary dance company created by the Department of Culture of La Universidad del Zulia in Maracaibo, Venezuela, and has been directed since its founding in 1969 by Marisol Ferrari. The letters L.U.Z., which stand for the university, also represent a play on words, since *luz* is also the Spanish word for light. The company incorporates classical and contemporary dance techniques and is composed of university students as well as graduates, professors, and invited guests. A primary focus of choreography performed by the company is the history of the peoples who make up the community of Latin American countries. Danza L.U.Z. has made several international tours to such countries as Colombia, Cuba, Mexico, Puerto Rico, Costa Rica, Nicaragua, Spain, France, Belgium, and Great Britain. In addition, it has toured throughout Venezuela, performing in all of Venezuela's dance festivals and a diversity of stage settings. A related activity of the company is the publication of the *Directorio Latinoamericano de Danza,* a listing of most of the folkloric, modern, and ballet companies, teachers, and choreographers throughout Latin America.

—N.D.B. & J.M.H.

Danza Teatro Abelardo Gameche

Danza Teatro Abelardo Gameche, a Venezuelan contemporary dance company, was created in 1984 by Abelardo Gameche, whose artistry was formed in part by his residency in New York City. There he studied the formal geometric patternings and the "chance" choreographic techniques of American teacher/choreographer Merce Cunningham.

— N.D.B. & J.M.H.

DANZAHOY

Danzahoy (Dancetoday) has been the Venezuelan contemporary dance company in residence at the Teatro "Teresa Carreño" since 1986, together with the **Ballet Nacional de Caracas.** The company was founded in 1980 and is directed by its founders, Luz and Adriana Urdaneta, the latter of whom was trained in the Martha Graham technique in Caracas and London. The company seeks to express a Latin American dance language, clearly reflected in its preference for specifically Latin American themes, choreographers (Carlos Orta, José Limón, Graciela Henríquez), and the composers who appear in its repertory listing. Architecture, set design, literary texts (by **Pablo Neruda,** Octavio Paz, and **Jorge Luis Borges**), the plastic arts, and film have influenced the company's more than thirty-six works. In addition, American Dance Theater choreographer Ana Sokolow, supported by Conac (the National Culture Commission), has created work for the company.

— N.D.B. & J.M.H.

MARIO DAVIDOVSKY

Mario Davidovsky, an avant-garde Argentinean composer, was born in 1935 in Médanos, in the province of Buenos Aires. He has composed ballet, chamber, theater, and film music but is best known for his work in the electronic medium. Following musical studies in Buenos Aires, where he was active in the Association of Young Composers, a group devoted to new music, he went to the United States in 1958. Two years later he received a Guggenheim Fellowship enabling him to study at the Columbia-Princeton Electronic Music Center, where he later became assistant director. Recognition for his work has included his being the first foreign national selected as composer of the year by the New York Academy of Arts and Letters and his winning of the Pulitzer Prize in 1971 for *Synchronism No. Six.* Davidovsky's *Synchronisms* series focuses on the use of electronic tape and traditional instruments: for example, no. 1 for flute; no. 2 for flute, clarinet, and violin; and no. 3 for cello.

REFERENCES:

Gerard Béhague, "Latin American Folk Music," in *Folk and Traditional Music of the Western Continents,* by Bruno Nettl, third

edition, revised and edited by Valerie Woodring Goertzen (Englewood Cliffs, N.J.: Prentice-Hall, 1990);

Vicente Gesualdo, *La música en la Argentina* (Buenos Aires: Editorial Stella, 1988);

Joseph Machlis, *Introduction to Contemporary Music,* second edition (New York: Norton, 1979).

— R.L.S.

DETECTIVE FICTION

The detective-novel genre was largely imported to Latin America from Britain in the nineteenth and early twentieth centuries and from the United States from the 1930s until the 1950s. During that decade national traditions, characterized by distinctive settings and social mores, emerged, especially in the Río de la Plata area, Mexico, and Cuba. In Argentina, particularly given the British cultural influence during the early years of the twentieth century, the detective novel flourished. The Argentinean detective novelist Leonardo Castellani (better known by his pseudonym Jerónimo del Rey), for example, began to publish in the 1930s and hit full stride in later decades with the publication of a series of stories featuring Padre Ducadelia, stories which are reminiscent of G. K. Chesterton's tales of Father Brown. Other more elitist writers such as **Jorge Luis Borges,** Manuel Peyrou, **Adolfo Bioy Casares,** and Enrique Anderson Imbert used the detective-novel genre in the 1940s to satirize **Juan Domingo Perón**'s populism. By the 1970s the *novela dura* (hard-boiled novel) had completely replaced the *relato problema* (enigma story) in Argentina. **Ricardo Piglia,** editor of Editorial Tiempo Contemporáneo's Serie Negra (Black Series), played a major role in popularizing this new type of detective fiction, which was earthier, with more sex and violence. (See also **Literatura Negra.**)

REFERENCE:

Amelia Simpson, *Detective Fiction from Latin America* (Rutherford, N.J.: Fairleigh Dickinson University Press, 1990).

— S.M.H.

DEVIL DANCES

The quasi-religious devil dances that once flourished throughout Latin America are now largely restricted to Oruro and Potosí, Bolivia; San Francisco de Yare, Venezuela; and the Guaharibo Indians of the upper Orinoco River basin. In San Francisco de Yare, the devil dances on the night of the Catholic feast day of Corpus Christi. Several devils, wearing devil masks, may dance to the sound of a side drum and a shaken

A modern-day performance of a devil dance in Oruro, Bolivia

maraca. Pilgrimages are made to the church, to an improvised representation of Calvary, and to the home of the person whose responsibility it is to organize the devil dance. Various other houses of important personages in the town are also visited. From among these, the devil chooses a person to whom he hands a stick with a handkerchief attached. The person chosen is required to tie a coin into a corner of the handkerchief as a response to the devil's begging. Predominant colors for the costumes are red and black; yellow and green are also common. White is never worn. Some of the devils wear a belt whose ends hang like a tail. Many have bells.

The Guaharibos of the upper Orinoco celebrate the Devil's Funeral by dancing and drinking. The men arrange themselves on one side and the women on the other. The men advance, drink, and retreat. The women then follow their example. The central figure in the dance is the tribal ruler, or "grandfather," assisted by two young boys as acolytes, one of whom carries a bundle of lighted sticks and the other an effigy of the devil. Small drums and reed instruments sound endlessly.

—N.D.B. & J.M.H.

GONZALO DÍAZ

The Chilean Gonzalo Díaz (1947–) is a member of the Avanzada group, a loose association of artists that uses nontraditional media, and an important exponent of **Conceptual Art** in Latin America. Born in Santiago, he studied at the Escuela de Bellas Artes of the Universidad de Chile during the 1960s. After graduating, he taught there, as well as at the Universidad Católica and in the Instituto de Arte Contemporáneo. In the late 1970s he joined the Avanzada group and adopted the subtle strategies of Conceptual Art in order to avoid state censorship while subverting the official discourse imposed by **Augusto Pinochet**'s dictatorship. Since the 1970s Díaz has worked with two media, painting and installations, through which he questions the validity of accepted popular myths by employing complex conceptual strategies based on deconstruction.

In his painting *La historia sentimental de la pintura chilena* (1982; The Sentimental History of Chilean Painting) Díaz presents as the main icon the figure of a Dutch woman, taken from the box of a widely used detergent, in order to denounce Chile's cultural dependence on Europe. In the installation *Marco/Banco de Pruebas* (1988; Frame/Testing Bench) Díaz places a series of neoclassical balusters in two rectangular boxes sitting on the floor and a third box with a single baluster on a bench under a canopy illuminated by a neon light. On the wall there are two paintings depicting images taken from consumer labels and magazine advertisements, which, according to the artist, suggest the state's conceptualization of Chile as a "cultural landscape." Díaz recontextualizes these objects and images in a new space designed to create multiple cultural and ideological connotations that are negotiated by the viewers. For instance, the baluster, which is cast in one box, inspected on the bench, and dried in the other box, represents the subjection of the individual to the power of the state.

REFERENCE:

Mari Carmen Ramírez, "Blueprint Circuits: Conceptual Art and Politics in Latin America," in *Latin American Artists of the Twentieth Century,* edited by Waldo Rasmussen, Fatima Bercht, and Elizabeth Ferrer (New York: Museum of Modern Art, 1993), pp. 156–167.

—F.B.N.

JORGE DÍAZ

Jorge Díaz (1930–) is a prolific Chilean playwright born of Spanish parents in Argentina. Díaz's early plays can be identified with the theater of the absurd. *El cepillo de dientes* (1961, rewritten in 1966; The Toothbrush) and *El velero en la botella* (1962; The Sailboat in the Bottle) turn on the problem of communication. The protagonists of the first — Díaz's signature play — are a He and a She who confront each other in a series of sexual games in which identity and communication are at stake. *El velero en la botella* uses a mute character as the embodiment of the failure to communicate. Other absurdist plays by Díaz are *Réquien por un girasol* (1962; Requiem for a Sunflower), set in a funeral home for animals, and *El lugar donde mueren los mamíferos* (1963; The Place Where Mammals Die), in which an implausible charity organization perpetuates itself by implausible and grotesque means.

In 1965 Díaz settled in Spain and wrote plays of political protest. *Topografía de un desnudo* (1967; Topography of a Nude) was inspired by the massacre of Brazilian slum dwellers and incorporates documentary elements; *Americaliente* (1971; Hotamerica) protests against U.S. imperialism in Latin America. In 1970 Díaz formed his own theater company and began acting in his plays. Teatro del Nuevo Mundo (New World Theater) toured schools, cultural institutes, and other venues, first in Spain and later throughout the world, performing political plays and children's theater. Díaz's most ambitious play of the 1980s was *Desde la sangre y el silencio, o Fulgor y muerte de Pablo Neruda* (1984; From Blood and Silence, or Splendor and Death of Pablo Neruda), commissioned by the Oxford Playhouse Theatre and based on the last four months of the life of **Pablo Neruda.** In an earlier play — *La puñeta* (1977; Up the Creek) — Díaz had paid homage to another Chilean poet, **Nicanor Parra.** More recently Díaz has shown concern for the harmful effects of consumer society on the culture of the young. The plays that belong to this cycle are *Andrea, El extraterrestre* (The Extraterrestrial) and *Todas las fiestas de mañana* (All Tomorrow's Parties). In 1985 Jorge Díaz won the Tirso de Molina prize for *Las cicatrices de la memoria* (The Scars of Memory), a play about family tensions in post-Franco Spain.

REFERENCE:

George W. Woodyard, "Jorge Díaz and the Liturgy of Violence," in *Dramatists in Revolt: The New Latin American Theater,* edited by Leon Lyday and Woodyard (Austin: University of Texas Press, 1976).

— R.G.M.

DICTATORSHIP NOVEL

The dictatorship novel is a thematic genre of Latin American narrative dating from the middle of the nineteenth century and conspicuously resurfacing in the 1970s, when several important novels dealing with dictatorship were published within two years of one another.

Domingo Faustino Sarmiento's *Facundo* (1845) inaugurated the dictatorship genre in Latin American narrative. *Facundo* is a hybrid work that ostensibly centers on the life and death of the regional Argentinean caudillo Facundo Quiroga (1793–1835), but the novel goes far beyond the chronicle of one man's life to inquire into the deep-seated causes of tyranny in the young Argentinean republic. Sarmiento posits the existence of two Argentinas, one civilized (identified with the Buenos Aires elite who look toward Europe for political and cultural values) and one barbarian (dispersed in the plains and villages of the interior of the country). *Facundo* is ultimately a liberal diatribe against the dictatorship of Juan Manuel de Rosas, a magnified version of the book's eponymous protagonist. Sarmiento, exiled in Chile when he wrote *Facundo,* explains Rosas's power in terms of the ascendancy of the archaic interior over the progressive ideals of his own coreligionists in the port city of Buenos Aires. Toward the end of the century, however, Sarmiento's thesis concerning dictatorship was overturned by Cuban José Martí, who argued that the enabling cause of de facto governments in Latin America was the liberal intelligentsia's failure to understand the cultural soil from which tyranny sprouted. Martí called for a new generation of political leaders more responsive to autochthonous realities and less concerned with imposing extraneous models on the emerging Latin American nations.

The interpretation of dictatorship as a cultural and political phenomenon is one variant of the modern novel of dictatorship. Another theme deals with the evolution of dictatorship over the course of Latin American history. Sarmiento's barbarian caudillo is replaced by the enlightened dictator and, in more recent times, by the military dictator who functions within a bureaucratic institutional framework.

The first modern dictatorship novel was Ramón del Valle Inclán's *Tirano Banderas* (1926; translated as *The Tyrant*), written by a Spaniard but set in an unspecified Latin American location. The novel was subtitled "Novela de tierra caliente" (Novel of the Tropics). Valle Inclán's dictator is a syncretic figure, departing from the tradition, which had tended to focus on specific historical figures and anticipating later works by **Gabriel García Márquez** and Alejo Carpentier.

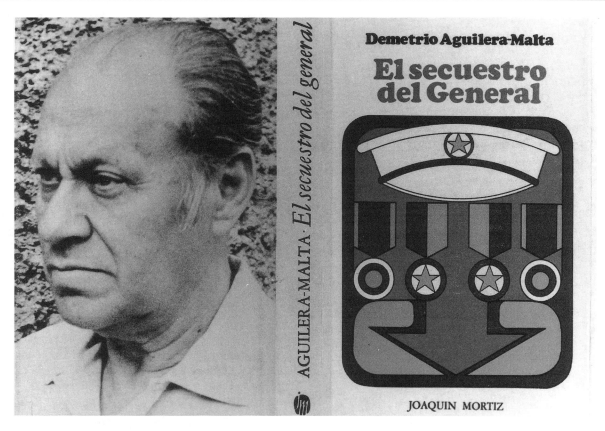

Dust jacket for Demetrio Aguilera-Malta's 1973 novel, about a fictional dictatorship that bears some resemblance to the Ecuadoran government of José María Velasco Ibarra

The first notable Latin American novel of dictatorship was Miguel Angel Asturias's *El Señor Presidente* (1946; translated), which focuses on the historical figure of Manuel Estrada Cabrera. The Guatemalan dictator is described as a mythical and satanic character whose lust for power corrupts an entire society. Asturias, who began to write *El Señor Presidente* in Paris during the heyday of Surrealism, developed an incantatory and hallucinatory style indebted as much to the Surrealist experiments with free association as to his discovery of Mayan mythology and literature. The novel is in the mode of the grotesque. Farce and melodramatic elements abound, and exaggeration and deformation characterize Asturias's presentation of events and people. Asturias, though, is unequivocal as to his interpretation of dictatorship, showing all the horrors that unbridled power brings to an impotent population.

In the 1970s the dictatorship genre boomed, beginning in 1974 with the twin publication of Carpentier's *El recurso del método* (translated as *Reasons of State*) and **Augusto Roa Bastos**'s *Yo el Supremo* (translated as *I, the Supreme*). The dictator portrayed by Carpentier is a generic and allegorical figure con-structed from bits and pieces of several historical tyrants (chiefly Cuba's Gerardo Machado and the Dominican Republic's Rafael Leonidas Trujillo) and is meant to be an ironic representation of the enlightened despot. He divides his time between Paris and his unnamed and turbulent native land, that is, between civilization and barbarism, between the refinements of culture and the cycles of revolutionary upheaval that he must put down if he is to hold on to power and finance his Parisian sojourns. Carpentier, however, dismantles the civilization/barbarism antithesis, showing how French history has been riddled with the same kind of violence afflicting the less fortunate lands of the tropics.

A year later García Márquez brought out *El otoño del patriarca* (1975; translated as *The Autumn of the Patriarch*), the quintessence of the Latin American neobaroque (or **magical realism**). The patriarch, like Carpentier's protagonist, is a composite of various historical figures and the embodiment of the barbarian chieftain. The language of García Márquez's novel, however, differs greatly from Carpentier's erudite style: one constantly hears the voice of the people, the orality of an illiterate culture that construes the dictator's power as mythical. This pervasive popular note and García Márquez's attempt to demystify the dictator are closely linked to the carnivalesque mode that characterizes the novel. Both Carpentier and García Márquez display an ambiguous attitude toward dictatorship. Their protagonists are anachronistic, folkloric figures by the mid 1970s, and this distance from immediate political reality allows the characters to be portrayed at the same time as charismatic cultural symbols and abhorrent, depraved tyrants.

Other dictatorship novels of the 1970s include René Avilés Fabila's *El gran solitario de palacio* (1971; The Great Recluse of Government House); **Demetrio Aguilera Malta**'s *El secuestro del general* (1973; translated as *Babelandia*); and **Arturo Uslar Pietri**'s *Oficio de difuntos* (1976; Mass for the Dead).

Historical dictators most often alluded to in fiction include the following: Manuel Estrada Cabrera (in power 1898–1920) was a corrupt Guatemalan dictator who assumed office when the president in power was assassinated and whose rule coincided with the heyday of the United Fruit Company in Central America. The situation of the Maya Indians deteriorated rapidly in this period. Cabrera was driven out by a revolution and is the model for Miguel Angel Asturias's *El Señor Presidente*.

José Gaspar Rodríguez de Francia, known as Dr. Francia (1814–1840), was a Paraguayan dictator who consolidated the independence of his nation by sealing it off from the outside world and avoiding the turmoil that beset neighboring countries. Francia kept the Church and the Creole aristocracy in check (sometimes by means of terror) and relied on the Indian masses for support, out of which he built a large army to reinforce the borders. While not the unscrupulous man his liberal enemies made him out to be, he was an authoritarian traditionalist and an intellectual who won the admiration of Thomas Carlyle in England. He is the model for Augusto Roa Bastos's *Yo el Supremo*.

Juan Vicente Gómez (1908–1935), the "tyrant of the Andes," was a Venezuelan despot who seized power when the ruling president was absent from the country and whose roots in the wild interior of the country added to his reputation for barbarism. Gómez was almost illiterate and never married yet had a large progeny. He effectively used repressive measures in dealing with his enemies and oversaw the rapid growth of the oil industry and the country's change from a pastoral society to an industrial economy. Student rebellions flourished under Gómez's rule, but the dictator died in office. He appears in **Miguel Otero Silva**'s *Fiebre* (1939; Fever), Gabriel García Márquez's *El otoño del patriarca*, and Arturo Uslar Pietri's *Oficio de difuntos*.

Gerardo Machado (1925–1933) was the head of the Cuban Liberal Party who became constitutional president but progressively hardened his rule. He suppressed civil liberties on several occasions, had the constitution amended to have his term extended, imprisoned and deported numerous opponents, and closed the national university. Machado was forced to resign and went into exile in the United States. He appears in Alejo Carpentier's *El recurso del método*.

Manuel Arturo Odría (1948–1956) was a conservative Peruvian general who assumed power by means of a coup and was noted for his suppression of sympathizers of APRA (Alianza Popular Revolucionaria Americana), the original and largest social democratic party in Latin America, whose leader spent five years as a political refugee in the Colombian embassy during Odría's government. Odría supported economic policies favoring exporters and foreign investors. Aided by his wife, he extended voting franchise to women in 1955 in order to increase his base of support. Odría developed a populist style in partial imitation of Gen. **Juan Domingo Perón** but lost power in an election. He appears in **Mario Vargas Llosa**'s *Conversación en la Catedral* (1969; translated as *Conversation in the Cathedral*).

Juan Domingo Perón (1946–1955, 1973–1974) was a populist Argentinean dictator who appears in Tomás Eloy Martínez's *La novela de Perón* (1985; translated as *The Perón Novel*) and **Julio Cortázar**'s *El examen* (1986; The Exam).

Augusto Pinochet (1973–1990) was a right-wing Chilean general who took power in a bloody coup against democratically elected Marxist president **Salvador Allende**. Pinochet appears in **José Donoso**'s *La desesperanza* (1986; translated as *Curfew*), Fernando Alegría's *El paso de los gansos* (1980; The Passage of the Geese), Poli Délano's *En este lugar sagrado* (1977; In This Sacred Place), **Antonio Skármeta**'s *Soñé que la nieve ardía* (1975; translated as *I Dreamt the Snow Was Burning*), and **Isabel Allende**'s *De amor y de sombra* (1984; translated as *Of Love and Shadows*).

Juan Manuel de Rosas (1835–1852), an Argentinean dictator known as "El Restaurador" (The Restorer), was instrumental in consolidating the Argentinean republic despite his many excesses and the factionalism he promoted between his Federalist Party and the Unitarios, the party of the liberal elite. Rosas created the *mazorca*, a feared secret police, and allowed himself all manner of excesses against his political enemies, many of whom had to go into exile. He favored landowners and the church. His portrait, decorated with a red ribbon, adorned the altars of church buildings in Buenos Aires. Suspected enemies of the dictator were forced to wear red in public. Rosas was overthrown in battle and left for exile in England. He is the model for Domingo F. Sarmiento's *Facundo* and José Mármol's *Amalia* (1851).

Anastasio Somoza Debayle (1967–1979) was the third and last member of the dynasty that ruled Nicaragua since 1933. He was a graduate of West Point and head of the National Guard, through which he terrorized enemies. Self-seeking and corrupt, Somoza profiteered from the international aid that poured into the country after a devastating earthquake that leveled Managua in 1972, and he controlled or had a stake in every profitable business in the country. His excesses promoted armed resistance. He was deposed by Sandinista guerrillas in 1979 and later assassinated in exile in Paraguay. He is the model for Antonio Skármeta's *La insurrección* (1982; translated as *The Insurrection*).

Rafael Leonidas Trujillo (1930–1961) was a Dominican dictator who used the army to assume power in a coup, reformed the constitution to perpetuate his regime, and was reelected several times but also allowed friends and relatives to be president for a period. Trujillo was a megalomaniac who renamed the capital city after himself and gave himself extravagant titles. He controlled every monopoly in the country as well as the press, employed repressive methods as a matter of course, and once massacred seven thousand Haitians who had entered the country to help cut sugarcane. Trujillo tried to assassinate the president of Venezuela in 1960 and was himself assassinated a year later. He figures in Alejo Carpentier's *El recurso del método,* Gabriel García Márquez's *El otoño del patriarca,* and Enrique Lafourcade's *La fiesta del rey Acab* (1959; King Acab's Party).

REFERENCE:

Carlos Pacheco, *Narrativa de la dictadura y crítica literaria* (Caracas: Fundación Centro de Estudios Latinoamericanos Rómulo Gallegos, 1987).

— R.G.M.

ELADIO DIESTE

The Uruguayan engineer Eladio Dieste (1917–) has revalued the use of brick as an efficient and versatile construction material, designing brick-based buildings of remarkable elegance and expressiveness. Dieste studied at the Facultad de Ingeniería (School of Engineering) at Montevideo's Universidad Nacional, where he later taught theoretical mechanics and structural analysis, on which he lectured in Argentina, Ecuador, Paraguay, and Colombia. In 1973 he became the director of the Taller de Ingeniería Civil (Civil Engineering Workshop).

Dieste has designed numerous industrial and commercial projects, but his best-known buildings are two churches built in small towns. His first "architectural" work, the Iglesia de Atlántida (1959) near Montevideo, features an undulating roof covered with shells of equal size and similarly undulating walls. This church, otherwise made of bare brick, embodies Dieste's ideas about architecture. He has denounced the unnecessary high cost of using advanced building technology just for the sake of imitating industrialized nations. Instead, he has advocated the most economic and rational use of local materials and workmanship, which in Uruguay means construction with bricks and concrete. In this church and in his other buildings, Dieste has demonstrated the superiority of brick as a material even over reinforced concrete: bricks are light, durable, and low-priced, and expressive in texture, capable of being molded into curved shapes; brick is also better suited to the local climate. Unrealized plans for the area in front of the Atlántida church had provided for an open space where people could meet, since one of Dieste's objectives has been to improve the sense of community through sensitive urbanization.

For the other church, the Iglesia de San Pedro in Durazno (1968), which had been partially destroyed by fire, Dieste followed the preestablished basilica plan with three naves and a presbytery tower whose simplicity recalls the understated style of Finnish architect Alvar Aalto. The lateral naves of the church are roofed with brick plaques and reinforced concrete. The central nave is not supported by columns, opening up the church's interior space, but rests on prestressed beams supported by reinforcing pillars on the facade and transept walls. Over the nave a double-pitched roof rests on small metal pillars that leave an open space in the clerestory through which natural light filters. On the atrium wall Dieste placed a remarkable rosette window built with concentric pentagons made of thin brick bands, subtly supported by metal rods. The altar is lit from above through a window on the presbytery tower, which adds to the quality of the light and gives the space a spiritual dimension. The simplicity of the brick textured walls and the use of perspective help to focus attention on the altar.

REFERENCE:

Galaor Carbonell, ed., *Eladio Dieste: La estructura cerámica,* Colección Somosur, no. 1 (Bogotá: Escala, 1987).

— F.B.N.

DIOS SE LO PAGUE

Dios se lo pague (1948; God Bless You) is a melodramatic movie by the Argentinean director Luis César

Amadori, considered one of the most significant films of the pre-1950 period. Set in downtown Buenos Aires, it features an intelligent beggar advising a woman who is down on her luck to seek love and fortune elsewhere; she receives tickets to the opera, and while she is there, a mysterious, aristocratic-looking man appears; a love affair ensues. In time, we realize that the mysterious man and the beggar are one and the same. *Dios se lo pague* is a subtle film which manages a convincing mixture of melodrama, the life of the down-and-out, and the stylized passion of opera; the film was nominated for an Oscar in 1948.

REFERENCE:

David William Foster, *Contemporary Argentine Cinema* (Columbia & London: University of Missouri Press, 1992).
— S.M.H.

EUGENIO DITTBORN

The Chilean Eugenio Dittborn (1943–) became a leader of the Avanzada group, a loose association of artists who used nontraditional media, and a well-known practitioner of **Conceptual Art** and Video Art in Latin America. Born in Santiago, Dittborn studied painting and printmaking in Chile and in Europe during the 1960s. In the late 1970s he joined the Avanzada group, whose members adopted the subtle strategies of Conceptual Art in order to avoid state censorship while subverting the official discourse imposed by **Augusto Pinochet**'s dictatorship.

In the context of Avanzada, Dittborn has produced his series of *Pinturas aeropostales* (Airmail Paintings), which feature photographs of marginalized people he finds in old periodicals and police files, such as the indigenous inhabitants of southern Chile and petty criminals. He rephotographs their images and accompanying captions, enlarges them, and prints them on brown wrapping paper or nonwoven synthetic fabric, which later is folded, placed in an envelope, and mailed to museums around the world. To the reproduced photographs Dittborn adds sketchy drawings, small objects, and subjective messages that undermine the official character of the photos. By recovering the memory of these forgotten people, Dittborn challenges the official version of history and suggests ideological messages that Chileans are able to read between the lines. When each work reaches its destination, the envelope is exhibited next to the unfolded painting to record the history of its travels. In this way Dittborn avoids the expensive process of sending artworks to Europe and the United States for exhibition. At the same time, he affirms the peripheral condition of his

Eugenio Dittborn unfolding his *Airmail Painting Number 96: Liquid Ashes* (1992) for an installation in Kassel, Germany

art and reveals the cultural control that the First World exerts over Latin America.

In the 1980s Dittborn also produced several Video Art pieces, such as *Historia de la física* (1983; History of Physics), which shows cases of extreme physical exertion, a theme related to representation of the human body, a significant subject in Chilean art since the 1970s.

REFERENCE:

Guy Brett and Sean Cubitt, *Camino Way: The Airmail Paintings of Eugenio Dittborn* (Santiago, Chile: Eugenio Dittborn, 1991).
— F.B.N.

JOSÉ DONOSO

José Donoso (1924–) is the most prominent Chilean novelist of the twentieth century and one of the select group of Latin American writers who achieved international renown in the 1960s. Chilean critics usually include Donoso's early works in the context of the "Generation of 1950," a group of middle- and upper-middle-class writers who changed the direction of Chilean fiction from nativism (**criollismo**) to a cosmopolitanism underscored by a renewed concern with artistic form.

Donoso's first novel, *Coronación* (1957; translated as *Coronation*), is a story of social decadence that grotesquely brings together characters from the idle bourgeoisie and the proletariat. The novel is one example among many in Donoso's fiction of the intertwining of masters and servants that undercuts the power of the master class (showing its dependence on the powerless) and reveals bourgeois repression. *Coronación* is ironic and grotesque at the same time with a touch of the existentialism then current in Latin American intellectual circles. In 1964 Donoso immigrated first to Mexico, then to the United States, and finally to Spain, where he settled in the Teruel region until 1980. In Mexico he wrote *El lugar sin límites* (1966; translated as *Hell Has No Limits*), a brilliant subversion of the Latin American **regionalist novel** and a provocative exploration of sexual ambiguity and of the violence implicit in sexual roles.

Donoso was in Spain when he published *El obsceno pájaro de la noche* (1970; translated as *The Obscene Bird of Night*), his great modern novel and the work that propelled Donoso to the first rank of Latin American novelists then making an impact beyond the confines of the Spanish language. *El obsceno pájaro de la noche* is hallucinatory and formally grotesque, a text laboriously pieced together from bits and pieces of its own material but unable or unwilling to disguise its sutures for the sake of cosmetic appearance. It is a deformation of conventional narrative and a grotesque parody of a central motif of modern fiction: the artist as hero. It is also Donoso's first exploration of the writer's fear of failure. Originally, *El obsceno pájaro de la noche* was to be a fable in the manner of Isak Dinesen, centering on the misshapen scion of an aristocratic couple who cannot bear the sight of their offspring and seclude him away from the eyes of the world in a family estate, which is then populated by freaks more repulsive than the firstborn, to maintain in him a sense of social superiority. This fable — to follow Donoso's account — was gradually deformed as darker presences (witches, vagrants, decrepit crones, and monsters) began to take over the creative process. Ultimately, the novel remained an experimental hybrid, torn between the classical simplicity of its original narrative model and the baroque convolutions of its search for an impossible synthesis. This hybrid form is functionally related to the presence of the failed author

José Donoso

within the novel. One of the representations of the novel-within-the-novel is the "imbunche," a mythological creature born with all its orifices sewn up — a macabre metaphor for a novel trapped in the imagination of a tortured writer.

Donoso's next major novel was a paradigm of the postmodern style. *Casa de campo* (1978; translated as *House in the Country*) is an ironic, self-conscious, and carnivalized allegory of the Chilean military coup of 1973 and an exploration, through a study of the aristocratic family, of the ideological repertory to which the military dictatorship could appeal in order to legitimize its authoritarian rule. The novel is set in the country residence of an extended oligarchic family where internal intrigues proliferate among the various factions: adults, children (all thirty-three of them), servants, the natives who mine gold, and the foreigners who market the family's gold throughout the world and wield the real power. All highly allegorical, the country house is the nation, the grown-ups are the landowners and traditional capitalists, the servants are the army, the madman in the attic is Marxist president **Salvador Allende,** the natives are the working class, and the children are split into reactionary and revolutionary factions. The novel plots the upturns and downturns of power and ends with an apocalyptic leveling of all social orders that is a call to cooperation in the face of institutional crisis.

In 1980 Donoso returned to Chile to await the publication of *El jardín de al lado* (1981; translated as *The Garden Next Door*), a sometimes bitter novel about a failed Latin American novelist in political exile (and in the midst of the **Boom**) whose family life crumbles all around him. Donoso handles the age-old topic of the novelist-within-the novel by means of a stunning reversal of perspective in the final chapter, when the novel's author turns out to be the wife of the male authorial figure and not the character (or narrator) who had assumed the guise of author throughout the course of the narrative. Sexual politics enriches the political connotations of the novel. Thematically, this novel touches on many important issues of the 1970s and is the fictional counterpart to Donoso's delightful *Historia personal del "boom"* (1972; translated as *The Spanish American "Boom": A Personal History*).

Upon his return to Chile, Donoso was actively involved in the theater and directed literary workshops attended by several of Chile's younger novelists. In 1986 he published his last novel to date, *La desesperanza* (1986; translated as *Curfew*), a somber work that directly confronts the Chilean political situation under the military regime. The form of this novel is classic in its tripartite division and in its observance of the canonical unities of time, place, and action. Its recurring icon is Arnold Böcklin's painting *Island of the Dead.* The story takes place in the twenty-four hours that elapse between the death of **Matilde Neruda** and her funeral. The novel is about political commitment and the future of Chile as a modern nation. In 1990 Donoso was awarded the National Prize for Literature.

REFERENCES:

Ricardo Gutiérrez Mouat, *José Donoso: Impostura e impostación* (Gaithersburg, Md.: Hispamérica, 1983);

Sharon Magnarelli, *Understanding José Donoso* (Columbia: University of South Carolina Press, 1993).

— R.G.M.

MIGUEL DONOSO PAREJA

An Ecuadoran writer born in Guayaquil in 1931, Miguel Donoso Pareja has authored the novels *Henry Black* (1969), *Nunca más el mar* (1981; The Sea Never

Again), and *Hoy empiezo a acordarme* (1993; Today I'm Beginning to Remember) and the short-story collections *El hombre que mataba a sus hijos* (1968; The Man Who Used to Kill His Children), *Lo mismo que el olvido* (1986; The Same As Oblivion), and *Todo lo que inventamos es cierto* (1990; Everything We Make Up Is True). In the early 1960s Donoso Pareja went into exile in Mexico and for eighteen years directed and coordinated literary workshops in the Mexican capital and in nearby cities such as Querétaro, Puebla, and San Luis Potosí, where he was recently awarded the first Ecuadoran *Casa de la Cultura* prize for the influential role he has played in Mexican and Latin American culture.

REFERENCE:

Renato Prada Oropeza, "Una incógnita obstinada: *Nunca más el mar,*" *Revista Iberoamericana,* 54 (July–December 1988): 917–931.

— R.G.M.

ARIEL DORFMAN

Chilean essayist, novelist, playwright, and poet Ariel Dorfman (1942–) is noted for his untiring defense of human rights in his country since the military takeover of 1973 and for his far-reaching critique of foreign cultural values that penetrate national cultures in Latin America through the influence of the mass entertainment media. Dorfman was a professor of literature at the University of Chile during the Marxist regime of **Salvador Allende** (1970–1973). He was a regular contributor to the literary column of an important news and culture magazine, hosted cultural programs on Chilean television, and sat on the advisory board of **Editorial Quimantú**, the government's publishing house. In 1973 Dorfman went into exile in Europe, and since 1980 he has spent a considerable amount of time in the United States, returning to Chile as often as circumstances allowed and resettling there in 1990, after the fall of the **Augusto Pinochet** regime. In the United States he became a regular contributor to *The New York Times* and the *Los Angeles Times* and was appointed to the faculty of Duke University.

Dorfman's most significant works are the political and cultural essays collected in *Para leer al Pato Donald* (1972; translated as *How To Read Donald Duck*), *The Empire's Old Clothes* (1983), and *Some Write to the Future* (1991); the novels *Viudas* (1981; translated as *Widows*) and *La última cancion de Manuel Sendero* (1982; translated as *The Last Song of Manuel Sendero*); *Pastel de choclo* (1986; translated as *Last Waltz in Santiago and Other Poems of Exile and Disappearance*), poems written mostly in Amsterdam between 1976 and 1980; and the play *La muerte y la doncella* (1992; translated as *Death and the Maiden*), whose Broadway premiere on 17 March 1992 was directed by Mike Nichols and starred Glenn Close, Richard Dreyfuss, and Gene Hackman.

All of Dorfman's literary output is closely identified with the Chilean political situation of the 1970s and 1980s. *Widows,* for example, is a novel of political terror set in Greece but obviously alluding to events in Chile. *Last Waltz in Santiago* is a series of dramatic monologues about the horror and pathos of the disappearances systematically perpetrated by the dictatorship against thousands of Chilean families. (The dramatic aspect of these poems led actresses such as Peggy Ashcroft and Meryl Streep to perform them in public. The first part of the collection was first published separately by Amnesty International.) *Death and the Maiden* is set in contemporary Chile as the nation treads the difficult path of democratic restoration and struggles with its guilt, with crimes unpunished in the decades of dictatorship that if brought to light in the new democratic regime could provoke a military backlash. Dorfman's most recent novel is *Konfidentz* (1994; translated).

REFERENCE:

Salvador A. Oropesa, *La obra de Ariel Dorfman: Ficción y crítica* (Madrid: Pliegos, 1992).

— R.G.M.

OSVALDO DRAGÚN

Contemporary Argentinean playwright Osvaldo Dragún (1929–) combines Brechtian and existentialist influences with sociopolitical themes. Dragún's first two plays are political renditions of historical themes. *La peste viene de Melos* (1956; The Plague Comes from Melos) dramatizes the Athenian siege of the small colony of Melos in 416 B.C. as a metaphor for the United States–led overthrow of the leftist Jacobo Arbenz regime in Guatemala in 1954. *Túpac Amaru* (1957) focuses on the Inca chief from the Peruvian highlands who in 1780 led a revolt against the colonial Spanish authorities.

The plays that consolidated Dragún's reputation are the *Historias para ser contadas* (1957; Stories To Be Told), a trilogy of one-act plays evocative both of Bertolt Brecht's estrangement techniques and of the commedia dell'arte style. The plays were performed on an empty stage by a limited number of actors enacting different roles (including that of raconteur) and included poems, songs, and dances. Their dramatic content is also reminiscent of the theater of the absurd. In

Historia de cómo nuestro amigo Panchito González se sintió responsable de la epidemia de peste en Africa del Sur (translated as *Story of How Our Friend Panchito González Felt Responsible for the Plague Epidemic in South Africa*), the protagonist takes a much-needed job in a packing plant that exports rat meat to South Africa. Panchito is rewarded by the municipal government for his contributions to the antirat campaign, but he also discovers that an episode of bubonic plague has broken out in South Africa. His ensuing guilt feelings make him an unproductive worker, and he is fired. *Historia de ... Panchito González* is available in English translation in *The Orgy: Modern One-Act Plays* (1974). In later plays such as *Los de la mesa diez* (1957; The Couple at Table Ten), *Historia de mi esquina* (1959; Story of My Corner), *El amasijo* (1968; The Hodgepodge), and *La historia del hombre que se convirtió en mono* (1979; The Story of the Man Who Became a Monkey), Dragún continued to explore the potential of the "historia" genre.

His international reputation was established when he was invited to Cuba in 1961 to direct drama seminars. In 1966 he was awarded the **Casa de las Américas** Prize for *Heroica de Buenos Aires* (Epic of Buenos Aires). Dragún lived in Spain between 1967 and 1972 writing television scripts. In 1981, back in Argentina, he helped create a theater collective known as Teatro Abierto (Open Theater) that attempted to breathe new life into the moribund national theater, overwhelmed by economic and political crises.

REFERENCES:

Frank Dauster, "Brecht y Dragún: Teoría y práctica," in his *Ensayos sobre teatro hispanoamericano* (Mexico: Secretaria de Educación Pública, 1975);

Gerardo Luzuriaga and Robert S. Rudder, eds., *The Orgy: Modern One-Act Plays* (Los Angeles: UCLA Latin American Center, University of California, 1974).

— R.G.M.

EMILIO DUHART

Emilio Duhart (1917–) is a leading Chilean architect. He completed his secondary studies in France and in 1943 graduated from the Universidad Católica in Santiago with a degree in architecture. He later obtained a master's in architecture from Harvard, where he studied with Walter Gropius. In 1952 he was in the studio of noted French architect Le Corbusier and working on the Chandigarh project for the Punjab states of India. From 1953 to 1960 Duhart was the director of the Instituto de Planificación de Urbanismo y Vivienda (Department of Housing and Urban Development) in

Santiago. He also taught at MIT in 1965 and at the School of Fine Arts in Paris since 1970.

One of Duhart's best-known projects is his building for the United Nations regional headquarters, the Comisión Económica Para América Latina (1966; Economic Commission for Latin America), or CEPAL, in Vitacura, a building considered to be an important example of international architecture in Chile. The horizontal emphasis of the main body of the building and the vertical direction of the snail-like tower over the conference hall echo the mountainous surrounding landscape and allow for a smooth integration of the building into its context. The whole structure hangs as a block from strong supports which rest on bedrock to minimize seismic damage. The different parts and functions of the building are clearly differentiated and con-

nected through an interior square patio: offices are in a circular area at the center, the meeting hall is in a diamond-shaped room, and the hall of conferences is under the dominant snail-like tower, reminiscent of the central tower in Le Corbusier's Assembly Building in Chandirgarh. Duhart also designed several housing developments in Huachipato-Talcahuano and Santiago, as well as important hotels in Castro and Ancud.

REFERENCES:

Damián Bayón and Paolo Gasparini, *Panorámica de la arquitectura latinoamerica* (Barcelona: Editorial Blume, 1977);

Leopoldo Castedo, *Historia del arte iberoamericano, 2: Siglo XIX. Siglo XX* (Madrid: Editorial Andrés Bello, Alianza Editorial, 1988).

—F.B.N.

E

Editorial Cartoons

Throughout the last two-thirds of the nineteenth century, the practice of publishing editorializing political caricatures gradually became widespread throughout Spanish America, largely inspired by mass-circulation cartoons in the United States. The independence movements (1810–1830) and the liberal reforms that continued to appear throughout the century created a new consciousness of the importance of fair government. Cartoons during the 1870–1910 period were explicit and often named the individuals and politicians satirized; for humor and context they also relied on classical mythology, a fact that suggests the elite nature of the intended readership.

In the twentieth century, however, the focus shifted and cartoonists began using everyday scenes and people as their subject matter. A good example of this trend was the Buenos Aires magazine *Caras y caretas* (circa 1890–circa 1920; Faces and Masks), which focused on everyday events such as getting caught in the rain or suffering the discomforts of public transportation. In Mexico City in the early decades of the twentieth century, Guadalupe José Posada reached a mass audience with his etchings of skeleton motifs satirizing establishments like the church and the landowning elite. In the 1940s there was a move toward Disney-influenced graphics with their exaggerated conventions for showing dismay or anger.

Buenos Aires and Mexico City have dominated cartoon publishing until the present day and have often attracted young talent from other countries, such as Uruguayan Hermenegildo Sábat, who moved to Buenos Aires in 1966. Post-1959 revolutionary Cuba uses cartoons for political ends; the cartoons in *Granma* (1965–1966), for example, a state-sponsored magazine, satirize Uncle Sam, the CIA, and international capitalism. The Bogotá *Alternativa* (circa 1975–circa 1985; Alternative), connected with Colombian novelist Gabriel García Márquez, concentrated its cartoons on human rights issues in Cuba and Central America.

Other important contemporary cartoonists are the Colombian Angarita, whose targets are ruthless social climbers; the Venezuelan Pedro León Zapata, whose humor is often local to Caracas; the Peruvian Giorg, whose cartoons published in the end section of the Lima magazine *Marka* (circa 1975–) satirize the obsession with gadgets in contemporary society; and the Argentinean Joaquín Salvador Lavado ("Quino"), whose targets are usually internationally known figures and whose cartoons are syndicated throughout the Hispanic world. (See also **Posters** and **Comic Strips and Books**.)

REFERENCES:

Naomi Lindstrom, "The Single-Panel Cartoon," in *Handbook of Latin American Popular Culture,* edited by Harold E. Hinds Jr. and Charles M. Tatum (Westport, Conn.: Greenwood Press, 1985), pp. 207–227;

William Rowe and Vivian Schelling, *Memory and Modernity: Popular Culture in Latin America* (London: Verso, 1991).
— S.M.H.

Editorial Quimantú

The Editorial Quimantú is the publishing house set up by the revolutionary government of President **Salvador Allende** in Chile that, following the precedent set by the revolutionary governments of Mexico and Cuba earlier in the century, churned out books in massive numbers in order to facilitate the spread of literacy and arguably an ideological message. When Allende was overthrown in September 1973, military authorities raided the publisher's warehouse and destroyed thousands of books that had been printed but not yet distributed. The name of the publishing house was changed from Editorial Quimantú (a name that linked the revolutionary state to the plight of Chile's surviving indigenes) to Editorial **Gabriela Mistral,** the Nobel laureate who was more acceptable to the counterrevolutionary state, as a symbol of "Chileanness."

— R.G.M.

Oscar Navarro, Nicanor Parra, and Jorge Edwards in the 1950s

JORGE EDWARDS

Chilean novelist and diplomat Jorge Edwards (1931–) explores the world of the Chilean middle class in his early writings — the volumes of short stories *El patio* (1952) and *Gente de la ciudad* (1961; City People) and the novel *El peso de la noche* (1965; The Weight of Night). Edwards is considered a member of the "Generation of 1950," a group of young middle-class writers whose work marked an important change in the direction of Chilean fiction. No longer indebted to the dominant trends in Chilean fiction in the first half of the century — **criollismo** and the proletarian novel — the younger writers introduced a whole new social class and a more refined type of narrative into the literary canon.

In 1970 Edwards was appointed Chilean chargé d'affaires in Cuba, with the task of normalizing diplomatic relations between the two countries. He was expelled the following year by Fidel Castro's government for his unsympathetic views of the Cuban revolution. This chain of events gave rise to Edwards's most famous — and controversial — book, *Persona Non Grata* (1973; translated), a chronicle of the author's experiences in Cuba that emphasizes the failings of the revolution and exposes the activities of the secret police and the climate of repression that enveloped intellectual and artistic production on the island. Edwards — who has described himself as a member of the democratic Left — was no less critical of Gen. **Augusto Pinochet**'s government in Chile, which expelled him from the diplomatic corps only a month after the coup of 1973.

In Spain, where the writer settled for the next five years, Edwards wrote *Los convidados de piedra* (1978; The Stone Guests), a novel about contemporary Chile set only a few months after the September coup and inspired by the story of the uninvited or absent guest who disrupts a banquet, a tale made popular by sixteenth-century Spanish playwright Tirso de Molina. In Edwards's novel, a group of aristocratic friends celebrate a birthday and reminisce about the past. History, politics, and personal lives are entwined by means of dialogue and first-person narration. The party prolongs itself until the small hours of the morning, when curfew is lifted and the revelers can go home.

Edwards has published three other novels to date: *El museo de cera* (1981; The Wax Museum), *La mujer imaginaria* (1985; The Imaginary Woman), and *El anfitrión* (1988; The Host), all of them dealing in different ways with the effects of the Chilean counterrevolution. He is also the author of an important biography of Chilean poet **Pablo Neruda,** *Adiós poeta* (1990; Farewell, Poet).

REFERENCES:

Kenneth Fleak, *The Chilean Short Story* (New York: Peter Lang, 1989);

Juan Andrés Piña, *Conversaciones con la narrativa chilena* (Santiago, Chile: Editorial Los Andes, 1991);

Mario Vargas Llosa, "Un francotirador tranquilo," in his *Contra viento y marea (1962–1982)* (Barcelona: Seix Barral, 1984).

— R.G.M.

CAMILO ALEJANDRO EGAS

Ecuadorian painter Camilo Alejandro Egas Silva (1899–1963) was one of the first in the Andean region to depict indigenous subjects. In Quito, Egas attended the Academia de Bellas Artes, and during the 1910s he studied in Rome and in Madrid, at the Real Academia de Bellas Artes de San Fernando. He also lived for a few years in Paris, where he exhibited paintings of native Ecuadorian themes in a style that betrayed his admiration for the Spaniard Ignacio Zuloaga. In 1925 Egas returned to Quito, where he taught at the Escuela

Directors Antonio Eguino (holding camera) and Jorge Sanjinés (right) with screenwriter Oscar Soria (center) during the filming of *Yawar Malku* (1970), released in the United States as *Blood of the Condor*

Normal de Quito and later became art director of the Teatro Nacional. In 1927 he established the Centro de Arte Egas, a meeting place for artists and intellectuals who rejected the dominant academic style.

Egas valued the native cultures of his country and saw them as a symbol of Ecuadorian nationalism. During the 1920s his paintings included images of archaeological artifacts and recognizable Ecuadorian landscapes. However, because Egas shared the positivists' belief that the advancement of the Indian would be achieved through assimilation to the dominant society, he showed his appreciation for the native people of Ecuador by Europeanizing them. In paintings such as *Ritual* (1922), Egas's representation of the Indian was also influenced by Zuloaga's figurative style, also reflected in the work of the Mexican Saturnino Herrán. Egas transformed his subjects into tall, muscular figures with European features, assuming poses reminiscent of Egyptian and classical art.

In 1927 Egas moved to New York and painted the mural *Festival* (1932) at the New School for Social Research. He taught painting there and in 1935 became the director of the art department, a post he held until his death. During this period Egas was influenced by Muralism and **Surrealism**: he became friends with José Clemente Orozco, who also painted a mural at the New

School, and met many of the Surrealists working in New York during World War II. There Egas developed a different indigenist style (one which had no effect on Ecuadorian art): in paintings such as *Dream of Ecuador* (1939) he shows a more Surrealistic and expressionistic use of monochrome tones and simplified shapes, marking a shift from the earlier idealization of native Ecuadorian life to a denunciation of the poverty of the Indian in the Andean regions.

REFERENCE:

Jacqueline Barnitz, *Latin American Artists in the U. S. before 1950* (Flushing: Godwin-Ternbach Museum, Queens College, 1981).
—F.B.N.

ANTONIO EGUINO

Bolivian cinematographer and movie director Antonio Eguino (circa 1940–) spent almost a decade in the United States, studying mechanical engineering, working in commercial photography, and going to film school. Back in Bolivia he joined the **Ukumau Group** in 1967 and was the cinematographer on *Yawar Malku* (1970; *Blood of the Condor*) and *El coraje del pueblo* (1971; also released as *The Courage of the People* and *The Night of San Juan*) under the direction of **Jorge**

Sanjinés. Commissioned by the Ovando government in 1969, he directed *Basta* (Enough), a short on the nationalization of Gulf Oil interests in Bolivia. In 1973 when Sanjinés was forced into exile, Eguino took on a leading role in the Ukumau Group, and, given the hostile political atmosphere of the time (the military dictator Col. Hugo Banzer Suárez ruled Bolivia with an iron fist from 1971 to 1978), he chose during this period to direct films that could be tolerated by the Bolivian Censorship Board. In 1973 he directed his first feature film, *Pueblo chico* (1974; Small Town), which focused on the story of a student who returns to his native village after studying abroad and which combines a veiled social critique with a love story. *Chuquiago* (1977), his second feature, uses four loosely connected dramatic episodes to represent different social strata in Bolivia's capital city (known as La Paz to the Spanish speakers and Chuquiago to the indigenous population); *Chuquiago* was the first film made by the Ukumau group to focus on the urban milieu, and it has been the most commercially successful film in Bolivian history. In La Paz alone, a city of 750,000 inhabitants, it attracted between 200,000 and 250,000 spectators. A more recent feature film by Eguino is *Amargo mar* (1984; Bitter Sea).

REFERENCES:

Julianne Burton, *Cinema and Social Change in Latin America: Conversations with Film-makers* (Austin: University of Texas Press, 1986);

Jorge A. Schnitman, *Film Industries in Latin America* (Norwood, N.J.: ABLEX, 1984).

— S.M.H.

DIAMELA ELTIT

The works of Chilean writer Diamela Eltit (1949–) evince a profound interest in the relation between language and politics. Eltit's "novels" do not conform to the expectations of realistic narrative but seem to be assembled instead with the fragments or the ruins of the novelistic tradition. The author herself speaks of her novels in terms of "textual bodies" in gestation and somewhat beyond the author's control. Indeed, the feminine body is a recurrent image in Eltit's texts. However, these texts are firmly rooted in a specific cultural and historical context and have a specific ideological function. They are emblems of resistance to the authoritarian impositions of Chile's military government in the 1970s and 1980s and to the neoliberal commercial ethic the regime fostered for two decades. Eltit remained in Chile through the worst years of military repression and witnessed firsthand the social contradictions involved in the implementation of a free-market economy and its regrettable effects, for example, the creation of a consumer society that excludes many poor Chileans and the standardization of cultural products through the channels of consumption.

The title of Eltit's first novel, *Lumpérica* (1983), is a neologism that refers to the Latin American "lumpen" and to its victimization at the hands of a military dictatorship in collusion with multinational capitalism. The text develops on a national scale a topic found in mystic writing, the "dark night of the soul." Its protagonist is "L. Iluminada," an allegorical female from the lumpen whose self-mutilation (the shearing of her hair) is a sacrificial and symbolic act of mourning. The female body also plays an important role in articulating the symbolic language of Eltit's second novel, *Por la patria* (1986; For the Fatherland), another national allegory concerned with the female's role in the institutional networks of power. *El cuarto mundo* (1988; The Fourth World) has a polyvalent title that refers to the world of the embryo in the mother's womb, to the enclosed world of the family dwelling, to the space of the text, and also to the economic and political issues associated with the "Third World." The final segment is a disenchanted protest against the perversion and ruin of the native city by foreign capital, alluding specifically to the Chilean "economic miracle" of the 1980s, though nothing in the novel's language or descriptions suggests so specific an identification. The passage works instead through subtle allusion to biblical topics (selling one's inheritance for a plate of lentils, money falling like manna from heaven, apocalyptic intimations) which are dramatically resolved in the last line by the identification of the author herself as the veiled protagonist of the novel and as the mother of a child who will go on sale because of her Third World race.

Eltit has also shown interest in surveying the marginal languages and bodies of the city. Her most unusual project to date is *El padre mío* (1989; Mine Father), a transcription of a former mental patient's monologue recorded on three separate occasions over the space of more than two years. Eltit found the character called "Padre Mío" in the streets of Santiago when she and a friend were looking for ways to document marginal urban practices constituting — as she states in the prologue — the photographic negative of bourgeois existence. Eltit's project is a **testimonial** of social anthropology that has parallels in contemporary United States commercial films such as *Nomads* (1986) and *Candyman* (1992). Eltit later published *Vaca sagrada* (1991; Sacred Cow).

REFERENCES:

Djelal Kadir, *The Other Writing,* chapter 9 (West Lafayette, Ind.: Purdue University Press, 1993);

Juan Andrés Piña, *Conversaciones con la narrativa chilena* (Santiago, Chile: Editorial Los Andes, 1991).

— R.G.M.

EQUIPO TERCER AÑO

The Equipo Tercer Año (The Third Year Team) was a film group which operated in Chile in 1973, the third and (as it turned out) last year of the presidential term of **Salvador Allende,** the only democratically elected Marxist president of a Latin American country. Members were Federico Elton, José Pino, **Patricio Guzmán, Angelina Vásquez,** and Jorge Müller, a cinematographer who worked with most of the directors of the period, in particular with Raúl Ruiz, and who "disappeared" with his companion, actress Carmen Bueno, in 1974. Ruiz and Müller are remembered for being the team which filmed Patricio Guzmán's epic, *La batalla de Chile* (1973; The Battle for Chile). With borrowed equipment and with film stock donated by the French filmmaker Chris Marker, they began shooting in February 1973. They filmed nearly every day for seven months and gained access to all sectors of society through various guises, accumulating extensive and almost unique coverage of the developing class struggle. When the coup took place in September of that year, the film stock was smuggled out of the country and edited in Cuba in the studios of the **Cuban Film Institute.** The film became Chile's most important testimony to the outside world and received worldwide distribution in the solidarity campaign.

REFERENCE:

John King, *Magical Reels: A History of Cinema in Latin America* (London: Verso, 1990).

— S.M.H.

PAZ ERRÁZURIZ

The work of Chilean photographer Paz Errázuriz (1944–) emphasizes the life of communities marginalized from mainstream society, including psychiatric patients, transvestites, and boxers from the slums. Errázuriz's early training was as a schoolteacher. During the 1960s she lived in England with her husband, who was studying literature at Cambridge. After her return to Chile, she continued teaching until she decided to become a photographer. She was apprentice to a friend who was an amateur and later to a commercial society photographer. Her early photographs were of children, first designed to please their parents, but then aimed at interesting and educating the children themselves. In 1973 she published her nursery book *Amalia,* based on photographs of a hen she had at home. The series editor **Isabel Allende** encouraged her to write the text too. In this project Errázuriz's objective was to explore an experimental approach to education she had observed in England and simultaneously show the limitations of the formal education dominant in Chile.

Becoming a professional was difficult for Errázuriz. Her work was not taken seriously at first because she was a woman. Nevertheless, she continued working and soon began to freelance for several publications such as *APSI.* She also joined the Asociación de Fotógrafos Independientes (AFI), an organization designed to give mutual support among photographers during the military dictatorship that took over in 1973 (see **Augusto Pinochet**). Professional photographers worked under difficult circumstances then, needing special permission from the state to work outside their studios. When Errázuriz began her project on psychiatric hospitals in 1981, she had to work in a semiclandestine manner. During the 1980s she continued, at some personal risk, to focus on marginal people of a kind often repressed by the military, as in her projects on circuses and gypsies, as well as female and male prostitutes. For several months she lived with female prostitutes and learned of their fears and feelings about their work. She also befriended the brothers Eve and Pilar, two male prostitutes who opened a window for her onto the world of transvestites. Her work with them ended when numerous transvestites "disappeared," tortured by the state — practically destroying their community in Santiago. She published their photographs in her book *La manzana de Adán* (1990; Adam's Apple) with text by Claudio Donoso.

Errázuriz's work also includes important series on boxers, tango dancers, and Chilean women, as well as photographs taken during International Women's Day in 1988, when the military attacked people who were participating in a peaceful demonstration; these photos were later published in the book *Chile From Within, 1973–1988* (1990). In 1991 she exhibited photographs of her adolescent son, taken once a month over a four-year period, at the Museo de Bellas Artes in Santiago, an institution which had censored her work during the dictatorship.

REFERENCE:

Paz Errázuriz, "Chilean Disguises," in *Desires and Disguises: Five Latin American Photographers,* translated and edited by Amanda Hopkinson (London & New York: Serpent's Tail, 1992), pp. 29–40.

— F.B.N.

El Espectador

El Espectador is the premier newspaper of Colombia; its first issue came out on 22 March 1887 in Medellín, and its founder was Fidel Cano, who named it after the pseudonym which Benjamin Franklin gave himself as a twenty-two-year-old publishing articles in the *Pennsylvania Gazette.* Although the government suspended publication for six months in 1887, *El Espectador* soon established a national reputation; it moved to Bogotá in 1891 and has remained there ever since. *El Espectador* has had some difficult times; it nearly went bankrupt as a result of the 1930s Depression caused by the 1929 Wall Street Crash, and it was unable to publish for three days as a result of the "bogotazo" (a civil uprising following the assassination of the leader of the Liberal Party on 9 April 1948). It has modified its printing practice over the years, becoming a morning paper in October 1955, and, since 1958, publishing two dailies, one morning and one evening edition. The Nobel prize–winning Colombian novelist, **Gabriel García Márquez,** wrote a film column for the paper in the 1950s. *El Espectador* is universally recognized as the daily which sets the highest standards for Colombian journalism, and it has won many international prizes; its circulation exceeds two hundred thousand.

REFERENCE:

Antonio Cacua Prada, *Historia del periodismo colombiano* (Bogotá, 1968).

— S.M.H.

Estudio de Danza Contemporánea Melo Tomsich

The Estudio de Danza Contemporánea Melo Tomsich in Cochabamba, Bolivia, exemplifies the search for the marriage of a specifically Bolivian cultural reality, past and present, with an authentic contemporary aesthetic statement. Its tenth anniversary statement (1988) begins with the somewhat obscure declaration that "Our times speak of conflict, tension, fighting; a historical responsibility is assumed by contemporary dance: that of making an instrument of investigation out of the body, which never repeats, but creates, launching itself into movement and space, like nuclei of life and of feeling."

The repertory includes *Games,* in which "the successive divergence of movements is a fundamental attribute of abstract dance." The company also performs *The Liberators,* which expresses "the idea of a central poem that brings together historical incidents, geographical conditions, the life and the struggles of our peoples" and "follows the thread of inspiration" of the great Chilean poet Pablo Neruda. *The Liberators* is an homage to the leaders of various Spanish American independence struggles — Cuauhtémoc, Lautaro, Caupolicán, Simon Bolívar, and José Francisco de San Martín — and it ends in a "fiesta of freedom."

— N.D.B. & J.M.H.

F

SARA FACIO

The Argentinean photographer Sara Facio (1932–) has made an important contribution to the appreciation of photography as an independent art in Argentina. She studied painting at the Escuela Nacional Bellas Artes in Buenos Aires, where she met Alicia D'Amico, her future collaborator. In 1955 she received a scholarship from the French government to study art history in Paris, but in Europe she became more interested in photography. After her return to Argentina in 1957, she became apprentice to Alicia D'Amico's father, the established photographer Luis D'Amico, who was also training his daughter. Facio continued her studies with Annemarie Heinrich, who taught her lighting, and later received a grant from Kodak to learn color processing at their laboratories in the United States.

In 1960 Sara Facio and Alicia D'Amico began a commercial studio in Buenos Aires. Their work included creative photography as well as freelance projects for periodical publications and advertisements. In 1963 they had their first exhibition, which consisted of portraits of Argentinean writers who had written self-descriptive captions for their photographs, a series later published as *Retratos y autoretratos* (1974; Portraits and Self-Portraits). In 1968 they published *Buenos Aires, Buenos Aires,* a book with photographs documenting the city and its inhabitants. Facio also worked as a photojournalist for the newspaper *La Nación* from 1966 to 1974. During those years her work turned toward more political issues. She recorded the funeral of **Juan Domingo Perón** in a series of poignant photographs she entitled *Funerales* (1974).

In 1973 Facio, Alicia D'Amico, and the Guatemalan photographer María Cristina Orive founded La Azotea Photographic Publishers, the first editorial house of its kind in Latin America. They introduced the work of other Latin American photographers into Argentina and Europe and actively supported the work of women photographers, who find it hard to gain recognition and employment both in national publications and international agencies. La Azotea organized exhibitions and published postcards, posters, and several books, including Facio and D'Amico's own projects, such as their book *Humanario* (1977), a sober and respectful look at patients with mental illnesses, with text by **Julio Cortázar.** In 1979 Facio helped to found the Asociación Argentina de Fotógrafos, created to provide mutual support and protection during the military dictatorship that had seized power in 1976. The association also made it possible for Facio and others to organize numerous exhibitions of important international photographers in Buenos Aires, while carefully avoiding any government sponsorship. In recent years Facio has worked on the series *Las hechiceras* (Enchantresses), featuring photographs of strong women she transforms with computer graphic technology.

REFERENCE:

Sara Facio, "The Streets of Buenos Aires," in *Desires and Disguises: Five Latin American Photographers,* translated and edited by Amanda Hopkinson (London & New York: Serpent's Tail, 1992), pp. 53–64.

—F.B.N.

FERNANDO FADER

Fernando Fader (1882–1935) was one of the most important **Impressionist** painters in Argentina. He spent part of his childhood in Europe, with the families of his German and French parents. In 1900 he began his artistic training at the Academy of Fine Arts of Munich, where he studied with Heinrich von Zügel. In 1904 Fader graduated with high honors, and his painting *La comida de los cerdos* (Feeding the Hogs) won the silver medal at the academy's exhibition that year. This painting also won the first prize at the International California Exposition held in San Francisco in 1915.

In 1904 Fader returned to Argentina and soon exhibited his work. He also participated in Nexus, an Impressionist group formed in 1907, which also included César Bernaldo Quirós and Pío Collivadino. After his affluent family's business failed in 1914, he became professor at the Academia Nacional de Bellas Artes but resigned in 1916 for reasons of health and moved to the province of Córdoba, where he lived until his death. Fader, who worked in a style reminiscent of von Zügel's, combined the rough treatment of surfaces, the realistic depiction of forms, and an interest in fleeting effects of light and atmospheric change. In this regard, one of the best examples of his work is the series *La vida de un día* (1917; The Life of a Day), which depicts the same landscape view of Córdoba but at different times of day. The subject he favored, the countryside and its inhabitants, became consecrated as the official themes of Argentinean national art until the avant-garde movements of the 1920s.

REFERENCE:

Marcelo Pacheco and Ana María Telesca, *Fernando Fader* (Buenos Aires: Museo Nacional de Bellas Artes, 1988).

— F.B.N.

FAVORABLES PARIS POEMA

Favorables Paris Poema was a poetry magazine founded in Paris in July 1926 by **César Vallejo** and Juan Larrea. The first issue includes an important manifesto by Vallejo, "Poesía nueva" (New Poetry), in which he cautions that the superficial use of new technical and cultural words (*cinema, telegraph, jazz band, engine, horsepower,* and *radio*) does not in and of itself constitute a new poetry. Modern poetry, Vallejo argues, can only arise from a new sensibility that has previously incorporated the lexicon of modern life, the "new relations and rhythms of things." Only one further issue of the magazine (October 1926) was published.

— R.G.M.

MACEDONIO FERNÁNDEZ

Generally known by his first name, Macedonio Fernández (1874–1952), the great eccentric of modern Argentinean letters and a powerful influence on Argentina's two greatest authors, **Jorge Luis Borges** and **Julio Cortázar,** was a legend in his own time. A recluse who never bothered to order his manuscripts or to muster the initiative necessary to publish them, he paid little attention to preserving what he wrote. He did write occasional letters and speeches meant to be read by others at literary banquets, some in his honor. The few books by Macedonio that circulated in his lifetime owed their published form to incessant cajoling by friends and admirers. This strange guru of the avant-garde was really "discovered" in the 1960s through an anthology of his writing prepared by Borges — who claimed him as his mentor — and published in 1961. The 1960s was the decade of the "new novel" in Latin America, a period of radical experimentation with narrative form, when Macedonio's speculations on the narrative genre — never conducted in a dogmatic or even systematic fashion — found fertile ground beyond a reduced group of adepts. Cortázar, for example, was not a member of the original Macedonio "cult" but found Macedonio's emphasis on the reader as the author's alter ego highly stimulating. His character Morelli in *Rayuela* (1963; translated as *Hopscotch*) appears to be a fictive rendition of Macedonio. Other aspects of Macedonio's thought are the absurdist logic of many of the author's witticisms and the espousal of philosophical irrationalism. Macedonio's preference for nonrealist writing (for writing, that is, that hampered the facile identification between reader and character and that was discontinuously structured) is also noteworthy.

Macedonio's aesthetic ruminations and dismantling of narrative conventions may be principally found in the 1966 edition of *Papeles de recienvenido* (Notes of a Newcomer) and *Museo de la novela de la Eterna* (1967; Museum of the Novel of the Eternal Woman). Both works are fragmentary not because they are incomplete but because their author avoided any semblance of conventional expository prose and cultivated truncated and digressive forms of expression. *Papeles de recienvenido,* furthermore, is a miscellany first assembled in 1929 and expanded in 1944, before assuming the "definitive" outline of the last edition (1966).

Macedonio Fernández also wrote a novel first published in 1974 — *Adriana Buenos Aires* (subtitled "Last Bad Novel") — and a collection of poems published in his lifetime, *Muerte es beldad* (1942; Death Is Beauty).

Inti, the Inca sun god, in the annual Inti Raymi (festival) in Cuzco, Peru

REFERENCE:

Naomi Lindstrom, *Macedonio Fernández* (Lincoln, Nebr.: Society of Spanish and Spanish American Studies, 1981).

                                                        — R.G.M.

FESTIVALS

Many South American festivals are descended from ancient, pre-Columbian pantheistic rituals. Among Andean groups, rituals for the Wiracocha (Father Sun), an Andean divinity, and for other guardian spirits were commonly performed through music and dance. Supplications to the Pachamama (Mother Earth) for planting and harvesting as well as celebrations for the marking of cattle and other practical matters were important occasions for ancient belief systems. Music was considered an important medium for communication with supernaturals and was an inherent ingredient of ceremonies. The musical heritage of antiquity may still be heard in the flutes and **sicu** of Aymara and Quechua Indians.

The many secular festivals that continue in popularity are quite varied. Normally these festivals include popular and folkloric musical ensembles as an additional attraction. For example, the Desfile de silleteros (Sedan Chair Parade) in Colombia is an an-nual event in which participants in period dress recall an earlier time and practice. Another annual Colombian festival is the *Desfile de los fundadores* (Founders' Parade), in which various fundamental trades are remembered and represented, such as those of woodcutter, muleteer, farmer, and domestic worker.

Since the arrival of the Europeans and the imposition of Catholic religious authority, many of the ancient festivals and celebrations have become syncretized with Christian observances. Patron saints' days, comparable in importance to birthday celebrations, are faithfully observed by individuals, communities, and whole nations. An example of a popularly observed feast day is that of San Juan Bautista (Saint John the Baptist). On the Víspera de San Juan (the eve of Saint John's Day, 23 June) the faithful participate in communal baths as a symbolic rite of purification. People with access to beaches bathe in the sea, accompanied by music and fireworks.

Villages and cities honor their patron saint through Fiestas Patronales, ten-day celebrations that resemble county fairs in North America. The fiestas are normally held in the plaza (the town square), surrounding the Catholic church, where the streets are filled with games of chance and booths with special shows featuring popular artists, musicians, and dancers performing free to the community. Folk music, played on traditional acoustic instruments, is often performed at the fiestas, but popular and commercial music employing modern instrumentation is increasingly prominent. It is through these local presentations that the majority of the population has the rare opportunity to see their favorite radio, television, and recording artists in person. (See also the entries on **Dances of Chile, Colombia, Paraguay, the Amazon Region, the Andean Region,** and the **Rio de la Plate Region.**)

REFERENCE:

Guillermo Abadía Morales, *Compendio general de folklore colombiano*, volume 112 (Bogotá: Biblioteca Banco Popular, 1983).

— R.L.S.

FICTION

As the new republics of the nineteenth century began to forge their separate identities, their writers tended to remain formally imitative of the styles of the old continent, while in their themes they increasingly sought to be different by highlighting local color. It would be well into the twentieth century before the novel achieved universal importance, but important developments in poetry were taking place as the century began.

The modern Spanish American novel was the result of a process that bore its earliest fruits in the 1940s and that culminated two decades later with the **Boom.** Prior to that time the novel was marked by **regionalism** and **Indigenism,** both grounded in the documentation of the distinctive social and natural traits that made up the author's national territory. From these tendencies, the modern novel effected a self-conscious break. Against the regionalist paradigm, the modern novel showed a propensity for the universal and the cosmopolitan. Against the social and utilitarian imperatives of the Indigenist novel, modern fiction claimed a fundamentally aesthetic legitimation. Thus, the modern novel has more significant affinities with the short-story genre (particularly in the form the latter took in the Río de la Plata area in the early decades of the century) and with avant-garde poetry than with the regionalist and indigenist fiction that preceded it. The beginnings of the modern novel coincided with the rise of anthropology as a discipline and with the predominance of **Surrealism** in the field of artistic ideas; the Surrealists themselves were deeply interested in the objects, discourses, and cultural practices studied by ethnographers. One of the early modern novelists was the Guatemalan Miguel Angel Asturias, the future Nobel Prize laureate who was inspired by his anthropological studies at the Sorbonne to translate the sacred book of the Mayas (the Popol Vuh) into Spanish. His own work blends an interest in the indigenous culture of Guatemala with Surrealist images and language. Another of the early modern novelists was the Cuban Alejo Carpentier, whose ethnographic interests and firsthand contact with the Surrealists in Paris ultimately led him to formulate the theory of **magical realism** in the prologue to his second novel *El reino de este mundo* (1949; translated as *The Kingdom of This World*). The gist of Carpentier's theory was that the distinctiveness of Latin American and Caribbean identity was to be found in the survival into historical times of archaic beliefs and cultural forms (derived from indigenous and African culture) that incarnate the Surrealist vision in terms more authentic and significant than those put forth in Surrealist experiments, for which Carpentier expressed nothing but disdain. Carpentier's influential third novel, *Los pasos perdidos* (1953; translated as *The Lost Steps*), may be read as an exploration of the contradictions inherent in the concept of magical realism, though this has since gained considerable currency as a term.

In the Southern Cone the influence of anthropology arrived in a more indirect fashion — through Sir James Frazer's *The Golden Bough* (1890–1915) — but made a deep imprint on **Jorge Luis Borges**'s theory of narrative, formulated in the essay "El arte narrativo y la magica" (1932; translated as "Narrative Art and Magic") and rehearsed in stories. Borges, who had a profound effect on the subsequent development of Latin American fiction as a whole, held that stories were autonomous structures ruled by magic causality and analogy. His emphasis on the formal autonomy of narrative texts and the brilliant experimentation that went along with it incarnated one of the key demands of literary modernity. Another was the claim to universality. The scope of Borges's cultural references, encompassing mainstream and obscure (and sometimes apocryphal) authors from every conceivable tradition, easily satisfied this second claim.

Borges was the most influential of a group of short-story writers who foreshadowed the advent of the modern Latin American novel. Other practitioners of the genre who paved the way for the modern novelists were **Leopoldo Lugones, Felisberto Hernández, Silvina Ocampo,** and **Horacio Quiroga,** all of whom challenged the conventions of literary realism. Detective, fantasy, and science-fiction stories broadened the scope of literary representation and showed that Latin American writers belonged in a cosmopolitan setting. In the 1950s and 1960s the Latin American short story continued its impressive evolution side by side with the development of the modern novel. In fact, there is scarcely a major novelist who did not also make signif-

Dust jacket for Juan Carlos Onetti's groundbreaking 1950 novel, which adapted the techniques of European and North American modernism to the cultural context of Onetti's native Uruguay

icant contributions to the short-story genre: **Juan Carlos Onetti, Julio Cortázar,** and **Augusto Roa Bastos,** not to mention their peers in Hispanic countries to the north, all made of the short story an independent genre and not a mere by-product of more elaborate novelistic projects. (Important contributions to the short story have also been made by later authors such as **Luisa Valenzuela** and **Cristina Peri Rossi.**)

Borges — the key figure of Latin American fiction — was also a reader and translator of James Joyce and Franz Kafka and was affiliated with the **Sur** group in Argentina, which was instrumental in disseminating modern European and U.S. fiction in Latin America. Many Spanish American writers who had been active in the 1950s and earlier, but who had worked in isolation from one another, would later discover that they all had been influenced by reading the same "high-modernist" authors, not only Joyce and Kafka, but also Marcel Proust, Virginia Woolf, Ernest Hemingway, Malcolm Lowry, F. Scott Fitzgerald, John Dos Passos, and especially William

Faulkner. Two of the most notable works of the 1950s were Juan Rulfo's *Pedro Páramo* (1955; translated) and Juan Carlos Onetti's *La vida breve* (1950; translated as *A Brief Life*), groundbreaking and influential novels that "translated" the literary idiom of high modernism into the cultural vernacular of Mexico and Uruguay, respectively. It is impossible to overstate the importance of international modernism in the evolution of modern Latin American fiction, but even older authors such as Honoré de Balzac, Gustave Flaubert, and Henry James played a major role in the formulation of a modern Latin American narrative style. Varied as the different regions and national traditions are, they are now more similar to each other and to their foreign models than to anything that might be described as a previous Latin American narrative tradition.

The 1950s was also the decade of existentialism in Latin America, and many novelists, particularly in the Southern Cone (Cortázar, **Ernesto Sábato,** Onetti, **José Donoso**), paid homage to the themes of alienation and moral degradation in their work. **Mario Vargas Llosa** was strongly influenced by both Jean-Paul Sartre and Albert Camus at different times: the former served him as the model of the public intellectual, while the latter was the source of some literary ideas and provided a more appealing political model once Sartre's influence had worn thin.

Because of the crucial role played by outside influences in the development of Latin American fiction, many writers have been vulnerable to the charge of "extraterritoriality" (if not vulgar imitation) made by Marxist and nationalist intellectuals. As their influence wanes, however, a debate that once seemed to boil mostly simmers today or has fully evaporated. The fact that Spanish American fiction has found widespread acceptance in the continent itself is sufficient proof that even the most "exotic" authors (such as Borges and Fuentes) are culturally rooted in the realities of Spanish America, however varied and foreign their sources may be.

In the 1970s and 1980s it became customary to speak of postmodern or **Post-Boom** fiction, terms which tend to be used in a chronological rather than in the properly categorical sense. Late–twentieth century fiction in Spanish America is less hermetic, less aesthetically ambitious, and more socially and politically rooted than was the fiction of the 1960s. Women writers are more visible than before, and testimonial narratives have been in vogue for two decades. The grand aesthetic syntheses of the 1960s have long been replaced by minimalism and by writing (such as that of **Manuel Puig**) steeped in the various genres of mass or popular culture. Carlos Fuentes once defined the modern novel in Latin America as the "critical synthesis of society." Postmodern novels remain to a large extent

Pedro Figari in his Paris studio, 1927

critical but have given up the synthetic structuring principle (see **Poetry** and **Theater**).

REFERENCES:

David William Foster, ed., *Handbook of Latin American Literature* (New York & London: Garland, 1992);

Donald L. Shaw, *Nueva narrative hispanoamericana* (Madrid: Cátedra, 1980);

Doris Sommer, *Foundational Fictions: The National Romances of Latin America* (Berkeley: University of California Press, 1991);

Martin Stabb, *In Quest of Identity* (Chapel Hill: University of North Carolina Press, 1967);

Philip Swanson, *Landmarks in Modern Latin American Fiction* (London & New York: Routledge, 1990).

— R.G.M.

PEDRO FIGARI

The Uruguayan Pedro Figari (1861–1938) was one of the first modern painters to work in the Río de la Plata area.

Although during the early part of his life Figari was a public defender and a member of the Chamber of Deputies, in 1886 he studied art with the Italian painter Godofredo Somavilla, and he became a part-time painter during the 1890s. Figari's public career also touched the arts: he was elected president of the cultural association called El Ateneo and in 1915 was appointed director of the Escuela Nacional de Artes y Oficios, a post he held until his resignation in 1917, when the school rejected his educational reforms. He published his aesthetic proposals in *El arte, la estética, y el ideal* (1912; Art, Aesthetics, and the Ideal). In 1921, at age sixty, Figari decided to become a professional painter and moved to Buenos Aires, where he joined the **Florida** movement and helped to found the Sociedad de Amigos del Arte, which supported modern art. He worked in Paris from 1925 to 1933 and later in Montevideo until his death.

Figari's early style was reminiscent of Somavilla's academicism but later he elaborated a personal and

La familia presidencial (1967; The Presidential Family), by Fernando Botero
(Museum of Modern Art, New York. Gift of Warren D. Benedek, 1967)

modern style by adopting and transforming the thick
impastos and decorative treatment of the surface of the
postimpressionist painters Pierre Bonnard and
Édouard Vuillard, whose works he saw in the collection of the Uruguayan artist Milo Beretta. Through
his painting Figari explored his family's and his own
memories of nineteenth-century traditional life in
Uruguay and Argentina. Interested in human solidarity as a way of life, Figari depicted people interacting in two recurrent situations: funerals and
dances. For instance, in *Media Caña Federal* (Federal
Media Caña Dance) the rich celebrate in an elegant salon adorned with red, the customary "federal" color, while in *Media Caña* (Media Caña
Dance) the same dance appears in a rural setting.
In his series of *Candomblé* dance paintings, Figari
recorded the surviving cultural traditions of the
few Uruguayans and Argentineans of African ancestry. Figari held the utopian belief that the poor,
the blacks, and the **gauchos** had simpler and truer
existences capable of recovering the harmony lost
in European life and thus engendering a new improved American culture.

REFERENCE:

Luis Camnitzer, "Pedro Figari," *Third Text,* 16/17 (Autumn–
   Winter 1991): 83–100.

—F.B.N.

FIGURATION SINCE THE 1970S

After the emergence of the **Neofiguration** movement
during the 1960s, figuration continued to be a strong
expressive mode in Latin America, often developing
side by side with **Geometric Abstraction** and **Conceptual Art.** There has also been an important connection
between Conceptual Art and figuration: several artists
such as **Gonzalo Díaz, Liliana Porter,** and **Beatriz
González** have worked with both trends, combining
them to the point of blurring their limits. In fact, since
the 1970s figuration in Spanish America has grown to
be richly diverse and of great contextual complexity; its
numerous figurative modes include the realism of the
Uruguayans **José Gamarra** and **Horacio Torres,** the
expressive distortions of the Colombians Beatriz
González and **Fernando Botero,** the quasi-conceptual

approach of the Argentinean Liliana Porter, and the enigmatic images of the Chilean **Nemesio Antúnez.**

Latin American artists, including Gamarra, Torres, Botero, González, and Porter, often appropriate or quote earlier European art as a way of consciously articulating their own place in the broader tradition of Western art, a tradition which for the most part has remained unappreciative of the work of Latin American artists. For instance, in his paintings Gamarra quoted landscapes produced by European artists traveling through the Americas during the eighteenth and nineteenth centuries, his aim being to show the perpetuation of Eurocentrism. Horacio Torres produced large paintings of nudes in an old-masterly manner reminiscent of Titian and Diego Velázquez, after he abandoned his earlier **Constructive Art** in the 1970s. Similarly, Botero has often quoted well-known paintings such as Hyacinthe Rigaud's *Portrait of Louis XIV.* Botero's new and characteristically blown-up version includes a self-portrait next to Louis XIV, thus affirming his double right to inherit European artistic traditions and to transform them for his own artistic ends, a strategy that had been part of Latin American art since the **avant-garde art of the 1920s.**

Among the major themes that have formed the repertoire of figurative artists since the 1970s are allusions to their political, social, and cultural circumstances. In his art Botero uses gentle satires of military men, priests, and bourgeois families as an effective critique of the political and social situation. Similarly, González reveals the massive influence of official portraits of well-known statesmen such as Simón Bolívar and Julio César Turbay Ayala by irreverently giving them the appearance of commercial art and placing them on the surface of ordinary household objects, such as shower curtains or living-room draperies. Porter has also explored the inner workings of cultural representations through a dual strategy: she juxtaposes real objects with their two-dimensional counterparts, creating witty deceptions that effectively undermine our ability to perceive reality, while at the same time using stereotypical objects such as Donald Duck toys and **Che Guevara** memorabilia which show how what was once real (a duck, a man) can become a powerful illusion. Porter's art has an open-ended structure that gives her work a sense of mystery. Antúnez, whose work shares this enigmatic quality, at times approaches the paradoxical juxtaposition of images that is characteristic of **Surrealism.** In his series *Manteles* (1980s; Tablecloths) he presents floating objects on a space defined by geometric patterns in a state of flux, while in his *Estadios* (late 1960s to early 1970s; Stadiums) series he imprisons multitudes of minute figures between translucent geometric planes.

In recent years figuration in Latin America has been given a boost by artists using neoexpressionist modes, such as the Argentinean Guillermo Kuitca and the Chilean Jorge Tacla.

REFERENCES:

Miguel Cervantes and others, *Mito y magia en América Latina: Los ochenta* (Monterrey, Mexico: Museo de Arte Contemporáneo, 1991);

Charles Merewether, "Displacement and the Reinvention of Identity," in *Latin American Artists of the Twentieth Century,* edited by Waldo Rasmussen, Fatima Bercht, and Elizabeth Ferrer (New York: Museum of Modern Art, 1993).

— F.B.N.

FLORIDA

The Florida group, also known as the Martín Fierro group, was an avant-garde group active in Buenos Aires from 1924 to 1927, associated with the magazine *Martín Fierro,* which was founded in 1924 by **Evar Méndez** and **Oliverio Girondo** and located on the affluent Florida Street. *Martín Fierro* included artists and writers who had participated in two preceding avant-garde magazines, *Prisma* and *Proa*: **Jorge Luis Borges, Norah Borges, Macedonio Fernández,** Eduardo González Lanuza, and Norah Lange. During the 1920s they joined the ranks of the Florida group, together with the artists **Pedro Figari, Emilio Pettoruti,** and **Xul Solar,** as well as the art critic and architect Alberto Prebisch. Most of the martinfierristas had middle- or upper-class origins, which allowed them to have artistic and literary training in Europe and direct exposure to modern art. The counterpart and rival of Florida is **Boedo,** a group who identified more readily with the working class and whose works deal more explicitly with social issues.

The first artists to introduce avant-garde forms and ideas to Buenos Aires were Pedro Figari and Norah Borges. Figari had been in Paris in 1913, where he adopted some of the technical and formal approaches of the French postimpressionists, and in 1921 he moved to Buenos Aires from his native Montevideo. Norah Borges, who was familiar with the work of the German expressionists and Spanish Ultraists, returned from Spain in 1921 and published her **Ultraist** woodcuts in *Prisma* and *Proa*. Her achievements were remarkable because of the limitations placed on women's work at the time. Both she and Figari compensated for the vanguardism of their styles by idealizing local turn-of-the-century traditions that had been marginalized by immigration and rapid urban growth. On the other hand, when Xul Solar and Pettoruti returned from Europe and joined Martín Fierro in 1924, they transformed the avant-garde discourses they had encountered in Europe into a celebration of Buenos Aires as a modern cosmopolis.

The artists of Florida shared common avant-garde attitudes: they attacked late Academicism and **Impressionism** as rhetorical vehicles for the dominant artistic elite, which still identified national art with folkloric themes. Through *Martín Fierro* they denounced official institutions as conservative and corrupt organizations that distorted the public's taste. The martinfierristas used the avant-garde strategies they had brought from Europe to renovate radically the dominant artistic, literary, and critical discourses and unsettle the self-satisfied attitudes of the public. For this reason Pettoruti's first exhibition at the Witcomb Gallery in 1924 caused an explosive reaction comparable to that of the 1913 Armory Show in New York. Conservative art critics called Pettoruti a "Futurist," a term they used pejoratively to mean both vanguardist and insane, and denounced his radical departure from reality as technical incompetence. The martinfierristas strongly defended him and later sponsored several exhibitions of modern art, often at the Sociedad de Amigos del Arte gallery. Other important examples of collaborative work between artists and writers were the illustrations that Norah Borges and Xul Solar produced for several of Jorge Luis Borges's books, such as *Luna de enfrente* (1925; Moon Across the Street) and *El idioma de los argentinos* (1928; The Language of the Argentineans). Although *Martín Fierro* dissolved in 1927, its members continued their avant-garde projects independently.

REFERENCES:

Jacqueline Barnitz, "The 'Martinfierristas' and Argentine Art of the Twenties," dissertation, City University of New York, 1986;

Daniel E. Nelson, "Five Central Figures in Argentine Avant-garde Art and Literature: Emilio Pettoruti, Xul Solar, Oliverio Girondo, Jorge Luis Borges, Norah Borges," dissertation, University of Texas, 1989.

—F.B.N.

FOLK MUSIC OF ARGENTINA

The principal musical traditions in Argentina developed from indigenous Andean cultures, Creole assimilations, and an enduring European heritage. Although regional and geographic factors bear on their origins, these traditions appear to encompass the musical interests of all Argentineans regardless of provincial loyalties.

The indigenous legacy is generated by the descendants of the Incas in the province of Jujuy, located in the northeastern, Andean region of Argentina. The **carnavalito** and the **huaiño** are representative of the animated dance genres commonly performed in religious and secular fiestas. These genres are also indigenous to Peru, Bolivia, and Ecuador, where the huaiño is more widely known as the "sanjuanito." The **triste,** a melancholic song often relating the pains of love, also demonstrates the Argentinean Andean heritage. With strong indigenous ties to Peru, Bolivia, and Ecuador, the triste has a long history, during which it has often been often confused with the **yaraví.** Both gained popularity in Argentina in the late nineteenth century.

Other indigenous musics of the north-central Andean zone include various versions of the **vidala** and the **baguala.** Both are traditional songs that were associated with rituals or festive celebrations. Typically expressing somber tenderness, the rhythms of these genres were chosen by the composer **Ariel Ramírez** for the opening Kyrie of his *Misa Criolla,* a setting of the Catholic Mass in traditional Argentinean rhythms.

The Creole musical traditions of Argentina emanate from a much greater territorial base than the northeastern mountainous region. The zamba, the national dance of Argentina, bears a close lineal kinship to popular folk dances: the zamacueca of Peru and the Chilean cueca.

REFERENCES:

Isabel Aretz, *El folklore musical argentino* (Buenos Aires: Ricordi Americana S.A.E.C., 1952);

Rodolfo Arizaga, *Enciclopedia de la música argentina* (Buenos Aires: Fondo Nacional de las Artes, 1971).

—R.L.S.

FOLK MUSIC OF COLOMBIA

Folk music in Colombia is particularly illustrative of the strong influence of the three principal ethnic groups that constitute the general populations of Latin America: indigenous, European, and African. Each musical tradition has been preserved to some degree, but much of the music of Colombia derives from varying degrees of cultural syncretism.

Analysts of traditional Colombian folk musics recognize at least four folkloric zones in which the music of one of the ethnic groups or mixtures tends to dominate: the Andean region; the Atlantic-Caribbean coast; the Pacific littoral; and the eastern plains. Some analysts justify a fifth zone by dividing the eastern plains region into two zones of separate indigenous influences: the eastern plains and the Orinoco-Amazon region. The various musics of Colombia are not exclusive to any region and commonly enjoy popularity in all of them. Regional and ethnic influences, however, tend to modify performance practice in the different regions.

Although indigenous tribes are present in each of the zones, indigenous music is most prominent in the eastern plains that border on the northwestern region of Venezuela and the Orinoco-Amazon zone that borders on southwestern Venezuela, northeastern Brazil, Peru, and northwestern Ecuador. The distinction between these two zones rests on the degree of racial and cultural miscegenation of Spanish colonists and indigenous tribes. In the eastern-plains region mestizo musics feature various combinations of indigenous and Spanish instruments, forms, and styles. The musics of the Orinoco-Amazon region, however, reflect a much stronger influence from indigenous tribes of Venezuela, Brazil, Peru, and Ecuador.

Perhaps the most typical music of the Colombian eastern plains is represented by the **joropo,** a song-dance genre not only shared with Venezuela, but one which became the Venezuelan national air and dance. With strong historical ties to the Gypsy **zapateo** from Andalusia, the mestizo elements of the joropo may be seen in the instruments that were traditionally used to accompany it in Colombia: the **cuatro,** requinto, and carraca. The cuatro and requinto are smaller and simpler versions of the **tiple,** an American adaptation of the Spanish guitar. The carraca is an indigenous instrument made from the jawbone of a cow and played rhythmically as a scraper.

In the sixteenth century the Atlantic coast of Colombia began to receive large numbers of slaves from Yoruba, Dahomeyan, and Bantu cultures. Although they could bring no instruments on slave ships, music was in their memory, and they soon discovered appropriate materials to reconstruct the **marimba,** various **membranophones,** and minor percussion instruments that have continued to characterize their musical culture. The mestizo presence has also maintained many European elements, but the strength and energy of African music appears to predominate through the cumbia (from cumbe, "dance of the negroes") and its variant, the porro (the name of a drum); the **currulao** (dance of slaves); the bullerenque (pubertal initiation rites for girls); the **lumbalú** (funeral ritual) and the merengue (imported from the Dominican Republic and Puerto Rico).

Many of the slaves from the Atlantic coastal region were selected for their physical strength and appearance to be transferred to the Pacific littoral for work in the mines and on plantations. In the isolated coastal areas they were able to preserve tribal rituals and music with only moderate pressure to assimilate European influences. The predominant rhythmic con-

tent of African-derived music in the south-central Pacific region came from the Atlantic coastal region with the currulao and related genres such as the pango (a magic and ritual celebration), the bambuco viejo (the old **bambuco**), and the abozao (a symbolic dance meaning "tied with a knot"). The rumba (from Cuba), the bunde (performed at a wake for a dead child), and the caderona (an erotic dance featuring hip and stomach movement) are also prominent examples. These dances are typically accompanied by regional instruments of African origin, such as the cununo hembra (female drum), the cununo macho (male drum), **marimba,** and shakers. When sung, the African call-and-response format alternates with dance. In the north-central zone, acculturated forms of the European mazurka, the contradanza, and the jota (derived from provincial dances of Aragon and Valencia but with a strong African flavor), the danza chocoana (related to the Cuban habanera), and the **polca** brincadita (polka danced briskly, skipping) are prominent. Also in this region the old Spanish **romance** has been preserved.

All of the folkloric musical manifestations of Colombia converge in the Andean region, but here the European influence predominates in genres such as the mazurka, polca, chotís (schottische), and the **vals,** all Creole genres indebted to European styles and combined with African and indigenous elements to represent the Colombian national image. Played with European and Creole instruments such as the tiple, guitar, **bandola,** requinto (a small guitar tuned higher for ornamental parts), violins, flutes, and pianos, Creole music of the Andean region resonates with elegance and sophistication. Among the Creole genres are the pasillo (a popular air in waltz time), the torbellino (a song-dance in lively 3/4 meter), the danza (from the Cuban **contradanza**), and the most representative of the Andean region, the bambuco.

REFERENCES:

Guillermo Abadía Morales, *Compendio general de folklore colombiano,* volume 112 (Bogotá: Biblioteca Banco Popular, 1983);

Octavio Marulanda, *El folclor de Colombia: Práctica de la indentidad cultural* (Bogotá: Artestudio Editores, 1984).
— R. L. S.

FOLLETÍN

A popular urban art form that came to prominence in the nineteenth century, the "folletín," or serial novel, was frowned on by elitist literary authors. In Spanish America, folletines normally were prevalent in large urban areas such as Lima, Mexico City, and Buenos Aires. There was a vast gap between the small print runs of "serious" literature, a thousand copies being not unusual, and the tens of thousands of copies sold of popular "criollista" literature (see **criollismo**). In Buenos Aires in 1882, for example, for a population of some three million, the total number of copies produced per day was more than three hundred thousand. The massive production of criollista texts in Argentina between the late nineteenth and early twentieth centuries served a public in transition between the country and the city, especially immigrants who had recently entered Argentina. Popular urban criollista literature, with its narratives of traditional rural types like the **gaucho,** offered them a sense of belonging. Many became literate by the reading of serial novels bought not only from bookshops but from kiosks or traveling salesmen. The time structure of the serial, continually interrupted by the wait for the next installment, generated a fragmented manner of reading, interrupted by everyday life and thus porous to its experiences. Particularly popular were cliffhangers and melodrama.

One famous author of folletines was Eduardo Gutiérrez; the best-known of his novels was *Juan Moreira* (1879), which was published in serial form by the newspaper *La Patria Argentina* and immediately thereafter in book form under the imprint of the same newspaper. *Juan Moreira* was presented as a pantomime in Buenos Aires in 1884, and the eponymous hero became a key figure in Argentinean circuses, where it was not uncommon for spectators to jump into the ring in order to defend him from the police. The folletines also included specialized women's serials, some of which reached a circulation of two hundred thousand copies. (See also **Movies from Books**.)

REFERENCE:

William Rowe and Vivian Schelling, *Memory and Modernity: Popular Culture in Latin America* (London: Verso, 1991).

— S.M.H.

Gonzalo Fonseca as a totem, circa 1958

GONZALO FONSECA

The Uruguayan sculptor Gonzalo Fonseca (1922–) was a member of the **Taller Torres-García.** After studying architecture for three years, Fonseca joined the Taller Torres-García in 1943 to continue his artistic training with **Joaquín Torres-García.** As a member of the taller, he participated in the mural project for the Saint Bois Hospital and worked in a variety of media, including furniture design. In 1945 Fonseca, who was particularly interested in ancient cultures, went with other members of the Taller Torres-García to Peru and Bolivia to study pre-Columbian art. After Torres-García's death in 1949, Fonseca traveled throughout Europe and the Near East, where he worked on several archeological digs. While in Spain during the 1950s, he learned pottery techniques, producing striking pieces in a style suggestive of the **Constructive Art** of the Taller Torres-García. He settled in New York in 1958; since 1970 he has alternated between New York and Carrara, Italy, where he produces his larger sculptural pieces.

In New York Fonseca redefined his style, retaining from Constructive Art the emphasis on orthogonal compositional structures and the fascination with the ancient past. During the 1960s Fonseca worked mainly with wood reliefs, as in *Katabasis Ship* (1963), but in the 1970s he began to produce three-dimensional stone sculptures such as the red travertine piece *Graneros III* (1971–1975; Granaries III). Fonseca intensifies the atavistic connotations of these miniature versions of an ancient ship and an archaic city through the inclusion of enigmatic signs and hanging fetishes and through the rough treatment of the wood and stone surfaces. Most of Fonseca's works include a variety of nonsensical architectural devices, such as unexplained windows, blind doors, and truncated ladders, suggesting a labyrinthine view of the universe often compared to that of **Jorge Luis Borges.**

REFERENCE:

Mari Carmen Ramírez, ed., *The Taller Torres-García: The School of the South and Its Legacy* (Austin: University of Texas Press, 1992).

—F.B.N.

LUCIO FONTANA

Lucio Fontana (1899–1968) is claimed by two countries: his native Argentina, where he lived in the 1920s and 1940s, and Italy, where he studied art and produced his most innovative artworks. Fontana was born in Rosario, in the province of Santa Fe, to a family of Italian immigrants and in 1905 was taken to Italy for his education. After serving in the military during World War I, he studied art at the Brera Academy in Milan and returned to Rosario in 1922. There he worked in his father's commercial sculpture studio. In 1928 Fontana enrolled again at the Brera Academy in order to study sculpture, exhibiting his early works at the First Venice Biennial. In the 1930s Fontana became interested in abstraction and joined the Abstraction-Creation group in Milan. He moved to Paris in 1936 and met Joan Miró, Tristan Tzara, and Constantin Brancusi. At the beginning of World War II Fontana sought refuge in Buenos Aires. Although by then he was producing neobaroque figurative sculptures, he followed the activities of the Argentinean concrete movements called **Asociación de Arte Concreto-Invención** and **Madí,** becoming friends with some of their members, such as **Tomás Maldonado,** who appreciated Fontana's direct experience of European abstract art. In 1946, with Jorge Romero Brest and **Emilio Pettoruti,** Fontana organized the Escuela de Arte Altamira, which encouraged modern visual theories. With his students there, Fontana issued his *Manifiesto blanco* (1946; White Manifesto), calling for a new art, which would be more suitable to the spirit of the modern world and capable of overcoming traditional conceptions of space by uniting matter, sound, motion, color, and space.

Fontana returned to Milan in 1947 and in the early 1950s issued six *Manifesti spaziale* (Spatial Manifestos), emphasizing the need for a new concept of space and the use of new materials. In 1949 he began his series of *Buchi,* such as *Spatial Concept (50 B 9)* (1950), an iron relief whose perforated surface questions the role of easel painting and undermines the separation between painting and sculpture. During the 1950s he continued to explore these issues in two important series: *Tagli* (Cuts), which were cut monochrome canvases, and *Atesse* (Expectations), which were slashed canvases. While his expressive surfaces show the influence of Informalism and other types of **Informal Abstraction,** his innovative use of materials, which he had observed in Madí, is a precedent for later developments in Europe and the United States, such as Minimalism and light art. For instance, in 1951, in collaboration with the architect Luciano Baldessari, he designed an environment containing 270 meters of spiral neon tubing, for the Ninth Milan Triennale. Fontana won international acclaim at the Venice Biennials: a retrospective exhibition of his work was organized in 1954, and he was awarded the Grand Prize for sculpture in 1966. The Guggenheim Museum organized a posthumous retrospective exhibit of his art in 1977.

REFERENCE:

Erika Billeter, "Between Tradition and Avant-Garde," in her *Lucio Fontana 1899–1968: A Retrospective* (New York: Guggenheim Museum, 1977).

—F.B.N.

RAQUEL FORNER

Raquel Forner (1902–) is an Argentinean painter who has expressed two major issues in her art: the desolation caused by war and the epic saga of space exploration. Forner was born in Buenos Aires to a family of Spanish immigrants. She graduated from the Academia Nacional de Bellas Artes in 1922 and studied with Othon Friesz in Paris from 1930 to 1931. When she returned to Buenos Aires, she helped to found a progressive art school, called Cursos Libres de Arte Plástico, with Alfredo Guttero, Pedro Domínguez Neira, and the sculptor Alfredo Bigatti, whom she married in 1936.

The Civil War in Spain and World War II deeply affected her and moved her to begin several series of paintings about the horrors of war, such as *Series de España* (1936–1939; Series about Spain), *Serie el drama* (1939–1945; The Drama Series), and *Serie de las rocas* (1947–1949; The Rocks Series). Her allegorical paintings show monumental female figures, sometimes emerging from the scorched earth. They symbolize hu-

Raquel Forner

tionship of the individual with the cosmos. In her *Serie de los astronautas* (1967–1970; Series of the Astronauts), the astronauts struggle with space monsters, which she calls "astroseres" (astrobeings), while in the *Serie de los mutantes* (1970s; Series of the Mutants), humanity is rescued by extraterrestrial beings. Forner has successfully exhibited in Buenos Aires and abroad, winning many prestigious awards.

REFERENCE:

Guillermo Whitelow, *Raquel Forner*, translated by Kenneth Parkin (Buenos Aires: Gaglianone, 1980).

— F.B.N.

FOTONOVELAS

Fotonovelas (photo novels) — romantic stories presented as balloon-captioned photographs — are, next to comic books (see **Comic Strips and Books**), the most widely distributed printed material in Latin America. Europe was the initial source of fotonovelas for Latin America. The first commercial fotonovela was published in Italy in 1945 by the del Duca brothers; its title, *Grand Hotel,* was borrowed from the 1932 Hollywood movie. The first fotonovelas sold in Spanish America came to the northern part of the continent from Spain and to the Southern Cone from Italy. During the relative economic prosperity of the 1950s and early 1960s, fotonovela production boomed in Argentina. As television grew in importance, dual productions of fotonovelas and **telenovelas** (soap operas) emerged; in the late 1960s and early 1970s in Peru, for example, a favorite soap opera, *Simplemente María* (Simply Mary), spun off a highly popular fotonovela to accompany it.

The fotonovela is distributed in Latin America by a tier system. For example, many fotonovelas are produced, printed, and distributed in Mexico City and then are shipped to Colombia, Central America, and the Caribbean. The issues go from major cities to minor ones, then to rural towns.

There are several noticeable genres of fotonovela. One of the standard types is the "fotonovela rosa" (see **Novela Rosa** — *rosa* means "pink"), which is populated by poor, pure women confronting rich, evil women to win the love of rich, cynical men who are forever torn between their base instincts (represented by the wiles of the evil, rich female) and their nobility (marriage, represented by the virtue of the poor heroine). Typical titles are *Novelas de amor* (Novels of Love) and *Secretos de corazón* (Secrets of the Heart).

Beginning in the late 1960s, but only becoming the norm by the mid 1970s, there emerged a new ver-

manity facing the power of death, hunger, and plague. In the background of her desolate landscapes, painted in somber colors, women plead as parachutists fall in the distance. Sometimes she includes sinister beings, half-human and half-stone. Her unusual symbolism and fragmentation of human figures connects her work to **Surrealism,** although she does not consider herself a surrealist.

During the 1950s the mood in Forner's work began to change. Her art became increasingly abstract, combining figuration with the textured surfaces, looser brush strokes, and bright color contrasts characteristic of **Neofiguration.** In 1957 she began her well-known *Series del espacio* (Series of Space), including cycles of paintings about the moon, astronauts in space, and extraterrestrial and mutant beings, reflecting a change from her focus on the world to an interest in the relasion of the fotonovela called the "fotonovela suave" (soft fotonovela), which, though based on the dilemma of the pink fotonovela (making a living versus finding true love) took a less Manichaean, more middle-class view, suggesting that these two options (money versus love) are ultimately compatible.

The third main genre of the fotonovela is the "fotonovela roja" (red fotonovela), which is more down-to-earth in theme and orientation than the pink fotonovela; typical titles are *Casos de la vida* (Real Life Stories) and *Pecado mortal* (Mortal Sin). Middle-class characters are practically absent from the red fotonovela; instead, the majority of the characters do not have stable jobs, they have darker hair and darker skins, and the setting has shifted to the poorer parts of town. Whereas the covers of the "fotonovela rosa" and the "fotonovela suave" strike a romantic and tender note, the "fotonovela roja" always has full body shots, with the women in the scantiest of clothes; female sexuality is portrayed as an irresistible temptation to men, leading toward sin and tragedy. The "roja" combines the morality tale of the importance of keeping to the straight and narrow path with photographs that approach soft-core pornography in their explicitness. The red fotonovela emphasizes tales of violence, family disintegration, and the destructive powers of sexuality, often in the form of rape and incest. In the lower-class neighborhoods of Lima, Bogotá, and Mexico City the "roja" fotonovela outsells the "rosa" and "suave" types.

The fourth main genre of fotonovela is the "fotonovela picaresca" (picaresque fotonovela), in which the focus is on overt sexuality. The "picaresca" genre exploits prurient photographs, uses lower-class models and settings, and totally separates sex from love. Apparently aimed at a thirteen-year-old male's imagination, the stories center around heroic young men whose recently revealed sexual powers drive women mad, causing generously endowed and scantily clad women, usually unnaturally blond and married to older, obviously impotent males, to fight each other for the chance of having sex with the hero. Typical titles are *Sexy risas* (Sexy Laughs) and *Fiebre de pasiones* (Fever of Passions).

REFERENCE:

Cornelia Butler Flora, "Photonovels," in *Handbook of Latin American Popular Culture,* edited by Harold E. Hinds Jr. and Charles M. Tatum (Westport, Conn.: Greenwood Press, 1985), pp. 151–171.

— S.M.H.

G

GAITAS

Gaitas are duct flutes typical of the Atlantic coastal region, especially in Colombia, and are not to be confused with the Spanish gaita, which is a kind of bagpipe. South American gaitas are made from cane tubes and have male and female versions. The female version may have five or six finger holes and is assigned the melodic role. The male version has only one open finger hole, providing low notes, which leaves one hand free to play **maracas** in a rhythmic accompaniment. The sound of the gaitas is produced by blowing through a mouthpiece made of a mixture of beeswax and coal dust. Embedded in the mouthpiece is a feather that reaches into the cane tube, forming a whistle. Male and female gaitas are often included in the cumbiamba, the ensemble that accompanies the cumbia.

Some indigenous peoples divide instruments into two categories, the "pure" and the "impure," the former used for religious purposes and the latter in fiestas. Since the gaitas are used to accompany an erotic dance, they are "impure."

REFERENCE:

Octavio Marulanda, *El folclor de colombia: Práctica de la identidad cultural* (Bogotá: Artestudio Editores, 1984).

— R.L.S.

EDUARDO GALEANO

A Uruguayan writer with a distinguished career in cultural and political journalism, which includes having been editor in chief of the Uruguayan weekly *Marcha* (1961–1964) and the Argentinean left-wing review *Crisis* (1973–1976), Eduardo Galeano (1940–) became widely known in 1971 with the publication of *Las venas abiertas de América Latina* (translated as *The Open Veins of Latin America*), a Marxist interpretation of Latin American economic history. More recently he has published the three volumes of *Memoria del fuego* (1982–1986; translated as *Memory of Fire*), an imaginative retelling of Latin American history that discards linear narrative and throws into question the very definition of historical meaning implicit in the narratives of official historians. Galeano selects fragments of the Latin American past and reinterprets their meaning stressing the themes of colonialism and liberation.

REFERENCES:

Raquel Angel, *Rebeldes y domesticados* (Buenos Aires: Edíciones El Cielo por Asalto, 1992);

Elisa T. Calabrese, ed. *Itinerarios entre la ficción y la historia* (Buenos Aires: GEL, 1993).

— R.G.M.

RÓMULO GALLEGOS

The towering Venezuelan novelist of the first half of the twentieth century and president of his country for a brief period in 1948, Rómulo Gallegos (1884–1969) was a political reformist with a strong interest in education before becoming an author. He taught high school in his mid thirties and in 1936 was appointed secretary of public education. His program called for a revitalization of humanism and an emphasis on the fine arts at a time when United States–influenced educational practices emphasized technical training and the development of marketable abilities.

Gallegos's great contribution to Latin American literature was *Doña Bárbara* (1929; translated). Set in the Venezuelan plains, the novel depicts the classic struggle between civilization (embodied by the male protagonist Santos Luzardo) and barbarism, incar-

Rómulo Gallegos

chooses to live with an Indian tribe but sends his son to be educated in the city. Thus, Gallegos resolves the antithesis between barbarism and civilization he had presented in *Doña Bárbara* and shows that he has reconsidered the value of these terms. "Barbarism" is no longer viewed as a social evil but is reinterpreted as an integral part of autochthonous Latin American reality.

Many public honors were bestowed on Gallegos after he returned to Venezuela in 1958 from one of several periods of exile, chief among them the creation of the **Premio Rómulo Gallegos de Novela** (Rómulo Gallegos International Novel Prize), instituted in 1964 and still the most prestigious award to which Spanish American novelists may aspire (see also **Regionalist Novel**).

REFERENCE:

Hugo Rodríguez Alcalá , *Nine Essays on Rómulo Gallegos* (Riverside, Cal.: Latin American Studies Program, University of California, 1979).

— R.G.M.

José Gamarra

Uruguayan painter José Gamarra (1934–) has worked with **Informal Abstraction** and realism and is an important example of **figuration since the 1970s.** He studied painting and graphic arts at the Escuela de Bellas Artes in Montevideo during the 1950s, settled in Brazil in 1959, and continued his studies in graphic art with Johnny Friedlaenden at Rio de Janeiro's Museo de Arte Moderna and his work in painting with the informal abstract artist Ibere Camargo at Praia Vermelha's Instituto de Bellas Artes. In 1960 Gamarra became a teacher at the Escola de Artes of the Fundação Armando Penteado. During the early 1960s, Gamarra's work, such as *Pintura M-626371,* shows an overall pattern of signs reminiscent of pre-Columbian petroglyphs. These symbols, drawn with thin lines over a dark textured surface, generally follow an orthogonal direction, which recalls the work of his fellow Uruguayan **Joaquín Torres-García,** who had earlier integrated ancient signs into a gridlike structure. In 1963 Gamarra settled in Paris, where he still lives. In 1967 he helped to found the Automat Group and began to study animation.

In the mid 1960s Gamarra became interested in figurative painting, producing landscapes which recreated the romanticized jungle scenes depicted by European traveling artists who visited the Americas during the eighteenth and nineteenth centuries, in search of exotic images to sell back home. Gamarra, who had never seen the jungle personally, based his paintings

nated in the novel's eponymous character. Though *Doña Bárbara* is a novel of ideas, its detailed description of the Venezuelan countryside and the attention paid by its author to character development make it compelling reading even today, long after its reputation was eclipsed by the emergence of the New Latin American Novel of the 1960s **Boom**.

Gallegos wrote two other important novels, *Cantaclaro* (1934) and *Canaima* (1935). The first is heavily indebted to nineteenth-century theories of environmental determinism, yet it tells the stories of the many characters molded by the natural forces of the plains in a poetic style without precedent in the naturalist novel. The novel's focus and organizing device is a traditional storyteller who in his wanderings gathers and transmits the various stories comprising the narrative. *Canaima* is set in the jungle and focuses on a protagonist, Marcos Vargas, who is the quintessential embodiment of his harsh environment, brutal and kind at the same time, impulsive but also imbued with a natural sense of justice. At the end of the novel he on photographs. He worked with a realistic style, paying close attention to minute details of flora and fauna. For this reason his paintings demand careful observation; the clues conveying the meaning of the work often appear submerged in the exuberance of Gamarra's archetypal jungle. In his painting *Cinq Siècles Après* (1986; Five Centuries Later), the European desire for an edenic and pristine "New World" becomes forever lost to the historical realities of domination and greed: in a distant clearing in the midst of luscious vegetation, two Europeans in fifteenth-century clothing seem to argue while two figures wearing loincloths, perhaps enslaved local inhabitants, wait with packages on their heads. The title indicates that this uneven distribution of power has not changed and continues to the present.

REFERENCE:

Holliday T. Day, "José Gamarra," in his *Art of the Fantastic: Latin America, 1920–1987* (Indianapolis: Indianapolis Museum of Art, 1987).

— F.B.N.

GRISELDA GAMBARO

An Argentinean playwright and author of prose narratives often related to her plays, Griselda Gambaro (1928–) portrays the central human relationship as one between victim and victimizer. For this reason critics associate her works with the theater of cruelty propounded by French dramatist Antonin Artaud. *Las paredes* (1963; The Walls), Gambaro's first dramatic work, has affinities with Franz Kafka's *The Trial* (1925). The protagonist (the Youth) is detained for unspecified offenses and subjected to an implacable interrogation by the Custodian and the Official until he loses his will and identity. The action takes place in a comfortably appointed room which is progressively stripped of its furniture and becomes bleaker as the interrogation progresses. English translations of *Las paredes* and two other plays by Gambaro were published as *Information for Foreigners* (1992).

El desatino (1964; The Blunder) — also the title of a short-story collection published in 1965 — relies for its effect on another metaphor with Kafkian overtones. A man wakes up one morning weighed down by an inexplicable iron object that immobilizes him throughout the play. He is surrounded by family and friends, yet his liberation is strangely postponed. When it finally comes (after several episodes involving guilt and sadism) the protagonist falls back in bed with his eyes wide open. In *El campo* (1967; The Camp) Gambaro superimposes to great dramatic effect the two meanings implicit in the Spanish title (though lost

in translation): the bucolic countryside — symbolized in the play by the offstage voices of children singing and peasants returning from the fields — and a Nazi death camp evoked by the characters' attire and demeanor and by the sadomasochistic relationship between the male and female protagonists. These plays by Gambaro anticipated the political reality of Argentina in the 1970s, the decade of the **Guerra Sucia** (Dirty War), when wanton acts of cruelty by the security forces against all manner of individuals suspected of collaborating with "the enemy" shocked the world.

Gambaro's prose fiction also develops the themes of cruelty and sexual violence, especially *Dios no nos quiere contentos* (1979; God Doesn't Want Us to be Happy) and *Ganarse la muerte* (1976; To Earn One's Dying), which was censored by the military authorities. Gambaro is also the author of an erotic novel, *Lo impenetrable* (1984; translated as *The Impenetrable Madame X*).

REFERENCE:

Evelyn Picón Garfield, *Women's Voices from Latin America: Interviews with Six Contemporary Authors* (Detroit: Wayne State University Press, 1985).

— R.G.M.

GABRIEL GARCÍA MÁRQUEZ

Gabriel García Márquez (1928–) is in all likelihood the best-known Spanish-language novelist in the world. He is a Latin American writer but in the distinct sense that his cultural axis is the Caribbean. García Márquez was born in the small Colombian town of Aracataca, near the colonial port city of Cartagena de Indias and not far from the Caribbean Sea. His novels are consistently set on the Caribbean coast of Colombia, no farther inland than the towns strung along the network of rivers that flow into the Caribbean. Like William Faulkner, García Márquez entered the stage of world literature from a region stigmatized by some as a cultural backwater and emphasized the eccentricity of his regional culture in a distinctly modern narrative idiom. García Márquez himself has pointed out that his knowledge of and infatuation with international modernism in the 1940s was a gift of the Caribbean, one made possible by the region's openness to cultural exchange, in sharp contrast to the academic and stifling culture of the nation's capital, Bogotá, isolated in its Andean location and looking more toward the past than to the future.

García Márquez's literary apprenticeship consists of several short stories, a novella, and two longer novels, a body of work that only rarely affords a glimpse

Gabriel García Márquez (center) at the Nobel Prize ceremony in Stockholm, 1982

of the novelist to come. The breakthrough for García Márquez came in 1967 with the publication in Buenos Aires of *Cien años de soledad* (translated as *One Hundred Years of Solitude*), the novel that consolidated the **Boom** of Latin American fiction in and beyond Latin America. The critical and popular success of this novel was resounding and immediate. After the French had declared the novelistic genre to be more or less moribund in the 1950s, *One Hundred Years of Solitude* seemed to anxious European and United States readers to be the narrative equivalent of the discovery of the New World, the rebirth of a form whose origins could be traced back to another Spanish-language classic: Miguel de Cervantes' *Don Quixote* (1605).

García Márquez's novel is a grand synthesis of Latin American history and culture that raises the twin issues of cultural identity and historical alienation. It is a carnivalesque fable of the origins and destiny of a continent plagued by colonialism and internecine warfare since its beginnings. The story is told from a domestic point of view that allows the reader access to myth and epic while demystifying the grandiosity of recorded events. The book is indebted to both popular and learned traditions, to oral storytelling with its peculiar blending of imagination and reality (a mixture

that caused many to label García Márquez's style **magical realism**), and to the most sophisticated novels of High Modernism. However, while one may hear echoes of Marcel Proust, Virginia Woolf, and Faulkner, this novel is more of a tribute to **Jorge Luis Borges** and to Mexican writer Juan Rulfo as well as an "archive" of Latin American texts, an intertextual recollection and summation of various historical and literary narratives and interpretive essays focusing on the problems of Latin American culture with the implicit purpose of founding a cultural tradition and restoring (or inventing) cultural identity.

García Márquez has published three other major novels to date. *El otoño del patriarca* (1975; translated as *The Autumn of the Patriarch*) — an inquiry into the myth of the Latin American dictator — was the immediate successor to *One Hundred Years of Solitude*. García Márquez was clearly concerned with avoiding the trap of self-plagiarism. Not only is the locale of the novel different from that of its predecessor but, more important, its style is notoriously experimental: the linear narrative of *One Hundred Years of Solitude* is abandoned for the sake of spiral or cyclical forms of plot construction. The sentences are long and tortuous and punctuated by fluid displacements in perspective. Yet both novels share the same "project," namely, the mythical exploration of Latin American culture. García Márquez's patriarch is a composite of actual historical dictators, and the anecdotes of which he is the protagonist are taken as much from the popular tradition of hearsay as from written sources. Thus, for all the novel's mythical hyperbole the patriarch is a figure firmly rooted in cultural reality. Understanding him, García Márquez implies, means understanding the culture that produced him.

With his next major effort García Márquez returned to the international best-seller lists. *El amor en los tiempos del cólera* (1985; translated as *Love in the Time of Cholera*) is a no-holds-barred celebration of undying love and of the romantic spirit in general. While the novel's literary model would seem to be Gustave Flaubert's *Sentimental Education* (1845, 1869), García Márquez incorporates several references to the courtship of his own parents and anchors the narrative firmly in Cartagena de Indias. The novel masterfully handles all the topics of romantic literature and is perhaps the author's most accessible and universal work to date. The very fact that it was so universal led to its being coolly received by some Latin American critics. Perhaps its greatest merit is its audacity in telling a love story in an epoch plagued by postmodern skepticism.

El general en su laberinto (1989; translated as *The General in His Labyrinto*) is perhaps the author's best work since *One Hundred Years of Solitude*. Focusing on the last weeks of Simón Bolívar's life, as the hero drifts down the Magdalena river to his final island exile, *The General in His Labyrinth* is yet another inquiry into a founding myth of Latin American identity. Unlike the mythical patriarch of the 1975 novel, however, García Márquez's Bolívar is thoroughly demystified and presented to the reader divested of all epic trappings, in all his human nakedness. The ire of official historians when the novel was published was predictable; yet García Márquez's sober meditation on the Liberator is a far more meaningful reflection on Latin American history than any attempt at hero worship.

García Márquez's other interests besides literature are politics, journalism, and film. As a political figure the Colombian author has been close to several Latin American and European presidents and has occasionally played informal brokerage roles from time to time. His socialist leanings and his continuing support for Fidel Castro's regime in Cuba are amply documented. García Márquez's journalistic writings stretch back over several decades. Standing above the mundane pieces typical of journalistic prose are several investigative reports and two book-length chronicles that approach the condition of imaginative literature:

Relato de un náufrago (1955; translated as *The Story of a Shipwrecked Sailor*) and *La aventura de Miguel Littín, clandestino en Chile* (1986; translated as *Clandestine in Chile: The Adventures of Miguel Littín*). One of García Márquez's shorter works, *Crónica de una muerte anunciada* (1981; translated as *Chronicle of a Death Foretold*), is a magnificent example of how close investigative journalism can be to fiction. In 1994 García Márquez published another short novel, also inspired by an experience he had while a reporter, watching a girl's remains being exhumed; he reconstructs a life for her in *Del amor y otros demonios* (translated as *Of Love and Other Demons*). Finally, García Márquez has contributed to Latin American cinema both artistically and financially. In the late 1980s he set up a foundation in Cuba for the production of Latin American films and donated six scripts that have been filmed by directors from various Hispanic countries including Spain. (See **Movies from Books** and **Nueva Fundación de Cine Latinoamericano**.)

Gabriel García Márquez was awarded the Nobel Prize for Literature in 1982.

REFERENCES:

Gene Bell-Villada, *García Márquez: The Man and His Work* (Chapel Hill: University of North Carolina Press, 1990);

Bernard McGuirk and Richard A. Cardwell, eds. *Gabriel García Márquez: New Readings* (Cambridge: Cambridge University Press, 1987);

Julio Ortega, *Gabriel García Márquez and the Powers of Fiction* (Austin: University of Texas Press, 1988).

— R.G.M.

CARLOS GARDEL

Carlos Gardel (1890–1935), the legendary interpreter of the **tango,** was born in Toulouse, France, to an unwed mother. Named Charles Romuald Gardes, he immigrated to Argentina with his mother, Marie Berthe Gardes, in 1893. Attracted to the music of the bistros of Buenos Aires, he began to play the guitar and learned to sing the improvised payadas (poems and music) of Argentinean folklore. As his repertoire expanded to include the popular **milonga,** zamba, and other Creole songs, so did his esteem among the patrons of Buenos Aires nightlife.

One of the first sound motion pictures produced in Argentina, directed by Eduardo Moreno, featured ten songs by Gardel, who soon realized the potential offered by the movies. His first film, *Melodía de arrabal* (1932; Suburban Melody), produced in France, featured a traveling theater group and a traveling tango band who happened to be in Paris at the same time. The movie was a great success, as were his later films,

Carlos Gardel

Cuesta abajo (1934; Downward Slope) and *El día que me quieras* (1935; The Day You Love Me). These films had an enormous impact in Latin America, spawning a number of similar formula films in Argentina, using the basic combination of comedy, melodrama, and song. Gardel was already a superstar before the advent of sound cinema, but the movies increased his status throughout Latin America, enabling Argentina to export its own versions of musical comedy throughout South and Central America.

A challenge to an artistic duel with a popular rival, José Razzano, began a long friendship and artistic partnership in the Gardel-Razzano Duo, which enjoyed extraordinary success and became the rage of Buenos Aires. Gardel's guitar technique could no longer satisfy the standard of performance required, but the finest guitarists in Argentina were anxious to accompany this prospering duo (see **Tango Guitarists**). Appearances in various parts of Argentina, as well as in Montevideo, Madrid, Barcelona, Paris, Cannes, Rio de Janeiro, and New York soon followed.

In 1924–1925 Razzano developed vocal problems and was forced to retire. Gardel continued touring in Europe as a soloist accompanied by three guitars, and in 1931 he signed a contract with Paramount to make feature-length films in Paris. After making four films Gardel left Paris for New York to continue making motion pictures with Paramount. In New York "El morocho" (a nickname he had acquired by virtue of his masculine vigor) was contracted by the National Broadcasting Company for programs for their eight-hundred-station network, for which Gardel sang many of his popular tangos in English.

In June 1935, during a concert tour of Central America, Venezuela, and Colombia, Gardel's terrible fear of flying was realized. As his plane was taking off from Medellín, it crashed into another plane and burned. The king of the tango was not among the five survivors.

Salvador Garmendia

REFERENCES:

John King, *Magical Reels: A History of Cinema in Latin America* (London: Verso, 1990);

Pedro Malavet Vega, *Cincuenta años no es nada* (San Juan, Puerto Rico: Editora Corripio, 1986);

Argentino Manrique Carriego, *No habrá más penas ni olvido: Carlos Gardel 50 años, 1935–1985* (Medellín: Editorial Percepcion, 1985).

— R.L.S. & S.M.H.

Salvador Garmendia

Venezuelan author Salvador Garmendia (1928–) is usually credited with introducing the problems of urban life into the literary narrative of his country with novels such as *Los pequeños seres* (1959; The Little Beings) and *Los habitantes* (1961; The Inhabitants). *Memorias de Altagracia* (1974; Memories of Altagracia), Garmendia's best-known work, transcends the social and existential focus of the earlier works and evokes the past of the town or barrio of Altagracia in a style that allows the coexistence of the natural and the supernatural, of fact and whimsical fantasy. The novel is loosely structured and some of its episodes could stand as independent short stories. Other novels by Garmendia are *Día de ceniza* (1964; Day of Ashes) and *El único lugar posible* (1981; The Only Possible Place).

REFERENCE:

Angel Rama, *Salvador Garmendia y la narrativa informalista* (Caracas: Universidad Central de Venezuala, 1975).

— R.G.M.

Gauchos

The gauchos were mestizo horsemen of the plains south and west of Buenos Aires whose appearance dates back to the seventeenth century. In the nineteenth century, gaucho culture disappeared as a result of government policies and economic changes. Gauchos were recruited by the army to fight against the pampa Indians, who were a constant threat to European settlements in the environs of Buenos Aires. The Indians were exterminated by Gen. Julío A. Roca in 1880 but not before the prolonged and bloody wars took a heavy toll in gaucho lives. As the pampa was made safe for European settlers, cattle ranching proliferated and displaced the gauchos from the land, often employing them as ranch hands in the large estates that dominated the economy of Argentina at the turn of the century. In the first years of the twentieth century nationalist intellectuals forged a myth of the gaucho centered on *Martín Fierro* (1872, 1879; translated), José Hernández's great epic poem narrating the vicissitudes of the eponymous gaucho hero, a poem which quickly became the cornerstone of Argentinean literature. The elevation of the gaucho to the status of national symbol is readily explained by the stream of European immigrants who came to the Rio de la Plata region at the end of the nineteenth century and who threatened the older Argentineans with a loss of cultural identity. In the nineteenth century an important strain of Argentinean literature was gauchesque poetry (of which the most important example is *Martín Fierro*), narrative poetry about the gauchos written by city intellectuals who imitated gaucho speech and cultural forms of expression, especially the "payada," an improvised song duel between two **payadors** armed with a guitar. **Jorge Luis Borges, Ricardo Güiraldes,** and Benito Lynch are among the twentieth-century writers who take up the figure of the gaucho from a variety of perspectives. Borges dwells on the knife duels that punctuated gaucho culture. Güiraldes creates a larger-than-life gaucho who mentors a wayward

Gauchos in traditional dress, including *rastras* (belts made from silver coins) and drinking *mate,* a strong tea made from the leaves and shoots of a tree in the holly family

youth from the city into the ways of the pampa. Lynch's gauchos, by contrast, are realistic.

REFERENCE:

Richard W. Slatta, *Gauchos and the Vanishing Frontier* (Lincoln: University of Nebraska Press, 1992).

— R.G.M.

GEOMETRIC ABSTRACTION

Geometric Abstraction is a term that generally refers to several geometry-based abstract modes, such as hard-edge abstraction, which includes Concrete Art, Constructivism, Generative Art, Op Art, Kinetic Art, and soft-edge abstraction, which has also been called Geometría Sensible (literally "Sensitive Geometry," but more usually known in English as "Lyrical Abstraction"). Geometric Abstraction has developed through-out Latin America since the 1940s, especially during periods of economic optimism and a utopian desire for modernization, which, in the case of Brazil, Mexico, and Venezuela, also took the form of important urbanization projects. Artists in Latin America often see Geometric Abstraction as a universal language with the power to connect their personal projects to a wider international exploration of abstraction, especially the kind of geometry-based art favored in Europe. Although Latin American artists frequently lived in New York and Paris and knew well which trends were fashionable, they chose as the starting point of their own projects the works of Piet Mondrian, Max Bill, and Georges Vantongerloo, whose art was no longer fashionable after World War II. **Joaquín Torres-García**'s **Constructive Art** is also an important antecedent; in spite of his rejection of complete abstraction, his encouragement of younger artists to pursue their own radical explorations paved the way for the development of abstract geometric movements in Latin America.

During the 1940s the **Asociación de Arte Concreto-Invención** and **Madí** groups were formed in Argentina, actively advocating an abstract art based on concrete plastic elements, such as lines, planes, and colors. After their demise many abstract artists continued working independently, while in 1952 others founded the Artistas Modernos de la Argentina (Modern Artists of Argentina), a group that included **Tomás Maldonado, Alfredo Hlito,** Enio Iommi, Lidy Prati, José Antonio Fernández-Muro, Sarah Grilo, and Miguel Ocampo. In 1952–1953 they exhibited their geometric abstract works in Buenos Aires, Amsterdam, and Rio de Janeiro, which further encouraged interest in concrete art in Brazil. The group dissolved in 1954, when Maldonado left for Europe. In 1959 **Eduardo Mac Entyre** and Miguel Angel Vidal founded the group Arte Generativo (Generative Art) in order to explore the dynamic qualities of geometry and achieve a sensation of motion through optical effects, which connects their search to op art. In the 1970s a new generation of artists, including Alejandro Puente, **César Paternosto,** and **Marcelo Bonevardi,** renewed the tradition of Constructive Art. After exploring different abstract modes, Puente and Paternosto evoke in their soft-edge paintings the sense of constructive geometry that underlies Inca art and architecture, in order to express their own cultural concerns. Bonevardi, on the other hand, emphasizes more universal metaphysical concerns in his painting constructions.

In Chile five young artists, including Matilde Pérez and Ramón Vergara Grez, formed the Grupo de los Cinco (Group of Five) in 1943; they sought to reject the dominant figurative style of the **Montparnasse Group** and work toward abstraction. By 1955 a new group called Rectángulo (Rectangle) was formed by Vergara Grez, who acted as its leader, and other artists who rejected both realistic art and **Informal Abstraction,** advocating instead a rational geometric art based on flatness and orthogonal compositions. They were further encouraged by the arrival in Chile in 1958 of the Cuban Mario Carreño, a well-known abstract geometric artist. In 1962 Rectángulo organized an international exhibition, Forma y Espacio (Form and Space), which in 1965 became the new name of Vergara Grez's group; the group then advocated integration of the arts into the context of everyday life. Matilde Pérez, who briefly participated in Rectángulo, is one of the few Chileans to explore Op Art and **Kinetic Art.**

In Venezuela the interest in Geometric Abstraction began in the 1940s, with the creation of the Taller Libre de Arte (Free Workshop of Art), which sponsored the controversial exhibitions of the **Asociación de Arte Concreto-Invención** (1948) and of **Alejandro Otero**'s first informal abstract series titled *Cafeteras* (1949; Coffee Pots). In Paris in 1950 Otero and others formed a group called Los Disidentes (the dissidents) and published *Revista Los Disidentes,* which they sent back to Caracas to attack its artistic conservatism and champion avant-garde trends. **Carlos Raúl Villanueva**'s design for the Ciudad Universitaria in Caracas (1950) further encouraged Geometric Abstraction in Venezuela. He integrated artworks of internationally recognized artists, such as Fernand Léger, Alexander Calder, and Victor Vasarely, with those of local artists, such as Otero and **Jesús Rafael Soto.** With the success of Otero's series *Colorritmos* (1955–1965; Color-Rhythms), Geometric Abstraction became an accepted artistic mode. Around the mid 1950s Soto and **Carlos Cruz-Diez** also introduced Kinetic Art, which explores the effects of optical and real movement in abstract geometric sculptures. It became Venezuela's dominant style during the 1960s and 1970s.

In Colombia Geometric Abstraction also emerged in the 1950s and early 1960s with artists working independently at home and abroad. In 1948 Marco Ospina exhibited his semiabstract paintings in Bogotá, featuring flat curvilinear areas of color. During the 1950s in the United States and Europe the sculptors **Eduardo Ramírez Villamizar** and **Edgar Negret** developed geometry-based vocabularies. In 1952 Ramírez Villamizar, who lived in Paris at the time, showed his abstract paintings in Bogotá. When Negret returned to Colombia in 1963, he worked with aluminum modules placed in sequence, constructing shapes which simultaneously evoked poetic, organic, and industrial qualities. Since the 1970s Ramírez Villamizar and Negret have included references to pre-Columbian art in their sculptures, linking their work to the tradition of Constructive Art. Other geometric abstract artists working in Colombia since the 1960s are Omar Rayo, Carlos Rojas, Fanny Sanin, Antonio Grass, and John Castles. Geometric Abstraction continues to be a strong tendency in the art of Latin America.

REFERENCES:

Aracy Amaral, "Abstract Constructivist Trends in Argentina, Brazil, Venezuela, and Colombia" in *Latin American Artists of the Twentieth Century,* edited by Waldo Rasmussen, Fatima Bercht, and Elizabeth Ferrer (New York: Museum of Modern Art, 1993): 86–99;

Guy Brett, "A Radical Leap" in *Art in Latin America: The Modern Era, 1820–1980,* by Dawn Ades, Brett, Stanton Loomis Catlin, and Rosemary O'Neill (New Haven & London: Yale University Press, 1989): 252–283.

— F.B.N.

Lobby poster for *Gerónima,* starring Luisa Calcumil

GERÓNIMA

Gerónima (1986), directed by Argentinean Raúl A. Tosso, is a feature-length treatment of the story of how the urban medical establishment destroyed an impoverished Mapuche Indian woman, Gerónima Sande, from south central Argentina. In the course of the film the viewer sees her at the mercy of a social-welfare system that functions erratically; she and her children are hospitalized, leading to even greater culture shock. When they finally return to their home in the desert, by a cruel twist of irony she and her children die as a result of their "innoculation" and the alien microbes from the hospital. This harrowing documentary concentrates not only on social but also on gender oppression.

REFERENCE:

David William Foster, *Contemporary Argentine Cinema* (Columbia & London: University of Missouri Press, 1992).

— S.M.H.

ALBERTO GINASTERA

One of the leading Latin American composers of the twentieth century, Alberto Ginastera (1916–1983) established his relationship with musical **nationalism** while still a student at the National Conservatory of Argentina. A year before his graduation with honors (1938) he wrote two works that signaled his early interest in what he termed "objective nationalism": *Danzas argentinas* (Argentinean Dances) for piano; and his ballet, *Panambí,* based on an Indian legend about a chief's daughter, Panambí, who marries the tribe's greatest hunter. A symphonic suite from *Panambí* was performed the same year of its composition in the great **Colón Theater** in Buenos Aires under the direction of Juan José Castro. The young composer was awarded the National Music Prize of Argentina in 1940 following a full production in the Colón Theater of the ballet in its original form. Within a year Ginastera received a commission from the Ballet Caravan in New York for *Estancia* (Ranch), a ballet based on scenes of Argentin-

Alberto Ginastera

ean rural life. The enthusiastic reception of his works encouraged a series of compositions that established his leadership of the nationalist group: *Obertura para el "Fausto" criollo* (1943; Overture for the Creole "Faust"); *Cinco canciones populares argentinas* (1943; Five Popular Argentinean Songs); *Las horas de una estancia* (1943; Time on a Ranch); and *Suite de danzas criollas* (1946; Suite of Creole Dances).

Ginastera visited the United States for the first time (1946) as the recipient of a Guggenheim Fellowship. During his stay the *Panambí* suite was given its first performance in New York by the NBC Symphony, conducted by Erich Kleiber. Over the years commissions by North American institutions and foundations nurtured interest in his music: the Sonata for Piano (Pittsburgh Festival, 1952); *Pampeana No. 3* (Louisville Orchestra, 1954); String Quartet No. 2 (Coolidge Foundation, 1958); *Cantata para América mágica* (Fromm Foundation, 1960); and a Violin Concerto

(1963), commissioned by the New York Philharmonic for the opening of Lincoln Center.

After an early nationalistic period Ginastera gradually evolved toward more-international styles in which avant-garde techniques such as the twelve-tone method appeared. Although he explored new techniques, he did not abandon traditional structures such as sonata form, theme and variations, and scherzo and trio.

His legacy as a music educator is as distinguished as his compositional career. Ginastera served on the faculty of the Argentinean National Conservatory of Music and Art (1941–1962); was cofounder and professor of the Conservatory of the Province of Buenos Aires (1948–1958); and also taught at the National University of La Plata (1958–1962). In 1958 he became founder and dean of the first university-level music program offering a doctorate in music at the Catholic University of Argentina. In 1963 he left to found and direct the *Centro Latinoamericano de Altos Estudios Musicales del Instituto Di Tella* (The Di Tella Institute Latin American Center for Advanced Musical Studies). Many of Latin America's foremost contemporary composers studied at the Di Tella Institute.

Ginastera's contributions to twentieth-century music have been widely recognized. He was a member of the National Academy of Fine Arts of Argentina, the Brazilian Academy of Music, and the American Academy of Arts and Sciences and served on committees of the International Society of Contemporary Music and the International Music Council in Paris.

REFERENCES:

"Alberto Ginastera" in *Composers of the Americas,* volume 1 (Washington, D.C.: Pan American Union, General Secretariat, Organization of American States, 1955);

Rodolfo Arizaga, *Enciclopedia de la música argentina* (Buenos Aires: Fondo Nacional de las Artes, 1971);

Gerard Béhague, *Music in Latin America: An Introduction* (Englewood Cliffs, N.J.: Prentice-Hall, 1979);

Vicente Gesualdo, *La música en la Argentina* (Buenos Aires: Editorial Stella, 1988).

— R.L.S.

OLIVERIO GIRONDO

The greatest poet and enfant terrible of the Argentinean avant-garde, Oliverio Girondo (1891–1967) celebrated the modern city, whose features he recorded through a lens that was new in Argentinean letters and that had significant parallels with the camera eye of filmmakers. He also filled his poetry with everyday objects excluded by conventional poetic language (for example, that of Romantics and **modernistas**) because he understood that the meaning of the avant-garde was the return of art to social and everyday practice. This conviction models not only the content of Girondo's poems but also the material form of his books and even colors their marketing. Thus, Girondo's first collection of poems, *Veinte poemas para ser leídos en el tranvía* (1925; Twenty Poems to Be Read in the Streetcar), appeared in a "streetcar edition" that sold for twenty cents. (The same collection had previously appeared in France in 1922.) In content, form, and mode of circulation these poems redefined the institutional situation of poetry during the heyday of the avant-garde. The poet had stepped down from his ivory tower (though without any illusions that he would take the world by storm), the poems were smart and showy and evoked the urban context of the reader, and the pact with the reader had also changed. The poet now acknowledged that the reader did not have the same leisure to savor poetry as aristocratic readers had in the past.

A few years later Girondo published *Espantapájaros* (1932; Scarecrow), and for fifteen days the author advertised the book by parading a scarecrow in a hearse through the streets of Buenos Aires. The result was that all five thousand copies of the book were sold in a month. Girondo's work culminates with *En la masmédula* (1956; In the Moremarrow), the neologism of the title serving as notice that the poet is now located at the core of poetry, inside words, and that the reader can no longer take for granted the stuff of language itself.

REFERENCE:

Jorge Schwartz, *Homenaje a Girondo* (Buenos Aires: Corregidor, 1987).

— R.G.M.

BEATRIZ GONZÁLEZ

In her figurative paintings and conceptual objects Colombian artist Beatriz González (1936–) often deals with the relationship between European and Latin American art and between high and popular culture. González studied art at the Universidad de los Andes in Bogotá, where she later taught. During the late 1950s she traveled through Europe and later visited the United States. In 1966 she studied graphic arts at the Van Beeldend Kunstein Academy in Rotterdam.

González makes satirical statements intended to subvert the view of Latin American art as marginal and derivative. She appropriates and transforms two types of visual sources: quotations from the history of Western art and popular images from Colombia. In her 1960s series based on Jan Vermeer's seventeenth-

century *The Lace Maker,* González studied Vermeer's use of color and form in order to formulate her own visual vocabulary: a simplified figurative style built from flat areas of bright colors evenly applied. In *La última mesa* (1970s; The Last Table) González painted her version of Leonardo da Vinci's *The Last Supper* on the top of a dining room table which had been decorated by a popular artisan. This piece of furniture, like many of the popular objects used by González, shows how European artworks often reach Latin America through secondary sources. By emphasizing the appropriative nature of her art, González turns it into an active statement of resistance and transformation that effectively opposes the view of Colombian art as submissively accepting external and internal sources. In *Decoración de interiores* (1981; Interior Decoration) González silk-screened onto a two-hundred-yard-long living-room drapery her version of a photographic image showing the former Colombian president Julio César Turbay Ayala hosting a party; while in her forty-foot frieze *Parrots* (1986), in bright orange and green, she painted the heads of four Colombian military men, whose faces are repeated as in a wallpaper pattern. González subjects these heroic or official figures to the irreverent appearance of commercial art and presents them within the ordinary context of household objects, an approach which links her work with both **Pop Art** and **Conceptual Art.**

REFERENCE:

Gloria Zea, *Beatriz González: Exposición retrospectiva* (Bogotá: Museo de Arte Moderno, 1984).

— F.B.N.

RICARDO GRAU

Ricardo Grau (1907–1970) was among the first Peruvian painters to reject **Indigenism** and foster later avant-garde styles. He spent the first part of his life in Europe, studying art in Brussels and later in Paris, where his teachers André Lhôte, Othon Friesz, and Fernand Léger, of the so-called School of Paris, introduced him to post-Cubist figuration. By the time Grau arrived in Lima in 1937, he had acquired a solid artistic foundation that offered an alternative to an eclectic group of artists who worked with figuration but rejected the thematic limitations of Indigenism. In 1945 he was appointed director of the Escuela Nacional de Bellas Artes (National School of Fine Arts), where he initiated progressive reforms aimed at ensuring the artistic autonomy of the faculty. He was dismissed by the conservative government of Gen. Manuel A. Odría but was later reappointed professor by the next director,

Manuel Ugarte, another progressive artist who continued Grau's reform program.

In the 1940s Grau began to experiment with textures and colors as independent plastic elements. After a short period of working in a style with some Surrealist characteristics, he turned to **Informal Abstraction** in the mid 1950s, continuing to emphasize color and texture. These stylistic changes in Grau's art were important because they made clear to the Peruvian public how a recognized artist could undergo a gradual artistic evolution that would culminate in Informal Abstraction, thus encouraging the acceptance of important abstract artists such as **Fernando de Szyszlo.**

REFERENCES:

Mirko Lauer, *Introducción a la pintura peruana del siglo XX* (Lima: Mosca Azul, 1976);

Teodoro Núñez Ureta, *Pintura contemporánea: Segunda parte* (Lima: Banco de Crédito del Perú, 1976).

— F.B.N.

GRUPO CHASKI

The Grupo Chaski (*chaski* is the Quechua word for messenger) is a cooperative of some thirty filmmakers, producers, and technicians in Peru. The group is a major distributor of Peruvian films, supplying commercial cinemas, universities, and trade unions. It has produced several important documentaries and features, including an ironic look at the Miss Universe competition in Peru (novelist **Mario Vargas Llosa** was one of the judges). Its most important feature to date, *Gregorio* (1984), traces the life of a young country boy forced by poverty to migrate to Lima, where he is caught up in a life of petty crime. The most recent feature, *Juliana* (1988), continues in the same vein, charting the picaresque adventures of a girl who disguises herself as a boy in order to become part of a gang of street beggars and entertainers.

REFERENCE:

John King, *Magical Reels: A History of Cinema in Latin America* (London & New York: Verso, 1990).

— S.M.H.

OSWALDO GUAYASAMÍN

Oswaldo Guayasamín (1919–) is one of the best-known Ecuadoran artists. Raised in poverty he paid for his studies at the Escuela Nacional de Bellas Artes in Quito by peddling his landscapes on the street. Guayasamín shared the descriptive and thematic approach of **Indigenism.** For this reason he joined the Galería Caspicara, directed by **Eduardo Kingman,** which attracted other indigenist artists. Nelson Rockefeller, then coordinator for inter-American affairs, visited his first individual exhibition and purchased several works, solving Guayasamín's financial difficulties. In 1943 he was invited by the United States to visit its main museums, where he admired the works of El Greco and Pablo Picasso. He also traveled to Mexico, where he studied mural painting with José Clemente Orozco. Guayasamín's style synthesized the simplification of form seen in Picasso and Orozco with the indigenist interest in the plight of the Indian and other marginalized groups. In 1945 he traveled through South America, making more than three thousand sketches of the native peoples he encountered. These sketches were used as the basis for a series of 103 paintings titled *El camino de lágrimas* (1951; The Road of Tears), most of them monumental allegories with strident emotional appeal. Another important series in Guayasamín's oeuvre is *The Age of Wrath*, which decries catastrophic world events, such as the Spanish Civil War and World War II. Guayasamín's art met with remarkable commercial success. His residence in Quito houses a splendid collection of pre-Columbian, colonial, and modern Latin American art.

REFERENCE:

Dorothy Chaplik, *Latin American Art: An Introduction to Works of the 20th Century* (Jefferson, N.C.: London: McFarland, 1989).

— F.B.N.

LA GUERRA SUCIA

The internal war waged by the Argentinean military against left-wing guerrillas between 1970 and 1982 has been termed *la guerra sucia* (the dirty war). The military campaign intensified in 1976 when the generals overthrew the civilian government of Isabel Martínez de Perón, Gen. **Juan Domingo Perón**'s second wife, who assumed the presidential office in the wake of Perón's death in July 1974. As a result of the military government's tactics more than six thousand people "disappeared" before the armed forces could claim a complete victory over terrorism in 1981, and more people disappeared thereafter. The systematic violation of human rights by the Argentinean junta reached excesses unheard of in the West since the Second World War: torture of political prisoners, officially directed death squads, press censorship, and a general climate of fear. The military targeted not only presumed guerrillas and their sympathizers and families but also journalists, psychiatrists, and labor leaders. Approximately

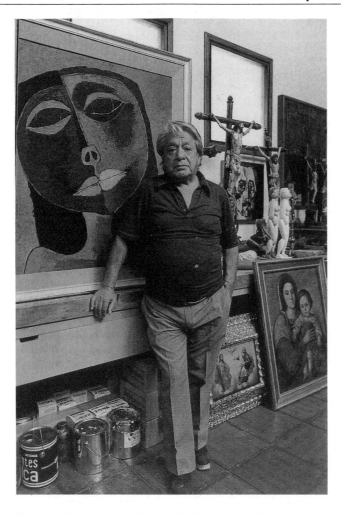

Oswaldo Guayasamín in his studio (photograph by Eduardo Gil)

one hundred journalists disappeared, kidnapped by security forces and probably murdered. Speaking out against the government was punishable by a ten-year jail term. Psychiatrists were suspect because they were often in touch with the shocked relatives of the disappeared. The labor movement in Argentina, perhaps the best organized and most powerful in Latin America, was dismantled, and social security programs were eliminated,

By 1982 the military regime had been discredited, and the economy was in shambles. President Leopoldo Galtieri (who had succeeded Gen. Jorge Videla as the country's strongman) decided to divert attention from the national crisis by staging a full-blown military attack on the Falkland Islands (known to Argentineans as **Las Malvinas**), a remote territory lying three hundred miles east of the Strait of Magellan and less than a thousand miles north of Antarctica, and claimed by Argentina but administered by the British. Galtieri's strategy turned into a national disaster when British forces eventually routed the poorly prepared Argentinean army. As a result of this fiasco the military stepped down from power, and Argentina became a democratic state.

The Dirty War is the subject of several contemporary Argentinean novels, stories, **testimonial narratives,** films, and plays. Among the disappeared — later certified to have been killed — was the writer and journalist Rodolfo Walsh, author of *Operación Masacre* (1957; translated as *Operation Massacre*), an account of the massacre of some terrorists jailed in a Patagonian cell, who were set up by prison authorities in order to be killed as they escaped.

In the interest of national reconciliation President Carlos Menem declared an amnesty in 1990 for former junta members convicted of human rights abuses.

REFERENCE:

Donald Clark Hodges, *Argentina's 'Dirty War': An Intellectual Biography* (Austin: University of Texas Press, 1991).

— R.G.M.

Members of the Chilean Movimiento de Izquierdo Revolucionaria (Leftist Revolutionary Movement), or MIR, carrying a Che Guevara banner in a parade

ERNESTO "CHE" GUEVARA

An Argentinean physician and revolutionary born in the city of Rosario, Ernesto Guevara (1927–1967), known as Che, is closely identified with the **Cuban Revolution.** Guevara was traveling through Guatemala in 1954, when the nationalist government of Jacobo Arbenz was overthrown by a right-wing military coup backed by the CIA. This experience radicalized the young bourgeois physician. Two years later Guevara met Fidel Castro in Mexico and helped him organize the Cuban Revolution.

In the early years of the Castro government Guevara was deeply involved in economic planning, first pushing for diversification to counter reliance on sugar exports, and, when this initiative failed, advancing a strategy of "moral incentives" to stimulate the economy and to eradicate all capitalist vestiges by doing away with material incentives for work and production. Guevara's economic conception was explicitly idealistic and required a "New Man," a socially conscious and self-sacrificing person fully described in "El socialismo y el hombre en Cuba" (So-

cialism and Man in Cuba), Guevara's 1965 essay originally published in *Granma,* the official organ of Castro's government. The New Man was to break with the capitalist conception of work by redefining it as a "social duty." Work would reflect the individual's humanity; it would no longer be performed out of need but in freedom. Volunteerism was an integral part of Guevara's vision, and indeed, after 1966, when Castro endorsed the moral-incentive approach to economic production, Cubans were mobilized on a massive scale to undertake various projects and, especially, to harvest the ten million tons of sugar that Castro had set as a goal for 1970.

"Proletarian internationalism" was another aspect of Guevara's thought that characterized the Cuban Revolution in the 1960s and beyond. Guevara had written that the true revolutionary cannot rest after the most urgent local affairs have been set in order but that he must continue to strive on a global scale to prevent the enemies of the revolution from striking back. In the 1960s Cuba was a beacon for revolutionaries who came to the island for training in guerrilla warfare. Guevara himself took the revo-

Ricardo Güiraldes

lutionary torch abroad. In October 1967 he was captured in Bolivia by counterinsurgency troops and executed.

Guevara's revolutionary idealism defined a whole decade in the West. The handsome face of the martyred "guerrillero" could be seen on thousands of posters, placards, and T-shirts in the massive student demonstrations of 1968 in Paris, Mexico City, the United States, and elsewhere. Guevara's status as pop icon was fleeting, but the landscape of Latin American intellectual and political culture in modern times would be incomplete without the figure of Che.

REFERENCE:

Andrew Sinclair, *Guevara* (London: Fontana, 1970).

— R.G.M.

RICARDO GÜIRALDES

Author of the classic **gaucho** novel of Argentinean literature, *Don Segundo Sombra* (1926; translated), Ricardo Güiraldes (1886–1927) was the son of a wealthy landowner and spent much of his life in France. His cultural heritage was essentially European, but his treatment of the gauchos and the pampa in his great novel is based on personal experience. *Don Segundo Sombra* is a bildungsroman and a nostalgic farewell to the gaucho traditions that for many Argentineans in the 1910s and 1920s incarnated the national spirit. Its protagonist is the adolescent Fabio Cáceres, an orphan and illegitimate son of a landowner who becomes attached to the gaucho Segundo Sombra and heads out to the plains with him. For five years the mentor

Patricio Guzmán in Paris during the French release of *La batalla de Chile* (The Battle of Chile), part 2

teaches Fabio the ways of the pampa, and the latter gradually becomes a gaucho. In the third part of the novel Fabio Cáceres returns to "civilization" to inherit property and write his experiences of the pampa, which have made him a better man, able to deal with his newfound economic responsibilities. The novel's style and technique are cosmopolitan and even avant-garde, but there are descriptions of typical rural scenes such as horse breaking, knife duels, and cattle stampedes that hark back to an older mode of literary representation.

Don Segundo Sombra embodies an Argentinean preoccupation with national identity common in the early twentieth century, a period in which roughly half of the inhabitants of Buenos Aires were of foreign extraction, European immigrants lured to Argentina by the promise of a better life and by the policies of Liberal governments going back to before the 1870s. Like other nationalist intellectuals before him, Güiraldes glorifies the gaucho by turning him into a mythic figure. Needless to say, the real-life existence of the gauchos in the nineteenth century (by the 1920s they were all but extinct) was far less poetic, their famed independence seriously compro-

mised by the proliferation of cattle ranches ("estancias") in the pampa which employed them as farmhands and peons. Güiraldes himself was a ranch owner. His gaucho myth attempts to dissolve the historical contradiction between landowners and peons while legitimizing the continued existence of the same exploitative economic relations, in the pursuit of a common national cause.

REFERENCE:

Giovanni Previtali, *Ricardo Güiraldes and* Don Segundo Sombra: *Life and Works* (New York: Hispanic Institute, 1963).

— R.G.M.

ALFONSO GUMUCIO DAGRÓN

Bolivian film director Alfonso Gumucio Dagrón (circa 1951–) has specialized in documentaries. After training as a filmmaker initially in Madrid and later in Paris, he worked at transferring his skills to peasant and workers' organizations in Mexico, Nicaragua, and intermittently in his native Bolivia, where adverse political circumstances have forced him to flee the country more than once. In addition to several documentary films, few of which have been intended for circulation outside the radius of their production site, Gumucio has published several books of poetry, a history of Bolivian filmmaking (*Historia del cine boliviano,* 1982), a survey of film censorship in Latin America (*Cine, censura y exilio en América Latina,* 1979), and a manual for workers' cinema (*El cine de los trabajadores,* 1981). He returned to Bolivia in 1985 to direct CIMCA, the Centro de Integración de Medios de Comunicación Alternativa (Alternative Mass Communications Coordination Center).

REFERENCE:

Julianne Burton, ed., *Cinema and Social Change in Latin America: Conversations with Latin American Filmmakers* (Austin: University of Texas Press, 1986).

— S.M.H.

the monumental three-part documentary *La batalla de Chile* (1975–1979; The Battle of Chile), studied filmmaking in Spain before returning to his native Chile with the electoral victory of the Popular Unity coalition in 1970. He directed two other documentaries, *El primer año* (1971; The First Year) and *La respuesta de octubre* (1972; October's Answer), before undertaking **La batalla de Chile,** his masterpiece, on the nature and consequences of political events in Chile during the last year of the government of **Salvador Allende**. Since the Chilean coup (1973) Guzmán has lived in France, Cuba, and Spain.

REFERENCE:

Julianne Burton, ed., *Cinema and Social Change in Latin America: Conversations with Latin American Filmmakers* (Austin: University of Texas Press, 1986).

— S.M.H.

PATRICIO GUZMÁN

Movie director Patricio Guzmán (circa 1947–), founder of the **Equipo Tercer Año,** the team that made

H

MARIO HANDLER

A Uruguayan movie director specializing in documentary shorts, Mario Handler (circa 1943–) studied film in Germany, Holland, and Czechoslovakia. His first major work was a portrait of a tramp he had befriended in the port area of Montevideo, *Carlos: Cine-retrato de un caminante* (1965; Carlos: Film-Portrait of a Tramp). He subsequently worked with **Ugo Ulive** on a documentary about the upcoming elections in Uruguay, *Elecciones* (1966; Elections). Handler later produced a six-minute short titled *Me gustan los estudiantes* (1968; I Like Students) for the Marcha Film Festival. Based on the student protest during the Conference of American Heads of State (which included Alfredo Stroessner from Paraguay, Artur de Costa e Silva from Brazil, and Gen. Juan Carlos Onganía from Argentina) held at Punta del Este in 1967, the documentary created a storm of protest. Handler made two documentaries in 1970: *Liber Arce, liberarse* (Liber Arce, Liberation), a silent film which followed the funeral cortege of the first student killed by the police in 1969, and *El problema de la carne* (The Meat Problem), which portrayed a mass strike of packinghouse workers. Though Handler's documentary shorts have not been distributed widely in North America, his work is significant because of its international flavor, despite the severe limitations produced by low production budgets. Forced abroad as a result of the military dictatorship of 1973, Handler nevertheless maintained a steady output of documentaries in the 1970s and 1980s.

REFERENCES:

Julianne Burton, ed., *Cinema and Social Change in Latin America: Conversations with Latin American Film-makers* (Austin: University of Texas Press, 1986);

John King, *Magical Reels: A History of Cinema in Latin America* (London & New York: Verso, 1990).

— S.M.H.

Uruguayan director Mario Handler at the Second International Festival of the New Latin American Cinema, Havana, Cuba, 1980 (photograph by Julianne Burton)

JAVIER HERAUD

A minor Peruvian poet killed in a skirmish with the Peruvian army at the age of twenty-one, Javier Heraud (1942–1963) sympathized with the Cuban Revolution (see **Cuban Revolution and Cultural Politics**) and accepted a scholarship from the Cuban government to study cinematography on the island. Heraud left Lima in March 1962; the following month he was receiving guerrilla training in the Cuban mountains and preparing to open a subversive front in the Peruvian jungle with a small band of comrades-at-arms. Shortly after Heraud covertly crossed the border from Bolivia into

Peru he was slaughtered by an army detachment as he drifted in a canoe down the Madre de Dios river, near Puerto Maldonado in southeastern Peru. To convey his conversion to the revolutionary faith and the acquisition of a new political identity, Heraud adopted a pseudonym (Rodrigo Machado) in July 1962 in Havana and wrote political poetry. A collection of his *Poemas* (Poems) was published by **Casa de las Américas** in 1967. The first *Poesías completas* (1973; Complete Poems) appeared in Lima. An updated edition, *Poesías completas y cartas* (Complete Poems and Letters), was published in 1976.

REFERENCE:

Javier Heraud, *Poesía completa,* edited by Javier Sologuren (Lima: Peisa, 1989).

— R.G.M.

FELISBERTO HERNÁNDEZ

Uruguayan author Felisberto Hernández (1902–1964) was neglected in his lifetime but was rediscovered in the 1970s. He was widely appreciated for the singular quality of his writings, which allude to the world of childhood and might be considered autobiographies did they not dwell mostly on a peculiar mode of perception that displaces the narrative emphasis of conventional autobiographical memoirs. Works such as *Por los tiempos de Clemente Colling* (1942; In the Times of Clemente Colling) — focusing on the blind piano teacher of the author's childhood — *El caballo perdido* (1943; The Lost Horse), and *Tierras de la memoria* (1965; Lands of Memory) are exercises in "creative" memory, in which the past is transformed and gains a new meaning in its re-creation in the present. In these works time is distended by perception, and memory becomes a sixth sense.

Hernández's most memorable texts are the stories of *Nadie encendía las lámparas* (1947; translated as *Piano Stories*), the short novel *Las hortensias* (1949; The Hortensias), and occasional stories written later, such as "El cocodrilo" (1951; The Crocodile) and "La casa inundada" (1960; The Flooded House). These narratives are as realistically detailed as they are absurd. With no regard for realistic verisimilitude, nor for the kind of believability attached to fantastic or marvelous stories, they introduce the reader into a fully realized logical discourse that is, however, impossible to accept as a rendering of normal events. Their logic is imaginary but coherent on its own, improvised terms. For example, "El cocodrilo" is the story of a man with artistic ambitions who wants to make a living as a concert pianist. (In real life Felisberto — as the writer is

usually known — did make a living for a while as an itinerant pianist, playing in provincial bars and concert halls.) Nevertheless, he must settle for peddling women's stockings because his artistic talent is not sufficiently marketable in the provincial circles in which he moves. By accident he comes upon an original commercial strategy: breaking into tears for no apparent reason and in public. Thus, he sells many pairs of stockings and finally receives an invitation to perform at the piano. The recital is successful, but afterward, alone in his hotel room, the pianist begins to cry tears that are no longer crocodile tears. The mask comes off to reveal the artist degraded by his public.

Other narratives, such as "La casa inundada" and *Las hortensias,* relate elaborate private rituals that seem to call for a psychological interpretation. *Las hortensias,* for instance, is about a man who develops a special liking for fashion mannequins and arranges his living room to look like a window shop. To complete the illusion he orders custom-made, life-size rubber dolls who eventually replace his wife and drive him mad. In "La casa inundada" the unconscious is amply represented by the symbol of water.

REFERENCE:

Francisco Lasarte, *Felisberto Hernández y la escritura de 'lo otro'* (Madrid: Insula, 1981).

— R.G.M.

ALBERTO HIDALGO

Alberto Hidalgo (1897–1967) was a Peruvian avant-garde poet. His first books, *Arenga lírica al emperador de Alemania* (1916; Lyrical Harangue to the German Emperor) and *Panopla lírica* (1917; Lyrical Panoply), were influenced by Italian Futurism. In 1922 he settled in Buenos Aires, and in 1925 he published *Simplismo: poemas inventados* (Simplism: Invented Poems), foregrounding his own avant-garde style. Simplismo implies the stripping down of poetic discourse to its metaphoric component. Both militant and nihilistic, it did not differ substantially from other, more-influential avant-garde projects. The following year Hidalgo, **Jorge Luis Borges,** and **Vicente Huidobro** wrote *Indice de la nueva poesía americana* (Index Of the New American Poetry), an important collection of avant-garde Latin American poetry whose historical significance has only increased with time.

Hidalgo also made incursions into Peruvian politics, first with a pamphlet dedicated to Víctor Raúl Haya de la Torre, the founder of the most influential Latin American social-democratic party, APRA (Alianza Popular Revolucionaria Americana). Later he

A scene from *La historia oficial* (1986; The Official Story), set in Buenos Aires during the Guerra Sucia (Dirty War) of 1976–1983

wrote *Porqué renuncié al APRA* (1954; Why I Quit APRA), a diatribe against the very same leader and his party. Hidalgo published more than twenty, mostly ephemeral, volumes of poetry, the last of which is *Volcandida* (1967; Volcandide). In the year of his death the Centro Editor de América Latina in Buenos Aires published *Antología personal,* a collection of his poetry.
— R.G.M.

LA HISTORIA OFICIAL

La historia oficial (1986; The Official Story), directed by Argentinean Luis Puenzo, tells the story of the **Guerra Sucia** (Dirty War), which swept Argentina between 1976 and 1983 and in which ten thousand to twenty thousand people designated "subversives" were "disappeared." The film focuses on the personal narratives of Roberto, a rich, shady businessman, of his wife, Alicia, and of their adopted child, Gaby. As the title makes clear, the main point of the movie is the distinction between the "Official Story" of what is happening during the Dirty War (namely, according to the establishment, nothing) and the "Unofficial Story" (the reality

of thousands of people being kidnapped and killed). The story is narrated through the eyes of Alicia, who not by chance is a history teacher and who gradually discovers, in detectivelike fashion, that her adopted child's natural mother was a "disappeared" subversive (she finds out by meeting Gaby's natural grandmother). A clever use of subtle sound effect is employed in *La historia oficial,* especially in the second half, when Alicia is drawing near the truth; the sound of steps in the hallways and the sound of cups or glasses making contact with tables are enhanced and made to reverberate as if to emphasize the hollowness of Alicia's life. The concluding scene of the film, in which Alicia "disappears" Gaby from Roberto and he retaliates by breaking her hand in the door, reveals that he is not only involved with the military cleanup schemes but also probably involved with the torturing as well. *La historia oficial,* a gripping, suspenseful movie which combines political and personal levels adeptly, won international recognition and an Oscar for best foreign film of 1986.

REFERENCE:

David William Foster, *Contemporary Argentine Cinema* (Columbia & London: University of Missouri Press, 1992).
— S.M.H.

ALFREDO HLITO

The Argentinean painter Alfredo Hlito (1923–) participated in the **Asociación de Arte Concreto-Invención** (AACI) and was later an advocate of abstract art. Hlito studied at the Escuela Nacional de Bellas Artes in Buenos Aires and in 1945 joined the AACI, participating in its exhibition at the Salón Peuser in 1946. Although Hlito's early paintings were stylistically close to **Joaquín Torres-García**'s work, his later works were concrete geometric compositions evocative of Georges Vantongerloo's art, such as *Curvas y series rectas* (1948; Curves and Straight-Line Series), featuring subtle shapes of pure colors on a white background. After the AACI dissolved, Hlito went to Europe in 1953. During his travels there he realized that during his concrete period he had rejected many artistic elements without fully exploring them. His geometric compositions became progressively more dynamic and expressive as he reintroduced color modulation into his work, which, by the end of the 1950s, became a vibrant pointillism of translucent colors.

From 1964 to 1973 Hlito lived in Mexico, where he worked as director of the Departamento de Artes Gráficas at the Editorial Universidad Nacional Autónoma de México and began to introduce drawing into his paintings, playing with dark lines and shapes placed on softly colored backgrounds. Soon Hlito's abstract forms began to approximate the proportions and the three-dimensionality of the human figure: for all their abstraction his paintings evoked a sense of human presence. After his return to Argentina in 1973, he produced the *Efigies* (Effigies) series, in which he used drawing and contrasts of light and dark areas to define his abstract forms. Eventually, these abstract effigies consolidated into more-cohesive vertical figures, and during the 1980s Hlito began to place them in a stagelike setting. In paintings such as *Iconostasis* (1982) he combined multiple effigies in a grid structure reminiscent of Torres-García's **Constructive Art.**

REFERENCE:

Aracy Amaral, "Abstract Constructivist Trends in Argentina, Brazil, Venezuela, and Colombia," in *Latin American Artists of the Twentieth Century,* edited by Waldo Rasmussen, Fatima Bercht, and Elizabeth Ferrer (New York: Museum of Modern Art, 1993), pp. 86–99.

— F.B.N.

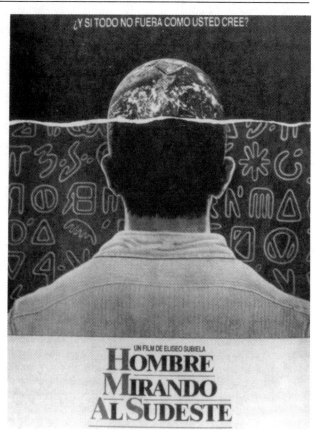

Movie poster for *Hombre mirando al sudeste* (1986), released in the United States as *Man Facing Southeast*. The line at the top says, "And what if nothing were as you think it to be?"

the story of Rantes Soto, a young man who comes under the treatment of a psychiatrist, Quinteros, in the Hospital Borda, a major institution, located on the outskirts of Buenos Aires. The film, set in the period of the redemocratization process in Argentina, follows the figure of Rantes as a nonconformist in an Argentina which is making the transition from fascism to democracy, although the former still permeates the latter. Though Rantes is insane, his story is emblematic of the alienated consciousness of the individual in Argentina in the 1980s.

REFERENCE:

David William Foster, *Contemporary Argentine Cinema* (Columbia & London: University of Missouri Press, 1992).

— S.M.H.

HOMBRE MIRANDO AL SUDESTE

Hombre mirando al sudeste (1986; *Man Facing Southeast*), directed by Eliseo Subiela, was a successful motion picture in Argentina and the United States and won important prizes in both Cuba and Spain. The movie is

HORA ZERO

Hora Zero (Zero Hour) was an iconoclastic group of Peruvian poets established in 1970 and influential throughout the decade. Their founding manifesto is a noisy excoriation of Peruvian poetry from which only three poets are exempted: **César Vallejo,** Edgardo Tello, and **Javier Heraud,** the last two known mostly as left-wing guerrillas who met an early death at the hands of the army. Its most prominent associate and founding member was Enrique Verástegui, an eclectic poet who mixes urban slang with Surrealist images and reminiscences of T. S. Eliot and Ezra Pound. Other members of the group were Carmen Ollé and Jorge Pimentel. The journal *Hora Zero,* also founded in 1970, ceased publication the following year.

— R.G.M.

HUAIÑO

In the anc \ient Quechua language the word *huaiño* refers to a social dance, soirée, or funeral dance. In current usage it refers to a lively song and dance form. Resembling the **carnavalito,** the huaiño may emphasize the pentatonic scale in its melodic progression or may employ mixed pentatonic, major, and minor modes. Its rhythm is lively, set in duple meter, and typically consists of two phrases that are repeated many times. Lyrics appear in strophic couplets expressing topics appropriate to the occasion. They may be sung in Spanish, Quechua, or both. Instrumental accompaniments may include **quenas, tarkas, charango, bombo,** violin, and diatonic harp. Original to the Andean altiplano, the huaiño (also found as *wainyio, huayno, huayñu,* and *guaiño*) is popular among the indigenous peoples of Peru, Bolivia, Ecuador, and Argentina. In Ecuador it goes under the name *sanjuanito.*

REFERENCES:

Isabel Aretz, *El folklore musical argentino* (Buenos Aires: Ricordi Americana SAEC, 1958);

Gerard Béhague, "Latin American Folk Music," in *Folk and Traditional Music of the Western Continents,* by Bruno Nettl, third edition, revised and edited by Valerie Woodring Goertzen (Englewood Cliffs, N.J.: Prentice-Hall, 1990);

Thomas Turino, "Music in Latin America," in *Excursions in World Music,* by Bruno Nettl, Charles Capwell, and others (Englewood Cliffs, N.J.: Prentice-Hall, 1992).

— R.L.S.

HUELVA FILM FESTIVAL

The Festival de Cine Iberoamericano, or Huelva Film Festival, founded in 1974 and held in southern Spain each autumn, is largely devoted to increasing awareness of Latin American cinema. In an industry dominated by the commercial interests of Hollywood, the distribution of films from other countries, even within their countries of origin, has often been limited and difficult. Censorship is another factor that has sometimes affected the showing of home-produced films in certain countries. Against this background the Huelva festival has become a major showcase for filmmakers from Latin America. Films about Latin America, even if produced elsewhere, can also be featured. About 90 percent of the support for the festival is public funding from Spain.

Each festival consists of an official film season and a competition with several categories and prizes. Principal among them are the Colón de Oro (Golden Columbus) prizes, worth some twenty-five thousand dollars each. There are two such prizes for full-length movies; one is awarded by an international professional jury, another following a vote by the audience. There are also Casa de las Américas prizes for shorts. Recent South American films to have won a Colón de Oro include *Juliana,* made by Fernando Espinosa and Alejandro Legaspi, Peru, and receiving both "colones" in 1989; *Yo, la peor de todas* (1990; I, the Worst of All of Them), by María Luisa Bemberg, Argentina; *Después de la tormenta* (1990; After the Storm), by Tristán Bauer, Argentina; *Disparen a matar* (1991; Shoot to Kill), by Carlos Azpurúa, Venezuela; *Las tumbas* (1991; The Tombs), by Javier Torre, Argentina; *La estrategia del caracol* (The Snail's Strategy) and *Aguilas no cazan moscas* (Eagles Do Not Hunt Flies), both by the Colombian Sergio Cabrera, and receiving prizes in 1993 and 1994, respectively.

— P.S.

VICENTE HUIDOBRO

Avant-garde poet and enfant terrible of the Chilean aristocracy, Vicente Huidobro (1893–1948) was the proponent of **creacionismo,** one of the many aesthetic creeds in vogue during the first part of the twentieth century advocating the autonomy of the poetic image. In the spirit of the European avant-garde, Huidobro was a poet without national borders. He wrote poetry and poetic manifestos in French and Spanish and lived for extended periods in Paris. Intent on carving for himself a prominent place among the artistic elite of the period, Huidobro engaged in polemical confrontations with other poets and was not above engineering publicity ploys of dubious taste. His creative talent, however, was commendable. Apart from inventing new poetic forms, Huidobro tried the painted poem (visually modeled texts meant to be exhibited in art galleries), brought together poetry and fashion by having brief texts sewn onto blouses sold to Parisian ladies, authored avant-garde novels, and even wrote a film

Vicente Huidobro and Juan Larrea in Les Sables-d'Olonne, France, 1924 (photograph by Gerardo Diego)

since Charles Baudelaire, namely, the increasing distance in the modern world between poetry and the public, which Huidobro tried to bridge by becoming a public figure himself.

Huidobro's reputation as a major poet is based on "Ecuatorial" (1918), a long poem reminiscent of Guillaume Apollinaire; *Poemas árticos* (1918; *Arctic Poems*), texts that embody the essence of "creacionismo"; and, above all, *Altazor* (1919), a book-length poem divided into seven cantos. *Altazor* dramatizes the death of modern poetry, if modern poetry is defined as the search for originality or the search for a specifically poetic language uncontaminated by everyday use and by poetic tradition. In this work Huidobro's poetic voice is anguished, lyrical, and playful at the same time. The final cantos are particularly striking for their word games and for staging the destruction of language.

Reference must also be made to the many poetic manifestos Huidobro wrote through the halcyon years of the avant-garde, because in spite of their partisan tone they show an intimate knowledge of modern poetry and a technical proficiency in the analysis of poetic images that go a long way toward endorsing Huidobro's view that the poet was the equal of the scientist in his field. In Latin America this claim of poetic expertise goes back to Rubén Darío (see **Modernismo**) and must be understood as an attempt to relegitimize a profession that was losing ground to the scientist's prestige in modern culture. Huidobro emphasized that, unlike the scientist, the poet expressed the totality of man.

REFERENCE:

René de Costa, *Vicente Huidobro: The Careers of a Poet* (New York: Oxford University Press, 1984).

— R.G.M.

script that won a ten-thousand-dollar prize in New York. Behind these sometimes frivolous activities there was a serious concern shared by every major poet

I

Juana de Ibarbourou

Uruguayan poet Juana de Ibarbourou (1895–1979) is conventionally included in the group of "poetisas" (women poets) who came into their own following the demise of **modernismo** and who turned away from the aestheticism of the modernist poets in the direction of a simplified poetic diction and a greater contact with nature. Ibarbourou reached the height of her literary fame in 1929 — ten years after the publication of her first collection of poetry, *Las lenguas de diamante* (The Diamond Tongues) — when she was acclaimed in a public ceremony in Montevideo and given the title "Juana de América." The third edition of Ibarbourou's complete works, *Obras completas* (edited by Dora Isella Russell, Madrid), appeared in 1967, the year she published her last volume of poetry, *Elegía* (Elegy).

REFERENCES:

Diego Córdoba, *Presencia y poemas de Juana de Ibarbourou* (Mexico: Beatriz de Silva, 1954);

Sidonia C. Rosenbaum, *Modern Women Poets of Spanish America* (New York: Hispanic Institute in the United States, 1945).
— R.G.M.

Juana de Ibarbourou

Idiophones

Idiophones, which add color to rhythmic patterns, are among the most primitive musical instruments still in use today; they are constructed from sonorous materials that may be made to sound in a variety of ways. Hand clapping and foot stamping were probably the first idiophones. Subsequently, many other sonorous materials with quite different sounds and pitches have been used. Varieties of woods, metals, glasses, vegetable matter, and even plastics are among the materials that are used for stamping, scraping, striking, plucking, and shaking. Instruments classified as idiophones include rattles, scrapers, stamping tubes, cymbals, xylophones, bells, gongs, pots, and claves (two cylindrical pieces of hardwood struck together to mark basic rhythmic patterns). Claves are common in the Caribbean but rare in South America, except in Venezuelan and Colombian music influenced by Antillean styles. Cowbells of different sizes are employed as idiophones to add color to rhythmic patterns. They are widely used in musical styles influenced by Afro-Cuban and Antillean sources. Sometimes referred to as *cencerro,* the cowbell has no clapper and is played with a thick drumstick.

— R.L.S.

IMPRESSIONISM AND POSTIMPRESSIONISM IN ART

Impressionism and Postimpressionism were introduced into Spanish America by artists who studied in Paris at the turn of the century — such as the Argentineans Martín Malharro and Faustino Brughetti, the Uruguayan **Pedro Figari,** the Colombian **Andrés de Santa María,** as well as the Venezuelans Emilio Boggio and **Armando Reverón** — and by the Argentinean **Fernando Fader,** who had studied in Munich. Although there were few contacts among most of these artists, upon their return to their native countries they followed a similar pattern of rejection of the dominant late-academic schools and of the Spanish modernist style popularized by Ignacio Zuloaga. At the same time, many Impressionists were encouraged by collectors who often bought the works of the Spanish plein-air painter Joaquín Sorolla.

In 1902 Malharro introduced Impressionism into Argentina. The style was later advocated by Nexus, a group of Impressionist artists formed in 1907, which included Fader, César Bernaldo Quirós, and Pío Collivadino. Fader, who worked in a style reminiscent of his German teacher Heinrich von Zügel, produced, like Claude Monet before him, a well-known series of paintings of the same landscape done at different times of the day in an effort to capture fleeting effects of light and atmospheric changes. The images he favored, the countryside and its inhabitants, became identified as the official themes of Argentinean national art when the members of Nexus gained control of the art market and most official art institutions, becoming professors and serving on juries for prizes and scholarships. Even the Postimpressionist **Pedro Figari,** whose art provided a bridge to the more radical avant-gardes of the 1920s, often worked with images of nineteenth-century rural life.

During the same period, the Chilean Juan Francisco González and Peruvians Daniel Hernández and Carlos Baca-Flor worked in a loose impressionistic style. González often painted flowers and views of local landscapes. In Colombia the most important Impressionist was Andrés de Santa María, who spent most of his life in Europe. From 1893 to 1911, when he was in Colombia, his Impressionist style became looser and more expressive, closer to Postimpressionism. In spite of his efforts to renew the art of Bogotá, his influence was neutralized by the unstable political situation. Impressionism was advocated in Venezuela by the Círculo de Bellas Artes, founded in 1912, as a means of opposing the dominant academic styles and in support of the work of artists such as Emilio Boggio (who lived in France most of his life), Rafael Monasterios, and Manuel Cabré. The Venezuelan Armando Reverón also began as an Impressionist but soon developed his light-filled landscapes into a personal and original version of Postimpressionism. During the 1920s Impressionism and related styles were quickly superseded by more-radical avant-garde developments in Argentina, Uruguay, and Chile and by styles influenced by Muralism and **Indigenism** in Peru, Colombia, and Venezuela.

REFERENCES:

Leopoldo Castedo, *A History of Latin American Art and Architecture: From Pre-Columbian Times to the Present,* translated and edited by Phyllis Freeman (New York & Washington, D.C.: Praeger, 1969);

Edward J. Sullivan, "Notes on the Birth of Modernity in Latin American Art," in *Latin American Artists of the Twentieth Century,* edited by Waldo Rasmussen, Fatima Bercht, and Elizabeth Ferrer (New York: Museum of Modern Art, 1993), pp. 18–37.

— F.B.N.

INDIGENISM IN ART

Indigenism was the first important tendency in twentieth-century art and literature to develop in the Andean regions of South America, home to large Indian populations. At the turn of the century, governments and intellectuals of the Andean nations began to reevaluate their earlier deprecatory attitudes toward the local indigenous and pre-Hispanic heritages. Their proposed solution to "unify" the multiple cultures of their nations was to assimilate the Indian peoples into the mainstream by "Europeanizing" them through education and eliminating marginality through economic and social measures. For instance, during the 1920s positivists such as Alfredo Espinosa Tamayo sought to redefine Ecuadoran national identity by determining the psychological traits of Ecuadoran peoples; marginal traits could therefore be "corrected" through education and replaced by those of the mainstream. After

Huanca Indian (1930), by José Sabogal (The Art Museum of the Americas, OAS, Washington, D.C., anonymous gift, 1976)

the Russian and Mexican revolutions, the influence of socialism and Marxism convinced many intellectuals, such as the Ecuadoran Agustín Cueva Tamariz, that social and economic inequalities had to be addressed as well. In Peru the need for national redefinition came during the period of "reconstruction" after the disastrous loss of the War of the Pacific against Chile in 1883. Peru had two equally strong cultural heritages: it had been the center of the Incan Empire and later the center of a colonial Spanish viceroyalty. This duality later translated into a dichotomy in Peruvian intellectual life: Hispanism versus Indigenism. While some thinkers lamented Peru's multiple identity, many saw in the "Indian" a symbol of national identity.

Defined as the reevaluation of the autochthonous and native heritages of the Andean region and the denunciation of the impoverished condition of the Indian peoples, Indigenism first appeared in literature. (See **Indigenism in Literature**.) In art the nationalism inherent in Indigenism encouraged practitioners to reject both academic and avant-garde solutions as "foreign" to the Americas. Influenced by Mexican Muralism, Indigenist artists worked in a conservative descriptive style that focused on a revolutionary appreci-

ation of native themes. In Peru Indigenism became established as an art movement in the 1920s, when **José Sabogal,** the leading Indigenist artist, was appointed professor and later director of the recently founded Escuela Nacional de Bellas Artes, a powerful position that allowed him to dominate the art scene for a long time. His aesthetic nationalism shaped the work of the first generation of artists to study at this school, including **Julia Codesido,** Ricardo Flores, Camilo Blas, and Enrique Camino Brent. Another group of Indigenists, among them **Jorge Vinatea Reinoso** and **Mario Urteaga,** worked independently of Sabogal's influence.

In Ecuador Indigenism developed during the 1930s, in a context of political unrest caused by tension between a government with fascist sympathies and a cultural intelligentsia with socialist tendencies which supported the cause of Indigenism. One of the first artists to work with indigenous subjects was **Camilo Egas,** who was further encouraged by the Mexican Muralist David Alfaro Siqueiros, who traveled to Ecuador several times during the 1930s. Indigenism was launched officially as a movement in 1939, when the writers Jorge Reyes, José Alfredo Llerena, and Alfredo Chávez founded the Salón de Mayo del Sindicato de Escritores y Artistas Ecuatorianos, fashioned on the model established by the Mexican Sindicato de Trabajadores Técnicos, Pintores y Escultores. The salón's first exhibition included works by the leading Indigenist artists: **Oswaldo Guayasamín, Eduardo Kingman Riofrío,** Diógenes Paredes, and others.

There were also Indigenist trends in Colombia, Venezuela, and Bolivia. In Colombia the leading Indigenist painters were Luis Alberto Acuña and Gómez Jaramillo, who like Sabogal and Kingman had firsthand knowledge of Mexican Muralism, and Pedro Nell Gómez, who also worked with local themes. In Venezuela, Héctor Poleo painted images of rural workers during the 1940s, giving them a monumental quality, and in Bolivia, Arturo Borda was a self-taught artist, a prolific writer, and a social activist whose Indigenist work was discovered later in the 1960s. As Indigenism became outdated, it was replaced by the abstract styles of the 1940s and 1950s.

REFERENCES:

Jacqueline Barnitz, *Abstract Currents in Ecuadorian Art* (New York: Center for Inter-American Relations, 1977);

Gilbert Chase, *Contemporary Art in Latin America* (New York: Free Press, 1970), pp. 113–114.

— F.B.N.

INDIGENISM IN LITERATURE

In its broadest sense, *indigenismo* relates to artistic endeavors that in some way portray the social conditions or worldview of the indigenous peoples of Latin America. (See **Indigenous Cultures**.) The term has particular importance in the study of art and literature and, naturally enough, for countries with significant Indian populations (Mexico, Guatemala, Ecuador, Peru, and Bolivia). Various ideological perspectives have been used in creating Indigenist art and literature.

As a literary genre, Indigenism may be said to have its roots in the chronicles written by Bartolomé de las Casas, a priest who championed the rights of oppressed Indians in early colonial times. However, the term is most often used in relation to modern novelists, and in this context the first significant manifestation is Clorinda Matto de Turner's *Aves sin nido* (1889; Birds Without Nests). Indigenism in literature bears a close relationship with indigenism in sociology and anthropology, that is, with the scientific study of the Indian tending toward the vindication of the original inhabitants of the "New World." It must be emphasized that Indigenist novels were not written by Indians themselves but by mestizo or white intellectuals speaking on their behalf. Such is the case, for example, of the author of this first Indigenist novel, the wife of a landowner whose argument in defense of the Quechua Indians is couched in the terms of nineteenth-century liberalism. Matto de Turner was acquainted with descendants of the Incas, but this knowledge did not prevent her from idealizing the Indians or from indulging in exotic landscape descriptions, as did her mentor, Manuel González Prada, a liberal intellectual from Lima who did not write novels but whose spirited pronouncements against Indian exploitation signal the transition from "Indianism" (the romantic idealization of the Indian) to Indigenism. **José Carlos Mariátegui** was the most influential Peruvian thinker of the early twentieth century and the first to make the case for the Indians in socialist terms, arguing that Indian exploitation was a function of landownership and that no solution that failed to envisage a radical transformation in the system of land tenure was viable. **José María Arguedas** (an ethnologist as well as a literary artist) was the novelist who most effectively represented the Indian world from within, as one who spent his early years among Indians and learned their language in childhood. He comes as close as an Indigenist writer can to being one with his subject. In the worst cases, the cultural distance between white urban author and Indigenist subject matter resulted in artificial novels more valuable for the social theses discussed than for their literary merits.

Indigenist writers were aware of their limitations in cultural representation and appealed to several different devices (all taken from indigenous cultures) for the sake of verisimilitude, such as the use of folk songs, legends, and myths; the presentation of conflict in terms of the whole collectivity; the construction of the plot by accumulation of events rather than by the conventional rules of European realism; and a different perception of time. Clearly, José María Arguedas was the most successful Indigenist writer in this formal sense, too, because in addition to the various techniques shared by Indigenist writers in general, Arguedas was able to write in a syncretic, Quechua-inflected Spanish that effectively communicated to the reader the lived experiences of the Indian characters. (The Guatemalan Miguel Angel Asturias also strove to achieve this syncretic effect by appealing to the Mayan repertory of legend and myth.) In general, since no indigenous culture has the narrative form known as the novel, Indigenist novels are more authentic to the extent that they are less recognizable as novels.

The term *Indigenism* is usually associated with the period 1920–1940 and with the Andean highlands, but it should be expanded to cover a wider temporal and spatial range. Not only was the first Indigenist novel published in 1889, but the work of José María Arguedas belongs to the second half of the century. The genre also flourished in Mexico and Guatemala, and in Peru it has continued to evolve in the works of **Manuel Scorza.** The best-known Indigenist novels are *Raza de bronce* (1919; Bronze Race), by Bolivian Alcides Arguedas; *Huasipungo* (1934; translated), by Ecuadoran Jorge Icaza; *El indio* (1935; The Indian), by Mexican Gregorio López y Fuentes; *El mundo es ancho y ajeno* (1940; translated as *Broad and Alien Is the World*), by Peruvian Ciro Alegría; *Hombres de maíz* (1949; translated as *Men of Maize*), by Miguel Angel Asturias; *Los ríos profundos* (1958; translated as *Deep Rivers*), by José María Arguedas; and *Balún-Canán* (1957) and *Oficio de Tinieblas* (1960; Rites of Darkness), by Mexican Rosario Castellanos.

An important mutation of the Indigenist genre is the late appearance of ethnographic narratives (**Testimonial Narrative**) that cut across the cultural and ethnic divide by seeming to allow the Indians themselves to speak. The first of these narratives was Ricardo Pozas's *Juan Pérez Jolote* (1948), a first-person account of the life of a Chamula Indian, originally published in an anthropological journal. The best-known of these ethnographic "autobiographies" is Elizabeth Burgos's transcription of interviews with a Mayan woman who went on to win the Nobel Peace Prize: *Me llamo Rigoberta Menchú y así me nació la conciencia* (1985; translated as *I, Rigoberta Menchú*).

REFERENCES:

René Prieto, *Miguel Angel Asturias' Archaeology of Return* (Cambridge: Cambridge University Press, 1993);

Angel Rama, *Transculturación narrativa en América Latina* (Mexico: Siglo XXI, 1982);

Julio Rodríguez-Luis, *Hermenéutica y praxis del indigenismo* (Mexico: Fondo de Cultura Economica, 1980).

— R.G.M. & P.S.

INDIGENOUS CULTURES

When one considers the demographic catastrophes that struck the Americas with the arrival of the Europeans, mostly due to epidemic diseases to which the natives had no resistance, it is notable that the indigenous peoples continue to constitute a substantial portion of the population in various countries. It is estimated that upon first contact with the Europeans the native peoples numbered seventeen million along the Andes and twelve million in lowland South America. Following the demographic collapse that occurred largely during the first century of the Spanish occupation, the surviving Indians assimilated to the European way of life, controlled by the Spanish priests and government officials, who also rapidly rewarded loyal Spanish subjects with grants of depopulated land for cultivation or mining. However, through strategies of assimilation and resistance indigenous peoples have persevered throughout five hundred years; their languages are the major cultural survivors, and they are the bridges to the future of the native peoples of South America. (See **Languages.**)

As can be seen by the numbers of Quechua and Guaraní speakers today, the indigenous languages with the best survival rates were those spoken by inhabitants of the mountains or the jungles. Colonizers tended to appropriate the coastal plains for themselves, liquidating the native populations and with them their languages. However, throughout the centuries the cultural resilience of indigenous peoples of the Americas has been remarkable when one takes into account demographic catastrophes, loss of lands and local political autonomy, the invasion of foreign technologies, agricultural practices and belief systems, and the devalued status accorded their cultures by national governments and fellow peoples. (See **Peoples and Races.**) Despite these factors, in South America the indigenous are still a majority of the population in Bolivia and a significant presence in Ecuador and Peru.

One may trace the indigenous preference for living in natural settings and their intimate connection with the land to the agriculturally based and highly developed precolonial indigenous societies. In South

An Aymara Indian woman weaving

America the most important indigenous civilization by the time the Spaniards arrived was that of the Incas. Their intensive agriculture, supplemented in part by hunting and gathering, created a way of life that depended on cultivation of the land for survival. With the arrival of the Europeans and their concept of private property, this way of life was deeply modified; however, the indigenous still living in rural areas revere nature as their provider and life-giving force, drawing also on Catholicism for a syncretism of deities. Various annual celebrations and festivities are held to honor and placate these deities, blending native elements in music and dance with more-formal Catholic traditions. The most impressive are those signaling the beginning of Lent, the immensely popular Carnival festivals that take place in various areas of South America, the more remarkable ones in Brazil, Bolivia, and northern Argentina. Participants practice with various groups throughout the year, creating an extensive repertoire of folk song and dance along with flamboyant and intricately designed costumes to celebrate their chosen historical, spiritual, or playful themes. Frequently, the participants also take a vow by which they must abide throughout Lent and at times throughout the year until the next Carnival, at which time they are either punished or rewarded as befits their cases.

The intimate relationship with nature is reflected in many of the crafts practiced by indigenous groups. Basketry is one of the more important arts and one that serves a variety of practical purposes. In lowland areas such as eastern Bolivia, long, slender palm leaves are

137

braided to form floor mats and sleeping mats; thicker mats serve as rafts. Various kinds of carrying baskets along with hammocks and fire fans are made from fresh-cut palm leaves. Palm straw is used by Patuso hat makers in Colombia. Leaf and grass fibers are used largely to make baskets and mats and in the tablelands in Quechua and Aymara territory to make hats. Peruvian natives of the Puna and those near Piura weave what have come to be known as Panama hats, using *paja taquilla* straw. Rushes and reeds that grow six to eight feet high and are used for walls, roofs, mattresses, rafts, and sails are valuable to the Aymara and Quechua who live in the region of Lake Titicaca in Peru and Bolivia. Natives in the Chaco area make huts of rush mats, sometimes used for sleeping or sitting. Roots and vines are also used for baskets and ropes.

Weaving, too, is practiced by various South American indigenous groups. Cotton was used for weaving by pre-Columbian Indians and is thought to have spread to various groups through Carib and Guaraní migration. Spinning is an extremely important part of the process, since fabric quality and durability depend largely on how well the yarn is spun. The Incas built suspension bridges of bark or fiber ropes that were spun together, two to three feet thick. Such bridges are still in use in certain areas, such as in Aymara territory. Among various Andean indigenous groups in Aymara, Quechua, and Chaco areas, wool and hair from llamas, alpacas, vicuñas, guanacos, and sheep are used to weave clothing, felted hats, hammocks, and blankets.

Pottery making is another important native craft and is practiced almost throughout the continent. Most South American pottery serves a practical purpose, as containers to prepare, serve, and store food and drink. Open bowls are found in all parts of South America where pottery is made. Ceramic forms other than containers include hollow and solid figurines, whistles, panpipes, and censers. Pottery was also used for ceremonial purposes and burial urns. Much of it represents the human condition: diseases, bodily functions, and social and sexual activities. After the arrival of the Europeans the art of pottery as an outlet for artistic or cosmological expression declined, especially the more ornate, ceremonial kind, which may reflect the diminishing of native cultural identity and pride that resulted from the European takeover. Somewhat ironically, today ornate pottery has been revived in part for foreign (including European) trade. However, the quality of pottery made for tourists is usually inferior to that of the pottery made for native purposes. (See **Indigenism in Art** and **Indigenism in Literature**.)

REFERENCES:

Eduardo H. Galeano, *Memory of Fire* (New York: Pantheon, 1985);

John E. Kicza, *The Indian in Latin American History: Resistance, Resilience, and Acculturation* (Wilmington, Del.: Scholarly Resources, 1993);

Julian Haynes Steward, ed., *Handbook of South American Indians,* volume 5 (Washington, D.C.: Smithsonian Institution, 1948).

— M.E.S. & P.S.

INFORMAL ABSTRACTION

Also called Informalism or Lyrical Abstraction, Informal Abstraction refers to the nongeometric abstract styles that emerged in art throughout South America during the 1950s. Informal Abstraction has antecedents in French and Spanish Informalism, and to a certain extent in North American Abstract Expressionism, but it often differs from these movements in its evocation, through colors and textures, of cultural meanings native to South America.

In Peru the path toward abstraction was prepared during the 1940s by an eclectic group of independent artists, among whom **Ricardo Grau** stands out. He acquired a solid artistic formation in Europe, worked in the figurative style of the School of Paris, and rejected the thematic approach of **Indigenism.** When he was appointed director of the Escuela Nacional de Bellas Artes in 1945, Grau instituted reforms later continued by Manuel Ugarte, to increase the school's artistic freedom. In spite of such progressive efforts, when **Fernando de Szyszlo** exhibited his abstract paintings for the first time in 1951, his work provoked a hostile reaction from the public and critics, who labeled it un-Peruvian and a tool of North American imperialism. In fact, de Szyszlo had not been influenced by the Abstract Expressionism of the United States so much as by French and Spanish Informalism. Furthermore, into his abstract work he successfully integrated the native myths and traditions of Peru. His example encouraged other abstract Peruvian artists such as Sabino Springett, Alberto Dávila, Emilio Rodríguez-Larraín, and Jorge Piqueras.

María Luisa Pacheco had a similar role in renovating the art of her native Bolivia and producing a type of Informal Abstraction with the power to evoke her homeland. Pacheco came in contact with postcubist figuration and Spanish Informalism while studying in Spain. After her return to La Paz in 1952, she cofounded the avant-garde Ocho Contemporáneos (Eight Contemporaries) group, whose objective was to renovate Bolivian art. Their 1953 exhibition in La Paz was attacked by many established Indigenist artists, but

Pacheco's later successes as an Informal Abstract artist in Latin America and New York encouraged other Bolivian abstract artists, such as Jorge Carrasco Núñez del Prado, Moisés Chire Barrientos, Oscar Pantoja, and Alfredo Da Silva.

In Ecuador the beginning of Informal Abstraction and the end of Indigenism occurred simultaneously during the war years with the arrival in Ecuador of foreign artists who worked in contemporary styles, such as Hans Michaelson, Lloyd Wulf, and Jan Schreuder. They became teachers of several artists who later turned to abstraction, including Araceli Gilbert, **Estuardo Maldonado, Enrique Tábara,** and Oswaldo Viteri. The first two exhibitions of abstract painting in Ecuador were in 1955, when Araceli Gilbert returned from Europe and exhibited works in a geometric abstract style, and in 1959, when Manuel Rendón exhibited semifigurative works in a style close to Informalism. Soon thereafter, many artists began to explore Informal Abstraction, including Aníbal Villacís, Tábara, and Viteri, who had become interested in Informalism while living in Spain. During the 1960s these and other artists formed the Grupo VAN (from *vanguard*), which exhibited at the Galería Siglo XX and issued a manifesto opposing institutionalized Indigenism. In 1968, when the Casa de la Cultura de Quito, headed by the leading indigenist **Oswaldo Guayasamín,** organized the First Quito Biennial, VAN organized its own Antibiennial in protest, and eventually artists and critics were forced to discuss openly and to accept new directions in Ecuadoran art.

In Argentina, Uruguay, and Chile, Informal Abstraction was introduced later than in the Andean area because of the strong influence of the **Taller Torres-García,** which rejected complete abstraction, and because of the emphasis on **Geometric Abstraction** favored by movements such as **Madí.** In fact, it was as a reaction against concrete and geometric styles that Informal Abstraction began in Argentina. It spread quickly during the late 1950s and 1960s, in spite of the critics' scorn, thanks to the activities of Mario Pucciarelli, **Kenneth Kemble,** Olga López, Alberto Greco, Fernando Maza, Luis Alberto Wells, Sarah Grilo, José Antonio Fernández-Muro, and Enrique Barilari, all of whom participated in numerous exhibitions. Their use of unorthodox materials eventually led to other movements, such as Arte Destructivo, **Otra Figuración, Pop Art, Assemblages,** and **Happenings.** In Uruguay the brothers Jorge and Carlos Paez Vilaró also worked with Informal Abstraction during the 1960s. In Chile the interest in this style began in 1960 with an exhibition of the work of several Spanish informalist artists and continued during 1962 and 1963, with the exhibitions of the Grupo Signo. This Informal

Abstract group included José Balmes, Gracia Barrios, Eduardo Martínez, and Alberto Pérez, all of whom, like the independent sculptor Carlos Ortuzar, opposed Geometric Abstract styles advocated by the Grupo Rectángulo. Initially, Ortuzar's work combined thick textures and pre-Columbian symbols; later he turned to **Conceptual Art,** blending sculpture with technology.

In Colombia Informal Abstraction was preceded by the abstract geometric styles of artists such as **Eduardo Ramírez Villamizar.** During the 1960s several artists worked with Informal Abstraction, such as Guillermo Wiedemann, Antonio Roda, Armando Villegas, and Judith Márquez, but later, with the exception of Wiedemann, they turned to figuration. **Alejandro Obregón,** one of the most important Colombian artists, also blended the abstract treatment of plastic elements with figuration, producing a semiabstract mode that is hard to categorize. Although Geometric Abstraction and **Kinetic Art** were stronger trends in Venezuela, Informal Abstraction was also represented there by several artists such as Luisa Richter, José María Cruxent, Mercedes Pardo, Humberto Jaime Sánchez, Angel Hurtado, Oswaldo Vigas, and Elsa Gramcko.

REFERENCES:

Félix Angel, "The Latin American Presence: Part I: The Abstract Spirit," in *The Latin American Spirit: Art and Artists in the United States, 1920–1970,* by Luis R. Cancel and others (New York: Bronx Museum of the Arts/Abrams, 1988), pp. 239–265;

Gilbert Chase, *Contemporary Art in Latin America: Painting, Graphic Art, Sculpture, Architecture* (New York: Free Press, 1970).

— F.B.N.

INSTITUTO SUPERIOR DE DANZA

The Instituto Superior de Danza of Venezuela provides training in various techniques and styles of contemporary dance. It also publishes the magazine *La danza* and sponsors the Festival de Jóvenes Coreógrafos (Young Choreographers' Festival). The festival has created an opportunity for choreographers and teachers from various countries to come together. The institute is supported by a local industrialist and dance aficionado. It has served as an incubator for rising young Venezuelan choreographers such as Luís Viana, Julie Barnsley, Carlos Orta, Abelardo Gameche, and Hercilia López, and for the companies **Acción Colectiva** and **Coreoarte.** The director of the institute is Carlos Paolillo, a noted dance journalist and researcher.

— N.D.B. & J.M.H.

Inti-Illimani performing for a crowd of workers

INTI-ILLIMANI

The most cosmopolitan and visible musical ensemble of the continuing **Nueva Canción** tradition, Inti-Illimani has remained in forced exile from Chile since the violent overthrow of the **Salvador Allende** government in 1973. Although Chilean in its composition, the ensemble has upheld the pan-Latin principle of Nueva Canción by performing music from a variety of musical cultures.

Beginning in 1967 as a student group, Inti-Illimani quickly attracted massive audiences of devoted fans in Chile. With the election of Allende, they became cultural ambassadors of the "New Chile" and were on a world tour when the government was overthrown. They have remained in exile in Rome ever

since. An extremely active group, Inti-Illimani has made many recordings and maintains a rigorous concert schedule. The group has appeared in more than forty-five countries on five continents, but their petitions to return to Chile have been denied.

REFERENCES:

Guillermo Barzuna, "De Atahualpa Yupanqui a Fito Páez: Génesis del oficio de cantor," *Escena,* Año 14, no. 30 (1992);

Gerard Béhague, "Popular Music in Latin America," *Studies in Latin American Popular Culture,* 5 (1986): 41–67;

Peter Manuel, *Popular Musics of the Non-Western World* (Oxford: Oxford University Press, 1988);

Albrecht Moreno, "Violeta Parra and La Nueva Canción chilena," *Studies in Latin American Popular Culture,* 5 (1986): 108–126.

— R.L.S.

J

ALFREDO JAAR

Alfredo Jaar (1956–), a Chilean **Conceptual Artist** of international recognition, was born in Chile and spent his childhood in Martinique. After returning to his native Santiago, he studied filmmaking at the Instituto Chileno-Norteamericano de Cultura and architecture at the Universidad de Chile. In 1982 Jaar moved to New York, where he produced a series of large installations combining his dual background in filmmaking and architecture. These complex works usually include his own photographs, light boxes reminiscent of minimal art sculptures, and a variety of objects such as mirrors, coins, and even water. The quiet elegance and slickness of Jaar's installations appeal to a public that has received a significant part of its visual education through sophisticated television and magazine commercials. However, Jaar effectively uses the strategies of advertisement to confront the viewers surreptitiously with serious political issues, such as the racial struggle in the United States, the effects of toxic waste exported from the First World to underdeveloped nations, and the plight of those who cross the Rio Grande in hope of a better or safer future in the United States.

When preparing an artwork, Jaar travels to the site represented in his piece and takes hundreds of photographs, from which he later selects only a few. For his installation *Oro en la mañana* (1986; Gold in the Morning) Jaar traveled to Brazil's Sierra Pelada and observed the life of the miners for several weeks. This installation includes large light boxes showing Jaar's photographic transparencies, which are placed in marginal areas of the wall: on the bottom, resting on the floor; in the corner; near the ceiling. In front of one of the light boxes on the floor there is a square bed of black nails with a smaller square of gold nails in the center. This piece uses the strategies of Conceptual Art and presents the viewer with a series of visual fragments that refer to an idea or concept that lies outside the confines of the work of art. In this case the symbolic components of the piece refer to the marginalization and poverty of the gold miners in the Sierra Pelada and their struggle for survival and perhaps a chance at prosperity. Jaar finances his installation projects through grants, such as the Guggenheim Fellowship (1985), the National Endowment for the Arts (1987), and the Deutscher Akademischer Austauschdienst Berliner Kunstlerprogram (1989).

REFERENCE:

Madeleine Grynsztejn, *Alfredo Jaar* (La Jolla, Cal.: La Jolla Museum of Contemporary Art, 1990).

—F.B.N.

VICTOR JARA

One of the most dedicated and popular leaders of the **Nueva Canción** movement in Chile, Victor Jara (1938–1973) was born in southern Chile, where, while working in the fields with his father and listening to his mother sing, he learned firsthand the rich folk traditions of his heritage. Jara was a successful theater director at the University of Chile in the 1960s, and his work was taken on tours throughout Latin America, the United States, and Great Britain. The developing song movement led by **Violeta Parra** captured his attention in the late 1960s, and he began to express his identity in the liberating ambience of Nueva Canción. Violeta Parra's initial interests were focused on the heritage of Chilean folksong; musical statements of a political nature evolved later. Jara soon became the master of political

141

Victor Jara performing above the ruins of Machu Picchu, Peru, July 1973 (photograph by Mariano Sanchez Macedo)

criticism through his music. Both Parra and Jara objected to the cultural invasion of the imported and trivial commercial music that dominated Chile to the exclusion of its national legacy. Jara's militancy targeted the plight of the nation's poor and the working class and reinforced their dignity. As the 1970 elections approached, Jara's music tended to celebrate the ideology of political figures associated with the radical left. During the ensuing presidency of Salvador Allende, Jara and others celebrated the idea of a new democracy, a new Chile. Their euphoria was short-lived; Allende's government was sacked in a military coup led by Gen. **Augusto Pinochet** on 11 September 1973. Jara and thousands of others were immediately arrested. Many "disappeared," and some were imprisoned; Jara's militancy was repaid with torture, and execution on 13 September.

REFERENCES:

Guillermo Barzuna, "De Atahualpa Yupanqui a Fito Paez: Génesis del Oficio de Cantor," *Escena*, Año 14, no. 30 (1992): 55–65;

Gerard Béhague, "Popular Music in Latin America," *Studies in Latin American Popular Culture*, 5 (1986);

Joan Jara, *Victor — An Unfinished Song* (London: Cape, 1983);

Peter Manuel, *Popular Musics of the Non-Western World* (Oxford: Oxford University Press, 1988);

Albrecht Moreno, "Violeta Parra and La Nueva Canción Chilena," *Studies in Latin American Popular Culture*, 5 (1986).
                                                              — R.L.S.

JOROPO

Recognized as one of the most typical folk dance/songs of Venezuela, the joropo is also important in the eastern plains region of Colombia. Venezuelan sources indicate that the joropo descended from the Spanish *fandango,* but there are clear African influences noticeable in the pronounced hip movements. It has also been claimed to be the same dance as the Colombian *pasillo,* a shortened **vals** (waltz) movement of Spanish origin, but no longer extant in Spain. The dance is accompanied by a simple melody with frequent pauses in the music filled by the rhythmic shuffling of the dancers' feet; this dance accents the movement of the feet. If the dancer wears shoes instead of the traditional toeless, rope-soled sandals, the steps are transformed into a brisk **zapateo.** The dance is performed by male-female couples in an open waltz position, with frequent breaks for the ostentatious solos of the man. For the most part, the man and the woman hold hands while facing each other; in a less common variation, they stand side by side, crossing arms to hold hands. An eighteenth-century description of the "xoropo" states that in some places this dance was one of extreme and distasteful gestures, with sweeping, stamping movements of the feet that were repugnant to people of intelligence. In addition, it was sacrilegiously danced at funeral wakes and over cadavers in homage to the dead. From this heritage the joropo came to be associated with festive occasions involving music, singing, and dancing.

Currently, the joropo is a popular genre of the northern rim of Hispanic South America. Its musical constant is a standard, fast 3/4 meter. Beyond the constancy of the meter, there are more than thirty "golpes," or rhythmic patterns, in addition to improvised variations that can be developed by accompanying instruments. Many of the golpes bear the names of animals or plants of the plains region, while others have names referring to different regions or to individual artists. The accompaniments provide strong contrapuntal accents in cross rhythms with the melody, which may sustain sung texts of quatrains in eight-syllable lines. Joropos may feature three or more contrasting musical sections in which different dance steps are performed: *valsiao* (waltz); *escobillao* (sweeping movement of the feet); and *zapateado* (stamping, tapping). Typical instruments accompanying the joropo include the **bandola,** the bandolín, the *capachos* (**maracas**), the **cuatro,** and occasionally the harp.

REFERENCES:

Octavio Marulanda, *El folclor de Colombia: Práctica de la identidad cultural* (Bogotá: Artestudio Editores, 1984);

Luis Felipe Ramón y Rivera, *La música folklórica de Venezuela,* second edition (Caracas: Monte Avila Editores C.A., 1977).
                                          — R.L.S., J.M.H. & N.D.B.

K

LEANDRO KATZ

Work in literature, theater, filmmaking, and **Conceptual Art** has characterized the career of Argentinean Leandro Katz (1942–). Katz began his artistic career in literature, first studying at the Universidad de Buenos Aires and later publishing several books of poetry, including *Puerto verano* (1960; Port Summer) and *Poemas* (1962; Poems), as well as the novel *Es una ola* (1968; It's a Wave) and an artist's book *Self-Hypnosis* (1975). From 1961 to 1965 Katz lived in Peru, Ecuador, and Mexico and finally settled in New York, where he studied at the Pratt Graphic Arts Center. In the early 1970s he established his own publishing house, called The Vanishing Rotating Triangle and participated in Charles Ludlam's Ridiculous Theatrical Company as an actor and a photographer. During this period Katz also began to explore the possibilities of film, eventually producing more than ten experimental and documentary films, which have been exhibited around the world. Among these are *Splits* (1978), based on **Jorge Luis Borges**'s short story "Emma Zunz"; *Metropotamia* (1982), designed to be projected by two synchronized projectors on the two-faceted surfaces of a zigzag-folded screen; and *El espejo en la luna* (1992; Mirror on the Moon), also inspired by a Borges short story, "The Aleph."

Katz's early conceptual installations were an extension of his interest in language. His *Word Column* (1970) consists of a large typewriter with a scroll typed with word lists. In later pieces he related natural objects, such as slightly varying achatinella shells or images of the changing faces of the moon, to letters of the alphabet. In the 1980s Katz produced several multimedia installations that questioned the nature of language and of cultural representations in more political terms: *The Judas Window* (1982) and *Orpheus Beheaded* (1983–1984) are examples. Since then he has worked on several long-term series. In *The Catherwood Project* Katz contrasts his own photographs of Mayan ruins with Frederick Catherwood's drawings of the same sites in order to explore issues of colonialist representation. In *El día que me quieras* (The Day You Love Me), based on a famous photograph of **Ernesto "Che" Guevara**'s dead body being exhibited to the press by the Bolivian armed forces, Katz reveals and subverts the manipulation of revolutionary idealism by the media and the state.

REFERENCE:

Susana Torruella Leval, "The Catherwood Project by Leandro Katz," *Review: Latin-American Literature and Arts* (January–June 1990): 10–13.

—F.B.N.

KENNETH KEMBLE

Kenneth Kemble (1923–) was one of the first artists to introduce **Informal Abstraction** in Argentina. He studied art in Buenos Aires and later in Paris during the early 1950s. After his return to Buenos Aires in 1956, Kemble rejected the emphasis on elegance and technique of **Geometric Abstraction** and worked simultaneously in three informal abstract styles: collages of unorthodox materials chosen for their tactile qualities, such as tree bark and used fabric; compositions of black shapes over white backgrounds, evocative of Japanese calligraphy; and large gestural paintings featuring thick impastos and graffiti. In 1959 Kemble participated with a small group of artists in the first exhibitions of Informal Abstraction. In spite of the negative critical response this group received, Informal Abstraction soon became fashionable, and many artists were forced to seek more-radical ways of expressing their rebellious opposition to any conventional or accepted styles. In 1960 Kemble, who was also an effective spokesman for radical art, organized Arte Destructivo (Destructive Art), an exhibition that featured half-destroyed ordinary objects and scandalized the public and the critics, paving the way for art movements such as **Pop Art, Assemblages, and Happenings.**

During the 1960s Kemble's work contrasted different materials and techniques, as in *Pequeño teatrito* (1963; Tiny Little Theater), which includes decorative paper, thick impastos, and geometric shapes. This emphasis on the fragmentary continued in the 1970s, when Kemble juxtaposed irregular pieces of canvas and paper which had been prepainted using different techniques; an example is his *Ocaso* (1971; Sunset). In 1962 Kemble was appointed professor of painting at the Escuela Superior de Bellas Artes Ernesto de la Cárcova; he later became the director of the Museo de Bellas Artes in the city of Luján.

REFERENCE:

Jorge López Anaya, "Kemble," in *Pintores argentinos del siglo XX,* no. 41 (Buenos Aires: Centro Editor de América Latina, 1981).

— F.B.N.

KINETIC ART

Kinetic Art takes the emphasis on virtual or optical motion of Op Art one step further, making real movement an integral part of the artwork. The first mobile sculptures were Marcel Duchamp's *Rotoreliefs* (1920), whose rotating, staggered glass panels produced the image of a solid circle, and Naum Gabo's *Kinetic Construction* (1920), in which a straight metal rod vibrates, becoming a luminous curvilinear space. These pieces were dependent on small, noisy engines, however, which discouraged artists from working with motion. In the 1930s Alexander Calder, from the United States, found a more elegant solution: his sculptures were mobiles activated simply by circulating air. In spite of Calder's pioneering work, Kinetic Art was not successful in the United States, but it enjoyed considerable support among European and Latin American artists working in Paris, such as the Swiss Jean Tinguely, the Argentineans **Gyula Kosice** and **Julio Le Parc,** the Chilean Matilde Pérez, and the Venezuelan **Jesús Rafael Soto.** During the late 1950s many artists interested in Kinetic Art combined the playfulness of Duchamp with the constructivist approach of Gabo and Calder. While Tinguely satirized technology through his whimsical self-destructive machines, Pérez, Soto, Le Parc, and Kosice preferred **Geometric Abstraction** and Constructivism as their points of departure. Most of these artists participated in the main international exhibi-

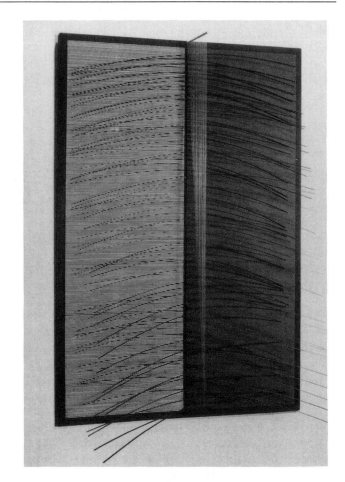

Oliva et negro (1966; Olive and Black), by Jesús Rafael Soto (Museum of Modern Art, Inter-American Fund, 1967)

tions of Op and Kinetic Art, *The Responsive Eye* (1964) in New York and *Lumière et Mouvement* (1967; Light and Movement) in Paris.

Kosice, cofounder of the Arturo and **Madí** groups, produced his first kinetic piece in 1944, the articulated wood sculpture *Royï,* inspired by **Joaquín Torres-García**'s modular toys. During the 1950s Kosice began his series of Plexiglas *Hydrosculptures,* which combine light, bubbles, movement, and sound with small motors that provide a light source and circulate water and oxygen. Similarly, Le Parc, who in the early 1960s participated in the Groupe de Recherche d'Art Visuel or GRAV (Group for Research in Visual Art), also experimented with light and movement. In Le Parc's *Mural de luz continua: Formas en contorsión* (1966; Mural of Continuous Light: Forms in Contortion) long, narrow metal plates are continuously contorted by electric motors to reflect the strategically placed spotlights in an ever-changing pattern that transforms the surrounding space. Matilde Pérez, who admired Le Parc's art, also worked in Paris during the early 1960s with sculptures combining movement and light sources powered by small motors.

Soto, like fellow Venezuelans **Alejandro Otero** and **Carlos Cruz-Diez,** became interested in the optical aspects of Geometric Abstraction in the 1950s. He went beyond optical motion to produce kinetic sculptures capable of both real movement and dynamic optical effects. In his *Oliva y negro* (1966; Olive and Black) the suspended metal strips move in front of a backboard painted with thin, parallel lines, producing intense moiré patterns. Le Parc and Soto were also interested in creating art capable of involving the public directly. GRAV's ludic activities *Day in the Street* (1966) and Soto's *Penetrable* (1969) exemplify the way Kinetic Art opened the doors to more participatory art forms such as **Pop Art, Assemblages and Happenings.**

REFERENCES:

Aracy Amaral, "Abstract Constructivist Trends in Argentina, Brazil, Venezuela, and Colombia," in *Latin American Artists of the Twentieth Century,* edited by Waldo Rasmussen, Fatima Bercht, and Elizabeth Ferrer (New York: Museum of Modern Art, 1993), pp. 86–99;

Daniel Wheeler, "Op, Kinetic, and Light Art," in his *Art Since Mid-Century: 1945 to the Present* (Englewood Cliffs, N.J.: Prentice-Hall / New York & Paris: Vendome Press, 1991), pp. 230–242.

— F.B.N.

EDUARDO KINGMAN

Eduardo Kingman Riofrío (1913–) is one of the leading Indigenist artists of Ecuador. He studied at the Escuela Nacional de Bellas Artes with the symbolist Víctor Mideros and in 1936 won the Premio Mariano Aguilera, the highest artistic award in Ecuador. During the 1930s, inspired by the social and artistic ideas of Peruvians **José Mariátegui** and **José Sabogal** and by the work of the Mexican Muralists, Kingman identified himself with **Indigenism** and left Quito to live among the native Ecuadorans who inspired his art. In his works Kingman focused on the human figure, depicted with unusually large hands, to describe the traditions and the suffering of native Ecuadorans.

In 1939 Kingman went to New York to study with the Ecuadoran **Camilo Egas**. There the two artists were commissioned for the mural decoration of the Ecuadoran Pavilion at the 1939 New York World's Fair. After returning to Quito in 1940, Kingman founded and directed the Galería Caspicara, where he was soon joined by other Indigenist artists, such as **Oswaldo Guayasamín.** In 1945 Kingman worked for the San Francisco Museum of Art on a scholarship; and after his return to Ecuador in 1947, he was appointed

director of the Museo de Arte Nacional. He later became director of the Patrimonio Artístico Nacional. During the 1950s Kingman's work became increasingly abstract.

REFERENCES:

Jacqueline Barnitz, *Abstract Currents in Ecuadorian Art* (New York: Center for Inter-American Relations, 1977);

Gilbert Chase, *Contemporary Art in Latin America* (New York: Free Press, 1970), pp. 113–114.

— F.B.N.

KLOAKA

The name of the Kloaka (Sewer) group of Peruvian poets of the early 1980s echoes Jack Kerouac's *The Subterraneans* (1958) and alludes to their identity as denizens of the underground. The most visible poet of the group was Roger Santiváñez (1956–), whose poetic persona has been compared to a character in Dennis Hopper's movie *Easy Rider* (1969). Santiváñez's poetry bears out this comparison to the extent that it is influenced by the style of the Beat Generation.

— R.G.M.

GYULA KOSICE

During the 1940s the Argentinean artist Gyula Kosice, born Fernando Falik (1924–), was the cofounder of the **Madí** group and later developed what he called hydrokinetic sculptures and hydrospatial architecture. Born in Hungary, Kosice was raised and educated in Argentina, where he studied art at the Academias Libres in Buenos Aires. In 1944 he joined the Arturo group, among whose objectives were to produce abstract works and explore the possibility of making movable sculptures, such as Kosice's *Röyi* (1944), inspired by **Joaquín Torres-García**'s modular wooden toys. Arturo eventually divided into two groups, the **Asociación de Arte Concreto-Invención** and the Movimiento de Arte Concreto-Invención, cofounded by Kosice and **Carmelo Arden Quin**. This last group organized three exhibitions in 1945 and the following year adopted the name Madí, a word perhaps invented by Kosice, who also wrote the "Madí Manifesto," describing his and Madí's objectives: to produce an art with freer compositional structures than those demanded by concrete art, and with a stronger emphasis on intuition and motion. Kosice responded with works such as *Estructura de aluminio Madí no. 3* (1946; *Madí Aluminum Structure No. 3*), made of neon lights, which shows his radical use of unorthodox materials. He par-

Gyula Kosice, Manuel Mujica Láinez, and Jorge Romero Brest

ticipated in Madí's exhibitions at the Instituto Francés de Estudios Superiores in Buenos Aires and the Salon des Réalités Nouvelles in Paris. In 1947 Kosice broke with Arden Quin and founded a new movement called Madinemsor, which published the magazine *Arte Madí Universal* until 1954.

During the 1950s Kosice moved to Paris and experimented with large-scale Plexiglas hydrokinetic sculptures, such as *Hidroescultura* (1970; *Hydrosculpture*), which often combined electric lighting and transparent bubblelike shapes, with water trapped or circulating through them. His purpose was to transform the sculptural medium into a living organism. Since the 1970s Kosice has developed descriptive designs and acrylic maquettes for one of his most radical projects, the Hydrospatial City, a scientifically based utopian plan for a city built with crystallized water in orbit around the earth.

REFERENCE:

Rafael Squirru, *Kosice* (Buenos Aires: Gaglianone, 1990).

— F.B.N.

L

LIBERTAD LAMARQUE

Known as *La Reina del Tango* (The Queen of Tango), Libertad Lamarque (1908–) began her singing career in the local theaters of Rosario de Santa Fe, Argentina, at the age of eight. At sixteen she moved to Buenos Aires and worked as an actress in the National Theater. Within the next two years she made her singing debut on radio with *La cumparsita* and in the National Theater with *El tatuaje,* both **tangos.** At the age of twenty she became an exclusive recording artist with RCA Argentina and within five years had recorded nearly one hundred songs.

Lamarque's extensive film career began in 1928 with *Caminito* (Little Road). In 1932 she starred in the first sound film made in Argentina, *Tango,* a film that featured many popular tango artists, including Azucena Maizani, Mercedes Simone, Osvaldo Fresedo, Edgardo Donato, Pedro Maffia, and Juan de Dios Filiberto. Other film successes include *El alma del bandoneón* (1934; The Soul of the **Bandoneón**), *Ayúdame a vivir* (1935; Help Me Live), and *Madreselva* (1938; Honeysuckle). An unpleasant experience during her film career involved Eva Duarte (later **Eva Perón,** the second wife of **Juan Domingo Perón**): an unfriendly relationship developed between them while filming *La cabalgata del circo* (The Circus Cavalcade) in 1945. Following additional films and highly successful concert tours throughout Latin America, Lamarque returned to Argentina in 1948 with expectations of continuing her career, but by order of Eva Perón she was denied permission to work as an artist. In 1949 she returned to New York and eventually chose to reside in Mexico.

In addition to her fame as "Queen of the Tango," Libertad Lamarque was also beloved for her interpretations of **boleros.** Among her most famous are "Te sigo esperando" (I'm Still Waiting for You), "O . . . " (Or . . .), "Volveré" (I Shall Return), and "Y . . . " (And . . .).

REFERENCES:

Pedro Malavet Vega, *Cincuenta años no es nada* (San Juan, Puerto Rico: Editora Corripio, 1986);

Jaime Rico Salazar, *Cien años de boleros* (Bogotá: Centro Editorial de Estudios Musicales, 1987).

—R.L.S.

LANGUAGES

Spanish is the official language of all the countries of South America save Brazil (Portuguese), French Guiana, Surinam (Dutch), and Guyana (English). In one or two countries (most notably, Paraguay) indigenous languages share official status with Spanish. Given the vast expanse of Spanish-speaking territory in the Americas, what is remarkable is the extent to which speakers of that language have the same linguistic habits. Among educated urban peoples (including those in Spain itself) the level of mutual intelligibility is high. Typically, the greatest differences are found among isolated, poorly educated peoples lacking communication with the outside.

At the time of the conquest, Spain was only beginning to cohere linguistically, having previously consisted of several largely independent kingdoms united at times in their struggle to expel Spain's own invaders, the "Moors." Thus, the speech of those who went to the Americas, people who came from various parts of Spain and who often were uneducated, was varied. In modern Spanish America it is possible to find many linguistic features that are antiquated or have long ago disappeared on the Iberian Peninsula. In addition, indigenous languages have had a marked influence on American Spanish, especially on its vocabulary (some indigenous words have even found their way, via Spanish, into English; *cigar(ette)* is an example). In some countries immigration in significant numbers from other countries, such as that of Italians into Argentina, has also been a factor in the evolution of dialects. Finally, there are a few cases of linguistic anachronisms, such as the survival of Welsh-speaking communities in Patagonia.

Determining how many dialects of Spanish there are depends on how finely one makes distinctions. The much-used classification done by the famous Dominican researcher Pedro Henríquez Ureña gives five; a later classification by José Pedro Rona lists twenty-three; neither is definitive. For present purposes, a number of illustrative observations may be made: many differences are related to pronunciation and particularly to the pronunciation of consonants; vowels tend to disappear, and consonants tend to be more precise in Mexico and in Andean areas (a phenomenon that has been attributed to indigenous influence and even to altitude); in lowland areas, especially around the Caribbean, the opposite is often the case; a large part of Argentina and Uruguay, together with certain parts of Central America, use antiquated and much-modified pronoun and verb forms (collectively known as *voseo*); in Bolivia, Colombia, Ecuador, and Peru the Spanish spoken is quite similar to that of Spain. In general, many Spanish speakers are able to guess the origins of a Chilean, a person from the Río de la Plata region, one from the Andean countries, one from the Caribbean and the areas bordering on it, a Central American, and a Mexican.

Spanish American countries have their own official national Academies of the Language, modeled on the one in Spain and in some ways more conservative, charged with respecting national differences but also preserving linguistic cohesion between the many territories of the Spanish-speaking world; through their publications, these academies give formal recognition to changes in the language. The achievements of Spanish American writers in the latter half of the twentieth century have greatly enhanced the position of American Spanish.

Although indigenous languages sometimes are considered official along with Spanish (Quechua, Guaraní), it is almost impossible to produce accurate numbers of speakers who belong to specific indigenous linguistic groups. Collecting such statistics is hampered by various factors, among them the inaccessibility and isolation of some communities and the difficulties of producing census lists when such a task is viewed by many people as a tool for government conscription, taxation, discrimination, and abuse. Under these circumstances, Quechua speakers, for instance, may not identify themselves as such since that would reveal Indian ethnicity and could leave them vulnerable to discriminatory treatment. For these reasons many of the numbers cited below should be considered estimates.

The most far-reaching of the lowland languages is Tupi-Guaraní, spoken in one of its many variant forms from the Guianas down to northern Argentina. Guaraní is by far the dominant variety. Unlike most other indigenous languages, Guaraní, at least, is respected in Paraguay, where 90 percent of the population speaks the language. Paraguay is the most bilingual country in South America, largely due to the efforts of Jesuit missionaries during the seventeenth and eighteenth centuries. The Guaraní that is spoken in the capital, Asunción, is modified by Spanish and is called Yopará. The number of the indigenous Guaraní is estimated at 40,000 out of 3 million Paraguayans; however, since most Paraguayans speak Guaraní, this number may not reflect an accurate count.

In the highlands the most extensive language is Quechua, spoken by about 8 million people in territories extending over three thousand kilometers of mountain ranges from southern Colombia to northern Chile and central Argentina. Quechua is classified into eight dialects. Originally the language of the Incas, its classical form is considered to be that of the former central capital of the Inca Empire, Cuzco. Quechua is the most widely spoken indigenous language in South America.

Around Lake Titicaca, bordering Peru and Bolivia, Aymara is spoken by about 500,000 people. Between Quechua and Aymara, it is estimated that the indigenous number 2.5 million out of a total population of 5.7 million in Bolivia and 3.5 million out of 16.6 million in Peru. In southern Chile among the Araucanian and Mapuche Indians it is estimated that 250,000 speak Mapuche. In northern South America variants of the Carib family are spoken. In lowland Colombia about 20,000 out of 25 million are considered native speakers; more are to be found in the Guianas (16,000 out of 1.35 million), Venezuela (98,000 out of 15 million), and northeastern Brazil. Arawak is spoken in one of its many forms in the west of the Amazon basin and nearer the Andes.

REFERENCES:

Rubén del Rosario, *El español de América* (Sharon, Conn.: Troutman Press, 1970);

Alonso Zamora Vicente, *Dialectología española* (Madrid: Editorial Gredos, 1974).

— P.S. & M.E.S.

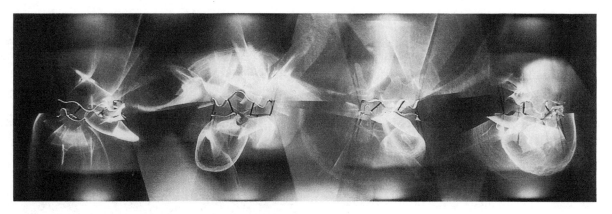

Mural de luz continua: Formas en contorsión (1966; Mural of Continuous Light: Forms in Contortion), by Julio Le Parc (Fundación Museo de Bellas Artes, Caracas)

JULIO LE PARC

The Argentinean artist Julio Le Parc (1928–) was a leading practitioner of **Kinetic Art,** also working with **Geometric Abstraction.** Le Parc studied art in Buenos Aires at the Escuela Nacional de Bellas Artes and later joined the Teatro de los Independientes, with which he was involved until the mid 1950s, when he returned to painting. In 1958 he received a scholarship from the French government to study in Paris, where he befriended the well-known Op artist Victor Vasarely and soon had the sponsorship of the Denise René Gallery, which supported radical and innovative art. Le Parc was then working in a Geometric Abstract style that showed his interest in the Argentinean **Asociación de Arte Concreto-Invención** and **Madí** movements and in the work of Vasarely. His paintings feature color progressions and simple geometric shapes that produced optical effects.

From 1960 to 1969 Le Parc participated in the Groupe de Recherche d'Art Visuel (Visual Art Research Group), or GRAV, which also included two of his friends from Buenos Aires, the Argentinean Horacio García Rossi and the Spaniard Francisco Sobrino, as well as the French artists Joel Stein, François Morellet, and Yvaral (who was Vasarely's son). GRAV's objective was to produce anonymous and collective art and emphasize the democratic appeal of an art based on optical perception. Le Parc contributed to the group with his mobiles, such as *Móvil transparente continuo* (1960; Continuous Transparent Mobile), whose small square metal plates are suspended from threads over a changing light, which they reflect when moved by aleatory forces. A similar concern underscores his series *Continuos luminosos* (Luminous Continuous), in works such as *Mural de luz continua: Formas en contorsión* (1966; Mural of Continuous Light: Forms in Contortion), featuring lights focused on narrow

metal plates that are twisted and turned by small motors, reflecting an ever-changing pattern of light and shadow on the white support. GRAV also sought the active participation of the viewer and organized installations of kinetic pieces which could be manipulated directly by the visitors. In addition Le Parc organized a series of art experiences: for instance, *Una jornada en la calle* (1966; Day in the Street), which took place in the streets of Paris; passers-by were invited to participate in activities such as walking with large square weights attached to their feet or wearing glasses that distorted vision in unusual ways. The active participation of the public connects this art with **Pop Art, Assemblages, and Happenings.**

In 1966 Le Parc won the Grand Prize for Painting at the Venice Biennial, an event which signaled the international acceptance of such radical art. Yet this award disturbed GRAV's ideal of collective and anonymous work, and a year or two later the group dissolved. Afterward, Le Parc returned to painting, and in works such as *Modulación 879* (1986; Modulation 879) he continued to explore issues of optical perception through methodical combinations of color, forms, and representations of simple geometric volumes.

REFERENCE:

Aracy Amaral, "Abstract Constructivist Trends in Argentina, Brazil, Venezuela, and Colombia," in *Latin American Artists of the Twentieth Century,* edited by Waldo Rasmussen, Fatima Bercht, and Elizabeth Ferrer (New York: Museum of Modern Art, 1993), pp. 86–99.

— F.B.N.

LIBERATION THEOLOGY

A movement within the Catholic and other Christian churches beginning in the mid 1960s and designed to make Christianity more relevant to social and political issues, liberation theology advocated political activism and radical social change. Liberation theologians, often at odds with ecclesiastical authorities, emphasized biblical motifs that could be interpreted as socially liberating (such as the escape of Israel from Egypt or the promise of a Kingdom of God that the oppressed would inherit) and integrated Marxist political theory with traditional Christian dogma. For liberation theologians, conditions of abject poverty constituted an "institutional sin" and had to be removed before the masses could have a significant relationship with God. The Peruvian theologian Gustavo Gutiérrez was one of the founders of the movement. Nicaraguan poet and priest Ernesto Cardenal is closely identified with the tenets of liberation theology in Latin America, especially through the founding of a religious commune in Solentiname (an island in Lake Nicaragua), where the Scriptures were read and discussed by humble fishermen in terms relevant to their everyday lives.

REFERENCE:

Rosino Gibellini, *Frontiers of Theology in Latin America* (New York: Orbis, 1979).

— R.G.M.

Luis Oyarzún, Enrique Lihn, and Jorge Palacios, early 1950s

ENRIQUE LIHN

Enrique Lihn (1929–1988) was the leading Chilean poet of the generation after **Nicanor Parra,** with whom he shares a demystified approach to the poet's métier and an important place in contemporary Latin American poetry.

Lihn's first important work was *La pieza oscura* (1963; The Dark Room), an existential poetic cycle in which the poet explores the relation between memory and poetic language and in which the theme of childhood's end stands out with particular poignancy. The collection also includes a poem denouncing the 1961 Bay of Pigs invasion of Cuba, a text that foreshadows many of the political poems Lihn wrote in subsequent years and his book *Escrito en Cuba* (1969; Written in Cuba).

In *La musiquilla de las pobres esferas* (1969; The Tune of the Ragged Spheres) Lihn addresses the dilemma of the contemporary poet and rejects the visionary poetry of his Romantic and Symbolist precursors for the sake of a modest poetic style firmly rooted on the little truths of everyday life: "I'm sick of that Alchemy of the Word, / poetry, let's get down back to earth." Two beliefs conspire in the poet's sometimes nostalgic, sometimes sarcastic repudiation of the grand poetic fictions of precursors such as **Pablo Neruda** and

Vicente Huidobro. One is the guilty conscience of a poet for whom poetry must be the testimony of the real and not the fabrication of myths; the other is Lihn's conviction that poetry will not transform history: "They [young poets] can laugh at magic safely enough / yet believe in a poem's a song's utility / A new world arises without any one of us. . . ." And yet for all of Lihn's demystification of poetry the collection includes "Porque escribí" (Because I Wrote), a stirring and passionate defense of the poet's vocation.

El Paseo Ahumada (1983; Ahumada Mall) includes Lihn's most compelling social poetry. The title refers to a pedestrian mall in downtown Santiago designed to showcase the prosperity brought about by the regime of Gen. **Augusto Pinochet.** But in 1981 the Chilean economy was devastated by a severe recession so that by 1983, 20 percent of the Chilean workforce was unemployed and another half-million people were subsisting on government-financed minimum-employment programs. Thus, the mall is a perverse symbol, a "Grand Theatre of national and popular cruelty," as the author wrote in his prologue to *El Paseo Ahumada,* "where all the tricks of survival are practiced. . . . The show begins when you arrive and doesn't stop when you leave. And we are all its co-authors, actors, and spectators." Lihn here refers to the peddlers, beggars, and prostitutes who try to eke out a living in Ahumada Mall under the watchful eye of the police. One of them is the "Penguin," a deformed street musician who becomes the addressee of several of the poems in the collection. The book originally appeared in tabloid form, and the poems' titles were made to look like sensational headlines.

Lihn's other major work of the same year, *Al bello aparecer de este lucero* (1983; Upon This Star Fairly Dawning), is a celebration of erotic love and of the poetry that through the ages has sung of love between man and woman. This was Lihn's only book to be originally published in the United States.

Enrique Lihn also wrote experimental novels such as *El arte de la palabra* (1980; The Art of Words). In 1966 he won the **Casa de las Américas** Prize in Cuba for *Poesía de paso* (Occasional Poetry). His poetry is best known to the American public through the New Directions anthology published in 1978 with the title *The Dark Room and Other Poems*.

REFERENCE:
Pedro Lastra, *Conversaciones con Enrique Lihn* (Xalapa, Mexico: Centro de Investigaciones Lingüístico-Literarias, Instituto de Investigaciones Humanísticas, Universidad Veracruzana, 1980).

— R.G.M.

LITERATURA NEGRA

Literatura Negra is a term applied to hard-boiled detective fiction, as opposed to the classic "closed room" mystery associated with Edgar Allan Poe, Agatha Christie, G. K. Chesterton, and Arthur Conan Doyle. After its heyday in the 1930s and 1940s in the United States, the hard-boiled genre made a strong showing in Argentina in the 1970s in the work of writers such as Mempo Giardinelli, Juan Carlos Martini, **Ricardo Piglia, Osvaldo Soriano,** and the Uruguayan Hiber Conteris. The epithet *negra* (black or dark) connotes the sordid social ambiance depicted in many of these crime stories. Its currency in Spanish probably derives from French, since the publisher Gallimard had issued the American classics of hard-boiled fiction in French under the collective rubric of *Série Noire.* In the 1970s the Argentinean publisher Editorial Tiempo Contemporáneo issued its own *Serie Negra* under the direction of Ricardo Piglia. Spanish-language translations of Dashiell Hammett, Raymond Chandler, and John MacDonald were widely available in cheap editions in Argentina and elsewhere long before the 1970s. The rebirth of the genre in Argentina coincided

with the period of the **Guerra Sucia** (Dirty War). The most significant manifestations of the private-eye genre in the Southern Cone use crime detection as a heuristic device to explore a society subjected to political repression and state terrorism. (See **Detective Fiction.**)

REFERENCE:
Mempo Giardinelli, *El género negro,* 2 volumes (Mexico: Universidad Autónoma Metropolitana, 1984).

— R.G.M.

MIGUEL LITTÍN

In 1969 Chilean director Miguel Littín (circa 1935–) released his best-known movie, *El chacal de Nahueltoro* (The Jackal of Nahueltoro), a true story of a man who murdered a homeless woman and her five children in an act of violence and drunkenness. The protagonist, played by **Nelson Villagra,** is arrested, put in prison, and executed.

During the presidency of **Salvador Allende** (1970–1973), Littín was named director of Chile Films, which concentrated on documentaries from archives and photographs but did not produce any feature-length films. Littín made his next film, *La tierra prometida* (1974; The Promised Land), which won the Prix Sadoul, outside the official structures of Chile Films, although the sound was made in the laboratories there. *La tierra prometida* extended the political focus of his previous work by contrasting state religion and the religion of the poor; the lead was again played by Villagra. Because of financial problems, Littín made his high-budget, internationalist, Third World epic *Actas de Marusia* (1975; Letters from Marusia) in Mexico. This film deals with a massacre that took place in Marusia, a once-British-owned nitrate mine in the north of Chile. With its portrayal of working-class mobilization and politicization, strike-breaking, and foreign imperialist influence, the film is meant as an analogy to the circumstances that led to the coup by **Augusto Pinochet**. One of the self-confessed main aims of Littín's work is to salvage popular culture and traditions, restoring their force and significance. Like **Jorge Sanjinés,** Littín strove to rescue history and turn it, through the medium of film, into an authentic record of the people's struggle.

REFERENCES:
Julianne Burton, ed., *Cinema and Social Change in Latin America: Conversations with Latin American Filmmakers* (Austin: University of Texas Press, 1986);
Michael Chanan, ed., *Chilean Cinema* (London: BFI, 1976).

— S.M.H.

Chilean filmmakers Miguel Littin, Héctor Rios, and Fernando Bellet on the set of *El chacal de Nahueltoro* (1969; The Jackal of Nahueltoro)

FRANCISCO LOMBARDI

Francisco Lombardi (circa 1945–) is the most commercially successful filmmaker in Peru. His first feature-length film, *Muerte al amanecer* (1977; Death at Dawn), proved to be a great box-office success and was seen by more than half a million people in Peru, becoming the first Peruvian film to cover its costs in the internal market. As in **El chacal de Nahueltoro** (1969; The Jackal of Nahueltoro) directed by **Miguel Littín,** the protagonist is a celebrated child murderer, the "monster of Armendáriz," and, again like Littín, Lombardi is concerned with analyzing the mechanisms of power in society. In his next film, *Muerte de un magnate* (1980; Death of a Magnate), Lombardi focused on a celebrated crime of violence in which an Indian gardener captured and killed an important businessman. He then turned to two adaptations of literary texts, *Maruja en el infierno* (1983; Maruja in Hell), which became the biggest box-office success in Peruvian history, and *La ciudad y los perros* (1986; The City and the Dogs), a faithful and violent rendering of **Mario Vargas Llosa**'s 1963 novel. In *La boca del lobo* (1988; The Mouth of the Wolf) Lombardi tells the story of Peru's principal guerrilla group, **Sendero Luminoso** (Shining Path). The setting is a small remote village under siege by the Shining Path. Sendero Luminoso is not mentioned; it is just there, terrorizing the villagers and mutilating and killing the soldiers who leave the encampment.

REFERENCE:

John King, *Magical Reels: A History of Cinema in Latin America* (London: Verso, 1990).

— S.M.H.

LEOPOLDO LUGONES

The dominant figure of Argentinean letters in the first three decades of the twentieth century, Leopoldo Lugones (1874–1938) was a protean writer who excelled in a variety of genres: poetry, short fiction, essay, translation, and journalism. He was a politically controversial figure, having converted from the anarchism and socialism of his youth to right-wing nationalism in his later years. He is remembered mostly for two books, a collection of fantastic tales titled *Las fuerzas extrañas* (1906; Strange Forces) and *Lunario sentimental* (1909; Sentimental Lunar Poems), a brilliant poetic work characterized by a burlesque tone and extravagant images that closes the cycle of **Modernismo** and announces the coming of the avantgarde. Lugones, however, did not continue on the

Leopoldo Lugones, 1911 (portrait by Vázquez Díaz; from
Gran Enciclopedia de España y America, volume 8, 1985)

road to avant-garde poetry. In 1910, the year in
which Argentineans celebrated the centenary of their
independence from Spain, he published *Odas
seculares* (Secular Odes), a work inspired by Horace
and dealing with Argentinean rural life and patriotic
themes. From this moment on Lugones became a
nationalist intellectual committed to the reinterpre-
tation of the Argentinean past, in an effort to dis-
credit liberal democracy and industrialization and to
counteract the cultural influence of the masses of
immigrants who had arrived in the country during
the previous decades. In *El payador* (1916; The
Singer of the Pampa) Lugones calls *Martín Fierro* —
José Hernández's narrative poem of 1876 — the Argentinean national epic and makes an impressive and
successful case for its canonization as the fountainhead of national values. Lugones cultivated the
nationalist vein (emphasizing ancestor worship and
the virtues of rural life) in much of the poetry he
published after 1910, particularly in the *Poemas
solariegos* (1927; Ancestral Poems) and in the posthumous *Romances de Río Seco* (1938; Ballads of the
Río Seco).

REFERENCE:

Jorge Luis Borges, *Leopoldo Lugones* (Buenos Aires: Editorial
Troquel, 1955).

— R.G.M.

LUMBALÚ

Lumbalú is a funeral ritual of the Pacific coastal
region of Colombia, practiced by Angolan slaves
brought to work on plantations and in mines during
the colonial era. The ceremony includes recited pray-
ers, songs, and specific drum rhythms of special significance. The death of a person is announced by the
assigned elder, who is playing a specific rhythmic
pattern, which is clapped by others in attendance. A
large, single-membraned drum is played by a descen-
dent of the Batá family (a religious sect). Texts are
recited in the Lumbalú dialect and in Spanish. When
the people have gathered, the song begins, accompanied by other drums. The soloist sings the verse, and
those in attendance answer with a collective refrain.

This ceremony may last for many hours until sufficient homage has been paid.

REFERENCE:

Octavio Marulanda, *El folclor de Colombia: Práctica de la identidad cultural* (Bogotá: Artestudio Editores, 1984).

—R.L.S.

LUNFARDO

Lunfardo refers to the slang of burglars and other petty criminals in late–nineteenth century Buenos Aires. The word *lunfardo* is a corruption of *Lombard,* a term that in the Middle Ages came to mean "burglar." (The Lombards — bankers and moneylenders — acquired a reputation second only to that of the Jews as usurious financiers. They were admitted to England, for example, but on the condition that they confine themselves to their own neighborhood, Lombard Street). Lunfardo slang, mostly of Italian origin, came with the immigrants who started to arrive in Buenos Aires in 1854. By the end of the 1870s lunfardo was a recognizable dialect of popular speech but limited to the criminal element. Later it was adopted by the compadres (the "tough guys" who proliferated in the outskirts of Buenos Aires) and made deep inroads into **tango** lyrics and other popular forms of culture such as the sainete (a form of one-act farce). In the 1920s lunfardo was part of the debate over national identity. In a lecture titled "El idioma de los argentinos" (The Language of the Argentineans), published in 1928 in a book of the same name, **Jorge Luis Borges** mocked lunfardo (the "evasive jargon of burglars," a "dialect specializing in infamy and lacking words of general intent") and refuted those nationalists who identified the dialect with the speech typical of Argentineans. Despite the hostility of cosmopolitan writers and intellectuals, the Academia Porteña del Lunfardo (Buenos Aires Lunfardo Academy) — a research center specializing in the study of Buenos Aires popular speech and culture — was established in December 1962.

REFERENCE:

Arturo López Peña, *El habla popular de Buenos Aires* (Buenos Aires: Editorial Freeland, 1972).

—R.G.M.

M

EDUARDO MAC ENTYRE

With Miguel Angel Vidal, the Argentinean Eduardo Mac Entyre (1929–) formulated the principles of Arte Generativo (Generative Art), which explores optical aspects of **Geometric Abstraction.** Mac Entyre studied technical drawing at the Universidad de la Boca in Buenos Aires and trained in academic techniques with artists such as Vidal and Victor Margariños. Although Mac Entyre's early works were figurative, during the 1950s he began a progressive cubistlike reduction of the elements of the visible world into schematic geometric shapes, as for instance in *Desnudo* (1950–1951; Nude) and *Tintero azul* (1953; Blue Inkwell). This process culminated in completely geometric works like *Composición* (1959; Composition), which features circles, curves, and straight lines, reflecting an interest in Geometric Abstraction present in Argentinean art since the 1940s.

In 1959 Mac Entyre and Vidal, together with the critic and collector Ignacio Pirovano, founded the Arte Generativo group, which issued a manifesto advocating an art generated by the displacement through space of lines and geometric figures, which in turn generate optical effects of movement and three-dimensional space. While Vidal worked with straight lines and polygons, Mac Entyre chose the circle because of its metaphysical and cosmic connotations. During the 1960s he created ethereal spirographlike designs, usually referred to as *Pintura generativa* (Generative Painting), with the use of special compasses and oil paint, preferring glowing colors against dark backgrounds. Since the mid 1970s he has worked with freer structures by fragmenting his circles into separate bands to form intricate patterns and using free-flowing curved lines painted with acrylics which shimmer like multicolored laser holograms in the dark. Mac Entyre has successfully exhibited his art throughout the Americas.

REFERENCE:

Rafael Squirru, *Eduardo Mac Entyre* (Buenos Aires: Gaglianone, 1981).

—F.B.N.

MADÍ

Madí and the **Asociación de Arte Concreto-Invención** (AACI) were groups of concrete artists active in Buenos Aires during the 1940s. They drew together the Uruguayans **Carmelo Arden Quin** and Roth Rothfuss, and the Argentineans Martín Blaszko, **Alfredo Hlito, Gyula Kosice,** Diyi Laañ, **Tomás Maldonado,** and Lidy Prati. The antecedents for both Madí and AACI are varied, including the European abstract avant-garde movements known as de Stijl, Bauhaus, Cercle et Carré, and Abstraction-Création, the artistic breakthroughs of the Uruguayan **Joaquín Torres-García,** and the abstract work of more-established Argentinean artists, such as **Emilio Pettoruti, Lucio Fontana,** and Juan del Prete. (Prete had participated personally in the activities of the French Abstraction-Création movement.) The artists of Madí, like their European counterparts, developed a completely abstract geometric art. It is called concrete because it is based on plastic elements, such as planes, colors, and lines, considered as concrete objects rather than tools to create the illusion of reality.

The activities of these concrete artists began in 1944 with the formation of the Arturo group, which included Arden Quin, Kosice, Maldonado, Prati, and Rothfuss. The artists' objective was to produce abstract works, redefine the relationship between the surface and frame of paintings through "cut-out" or "shaped" frames, and explore the possibility of making articulated sculptures, such as Kosice's *Röyi*. In 1945 Arturo

Madí Neon, No. 3 (1946), by Gyula Kosice (Musée de Grenoble, France)

separated into two groups, the Movimiento de Arte Concreto-Invención, founded by Arden Quin and including Blaszko, Kosice, Laañ, Rothfuss, and **Grete Stern,** and the Asociación de Arte Concreto-Invención, formed by Espinosa, Hlito, Maldonado, and Prati. Arden Quin and Kosice's group had three exhibitions in 1945. Since they were rejected by established galleries, their first exhibition was on a sidewalk in downtown Buenos Aires, and the other two were at the private residences of Dr. Enrique Pichón Riviere and photographer Grete Stern. In 1946 this group adopted the name of Madí. (Perhaps invented by Kosice, the word had no specific meaning.)

Unlike the emphasis of the AACI, that of Madí was not on rationality, but on a more playful and intuitive approach that favored freer structures and compositions. The first Madí exhibition at the Instituto Francés de Estudios Superiores included works by Rothfuss, Kosice, Arden Quin, and Blaszko, revealing their interest in breaking with the traditional two-dimensional support in favor of broken planes, curved

surfaces, cut-out frames, and articulated surfaces. Kosice, one of the main forces behind Madí, experimented in this period with articulated sculptures and radically new materials, such as neon lights and Plexiglas. In 1947 Arden Quin broke conceptually with Kosice and abandoned Madí. Settling in Paris, he formed a parallel Madí group which had some success, while Kosice founded a new movement called Madinemsor in Buenos Aires. Despite the demise of the original Madí movement in Buenos Aires, its members participated as a group in several exhibitions thereafter, such as at the Salon des Réalités Nouvelles in Paris and the Salón de nuevas realidades, arte abstracto, concreto, no figurativo in Buenos Aires.

REFERENCES:

Aracy Amaral, "Abstract Constructivist Trends in Argentina, Brazil, Venezuela, and Colombia," in *Latin American Artists of the Twentieth Century,* edited by Waldo Rasmussen, Fatima Bercht, and Elizabeth Ferrer (New York: Museum of Modern Art, 1993), pp. 86–99;

Gyula Kosice, *Arte Madí* (Buenos Aires: Gaglianone, 1983).
                                                        — F.B.N.

MADRES DE LA PLAZA DE MAYO

The mothers of the "disappeared" in the Argentinean **Guerra Sucia** (1970–1982; Dirty War) were known as the Madres de la Plaza de Mayo because they gathered weekly in the Plaza de Mayo in the center of Buenos Aires to protest the disappearance of their relatives and to demand information as to their whereabouts. The mothers' activities began in the early days of the war and did not cease with the downfall of the military government in 1982. The mothers became an icon to the international media, in which they were shown with scarves tied around their heads and with placards bearing the names and photographs of their missing relatives.

REFERENCE:

Jo Fisher, *Mothers of the Disappeared* (Boston: South End Press, 1989).
                                                        — R.G.M.

MAGICAL REALISM

Magical realism generally means fiction that does not distinguish between realistic and nonrealistic events, fiction in which the supernatural, the mythical, or the implausible are assimilated to the cognitive structure of reality without a perceptive break in the narrator's or characters' consciousness. Magical realism is a style

Mothers demonstrating in the Plaza de Mayo, Buenos Aires, for the return of relatives taken prisoner by the military government of Argentina during the years 1970–1982. The sign at front says, "We demand the return alive of the detained and disappeared."

associated with Latin American fiction especially in the 1960s and after. The concept raises the issue of cultural authenticity, sometimes in ways not intended by its proponents. The history of magical realism as an idea is in itself disjointed and inorganic.

The term was first proposed by art critic and historian Franz Roh in his book *Nach Expressionismus (Magischer Realismus)* (1925) in reference to German post-Expressionism. Roh's theory was that post-Expressionist painters sought to represent concrete and palpable objects in such a way that they revealed their hidden mystery through their very physical existence. Like the later proponents of magical realism, Roh vacillates between an ontological and a phenomenological approach to the concept; that is, he never resolves the question whether objects are miraculous in themselves or whether it is the artist's perception that endows them with a magical quality.

The term reappears in the work of another European aesthetician, Massimo Bontempelli, who in his book *L'avventura novecentista* (1938; The Nineteenth Century) refers to magical realism as an attempt to go beyond the aesthetics of Futurism by appealing to the fantastic. The appeal to fantasy, however, is firmly

grounded on the representation of the visible and concrete. Neither of these approaches to magical realism is linked to Latin American art or literature.

The first Latin American postulation of magical realism is that of **Arturo Uslar Pietri**, who in his *Letras y hombres de Venezuela* (1948; Literature and Folks of Venezuela) uses the concept in relation to the "poetic decipherment" or "poetic negation of reality" in the context of the Venezuelan short story of the 1930s and 1940s. Uslar Pietri had met Bontempelli in Europe and may have adapted the latter's notion of magical realism to a specifically Latin American situation. Nevertheless, it is difficult to apply Uslar Pietri's version of magical realism to the modern Latin American novel.

In a 1954 lecture ("Magical Realism in Spanish American Fiction"), published the following year in the journal *Hispania,* the critic Angel Flores proposes the term *magical realism* as a solution to the problem of ordering Latin American literary movements according to European categories and traces its genealogy to a double origin: the realism of nineteenth century European and Latin American fiction and the fabulous chronicles of discovery and conquest sent back to Europe by the first explorers of the New World.

These two strands — realism and fantasy — come together in contemporary magical realism. Flores's paper has some merit but it fails to discriminate between literature inspired by French Symbolism and Parnassianism, fantastic literature, and magical realism per se; not surprisingly, Flores's list of magical realist authors is a hodgepodge of styles and names. Flores also fails to make any reference to Uslar Pietri's use of the term "magic realism," an omission that forcefully underscores the historical discontinuity of the notion.

The one version of magical realism that serves as the prologue to the new Latin American novel was put forth by the Cuban writer Alejo Carpentier in an essay first published in the Venezuelan daily *El Nacional* (1948) and titled "De lo real maravilloso americano" ("On the Marvelous Real in America"). Carpentier's concern is the originality of Latin American culture, traditionally compromised by the weight and prestige of European models, which Latin American writers and artists have often followed in seeking to express themselves. Carpentier, whose father was French and who lived for many years in Paris before "discovering" the Caribbean and the Venezuelan jungles, derives his notion of the marvelous from a critique of the French Surrealists. He charges that the Surrealists aimed to provoke marvelous epiphanies by devices (such as dreams, delirium, madness, games like the "exquisite corpse," and trances), that ultimately seemed artificial, contrived, even "bureaucratic," while the very same experience that was sought as the basis of the Surrealist aesthetic was available in natural form in Latin America, a region whose history and culture (and natural environment) are alien to European forms of representation.

Carpentier does not do away with Europe in order to found or invent an original Latin American identity; on the contrary, without a European perspective such a cultural invention would not be possible. For Carpentier, magical realism is the mixture of elements from heterogeneous cultures that form a new historical entity in a natural environment beyond the imaginings of the European mind. In other words, Carpentier's marvelous realism is what happens to European culture when it is transplanted to America, either in the form of a European observer able to attest the American difference or in the guise of artifacts, institutions, and beliefs which either seem out of place in their new environment or undergo a startling metamorphosis. Religious syncretism and the Napoleonic court of Henri Christophe of Haiti, the first black king in the Americas, are examples of Carpentier's brand of magical realism.

Carpentier, then, legitimizes the intellectual invention of magical realism in terms of the search for cultural identity and authenticity. He also demonstrates a powerful historical consciousness that grounds the originality of Latin America literally in its historical origins, while not ignoring the fact that the European presence in the New World is the equivalent of colonialism. In fact, magical realism is a cultural response to colonialism, an affirmation of identity both against and partially thanks to the colonial master.

Even in Carpentier's version, however, magical realism has been viewed with suspicion in Latin America. Carpentier's novels demonstrate the collapse of the concept under the weight of its own contradictions: in what aspect of the real is the marvelous located? In the objective, empirical world itself (the ontological approach) or in the perceiver (the phenomenological one)? If in the perceiver, then who is this subject? The foreigner? Or the credulous naïf, as Carpentier himself suggests? If the foreigner, then the cultural authenticity of magical realism loses all credibility; if the naïf, then what role can legitimately be played by an intellectual such as Carpentier? Can such an intellectual put forth the concept in good faith?

The concept of magical realism, furthermore, has been attacked by the Left as an aestheticization of poverty and of the neocolonial status of the Caribbean and Latin America in general. It has been ridiculed by others as an exotic label stuck by United States and European publishers on cultural artifacts from Latin America that have penetrated foreign markets but have made no dent on foreign consciousness. It has also been derided as plainly naive because it revives the stereotype of Latin America as the site of Nature in opposition to Europe as the site of Culture.

If magical realism has any future as a serious intellectual concept, it is in the realm of literary theory. Carpentier's version of the idea was inherited and modified by **Gabriel García Márquez** in "Fantasía y creación artística en América Latina y el Caribe" (Fantasy and Artistic Creation in Latin America and the Caribbean), a short article originally published in Mexico in 1979. While reaffirming Carpentier's emphasis on magical realism as a variation on the theme of Latin American identity and restating the link between the concept and the early chronicles of discovery, García Márquez shifts the field of pertinence of magical realism from the cultural to the literary and the tone of its postulation from the transcendental to the carnivalesque. For him the problem of magical realism (which, incidentally, he never refers to as such) is a literary problem: how can the writer make believable the unbelievable components of Latin American history, culture, and nature? Carpentier had placed the question of belief at the center of the "marvelous real" by saying that faith would determine the validity of the concept.

García Márquez turns the issue of faith into the literary problem of verisimilitude. He intimates that Latin America is already a novel and one that exceeds the canon of verisimilitude established by realism. Whether one believes or not that Latin American reality is marvelous or magical, the issue raised by García Márquez is compelling because it involves the more general problem of the relation between traditional literary forms (in this case, the novel) and the new contents that such a form — itself a product of social history — is or is not able to represent. Can one write about Latin America, or as a Latin American, in a genre developed for and by the European bourgeoisie of the last century?

Apart from Carpentier and García Márquez, other writers associated with magical realism are **Isabel Allende,** Miguel Angel Asturias, Juan Rulfo, **Demetrio Aguilera Malta,** and the Brazilian novelist Jorge Amado.

REFERENCE:

Irlemar Chiampi, *El realismo maravilloso* (Caracas: Monte Avila, 1983).

— R.G.M.

ESTUARDO MALDONADO

The art of Ecuadoran Estuardo Maldonado (1930–) has synthesized interests in **Geometric Abstraction,** optical effects, and indigenous Andean patterns. Maldonado studied art in Guayaquil and later in Rome, where he attended the Academy of Fine Arts. After traveling throughout the Americas and Europe, in 1966 he won the first National Prize for Young Artists at the Palazzo delle Esposizioni in Rome. He was later appointed an organizer of the thirty-second Venice Biennial and official representative of the Casa de la Cultura Ecuatoriana at the Primera Bienal Latinoamericana in Quito.

During the 1960s Maldonado's art revealed his interest in reflecting his Latin American roots through abstract means. In *Pictografía* (1963; Pictography) he combines an expressive treatment of color and texture reminiscent of **Informal Abstraction** with pre-Columbian schematic signs arranged in an intricate orthogonal pattern evocative of **Joaquín Torres-García**'s art, which Maldonado greatly admires. Afterward, Maldonado became increasingly interested in dynamic optical effects produced by color interactions. By the 1970s he had found stainless steel to be a vehicle rich in expressive possibilities, using it as support and surface of his two-dimensional works. For instance, in *Estructura modular 32* (1976; Modular Structure 32)

Maldonado uses an intricate geometric design, reminiscent of indigenous Andean patterns, to produce shimmering optical effects, while in *Estructura modular 26* (1977) he contrasts shiny and opaque surfaces in subtle purples and violets, whose reflective qualities and hues change according to the viewer's perspective. Maldonado has successfully exhibited his art throughout the Americas and Europe.

REFERENCE:

Catálogo General: Colección Pintura y Escultura Latinoamericana (Caracas: Museo de Bellas Artes, 1979), pp. 122–125; 311.

— F.B.N.

TOMÁS MALDONADO

The Argentinean Tomás Maldonado (1922–) was a leading participant in the **Asociación de Arte Concreto-Invención** (AACI) and later a distinguished professor of design in Europe. After graduating from the Academia de Bellas Artes in Buenos Aires, Maldonado met **Carmelo Arden Quin,** with whom he shared an interest in concrete art. In 1944 they founded a review called *Arturo*, which attracted artists with similar concerns, such as **Gyula Kosice,** Manuel Espinosa, **Alfredo Hlito,** Enio Iommi, Lidy Prati (Maldonado's wife), and the poet Edgar Bayley (Maldonado's brother). By 1945 ideological disagreements had divided the members of *Arturo* into two separate groups: the AACI, led by Maldonado, and **Madí,** cofounded by Kosice and Arden Quin. Maldonado's works helped define the aims of the AACI: his "cut out" canvases were based on rational structures and concrete plastic elements, such as lines, hard-edged shapes, and primary colors. In 1948 Maldonado traveled to Europe, where he met the artists Max Bill and Georges Vantongerloo. On returning to Buenos Aires, Maldonado founded the *Nueva Visión* magazine, wrote a book about Bill, and participated in Artistas Modernos de la Argentina, a group which advocated **Geometric Abstraction.** During this period Maldonado's paintings, such as *Construcción de 2 elementos* (1953; Construction with 2 Elements), featured thin lines forming subtle rectangular patterns over flat backgrounds, and a limited range of colors.

Maldonado returned to Europe in 1956 when he was invited by Bill to be a professor at the Hochschule für Gestaltung in Ulm. In 1964 he became the school's director. By then Maldonado had stopped painting to dedicate himself to writing and teaching the principles of design, first in Ulm and later as the Lethaby Lecturer at the Royal College of Art in London. In 1967 Maldonado moved to Italy; he won the Design Medal

Eduardo Mallea

from the Society of Industrial Artists and Designers in 1968 and became Professor of Environmental Planning at the Universitá di Bologna in 1971.

REFERENCE:

Aracy Amaral, "Abstract Constructivist Trends in Argentina, Brazil, Venezuela, and Colombia," in *Latin American Artists of the Twentieth Century,* edited by Waldo Rasmussen, Fatima Bercht, and Elizabeth Ferrer (New York: Museum of Modern Art, 1993), pp. 86–99.

— F.B.N.

EDUARDO MALLEA

An important Argentinean novelist, Eduardo Mallea (1903–1982) produced an unusual amalgam of philosophical speculation and telluric nationalism grounded in a strong sense of ethics. Through spiritual crises reasoned in a philosophical way, Mallea's characters find a renewed affiliation with the soil on which they were born. Mallea's novels search for what the author called the "invisible Argentina" and are full of existential anguish. Mallea's best-known works are the novels *Fiesta en noviembre* (1938; translated as *Fiesta in November*), *La bahía de silencio* (1940; translated as *The Bay of Silence*), and *Todo verdor perecerá* (1941; translated as *All Green Shall Perish*); the stories in *La ciudad junto al río inmóvil* (1936; The City by the Motionless River), and the essay *Historia de una pasión argentina* (1935; History of an Argentinean Passion).

REFERENCE:

John H. R. Polt, *The Writings of Eduardo Mallea* (Berkeley: University of California Press, 1959).

— R.G.M.

LAS MALVINAS (FALKLANDS)

Las Malvinas are a windswept group of islands located some three hundred miles east of the Straits of Magellan. The first European visitors were the British, who arrived in 1592 and named them the Falklands. In 1764 they were taken by the French (who called them Iles Malouines); the islands were later ceded to Spain. After further changes of dominion, the British reasserted their claim to what they call the Falklands in 1832. Argentina, however, did not recognize British authority. The Falklands are inhabited almost exclusively by people of British descent and were of greatest interest to sheep farmers and birdwatchers until 1982, when Argentina invaded them. The Argentinean forces, comprised mainly of inexperienced conscripts, were defeated by a British army consisting entirely of professionals. The Falklands War was a means for the generals of the ruling Argentinean junta as well as British prime minister Margaret Thatcher to divert attention from their problems at home. A conflict between two nations with strong cultural and economic ties, the war disrupted international relations in Europe and the Americas and cost many lives.

— P.S.

MANDRÁGORA

La mandrágora (The Mandrake Root) is the name of a Surrealist group that flourished in Chile during the late 1930s and early 1940s. Its best-known member was the poet Braulio Arenas. Between 1938 and 1943 the group published seven issues of a journal, *La mandrágora*.

— R.G.M.

MARACAS

Various types of vessels containing beads, pebbles, shells, seeds, and other small objects have been used to make the shaken percussion instruments called maracas in Latin American music. The vessels are typically made from easily accessible materials such as gourds or clay, but may be constructed of solid wooden parts or metal. Even dried seed pods, such as are produced by the royal poinciana tree, can provide a natural instrument. Maracas are commonly played in pairs when part of an ensemble percussion section. Among indigenous tribes a single maraca is commonly used by the shaman and may be adorned with feathers or other objects and include symbolic drawings or carvings. The maracas used by popular nightclub orchestras are typically decorated with colorful designs.

Different names identify the maraca in various parts of Latin America: *alfandoque, carángano,* or *guazá* in Colombia; *chinchín* in Guatemala; *dadoo* in Venezuela; *huada* or *wada* in Chile; *maruga* in Cuba; and *sonaja* in Mexico.

— R.L.S.

MARCHA

Marcha, founded in June 1939 by veteran journalist Carlos Quijano, was the most important cultural and political Uruguayan weekly of the twentieth century and one of a handful of Latin American journals whose influence extended throughout the continent. Its editorial staff included intellectual figures of the stature of **Juan Carlos Onetti** and **Angel Rama.** Its declaration of principles stated that *Marcha* would be a paragon of modern journalism, each issue comprising a variety of sections seeking to synthesize the political, literary, economic, and artistic activities of the week. "It will not be the organ of any political camp but it will fight against fascism, racism, dictatorship, and every other form of reaction, defending culture, democracy, and freedom of speech." The journal's political line may be described as social democratic, and during the Cold War its main political concern was U.S. imperialism in Latin America. Its cultural pages included book reviews (originally by Onetti under the pseudonym "Periquito el Aguador") and reviews of theatrical performances, painting exhibitions, concerts, and poetry recitals. *Marcha* ceased publication in 1969.

REFERENCE:

Hugo Alfaro, ed., *Antología de 'Marcha' (1939)* (Montevideo: Biblioteca de Marcha, 1970).

— R.G.M.

JOSÉ CARLOS MARIÁTEGUI

An influential Peruvian intellectual, José Carlos Mariátegui (1894–1930) was the founder of the Peruvian Socialist Party (1928), editor of the literary journal *Amauta* (founded in 1926), and author of *Siete ensayos de interpretación de la realidad peruana* (1928; trans-

José Carlos Mariátegui, circa 1915–1916

lated as *Seven Interpretative Essays on Peruvian Reality*), a Marxist analysis of Peruvian problems and one of the fundamental books of the Latin American intelligentsia in the twentieth century.

Mariátegui was the illegitimate but recognized child of a landowner. His early years were spent with his mother and were marked by sickness and poverty. He was largely self-taught, but by the age of nineteen he had already become a journalist and was shortly to launch his first publishing venture, *La Razón,* a working-class daily promptly closed down by the government. After a European sojourn (1919–1923) during which he embraced Marxism, Mariátegui became a political activist and a proponent of avant-garde ideas in art and literature, writing articles for various publications and founding his own journal and publishing house. In 1924 he suffered the amputation of a leg. At the time of his death six years later, his dream of a socialist Peru remained as elusive as ever.

Mariátegui's analysis of Peru's Indian question is forceful. After discarding the solutions endorsed by the liberal elite and the Church, Mariátegui locates the serious problems affecting the indigenous population in the system of land ownership prevalent in the Andes, where a few landowners ("gamonales") hoard the available land and create massive dispossession among the Indian serfs. Therefore, the solution to the problem is a radical agrarian reform that would improve the Indians' socioeconomic status by restoring their communal lands.

Mariátegui's thought is still vigorous in contemporary Peru and has been appropriated by the radical Left, specifically by the Tupac Amaru Revolutionary Movement, a guerrilla group that has operated in urban areas since the mid 1980s and that draws its program from Mariátegui's ideas.

REFERENCES:

Eugenio Chang-Rodríguez, *Poética e ideología en José Carlos Mariátegui* (Madrid: J. Porrúz Turranzas, 1983);

Jesús Chavarría, *José Carlos Mariátegui and the Rise of Modern Peru* (Albuquerque: University of New Mexico Press, 1979).
— R.G.M.

Dancers performing the marinera, the national dance of Peru

MARIMBA

Although the marimba is more widely found in Central America, it is one of the most important musical instruments of the Pacific coast of Colombia and Ecuador. The top frame, in the form of a trapezoid, contains the wooden keys. Below the keys are tubes, often constructed of palm bark or bamboo tubes, which serve as resonators. Open at the top beneath the keys, the resonators are closed at the bottom. All is held in place by handmade ropes or vines. The instrument is normally supported on wooden legs. In rural areas, however, it is often hung from the ceiling in the home or even from a tree in the yard. Polished sticks with bulbs of crude latex are used to play the marimba. In Colombia two people play the instrument; one plays treble parts at the small end, and the other accompanies with the lower parts at the large end. They often face each other while playing. The marimba is the primary instrument of the **currulao,** popular on the Pacific coast.

REFERENCE:

Octavio Marulanda, *El folclor de Colombia: Práctica de la identidad cultural* (Bogotá: Artestudio Editores, 1984).
— R.L.S.

MARINERA

A Peruvian national dance, the marinera was originally called the chilena, owning to its Chilean origins, until political trouble between those two countries led to it being renamed. A dance of African origin (for the slave trade found its way to the Pacific coast of South America as well as the Caribbean and Atlantic coasts), the marinera differs from the cueca only in that it is performed more quickly, owing, perhaps, to the higher and cooler climate. Extremely bright colors in the wool costume — jacket, cap, and leggings for the man and the woman; baggy trousers and a poncho for the man; a long dress for the woman — also differentiate it not only from its African but also from its Chilean origins.
— N.D.B. & J.M.H.

MARISOL

Marisol Escobar (1930–), who uses only her first name professionally, has been recognized as an important sculptor in the United States and Latin America.

She was born in Paris and raised in Caracas by her Venezuelan parents. From 1949 to 1950 she studied art in Paris, at the Ecole des Beaux-Arts and at the Académie Julien. Afterward she settled in New York, where she studied at the Art Students' League, the New School for Social Research, and at Hans Hofmann School of Fine Arts. She successfully exhibited her work at the Sidney Janis and other galleries interested in **Pop Art, Assemblages, and Happenings.** During the 1960s she actively participated in the Pop Art movement, becoming friends with Andy Warhol and appearing in his movies *Kiss* (1963) and *13 Most Beautiful Women* (1964).

Since the mid 1950s Marisol has constructed whimsical life-size sculptures out of vertical boxlike blocks of wood and found objects. In her works she represents social stereotypes with satirical intent, as in her installation *The Party* (1965–1966), which includes a wide selection of characters, ranging from extravagantly dressed socialites to uniformed maids and butlers. Marisol emphasizes the human quality of each figure by attaching a plaster cast of her own face to each head. In the case of her caricatures of modern leaders, such as *Charles de Gaulle* (1965) and *LBJ* (1967), and in her 1980s series on prominent artists, she paints the model's face on the upper part of the sculpture. Marisol completes the personality of her sculptures by attaching to them discarded objects and accessories, which further accents the innovative tension between the flatness of the surfaces and the three-dimensionality of her figures. During the 1970s she also produced a series of erotic prints and drawings based on tracings of her own body.

REFERENCE:

Nancy Grove, *Magical Mixtures: Marisol Portrait Sculpture* (Washington, D.C.: National Portrait Gallery, Smithsonian Institution, 1991).

— F.B.N.

Martín Fierro

The most important avant-garde journal in Argentina, founded in February 1924 and directed by Evar Méndez, was named *Martín Fierro* after the Argentinean national poem, a fact that signals the journal's nationalist line. It was the third periodical to bear this name. The first "Martín Fierro" was the literary supplement to an anarchist paper (1904–1905); the second, also directed by Evar Méndez, published only three issues in 1919. The relationship between the early avatars of the journal and its "definitive" version of 1924 is merely external. The avowed purpose of the third *Martín Fierro* was to create a new literary culture in

Women Leaning (1966–1967), by Marisol (Chicago Public Library Cultural Center)

Argentina, which it did by challenging prevailing aesthetic values, the philistinism of the culture industry, and the mechanisms of the literary institution, such as the way of bestowing prizes and other public honors on writers. The Martín Fierro Group promoted new "institutions" such as writers' gatherings at cafés and restaurants (gatherings which for the first time included women) and loud debates on literary and cultural themes, with the aim of attracting public attention. However, the journal was politically and culturally moderate, unlike many of its European and Latin American counterparts. Its irreverent humor and its thirst for novelty never challenged basic social institutions (such as family and Church) or questioned the principle of authority, a stance partially explained by the need of younger writers to rely on state patronage for economic protection and advancement. Writers linked to the journal include **Jorge Luis, Macedonio Fernández, Ricardo Güiraldes, Oliverio Girondo,** and Evaristo Carriego. The final issue of *Martín Fierro* was published in 1927.

REFERENCE:

Eduardo González Lanuza, *Los martinfierristas* (Buenos Aires: Ediciones Culturales Argentinas, 1961).

— R.G.M.

Ezequiel Martínez Estrada speaking at the Casa de las Américas, in Havana, Cuba

EZEQUIEL MARTÍNEZ ESTRADA

An eclectic and controversial Argentinean essayist, Ezequiel Martínez Estrada (1895–1964) is noted mostly for three of his works: *Radiografía de la pampa* (1938; translated as *X-Ray of the Pampa*), *La cabeza de Goliat* (1940; The Head of Goliath), and *Muerte y transfiguración de Martín Fierro* (1948; Death and Transfiguration of Martín Fierro). All three focus on related aspects of the Argentinean national experience.

Radiografía de la pampa is an idiosyncratic and pessimistic meditation on Argentinean history and an implacable critique of the nineteenth-century liberal elite that had sought to replace the "barbarism" of the **gaucho** with European political and cultural imports. According to Martínez Estrada, the "foreign idols" never took hold, and the gaucho remains the greatest symbol of the Argentinean nation. The visionary tone of the book led some critics to characterize its author as a prophet of doom. *La cabeza de Goliat* is a reflection on Buenos Aires, a city which Martínez Estrada views as disproportionate in relation to the rest of the

country and as a megalopolis whose life is no longer rooted in the natural soil that alone could endow it with vitality. The author, however, celebrates some of the people and places in the city that have retained an authentic essence. More generally, the book is a critique of modern urban civilization for severing the bonds between people as well as between people and their earthbound roots. *Muerte y transfiguración de Martín Fierro* centers on the classic work of Argentinean literature — the epic poem *Martín Fierro* (two parts, 1872; 1879) — and restates the interpretation of the gaucho that Martínez Estrada had advanced in *Radiografía de la pampa*. For him the prototype of Argentinean national identity is an avatar of the "shamed son" of modern psychology, procreated by means of rape, orphaned of both Indian mother and Spanish father, and exploited and eventually destroyed by the policies of "progressive" governments intent on shaping the country according to a European blueprint.

Martínez Estrada's empathy with the dispossessed is reflected in the thinker's early support for the **Cuban Revolution.**

REFERENCE:

Peter G. Earle, *Prophet in the Wilderness* (Austin: University of Texas Press, 1971).

— R.G.M.

ROBERTO MATTA

Chilean artist Roberto Sebastián Antonio Matta Echaurren (1912–), internationally recognized as one of the most important **Surrealists,** graduated from the Universidad Católica with a degree in architecture. In 1933 he left Santiago for Paris, where his fluency in French and English facilitated his access into avant-garde circles. Matta soon became a freelance drafts-man for French architect Le Corbusier and on a holi-day trip to Spain met Federico García Lorca and Salva-dor Dalí, who later introduced him to André Breton, the leader of the Surrealist movement. Encouraged by his friend the English artist Gordon Onslow Ford, Matta abandoned architecture and began to experi-ment with automatist drawings, which he called "psy-chological morphologies." His purpose was to express his interest in esoteric notions about the "fourth di-mension" and the creation of the world. Matta began painting around 1938, and Breton soon invited him to join the Surrealist movement. They both shared a keen enthusiasm for the visionary poem *Les chants de Maldoror,* written by the Uruguayan-born Comte de Lautréamont (Isidore-Lucien Ducasse).

At the beginning of World War II, many Sur-realists, including Matta, left Paris for New York, where once again Matta's command of the language allowed him to connect in a short time with the princi-pal members of the incipient New York School. He actively proselytized in favor of Surrealism, organizing exercises in automatism in his studio for his friends Arshile Gorky, Jackson Pollock, and Robert Moth-erwell. Matta had a strong influence on the art of these Abstract Expressionists because in his work they saw a way to free themselves from Cubism. Matta was also well received by curators, critics, and dealers. He showed his paintings at the Julien Levy Gallery and was included in important exhibitions, such as *Artists in Exile* and *The First Papers of Surrealism.* By then his semiabstract works, such as *Ecoutez Vivre* (1941; Lis-ten to Living) and *Le vertige d'Eros* (1944; The Vertigo of Eros), evoked both an interior mindscape and the primordial cosmic chaos from which life forces vio-lently precipitate the creation of the universe. During the mid 1940s he began to introduce — in paintings such as *Wound Interrogation* (1948) — anthropomor-phic monsterlike figures involved in strange violent rit-uals with erotic connotations. Matta returned to Eu-

Roberto Matta with two early works, 1941. The painting be-hind him is *Rocks* (1940)

rope in 1948 and associated with the Situationists. Dur-ing the 1960s and 1970s he became interested in polit-ical activities and traveled to Cuba, South America, and Africa. He became a French citizen and lives in Paris.

REFERENCE:

Valerie Fletcher, ed., *Crosscurrents of Modernism: Four Latin American Pioneers: Diego Rivera, Joaquín Torres-García, Wifredo Lam, Matta* (Washington, D.C.: Hirshhorn Museum and Sculpture Garden, 1992).

— F.B.N.

MEMBRANOPHONES

Membranophones exist in great variety and are among the most widely used instruments in Latin American music. The name derives from the stretched animal skin or membrane that is fitted to a drum frame. The thickness and tension of the membrane determine the pitch of the sound. The properties of the drum frame or vessel determine the quality of sound and its resonance. As the membrane is struck by hand or stick, its vibrations cause the air within the drum and the drum itself to vibrate, thus producing the sound. Drum categories include tubular drums, vessel drums, and frame drums. Tubular drums may feature different shapes: conical, cylindrical, or barrel. Friction drums are also used in South America. Latin American drums may be very small, held in the hand, or may be made from large tree trunks several meters in length. They may have one head (membrane), as is the case with the conga drums, large conical drums generally ascribed to Afro-Cuban origin and used especially in religious cult music, or two heads, as with the tambora. The drums may be played by two hands, two sticks, or a combination of hand and stick. Andean music typically features only one drum, the **bombo.** African-influenced music tends to use several different types of drums: **bongos,** congas, and batá drums.

Drums frequently have strong religious ties and, especially among African American groups, represent spiritual symbolism. Certain rhythmic patterns played on drums are also closely associated with specific spiritual values. Indigenous drums often bear symbolic paintings or carvings that relate the instrument to extramusical values. Some African traditions require that only the maker of the instrument play it or that only a member of a certain religious sect use specific drums.

— R.L.S.

OCTAVIO MENESES

Chilean choreographer Octavio Meneses is a graduate in acting of the Theater School of the University of Chile. Meneses left theater for the field of dance after seeing the company of German Expressionist dance-theater choreographer Pina Bausch perform at Santiago's Municipal Theater. He studied dance-theater with the Lavoro group in Rome and performed in street theater in Italy and Spain. His artistic statement lists mime, pantomime, phonomime, theater-dance, and belief in Chile and in Chilean art as influences on the development of his career. He has created choreography for eleven theater works, including *Woyzeck,* and is a teacher of dance, corporal expression, and theater.

— N.D.B. & J.M.H.

TUNUNA MERCADO

Argentinean writer Tununa Mercado (1939–), one of the leading feminine voices in Latin American narra-

tive, was born in the provincial city of Córdoba and moved to Buenos Aires in 1963 to be a journalist. Her first work of fiction is a collection of stories, *Celebrar a la mujer como una pascua* (1967; To Celebrate Woman Like a Fiesta). Almost twenty years elapsed before Mercado published another book. During this time she lived in France and Mexico as a political exile. The stories in *Canon de alcoba* (1988; Bedroom Canon) and the autobiographical narrative *En estado de memoria* (1990; In a State of Memory) consolidated her reputation in Argentina, where she now lives, and abroad. These works shun canonical genres and straddle the domains of the short story, the novel, and autobiography. They are written in a subtle and intensely introspective style that reduces external description to a minimum and concentrates on psychological analysis and on the small epiphanies that the details of daily life can disclose. The themes most readily associated with Mercado's works are memory, desire, and the ravages of exile. Indeed, *En estado de memoria* is an unequaled exposition of the exile's predicament.

REFERENCE:

Guillermo Saavedra, *La curiosidad impertinente: Entrevistas con narradores argentinos* (Buenos Aires: Beatriz Viterbo Editora, 1993).

— R.G.M.

MILONGA

The Argentinean revolutionary spirit of the early nineteenth century broke the artificial barriers that had separated the ruling upper classes from the Creole masses. Revolutionary songs of the cities spread throughout the country and inspired a new wave of songs, milongas, by the famous Argentinean **payadors,** whose long tradition of **gaucho** songs had documented their lonely lives in the pampas. Earlier in the colonial era the song literature was more or less limited to religious and romantic songs of the Spanish tradition. The revolutionary sense of freedom and national identity found an enthusiastic outlet in music that celebrated the reality of life. Scattered across the vast pampas were cantinas where gauchos gathered to be refreshed, drink wine and other spirits, and enjoy human contact. Because the gauchos were encouraged to drink more when there was music, the cantinas maintained payadors to entertain them. The payadors created narratives that were often sentimental yet replete with images and scenes of rural life, animals, and the deserted land. Their frequently improvised lyrics were unpolished, showing little concern for poetic correctness or proper rhyme. **Zambas, bagualas,** and **vidalas** were popular in the repertoire of the payador.

The term *milonga* comes from the Bunda dialect of blacks from Angola who inhabited the Río de la Plata region. Originally, the term encompassed such meanings as "words," "verbiage," "question," and "confusion of ideas." The popularity of the Cuban *habanera* in the ports of Montevideo and Buenos Aires began a process of fusion and syncretization in Argentinean music that eventually produced not only the milonga but also the **tango.** The milonga became immensely popular in urban centers as well as in rural areas. In the musical nationalism of cultivated art music that followed, the milonga was featured in works by luminaries such as Julián Aguirre and **Alberto Williams.**

The death of **Atahualpa Yupanqui** in May 1993 brought to a close the illustrious life of the world's most beloved and talented payador. His worldwide tours, numerous recordings, and television appearances endeared him to generations of aficionados of the milonga.

REFERENCES:

Isabel Aretz, *El folklore musical argentino* (Buenos Aires: Ricordi Americana, 1952);

Rodolfo Arizaga, *Enciclopedia de la música argentina* (Buenos Aires: Fondo Nacional de las Artes, 1971).

— R.L.S.

Marta Minujín

The Argentinean artist Marta Minujín (1943–) is one of the main exponents of **Pop Art, Assemblages, and Happenings** in Latin America. She studied at the Escuela Superior de Bellas Artes in Buenos Aires and worked in Paris until 1964, becoming interested in the writings of Pierre Restany and Marshall McLuhan. By then she was already producing works such as *The Destruction* (1963), in which participants were invited to destroy her earlier pieces and build new ones with the fragments, which were then burned. Minujín believes that traditional art is too static to reach observers immersed in modern life, and therefore art must come alive. For her, the work of art is the experience of the participant, rather than being the materials of which her pieces are composed. After returning to Argentina, she produced her well-known work *La menesunda* (1965; The Confusion), in collaboration with other artists at the Instituto Di Tella; this work was a complex mazelike installation which exposed the numerous visitors to multisensory experiences, including flickering neon lights, loud televisions, and powerful smells. Minujín also explored the relationship of technology, communication, and behavior in pieces such as *Simultaneity on Simultaneity* (1966), organized

with Wolf Vostell and Allan Kaprow, and *Minúfono* (1967), a telephone booth that played back the users' voices, showed their faces on a screen, and blew smoke and air on them.

Minujín lived in New York during the late 1960s and was a guest artist at the Corcoran School of Art in Washington, D.C., from 1970 to 1974. After her return to Buenos Aires she began a series of ephemeral projects of monumental proportions, involving massive participation by the public. With the purpose of deconstructing stereotypes and modifying collective behavior, she re-created large public monuments such as the Buenos Aires Obelisk, which she covered with loaves of sweet bread, then toppling it and distributing the loaves to the public. She produced similar projects in Medellín, São Paulo, New York, and Dublin. Since the 1980s Minujín has focused on sculpture, such as her *Venus cayendo* (1981; Venus Falling), which questions our concept of space and the classical understanding of form.

REFERENCE:

Jorge Glusberg, "Marta Minujín," in his *Del Pop-Art a la Nueva Imagen* (Buenos Aires: Ediciones de Arte Gaglianone, 1985), pp. 321–356.

— F.B.N.

Gabriela Mistral

Gabriela Mistral, the pen name of Lucila Godoy Alcayaga (1889–1957), the first Latin American writer to be awarded the Nobel Prize (1945), was born in a small town in northern Chile and was a schoolteacher (later a college professor in the United States) until 1935, when the Chilean Congress named her consul for life. She first acquired poetic fame in 1914 when she won a poetry contest in Santiago with her "Sonetos de la muerte" (Sonnets of Death), a brief but enduring cycle of poems inspired by the suicide of a young male acquaintance in 1909. Her first published collection of poems, *Desolación* (Desolation), appeared in the United States in 1922. Mistral's continental reputation was assured when the Mexican education minister, José Vasconcelos, invited her to Mexico in the early 1920s to contribute to the educational reforms implemented by the revolutionary government of Alvaro Obregón. She traveled through Mexico, setting up public libraries in remote locations and beginning a peripatetic existence. She lived in Brazil during World War II, and she died in New York, where she had been the Chilean representative to the United Nations since 1953.

Gabriela Mistral receiving the Nobel Prize for Literature from King Gustav V of Sweden, 1945

Gabriela Mistral published three other collections of poetry: *Ternura* (1924; Tenderness), *Tala* (1938; Felling), and *Lagar* (1954; Wine Press). In spite of her admiration for Rubén Darío, Mistral never embraced the cosmopolitan style of **Modernismo,** preferring instead a more traditional poetic idiom better suited to the expression of her artistic perceptions: earthly existence as a vale of tears, love for the poor, maternal love, and the description of regional landscapes. Mistral's poetry is supervised by a poetic persona that combines the archetypes of mother and teacher and never loses sight of regional culture, whose values and language (including those of the Old Testament) permeate it.

REFERENCES:

Marjorie Agosin, ed., *A Gabriela Mistral Reader,* translated by Maria Giachetti (Fredonia, N.Y.: White Pine Press, 1993);

Margot Arce de Vásquez, *Gabriela Mistral: The Poet and Her Work,* translated by Helene Massio Anderson (New York: New York University Press, 1964).

— R.G.M.

MITO

The Colombian literary review *Mito* (1955–1962) was founded by Jorge Gaitán Durán, whose goal was the modernization of national culture at a time when Colombia was suffering from the effects of **La Violencia** and a repressive military dictatorship. The review published original contributions and translations by noted national, Latin American, and European figures and works by younger writers — such as **Gabriel García Márquez** — who were soon to come into their own.

— R.G.M.

MODERN DANCE FESTIVALS

There are important dance festivals in several countries of Spanish-speaking South America. Those in Venezuela include the Temporada Latinoamericana de Danza de Caracas (Latin American Dance Season of Caracas), the Festival of Young Choreographers (see **Instituto Superior de Danza**), the Festival of Postmodern Dance at the International Workshop for Experimental Dance, and the International Meeting of Creators (all in Caracas). Argentina has the Danza Abierta (Open Dance), Otras Danzas (Other Dances), Teatro Presidente Alvear (all in Buenos Aires), and the Danza Libre (Free Dance) Festival of Corrientes. Bolivia has De Arte (About Art, a festival in which dance is one of several artistic activities), the International and National Festival of Culture in Sucre, and in La Paz the María Luisa Pacheco Festival, the Entrada del Gran Poder (Entrance of the Great Power, a traditional folkloric festival), and the University Folkloric Festival.

— N.D.B. & J.M.H.

MODERNISMO

A Spanish American literary movement of the late nineteenth century in prose and poetry, Modernismo marked the beginning of a distinctly Spanish American literary culture, founded not on indigenous but on cosmopolitan (especially French) artistic forms. It is important to note that modernismo is not equivalent to Anglo-American or to Brazilian modernism, movements that formally and chronologically correspond to the period of the Spanish American avant-garde.

The "modernity" of Spanish American modernistas is that of the French Romantics, Parnassians, and Symbolists. In France these styles followed each other in sequence, but in Spanish America they arrived simultaneously and were mixed in original ways. Modernista prose dates back to the early 1880s, and its most characteristic genre was the "crónica," a journalistic chronicle of artistic worth that ranged in content from a lecture by Oscar Wilde in New York to the latest technological invention. The Guatemalan Enrique Gómez Carrillo (1873–1927) was the master of the genre, but many other writers cultivated it with assiduity, among them José Martí (Cuba; 1853–1895), Manuel Gutiérrez Nájera (Mexico; 1859–1895), and Julián del Casal (Cuba; 1863–1893). Another prose genre favored by the modernistas was the "cuento azul," a whimsical tale modeled on those of French authors like Catulle Mendès and Alphonse Daudet.

In poetry, Modernismo is associated above all with the figure of Rubén Darío (Nicaragua; 1867–1916), the founder of Spanish American poetry and the outstanding literary artist of the turn of the century. Darío's first important book, *Azul* (1888; Azure), marks the onset of Modernismo and includes both poetry and prose. *Prosas profanas* (1896; Profane Hymns) represents the zenith of the initial, purely aesthetic phase of the movement, whose most frequent symbols are the swan, the fleur-de-lis, and the peacock. After the Spanish-American War (1898) and the concomitant rise of the United States as an imperialist power in Latin America, Darío turned in his third great book — *Cantos de vida y esperanza* (1905; Songs of Life and Hope) — to political themes, though he never ceased to be first and foremost a poet concerned with the invention of new forms and rhythms. In *Cantos de vida y esperanza,* the work that marks the end of the heyday of Modernismo, Darío also reverts to the Spanish tradition, seeking to reestablish a cultural continuity with the "Mother Country" spurred by Spain's loss of her last possessions in the New World.

In spite of the exoticism of Modernismo's cultural references and images (drawn from Greek and Teutonic mythology and from French reminiscences of pre-revolutionary Versailles), the movement is an organic though contradictory product of specifically Spanish American political, economic, and cultural conditions. The refinement and sheer luxury of the poetic objects and ambiences evoked by modernista poetry may be read as a sublimation of the materialism that characterized the incipient Spanish American bourgeoisie. The delicately wrought silk screens of the poems, the ample and ornate gardens with their statues and fountains, the desirable women, and other attractions of this ilk were possessions that money could buy and therefore were "understood" by the bourgeois reader; but they were also objects of art, beautiful things valuable in themselves and not only in terms of their exchange value, and this implication the crass bourgeois could never hope to understand. There is a necessary

analogy between the integration of the Latin American economies into the world market at the turn of the century and the rise of Modernismo as a cultural ideal. Both of these dynamics are exogenous and depend on foreign capital, not just money but also symbolic capital of the kind normally attached to the production of culture. The exportation of primary raw materials by economic producers (beef, hides, tin, copper, coffee, bananas, sugar, hemp) is part of the same cycle as the importation of symbolic goods carried out by modernista poets.

More significantly, the aesthetic principles of modernista poetry and the very forms and language of the poems reflect the new and specifically modern situation of the Spanish American poet around 1900. The gradual modernization of Latin American societies and the concomitant division of labor it promoted divorced poetic discourse from the traditional forms of cultural authority it had enjoyed in the earlier part of the nineteenth century, a process visible in the rise of philological studies (which contributed to making language and literature a separate and specialized field of inquiry) and even in the class allegiance of turn-of-the-century poets and novelists, who ceased to belong automatically to the ruling classes. Literature had been an avocation in the middle of the nineteenth century, but as more and more legislators and politicians were forced to specialize in their own disciplines literature became a separate vocation by the end of the century, only rarely practiced on the side by those with more urgent things to do. Darío knew he had to conjure up a new public for his poetry and that this public would have to come from the same bourgeois class he excoriated. His technical refinements, his deliberate use of rare words, his occasional hermeticism, his display of cultural knowledge, his insistence on individuality and originality, his evasive themes — in short, all Darío's attributes — can be explained as a response to the real situation of poetry in his time. The modern poet was an expert in a newly differentiated cultural domain and had to acquire the tools of the profession by dint of study in order to practice that profession legitimately. He was alone — devoid of a ready-made poetic idiom inherited from tradition and devoid of a public — and therefore compelled to develop an original poetic individuality. In this light, the modernistas' flights of fancy and their creation of a purely imaginary space in their poetry may be interpreted as the desire to transcend the difficult situation of the modern poet.

Other modernista poets were José Asunción Silva (Colombia; 1865–1896), Ricardo Jaimes Freyre (Bolivia; 1868–1933), Amado Nervo (Mexico; 1870–1919), Guillermo Valencia (Colombia; 1873–1943), José Santos Chocano (Peru; 1875–1934), Julio Herrera y Reissig

(Uruguay; 1875–1910), and **Leopoldo Lugones** (Argentina; 1874–1938). The last two mark the boundary of Modernismo because their deliberately exaggerated and often parodic work shows that they were self-consciously working with exhausted poetic forms.

REFERENCES:

Aníbal González, *La crónica modernista hispanoamericana* (Madrid: Gredos, 1983);

Rafael Gutiérrez Girardot, *Modernismo: Supuestos históricos y culturales* (Mexico: Fondo de Cultura Económica, 1988);

Max Henríquez Ureña, *Breve historia del modernismo* (Mexico: Fondo de Cultura Económica, 1954);

Angel Rama, *Rubén Darío y el modernismo* (Caracas: Ediciones de la Biblioteca de la Universidad Central de Venezuela, 1970).

— R.G.M.

MONTPARNASSE GROUP

The Chilean Montparnasse Group was composed of painters who went to Paris during the late 1920s on government grants to study art and assimilate the principles of modernism. In 1928 Minister of Public Instruction Pablo Ramírez considered Chilean painting incapable of transcending exhausted academic and **impressionist** styles and drastically in need of renewal. For this reason he closed the Escuela Nacional de Bellas Artes (National School of Fine Arts) for two years and gave grants to about thirty promising artists to study the most recent developments in Paris. Among these students were Julio Ortiz de Zárate, Camilo Mori, Luis Vargas Rosas, and José Perotti. In 1930 Ramírez founded the Facultad de Bellas Artes of the Universidad de Chile and hired as faculty some of the artists who had been trained in Europe. Part of their mandate was to organize and adjudicate an annual official exhibition of Chilean painting.

The modernism these artists introduced into Santiago was relative. Many of them worked in styles reminiscent of Paul Cézanne's, producing pieces that were still conservative in relation to more-modern movements such as Cubism or Constructivism. The members of the Montparnasse Group considered art to be based on plastic values and thus independent from its role as a means of representing reality; such independence was an important modernist principle. Although Pablo E. Burchard, the leader of the group, had not accompanied the other artists to Europe, he creatively assimilated the new approach, working with a bold sense of color reminiscent of Fauvism. Another important member of this group was Carlos Mori, who worked in a semiabstract style that also emphasized color.

The teachings of the Montparnasse Group strongly influenced the next important group of Chilean painters, the Generation of 1940, which included Israel Roa, Carlos Pedrazza, Raul Santelices, and Sergio Montecino, who painted in a style that recalls Fauvism, making color central to their art.

REFERENCE:

Gilbert Chase, *Contemporary Art in Latin America: Painting, Graphic Art, Sculpture and Architecture* (New York: Free Press, 1970), pp. 120–121.

— F.B.N.

CÉSAR MORO

César Moro was the pseudonym of Alfredo Quispez Asín (1903–1956), chief Peruvian Surrealist poet and author of *La tortuga ecuestre* (1957; The Equestrian Turtle), written in Spanish, and of other plaquettes written in French, including *Le Château de Grisou* (1943; The Gas Chateau) and *Amour à mort* (1957; Love until Death). The first volume of *Obra poética* (Complete Poems), a bilingual edition of all his poems, appeared in Lima in 1980.

REFERENCE:

James Higgins, *The Poet in Peru* (Liverpool: Francis Cairns, 1982).

— R.G.M.

MOVIES FROM BOOKS

There have been many movie versions of important twentieth-century Spanish American books. Some are rather wooden, such as the version of **Ricardo Güiraldes**'s *Don Segundo Sombra* (1926) directed by Manuel Antín and produced in 1969 (the actors were Juan Carballido, Juan Carlos Gené, Soledad Silveyra, and Alejandro Boero). **Gabriel García Márquez**'s short story "En este pueblo no hay ladrones" (translated as "In This Town There Are No Thieves") was adapted for the screen by Mexican directors Alberto Isaac and García Riera in 1964; it was entered in a competition sponsored by the Sindicato de Trabajadores de la Industria Cinematográfica (Union of Cinema Industry Employees) and was awarded second prize.

Guillermo Cabrera Infante's novel *Tres tristes tigres* (1966; translated as *Three Trapped Tigers*) was transposed to the big screen by Chilean director **Raúl Ruiz** in 1968. Dedicated to the Chilean poet **Nicanor Parra,** this film established Ruiz as the most experimental cineaste of his generation. (The sad/trapped tigers of the title are the petty-bourgeois protagonists

A scene from *Martín Fierro* (1969), Leopoldo Torre Nilsson's movie version of José Hernández's epic poem (1872, 1879) about the gauchos of Argentina

who hang out in bars talking about everything and nothing, unable to relate to the changing realities of society).

In Peru three directors of the Cuzco School, Eulogio Nishiyama, Luis Figueroa, and César Villanueva, produced *Jarawi* (1966), a feature-length documentary/fiction based on a short story by the Peruvian novelist **José María Arguedas.** Figueroa, cofounder of the Cuzco School, adapted **Ciro Alegría**'s novel *Los perros hambrientos* (1939; revised, 1942; The Hungry Dogs) for the screen in 1976 and Arguedas's novel *Yawar Fiesta* (1941; translated) in 1980. In Ecuador, Gustavo Guayasamín directed *El cielo para la Cushi, caraju* (1975; Cushi Goes to Heaven, Dammit), based on Ecuador's famous indigenist novel, *Huasipungo* (1934; translated), by Jorge Icaza.

Mario Vargas Llosa's novel *La ciudad y los perros* (1963; translated as *The Time of the Hero*) became a dramatic film in the hands of director Francisco J. Lombardi in 1986, though it lost some of its narrative refinements in the process. The film version (1976) of another Vargas Llosa novel, *Pantaleón y las visitadoras* (1973; translated as *Captain Pantoja and the Special Service*), in which the author himself made a fleeting appearance, was tedious. The same cannot be said of *Tune in Tomorrow* (1990), which moved the farcical soap-opera style of *La tía Julia y el escribidor* (1977; translated as *Aunt Julia and the Scriptwriter*) to New Orleans.

Fernando Solanas directed a film based on José Hernández's nineteenth-century poem about the gau-

cho way of life, *Martín Fierro,* with the title *Los hijos de Fierro* (1979; The Sons of Fierro). Another based on the same poem was made by **Torre Nilsson** in 1969. Solanas's film, which had some success in international circles, used the poem as a backdrop to explore Peronist militancy in the years between 1955 and 1973.

The novels of **Manuel Puig,** themselves inspired in good part by films, have been filmed; for example, *Boquitas pintadas* (1969; translated as *Heartbreak Tango*) was directed by Torre Nilsson. By far the most successful movie based on a work by Puig has been the English-language version of *El beso de la mujer araña* (1976; translated as *Kiss of the Spider Woman*), released in 1985. Theatrical and musical versions have also been popular.

Chilean director **Miguel Littín** made two movies from literary works in the late 1970s: *El recurso del método* (Reasons of State), filmed in 1977 and based on Alejo Carpentier's 1974 novel, and *La viuda de Montiel* (Montiel's Widow), released in 1979, a rather drawn-out adaptation of one of García Márquez's short stories. Much more successful was *Letters from the Park,* released in 1988, based on García Márquez's novel *El amor en los tiempos del cólera* (1985; translated as *Love in the Time of Cholera*) and directed by Cuban Tomás Gutierrez Alea; the screenplay was by Eliseo Alberto Diego and García Márquez, and the movie starred Víctor Laplace, Ivonne López, and Miguel Paneque. *Letters from the Park* is an imaginative rendering of García Márquez's novel and was described as "a charming and humorous romance" by the

San Francisco Chronicle. The English-language movie (1987), directed by Francesco Rosi and based on García Márquez's *Crónica de una muerte anunciada* (1981; translated as *Chronicle of a Death Foretold*), was only partially successful. ***No habrá más penas ni olvido*** (1983; A Funny, Dirty Little War), based on Osvaldo Soriano's 1980 novel, was directed by Argentinean Héctor Olivera.

The House of Spirits, directed by the Dane Billie August and starring Meryl Streep, Jeremy Irons, Glenn Close, and Winona Ryder, is based on **Isabel Allende**'s novel *La casa de los espíritus* (1982). Widely distributed, it opened in England in December 1993 and was released in the United States in early 1994. In England, the United States, and Mexico, where it was showing in the summer of 1994, the film was greeted rather frostily by the general public. The reviews were mixed; one reviewer in the Mexican magazine *Proceso,* for example, called the film a "distortion of magical realism."

REFERENCES:

John King, *Magical Reels: A History of Cinema in Latin America* (London: Verso, 1990);

Charles Ramírez Berg, *Cinema of Solitude: A Critical Study of Mexican Film, 1967–1983* (Austin: University of Texas Press, 1992).

— S.M.H. & P.S.

MANUEL MUJICA LÁINEZ

The cosmopolitan Argentinean writer Manuel Mujica Láinez (1910–1984) is admired for his aesthetically refined novels, especially *Bomarzo* (1962; translated), which he wrote after visiting the duke of Orsini's enclave in Viterbo at the end of the 1950s. *Bomarzo* is a richly stylized historical novel dealing with the intellectual contradictions of the Italian Renaissance and with a contradictory protagonist: the duke of Orsini, a hunchback of the utmost aesthetic refinement who seeks to synthesize opposites such as Christianity and paganism, God and the Devil, beauty and misery. It is perhaps the only Mannerist novel in Latin American literature, if by Mannerism one means the display of artificial beauty and trompe l'oeil effects. The ending of the novel suggests that the duke has achieved the immortality he was seeking and that he is the author of the novel the reader holds in his hands, a device that works because the narrative is cast in the form of a memoir. *Bomarzo* earned Mujica Láinez the National Prize for Literature in 1963 and was subsequently made into an opera by Argentinean composer **Alberto Ginastera.** Other notable works by Mujica Láinez include *La casa* (1957; The House), the last of a quartet of novels dealing with the Buenos Aires aristocracy; *El unicornio* (1965; translated as *The Wandering Unicorn*), in which the legendary figure Melusine recounts her love for the Knight of the Unicorn; and *El laberinto* (1974; The Labyrinth), a narrative modeled on the picaresque genre, whose protagonist crosses the Atlantic in search of Eldorado. Apart from his many novels, Mujica Láinez also wrote art criticism for the daily *La Nación* and translated fifty of Shakespeare's sonnets into Spanish.

REFERENCE:

George O. Schanzer, *The Persistence of Human Passions: Manuel Mujica Láinez's Satirical Neo-Modernism* (London: Tamesis Books, 1986).

— R.G.M.

LA MURALLA VERDE

La muralla verde (1970; The Green Wall), directed by Peruvian Armando Robles, is one of the most celebrated Latin American movies of the 1970s. It tells the story of a young married couple who, tired of life in the city, decide to move to a homestead in the Peruvian jungle. After a great deal of effort, they eventually overcome the nightmarish bureaucracy of Lima, buy the land, and build the house of their dreams. Tragedy strikes, however, when their son is bitten by a snake and, despite his parents' desperate attempt to transport him quickly to the nearest medical facilities, dies. Their idyll crumbles. The film concentrates on the struggle between the lifestyles of the city and the jungle, a struggle which is mediated by the politician who happens to be canvassing for votes in the area at that time. Visually, the cuts suggest that his winding political cavalcade is as poisonous for the people whose votes he seeks as the snake which kills the child. The tragedy of the film is made all the more poignant by the exquisite filming (by Robles's brother, Mario) of the physical environment of the Peruvian jungle. The film's final sequence, an almost wordless funeral, is both moving and haunting. The couple is played by Sandra Riva and Mexican star Julio Alemán.

— S.M.H.

H. A. MURENA

Argentinean essayist H. A. Murena (1923–) is best known for *El pecado original de América* (1958; [Latin] America's Original Sin), one of the many works by Spanish American essayists dealing with the issue of cultural identity. Like Octavio Paz in *El Laberinto de la soledad* (*The Labyrinth of Solitude*), Murena (whose real name is Héctor Alberto Alvarez) is heavily indebted to existentialist topics such as anguish, solitude, authenticity, and alienation. For Murena the condition of the Argentinean (and of Americans by extension) is defined by dispossession. Murena's American left history behind when he left Europe in order to be a citizen of the New World. Being historically and culturally dispossessed, Americans look back toward Europe with impossible nostalgia at the same time as they try to escape by any means possible from the frightful awareness of solitude in the vast natural stage of America. Nature does afford Murena's ahistorical subject a possibility of self-realization; yet the relationship between people and Nature must not be antithetical (as described in certain **regionalist novels**) but dialectical (as it sometimes is in the poetry of **Pablo Neruda**). Murena predicates cultural identity and ontological authenticity on the American's ability to absorb and be absorbed by Nature.

REFERENCE:

Martin S. Stabb, *In Quest Of Identity* (Chapel Hill: University of North Carolina Press, 1967).

— R.G.M.

Music

Latin America reverberates with the sounds of music that reveals an intricate mosaic of indigenous, foreign, and syncretic sonorities. Some Latin American music — such as ceremonial and festival music — has remained practically unchanged for hundreds of years, preserved primarily by indigenous groups. The ancient musics are proudly preserved, sometimes separately, sometimes through fusion with newer musics of the electronic age. Other examples demonstrate the evolution of Latin American music through its exposure to the influences of urban centers, the commercial recording industry, radio, motion pictures, television, and international tourism.

Since the Spanish explorations of the fifteenth century, an almost continuous flow of immigrants has brought other musical traditions to South America. Although Spain exerted the strongest European influence on Latin American musical cultures, a significant influx of Italians, Germans, and Portuguese also enriched the musical palette. At times these foreign musics have fused with indigenous music; at other times their original character has been preserved intact. European guitars, harps, and accordions, for example, often retained their original physical forms and musical functions, but many instruments were modified in order to respond to the material resources and musical needs of diverse populations in the New World. European forms and styles of music such as the **romance,** the **polca,** and the **vals** (waltz) were also preserved in original and modified versions.

A quite different and exceptionally strong musical tradition came with the African slaves whose descendants are still concentrated along the coastal lowlands, especially of the Caribbean. As is the case with European musical cultures, the African presence in the Americas has been one of great diversity; slaves were brought from many cultures which were marked by different languages, traditions, and musics.

During thousands of years of pre-Columbian migrations, native South Americans found homelands in which distinctive cultures gradually emerged within tribal groups, villages, and empires. In recent years, seminomadic groups have been discovered, groups which apparently have had little or no interaction with foreign cultures. Living in isolated regions, especially the Amazon basin, their social and cultural development appears to have been frozen in pre-Columbian time. A lack of interaction with the Spanish and African communities of South America, as well as a severe decline in their populations, has diminished the prominence of seminomadic indigenous musical practice in discussions of Latin American music; nevertheless, to understand current musical cultures of Latin America, we may ignore neither indigenous music of the present nor its influential past.

Attempts have been made to classify the major regions populated by South American Indians, based on geography and cultural variations, and there has been speculation regarding the numbers and types of languages spoken (see **Languages**). Ethnomusicologists, however, have not produced a classification of musical styles. Although certain similarities among musical styles may be found, particular features serve more to distinguish than to unify them.

Music among the indigenes is generally related to specific cultural functions. Planting songs, mourning songs, curing chants, and musical supplications to supernaturals are commonly performed. Indigenous musics are typically monophonic: in other words, they feature a single melody sung in unison. Cultures with less refined social and political systems tend to develop less sophisticated musical systems. Thus, some of the more remote groups of the Amazon region employ music of only one or two notes while others, such as the Jíbaro tribes of Ecuador, employ more-elaborate systems. Mobility is another factor affecting indigenous music: groups who migrate regularly in search of food sources are somewhat limited in the sophistication of their musical needs as well as in the number, size, and quality

Quechua Indians in the Cuzco area of Peru playing violin, harp, and quena

of instruments that can be easily transported and safely preserved in unforgiving climates. Also significant is isolation: those who have continued to live far from contact with outside influences have retained the attributes of native musical expression with minimal, if any, European or other foreign influence. Consequently, specialists tend to distinguish indigenous music by the presence or absence of European elements.

Civilizations such as those that culminated with the great Inca empire developed relatively stable societies with permanent, sheltered ceremonial and living sites, and their musical accouterments tended to reflect their more-elaborate lifestyles and greater degree of technological advancement. In these societies the greatest social and cultural contact with the Europeans occurred, and it is in them that we still see acculturation in progress.

Indigenous instruments are normally constructed or adapted from materials which are accessible in the regions where specific groups live. Normally, the instruments are closely associated with particular traditions and customs and tend to resist change. Numerous percussion instruments, from the simplest **idiophones** to more sophisticated **membranophones,** provide a rhythmic foundation for songs and dances. Rocks, shells, seeds, animal bones, sticks, gourds, and similar materials are examples of idiophones used in abundance. Drums of different shapes and sizes requiring animal skins, membranophones are practically insepa-

rable from indigenous musics. The category of aerophones incorporates all types of instruments that produce sound by the movement of air; flutes of many types made from a variety of materials constitute the largest group. **Chordophones** are stringed instruments that gained popularity among tribes interacting with European and African cultures, but they are not common among remote nomadic groups. Indigenous musical instruments are normally endowed with an elaborate symbolism in their form, in the sounds they produce, and in the sexual roles they represent. The shape and construction of the instrument may explicitly describe what it represents: the flute as a phallic symbol or the conch-shell trumpet as a vaginal symbol, for example. The skin-head drum and drumstick typically convey a sexually symbolic creative union.

We do not know with precision how pre-Columbian music sounded. The Catholic Church generally condemned indigenous music because of its close association with pagan rituals and ceremonies; consequently, the colonial authorities made no attempt to preserve it. On the contrary, the conscious effort of the Catholic Church was to replace native musics with European genres, especially with liturgical and sacred music. Indeed, the Catholic Church in colonial South America exerted a powerful and pervasive influence over all areas of daily life. Music was a principal feature of Catholic services and became one of the clergy's most effective tools for the conversion of native populations. There are numerous accounts of the attraction that European music and instruments held for Native Americans throughout the Americas.

Cathedrals, requiring extensive musical provision, were established in the important colonial cities of the early colonial period. Among them were Cartagena and Bogotá in Colombia, Quito in Ecuador, La Plata (now Sucre) in Bolivia, and Cuzco and Lima in Peru. Spanish singers, instrumentalists, composers, and teachers were appointed to ensure that the quantity and quality of music required for daily services would be available. Pipe organs and stringed and wind instruments were brought from Spain to be used in services and for musical instruction. Considerable effort was made to teach the indigenous hopefuls and a growing Creole society not only to sing the liturgy of the church but also to play its instruments and even to compose polyphonic music. Jesuit and Franciscan missionaries in South America placed special emphasis on music by providing instruction in Gregorian chant and, subsequently, vocal polyphony. Singing schools, choirs, and small orchestras were set up to serve the musical needs of Catholic services, especially in Argentina, Bolivia, Colombia, Ecuador, and Paraguay. In Peru descendants of the Inca nobility were provided special opportunities to learn European musical styles. By the early eighteenth century South American musicians were being favorably compared with their European counterparts for the quality of performances.

Music in the cathedrals differed from that of the missions. The cathedrals, which were economically privileged, employed trained European musicians who were augmented by Native American converts. These cathedral centers became vast repositories of music and manuscripts that nowadays make possible performances of an abundant musical heritage. The cathedrals featured elaborate musical services that were overwhelmingly European in origin. Cathedral musicians also often provided European music for social occasions in the community, eventually leading to the establishment of secular, classical music traditions in the urban centers. Priests in the early Catholic missions, often located in remote areas, were of necessity more involved personally with teaching than were their counterparts in the cathedrals. Without sacrificing the norms of Catholic liturgy (Gregorian chant, psalms, and antiphons), mission music tended to exhibit a greater degree of compromise with native musical traditions than did cathedral music. Missionaries taught the indigenes nonliturgical hymns and songs of praise, which, when combined with native musical traits, led to the development of a syncretic South American folk music.

The secular music of the European colonials included both vocal and instrumental genres and focused on theatrical music, songs of romance, history, adventure, and dances. Public and private musical entertainments included an increasing mixture of European and indigenous elements. Early in the colonial era native Americans and Creoles began to construct imitations of European instruments, a practice that continues to the present. Handmade violins, harps, and unique versions of Spanish guitars proliferated in those areas where there was close association between Europeans and indigenous people. Gradually, these instruments were used for musics that incorporated mixed European and indigenous elements.

Colonial attempts to enslave Indian populations as a potential workforce in Latin America had mixed results. Although large numbers of Indians were in fact enslaved, and many died as a consequence of maltreatment and European diseases, others refused to serve, sometimes relocating to more remote areas or even committing suicide. African slavery was introduced into the Caribbean by the mid sixteenth century to provide a reliable workforce for mining and agriculture. Gradually spreading to South America, especially to the coastal regions, the slaves, who were primarily from West Africa, brought with them yet other foreign cultures that influenced South American music. References to African influences on Latin American music sometimes fail to mention the immense variety of African cultures transported to the Americas. Slave traders had no interest in maintaining the cultural integrity of tribal groups. On the contrary, individuals with different tribal customs, languages, and musics were mixed. Communication among them was often extremely limited, if not impossible, except through the language of their eventual owners.

The largest concentrations of African descendants in Spanish-speaking South America are found in Colombia, Ecuador, and Venezuela. There, the impact on musical culture is particularly strong; furthermore, the proximity of these areas to Afro-Antillean musical cultures of the Caribbean has provided for continuous exchange and interaction. African and mulatto populations are also found in other South American countries, but, with the exception of Brazil, their numbers are small when compared to other ethnic groups. Therefore, while their musical practices may be quite varied, their influence on the musical culture of the majority has been limited.

The African musical presence is expressed through characteristic melodic and rhythmic configurations, African-derived instruments, the prominence of percussion accompaniments, and certain performance procedures such as the call-and-response format that features a soloist's statement followed by a communal response. Among the popular older genres performed in social and other festivities in Colombia are the **cumbia,** the **currulao,** the **bambuco** viejo, and the **lumbalú.** More-recent popular genres imported from the Antilles islands include salsa, merengue, and reggae in both English and Hispanic versions. Another of the major contributions of West Africa to Latin American music may be observed in the number and variety of instruments that were re-created in the Americas. Forbidden to bring personal possessions with them as slaves, Africans and their descendants in the Americas reconstructed instruments similar to those of their homelands from available materials in their new surroundings. Single- and double-skin drums in various shapes and sizes figure prominently in music throughout Latin America. Not all are African-derived; many types of drums originated with South American Indians, but the conga drums, the **bongos,** and the tambora are of African origin, and many of them are related to worship ceremonies of African American religious cults: candomblé in Brazil, Santería in the Antilles, and voodoo in Haiti are religious traditions of the Yoruba and Bantu still practiced by many descendants of West Africans. Other percussion instruments are claves (two short sticks of hardwood struck together), cowbells, and the **marimba,** a percussion instrument capable of both melodic and harmonic roles and one prominent throughout Mesoamerica and the Pacific coasts of Colombia and Ecuador. Although Central America claims credit for having invented the marimba (and it is the national instrument of Guatemala), most scholars believe it is a descendant of the African xylophone.

Perhaps the most pervasive African influence on Latin American music has been in rhythm. Not confined to the traditional European sense of rhythmic order, African rhythms tend to employ a variety of procedures simultaneously, including mixed meters, polyrhythms within a single meter, and syncopation. These rhythmic devices provide a series of accents, both on and off the beat, and the appearance of accents in unexpected places of the melodic/harmonic progression subverts the regularity of the European measure. To add to the complexity, African-derived melodic progressions in Latin American music incorporate many similar procedures to those common in African rhythms.

Despite their independent origins, various syncretisms were possible between the indigenous and foreign musical cultures because there were many compatibilities within their musical systems and similarities of musical function in their cultures. In general, indigenous, European, and African societies all placed high value on their musical cultures. All employed music for social and religious purposes and all supported both vocal and instrumental genres. These similarities facilitated the confluence of musical traditions to form Creole musics. The term *Creole musics* refers to genres of music in the Americas that have been produced and preserved by populations of mixed ethnic and cultural origins. While the term has been used to identify the music of Latin American–born descendants of Europeans, today its meaning is often less specific and may refer to the products of those descended from any of the ethnic groups born in the Americas.

European missionary zeal enforced acceptance of Catholic Church music among Creole societies, generating a tradition of composition in European styles among native-born composers, one of which is still very much in evidence. Yet, in spite of often-intolerant Church policies, indigenous and African communities preserved their own versions of religious music for worship and healing, sometimes practicing in secret and at other times disguising them under Christian paraphernalia. Secular music was apparently of less concern to the Catholic Church as long as it did not seem to contribute to immoral or illegal behavior; but in any case it was often beyond Catholic control, especially in isolated missions.

Gradually, the Indians and the growing mestizo populations were able to exercise more freedom of expression regarding preferred forms and styles of music for entertainment. In addition, increasing numbers of colonists maintained a healthy interest in European secular music for their own pleasure and entertainment. Their dances and songs, such as the waltz and the **romance,** eventually blended with indigenous and African elements in a process of acculturation that resulted in various mestizo musical cultures. In Andean music, for example, the **huaiño,** a pre-Columbian funeral dance among the Quechua Indians, is today a lively secular song-dance form featuring European metrical and phrase organization and, at times, combining Spanish, Quechua, or Aymara lyrics. In addition, the pentatonic scale, featured in many Andean indigenous melodies, combined with European major and minor modes and gradually produced a syncretism of melodic and harmonic practice. Similar examples of the fusion of musical features from various cultures may be seen in the **yaraví,** the **triste,** and the **bailecito,** distinctive song-dance forms of the Andes; in the **tango** and **milonga,** Argentinean music of the Río de la Plata region; in the Chilean cueca; in the Venezuelan **joropo** and vals; and in the cumbia and bambuco of Colombia.

Individual examples of these syncretic musics seldom feature musical equality of the constituent cultures; more common is a subtle predominance of one culture accompanied by a mixture of elements from the other principal sources. The lyrics of most Creole musics generally follow forms and styles of European models, frequently depending upon rhymed couplets for verses and refrains. Verses are typically sung by a soloist, sometimes two soloists in alternation, followed by a choral or communal refrain. Lyrics are most frequently in Spanish but may be performed in indigenous languages such as Quechua and Aymara, or in mixtures of languages. The melodic progressions of Creole musics represent a subtle blend of European major and minor modes mixed with indigenous modes. The verse melodies are most often followed by unison refrains, but simple harmonizations may be improvised by the communal chorus. Harmonic accompaniments reflect typical European practice but are restricted to a limited harmonic vocabulary. A true image of the syncretism inherent in mestizo musics may be seen in the instruments employed. Indigenous flutes (**quenas**), panpipes (**sicus**), drums (**bombos**), rattles, and scrapers are combined with instruments derived from European models, such as the Andean **charango,** the Venezuelan **cuatro,** the Colombian **tiple,** and the Río de la Plata region's **bandoneón.**

The repertories of Creole musics are the largest and most prominent in Latin America. In addition to their pervasive role in South American everyday life and in **festivals** and celebrations, these musics are now easily accessible to worldwide audiences through numerous recordings and live performances. With the exception of certain remote tribal musics and some cultivated art music of the European tradition, it would be difficult to identify current musics in Latin America that reflect pure ethnic practice, devoid of influence from other cultural groups. There are, however, genres of music, institutions, and activities that preserve a predominantly European, indigenous, or African heritage. Most Latin American republics, for example, support symphony orchestras, chamber ensembles, opera, and conservatories of music in the cultivated art-music tradition.

As was the case with other cultural manifestations, particularly literature, the preferred musical styles for Creole activities, whether religious or secular, for a long time mirrored those of Europe, although somewhat belatedly and sometimes by as much as a hundred years. Renaissance polyphonic styles in sacred music, for example, were still in vogue in South America until the middle of the eighteenth century. In art music, all of the prevailing European musical styles (preclassical, classical, Romantic, impressionistic, neoclassical, atonal, and polytonal) found adherents among South American composers and performers. The dependency on European models has lasted well into the twentieth century, but there have been important alternative tendencies, among them **nationalism.** Nationalism (which has its counterparts in literature and art) relied on obvious references to local resources, such as indigenous themes, instruments, legends, or dances, and used them in a traditional European format (symphony, suite, sonata, opera). Andean nationalism, for example, was represented by Colombia's **Guillermo Uribe-Holguín** (1880-1971), Bolivia's José María Velasco Maidana (1900–), Chile's Carlos Lavín (1883–1962), and Peru's **Teodoro Valcárcel** (1902–1942), all of whom incorporated nationalistic indigenous elements into their music destined for the concert hall. In Argentina **Felipe Boero** (1880–1958) and **Alberto Ginastera** (1916–1983) were recognized respectively for their nationalistic operas and ballets. The creative mind of the composer, however, is seldom wont to dwell forever in a single style: composers tend to explore new structures, new sonorities, new means of communicating with contemporary audiences. Attempts to place labels on South American composers tend to run aground because, even if a composer wrote nationalistic music, he may well also have composed in a more cosmopolitan style and perhaps ventured into experimental music as well. Many South American composers developed beyond nationalistic interests and sought to communicate with a larger, cosmopolitan audience through other means. Influenced by French Impressionism, twelve-tone composition, and neoclassicism, they began to reveal a closer relationship to the new Western European musical aesthetics. Among the leaders were Chile's Alfonso Letelier (1912–) and **Juan Orrego-Salas** (1919–) and Argentina's **Juan Carlos Paz** (1901–1972).

Following World War II, improved electronic communications and means of travel empowered South American composers with easier access to the avant-garde movements. Polytonality, atonality, serial techniques, and the electronic synthesizer have all been explored and exploited by contemporary South American composers. At the same time, more international venues have become accessible to Latin American musicians, owing to an increasing interest in world music cultures. International performances have brought worldwide attention to otherwise unfamiliar composers. In addition to greater exposure to international audiences, the *Inter-American Music Bulletin,* published by the **Organization of American States** (OAS), has served to document publicly the achievements of Latin American composers. Throughout this century, but especially since World War II, the musics of Latin America have enjoyed wide exposure in global markets; most cabaret musicians today find it profitable to maintain at least a partial repertoire of Latin music. Music in Latin America continues to evolve through the absorption and modification of foreign musical influences. Although traditional folk musics are preserved with care and affection, Latin rock, jazz, and reggae are popular genres that attract large followings and increasingly occupy the attention of the young. For decades in the twentieth century, recorded music from the United States flooded the radios, motion pictures, television, private homes, and educational institutions of South America. Today there is a more-equitable exchange. North America's popular, commercial, and art musics reveal strong influences from South America. (See also **Dance.**)

—R.L.S.

ALVARO MUTIS

Colombian poet and storyteller Alvaro Mutis (1923–) creates works that are steeped in the primary sources of imaginative literature (such as marvelous accounts of foreign places or of everyday reality found in traditional narratives like *The Arabian Nights*) as well as in a peculiarly modern angst prompted by the ubiquitous presence of death and decay. In his second poetry collection — *Los elementos del desastre* (1953; The Elements of Disaster) — Mutis created a character, Maqroll el gaviero (Maqroll the Lookout), who has some similarities with Joseph Conrad's Marlow and who has functioned as the author's alter ego in many of his subsequent books. Maqroll is the experienced observer often hurled into a dismal, hopelessly tangled world. In the 1950s Mutis was part of the group of young poets set on renovating Colombian literature, a group that came together in connection with a review called *Mito.* He is also a close friend of **Gabriel García Márquez,** who dedicated his novel *El general en su laberinto* (1989; translated as *The General in His Labyrinth*) to Mutis in return for his having given García Márquez the idea for it. The imprint of Mutis in García Márquez's novel is not hard to find: *The General in His Labyrinth* narrates Simón Bolívar's last journey down the Magdalena River toward exile and death; the river or ocean journey is a recurrent motif in Mutis's own work.

The poetic production of Mutis's first two decades is collected in *Summa de Maqroll el gaviero* (1973). Subsequent works of poetry are *Caravansary* (1982), *Los emisarios* (1984; The Emissaries), and *Crónica y alabanza del reino* (1985; Chronicle and Praise of the Kingdom). Mutis's best-known novels are his first, *La mansión de Araucaíma* (1973), and *La nieve del Almirante* (1986; translated as *The Snow of the Admiral*). The English version of the latter is included in *Maqroll: Three Novellas* (1992). Mutis was awarded the Premio Nacional de Literatura de Colombia in 1983. He has lived in Mexico since the 1950s.

REFERENCE:

J. G. Cobo Borda, *Alvaro Mutis* (Bogotá: Procultura, 1989).

—R.G.M.

N

LA NACIÓN

Founded in 1870, *La Nación,* a noted national Argentinean newspaper, is arguably the most important newspaper currently published in South America and holds the record for longevity in Latin America. Its longevity is due in no small degree to its being a family business passed on from generation to generation; the present director, Bartolomé Mitre, is a direct descendant of the nineteenth-century president who founded the newspaper (also named Bartolomé Mitre). *La Nación* became more independent of the government line when editorship fell to the grandsons of its founder, Luis Mitre and Jorge A. Mitre, in 1909. It has clung to its independence doggedly despite rough times, when President **Juan Domingo Perón,** irritated by the daily's criticism of his policies, forced it to cut its circulation and to reduce its pages to a maximum of five, a prohibition which was lifted in 1955. Having weathered a rocky period during the **Guerra Sucia** (Dirty War) of 1976–1983, *La Nación* continues to assert itself as a serious world news–oriented daily with sections on sports, business, culture, and literature.

REFERENCE:

Robert N. Pierce and Kurt Kent, "Newspapers," in *Handbook of Latin American Popular Culture,* edited by Harold E. Hinds Jr. and Charles M. Tatum (Westport, Conn.: Greenwood Press, 1985), pp. 229–250.

— S.M.H.

NADAÍSMO

The poetic movement Nadaísmo, founded by Gonzalo Arango in Medellín, Colombia, in 1958, was composed of lower-middle-class youths disaffected with all as- pects of Colombian society. The group's name suggests nihilism and echoes the Dadaism of the earlier European avant-garde. The Nadaístas, who shared a radical cultural attitude, had lived through the most traumatic decade in recent Colombian history, the decade of **La Violencia** (1948–1958), a violent and protracted civil war that resulted in the deaths of hundreds of thousands of mostly rural inhabitants. Nadaísmo gained a national, as opposed to regional, scope in the early 1960s, when the original Nadaístas "toured" several Colombian cities, picking up many adherents in Cali. The group's public shenanigans were colorful, to say the least. In Cali they suggested that the bust of Jorge Isaacs (the author of the classic nineteenth-century Colombian novel *María*) might be replaced by one of French movie star Brigitte Bardot. The members of the group also shocked the public by dwelling on the virtues of free love and hallucinogenic drugs. On a less frivolous note, Arango was thrown in prison for directing a vitriolic manifesto against the hierarchs of the Catholic Church when they convened in Medellín in 1959. (A posthumous collection of his "prophecies," uttered in earnest, is in fact titled *Memorias de un presidiario nadaísta* [1991; Memoirs of a Nadaísta Convict].) Nadaísmo acquired an "official" profile in 1963, when *13 poetas nadaístas* was published, an anthology that grouped thirteen poets affiliated to the movement. The anthology includes poetry by Arango, Mario Rivero, Elmo Valencia, Eduardo Escobar, Alberto Escobar, Jaime Jaramillo Escobar (also known as X-504), Darío Lemos, and Jota Mario and prose by Humberto Navarro, Amilcar Osorio, and Jaime Espinel. A few other names were added to the Nadaísta roster three years later upon the publication of *De la nada al nadaísmo* (From Nothingness to Nadaism). In the early 1970s, and somewhat belatedly, the movement had its own journal, *Nadaísmo 70,* which lasted for only eight issues. Nadaísta poetry was iconoclastic, sardonic, and often prosaic.

Arango's poetry is collected in *Obra negra* (1974; Black Opus). Other important books by Nadaístas are *Los poemas de la ofensa* (1968; Poems on the Offensive), by X-504; Eduardo Escobar's *Invención de la uva* (1966; Invention of the Grape) and *Monólogos de Noé* (1967; Monologues of Noah); and *El poeta de vidrio* (The Glass Poet), by Armando Romero, collected in *Del aire a la mano* (1983; From Air to Hand).

— R.G.M.

NATIONALISM IN MUSIC

Nationalism is an important and distinctive tendency in the tradition of cultivated art (classical) music in South America. Prevalent in the first three decades of the century, nationalism may be thought of as a musical counterpart of **regionalism** and **Indigenism** in literature and art; like them, nationalism relied on obvious references to local resources, such as indigenous themes, instruments, legends, or dances, though often using these things in a traditional European format (symphony, suite, sonata, opera). Notable figures in Andean nationalism, for example, were **Guillermo Uribe-Holguín** (Colombia), José María Velasco Maidana (Bolivia), and **Teodoro Valcárcel** (Peru), all of whom incorporated indigenous elements of nationalistic value into their concert-hall music. The main figure in Chile was Carlos Lavín; in Argentina **Felipe Boero** and **Alberto Ginastera,** who coined the term *objective nationalism,* were recognized respectively for their nationalistic operas and ballets. For many such composers, however, nationalism was only one of several phases in their careers.

REFERENCE:

Gerard Béhague, *Music in Latin America: An Introduction* (Englewood Cliffs, N.J.: Prentice-Hall, 1979).

— P.S.

EDGAR NEGRET

The Colombian sculptor Edgar Negret (1920–) has stretched the limits of **Geometric Abstraction** by working with aluminum modules that simultaneously evoke poetic, organic, and industrial qualities. After studying art in Colombia, Negret went to New York in 1948. There he produced highly stylized linear sculptures made of steel in a manner reminiscent of

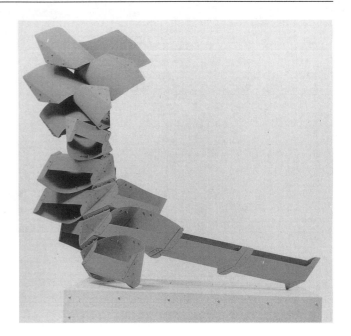

Escalera (1972; Staircase), by Edgar Negret (Collection Hanoj Pérez, Bogotá)

the wire sculptures by U.S. artist Alexander Calder. Negret settled in Paris during the early 1950s and met the Venezuelans **Alejandro Otero** and **Jesús Rafael Soto,** whose art encouraged him to continue exploring abstract modes. While in Spain he became fascinated with Antoni Gaudí's wrought-iron works and began to produce welded iron pieces. By the time he returned to New York in 1955, he was working with modular sculptures made of thin sheets of aluminum joined together with nuts and bolts, as in his series *Aparatos Mágicos* (1955–1965; Magic Apparatuses). He balanced the coldness of the industrial materials of his nonfunctioning machines by using playful combinations of shapes and colors.

In 1963 Negret returned to Bogotá and began teaching at the Universidad de los Andes. In his sculptures he arranged the aluminum modules in sequences in order to create shapes that simultaneously emphasize organic and industrial qualities, as in *Acoplamiento* (1966–1971; Coupling). In his sculptures Negret often includes references to pre-Columbian art, something that links his work to the tradition of **Constructive Art.** During the 1970s, in works such as *Navegador III* (1971; Navigator III), he also emphasized the themes of space travel and fantastic architecture, while in more-recent pieces, such as *Libélula* (1983; Dragonfly), he favored a more organic approach to art. In 1983 Negret founded a museum to house his own art in his native Popayán.

REFERENCE:

Aracy Amaral, "Abstract Constructivist Trends in Argentina, Brazil, Venezuela, and Colombia," in *Latin American Artists of the Twentieth Century,* edited by Waldo Rasmussen, Fatima Bercht, and Elizabeth Ferrer (New York: Museum of Modern Art, 1993), pp. 86–99.

—F.B.N.

NEO-AVANT-GARDE POETRY

Neo-avant-garde poetry is a convenient term to refer to the various avant-garde groups that dotted the Latin American cultural landscape in the 1960s and later. In spite of their juvenile excesses and often pamphleteering poetry, these groups were important as proving grounds for writers who later developed their own individual voices, or because they reinvigorated more than one moribund cultural tradition. As befits any self-respecting avant-garde movement, these neo-avant-garde groups railed against the literary past and the social establishment.

—R.G.M.

NEOFIGURATION

Neofiguration (also called *New Figuration,* a term coined in Paris by Michel Ragon) refers to a generalized trend toward figuration and the representation of the human figure that emerged in Europe, the United States, and Latin America during the 1950s. Many of the European artists who worked in neofigurative styles, such as the members of the COBRA group, Jean Dubuffet, and Francis Bacon, expressed existentialist concerns relating to the place of the individual in the unsettling context of postwar Europe. In Latin America the industrialization and urban growth of the 1940s and 1950s resulted in an increasingly alienating urban lifestyle, which also made artists receptive to existentialist ideas. Neofiguration became an important trend first in Mexico, with the work of José Luis Cuevas and the Nueva Presencia group, and soon thereafter in Argentina and Venezuela.

In Argentina neofiguration was developed in the early 1960s by the members of the **Otra Figuración** group, which included Ernesto Deira, Rómulo Macció, **Luis Felipe Noé** and **Jorge de la Vega,** and in the art of **Antonio Berni,** who had worked in realist modes since the 1930s. These artists attacked traditional views of art prevalent in Argentina, such as notions of "good taste," careful execution, and the dichotomy between abstraction and figuration. They blended the spontaneous manner and preference for thick textural surfaces of **Informal Abstraction** with figuration, an approach that in the case of Otra Figuración resulted in monsterlike images of alienated beings. Berni, however, made his figuration expressionistic by collaging trash and discarded objects on the canvas or support. Consequently, his art is hard to classify, since it shares characteristics with Pop Art and Assemblages; in fact, neofiguration coexisted during the 1960s with the development of **Pop Art, Assemblages, and Happenings,** and artists such as Noé and Berni often explored several styles simultaneously in their work.

Another common feature in the work of Argentinean neofigurative artists is frequent reference to social and political issues, something that ties their general interest in human nature to a specific historical context. Similarly, the Venezuelan **Jacobo Borges** synthesized figurative elements with Informal Abstract techniques in order to question the authority of repressive governments and the role played by the media in legitimizing state power and perpetuating social stereotypes. After experimenting with Pop Art, Assemblages, and Happenings during the late 1960s, his work became concerned with deeper psychological explorations.

REFERENCE:

Jacqueline Barnitz, "New Figuration, Pop, and Assemblage in the 1960s and 1970s," in *Latin American Artists of the Twentieth Century,* edited by Waldo Rasmussen, Fatima Bercht, and Elizabeth Ferrer (New York: Museum of Modern Art, 1993), pp. 122–133.

—F.B.N.

MATILDE NERUDA

The third and last wife of poet **Pablo Neruda,** Matilde Urrutia (1912–1985) met the poet in 1946 and married him in 1955. The relationship of the poet and his "muse" was the greatest romance in Chilean literature, signed and sealed by Neruda's dedication of his *Cien sonetos de amor* (1959; One Hundred Love Sonnets) to his wife. Matilde Neruda reluctantly became a public figure and political symbol of resistance after the death of the poet in September 1973, less than two weeks after the military coup that brought Gen. **Augusto Pinochet** to power. She died in January 1985, having seen to the preservation for posterity of the poet's manuscripts, rare books, and other personal effects that now make up the Neruda estate. Leading Chilean novelist **José Donoso** paid homage to Neruda's widow by centering his novel *La desesperanza* (1986; translated as *Curfew*) on the twenty-four hours that elapsed between her death and her funeral.

—R.G.M.

Juanito dormido (1978; Juanito Sleeping), by Antonio Berni (from Oriana
Baddeley and Valerie Fraser, *Drawing the Line*, 1989)

PABLO NERUDA

Pablo Neruda (1904–1973) was born Ricardo Neftalí
Reyes Basoalto. The son of a railroad worker and born
on the southernmost Chilean frontier, he was destined
to become perhaps the most widely read poet in the
Spanish language. In his early teens Neruda was already confident that he would be a poet; the first poem
he sent to be published was signed "Pablo Neruda," a
name he found at random in a literary magazine
(where there was a story by the Czech writer Jan
Neruda) and filched in order to avoid paternal wrath
for engaging in the lowly endeavor of poetry. It was not
until 1946, when his father was dead, that Neruda le-
gally changed his name to that of his Czech alter ego.

Neruda moved to Santiago, the Chilean capital,
in his midteens and in 1924 published a thin book that
made him an instant celebrity: *Veinte poemas de amor
y una canción desesperada* (translated as *Twenty Love
Poems and a Song of Despair*), a masterpiece of youthful romantic love that for decades has been an indis-
pensable aid to courtship and other amatory rituals.
The poetry is fresh and sensual, metaphorically auda-
cious, and free of rhetorical clichés.

For all the success of his book, however, Neruda
lived in poverty as he attended the university by day
and the bohemian dens, where other indigent young
poets passed the time in revelry and reverie, at night.
At this time Neruda was writing some of the poetically
revolutionary texts that would later make up *Residencia en la tierra* (1933; translated as *Residence on Earth*),
his great Surrealist meditation on alienation and melancholy. These feelings were aggravated when the poet
departed for the Far East in 1927 to occupy the position of honorary consul in Rangoon, Colombo, Batavia
(present-day Djakarta), and Singapore. Neruda spent

Pablo and Matilde Neruda

five lonely years abroad; his experience is reflected in the hermetic poetry he wrote in the inhospitable and colonial East during this period. The first edition of *Residencia en la tierra* was published in Santiago; a second and enlarged edition in two volumes followed in Madrid in 1935 and included poems written after Neruda's return to Chile; a third and final volume appeared in Buenos Aires in 1947, comprising poems written up to 1945.

The *Residencia en la tierra* cycle represents a formal break with Neruda's previous neo-Romanticism and marks the inception and elaboration of a poetics of "impure poetry," which sets out to subvert the various theories of pure poetry then in vogue, particularly the theory and practice of the reigning Spanish poet of the period, Juan Ramón Jiménez. Neruda's "unpoetic" and dissonant language, his Surrealist images, and the chaotic syntax of many of his verses were not only an attempt to render his existential anguish faithfully but also a conscious effort to found a new kind of poetry through the destruction of traditional forms. There is a note of poetic anguish in the work born from the poet's inability to respond with the appropriate prophetic voice to the demands of the self and the world. The prophetic response thwarted in *Residencia en la*

tierra manifests itself in Neruda's next major work, *Canto general* (1950; translated).

In the second half of the 1930s the isolated protagonist of the *Residencia en la tierra* poems is overrun by History. The most dramatic shift in Neruda's poetic trajectory begins with the Spanish Civil War (1936–1939), which Neruda witnessed firsthand in Madrid in his official consular capacity and also in his unofficial role as poet and intellectual. As consul he was responsible for arranging the resettlement in Chile of hundreds of Republican refugees; as poet he left a burning indictment of Franco's uprising in *España en el corazón* (translated as *Spain in the Heart*), a short volume of war poems first published in 1937 in Spain. From that point on Neruda was a public poet, and his life and his poetry were inextricably bound with historical events.

During World War II Neruda was consul in Mexico, where he provoked the local authorities by posting his "Song to Stalingrad" in public places. The authorities responded by expelling the poet from the country for contravening Mexico's neutral stand. In 1945, once again back in Chile, Neruda joined the Communist Party and successfully ran for the senate but was promptly impeached for publicly calling the president a traitor. An arrest order was issued, and Neruda went into hiding. More than a year later (in 1949) he was fortunate to escape to Europe via Argentina.

In this tumultuous decade Neruda finished his *Canto general,* an epic and encyclopedic account of Latin America from creation to the present that exalts its geography even as it excoriates its history as a tale of oppression of the many by the few. Some of the fifteen cantos of the poem are a chronicle of Neruda's times, and one of its protagonists is the chronicler himself. The most compelling and memorable section of *Canto general* is "The Heights of Machu Picchu," a poem of almost mystical intensity that narrates the poet's ascent to the ruins of the fabled Inca citadel. Upon reaching the summit, the poet makes a vow to speak for the city's dead and for the living of today, engaged in the same struggle against oppression as their indigenous ancestors. With *Canto general* Neruda becomes a Latin American Walt Whitman, a poet of continental dimensions able to handle the prophetic tone convincingly.

Neruda was also a master of the minimalist style, as he showed in *Odas elementales* (1954; Elemental Odes), an extraordinary collection of informal odes demystifying the poet's role and celebrating the objects and substances of everyday life. Neruda's at times playful metaphoric elaboration of things such as artichokes and woolen socks did not mean a retreat from the political front (other political books followed later) but an attempt to widen the circle of poetry readers. Three other books of odes followed in the 1950s.

In 1969 the Chilean Communist Party backed Neruda's candidacy for the presidential elections of the following year, but in early 1970, and much to the poet's relief, the unified Left settled on **Salvador Allende** instead. Allende won the elections and appointed Neruda ambassador to France in the same year that the poet was awarded the Nobel Prize for literature (1971). On 11 September 1973 a bloody military coup overthrew the Allende government and dealt a final blow to Neruda's dream of a socialist Chile. The poet died a few days later. Among the most significant works of Neruda's final years is the autobiographical *Memorial de Isla Negra* (1964).

REFERENCES:

René de Costa, *The Poetry of Pablo Neruda* (Cambridge, Mass.: Harvard University Press, 1979);

Volodia Teitelboim, *Neruda: A Personal Biography,* translated by Beverly J. DeLong-Tonelli (Austin: University of Texas Press, 1991).

— R.G.M.

NEW LATIN AMERICAN CINEMA

The most sophisticated type of urban popular culture, and the closest to the discourse of literature, is the movie. The first film showing in Spanish America occurred in Mexico City in August 1886, and films were being made in Cuba as early as 1896. The development of Spanish American film during the early silent era paralleled developments outside the region (for example, emphasis on travelogues and documentaries), and sound films came to Spanish America at roughly the same time as to the rest of the world; thus, talkies were being produced by the 1930s. By the 1940s and 1950s, and particularly in northern South America and Central America, the market was saturated with a mix of Mexican and North American entertainment films. Toward the end of the 1950s, however, this cultural dependence was cast off, and a new movement, called the New Latin American Cinema, emerged.

Since the early 1950s young directors in Latin America had been searching for ways to express a political vision of reality firmly rooted in the social reality of Latin America; examples are the filmmakers of the Documentary Film School of Santa Fé (Argentina), the **Ukumau** group (Bolivia), the *cinema nôvo* (Brazil), as well as equivalent groups in Cuba, Colombia, Chile, Uruguay, and Venezuela. These groups finally bore fruit in the form of the historical first international festival of Latin American cinema held in 1967 in **Viña del Mar,** Chile. Headed by Aldo Francia, the festival promoted extensive exchanges among filmmakers from Argentina, Brazil, Bolivia, Cuba, Chile, Uruguay, and Venezuela, most of whom met there for the first time. At this festival the term and the movement *New Latin American Cinema* was born. In the declaration signed by filmmakers at the conclusion of the festival, the new movement expressed its espousal of three basic principles: the development of national culture and rejection of imperialism, the adoption of a continental perspective that would further the integration of a Great Latin American Nation, and the use of cinema as a means of raising the consciousness of the popular masses. As a result of this important gathering of Latin American filmmakers, Latin American cinema began gradually to receive more and more coverage at other international film festivals, especially in Europe. In 1968, following the success of the meeting in Viña del Mar, a film festival was held in Mérida, Venezuela, organized by the University of the Andes and entitled the First Convention of Latin American Documentary Film. The main attraction was the enthusiastically received Argentinean documentary *La hora de los hornos* (1966–1969; The Hour of the Furnaces) by Fernando Solanas, codirected with Octavio Getino. Also shown was the documentary *Chircales* (The Brickmakers), directed by **Jorge Silva** and **Marta Rodríguez.**

Viña del Mar hosted the Second Festival of New Cinema, which was far more extensive than the 1967 festival, with 110 short films and features representing ten countries. Some of the Chilean films shown were *El chacal de Nahueltoro* (1968; The Jackal of Nahueltoro), by **Miguel Littín,** *Valparaíso mi amor* (1968; Valparaíso My Love), by Aldo Francia, and *Tres tristes tigres* (1969; Three Trapped Tigers), by **Raul Ruiz.** By 1970 the New Latin American Cinema had already established itself as a revolutionary cinema movement. The notoriety of the movement helped to attract outside sponsorship; RAI-TV, the Italian state-run broadcasting system, coproduced a series of films titled *Latin America Seen by Its Filmmakers,* with Eduardo Pallero (Argentina) and **Walter Achugar** (Uruguay) as managing producers, a project that resulted in one of the most innovative films ever to come out of Latin America, *El coraje del pueblo* (1971; The Courage of the People), by **Jorge Sanjinés** and the Ukumau group of Bolivia.

The growth of the movement was interrupted during the 1970s by a series of military coups which rocked Latin America (**Augusto Pinochet** in Chile in 1973; the military takeover in Argentina in 1976). Some film directors associated with the New Latin American Cinema "disappeared": Jorge Müller and Carmen Bueno (Chile, 1974) and Raymond Gleyzer and Rodolfo Walsh (Argentina, 1976). Others were forced into exile (including Sanjinés, Solanas, and Ruiz). From 1979 until 1991 the festival of the New Latin American Cinema was organized and hosted by the Cuban Film Institute in Havana, Cuba, giving a degree of stability to the movement. During the 1980s these annual festivals, attended by filmmakers and critics, provided an international forum for film retrospectives, a showcase for the work of promising directors, and an opportunity for the dissemination and discussion of new ideas about Latin American cinema.

REFERENCE:

Zuzana M. Pick, *The New Latin American Cinema* (Austin: University of Texas Press, 1993).

— S.M.H.

NEWSPAPERS AND MAGAZINES

Throughout its history, the press has been both a vehicle for and evidence of the linkage of Spanish America to Europe and the United States. The nations of Spanish America have contained nuclei of literates who were aware of Western journalistic standards and demanded newspapers and magazines roughly resembling those of Paris, Madrid, New York, and London. Before 1900 the press was primarily an instrument by which other institutions achieved their ends; in the twentieth century, however, it began to develop an identity of its own, separate from political, religious, and economic institutions. Although radio is the most widely used mass medium, in terms of political impact the large daily newspapers are most important; they are read by the civic leaders who shape public life.

There have been five historical phases of the press in Spanish America: prejournalism (1539–1790), the founding period (1790–1820), the factional press (1820–1900), the transition to modernism (1900–1960), and the modern period (since 1960). In Mexico, for example, the first periodical publication, or gazette, *La Gaceta de México* (The Mexican Gazette), founded in 1722 by Juan Ignacio de Castoreña, was a court gazette licensed and in some cases published by the local viceroy and, by extension, the Spanish Crown. Typically *La Gaceta de México* contained official announcements about Spain and the colonies and information about religious festivals. With the advent of the independence movements in the three decades following 1790 all the larger countries saw the birth of newspapers. The nineteenth century witnessed an explosion in the numbers of newspaper titles published in Spanish America, although their circulations were generally small and their lives short. Most of today's leading newspapers were founded during this period: *La Prensa* and **La Nación** of Buenos Aires, *El Mercurio* of Santiago de Chile, *El Día* of Montevideo, *El Comercio* of Lima, and *El Espectador* of Bogotá.

In the twentieth century newspapers underwent a technological revolution: presses progressed from steam to electricity, type was set by machine instead of by hand, relatively cheap wood-pulp paper replaced rag bond, and the telephone, telegraph, and cable opened up communications on a global scale not hitherto seen. In Spanish America the corresponding drop in their price meant that they soon achieved mass appeal, although not as extensively as in Europe or the United States. In the 1960s, largely as a result of influence from the New Journalism of the United States, journalism was professionalized; correspondents were sent abroad, new buildings were put up, and newspaper contents were modernized. For the first time editors began looking at the "other side" of life, such as life in the city slums.

These changes were halted in the 1970s with the advent of an era of dictatorship; in many cases newspapers were muzzled and regulations on advertising

A vendor selling the Argentinean newspaper *La Prensa* in 1956, after the fall
of Juan Domingo Perón's government freed the paper from official
censorship

were imposed (see **Censorship**). In Uruguay during
1973–1984 the military dictatorship closed down
newspapers and denied the public access to back
numbers of leading newspapers housed in the national library. During the **Guerra Sucia** (Dirty War)
in Argentina (1976–1983) seventy-two journalists
"disappeared" and were probably murdered, hundreds were jailed, and many fled into exile. The
quota of foreign news allowed in any Argentinean
newspaper was reduced. In Peru, Santa Claus was
outlawed as an example of United States cultural
imperialism. In the 1980s and 1990s the press has
been somewhat liberalized, thus matching the new
mood of democracy that swept through Spanish
America once the military retreated from the corridors of power.

By comparing the individual characteristics of
newspapers in Argentina, Colombia, and Peru, one
can derive a fairly clear image of the diversity of the
press in Spanish America. In Argentina, for example,
as in Mexico, the national press is dominated by
newspapers published in the capital. The three most
important, high-quality dailies in Buenos Aires are

La Nación (founded in 1870 by the president of Argentina, Bartolomé Mitre), *La Prensa,* and *Clarín.*
(There is also an English-language newspaper published in Buenos Aires.) In Peru the situation is
rather different; as elsewhere in the Americas, newspaper editorials have been used to promote the political candidacy of friends, or contrariwise to
blacken the reputation of an enemy. The so-called
gacetilleros, social commentators who published
their opinions in the local press, had a heyday at the
end of the nineteenth century but died out as the
modern era of professionalized journalism dawned.
The twentieth century witnessed a movement away
from politicking toward an emphasis on paid collaboration, increased circulation, lower per-unit prices,
more interviews, more social gossip, and more business information and advertising. A curious practice
emerged at the turn of the twentieth century; in
order to steal the thunder of antigovernment pamphlets and confuse their readers, governments were
known to publish pamphlets with exactly the same
title but exactly the opposite content: *Don Lunes*
(1919), for example, to counteract *Don Lunes*

(1919). Despite the impression of ephemerality, there have been some luminous exceptions, such as *El Comercio,* the daily with the largest national circulation, published in Lima, which published its first issue on 4 May 1839, and the Peruvian *La Prensa,* which was founded in 1903 by Pedro de Osma. The most important newspaper of Colombia, published in Bogotá, is *El Espectador;* other important dailies published in Bogotá are *Diario Económico* (founded 1963), *El Espacio* (founded 1965), *El Siglo* (founded 1936), *El Tiempo* (founded 1911), *El Vespertino* (founded 1964), and *La República* (founded 1954). Bogotá does not have the monopoly on newspaper production; other Colombian cities (Barranquilla, Bucaramanga, Cali, Cartagena, Medellín, and Pereira) publish three or more dailies each.

Of the 977 daily newspapers in the twenty-three Latin American republics and dominions, perhaps twenty dailies in twelve countries rate as journalistically first-rate in terms of scope and variety of news coverage of their own nations. They include *La Prensa, La Nación,* and *Clarín* in Argentina; *El Tiempo* and *El Espectador* in Colombia; *El Comercio* in Peru; *El Mercurio* in Chile; and *El Día* in Uruguay. Associated Press, United Press International, Reuters of Britain, Agence France-Presses, Efe of Spain, ANSA of Italy, DPA of West Germany, and Prensa Latina of Cuba all have client newspapers, broadcasting stations, networks, and magazines all over Latin America. Mexico, Brazil, and Argentina each have national news services. Since 1970 leading Latin American daily newspapers cooperatively have maintained LATIN, a regional news agency serving papers in every Latin American republic except Cuba. Despite this international focus, the major newspapers and other media in Latin America publish far more news about their own countries and more world news than they carry about other Latin American nations.

As for magazines, in Argentina a quality weekly, *Veritas,* founded in January 1931 by the late F. Antonio Rizzuto, concentrates on economics and finance. Another leading Argentinean newsmagazine also stresses business affairs: *5 Areas* appears twice a month, covering industry, finance, labor relations, and commerce. One weekly Argentinean magazine with general news coverage is *Análisis-Confirmado,* published by Fernando Morduchowicz; it has a *Time* format.

Peru has two elite weeklies. *Caretas,* which probes economic and social problems and is politically liberal, is published by Enrique Zileri, one of Peru's most distinguished journalists. *Oiga,* published by Francisco Iguarta, is to the political Left of *Caretas* and is a vigorous critic of the government. Peru's weekly newsmagazine field also has *Opinión Libre,* politically conservative; *Marka,* which supports the Marxist Left, edited and published by Jorge Flores; and *ABC,* the organ of the Aprista political party, made up of moderates and conservatives who are prolabor.

Venezuela has one of Latin America's leading weekly newsmagazines, *Resumen,* which is influential in Venezuela's national life and read by leaders of both major political parties as well as civic leaders. Publisher Jorge Olavarría investigates any hints of corruption in government. *Resumen* has an impact greater than its circulation of 170,000 might indicate because each university, school, and public library preserves its back issues for reference.

The leading newsmagazine in Chile, *Qué Pasa,* published in Santiago by Emilio Sanfuentes, carries more details than its rivals about economic problems and restrictions on opposition politicians. It also translates foreign criticism of Chilean policies found in the *Washington Post.* The other two Santiago magazines, *Hoy* and *Mensaje,* are milder in their antigovernment coverage, emphasizing more-general news of the republic. *Ercilla* has also been a serious contributor.

Circulating in every Latin American nation except Cuba, the weekly newsmagazine *Visión* is read by more than 300,000 Latin Americans who shape public opinion. Founded in 1950, *Visión* was published by Alberto Lleras Camargo, president of Colombia until 1979. It is now published by Mariano Grondona, who continues its traditions of journalistic objectivity with factual backgrounding of major events in Latin America. With a *Time* magazine format of news categories — world politics, finance, labor, and fine arts — *Visión* usually runs to eighty-four pages. From time to time it reports on criminal-justice trends, fuel and energy problems, or foreign trade in Latin America. *Visión* has editorial offices in Mexico City, Bogotá, Buenos Aires, Santiago, and Washington. (See also **Photography.**)

REFERENCES:

Marvin Alisky, "Latin America," in *Global Journalism,* edited by John C. Merrill (New York: Longman, 1983), pp. 249–301;

Antonio Cacua Prada, *Historia del periodismo colombiano* (Bogotá, 1968);

Robert N. Pierce and Kurt Kent, "Newspapers," in *Handbook of Latin American Popular Culture,* edited by Harold E. Hinds Jr. and Charles M. Tatum (Westport, Conn.: Greenwood Press, 1985), pp. 229–250;

Raúl Porras Barrenchea, *El periodismo en el Perú* (Lima: Miraflores, 1970).

— S.M.H.

Federico Luppi and Rodolfo Ranni as Peronists in *No habrá más penas ni olvido* (1983; A Funny, Dirty Little War)

NO HABRÁ MÁS PENAS NI OLVIDO

No habrá más penas ni olvido (1983; A Funny, Dirty Little War), directed by Argentinean Héctor Olivera, is based on Osvaldo Soriano's 1980 novel of the same name (translated into English in 1986). Set in 1974 in Colonia Vela, a small town in La Pampa province, the movie deals with an order from on high to purge the municipal delegate for being an infiltrator, namely, a Communist sympathizer who has infiltrated the party of **Juan Domingo Perón.** Olivera's movie is a scathing and funny indictment of the liquidation of left-wing Peronist elements by the old power guard within the party and its neofascist allies. Like *Camila,* it uses the struggles of a past epoch to criticize the excesses of the **Guerra Sucia** (Dirty War) of 1976–1983, from which Argentina had just emerged, and in which subversives had been mercilessly "disappeared" by the military forces.

REFERENCE:

David William Foster, *Contemporary Argentine Cinema* (Columbia & London: University of Missouri Press, 1992).

— S.M.H.

LUIS FELIPE NOÉ

Argentinean artist Luis Felipe Noé (1933–   ), who lives and works in Buenos Aires, was a member of the **Otra Figuración** group. During the early 1950s Noé studied law at the Universidad de Buenos Aires and painting in Horacio Butler's workshop. After abandoning the study of law, he worked as a journalist until he began exhibiting his art. In the early 1960s he joined the Otra Figuración group. Although he shared their interest in **neofiguration,** he was particularly concerned with exploring the idea of chaos as the primary state of the universe. Noé believed that the individual is immersed in a chaotic world in which people and objects become confused. In paintings such as *Convocación a la barbarie* (1961; Call to Barbarism) dark heavy impastos fuse together grotesque figures alluding to the unstable political situation in Argentina during the late 1950s and to the regime of the infamous nineteenth-century dictator Juan Manuel de Rosas. In 1962 Noé changed his vision of chaos in favor of a tension or opposition between forces. As a result his work became increasingly fragmented, until he produced *Así es la vida, señorita* (1965; That's Life, Miss), a three-dimensional assemblage (see **Pop Art, Assemblages and Happenings**) of unframed canvases, cutout figures, and empty stretchers. This work posed deep structural problems that Noé was unable to resolve, so he stopped painting for ten years and began writing.

In 1975 his vision shifted from one of chaos as a destructive force to chaos as a positive impulse, able to generate nature and the surrounding world, a view that is reflected in his paintings condemning the Spanish conquerors' violation of nature in the Americas. His style, although still combining abstract and figurative elements, became more linear, activating the surface of his paintings through a maze of vibrating lines that symbolize the chaotic energy of nature. During the 1980s Noé rejected theoretical constraints and readily incorporated all of his experiences into his work. In *La última ola* (1985; The Last Wave), he combined an abstract view of nature with his interest in subverting the illusive structure of the canvas, part of which is lifted to reveal another stratum of paint underneath.

REFERENCE:

Mercedes Casanegra, *El color y las artes plásticas: Luis Felipe Noé* (Buenos Aires: Alba, 1988).

— F.B.N.

NOSOTROS

The leading cultural magazine of Argentina in the first decades of the century, *Nosotros* was founded and directed by Roberto Giusti and Alfredo Bianchi. It focused on literature and the arts and helped to make known foreign authors (such as James Joyce and Marcel Proust) in the early 1920s. Its editorial line was eclectic, but as the "little magazines" of the 1920s siphoned off the avant-garde public, *Nosotros* came to be identified with the establishment (**Leopoldo Lugones,** Ricardo Rojas, Manuel Gálvez, Enrique Banchs, and others). It published a total of 390 issues between 1907 and 1943, though it ceased to publish between 1934 and 1936.

REFERENCE:

Noemí Ulla, *La revista 'Nosotros'* (Buenos Aires: Galerna, 1969).

— R.G.M.

NOVELA ROSA

The novela rosa, or sentimental romance, is as much a part of mass culture in Latin America as Harlequin romances are in the United States. The novela rosa is an international genre marketed in the form of novels but also available in other forms of mass cultural production:

fotonovelas, radio, and television soap operas (**telenovelas**). The most prolific author of sentimental novels in Spanish — a veritable one-woman industry — is the Spaniard María del Socorro Tellado López (1926–), better known to her millions of readers as Corín Tellado, whose products began to flood the Hispanic book industry in the 1940s and have yet to dry up. The Spanish *novela rosa* (pink novel), however, predates its most consistent practitioner by two decades and has evolved in accordance with the needs of its preferentially female readership. Through all the changes some invariants remain: the exclusive focus on romantic love with the appropriate happy ending; the lack of social or historical analysis; the psychological function ("wishful thinking" or compensatory fantasies) that the genre supplies; and narrative techniques derived from the most rudimentary nineteenth-century realism.

REFERENCE:

José Luis Méndez, "The Novels of Corín Tellado," *Studies in Latin American Popular Culture,* 5 (1986): 31–40.

— R.G.M.

NUEVA CANCIÓN

Originating in Chile in the works of **Violeta Parra, Victor Jara,** Patricio Manns, **Inti-Illimani,** and Quilapayún, the Nueva Canción, or New Song, movement of the second half of the twentieth century represents a concerted effort to endow poor and working-class people with a renewed perception of their inherent worth, dignity, and values, as expressed in their own folk-song repertoire. The various elements of the movement include the creation of an initial consciousness of self-worth; an aggressive nationalism rooted in folklore; and resistance to social, political, and economic oppression.

Related to other, concurrent song movements in the hemisphere — "protest songs" in the United States, *nueva trova* in Cuba — the New Song movement in Chile symbolized the reaction of the poor and working classes to an elitist social structure and a repressive political system. In the early years of the movement Parra recognized that the masses lacked a sense of self-esteem, due in part to an official interest in imported icons of European and North American cultures, especially in music. Radio broadcasts, for example, featured mainly popular and commercial music from abroad. In her performances Parra revealed the latent power of folk music to reinforce a sense of pride and cultural identity among the disenfranchised. Numerous urban musicians abandoned careers based on imported "entertainment music" to join her cause.

The groundswell of support for the movement soon spread beyond Chile's borders, becoming a mas-

Violeta Parra, one of the founders of the Nueva Canción (New Song) movement in Chile

sive Pan-Latin expression that has been tailored to accommodate various local conditions. Nueva Canción continues to be viable, refusing to yield to political repression and occasional public apathy.

REFERENCES:

Guillermo Barzuna, "De Atahualpa Yupanqui a Fito Páez: Génesis del oficio de cantor," *Escena,* 14, no. 30 (1992);

Gerard Béhague, "Popular Music in Latin America," *Studies in Latin American Popular Culture,* 5 (1986): 41–67;

Peter Manuel, *Popular Musics of the Non-Western World* (Oxford: Oxford University Press, 1988);

Albrecht Moreno, "Violeta Parra and La Nueva Canción Chilena," *Studies in Latin American Popular Culture,* 5 (1986): 108–126.

— R.L.S.

NUEVA FUNDACIÓN DE CINE LATINOAMERICANO

The **Cuban Revolution** of 1959 brought sweeping changes to the Cuban movie industry, one of which was the establishment of a government agency, the Instituto Cubano del Arte e Industria Cinematográficas (ICAIC), to organize and regulate the production, distribution, and exhibition of films. One of the most innovative developments of the ICAIC during the 1980s was the Nueva Fundación de Cine Latinoamericano (New Latin American Film Foundation), established in Havana by Nobel Prize–winning Colombian novelist **Gabriel García Márquez** in 1985. The foundation published a three-part collection of documents and manifestos called *Hojas del cine* (Cinema Section). García Márquez's aim was to promote a cinema capable of capturing the whole Latin American market, and the result was a series of successful coproductions with Televisión Española — including *Letters from the Park* (1988), directed by Tomás Gutiérrez Alea, and *Sandino* (1990), by **Miguel Littín.** Other successful projects — such as *Técnicas de duelo* (1988; A Matter of Honor), directed by Sergio Cabrera — were undertaken with FOCINE, or the Fondo de Fomento Cinematográfico (Fund for Cinematic Development), in Colombia.

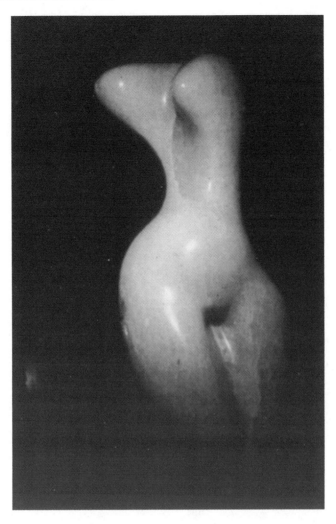

Torso, by Marina Núñez del Prado (from *Gran enciclopedia de España y America*, volume 9, 1986)

REFERENCES:

John King, *Magical Reels: A History of Cinema in Latin America* (London: Verso, 1990);

Márquez. Tales Beyond Solitude. Profile of a Writer, directed by Holly Aylett, Luna Films, 1989;

Zuzana M. Pick, *The New Latin American Cinema: A Continental Project* (Austin: University of Texas Press, 1993).

— S.M.H.

MARINA NÚÑEZ DEL PRADO

The Bolivian sculptor Marina Núñez del Prado (1910–) focuses her art on indigenous Andean traditions. Born in La Paz, she studied at the local Academia de Bellas Artes from 1927 to 1929; after graduating, she was appointed professor of sculpture at the same academy. Her sculptures at the time, such as *Danza de Cholas* (1937; Cholas Dancing) and *Huaka Tokori* (1937), portraying a ritual fertility dance, were based on her studies of Bolivian native popular music and dance. During the 1940s Núñez del Prado settled in New York, initially with a grant from the American Association of University Women. She received an honorary doctorate from Russell Sage College of Troy, New York, and participated in several exhibitions, opportunities created in part by the Good Neighbor Policy. She returned to Bolivia in 1949.

Although Núñez del Prado's interest in native Andean themes links her to **Indigenism,** her semifigurative style connects her work with the **Informal Abstraction** of her compatriot **María Luisa Pacheco** and even with **neofiguration.** In *Tercera luna* (Third Moon) she presents a flowing horizontal female body, suggesting love, procreation, and motherhood, themes which often appear in her oeuvre. Its semifigurative style, with its organic quality and elimination of detail, betrays her admiration for Constantin Brancusi, whose studio she visited when she traveled through Europe in the early 1950s.

Núñez del Prado paid special attention to her materials, preferring to work, as her themes dictated, with beautiful native stones and woods, such as basalt, black granite, comanche granite (named after a local river), white onyx, and guayacán wood. For instance, her *Venus negra* (1958; Black Venus) emphasizes the rich darkness of basalt, while the *Venus blanca* (1960; White Venus) is made of white onyx of spectacular quality. In 1972 Núñez del Prado was appointed Professor Emerita of Art by the Universidad Nacional Mayor de San Andrés in La Paz.

REFERENCE:

Gilbert Chase, *Contemporary Art in Latin America: Painting, Graphic Art, Sculpture, Architecture* (New York: Free Press, 1970), pp. 119–120.

— F.B.N.

O

ALEJANDRO OBREGÓN

Alejandro Obregón (1920–) is a leading Colombian painter. He was born in Barcelona and raised in Barranquilla, on the Caribbean coast of Colombia. During the late 1930s he studied art in Spain and France and at the Boston School of Fine Arts. In 1949, soon after he was appointed director of the Escuela de Bellas Artes in Bogotá, he left for France. He returned to Colombia in 1954 and later settled in the city of Cartagena.

During the 1950s Obregón developed a personal semiabstract style, inspired by the combination of abstract and figurative elements found in the work of Mexican artist Rufino Tamayo and by the textural surfaces and expressive colors of **Informal Abstraction.** In works such as *Cattle Drowning in the Magdalena River* (1955), Obregón heightens the tension between abstraction and figuration (see **Neofiguration**) by suggesting recognizable figures through abstract markings and by creating a sense of volume through the overlapping of flat planes. Although Obregón produced several paintings that comment negatively on the political violence in Colombia during the 1950s, such as *The Wake* (1956) and *Mourning for a Dead Student* (1956), his favorite themes have been the flora and fauna of Colombia, the landscape of the Caribbean coast, and views of the Andes and its inhabitants, including the condor, Colombia's national symbol. Obregón's art had a great impact in Colombian circles, helping to liberate his country's art from the last vestiges of **Indigenism.**

REFERENCE:

Félix Angel, "The Latin American Presence: Part II: Reality and Figuration," in *The Latin American Spirit: Art and Artists in the United States, 1920–70*, by Luis Cancel and others (New York: Bronx Museum of the Arts/Abrams, 1988), pp. 265–282.
— F.B.N.

Cattle Drowning in the Magdalena River (1955), by Alejandro Obregón (Museum of Fine Arts, Houston, Texas)

SILVINA OCAMPO

Closely identified with her older sister **Victoria Ocampo** and with the journal *Sur,* Silvina Ocampo (1903–1993) is overshadowed by writers of the stature of **Jorge Luis Borges** and **Adolfo Bioy Casares** (whom she met in 1933 and married seven years later); yet she

Igor Stravinsky, Victoria Ocampo, and Souline Stravinsky in Argentina, 1936

has her own distinctive literary voice. She is best known as an author of short stories. Her first important collection was *Autobiografía de Irene* (1948; Irene's Autobiography), followed a decade later by *Las furias* (1959; The Furies), brief narratives that frame the world of childhood and adolescence in a peculiarly intense way and focus on raw emotions such as jealousy and hate. The brazen narrative tone and the juxtaposition of childhood innocence and destructive emotions that result in vicious acts endow these stories with an atmosphere of their own. Other books by Ocampo include *Las invitadas* (1961; The Guests), *Los días de la noche* (1970; The Days of Night), and *Cornelia frente al espejo* (1988; Cornelia in Front of the Mirror). Silvina Ocampo also published poetry and children's stories and was one of the authors of the *Antología de la literatura fantástica* (1940; Anthology of Fantastic Literature), a landmark in the development of the fantastic genre in Argentina and throughout Latin America.

REFERENCE:

Noemí Ulla, *Encuentros con Silvina Ocampo* (Buenos Aires: Editorial de Belgrano, 1982).

— R.G.M.

VICTORIA OCAMPO

An Argentinean literary figure and patron of the arts, Victoria Ocampo (1890–1979) founded the review *Sur* in 1931 and financed it for decades with her personal wealth. Ocampo was born into a patrician family with deep roots in Argentinean history and grew up in a privileged environment that included regular trips to Paris. She was educated at home and in French with her five sisters. (Ocampo wrote in Spanish, but she was aided by a translator until she was forty.) She married briefly in 1913, published her first literary article in 1920, and hosted many important European and U.S. writers in her family villa near Buenos Aires, among them Spanish philosopher José Ortega y Gasset, whose *Revista de Occidente* was one of the models for *Sur*. Ocampo's network of personal contacts in Europe was impressive and did much to establish her magazine from the beginning as the major cultural institution of its time. The inaugural issue contained work by Pablo Picasso, Jules Supervielle, Drieu la Rochelle, Waldo Frank, Alfonso Reyes, Walter Gropius, and Swiss conductor-composer Ernest Ansermet, in addition to articles by **Jorge Luis Borges,** Ocampo herself, and a posthumous contribution by **Ricardo Güiraldes.** Victoria Ocampo's own writings are collected in the ten-volume series *Testimonios* (1935–1977; Testimonies) and in the several volumes of her autobiography, the first of which was published the year of her death. She also published essays on Emily Brontë and Virginia Woolf and a book on the feminine condition, *La mujer y su expresión* (1936; Woman and Her Expression).

REFERENCE:

Doris Meyer, *Victoria Ocampo: Against the Wind and the Tide* (New York: Braziller, 1979).

— R.G.M.

JUAN CARLOS ONETTI

Uruguay's most important literary figure and one of the major precursors of the **Boom,** Juan Carlos Onetti (1909–1994) was born in Montevideo and, until 1975, when he immigrated to Spain, lived alternately in his native city and in Buenos Aires, on the opposite shore of the Río de la Plata. In 1939 Onetti became managing

Juan Carlos Onetti, 1945

editor of the important weekly *Marcha,* founded that year in Montevideo; he also published his first novel, *El pozo* (translated as *The Pit*), in a limited edition of 500 copies. In 1943 Onetti settled for a few years in Buenos Aires, where he earned a living as a journalist while he continued to write and publish stories and novels, among them *La vida breve* (1950; translated as *A Brief Life*), his groundbreaking work. In 1955 Onetti returned to Montevideo and married Dorotea Muhr, his fourth wife. Two years later he was appointed director of Municipal Libraries, a position he held until 1974, when the military government briefly sent him and other intellectuals to jail on a charge of "pornography." (The jailed group had been members of a literary jury who had awarded a prize to a story disliked by the military censors.) In Spain in 1980 Onetti was awarded the most coveted prize in the Hispanic world, the **Premio Miguel de Cervantes,** to be followed in 1985 by the Uruguayan National Grand Prix for Literature.

Onetti is a master of all the genres of prose fiction: novels, novellas, and short stories. The same vision and technical devices underlie the whole of his narrative, which combines existentialist alienation and the Sartrean feeling of nausea with a profound inquiry into the nature of fiction as an imaginary reprieve from the human condition. In general, Onetti's texts are am-

biguous and deliberately imprecise; the events of the story are rarely known in advance and must be inferred by the narrator or narrators and by the reader, a process that easily blurs the line between fact and fiction. This conjectural approach to narrative also highlights the importance of gossip in Onetti's fiction. (In this sense both Marcel Proust and Henry James come to mind as forerunners of the Uruguayan author). Onetti's characters, moreover, are indeterminate, only barely sketched in, their proper names often missing and replaced by nicknames or personal pronouns. They are as indifferent in their existential outlook as is the implicit author's approach to their characterization. A favorite situation of Onetti's is the arrival of a stranger in town and the subsequent fabrication of a story explaining the character's past and his or her motives in the present. Such is the case with "Historia del Caballero de la Rosa y de la Virgen encinta que vino de Liliput" (1956; Story of the Knight of the Rose and of the Pregnant Virgin Who Came from Lilliput) — one of the author's most representative stories — and with *Los adioses* (1954; translated as *The Goodbyes*) and *Para una tumba sin nombre* (1959; For a Nameless Grave), two of his best short novels. The former deals with an anonymous patient who arrives in a mountain sanatorium to recover from tuberculosis and who becomes the object of the narrator's speculations. Two women take turns visiting the former basketball player (the only fact the reader can accept with certainty until the end of the story), and the narrator speculates that they are rivals and partners in a ménage à trois. The narrator — a grocery-store clerk who handles the protagonist's mail — withholds two letters from the patient and reads them when the latter commits suicide, only to discover that the older woman was the deceased's wife and the younger one his daughter from a previous marriage. The narrator's know-it-all vanity suffers a devastating blow with this information. The irony is that the narrator is less indifferent to the human tragedy unfolding in his domain than is the protagonist of the tragedy himself.

Para una tumba sin nombre is more grotesque and more experimental than *Los adioses*. As the text says, the story "could be told a thousand times in different ways" because the instance of storytelling becomes more significant than the content or truth of the tale. What sets the different purveyors of the "truth" in motion is the bizarre spectacle of a funeral procession featuring a coach pulled by pygmy horses and an entourage composed of a local youth and a lame goat. Various characters become narrators, contradicting and upstaging one another in their attempts to identify the deceased (she is given three different identities), to justify her life and explain her death, and to generate hypotheses to account for the goat. In the end there is no single truth, but the various "lies" devised by the townspeople can be integrated at a higher level into the theme or motif of the scapegoat.

Among Onetti's many novels three deserve special mention as the ones that have catapulted the author's name beyond the confines of Latin American fiction. *La vida breve* marks a turning point in Onetti's production because of its complexity and because it introduces the setting and characters that recur in later novels and stories. The novel is set in the fictional town of Santa María, a provincial riverside location that has been compared to Faulkner's Yoknapatawpha County. (There are other significant parallels between Faulkner and Onetti, such as the handling of point of view and the eccentricity of some of the characters.) The novel's title alludes to the French song "La vie est brève / un peu d'amour / un peu de rêve / et puis bonjour" (Life is short / a little love / a little dream / and then good-bye) and, therefore, both to the brevity of life and to the fictions woven by the human imagination to overcome the sense of dread. *La vida breve* is writing-within-writing, a baroque construction where author and characters, reality and fiction, lose their boundaries and commingle. Its protagonist is a scriptwriter who projects himself onto two fictitious identities. The script is set in the fictitious Santa María, but

at the end of the novel the author flees to the city of his imagination, while one of the imaginary characters flees to Buenos Aires. The labyrinthine construction of the novel is not gratuitous; the theme of writing as salvation from existential anguish motivates the structural ambiguities.

The protagonist of both *El astillero* (1961; translated as *The Shipyard*) and *Juntacadáveres* (1964; translated as *Body Snatcher*) is Larsen, a character who also makes a fleeting and anonymous appearance toward the end of *La vida breve*. Here he is expelled from the town along with his retinue of prostitutes; in *El astillero* Larsen returns to Santa María five years later in order to vindicate himself. He becomes the manager of a bankrupt shipyard and pretends that the job is real and not a farce. He plays the role of manager, charges imaginary salaries to the company books, and prepares impossible budgets. In a parody of romantic love Larsen also courts the boss's mad daughter, Angélica Inés, who reappears in Onetti's later novel, *Cuando ya no importe* (1993; When It No Longer Matters). All of this role-playing is a fiction that keeps the protagonist from falling into the existential abyss of old age and, ultimately, death. The novel has two endings from which the reader is free to choose, both equally pessimistic.

Juntacadáveres is set earlier than *La vida breve*, according to the internal chronology of Santa María. Larsen arrives in town with three decrepit whores and opens a brothel that for one hundred days titillates the locals until the authorities intervene and banish him. This story is interwoven with two others that have the same unhappy ending. Once again, for all the characters involved in these desperate projects, the trappings of fiction (invention, simulation, dissimulation, role-playing, imaginings) are the only recourse against nihilism. There is an artistic conscience attached to even the vilest of characters, which is a reflection of the author (of the artist) caught in the same existential trap as his characters.

Onetti published four other novels after 1964. His stories were collected in 1967 and published in Buenos Aires as *Cuentos completos*.

REFERENCES:

Djelal Kadir, *Juan Carlos Onetti* (Boston: Twayne, 1977);

Hugo Verani, ed., *Juan Carlos Onetti: El escritor ante la crítica* (Madrid: Taurus, 1987).

— R.G.M.

ORGANIZATION OF AMERICAN STATES

Founded on 30 April 1948 at the Ninth Pan-American Conference in Bogotá, the Organization of American

States (OAS) has become the most influential agency for peace, security, and cooperation among the nations of the Americas. Among the areas of cooperation, the emphasis on cultural affairs has been an effective instrument for cultural exchange, as evidenced in the publication *Américas,* a bimonthly magazine in English and Spanish.

This agency has been particularly supportive of the performing arts. For example, its music department has served to increase awareness and appreciation of the various musical cultures by publishing *Composers of the Americas,* a series that provides biographical data and catalogues of the works of composers (1955–1972), and the *Inter American Music Bulletin* (1957–1973), with articles on current events, concerts, festivals, and contests. The OAS has also sponsored nine Inter-American Music Festivals in Washington, D.C., from 1958 to 1978 and more than one hundred world premieres of Latin American music. Additional international efforts by the OAS include three Festivals of Music of the Americas and Spain (1960–1970) presented in Madrid.

REFERENCES:

Composers of the Americas (Washington, D.C.: Pan American Union, General Secretariat, Organization of American States, 1955–1972);

Inter American Music Bulletin (Washington, D.C.: Pan American Union, General Secretariat, Organization of American States, 1957–1973).

— R.L.S.

JUAN ORREGO-SALAS

Born in Santiago, Chile, Juan Orrego-Salas (1919–) graduated from the Catholic University in architecture but abandoned that career in order to devote his varied talents to music. After completing musical studies at the National Conservatory with Pedro Umberto Allende and **Domingo Santa Cruz,** he conducted the Santiago Catholic University Choir and lectured in music history at the National Conservatory. Two years of graduate study in the United States (1944–1946) were made possible through Rockefeller and Guggenheim fellowships. In the United States he studied composition with Randall Thompson and Aaron Copland and musicology with Paul Henry Lang and George Herzog. Following his studies in the United States, he returned to Chile as professor of music history and composition. Upon his return he immersed himself in projects that had been developed by his former teacher, Santa Cruz. He served as secretary of the Institute of Musical Research of the Faculty of Musical Arts and Sciences at the University of Chile, music critic for the newspaper

El Mercurio, editor of the *Revista Musical Chilena,* secretary of the National Association of Composers, secretary of the Chilean branch of the International Society of Contemporary Music, and director of the Institute of Musical Extension of the University of Chile.

In 1961 he became director of the Latin American Music Center and professor of composition at Indiana University, where he was instrumental in acquiring one of the largest library collections of Latin American music in the Western Hemisphere. Dr. Orrego-Salas was also the major contributor of articles related to Latin America in the *Harvard Dictionary of Music.* He retired from Indiana University in 1987 but has continued to be active as a composer. Orrego-Salas has produced a large catalogue of original compositions, many of which were commissioned works, while others were dedicated to specific teachers, composers, and performing artists. For example, the *Pastoral y scherzo* (for violin and piano) was dedicated to Copland; *Romances pastorales* (for four-part chorus) was dedicated to Thompson; and *Primera sinfonía* was dedicated to Santa Cruz. Other works were dedicated to the composers **Alberto Ginastera** and Alfonso Letelier and to Alejandro Barletta, the Argentinean virtuoso of the **bandoneón** (*Suite para bandoneón*). Among Orrego-Salas's commissioned works are several written for performances at the Inter American Music Festivals sponsored by the **Organization of American States.**

Stylistically, Orrego-Salas has tended to reveal a preference for neoclassical procedures, especially well-delineated contrapuntal lines. Although his music is generally conceived within the tonal system, it has tended to progress toward increasing chromaticism and more-striking dissonance. His catalogue of works contains a wide variety of genres, including chamber works for various combinations of instruments, choral music, dramatic works (ballet, opera, and oratorio), piano works, art songs, and orchestral music.

REFERENCES:

Gerard Béhague, *Latin American Music: An Introduction* (Englewood Cliffs, N.J.: Prentice-Hall, 1979);

Composers of the Americas, volume 1 (Washington, D.C.: Pan American Union, General Secretariat, Organization of American States, 1955).

— R.L.S.

ALEJANDRO OTERO

Alejandro Otero (1921–), one of the most important Venezuelan artists, worked in a variety of artistic modes, ranging from Geometric Abstract paintings and monumental sculptures to Informal Abstract collages.

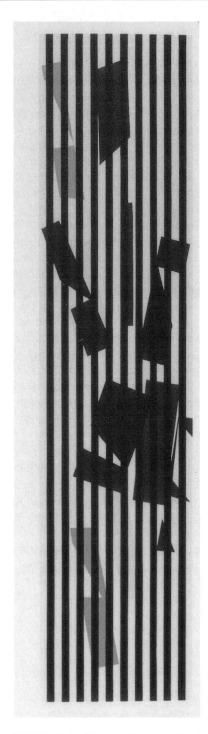

Colorritmo, 1 (1955; Color-Rhythm, 1), by Alejandro Otero (Museum of Modern Art, New York, Inter-American Fund, 1956)

In the 1940s Otero studied in Caracas and later in Paris. He arrived at **Informal Abstraction** by gradually reducing images of everyday objects to lines and areas of colors, as in *La cafetera roja* (1948; The Red Coffee-

pot), in which the coffeepot becomes a vertical red spot surrounded by blue lines and irregular areas of expressive brushwork. Otero exhibited his series *Cafeteras* in Caracas in 1948, but their abstraction created a scandal. He returned to Paris and joined the group called "los disidentes" (the dissidents), intent on renewing Venezuelan art through the publication of a magazine that they made available in Caracas. After a visit to Holland in 1950 to see Piet Mondrian's art, Otero switched to **Geometric Abstraction.** At first, he experimented with collages of overlapping colored bars, but in 1955 he began his well-known series *Colorritmos* (Color-Rhythms), which feature parallel vertical black bars that seem to trap colored shapes and halt their free-floating movement, thus creating an effect of spatial tension. By then Otero had returned to Caracas, where he taught at the Escuela de Artes Plásticas y Aplicadas and participated in the decoration project of Caracas's Ciudad Universitaria.

From 1960 to 1964 Otero lived in Paris and changed his style. Finding his *Colorritmos* too "elaborate," he again switched to Informal Abstraction and began working with rough textural surfaces and collages — such as *Bonjour M. Braque* (1961; Good Morning Mr. Braque) — which often include keys, nails, handwritten letters, and postage stamps. Upon his return to Venezuela, Otero was appointed vice president of the Instituto Nacional de Cultura y Bellas Artes in Caracas and in 1976 became president of the Comisión Especial de Artes Plásticas del Consejo Nacional de la Cultura. In addition to his official duties, Otero also produced abstract geometric sculptures. In 1971 he received a Guggenheim Fellowship to work at the Massachusetts Institute of Technology, where he experimented with "spatial sculptures," three-dimensional geometric grids determined by vertical and horizontal metal bars, which were intended as public monumental sculptures, such as *Ala Solar* (Solar Wing), built in Bogotá in 1975 under commission from the Colombian government.

REFERENCES:

Alejandro Otero (Caracas: Museo de Arte Contemporaneo de Caracas, 1985);

Jerry M. Davill and others, *Alejandro Otero: A Restrospective Exhibition* (Austin: Michener Galleries, University of Texas at Austin, 1975).

— F.B.N.

MIGUEL OTERO SILVA

Venezuelan novelist Miguel Otero Silva (1908–) traces the social, economic, and political history of his country through the 1960s. His first novel, *Fiebre*

Introducción a la esperanza (1963; Introduction to Hope), by Luis Felipe Noé (Museo
Nacional de Bellas Artes, Buenos Aires)

(1939; Fever), deals with a 1928 student revolt against
the dictatorship of Gen. Juan Vicente Gómez (see **Dictatorship Novel**). *Fiebre* was significantly revised in
1971, at which time the author tacked on a prologue
characterizing the novel as the impetuous product of
a student in his twenties who had not yet read "a
single page by Faulkner, Joyce, Kafka, not even by
Proust." Otero Silva's next novel, *Casas muertas*
(1955; Dead Houses), is a more accomplished
work that gave the author an international reputation. It narrates the decadence of an old rural
town left behind by economic progress, which in
Venezuela has been mostly fueled by oil. Otero
Silva's third novel, *Oficina No. 1* (1961; Office No.
1), deals precisely with this theme by focusing on
a new town brought to life by the oil fields in
which it sits. Otero Silva's later novels take leave
from the immediacy of Venezuelan contemporary
history. *Lope de Aguirre, príncipe de la libertad*
(1979; Lope de Aguirre, Prince of Freedom) is a
historical novel based on the life of the conquistador who in the sixteenth century rose against the
Spanish monarchy and wreaked havoc on the

shores of the Orinoco and Amazon rivers until he was
captured and executed in Venezuela by a Spanish official. The novel makes a social statement concerning the
violence implicit in economic development. Otero's
La piedra que era Cristo (1984; The Bedrock that
Was Christ) is based on the life of Christ.

REFERENCE:

Alexis Márquez Rodríguez, *Historia y ficción en la novela
    venezolana* (Caracas: Monte Avila, 1990).

                                                             — R.G.M.

Otra Figuración

During the early 1960s the Argentineans Ernesto
Deira, Rómulo Macció, **Luis Felipe Noé,** and **Jorge de
la Vega,** members of the **Otra Figuración** (Other Figuration) group, worked in a mode of figuration called
Neofiguration, which had been present in Europe, the
United States, and Latin America since the 1950s. They
aimed to overcome the traditional dichotomy of figuration versus abstraction by blending figuration with the

reliance on clear structures of **Geometric Abstraction** and the latest developments of **Informal Abstraction,** such as its emphasis on textured surfaces and spontaneity of execution. At the same time they hoped to reject the traditional but limiting notions of good taste, structural unity, and careful execution often found in Argentinean art. They also wanted to reaffirm the psychological and ideological possibilities of the human figure as a vehicle for expressing the artist's existentialist preoccupations with the alienating effects of mass society on the individual.

These four artists first exhibited together in Buenos Aires in 1961 at an open show titled *Otra Figuración,* a name derived from the term *art autre,* used by the French critic Michel Tapie in the 1950s. After working for a few months in Paris, they shared a studio in Buenos Aires and often contributed to the production of one another's paintings. Their group shows received harsh reviews from most critics but soon won the support of many other artists. Otra Figuración began to disband in 1963 and had its last group exhibition in 1965.

REFERENCES:

Jacqueline Barnitz, "New Figuration, Pop, and Assemblage in the 1960s and 1970s," in *Latin American Artists of the Twentieth Century,* edited by Waldo Rasmussen, Fatima Bercht, and Elizabeth Ferrer (New York: Museum of Modern Art, 1993), pp. 122–133;

Aldo Pellegrini, *Panorama de la pintura argentina contemporánea* (Buenos Aires: Paidós, 1967).

— F.B.N.

OTRA HISTORIA DE AMOR

Otra historia de amor (1985; Another Love Story), directed by Argentinean Américo Ortiz Zárate, is set during the period of redemocratization in Argentina. The movie deals with a homosexual love affair (the "otherness" of the title) between two individuals who have letters for names (Z and Y). Y is married; when his wife finds out (from a disgruntled coworker) about his homoerotic affair, she files for formal separation. Ortiz Zárate attempts to legitimize homosexuality in nonradical terms by handling the topic discreetly, both in its conflicts with dominant heterosexism and, in cinematic terms, in its details as a form of erotic passion.

REFERENCE:

David William Foster, *Contemporary Argentine Cinema* (Columbia & London: University of Missouri Press, 1992).

— S.M.H.

P

MARÍA LUISA PACHECO

Artist María Luisa Pacheco (1919–1982) was instrumental in the introduction of **Informal Abstraction** in her native Bolivia during the 1960s. She studied in La Paz and later in Madrid, where she came into contact with Spanish Informalism. After 1952, when she returned to Bolivia, she emphasized color and textural qualities in post-Cubist figurative paintings dealing with themes of social significance (See **Neofiguration**). The following year she cofounded the Ocho Contemporáneos group, whose objective was the renovation of Bolivian art. Although the group's exhibition in 1953 was attacked by the supporters of **Indigenism,** Ocho Contemporáneos represented Bolivia in the II Bienal de São Paulo. In 1956 Pacheco settled in New York and later became a United States citizen. She received consecutive Guggenheim Fellowships from 1958 to 1960.

In New York, Pacheco was exposed to Abstract Expressionism, which encouraged her to produce completely abstract work. During the 1960s she collaged into her paintings highly textured surfaces such as plywood and corrugated cardboard, which she combined with translucent planes of gray, earth, and blue tones. The harsh mood, rugged texture, and luminous atmosphere of paintings such as *Catavi* (1974) subtly evoke the austere landscape of the Andes. Pacheco titled this and other works in Aymara, an indigenous Bolivian language, in order to avoid any descriptive association and emphasize her main objective: the plastic treatment of the work. She successfully exhibited in New York, in her native country, and throughout Latin America, thereby encouraging the development of abstraction in Bolivia.

Composición (1960; Composition), by Maria Luisa Pacheco (Art Museum of the Americas, OAS, Washington, D.C., Purchase Fund, 1960)

REFERENCE:

Felix Angel, "La obra de María Luisa Pacheco," translated by Bryan J. Mallet as "The Work of María Luisa Pacheco," *Arte en Colombia,* no. 40 (May 1989): 52–60, 135–138.
—F.B.N.

PARALITERATURE

Some literary works explicitly employ and rework material derived from popular culture, particularly in the latter part of the twentieth century, partly in reaction to the hermeticism of **Boom** writers. One example of this paraliterature is the use by **Jorge Luis Borges** and

Adolfo Bioy Casares of the detective novel enigma motif in their *Seis problemas para don Isidro Parodi* (1942; Six Problems for Don Isidro Parodi). Another typical example is the use of political documentary material in documentary narrative. Perhaps the most widely known form of paraliterature is the utilization of popular and mass culture media in literature, as in Argentinean novelist **Manuel Puig**'s novels *La traición de Rita Hayworth* (1968; translated as *Betrayed by Rita Hayworth*), *Boquitas pintadas* (1973; translated as *Heartbreak Tango*), and *El beso de la mujer araña* (1976; translated as *Kiss of the Spider Woman*), which employ sentimental motifs from Hollywood films and popular songs as a framework which motivates the characters' emotional lives. Other examples of the use of paraliterature are **Julio Cortázar**'s *Fantomas contra los vampiros multinacionales* (1975; Fantomas against the Multinational Vampires), which uses **comics; Mario Vargas Llosa**'s *La tía Julia y el escribidor* (1981; translated as *Aunt Julia and the Scriptwriter*), which alludes to **telenovelas; Gustavo Sainz**'s *Gazapo* (1965), and **Luis Rafael Sánchez**'s *La guaracha del macho Camacho* (1976; Macho Camacho's Beat), both of which use pop-music culture. (See also **Movies from Books.**)

REFERENCES:

William Rowe and Vivian Schelling, *Memory and Modernity: Popular Culture in Latin America* (London: Verso, 1991);

Chuck Tatum, "Paraliterature," in *Handbook of Latin American Literature,* edited by David William Foster (New York & London: Garland, 1992): 687–728.

— S.M.H.

Nicanor Parra

Catalina Parra

The Chilean Catalina Parra (1940–) is a conceptual artist who has worked in Germany, Chile, and the United States. Parra's father is the famous poet **Nicanor Parra,** and her aunt was the prominent musician **Violeta Parra.** From 1968 to 1973 Parra lived in Germany, where she became interested in Dada art and began to study the ideas and artistic techniques of Dadaists such as John Hartfield. In 1969 Parra saw the *Information* exhibition at Basel and was impressed by British Pop Art, which used Dadaist strategies to satirize the mass media. Soon Parra began to produce collages with a variety of printed materials, organizing her fragmented images in orderly, gridlike compositions, such as *Nina* (1969).

In 1972, after her return to Chile, Parra began clipping articles from the conservative newspaper *El Mercurio* which referred to the upheaval that eventually culminated in the 1973 military coup. With these clippings she produced a notebook of political collages. Although Parra was closely connected with important conceptual artists such as **Eugenio Dittborn** and Carlos Leppe, she worked privately and did not show her work until 1977. Her first Chilean exhibition was called *Imbunches,* after an Araucanian myth in which a child's orifices had to be sewn shut to prevent evil from escaping. Her conceptual pieces, like most Chilean **Conceptual Art,** are oblique metaphors of the fearful effects of state terrorism and can only be understood by reading between the lines. In her collage *Diariamente* (1977; Daily) the visual fragments, including an advertisement for *El Mercurio* and pieces of its obituary page, are sewn together with large stitches, to symbolize the evil that is kept from being expressed. In 1980 Parra received a Guggenheim Fellowship and moved to New York where she produced more openly political pieces on a variety of subjects, such as United

States interventions in Latin America and environmental issues. For instance, in her collage *What's It To You?* (1982) Parra uses fragments of texts and images from *The New York Times* (a common source in her work), gauze, and stitching to denounce the covert war in Central America.

REFERENCE:

Julia P. Herzberg and Ronald Christ, *Catalina Parra in Retrospect* (The Bronx, N.Y.: Lehman College Art Gallery, 1991).
— F.B.N.

NICANOR PARRA

Poet Nicanor Parra (1914–) was a member of a family well known in Chile for its commitment to and diffusion of national folklore. His sister **Violeta Parra,** his nephew Angel Parra, and niece Isabel Parra are composers and folksingers of national and international stature. When his "antipoems" came out in 1954, Nicanor Parra was heralded as the successor to **Pablo Neruda.** Neruda had just published a book of epic proportions (*Canto general*) and was about to undergo his own transition toward a kind of poetic minimalism. This transitional moment in Chilean poetry was deftly exploited by Parra and provides the context for his emergence as a major poet who was soon to be read throughout Latin America and in the United States, where his poems were translated by Allen Ginsberg, Lawrence Ferlinghetti, and others.

Parra's antipoetry must not be considered a monolithic style impervious to its own evolutionary dynamics. The earlier poems of *Poemas y antipoemas* (1954; translated as *Poems and Antipoems*) may be approximately described as Surrealist narrative monologues entrusted to an idiosyncratic and eccentric speaker whose attitude toward the "human condition" is mainly sarcastic. Parra's Surrealism, however, is not the international or "literary" kind but a Creole Surrealism written in a conversational tone and heavily inflected by Chilean idiomatic usage.

A later work, *Artefactos* (1972; Gadgets), consists of aphorisms, many of which are political. The book coincides with a critical period in Chilean history. Marxist president **Salvador Allende** had been democratically elected two years earlier and was soon to be violently overthrown by a military coup supported by the United States. Parra displays a marked skepticism toward both antagonists of the Cold War and was accordingly criticized by leftists and rightists alike.

In *Sermones y prédicas del Cristo de Elqui* (1977; translated as *Sermons and Homilies of the Christ of Elqui*) and *Nuevos sermones y prédicas del Cristo de*

Teresa de la Parra

Elqui (1979; translated as *New Sermons and Homilies of the Christ of Elqui*) Parra dons the mask of an itinerant preacher in order to expound in a peculiarly absurd way on politics and on an array of other topics ranging from metaphysics to hygiene. Parra's character or persona is based on a historical figure (Domingo Zárate Vega) who roamed the Chilean countryside in the first half of the twentieth century. Parra's impersonation of this bizarre preacher may have a political origin, since the "sermons," some of which are tracts of political criticism, appeared at a time of inflexible military censorship when the **Augusto Pinochet** dictatorship had already jailed, murdered, "disappeared," or exiled thousands of opponents. It was common for Chilean literature in the 1970s and 1980s to camouflage political content and thus avoid direct engagement with the military censors.

In the late 1980s Parra took up the cause of ecology and began to publish his "ecopoems."

REFERENCE:

Edith Grossman, *The Antipoetry of Nicanor Parra* (New York: New York University Press, 1975).

— R.G.M.

Teresa de la Parra

The first major woman writer of Venezuela, Teresa de la Parra (1889–1936) wrote two books: *Ifigenia (Diario de una señorita que escribió porque se fastidiaba)* (1924; Iphigenia: Diary of a Bored Young Lady) and *Las memorias de Mamá Blanca* (1929; *Mama Blanca's Memoirs*). The first is a novel about the daughter of a wealthy Venezuelan family who returns to Caracas from Paris and finds it difficult to adjust to the traditional values and roles imposed on women. The heroine ultimately gives up her romantic striving for liberation and submits to the traditional role of wife and mother. Teresa de la Parra's second book purports to be the memoirs of Mamá Blanca, a septuagenarian who narrates the experiences of her childhood and bridges Venezuela's idyllic colonial past and its industrial present. The text of the memoirs is said to have been bequeathed to the "editor" on Mamá Blanca's deathbed. Both these works are recognizably autobiographical. Born in Paris, Teresa de la Parra grew up on a sugar plantation outside Caracas and moved again to Paris in the mid 1920s. She died of tuberculosis.

REFERENCE:

Teresa de la Parra, *Mamá Blanca's Memoirs,* critical edition (Pittsburgh: University of Pittsburgh Press, 1993).

— R.G.M.

Violeta Parra

The founder and leader of a cultural movement that sought to reassert the value of the Chilean poor and working classes through the music and poetry of the **Nueva Canción,** Violeta Parra (1917–1967), the daughter of a poor school music teacher and a peasant woman, became the singer-poet of an alternative popular music that expressed the hope of millions who were politically, economically, and socially oppressed.

During childhood she learned the folklore of Chile's countryside firsthand. As a young professional singer in bars and other popular venues, she succumbed to existing popular musical tastes that were dictated by radio and film, many of them imported. Violeta's brother, the poet **Nicanor Parra,** focused her attention once more on Chilean folklore. Her subsequent research and rededication to the values of her

people led to a new awareness of the inequities of their lives. She was, eventually, to compile more than three thousand songs from the different regions of Chile, songs that she not only gathered but also performed on national radio broadcasts and for regional audiences. Chile, as a nation, began to learn the social values of its national folk heritage and to recognize the political injustices of its elitist class system. After a successful trip to record in France (1954–1956), Violeta returned to release her first album in Chile, *El Folklore de Chile.* Although most of the songs included in her early recordings and performances were merely transmissions from folksingers she had met in the countryside, she soon began to render songs that were critical of the establishment. Among other musicians who began to follow her example were Patricio Manns; Rolando Alarcón; the Quilapayún and **Inti-Illimani** groups; **Víctor Jara;** and her own children, Angel and Isabel Parra. In 1964 Manns, Alarcón, Angel, and Isabel opened a folk café (La Peña de los Parras) that served as a catalyst for Nueva Canción until the 1973 assassination of President **Salvador Allende,** whose government the group had supported. Within days of Allende's death, Víctor Jara was tortured and executed; Angel Parra and Patricio Manns were sent to concentration camps; Isabel Parra, Quilapayún, and **Inti-Illimani** were out of the country on tour and remained in exile during the **Augusto Pinochet** regime. Violeta's death six years earlier had spared her from witnessing the tragedy.

Violeta Parra received prizes at the Youth Festival in Finland; gave recitals at UNESCO headquarters at the Théâtre des Nations in Paris; and had an exhibition of her art work and performed in Geneva. She also published a book, *Poésie populaire des Andes* (1965; Popular Poetry of the Andes), in France; she was the subject of a documentary television film in Switzerland; and she had a one-woman exhibit of her artwork at the Louvre in Paris. In Chile, however, she suffered from personal and economic problems; depression was revealed in her music and in her attempts to end her life. Shortly after the release of one of her most successful and popular recordings, "Gracias a la vida" (Thanks to Life), in 1967, she took her own life. With Violeta Parra's dedicated leadership, a new generation was molded to continue the trajectory of Nueva Canción from being based on Chilean folklore to becoming a pan-Latin song movement that permeated the Western Hemisphere. She founded La Carpa de la Reina, a center for folk music providing an alternative musical resource for urban musicians who joined the struggle against imported and tasteless commercial music. Nueva Canción continues and among its most fervent messengers are Parra's own progeny, Isabel and Angel.

REFERENCES:

Guillermo Barzuna, "De Atahualpa Yupanqui a Fito Paez: Génesis del oficio de cantor," *Escena,* Año 14, no. 30 (1992): 56–60;

Gerard Béhague, "Popular Music in Latin America," *Studies in Latin American Popular Culture,* 5 (1986): 41–67;

Juan Armando Epple, "Entretien avec Angel Parra," *Caravelle: Cahiers du Monde Hispanique et Luso-Brésilien,* 48 (1987);

Peter Manuel, *Popular Musics of the Non-Western World* (Oxford: Oxford University Press, 1988): 121–126;

Albrecht Moreno, "Violeta Parra and la Nueva Canción Chilena," *Studies in Latin American Popular Culture,* 5 (1986): 110–126.
                                                                                                      — R.L.S.

PASAJEROS DE UNA PESADILLA

Pasajeros de una pesadilla (1984; Passengers in a Nightmare), directed by Argentinean Fernando Ayala, is ostensibly a film based on the unpublished account of Pablo Schokendler, who was in prison during the period portrayed in the movie, accused and subsequently convicted along with his brother, Sergio, of murdering their parents. Ayala constructed his film around the Schokendler crime as an allegory of the corruption, violence, and dissoluteness of Argentinean society during the **Guerra Sucia.** Like Roberto in *La historia oficial* (1986; The Official Story), the father of the Schokendler family is involved in shady business interests that overlap with those of the military. The difference is that in Ayala's film other issues are also invoked, such as race and gender (Schokendler is Jewish and homosexual).

REFERENCE:

David William Foster, *Contemporary Argentine Cinema* (Columbia & London: University of Missouri Press, 1992).
                                                                                                      — S.M.H.

CÉSAR PATERNOSTO

The Argentinean artist César Paternosto (1931–) has worked with different abstract styles ranging from **Informal Abstraction** to **Geometric Abstraction** and has formulated an art rooted in the Americas. During the 1950s Paternosto studied law and later attended the Escuela de Bellas Artes in his native city of La Plata, near Buenos Aires. In 1961 he joined the informal abstract Grupo SI, founded by his friend Alejandro Puente, but he went beyond their concern with color and texture by employing figurative symbols inspired by the native pottery of northern Argentina. Soon Paternosto became interested in Geometric Abstraction, initially depicting simple geometric figures in a soft-edge style, often called "Geometría Sensible" because of its expressiveness, but later turning toward more dynamic hard-edge compositions combining shaped canvases and brightly colored surfaces. After Paternosto won awards at the III Bienal Americana de Arte in Córdoba and at the Instituto Di Tella in Buenos Aires, he moved to New York in 1967.

In the late 1960s Paternosto produced the series *Oblique Vision* (1969), consisting of deep, unframed stretchers whose fronts were completely white and whose sides were painted in different tones so as to reflect subtle auras of color onto the supporting wall. By the late 1970s Paternosto had become dissatisfied with the expressive limitations of this approach and had grown interested in the type of symbolic and metaphysical geometry found in Inca arts and crafts. He undertook several research trips to Bolivia and Peru, which culminated in the publication of a book on Inca sculpture titled *Piedra abstracta* (1989; Abstract Stone). Moreover, as a way of expressing his Latin American cultural identity he consciously began to introduce recognizable textures, colors, and austere patterns found in Inca textiles and stone work into abstract geometric paintings such as *Trilce II* (1980) and *T'Oqapu* (1982). He also found in **Joaquín Torres-García**'s writings a source of inspiration that links his art with the Americanist project of **Constructive Art.**

REFERENCE:

Mari Carmen Ramírez, "Re-positioning the South: The Legacy of the Taller Torres-García in Contemporary Latin American Art," in her *El Taller Torres-García: The School of the South and its Legacy* (Austin: Published for the Archer M. Huntington Gallery by the University of Texas Press, 1992).
                                                                                                      — F.B.N.

ANNA PAVLOVA

The Russian superstar ballerina Anna Pavlova toured South America for the first time in 1917. In Valparaíso, Chile, she presented a repertoire consisting of *Chopiniana, Bacchanale, Minuet, Pavlova Gavotte, Pastorale, Walpurgis Night, Magic Flute,* and *Giselle.* Audiences were reportedly overflowing. Her company also performed in Santiago, Chile; Lima, Peru; Caracas, Venezuela; Buenos Aires, Argentina; and three cities in Brazil. In 1918 she returned to South America with a larger company, sixty-five dancers, and an increased repertoire. The dancers

Payadors of Argentina

were drawn from Russia, England, France, the United States, Poland, and elsewhere. In Lima they were celebrated as the "Pavlovitas," or the "little Pavlovas." Elsewhere in Latin America, the company performed in Mexico, Puerto Rico, and Cuba, where a revolution forced a sudden rebooking into Panama, Costa Rica, and Ecuador. Owing to Pavlova's superstar status, the size of the company, and the infrequency of visits from well-known dance companies, these tours became legendary. No other foreign dance companies visited South America until the **Ballets Kurt Jooss** and the Ballets Russes de Monte Carlo arrived in the 1940s.

—J.M.H. & N.D.B.

PAYADORS

Payadors are singers of a particular type of patriotic song (payada) that developed in Argentina following the war of independence (1816). They reflected the new identity of the republic and new relationships within society: the imagined distance between political and social leaders and the general population was thought to have been reduced. A new awareness of rural, national traditions, especially of the **gauchos,** produced an ambience of cultural liberation paralleling the political one.

The early payadas focused on patriotism through the cielito, a song-dance in 3/4 waltzlike meter that became the sonorous vehicle of nationalism. Accompanied by guitar, the song form consisted of rhymed couplets that were thematically varied. The term *cielito* has been used ambiguously in Argentinean folklore referring to a song type, a dance type, and to the lively section of other genres such as the Montonero minuet and the Pericón. Musically, the cielito could be sung or played by an instrument such as the piano, accompanied by the guitar. The musical and poetic expression of payadors is not an erudite art. Rather it represents the spontaneous inspiration of rustic poet-singers whose view of life and circumstance is based on their own experiences and perceptions.

The best-known payador of the twentieth century is, without doubt, **Atahualpa Yupanqui,** whose numerous recordings, international tours, and television appearances developed a worldwide audience for the genre. "Don Ata," as he was affectionately called, expanded the payada by incorporating various folk genres into the repertory, such as the **baguala, vidala, milonga,** chacarera, and pampa.

REFERENCES:

Isabel Aretz, *El folklore musical argentino* (Buenos Aires: Ricordi Americana S.A.E.C., 1952);

Rodolfo Arizaga, *Enciclopedia de la música argentina* (Buenos Aires: Fondo Nacional de las Artes, 1971).

—R.L.S.

JUAN CARLOS PAZ

A devotee of avant-garde alternatives to traditional music, Juan Carlos Paz (1901–1972) participated in and led several "new music" groups in Argentina. Among the first in Latin America to adopt radical European trends in music, Paz was instrumental in the formation of *Grupo Renovación* and *Conciertos de Nueva Música,* finally creating his own group, *Agrupación Nueva Música.* Following early interest in the European neoclassical style, he became an ardent advocate of the twelve-tone method of composition in the 1930s, becoming one of the first Latin

Juan Carlos Paz

American supporters of Arnold Schoenberg's "Viennese School." Titles of works written in the mid 1930s reflect his new interest: *Primera composición en los 12 tonos* (First Composition in 12 Tones), *Segunda composición* (Second Composition), *Diez piezas sobre una serie de los 12 tonos* (Ten Pieces on a Series of 12 Tones), and *Tercera composición en los 12 tonos* (Third Composition in 12 Tones). Later in his life Paz went beyond the twelve-tone method to explore a free, total chromaticism that was not limited to any particular compositional point of view, also incorporating an interest in Oriental music.

REFERENCES:

Rodolfo Arizaga, *Enciclopedia de la música argentina* (Buenos Aires: Fondo Nacional de las Artes, 1971);

Gerard Béhague, *Music in Latin America: An Introduction* (Englewood Cliffs, N.J.: Prentice-Hall, 1979);

Composers of the Americas, volume 4 (Washington, D.C.: Pan American Union, General Secretariat, Organization of American States, 1958).

— R.L.S.

ALDO PELLEGRINI

Aldo Pellegrini (1903–) was the founder of Argentinean Surrealism (1926) and editor (under the pseudonym Adolfo Este) of the occasional review *Que* (two issues, 1928 and 1930). In the 1950s Pellegrini and poet Enrique Molina formed a group dedicated to the defense of the Surrealist aesthetic and centered on another review, *A partir de cero* (Starting from Zero). That review, which lasted until 1958, was instrumental in bringing several new poets to the attention of the public.

— R.G.M. & P.S.

PEOPLES AND RACES

The three principal groups upon which the population of Spanish American countries is based are peoples of European origin (beginning with the arrival of the conquistadors from Spain and continuing in diverse waves of immigration from Spain and other countries); peoples descended from slaves brought from Africa; and indigenous peoples. (See **Indigenous Cultures.**) In some areas there are also significant Arab and Oriental elements. The mingling of races is a widespread phenomenon in Latin America, dating back to the earliest colonial times; having mixed blood can be a source of pride.

Some of the terms that have arisen to designate race and ethnicity can be used pejoratively, but it is important to note that they do not always have negative overtones. The Spanish American "Indians" sometimes prefer to be called *indígenas* rather than *indios,* and they might use *ladinos* to refer to everyone else. The term *criollo* refers to a person of European blood, though born in Latin America, but it is sometimes applied more loosely to anyone born in the Americas. *Mestizo* refers to a mixture of criollo and indigenous blood. *Mulato* refers to a mixture of white and black ("negro") blood. A related term, though geographically more confined, is *cholo,* designating a mixture of black and Indian. *Gringo,* whose origins are not wholly clear, may be applied to any foreigner, though it tends to refer to North Americans.

Today the majority of the peoples of Latin America are mestizo, although the degrees of miscegenation are varied. Many people reflect their racial heritage in

Cristina Peri Rossi, circa 1988 (photograph by Guillermina Puig)

their physical characteristics; however, the distinctions between what are considered native and nonnative peoples rests to a large extent on questions of ethnicity rather than race. The most obvious exceptions are those indigenous peoples who live relatively isolated in remote areas; other exceptions are certain areas of South America that continue to have a majority or near majority of indigenous people, such as Bolivia and Peru. In these countries, however, racial intermarriage and ethnic blending have occurred to such a degree that it is difficult to label individuals as Indian or non-Indian by race; rather, their ethnic identity is determined by where they live, their relationship to the land, the language or **languages** they speak, the food they eat, their principal sources of economic sustenance, their clothing, their crafts, or their spiritual beliefs. Therefore an individual who is considered native may have the same racial heritage as one who is not. Because race and ethnicity in Latin America are inextricably connected to class, indigenous groups are also largely identified with the more impoverished sectors of various societies.

— P.S. & M.E.S.

CRISTINA PERI ROSSI

Uruguayan writer Cristina Peri Rossi (1941–) is best known for her often allegorical stories and novels dealing with existential, psychological, and erotic themes. Peri Rossi's first book, *Viviendo* (1963; Living), is a collection of three stories dealing with female protagonists in various degrees of existential torpor. Another collection of stories followed, *Los museos abandonados* (1968; The Abandoned Museums), four pieces that use classical mythology and allegory to express modern existential concerns, particularly those related to personal freedom and the passing of time. Peri Rossi's first novel, *El libro de mis primos* (1969; The Book of My Cousins), which won the prestigious **Marcha** award prior to its publication, is an original hybrid of poetry and prose designed to reinforce the theme of man's alienation in the modern world. As the author states in the prologue to a later edition, modern man can only recompose his image through ambiguity and confusion, a predicament formally signified in the book by the generic break with conventional narrative. Peri Rossi's last work to be published in Montevideo is

Indicios pánicos (1970; Panic Signs), a miscellany of poetry and prose unified by the idea that reality is a palimpsest that can be read on many levels. The book is a fragmented response (ironic, dramatic, hallucinatory) to the many signs surrounding the writer, especially those that pointed in the direction of the political crisis that overtook Uruguay in 1973, when the military staged a violent coup and began a systematic repression of the opposition.

In 1974 Peri Rossi settled in Barcelona. Her first work published in Spain was *La tarde del dinosaurio* (1976; The Dinosaur's Afternoon), a book of stories centered on the world of childhood and adolescence, followed by another collection of stories, *La rebelión de los niños* (1980; The Children's Rebellion). The title story dates from 1971 and eerily foreshadows the internal war shortly to be waged by the Uruguayan military. *El museo de los esfuerzos inútiles* (1983; The Museum of Useless Endeavors), a collection of brief narrative pieces and longer stories, is one of Peri Rossi's better-known works. One of the "endeavors" of the author's museum is "Session," a piece in which a psychoanalyst places a call to one of his patients in order to discuss his (the analyst's) anguish upon discovering his wife's second lover. Fifty minutes later he reminds the patient that his (the patient's) session is over and that it will resume the following day at his (the analyst's) office. Throughout the conversation the patient gropes all around his apartment and under the bed for "reality," which he had briefly managed to trap in a glass. *El museo de los esfuerzos inútiles* also includes "Instructions to Get Out of Bed," a piece inspired by **Julio Cortázar**'s *Historias de cronopios y famas* (1962; translated as *Cronopios and Famas*). Cortázar is one of the most consistent influences on Peri Rossi's fiction.

As opposed to the condensed intensity of Peri Rossi's shorter fiction, the author's novels are loosely plotted and amount essentially to a string of interconnected fragments unfolding in multiple temporal planes. They can be explicitly allegorical, like *La nave de los locos* (1984; translated as *The Ship of Fools: A Novel*), which uses a traditional motif to organize the experience of exile. The main symbol in this novel is a medieval tapestry called "Creation," and the novel's protagonist is a man devoid of individuality and known as "X" for "Extranjero" ("stranger," "foreigner"). A more recent novel is *Solitario de amor* (1988; Love Solitaire), which explores erotic passion through a lover's monologue. Perhaps the author's most successful effort to date is the short-story collection *Una pasión prohibida* (1986; translated as *A Forbidden Passion*), a book that pays tribute, in Peri Rossi's own words, to man's "fever of passion and the great and small failures in the attainment of its objective."

REFERENCE:

Mabel Moraña, *Memorias de la generación fantasma* (Montevideo: Monte Sexto, 1988).

— R.G.M.

EVA PERÓN

The wife of Gen. **Juan Domingo Perón,** Eva Perón (1919–1952), who in her later years became known as Evita, was born María Eva Duarte in the small town of Los Toldos, 150 miles west of Buenos Aires. She was born out of wedlock, and her childhood was poor and difficult. At the age of fifteen she went to the capital to become an actress. At twenty-five she met Perón and became his mistress, marrying him in October 1945, the year before the general was elected president for the first time.

The first couple were a powerful political machine. Evita's resentment against the rich accorded well with her husband's populism and appealed to his constituency, largely made up of the working class and the cabecitas negras (literally translated as "black heads"), the lumpen from the country's interior who became a conspicuous presence in Buenos Aires in the early 1950s. Evita never occupied an official position in Perón's government (she thought of running for the vice presidency in 1951, but the military opposed her); yet her power was greater than that of any of Perón's ministers. Her influence over the labor movement was considerable, and through the Eva Perón Foundation, a charitable institution that promoted public welfare at the expense of the well-to-do, Evita gained the undying gratitude of the masses, to whom she dispensed money and favors with seemingly endless largesse. Evita's prestige was at its zenith when she toured Europe in 1947 (the year women were given the vote in Argentina). Soon afterward she began to suffer from cancer of the uterus and wasted away for four years until her death in 1952, still young and glamorous. A year earlier General Perón had been reelected with the massive support of women voters, a further indication of Evita's central role in the Peronist government.

Evita's early death, however, contributed to the creation of her legend as a saintly and tragic woman — a martyr — dedicated in body and soul to the struggles of the poor. Her body was embalmed by a Spanish specialist and displayed to the multitudes in the Ministry of Labor. After General Perón fell from power in 1955, Evita's body was secretly buried in Milan, Italy. It was exhumed in 1971 and transported to Madrid, where General Perón was living in exile. In 1974 it was finally returned to Buenos Aires and reburied in the Recoleta Cemetery.

Juan Domingo and Eva Perón on the day of his inauguration to his second term as president of Argentina, June 1952 (UPI/Bettmann)

REFERENCE:

John Barnes, *Evita, First Lady: A Biography of Eva Perón* (New York: Grove, 1978).

— R.G.M.

JUAN DOMINGO PERÓN

Juan Domingo Perón (1895–1974), who was in power in Argentina during the periods 1946–1955 and 1973–1974, was a populist dictator and perhaps the most noted political figure in Latin America along with Fidel Castro since World War II. His power base was the army, and his policies (collectively known as justicialismo) consistently favored labor and the lower classes known as descamisados (the shirtless) or cabecitas negras (literally translated as "black heads"). Perón nationalized banking and clamped down on the press. An admirer of Benito Mussolini, he was the antagonist of the liberal intelligentsia to which writers such as **Jorge Luis Borges** and **Julio Cortázar** be-

longed. Massive demonstrations and riots were common in his first period of office.

In 1945 Perón married **Eva Duarte Perón,** who was to become an invaluable ally even after her death from cancer in 1952. Perón was first deposed by a navy revolt with the support of segments of the army. His second term was a failure and ended with his death in office.

Perón's rule inspired a good deal of artistic protest activity, including some **dictatorship novels.**

— R.G.M.

PERROS DE LA NOCHE

Perros de la noche (1986; The Dogs of Night), directed by Argentinean Teo Kofman, is based on Enrique Medina's novel of the same title. The movie deals with a handful of down-and-outs who live in the slums on the outskirts of Buenos Aires; it focuses on Mecha and

Quintet (1927), by Emilio Pettoruti (San Francisco Museum of Art)

Mingo, the young adult children of a woman who has just died. Without their mother's support they now have to fend for themselves in a hostile world. Mecha accepts odd domestic jobs, while Mingo gets involved in petty crime. After serving a prison sentence, Mingo attempts to earn a living through his sister by having her work as a dance-hall artist/stripper/prostitute (the dividing line is vague). Finally, the sister, Mecha, rebels against her brother and leaves him to fend for himself.

REFERENCE:

David William Foster, *Contemporary Argentine Cinema* (Columbia & London: University of Missouri Press, 1992).
                                                        — S.M.H.

EMILIO PETTORUTI

Emilio Pettoruti (1892–1971), one of the leading figures in the introduction of modern art into Argentina, achieved great public success during his lifetime. Like his friend **Xul Solar,** Pettoruti spent his formative years in Europe, mainly in Italy, where he became interested in Futurism and Cubism. Early abstract compositions such as *Harmony-Movement-Space* (1914)

and *The Blue Grotto of Capri* (1918) reflect Pettoruti's exploration of the effects of light and objects in motion that fascinated the futurists, while works such as *Lacerba* (1915) reveal his use of collage techniques, flattened shapes, and multiperspectival space characteristic of Cubism. He accomplished an original and poetic synthesis of both aesthetics in a series of portraits, such as *Pensive Woman* (1920), in which he combined the Cubists' preference for stable geometric structures with the futurists' emphasis on color and light.

When Pettoruti returned to Argentina in 1924, he joined the **Florida** movement and displayed his European works at the Witcomb Gallery in a memorable exhibition that scandalized many well-established but retrograde artists and critics who felt threatened by the radical vanguardism that Florida advocated and Pettoruti so efficiently promoted. During the 1920s and 1930s Pettoruti produced a series of paintings about musicians and harlequins, such as *Quintet* (1927), in which he transformed Cubism into an emblematic expression of the urban culture of Buenos Aires, the tango band. *Argentinean Sun* (1941) represents another important theme in Pettoruti's oeuvre, the still life. In this painting the plastic independence of the flat geometric shapes, color planes, and light effects is concretized in the representation of light as a solid, tangible form. During the last two decades of Pettoruti's life, these elements broke free in paintings such as *Marine Sunset II* (1953) and became abstract, elegant shapes of crystalized light and color.

REFERENCES:

C. Córdova Iturburu, *Pettoruti* (Buenos Aires: Academia Nacional de Bellas Artes, 1980);

Emilio Pettoruti, *Un pintor ante el espejo* (Buenos Aires: Solar-Hachette, 1968).
                                                        — F.B.N.

PHOTOGRAPHY

According to the Brazilian researcher Boris Kossoy, photography was born in Hercule Florence's improvised laboratory in the interior of the State of São Paulo, Brazil. Although his conclusions have often been disputed by the French, Kossoy established that in 1833 Florence successfully retained images by using urine as a fixing agent and that this discovery was acknowledged by other early photographers, including Joseph-Nicéphore Niepce, Louis-Jacques-Mandé Daguerre, and William Henry Fox Talbot. In spite of such early interest in photographic processes in Brazil, photography did not become a significant medium in Spanish America until the 1840s, when European itinerant photographers such as William Helsby in Chile, John Bennet in Colombia, and Ral Rosti in Venezuela introduced the daguerrotype. Occasionally, these professionals established temporary daguerrotype studios and trained local assistants to aid them in the production of portraits, mainly of the upper classes.

With the introduction of photography on paper in the 1860s, new and luxurious commercial photographic studios began to emerge throughout Latin America, many as franchises of foreign companies. Their commercial success relied on the production of portraits, cartes-de-visite (which were popular in all social classes), and postcards, often sold in Europe. During the last decades of the nineteenth century, Spanish American photographers such as the Argentinean Benito Pannunzi, the Colombians Demetrio Paredes and **Melitón Rodríguez,** and the Venezuelan Próspero Rey broke away from the tendency of their European colleagues to present melodramatic and exotic views of the Americas. Since then, local professionals have recorded the world around them with simplicity and austerity, ranging from events of everyday life to great historical moments: in Argentina up until the 1930s, Fernando Paillet photographed people at work and in bars, at social and sporting events, while in 1866 W. Bati recorded the atrocities of the War of Paraguay, and the Chilean Jorge Allan photographed the destruction caused by the Valparaíso earthquake of 1906.

At the beginning of the twentieth century, creative photography and its appeal to a wider public were further encouraged through the establishment of supporting institutions. Already in 1853 the Frenchman Victor Deroche had introduced photography at Chile's National Exhibition. By 1889 the importance of the new medium was also recognized in Buenos Aires with the founding of the Primera Sociedad Fotográfica de Aficionados (First Amateur Photographic Association) and in Venezuela with the publication in 1918 of a manual on photography written by F. M. Steadman. Until the 1970s the role of providing technical training for amateurs fell to the Foto Club. The first Foto Clubs were founded in Valparaíso in 1902, in Santiago in 1904, and in Buenos Aires in 1936. They also organized exhibitions and photo competitions. As photography became an increasingly widespread medium, avant-garde photographers introduced important changes in their aesthetic criteria; among these photographers was the Mexican Manuel Alvarez Bravo, one of the first artists to explore the possibilities of photography. Considered the father of Latin American photography because of the significant influence his work has had on younger generations, Alvarez Bravo helped to establish photography as a creative medium independent

of the other arts. Important avant-garde photographers in Spanish America were **Grete Stern** and Horacio Coppola in Argentina; Melitón Rodríguez, Jorge Obando, and Benjamín de la Calle in Colombia; and **Martín Chambi** in Peru.

Between World Wars I and II many photographers — including Franz van Riel, Annemarie Heinrich, Anatole Saderman, and Grete Stern — left Europe and settled in Argentina. They produced high-quality work and supported the formation of new photographic associations, such as the Carpeta de los Diez group. In the 1940s Spanish American photographers began to organize professional organizations, such as Argentina's Sociedad de Fotógrafos Profesionales, in order to secure needed chemicals and equipment, which were in short supply during and after the war. The same motivation applies to the amateurs and their association in Foto Clubs, which began to take a dominant role in creative photography during the 1960s. In Argentina and Chile these clubs virtually turned into academies, for in them were important photographers such as Juan Di Sandro in Buenos Aires and Lincoyán Parada and Luis Enrique Alfonso in Santiago, people who lectured to amateurs and beginners. Most professional photographers, on the other hand, were apprentices in the studios of already-established colleagues.

There are few employment options open to creative photographers in Spanish America: they must either teach; work in a commercial studio, photographic archive, or advertising agency; or do press photography. However, most press agencies in the United States and Europe have seldom employed or properly credited Latin American photojournalists; therefore, much of their remarkable work has not been known outside the region.

Press photography has developed in Spanish America since the turn of the century. In general it is characterized by a preference for black-and-white images and the use of wide lenses that capture detail in the foreground but still give a wide view of the surrounding context. In Venezuela the press began to reproduce photographs in 1889. In Argentina photojournalism developed at the same time as the progressive politics of the Partido Radical; in 1898 the magazine *Caras y Caretas* began publishing numerous photographs by José de Arce, who recorded the struggles of the working class, while in 1914 the conservative newspaper *La Nación* hired Juan Di Sandro as its photographer. In the 1900s Chile's weekly *Sucesos* introduced a section of "Fotografía Artística," while the *Diario Ilustrado* organized a contest of snapshots, and the publications *El Mercurio* and *Zig-Zag* held exhibitions of photography. Similarly, during the 1910s many Colombian publications began to publish photographs;

among them were *El Gráfico, Cromos, Pan,* and *Mundo al Día,* with regular collaborations by J. N. Gómez, Luis Lara, and Benjamín de la Calle. Gómez also owned a prestigious studio and recorded life in Bogotá, from portraits of influential people to social and religious events. His photographs were often used in local magazines and periodicals.

Press photography became increasingly important as a way of documenting social issues during the economic depression of the 1930s. Like Dorothea Lange and Walker Evans, photographers thoughout Latin America recorded the terrible effects of this economic crisis, the ensuing poverty, and the political instability: from César Sandino's rebellion in Nicaragua, to Gerardo Machado's fall in Cuba; the attempted murder of Rafael Reyes, which Luis Lara photographed in Colombia; and the assassination of Jorge Eliécer Gaitán, recorded by Luis B. Gaitán (a.k.a. Lunga). However, the image of Latin America seen worldwide in the 1940s and especially during the Cold War was not produced by local photographers but created by foreign professionals working for international press agencies which presented a "sanitized" version of the social and political conditions as well as of the regular military and economic penetrations of the United States into the area. Latin American photojournalists, such as the Chileans Helen Hughes and Sergio Larrain and the Guatemalan María Cristina Orive, were among the first to be recognized and hired by international press organizations in the 1960s and 1970s.

During the military dictatorships of the 1970s, photojournalists created associations independent of official institutions in order to provide mutual support and achieve some degree of protection while reporting in difficult circumstances. In Chile, after the military coup of 1973, the work of many photographers was censored by the media (see **Censorship**) and even by institutions such as Santiago's Museo de Bellas Artes (Fine Arts Museum). In 1981 the Asociación de Fotógrafos Independientes (AFI) was founded, an organization which functions like a union and encourages the appreciation of photography through publications and numerous exhibitions, such as the one held in honor of the photographer Rodrígo Rojas, killed in an incident in which the armed forces were involved. Among AFI's members are Claudio Bertoni, **Paz Errázuriz,** Patricio Guzmán Campos, Alvaro Hoppe, Helen Hughes, Héctor López, and Luis (Lucho) Poirot. As in Chile, photojournalists in Argentina had to have special permission to work outside their studios after the military takeover of 1976. The Asociación Argentina de Fotógrafos was founded in Buenos Aires in 1979, for reasons similar to those that had led to the creation of the AFI in Chile.

Since the 1970s there have been several concerted efforts to research and establish a history of Latin American photography and determine the main issues affecting this medium, a project which is still in its early stages. In order to disseminate the work of Latin American photographers, in 1973 three photographers — the Guatemalan María Cristina Orive and the Argentineans **Sara Facio** and Alicia D'Amico — founded La Azotea, a photographic publishing house in Buenos Aires, the first of its kind in Latin America. They have published postcards, posters, and books of the work of Latin American photographers, especially women. Since the 1980s they have also organized exhibitions of internationally known professionals. In Venezuela there have been significant efforts to keep track of the development of photography, such as the establishment of the Fundación para el Rescate del Archivo Documental Venezolano (a national archive of documentary materials), founded in 1977, and several important publications by Clara Posani, Josune Dorronsoro, Rafael Pineda, and Carlos Abreu. With the aim of giving the medium the place it deserves and improving the general understanding of photography, the Consejo Mexicano de Fotografía, which was founded in 1976, organized two important colloquia (1978 and 1981), accompanied by the first continental exhibitions of Latin American photography. Since these events and others in Havana in 1984 and Quito in 1990, many photographers in Latin America have become more aware of the social and cultural importance of their work, which in turn has resulted both in an increase in strategic agreements among them and in greater international recognition.

REFERENCES:

Conselho Mexicano de Fotografia, *Feito na América Latina: II Colóquio Latino-Americano de Fotografia,* translated by Alencar Guimarães and Maria Aparecida Roncato (São Paulo: FUNARTE, Instituto Nacional de Fotografia, 1987);

Fotografie Lateinamerika: Von 1860 bis heute (Zurich: Kunsthaus Zürich, 1981);

María Eugenia Haya, "Photography in Latin America," *Aperture* (Winter 1987): 58–69.

— F.B.N.

ASTOR PIAZZOLA

Born to Italian immigrant parents in Mar del Plata, Astor Piazzola (1921–1992) became one of Argentina's most popular composers and virtuosi on the **bandoneón.** Taken to New York in 1924 by his parents, he met **Carlos Gardel** and was given a child's role in one of Gardel's films. As an adult, Piazzola wrote successful arrangements of **tangos** for various artists and

Astor Piazzola (right) playing the bandoneón to accompany Italian singer Milva during a performance of his tango music, Paris, 1984 (AP/Wide World)

produced originals, including *La balada para un loco* (Ballad for a Crazy Man), *Balada para mi muerte* (Ballad for My Death), and *Tango de ángel* (Angel's Tango).

Piazzola won many prizes and scholarships that afforded him opportunities to study with outstanding teachers and composers: in Paris with the influential Nadia Boulanger; with Bela Wilda, a student of Sergei Rachmaninov; with Raúl Spivak, distinguished concert pianist, conductor, and professor at the National Conservatory; and with **Alberto Ginastera.** His ambition, his talent, and the influence of such renowned artists led him to explore new directions in music, especially in the evolution of the tango.

Piazzola developed a double identity in the Argentinean musical panorama. His widespread acceptance as a popular musician and composer was paralleled by the esteem in which he was held among classical audiences. His modernizing innovations with the tango divided his audiences: traditionalists thought his new directions were offensive and heretical; others saw his enriched musical language as a revitalizing force for a tradition that had begun to wane. Among his classically oriented works are *Suite* (1943), *Rapsodia porteña* for orchestra (1948), *Buenos Aires* — three symphonic movements — (1951), *Sinfonía de Buenos Aires* (1953), *Sinfonietta* for chamber orchestra (1953), and the *Concierto* for bandoneón, piano, strings, and percussion (1979). Piazzola died in 1992, the same year in which *The Vienna Concert,* a live recording of a mid-1980's performance by Piazzola and his "Quinteto Tango Nuevo," was released.

REFERENCES:

Rodolfo Arizaga, *Enciclopedia de la música argentina* (Buenos Aires: Fondo Nacional de las Artes, 1971);

Vicente Gesualdo, *La música en la Argentina* (Buenos Aires: Editorial Stella, 1988);

Mark Holston, "Music Notes," *Americas,* 44, no. 6 (1992): 56.

— R.L.S.

PIEDRA Y CIELO

The Piedra y Cielo movement in Colombian poetry was founded by Jorge Rojas and Eduardo Carranza in the late 1930s. Directed against the excesses of the avant-garde, Piedra y Cielo (which means "Stone and Sky") evokes the essential simplicity of the elemental objects of nature from which poetry should take its cue. The main influence on these poets was the Spanish master Juan Ramón Jiménez, who cultivated pure poetry in traditional verse forms. Rojas is the author of *Rosa de agua* (1941; Rose of Water), and Carranza collected his poems in *Los pasos cantados* (1970; The Chanted Steps).

— R.G.M.

RICARDO PIGLIA

Argentinean Ricardo Piglia (1941–) writes fiction that is a conscious reflection on modern Argentinean literature and on literary representation in general. Piglia's novels and stories partake of the activities of the literary sleuth and exploit the critical and theoretical possibilities of writing and reading (reversible categories in much of postmodern fiction) by means of innovative structural metaphors which raise questions about the organization of narrative meaning, the relationship between subjectivity and narrative, and between fiction on the one hand and history and politics on the other. The Argentinean writers of greatest significance for Piglia's work are **Jorge Luis Borges, Macedonio Fernández,** and **Roberto Arlt.**

Piglia has published three books of short narratives, two novels, and a collection of critical essays. His first collection of stories, *La invasión* (1967; The Invasion), won the **Casa de las Américas** Prize. His second, *Nombre falso* (1975; False Name), established his reputation as one of the most original writers in Latin America in the latter part of the century. Piglia's first novel, *Respiración artificial* (1980; Artificial Respiration), was enthusiastically received by the critics and has generated a substantial number of reviews and academic articles, partially because it includes a polemical interpretation of Argentinean literature. Piglia's second novel, *La ciudad ausente* (1992; The Absent City), was eagerly awaited by the reading public before its publication. One of its discarded fragments, "Prisión perpetua" (Life Sentence), served as the title story of a collection published in 1988, one that includes previously published stories. *Crítica y ficción* (1990; Criticism and Fiction) is the title of Piglia's collected critical essays on literary theory and Argentinean literature.

Piglia has also made important editorial contributions to Argentinean literary culture. In the 1970s he directed the "Serie Negra" (a collection of hard-boiled detective novels) for the Editorial Tiempo Contemporáneo of Buenos Aires (see **Literatura Negra**). He also edited a collection of Argentinean autobiographical fragments which spanned 150 years of national history and literature, *Yo* (1968; I). Finally, in *La Argentina en pedazos* (1993; Argentina in Pieces) he put together an anthology of literary pieces (illustrated with expressionist cartoons) dealing with the theme of violence in Argentinean history.

REFERENCES:

Héctor Mario Cavallari, "La escritura (en el/del) rizoma: *Respiración artificial*," *La práctica de la escritura* (Concepción, Chile: LAR, 1990);

Ellen McCracken, "Metaplagiarism and the Critic's Role as Detective: Ricardo Piglia's Reinvention of Roberto Arlt," *PMLA*, 106 (October 1991): 1071–1082;

Johnny Payne, "Epistolary Fiction and Intellectual Life in a Shattered Culture: Ricardo Piglia and John Barth," *Tri-Quarterly* (Winter 1990–1991): 171–205.

— R.G.M.

AUGUSTO PINOCHET

Gen. Augusto Pinochet (1915–) took power in a bloody right-wing coup against democratically elected Marxist president **Salvador Allende** and was in power in Chile from 1973 to 1988. Pinochet closed down the congress as part of a larger plan to destroy the country's political system. Thousands of political prisoners were tortured and "disappeared" during his regime. The massive repression was masterminded in the mid 1970s by DINA, the National Intelligence Directorate, whose agents also operated abroad, hunting down prominent opponents of the regime.

General Pinochet promoted neoliberal economic policies designed by a team of United States–trained Chilean economists known as the "Chicago Boys." He reformed the constitution in 1980 with the aim of self-perpetuation; however, eight years later he was rejected by voters in a plebiscite. Nevertheless, Pinochet continued to preside over Chile's National Security Council.

— R.G.M. & P.S.

ALEJANDRA PIZARNIK

An Argentinean writer and heir to the Symbolists and Surrealists, Alejandra Pizarnik (1936–1972) capped an extended poetic meditation on death and madness with

Augusto Pinochet (seated at center) and members of his government

her suicide while on leave from a psychiatric clinic. Pizarnik studied at the University of Buenos Aires and later at the Sorbonne. Between 1960 and 1964 she lived in Paris, where she made the acquaintance of **Julio Cortázar** and worked as a translator of French poetry for various publishers. Like many modern poets, Pizarnik was haunted by the search for plenitude and wholeness and distressed by the inability of language to hold onto meaning. The "leak" of meaning from linguistic structures made it impossible to establish a stable subjective domain, and yet linguistic discourse is the only "being" a poet has. The compromise between language and silence in Pizarnik's poetry is effected by a fragmentary style of which the poet was acutely conscious: "My imaginary contents are so fragmentary, so divorced from the real, that I fear, in short, I might be giving birth only to monsters."

Pizarnik's most haunting work is *Extracción de la piedra de la locura* (1968; Extraction of the Stone of Madness), whose title refers to a medieval belief that madness was caused by a "bump" — a stone — lodged in the brain and protruding from the victim's forehead. This work is a mixture of brief poems, poetic fragments, prose poems, and aphorisms.

REFERENCE:

Frank Graziano, ed., *Alejandra Pizarnik: A Profile,* translated by Maria Rosa Fort and Graziano, with the assistance of Suzanne Jill Levine (Durango, Colo.: Logbridge-Rhodes, 1987).

— R.G.M.

POETRY

Modern literature in Spanish America began with "modernista" poetry near the close of the nineteenth century. **Modernismo** (a movement not equivalent either chronologically or in terms of literary content to Anglo-American or European modernism) was the Spanish American synthesis of the most innovative currents of French poetry — Romanticism, Parnassianism, and Symbolism — and represented a break with the civic and declamatory poetry written by Spanish American poets since independence from Spain in the early nineteenth century. The initial stage of modernismo was programmatically aesthetic, emphasizing the cult of beauty for its own sake and the plastic and musical values of poetic language. The second stage, sometimes called "mundonovismo" ("New Worldism")

Alejandra Pizarnik (right) and Olga Orozco in Paris, 1962

and dating from the Spanish-American War of 1898, was characterized by a concern with the cultural identity of Spanish America. Both stages are present in the poetry of the Nicaraguan Rubén Darío (1867–1916), the greatest poet of the period and the founder of modern Spanish American poetry. His *Prosas profanas* (1896; Profane Hymns) marks the high point of aesthetic modernismo, while his *Cantos de vida y esperanza* (1905; Songs of Life and Hope), together with **José Enrique Rodó**'s essay *Ariel* (1900), are the most important examples of the later modernista style. Before coming to an end, modernismo went through a final phase represented by the work of **Julio Herrera y Reissig** and **Leopoldo Lugones,** "mannerist" poets who turned modernista style against itself through parody and exaggeration.

The years immediately following the death of Darío were characterized by the introduction of Euro-

pean avant-garde poetry into Spanish America, a process initiated by **Vicente Huidobro** and **Jorge Luis Borges** and consolidated in 1921, by which time Huidobro's *Poemas árticos* (1918; translated as *Arctic Poems*) and Borges's Ultraist manifesto had been published. Huidobro's brand of avant-garde poetry was called **Creacionismo** and had close affinities with French Cubism; **Ultraísmo** was an eclectic movement that called for poetry to go beyond its traditional horizons in search of that elusive quality known as modernity. Both attacked the formal tenets of modernismo: rhyme, meter, ornamental descriptions, elaborate syntactic constructions, poetic structure, verbal melody, and display of a confessional persona. Nevertheless, both implicitly carried forward other aspects of Darío's movement, including the claim that poetic discourse was autonomous and specific and the cosmopolitan aura that enveloped modernista poetry. The avant-garde, after all, was merely an acceleration of the same modernizing impulse that had driven late-nineteenth-century poetry to insert Spanish American poetry into a "universal" framework. Huidobro reaffirmed the sovereign nature of poetic creation and rejected the notion that poetic images represent previously created objects. Borges was equally forceful in stripping poetic discourse down to its essential component: images. Borges, like all avant-garde theoreticians, focused on images because they constitute the differential element of poetry.

After 1924 — the date of André Breton's first manifesto — Surrealism was the most influential avant-garde movement in Spanish America, deeply affecting poets like Octavio Paz, **César Moro,** and the early work of **Pablo Neruda,** specifically his *Residencia en la tierra* (1933; translated as *Residence on Earth*). Even poets who disagreed with Surrealism (including Huidobro) were compelled to take a public stance regarding Breton's movement, so strong was the hegemony of Surrealism in the 1920s and 1930s. Among the disaffected was **César Vallejo,** a figure central to Spanish American poetry but tangential in relation to the European "isms" of the 1910s and 1920s. Vallejo was a regional poet from the Peruvian hinterland who negotiated the innovations of the avant-garde without affiliating himself with any of the styles in vogue. His brand of avant-garde poetry contrasts with that of the majority of his fellow Spanish American poets. Whereas Huidobro, Neruda, Paz, and Moro cultivated a cosmopolitan poetic style in which signs of cultural identity were either nonexistent or secondary, Vallejo's poetry remained rooted in the culture of his Andean homeland. Many of the writers who kept their distance from the avant-garde were regional poets who resisted the onslaught of European fashions. The period immediately following modernismo (but not involving the avant-garde movements) has sometimes been called "postmodernismo"; important in relation to this catch-all category is the poet **Enrique González Martínez** (especially his sonnet demanding that the swan's neck be wrung, the swan being a standard modernista symbol of beauty) and the work of the "poetisas," female poets such as **Alfonsina Storni, Juana de Ibarbourou, Delmira Agustini,** and **Gabriela Mistral**.

The period dominated by the avant-garde came to an end with the Spanish Civil War of 1936–1939, a conflagration that redefined the poetic orientation of some of the major figures of Spanish American poetry. Poets as dissimilar as Neruda, Vallejo, Paz, and Guillén wrote important works inspired by the Spanish war in a new, politically committed vein. The solidarity of these poets with the Republican cause and their forceful stance against fascism brought to an end the self-absorption typical of experimental poets and reconnected them with a segment of the reading public. Avant-garde poetry itself, however, did not die out at the end of the 1930s. In subsequent decades groups of aesthetically (and often politically) militant poets continued to emerge all over Spanish America, but their poetic models and objectives were no longer those that had inspired their predecessors. Among notable new influences was that of the Beat poets of the United States.

The leading poets to emerge in Spanish America following the avant-garde were **Nicanor Parra** and Ernesto Cardenal. The former demystified the poetic myths of Surrealism and toned down the elevated rhetoric of his compatriot Neruda by means of an ironic style grounded on colloquial language. Parra seemed to carry on a dialogue with the reader, whereas Neruda sometimes spoke to the reader from the Olympian heights earlier reserved for Romantic poets. Colloquial language also characterized the poetry of Cardenal, whose work integrates traditional poetic forms (such as the epigrams of Roman poetry) with contemporary themes (political repression), and biblical language (derived from Psalms or Revelation) with twentieth-century concerns such as multinational capitalism, the hydrogen bomb, and Marilyn Monroe. Many contemporary South American poets, for example **Enrique Lihn** and **Antonio Cisneros,** share the informal relationship with the reader inaugurated by Parra and Cardenal. (See **Fiction** and **Theater.**)

REFERENCES:

Gordon Brotherston, *Latin American Poetry: Origins and Presence* (Cambridge: Cambridge University Press, 1975);

Frederick S. Stimson, *The New Schools of Spanish American Poetry* (Madrid: Castalia, 1970);

Saúl Yurkievich, *Fundadores de la nueva poesía latinoamericana* (Barcelona: Barral, 1971).

— R.G.M.

POLCA

The polca (polka) came to the Americas with the heavy European immigration that began in the nineteenth century. It became a popular dance in both North and South America, but in Latin America it was subjected to various local adaptations. In Mexico, for example, the polka exists as a separate genre but also provides the rhythmic basis for the *corrido* and the *canción*. An adaptation of the polka in Paraguay is the triplet rhythm of the accompaniment against the binary meter of the melody. It is a popular dance in Argentina, Paraguay, Uruguay, and (in various versions) Colombia.

REFERENCES:

Rodolfo Arizaga, *Enciclopedia de la música argentina* (Buenos Aires: Fondo Nacional de las Artes, 1971);

Vicente Gesualdo, *La música en la Argentina* (Buenos Aires: Editorial Stella, 1988);

Octavio Marulanda, *El folclor de Colombia: Práctica de la identidad cultural* (Bogotá: Artestudio Editores, 1984).

—R.L.S.

POP ART, ASSEMBLAGES, AND HAPPENINGS

In Latin America Pop Art, Assemblages, and Happenings are closely related art forms. During the 1960s and early 1970s the artists who produced assembled collages and sculptures, three-dimensional installations, and Happenings, in which the audience actively participated, often called their work Pop Art. In the United States Pop Art was generally based on neutral images of mass-produced commodities, such as Andy Warhol's *Campbell's Soup Cans,* whereas in Latin America this art form focused instead on popular images that carried multiple cultural and ideological connotations, such as **Marta Minujín**'s *El batacazo* (1965; The Long Shot).

In Buenos Aires several artists defined their work as Pop Art, including Minujín, Delia Cancela, Pablo Mesejeán, Dalila Puzzovio, Alfredo Rodríguez Arias, Rubén Santantonín, and Juan Stoppani. Others, such as **Antonio Berni,** Alberto Heredia, and the **Otra Figuración** group, did not use the label Pop Art, but during the 1960s they included visual references to popular culture and thrown-away everyday objects in their collages and assemblages. This neo-Dadaist approach had begun to be explored in Buenos Aires in 1960, in the Arte Destructivo exhibition organized by **Kenneth Kemble,** an exhibition which later encouraged pop artists to fabricate art "objects" with refuse, as exemplified by Puzzovio's *La carretilla de gas* (1964; The Gas Cart), loaded with used plaster casts. Many Argentinean pop artists also worked with installations, created by placing a variety of sculptures, everyday objects, or discarded things in a room-sized environment, which then becomes a single complex assemblage in which the public can circulate. An example was Robert Plate's *El baño* (1968; The Bathroom), which was censored by the police after the public wrote obscenities on its walls. Minujín also worked with technology in *Simultaneity on Simultaneity,* part of the *Happening in Three Countries,* organized with Wolf Vostell in Berlin and Allan Kaprow in New York (1966), which used radio and television as a means of simultaneous international communica-

tion. The Groupe de Recherche d'Art Visuel, an experimental group active in Paris during the 1960s, which included the Argentineans **Julio Le Parc** and Horacio García Rossi, also explored the active participation of the spectator in their art experiences, such as *Day in the Street* (1966), which took place in different street sites in Paris.

From the 1960s Chilean Pop Art took the form of highly politicized collages and assemblages produced by artists such as Francisco Brugnoli, Hugo Marín, Alberto Pérez, Juan Pablo Langlis, Guillermo Núñez, and Valentina Cruz. Among the earlier examples were Marín's collages of discarded objects, such as pieces of old furniture, rags, and carbonized wood, which symbolized the marginality of the more indigent sectors of society. The uncompromising poverty of this art (in the sense of the Italian "Arte Povera" of the 1960s) shocked the public in 1968, when Pérez exhibited his series *Barricada* (Barricade), constructed as wooden sheds holding photographs, including one of **Ernesto "Che" Guevara**'s dead body. The emphasis on radical protest in Pop Art continued during the 1970s, in spite of the fact that after 1973 Chile's military dictators imposed strict **censorship**, which cost Núñez several years of imprisonment for exhibiting a series of bird cages containing objects like bread and flowers. Pop Art's use of poor materials and ephemeral structures also characterized **Conceptual Art,** making it difficult to differentiate one form from the other.

In Colombia Pop Art had numerous adherents; as in Argentina and Chile, their purpose was often political and social commentary. Pop Art was introduced by **Bernardo Salcedo** in the mid 1960s through a series of collages including advertising photographs and boxlike assemblages made of industrial objects. During the 1970s Salcedo's work turned increasingly toward Conceptual Art. Jorge Madriñán and **Beatriz González** also used popular images in their work. In Madriñán's assemblage *Carmen la violenta* (Carmen the Violent) he included a popular print and other household items, while González used a photograph disseminated by the press as the focus of her painting *Los suicidas del Sisga* (1965; The Suicides of the Sisga), executed in a flat, figurative style reminiscent of that of the American painter Alex Katz. In the 1970s González also painted flat images with political content on household objects and on various pieces of furniture. Often associated with Pop Art are **Fernando Botero,** whose whimsical, inflated style caricatures Colombian society, and Santiago Cárdenas, whose paintings and drawings realistically portray every-

The Simulacrum (1991), by Liliana Porter (Collection of the artist)

day objects placed in orderly isolation in bare architectural settings. Hernando del Villar, Ana Mercedes Hoyos, and Javier Restrepo worked during the 1960s and 1970s with styles inspired by graphic design and comic strips (see **Comic Strips and Books**).

In Venezuela the **Neofigurative** artist **Jacobo Borges** often used images created by the press in order to reveal the complicity between the media and the Venezuelan government. In 1966 he stopped painting and for several years participated in the production of *Imágenes de Caracas* (Images of Caracas), a multimedia event presented as an installation/Happening in which the audience was immersed, to be confronted with audiovisual effects created by props, lights, and fragmented film projections. The purpose of this Happening was to make the public aware of the power relations present in everyday life. The Venezuelan **Marisol,** who has lived in New York since 1950, also works with social contents in assemblages featuring portraits and social stereotypes which she constructs with wood and objets trouvés.

REFERENCE:

Jacqueline Barnitz, "New Figuration, Pop, and Assemblage in the 1960s and 1970s," in *Latin American Artists of the Twentieth Century,* edited by Waldo Rasmussen, Fatima Bercht, and Elizabeth Ferrer (New York: Museum of Modern Art, 1993), pp. 122–133.

— F.B.N.

POP OCCULT LITERATURE

Popular occult literature is marketed in Spanish America as elsewhere in a mass-produced consumer form. It also has the same type of fixations as elsewhere: "psi" research, mysticism, out-of-body travel, prophecy, spells, apocalyptic thought, and heresy. Two important authors in this genre are the Chilean Elcira Pinticart de W. and Luis Eduardo Pérez Pereyra. Pinticart's *El cultivo de las rosas* (1977; The Growing of the Roses) describes the author's parapsychological discoveries, which pertain to prophecy and to her beliefs about her psychic awareness of natural phenomena. Pérez Pereyra, on the other hand, as an alternative to traditional Christian beliefs, takes a theosophist position that only a few enlightened individuals are endowed with truth and that only they can lead the masses to enlightenment.

REFERENCE:

Chuck Tatum, "Paraliterature," in *Handbook of Latin American Literature,* edited by David William Foster (New York & London: Garland, 1992), pp. 687–728.

— S.M.H.

LILIANA PORTER

Argentinean Liliana Porter (1941–) is one of the most innovative figurative artists to emerge in Latin America since the 1960s. (See **Figuration since the 1970s**.) She studied art in Buenos Aires, Mexico City, and New York, where she has lived since 1964. She cofounded the New York Graphic Workshop (1965–1970) with **Luis Camnitzer** (her husband at the time) and participated in the experimental activities of the workshop, which are related to **Conceptual Art.** In the 1960s Porter transformed the human figures that characterized her earlier expressionist style into a series of dark silhouettes which she later combined with printed images of wrinkles.

During the 1970s Porter began exploring the paradoxical quality of representation as a visual duplicate of reality. In deceptively simple installations she contrasted real objects — such as wrinkled paper, nails, strings, apples, and lemons — with their two-dimensional images. She further refined this approach in 1975, when she began appropriating René Magritte's art to explore the tension between reality and illusion. In her print *The Great War* (1975) Porter presents a real apple resting on a painting by Magritte showing a man whose face is covered by an apple. By contrasting the real, painted, and printed apples, Porter generates a multilayered reality that reminds one of some of the stories by her favorite author, **Jorge Luis Borges.** In the 1980s Porter extended her artistic vocabulary by appropriating the work of other writers and artists such as Lewis Carroll and Roy Lichtenstein and including autobiographical references in the form of visual fragments: art quotations, postcards, images of books, toys, or pieces torn from printed texts. Porter directly glues these objects and silk-screens their images onto white canvases or wall installations, following a textlike format or a still-life composition. In works such as *Triptych* (1986) and *The Simulacrum* (1991) the juxtaposition of real objects with their two-dimensional counterparts creates witty deceptions that not only effectively subvert the limit between the real and the imaginary but also comment on the very nature of cultural representations. Porter's art has an open-ended quality that generates multiple meanings, some of which express her cultural identity as a Latin American artist.

REFERENCE:

Mari Carmen Ramírez, Marisol Nieves, and Charles Merewether, *Liliana Porter: Fragments of the Journey* (New York: Bronx Museum of the Arts, 1992).

— F.B.N.

ABEL POSSE

In his 1971 novel *La boca del tigre* (The Tiger's Mouth) the Argentinean writer Abel Posse (1936–) reveals a pessimistic attitude when faced with the crisis of modern humanity, reminiscent of the work of **Ernesto Sábato.** *Daimón*, however, published ten years later, is a complex allegorical novel based on the mythical figure of Lope de Aguirre; in a search for the essence of Spanish America, a ghostly Aguirre looks back from an indigenous viewpoint on his colonial past. Aguirre has been the subject of several artistic re-creations, including **Miguel Otero Silva**'s *Lope de Aguirre: Príncipe de la libertad* (1979; Lope de Aguirre: Prince of Freedom) and **Arturo Uslar Pietri**'s *El camino de El Dorado* (1947; The Road to Eldorado). The novel that has won greatest recognition for Posse is *Los perros del paraíso* (1983; The Dogs of Paradise), which was awarded the **Premio Rómulo Gallegos de Novela;** this novel, again, is concerned with the colonial era, focusing on the figure of Columbus. Also by Posse is *Los demonios ocultos* (1988; The Hidden Demons), which delves into the roots of Argentinean fascism.

— P.S.

POST-BOOM

Some critics refer to the evolution of the Latin American novel since its heyday in the 1960s (**Boom**) as the Post-Boom. Although it has no agreed-upon meaning, leftist critics have used the term to revalidate a type of populist fiction made unfashionable by the cosmopolitanism of the Boom. Others have pointed to formal simplicity as the hallmark of the Post-Boom novel, as evidenced, for example, by the restoration of linear narrative and the scaling down of the representation of authorial consciousness, which played a central role in modern novels such as **Julio Cortázar**'s *Rayuela* (1963; translated as *Hopscotch*) and **José Donoso**'s *El obsceno pájaro de la noche* (1970; translated as *The Obscene Bird of Night*). Still others have spoken of a kind of Latin American "minimalism" in opposition to the totalizing ambitions of the Boom novel. The term *Post-Boom* is further complicated by its implied relation to postmodernism, an overarching notion issuing from cultural changes in Europe and in the United States, whose relevance to Latin American criticism is a matter of debate. What is clear is that the high-literary aesthetics of the modern novel have undergone profound modifications in the last two decades, resulting from the incorporation of mass cultural forms (film, melodrama, thrillers, forensic journalism, and popular music).

REFERENCE:

Ricardo Gutiérrez Mouat, "La narrativa latinoamericana del posboom," *Revista Interamericana de Bibliografía,* 38, no. 1 (1988): 3–10.

— R.G.M.

REFERENCES:

Lyman Chaffee, "The Popular Culture Political Persuasion in Paraguay: Communication and Public Art," *Studies in Latin American Popular Culture,* 9 (1990): 127–148;

Chuck Tatum, "Paraliterature," in *Handbook of Latin American Literature,* edited by David William Foster (New York & London: Garland, 1992), pp. 687–728.

— S.M.H.

POSTERS

Posters, a public form of popular culture, are often found on building walls in Latin America, and they are meant to be read by passersby, designed with a specific audience in mind and containing a political or social message expressed explicitly and overtly. The first recorded examples of poster culture in the New World are the anonymous messages called *pasquines* written on walls in Mexico during Hernán Cortés's military campaign there (1519–1522) and which were highly critical of his actions; these *pasquines* are the distant descendants of the political graffiti and posters which adorn the walls and billboards of Latin American cities in the twentieth century.

Colombian author **Gabriel García Márquez** illustrates the use of *pasquines* as a form of protest in one of his early novels, *La mala hora* (1962; translated as *In Evil Hour*). Contemporary Argentina provides a rich source of poster art arising from the political turmoil of the last twenty years; posters provide a means of communicating directly with the city's politicized masses, and their messages are informative (they relate narratives of injustice) and performative (they call the people to rally around a new set of ideals).

A different scenario is suggested by contemporary Paraguay, one of the least politicized countries in the Southern Cone, due mainly to the dominance of the authoritarian regime of Gen. Alfredo Stroessner. Because of the extreme risk of affixing posters to public walls, one tends to find displayed only officially sanctioned posters sponsored by approved political parties.

Posters were also common in Cuba, Chile, and Nicaragua at various times during the 1970s and 1980s. In Cuba posters sponsored by the Castro government have as a dominant message Latin American unity in resistance against imperialism. The Chilean Popular Unity government of **Salvador Allende** published posters from 1970 to 1973, but they were less uniform than the Cuban type and were generally not made available to as large a public. The Nicaraguan revolutionary government also used posters but seemed to prefer larger-format wall murals, in the Mexican muralist tradition, displayed on highway billboards where they could be seen by passing motorists and pedestrians.

POSTMODERN DANCE

Large increases in the number of Latin Americans moving to the United States during the post–World War II era and the reputation of New York City as the dance capital of the world account, in part, for the explosive growth of postmodern dance in Latin America. Tours to South America by German expressionist/postmodern choreographer Pina Bausch have also had an influence. The reputation of New York City makes it a mecca for large numbers of Latin American dance artists wishing to explore postmodern training and performance. Despite differences in national, political, and class backgrounds, Latinos in New York share a sense of unity because of their differences from mainstream culture and because of shared language and cultural values. Many are also acutely aware of the economic and political inequalities between the United States and Latin America. Their choreography, therefore, assumes the function of criticizing culture in general, as well as defining their personal and political identities as mestizo, as "underdeveloped," or as "American" in a broad sense. Their works focus on the politically conscious awareness of their role in bridging the gap between the Old and the New Worlds. Once trained and exposed professionally in New York, these choreographers — including Ecuadorans Wilson Pico and Susana Reyes — frequently return to their countries or cultures of origin to test the theories or works in the cultural crucibles which inspired their work.

— J.M.H. & N.D.B.

PREMIO BIBLIOTECA BREVE DE NOVELA

An annual prize for unpublished novels awarded during the years 1957–1972 by the Spanish publishing house Seix Barral, the **Premio Biblioteca Breve de Novela,** along with Seix Barral itself, played a crucial role in the Latin American **Boom.** In 1962 the Boom was first heard when the prize was awarded to **Mario Vargas Llosa**'s first novel, *La ciudad y los perros* (translated as *The Time of the Hero*). Other Latin

King Juan Carlos of Spain awarding the Premio Miguel de Cervantes de Literatura to Ernesto Sábato, April 1985

American novelists who won the Biblioteca Breve are the Cuban Guillermo Cabrera Infante (*Tres tristes tigres,* 1964; translated as *Three Trapped Tigers*) and the Mexican Carlos Fuentes (*Cambio de piel,* 1967; translated as *A Change of Skin*). **José Donoso** was to have been the recipient of the 1970 edition of the prize for *El obsceno pájaro de la noche* (translated as *The Obscene Bird of Night*), but that year the prize was declared null and void as the result of an internal quarrel in Seix Barral.

— R.G.M.

PREMIO MIGUEL DE CERVANTES DE LITERATURA

The most prestigious award for Spanish-language writers, the Premio Miguel de Cervantes de Literatura, was established in Spain in 1975 and granted for the first time the following year. It has the purpose of recognizing writers from Spain and Spanish America as members of the same cultural community. The prize, under the auspices of the Spanish Ministry of Culture, carries a large honorarium and is awarded yearly in a formal ceremony attended by the king of Spain in Alcalá de

Henares, the birthplace of Miguel de Cervantes. Candidates are nominated by the Spanish Royal Academy of Language, by the national academies of Spanish-speaking countries, and by previous winners. The Spanish American authors who have won the award include Alejo Carpentier (1977), **Jorge Luis Borges** (1979), **Juan Carlos Onetti** (1980), Octavio Paz (1981), **Ernesto Sábato** (1984), Carlos Fuentes (1987), **Augusto Roa Bastos** (1989), **Adolfo Bioy Casares** (1990), Dulce María Loynaz (1992), and **Mario Vargas Llosa** (1994). This prize should not be confused with the earlier and now defunct Premio Miguel de Cervantes.

— R.G.M.

PREMIO RÓMULO GALLEGOS DE NOVELA

The most prestigious Latin American prize awarded to novelists, the Premio Rómulo Gallegos de Novela, is named after the eminent Venezuelan writer and former president of the republic **Rómulo Gallegos,** author of *Doña Bárbara* (1929) and *Canaima* (1935). It was instituted in 1964 (while Gallegos was still alive) and was awarded for the first time in 1967 to **Mario Vargas**

Llosa for *La casa verde*. Originally, the prize was intended as a quinquennial affair. In 1972 it was awarded to **Gabriel García Márquez** for *Cien años de soledad* and in 1977 to the Mexican Carlos Fuentes for *Terra Nostra*. The next two went to Fernando del Paso (for *Palinuro de México*, 1982) and **Abel Posse** (for *Los perros del paraíso*, 1987). In the late 1980s the prize began to be awarded every two years. In 1989 it went to **Manuel Mejía Vallejo** for *La casa de dos palmas*, in 1991 to **Arturo Uslar Pietri** for *La visita en el tiempo*, and in 1993 the Rómulo Gallegos was awarded to Mempo Giardinelli for *El santo oficio de la memoria*. In the early 1990s the prize carried an honorarium of eleven thousand dollars plus a guaranteed edition of twenty-five thousand copies of the winning novel.

— R.G.M.

PUBLISHERS

While publishing houses are to be found in most of the principal cities, the places which dominate Hispanic publishing are Buenos Aires, Mexico City, Barcelona, and Madrid. From one or more of these cities come many of the books destined for the Hispanic world at large, a huge market (by the end of the twentieth century the relevant population may be in the region of four hundred million). Reading is a pastime for many Hispanics, although illiteracy continues to be at significant levels in many regions of Spanish America, and thus a part of the market is potential. Bookshops often serve as social meeting places, and sometimes poetry readings are held in them. Books of all sorts are commonly on sale at street kiosks, often in inexpensive editions. Publishing is an international business, and it is common to see cooperative ventures by consortia of publishing houses, for example Alianza (Madrid) in conjunction with Emecé (Buenos Aires). Many Spanish American writers are published by Spanish publishers: such publishers include Seix Barral, a particularly significant force during the developing years of the **Boom,** Alfaguara, Alianza, and Plaza y Janés. In Spanish America the main publishers are Sudamericana, Losada, Emecé, Monte Avila, Siglo XXI, Joaquín Mortiz, Fondo de Cultura Económica, and Casa de las Américas. Mondadori is an Italian firm publishing quality editions from Madrid. It is also worth noting the role of Ediciones del Norte, which, while based in Hanover, New Hampshire, has done much to bring the work of new Hispanic writers to prominence. (See also **Colección Archivos** and **Biblioteca Ayacucho.**)

— P.S.

MANUEL PUIG

One of the younger writers associated with the Latin American **Boom** of the 1960s, Manuel Puig (1932–1990) is the main transitional figure between the modern Latin American novel, characterized by the assimilation of European and United States "high modernism," and its postmodern sequel. At the same time as his contemporaries were adapting the literary culture of international modernism to the specific needs of Latin American fiction, Puig was working with models derived from mass culture and particularly from film. (In the 1950s Puig obtained a fellowship to study film directing in Rome and began his literary career by writing screenplays.) He was not alone in his devotion to film as an alternative narrative model; the Cuban Guillermo Cabrera Infante was also an avid film buff, and **Mario Vargas Llosa** has detailed the influence of the cowboy-film genre on the making of *La casa verde,* one of the major novels of the Boom. No other writer, however, has so systematically and single-mindedly "translated" the novel into the medium of film and vice versa.

Puig was born in a small town in the province of Buenos Aires, where his first two novels are set. Both *La traición de Rita Hayworth* (1968; revised edition, 1976; translated as *Betrayed by Rita Hayworth*) and *Boquitas pintadas* (1969; translated as *Heartbreak Tango*) dispense with conventional narrative structure and appeal instead to a wide array of experimental forms to advance the plot and present characters and thematic motifs: anonymous monologues identified and differentiated by stylistic features, one-way dialogues, the journals or notebooks of certain characters, letters, fragments quoted from sentimental magazines, **tango** lyrics, plot synopses of the characters' favorite films, and forensic files. In addition, both of these novels ultimately deal with the unsettling gap between the glamorized world of Hollywood films and the drab everyday world of the provincial petit bourgeois. The imprint of the film industry on Puig's first novel is evident from the title; *Boquitas pintadas,* however, takes its title from a tango and is subtitled **folletín** (serial). Thus, Puig remotivates the literary pact between author and reader by appealing to mass cultural forms.

Puig's first two novels may be described as polyphonic collages, that is, as a complex arrangement of narrative materials pinned to specific but often anonymous voices that engage one another in a rich interplay of information. In subsequent novels Puig simplifies his narrative structures, which acquire a binary or antithetical character. *The Buenos Aires Affair* (1973), a detective novel, is structured around two characters, a male sadist and a female masochist. The novel, which

Manuel Puig

was considered pornographic and banned in Argentina, foreshadows Puig's most successful effort, *El beso de la mujer araña* (1976; translated as *Kiss of the Spider Woman*), not only in its antithetical structure but also in the parodic use of psychoanalytic jargon to explain the characters' motivation. *El beso de la mujer araña* deals with the relationship between two prisoners in Argentina during the **Guerra Sucia** (Dirty War), a homosexual detained for child molestation and a guerrilla caught during a government raid. The prison authorities strike a deal with the child molester, coercing him to gather information from his cellmate about the activities of the latter's guerrilla band. In the novel's climax the prisoners undergo a symbolic exchange of identities which results in the homosexual dying for a political cause. Significantly, the revolutionary learns about his cellmate's world through the films that the latter wistfully recounts, some of them actual Hollywood productions (like *The Cat People* and *I Walked with a Zombie*) and others made up by the author.

These narratives provide a buffer zone where the antithetical characters lay down their preconceptions and empathize with one another. Not surprisingly, *El beso de la mujer araña* itself became a film in 1985, the most successful film rendition ever made of a Latin American novel. It also exists as a play and in a musical version.

Puig's next book, *Pubis angelical* (1979; translated), was a political science-fiction fantasy structured as a counterpoint between two stories belonging to different genres and set in different time frames. It relies on dialogue and extracts from the protagonist's diary as well as on objective narrative. *Maldición eterna a quien lea estas páginas* (1980; translated as *An Eternal Curse on the Reader of These Pages*) once again makes use of the psychoanalytical paradigm since it is a dialogue between two characters, an Argentinean political exile confined to a wheelchair and a young American, engaged in mutual analysis. The novel is set in New York (where Puig was living in the late 1970s)

225

and is supposed to be the translation of materials in English stemming from the interviews that Puig conducted with a young man he met at a public pool.

Puig's last two novels take place in Brazil, where the writer spent some of his final years. *Sangre de amor correspondido* (1982; translated as *Blood of Requited Love*) is an ambiguous story of youthful passion that takes place in a provincial setting and is protagonized by a small-time Don Juan vaguely reminiscent of the one in *Boquitas pintadas*. *Cae la noche tropical* (1988; translated as *Tropical Night Falling*) is sustained by the conversations and epistolary communications between two elderly sisters. Its tone and content allude to mass cultural genres like Harlequin romances and soap operas. Puig also wrote two plays (including the adaptation of *El beso de la mujer araña*) and two film scripts,

"La cara del villano" (The Villain's Face) and "Recuerdo de Tijuana" (Souvenir from Tijuana). The film scripts, which had been published in Italian five years earlier, appeared together in Spanish in 1985.

Manuel Puig was awarded the fourth Curzio Malaparte Prize (earlier awarded to Saul Bellow, Anthony Burgess, and Nadine Gordimer) in 1987. He died of complications following surgery in Mexico in July 1990.

REFERENCES:

Pamela Bacarisse, *The Necessary Dream: A Study of the Novels of Manuel Puig* (Totowa, N.J.: Barnes & Noble, 1988);

Lucille Kerr, *Suspended Fictions: Reading Novels by Manuel Puig* (Urbana: University of Illinois Press, 1987).

—R.G.M.

Q

QUENA

The quena is an end-blown flute used widely in the Andean and surrounding areas and descended from the ancient Inca civilization. The phallic symbolism of the quena indicated fertility. Early instruments were made of bone, which was believed to have magical properties. Later instruments were made of cane, with five to six finger holes on top and one underneath for octave transposition. In the past only men were authorized to play quenas. They are among the most versatile melodic **aerophones** and are made in different sizes, lengths, and keys. Quenas are often played in pairs as first and second parts. Ensembles that feature them typically include **charango**, **bombo**, and **sicu**.

REFERENCES:

Gerard Béhague, "Latin American Folk Music," in *Folk and Traditional Music of the Western Continents,* by Bruno Nettl, third edition, revised and edited by Valerie Woodring Goertzen (Englewood Cliffs, N.J.: Prentice-Hall, 1990);

Américo Valencia Chacón, *El siku o zampoña — The Altiplano Bipolar Siku: Study and Projection of Peruvian Panpipe Orchestras* (Lima: Centro de Investigación y Desarrollo de la Música Peruana, 1989).

— R.L.S.

Horacio Quiroga

HORACIO QUIROGA

An early master of the Latin American short story, Horacio Quiroga (1878–1937), born in Uruguay, was a tragic figure. Fatal accidents and suicides dogged him: his father was accidentally killed by a hunting rifle, a mishap that uncannily repeated itself in Quiroga's adolescence when the writer himself discharged a gun that killed his best friend. Quiroga also witnessed the suicide of his stepfather and of his first wife, whom Quiroga had taken to live in the wilderness. The writer ended his own life after he discovered he was afflicted with a terminal disease.

Quiroga was also a literary anomaly. He started out as a decadent modernista poet (see **Modernismo**) but soon broke ranks with the aesthetes of the day in order to write stories that gradually lost their aesthetic baggage and became naked and sometimes brutal descriptions of life and death in a primitive environment. A perennial outsider in Buenos Aires, where he lived most of his life, Quiroga effected a radical break with the various literary cliques of the Argentinean capital when he settled in 1909 in Misiones, a scarcely populated jungle territory in northern Argentina, where Jesuit missions had operated in the eighteenth century. Quiroga spent two significant periods of his life as a colonist (1909–1916 and 1932–1936). His experiences in the jungle, although economic failures, provided the content for his most representative stories. His work, published in various magazines and periodicals in Buenos Aires and collected in books such as *Cuentos de amor, de locura y de muerte* (1917; Tales of Love, Madness, and Death), *Cuentos de la selva* (1918; translated as *South American Jungle Tales*), *Anaconda* (1921), *El desierto* (1924; The Desert), and *Los desterrados* (1926; The Exiles), shows the imprint of authors such as Edgar Allan Poe, Guy de Maupassant, Rudyard Kipling, and Jack London. *Cuentos de la selva* was translated into English only a year after its original publication in Spanish and reprinted in 1940 and 1951, decades before Latin American fiction became fashionable abroad, perhaps because of its familiarity to readers of Kipling's *The Jungle Book* (1894) and *Just So Stories* (1902). Like Kipling's stories, Quiroga's tales were meant for children and feature a whole range of animal protagonists. Quiroga's last collection of short stories, *Más allá* (1935; Beyond), deals with supernatural themes and is heavily influenced by the movies. Quiroga, like other writers of the period, including **Jorge Luis Borges,** was a film reviewer and was fascinated by many facets of the Hollywood film industry.

The predominant theme in Quiroga's stories is death, often in the context of man's struggle against nature. In stories such as "A la deriva" (Adrift), "El hombre muerto" (The Dead Man), and "El hijo" (The Son), death overcomes the protagonists as they go about their routine chores in the jungle. At other times the protagonists are entrepreneurs whose projects and lives go awry in a hostile setting they cannot tame. In "Los destiladores de naranja" (The Orange Distillers), for example, psychological deterioration leading to accidental homicide follows the failure of the entrepreneurial project alluded to in the title. This story exemplifies Quiroga's use of realistic detail (in this case technical), which endows even his weaker jungle stories with an unusual type of verisimilitude. Many of Quiroga's Misiones stories are character sketches of the eccentric types who are driven to the jungle to count out their days or to prosper. These eccentrics are often foreigners and immigrants who have opted for

the outback instead of the city in their striving for economic advancement ("Los desterrados," "Los inmigrantes"). Occasionally Quiroga delved into social realism, as in "Los mensú," which describes the hopeless existence of peons on the local plantations.

For Quiroga there was no real difference between the manual labor needed to prevail in the jungle and the intellectual labor required to produce literary works. His stories are as rough-hewn as the canoes or shacks he built with his hands. He was a literary pioneer no less than a colonist hoping to get a good return on his investment of capital and labor. In fact, for many years Quiroga kept a journal recording the income he received for each of his publications, a significant quirk in that it underscores the sense of professionalism with which Quiroga approached literary production. This concern for pecuniary compensation rubbed many of his Buenos Aires colleagues the wrong way. For the **Martín Fierro** group, for example, Quiroga was the "savage" of one of his stories, a hirsute pioneer with no regard for fine literature, and a literary merchant to boot.

Quiroga was a professional writer at a time when copyright laws and laws protecting intellectual property were recent and not duly enforced. In a sense he was more modern (or at least less anachronistic) than "gentleman" writers such as Borges or **Adolfo Bioy Casares,** who were reluctant to assign commercial value to literary products. Quiroga's poetics of the short story (which significantly coincides with Poe's narrative theories) came in part as a response to the modern writer's dependence on the market. His emphasis on brief and concentrated narratives with calculated rhetorical effects reveals the constraints set by journal or newspaper publishers on the allowable length of stories. Quiroga wrote for the public of his time, not for posterity, as many modernists chose to do on finding themselves faced with the growth of mass culture in industrial societies.

However, Quiroga's work continues to be read today — at least that part of his work that most resembles Poe, such as "El almohadón de plumas" (The Feather Pillow), "El crimen del otro" (The Other's Crime), "La gallina degollada" (The Decapitated Chicken), and the stories set in Misiones, whose realism, pathos, and eccentricity remain unmatched. Two recent translations in English attest to Quiroga's durability: *The Decapitated Chicken and Other Stories* (1976) and *The Exiles and Other Stories* (1987).

REFERENCE:

Emir Rodríguez Monegal, *El desterrado: Vida y obra de Horacio Quiroga* (Buenos Aires: Losada, 1968).

— R.G.M.

R

RADIO AND TELEVISION

A 1983 survey of broadcasting revealed a radio in daily use for every 3.5 Latin Americans and a television in daily use for every 7.5. The broadcasting media pervade all social levels of Latin American life from the rich and famous to the poor and ignored. The media even reach shantytown dwellers; the survey showed that 86 percent of slum dwellers in Lima, Peru, and 91 percent of those in Guayaquil, Ecuador, for example, owned a radio receiver; the same study found that among the shantytown dwellers of Guayaquil, 88 percent regularly listened to the radio, while 85 percent said they read newspapers and 47 percent said they read magazines.

At the other extreme, Argentina, for example, with 9 million radios and 5 million television sets in daily use has both media in almost all its households. The networks are split between the commercial sector and the noncommercial government sector. The Argentinean government owns the Buenos Aires television stations broadcasting on channels 9, 11, and 13, as well as their networks serving thirty provincial television stations; the government also owns channel 8 in Mar del Plata and channel 7 in Mendoza. Seven of the provincial television stations belong to public universities or city governments.

In Peru the government owns 25 percent of the privately operated commercial radio stations. For music and entertainment, including soap operas, Lima's private stations Radio Central, Radio Miraflores, Radio Excelsior, and Radio Crónica compete for the largest audiences. Recent evidence suggests that radio broadcasting in Peru preserves rather than destroys traditional cultural practices of the Andean communities.

In Colombia the government's National Institute of Radio and Television, called Inravisión, operates the two commercial video networks of thirty provincial stations anchored by channels 7 and 9 in Bogotá and the educational network headed by channel 11. In 1985 a new channel, Tele-Antioquía, financed equally by Inravisión and the regional development corporation of Antioquía, was established, and other provincial channels soon followed suit.

In Venezuela more than 250 privately owned commercial radio stations compete fiercely for their audiences. The four television channels in Caracas and their respective networks in provincial cities put 1.7 million television sets in daily use for a republic with 14 million people.

In Ecuador most of the 228 AM, 52 shortwave, and 8 FM radio stations are privately owned commercial outlets; sixteen television stations, with programming from channels in Quito and Guayaquil, serve the republic.

Paraguay has three commercial stations, which are censored by the government. The Asunción station Radio Guaraní broadcasts in Guaraní, the Indian language much of the population speaks in addition to Spanish.

In Bolivia the government owns the ENT network of commercial television stations in La Paz and five provincial cities.

In Chile there are 3 million television sets and 4 million radios for a population of only 11 million. The three television stations in Santiago — channels 4, 9, and 13 — are owned by Valparaíso Catholic University, the University of Chile, and Santiago Catholic University, but the national network of twenty-three stations is owned by the government. The Chilean government Radio Nacional in Santiago anchors a nation-

A Bolivian radio announcer wearing a traditional *chullo* (photograph by Caroline Penn). Bolivian radio stations broadcast programs in the Indian languages Quechua and Aymara, as well as in Spanish.

wide network of twenty-five stations, which function as commercial outlets.

Like Chile and Argentina, Uruguay enjoys a high ratio of media outlets per household. In Montevideo, where approximately 96 percent of houses have at least one television set, there are three commercial television stations (channels 4, 10, and 12) and one owned by the state (channel 5).

As early as 1925, only five years after the first regular broadcasting license was issued in the United States, regular broadcasts were established in Mexico. The growth of radio in Colombia may serve as an illustration of how development occurred in South America. By the end of the 1920s La Voz de Barranquilla was inaugurated in Colombia. Shortly thereafter, La Voz de Bogotá and Radio Boyacá in Tunja were added. In the following years similar stations were established in other Colombian cities: Manizales, Medellín, and Cartagena. In 1940 the first radio network, Cadena Azul Bayer, was established with twenty-three affiliates in Colombia. A second network, Cadena Bolívar, was established in Medellín in

1941. As broadcast media technology became accessible and radio stations proliferated throughout Latin America, and in view of the prohibitive cost of phonographs, the marketing of music became profitable. In 1940 the KRESTO organization from Buenos Aires, producers of a popular chocolate beverage, began to sponsor presentations of artists who, because of the high costs, were otherwise unavailable to the nascent Colombian radio industry. This new accessibility to mass audiences created a new order of internationally known Latin American popular musicians. However, the difficult global economic conditions around World War II contributed to a temporary decline in radio networks. Radio and television programming of music has often responded to public tastes for romantic popular music emanating from Mexico, Cuba, and Puerto Rico. The most popular early genres for broadcast have included the bolero, son, and danzón, all of which have exerted strong influence in the northern republics of Colombia and Venezuela. In the south, Argentina and Chile received recordings of popular artists directly from the RCA studios in Camden, New Jersey.

Television is present in all Spanish American nations. In most Spanish American countries it is predominantly a commercial enterprise, run by private companies and supported by advertising revenue. As a result television programming is most often oriented toward entertainment rather than education. Despite varying government controls, television tends not to be an instrument of the state in Spanish America to the degree that it is in many Third World countries. It also began early compared with other developing countries.

Mexico and Cuba inaugurated television broadcasting in 1950. Argentina followed in 1951, Venezuela in 1952, Chile in 1954, Nicaragua in 1955, Uruguay in 1956, Peru in 1958, Paraguay in 1965, Bolivia in 1979, and, finally, Belize in 1981. In most Spanish American countries television started in one or two major cities and then gradually spread to smaller cities and even rural areas. While it developed in most countries as a commercial system, some countries (Cuba, Nicaragua after the revolution) nationalized television stations, while others (Colombia, Peru, and Argentina) have sought a balance between noncommercial and commercial forms of broadcasting.

Chile presents an interestingly individual case. During **Salvador Allende**'s presidency (1970–1973), for example, there were four channels, three of them housed in the capital and the fourth in the city of Valparaíso. The three Santiago channels were state run or partially state run; channel 7 was run by Allende's Popular Unity political party, channel 13 by the Catholic University, and channel 9 by the University of Chile. After the 1973 putsch, however, a mixture of state-run and commercial television emerged.

In many countries commercial television broadcasting was set up or developed in cooperation with U.S. television networks. In Venezuela, for example, as in Mexico, there are government stations, but they attract only a small audience, and television is, broadly speaking, in the hands of commercial trusts, in effect the sleeping partners of North American television companies such as CBS, ABC, and NBC. Most Spanish American commercial television stations continue to depend to some degree on advertising revenues from foreign or multinational corporations.

The story of Argentina's television is in many ways typical of the trends of television in the other countries of South America. With a population of more than 30 million and a degree of urbanization of 79 percent, Argentina is among the ten most urbanized countries in the world. Argentina experienced a television boom in the 1960s and 1970s: the number

of television sets jumped from 800,000 in 1960 to 4,080,000 in 1973. In the early 1960s Argentina was a heavy importer of American television film material, but this situation gradually changed, and in the 1990s there is a relatively low proportion of imported programs. By 1973 approximately 92.5 percent of the homes in Buenos Aires had television sets, and the average viewing time (for persons over six years old) was two hours and forty-nine minutes per day. Argentinean television has developed as an "entertaining" rather than "informing" medium, carefully avoiding the use of explicitly political or editorial comments, a tendency which became particularly evident during the **Guerra Sucia** (Dirty War) of 1976–1983. One area where there has been enormous growth in Argentina is the **telenovela,** and Argentina now competes effectively with Mexico, which for many years dominated the soap-opera market in the Spanish-speaking countries of Latin America.

Throughout most of South America broadcasters often rely on imported programs, usually from the United States, as a source of low-cost broadcast fare, but this dependence has diminished throughout the 1980s and 1990s. Many North American program genres have been transplanted to Latin America, such as variety shows, soap operas, game shows, music reviews, and interview programs. Comedy is one of the most idiosyncratic forms of popular culture and one of the most likely to be produced locally.

REFERENCES:

Marvin Alisky, "Latin America," in *Global Journalism,* edited by John C. Merrill (New York: Longman, 1983), pp. 249–301;

Fred V. Bales, *Comparing Media Use and Political Orientation among Squatter Settlers of the Latin American Countries,* Research Paper Series no. 13 (Albuquerque: Latin American Institute, University of New Mexico, 1983);

Azriel Bibliowicz, "Be Happy Because Your Father Isn't Your Father: An Analysis of Columbian *Telenovelas,*" *Journal of Popular Culture,* 14 (Winter 1980): 476–485;

Betsy J. Blosser, "Through the *Pantalla Uruguaya* (Uruguayan Screen): The Television Environment for Children in Uruguay," in *Studies in Latin American Popular Culture,* 9 (1990): 149–168;

Michael Chanan, ed., *Chilean Cinema* (London: BFI, 1976);

Elizabeth Fox, ed., *Media and Politics in Latin America: The Struggle for Democracy* (London: Sage, 1988);

José A. Lloréns, "Andean Voices on Lima Airwaves: Highland Migrants and Radio Broadcasting in Peru," *Studies in Latin American Popular Culture,* 10 (1991): 178–189;

William Rowe and Vivian Schelling, *Memory and Modernity: Popular Culture in Latin America* (London: Verso, 1991);

Joseph Straubhaar, "Television," in *Handbook of Latin American Popular Culture,* edited by Harold E. Hinds Jr. and Charles M. Tatum (Westport, Conn.: Greenwood Press, 1985), pp. 111–134.

— S.M.H.

ANGEL RAMA

Uruguayan intellectual and literary critic Angel Rama (1926–1983) wrote important essays on major Latin American writers, such as José Martí, Rubén Darío, **José María Arguedas,** and **Gabriel García Márquez.** His many publications in periodicals and newspapers throughout Latin America constitute one of the most original and far-reaching reflections on Latin American culture in the second half of the twentieth century. If his work can be reduced to one central theme, it is the theme of modernization and the cultural effects that this socioeconomic process has had in Latin America. In addition to the influence of his ideas, Rama held several important editorial posts in his native country and, later, in exile. He was the literary director of *Marcha* between 1958 and 1968 and the director of Uruguay's leading publishing house, Editorial Arca. Later he was a cofounder of the literary journal *Escritura* in Caracas, and in that same city he directed the collection of Latin American classics known as the **Biblioteca Ayacucho.** At the time of his death in a plane crash (which also took the life of his wife **Marta Traba**) Rama was a professor at the University of Maryland.

Rama compiled many of his periodical articles (often revising them and aiming for organic coherence) in book form. His most significant books are *Rubén Darío y el modernismo: Circunstancia socio-económica de un arte americano* (1970; Rubén Darío and **Modernismo:** The Socio-Economic Circumstances of an American Art), *Transculturación narrativa en América Latina* (1982; Narrative Transculturation in Latin America), and the posthumously published *La ciudad letrada* (1984; The City of Letters). In the first of these books Rama places the founder of modern Latin American poetry within his economic context and shows how Darío's forms and themes relate to the primary export economic model that at the turn of the century defined the role of Latin America in the world market. In *Transculturación narrativa en América Latina* Rama focuses on the Peruvian writer José María Arguedas and discusses his work in terms of "transculturation," a concept devised by Cuban cultural anthropologist Fernando Ortiz that designates the process whereby a regional culture responds to the influence of a hegemonic one without losing its identity. *La ciudad letrada* is an ambitious synthetic work that shows how the concentration of state power in the hands of urban bureaucrats, beginning in colonial times, affected the institutional development of literature in Latin America. Throughout his work Rama showed an unfaltering concern for the cultural unity and identity of Latin American history.

REFERENCE:

Angel Rama, *La crítica de la cultura en América Latina,* edited by Saúl Sosnowski and Tomás Eloy Martínez (Caracas: Ayacucho, 1985).

— R.G.M.

ARIEL RAMÍREZ

One of the most internationally known Argentinean composers, Ariel Ramírez (1921–), has focused his attention on interpretations of Argentinean folk music. His *Misa Criolla* (1964; Creole Mass), written for soloists, chorus, and regional instruments, features popular folk genres for the five parts of the Ordinary of the Catholic Mass: *Kyrie* — **vidala** and **baguala;** *Gloria* — **carnavalito;** *Credo* — chacarera trunca; *Sanctus* — Carnaval of Cochabamba; *Agnus Dei* — Solemn style of the Pampa. Ramírez's emphasis on folk music in this piece reflects the changes in Catholic liturgy effected by the Second Vatican Council, allowing vernacular languages and music in place of Latin and the traditional musical repertory. The work has been performed many times in South America, Europe, and the United States (including Avery Fisher Hall at Lincoln Center and Saint Patrick's Cathedral in New York). Millions of copies of the original recording of *Misa Criolla* have been sold internationally.

Prior to the success of *Misa Criolla,* Ramírez was known in South America and Europe as a pianist, composer, and conductor. In the early 1950s he directed a touring ensemble that specialized in Argentinean music and gave concerts at universities in Spain, England, Italy, and Germany. In addition to songs, he has written a cantata, *Navidad Nuestra* (Our Christmas), for soloists, chorus, and orchestra as well as film scores for *Los inundados* (1961; The Inundated) and *Martín Fierro* (1968).

REFERENCE:

Vicente Gesualdo, *La música en la Argentina* (Buenos Aires: Editorial Stella, 1988).

— R.L.S.

EDUARDO RAMÍREZ VILLAMIZAR

Eduardo Ramírez Villamizar (1923–) was one of the first artists to introduce **Geometric Abstraction** in Colombia. He studied art in Bogotá and later in Paris during the 1950s, producing paintings with flat areas of color and orthogonal compositions, which he exhibited in Bogotá in 1952. After he received a Guggenheim Fellowship in 1958, Ramírez Villamizar went to New

16 Torres (1972; 16 Towers), by Eduardo Ramírez Villamizar

York and began a series of sculptural reliefs in wood or cardboard, including *Homage to Vivaldi* (1963), which features vertical lines with horizontal accents and subtle interplays of light and shadow. He went back to Colombia in 1960 to become a professor at the Escuela de Bellas Artes in Bogotá; on his return to New York in 1964 he taught in the art education department of New York University.

Since the 1960s Ramírez Villamizar has experimented with many materials, such as concrete, painted metal, and oxidized iron. In 1972 he produced his well-known monumental sculpture *16 Torres* (16 Towers), whose concrete pylons, measuring twenty-three feet high, create a severe vertical rhythm of light and shadow and positive and negative spaces. In 1984 he began working exclusively with oxidized iron in many sculptures inspired by his visits to pre-Columbian sites, such as the series *Recuerdos de Machu Picchu* (Memories of Machu Picchu), which consists of large iron constructions with powerful shapes evocative of Inca geometric patterns. This synthesis of abstract geometric forms and pre-Hispanic references links Ramírez Villamizar's art to the tradition of **Constructive Art.**

REFERENCE:

Nelly Perazzo, "Constructivism and Geometric Abstraction," in *The Latin American Spirit: Art and Artists in the United States, 1920–70,* by Luis Cancel and others (New York: Bronx Museum of the Arts, Abrams, 1988), pp. 106–151.

— F.B.N.

REDE LATINO AMERICANA DE PRODUCTORES INDEPENDENTES DE ARTE CONTEMPORÂNEA

The Rede Latino Americana de Productores Independentes de Arte Contemporânea (Network of Independent Producers of Contemporary Art — a title which deliberately mixes Spanish and Portuguese) was created to support tours by contemporary performing artists within Latin America. With a central office in Paraty, Rio de Janeiro State, Brazil, the network, which receives financial support from the Rockefeller Foundation, has two branches in Argentina, six in Brazil, and others in Bolivia, Chile, Colombia, Mexico, Paraguay, Peru, and Venezuela. There is one center in the United States, at Miami-Dade Community College in Florida. By creating a touring circuit throughout

Latin America, the network helps artists and artistic groups become financially stable and acquire professional skills.

— N.D.B. & J.M.H.

REGIONALISM IN LITERATURE

Regionalism is a thematic category applied to certain novels of the second quarter of the twentieth century written by urban intellectuals but set in the hinterland. These novels harked back to the early–nineteenth century dichotomy between civilization and barbarism that structured the political and economic discourse of the liberal intelligentsia and whose most influential expression was Domingo Faustino Sarmiento's *Facundo* (1845; translated). For writers such as Sarmiento the main obstacle to progress was the backwardness of the regions beyond the control of the city, regions whose isolation bred contempt for the rule of law and customs inimical to civilized society. Regionalist novelists set out to chart the hinterland in their works and staged dramatic conflicts pitting the representatives of civilized values against the forces of evil, usually incarnated in the natural environment. In fact, Nature tended to be the protagonist of these novels, its imposing presence dwarfing or determining the human conflicts. The most representative regionalist novels are **Rómulo Gallegos**'s *Doña Bárbara* (1929; translated), **José Eustasio Rivera**'s *La vorágine* (1924; translated as *The Vortex*), and **Ricardo Güiraldes**'s *Don Segundo Sombra* (1926; translated), set, respectively, in the Venezuelan plains, the Colombian jungle, and the Argentinean pampa.

The regionalist novel is also known as novela de la tierra (novel of the earth, or telluric novel) and as a literary category overlaps with **Criollismo** and **Indigenismo.** The overwhelming power of the natural environment, most viciously represented in Rivera's *La vorágine,* where the jungle morally deforms and devours men, distinguishes regionalist novels from the criollista, which above all highlight national types and "essences." In the great regionalist novels, furthermore, a specific political and economic program lurks underneath the narrative surface and is sometimes revealed allegorically, as in Gallegos's *Doña Bárbara,* where the main conflict is between the eponymous character, representing barbarism, and Santos Luzardo, the young lawyer from the city, whose name combines the saintly with the enlightened. Before defeating Doña Bárbara, her antagonist must allow his character to be partially shaped by the barbaric values of the plains. Thus, he tames Doña Bárbara and brings her back to the fold. The novel is a melodramatic romance that ends with the union between Santos Luzardo and Marisela, Doña Bárbara's bastard daughter who inherits her mother's estate. This coupling stands for the creation of a national family grounded on civilized values such as property rights, the rule of law, education, and productive work.

In contrast to Gallegos's romantic vision of Venezuela's future, *La vorágine* is a journey to the "heart of darkness" from which the protagonist does not return. The poet Arturo Cova flees into the Colombian jungle with the woman he dishonored, and as he comes in contact with the brutality of the jungle itself and of its human denizens (particularly the dehumanized workers of the rubber plantations), he gradually loses his mind. In the end he is "devoured by the jungle," as the consul's cable reads in the epilogue. Since Rivera's only other work is a collection of idyllic sonnets called *Tierra de promisión* (1921; Promised Land), *La vorágine* may be read as the failure of the liberal idyll in the Colombian hinterland.

Güiraldes's pampa can also be a frightening environment, but in *Don Segundo Sombra* the pampa functions as a stage for a rite of passage that brings together several contradictions: between the city and the countryside, between Argentina's barbarous past and its civilized future based on a rational management of the land (Güiraldes was a wealthy landowner), and between European culture and Argentinean nationalism. The novel's penchant for harmonizing cultural, political, and economic contradictions equates it with the national romances of the nineteenth century, works that articulated a specific national project in terms of romantic liaisons and exemplary marriages.

This generic affiliation brings into question the meaning of regionalism as a category of literary history. Regionalist novels are "novels of the earth," but they can also be discussed in terms of the Romantic and Naturalist paradigms they invoke or in terms of their ideological function, not the least of which was to facilitate the expansion of the state to remote territories where its authority was feeble. At any rate, succeeding generations of writers discarded the regionalist novel as anachronistic and looked to more-cosmopolitan literary models for inspiration.

REFERENCE:

Carlos J. Alonso, *The Spanish American Regional Novel* (Cambridge: Cambridge University Press, 1990).

— R.G.M.

ARMANDO REVERÓN

The Venezuelan Armando Reverón (1889–1954) is an unusual figure in Latin America for the isolation in which he developed his art. Reverón began his training at the Academy of Fine Arts of Caracas, where he participated in the 1909 student strike against its retrograde educational program. After graduation Reverón won a scholarship to study at the Academy of San Fernando in Madrid, where he became interested in the paintings of Diego Velázquez, Francisco Goya, and Ignacio Zuloaga.

Reverón returned to Caracas in 1915 and joined the Circle of Fine Arts, whose artists advocated **Impressionism** and supported plein-air painting in order to capture directly the effects of tropical light. Reverón learned impressionistic techniques from two painters who had recently arrived in Caracas from Europe, the Romanian Samys Mützner and the Venezuelan Emilio Boggio. His friendship with the Russian Nicolas Ferdinandov, a symbolist painter who often used blue in his works, also had an effect on his art: Reverón began to work with thin textures, impressionistic brush strokes, and layers of luminous blues. In this "blue period" he focused on two recurrent themes: landscapes of coastal areas of Venezuela and human figures, as for instance *Figura bajo un uvero* (1920; Figure under a Grape Arbor).

In 1921 Reverón decided to withdraw from the conservative society of Caracas and settle in Macuto, a small village on the Caribbean coast of Venezuela. He lived there the rest of his life in increasing isolation with only the company of Juanita Ríos, his lifelong partner. He continued to paint marine landscapes using natural materials he prepared himself. Fascinated by the effects of light, he progressively eliminated all colors except whites and translucent grays from his palette. In this "white period" Reverón subordinated all forms to the powerful luminosity of the tropics, for example *Cocoteros en la playa* (1926; Coconut Trees on the Beach), in which the trees became dematerialized by the bleaching sun.

During the 1930s Reverón began to use the sepia color of unprimed canvas as part of his work. Sensual nudes such as *Maja* (1939) became the predominant theme. Because Juanita Ríos was often the only available model, he also used several life-size rag dolls he and Ríos fabricated. Toward the end of his life Reverón again emphasized the theme of landscape, reintroducing some colors and using a more ritualistic, dynamic, and almost graphiclike execution. One such work is *Palmera* (circa 1944; Palm Tree). In the late 1930s his work slowly began to be discovered and appreciated by the Venezuelan public through a series of exhibitions organized by Reverón's friends in Caracas.

REFERENCE:

Rina Carvajal, "Armando Reverón," in *Latin American Artists of the Twentieth Century,* edited by Waldo Rasmussen, Fatima Bercht, and Elizabeth Ferrer (New York: Museum of Modern Art, 1993), pp. 40–45.

—F.B.N.

JULIO RAMÓN RIBEYRO

A Peruvian author of stories, novels, and plays, Julio Ramón Ribeyro (1929–1994) rose to eminence in the 1950s during the height of existentialism and the emergence of urban narrative in Peru. Ribeyro is not exclusively an urban author, but his best novel, *Los geniecillos dominicales* (1965; Weekend Geniuses), is an ironic portrait of the Lima intellectual and artistic establishment (the "Generation of 1950") from the standpoint of a writer more responsible than his brethren. Ribeyro's other well-known novel is *Crónica de San Gabriel* (1960; Chronicle of San Gabriel), a kind of bildungsroman, or education novel, in which a young urban protagonist must learn to deal with a host of new experiences that result from his visit to a hacienda in the Peruvian highlands. Ribeyro's short stories up to 1977 were collected in three volumes as *La palabra del mudo* (1973–1977; The Speech of the Mute). *La juventud en la otra ribera* (1983; Youth on the Other Shore) is a later collection of stories. Among the author's plays, *Vida y pasión de Santiago el pasajero* (1959; Life and Passion of Santiago the Passenger) and *Atusparia* (1981) deserve mention. The first deals with an eighteenth-century visionary who believed he had discovered the secret of flying. Ribeyro uses this historical information, gleaned from one of Ricardo Palma's *Tradiciones peruanas* (a nineteenth-century collection of traditional Peruvian stories), as a metaphor for the artist's flights of imagination and transcendental yearnings.

REFERENCE:

Wolfgang Luchting, *Estudiando a Julio Ramón Ribeyro* (Frankfurt: Vervuert, 1988).

—R.G.M.

JOSÉ EUSTASIO RIVERA

Colombian writer José Eustasio Rivera (1888–1928) is best known for *La vorágine* (1924; *The Vortex*), the preeminent Colombian novel before **Gabriel García Márquez**'s *Cien años de soledad* (1967; translated as *One Hundred Years of Solitude*). On the eve of the novel's publication Rivera took out a newspaper advertisement alerting future readers to the fact that *La vorágine* deals with a neglected and troublesome aspect of national life: "slavery in the rubber fields in the

Dust jacket for José Eustasio Rivera's best-known novel, in which he spoke out against the exploitation of workers on rubber plantations in Colombia, Venezuela, and Brazil

jungles of Colombia, Venezuela, and Brazil." Only two years prior to the novel's publication, Rivera had penetrated into the interior of the Amazon jungle in his official capacity as secretary of the Colombian Boundary Commission, and there he witnessed firsthand the workings of the rubber industry. The exploitation of the *caucheros* (rubber workers) horrified him and motivated him to speak out against the lack of any government control over this modern form of slavery. The novel's documentary trappings — including a fictitious consular letter acknowledging the protagonist's disappearance in the jungle and material describing the invasion of Colombian territory by Peruvian soldiers and colonists — left no doubt that Rivera meant to address his work to the proper government authorities.

La vorágine became an overnight sensation despite its truculence and melodramatic excesses. Rivera's only other published work is a series of fifty-five sonnets entitled *Tierra de promisión* (1921; The Promised Land). The contrast between Rivera's two books is pointed, since both deal with Colombia's lush tropical landscapes. In the poems the tropics are described as an idyllic space ripe for romance and adventure and as a cornucopia of national wealth; in the novel, on the other hand, the plains of the Casanare in southeastern Colombia and the Amazon jungle around the Orinoco are seen as a barbaric environment that vitiates and devours the men and women trapped in its hold. Rivera was aware of the contrast and portrayed the protagonist of *La vorágine* as a deluded romantic visionary who is fated to experience the horrors of the jungle in person. The novel may be interpreted in several ways, one of which is as the clash between the "civilized" urban intellectual and the primitive hinterland of the national territory, one of the recurring motifs of Latin American literary and cultural history.

José Eustasio Rivera died in New York (apparently of the belated effects of malaria) as he was helping to prepare the English translation of his masterpiece. (See also **Regionalism in Literature**.)

REFERENCE:

Eduardo Neale-Silva, *Horizonte humano: Vida de José Eustasio Rivera* (Mexico: Fondo de Cultura Económica, 1960; Madison: University of Wisconsin Press, 1960).

— R.G.M.

AUGUSTO ROA BASTOS

The great literary figure of Paraguay, Augusto Roa Bastos (1917–) was born in Asunción in 1917 but grew up on a rural sugar plantation where his father was a clerk. In the countryside Roa learned the country's indigenous language Guaraní (see **Languages**) and absorbed some of the oral traditions that would later play roles in his novels and stories. In the capital Roa's formal schooling was interrupted by the Chaco War, intermittently fought by Bolivia and Paraguay between 1928 and 1935. Roa volunteered and was assigned to the rear guard to look after enemy prisoners. In 1942 he became a journalist for an Asunción newspaper and was later promoted to editor in chief but had to flee the country when a dictatorial government confiscated the newspaper in 1947. Roa went into exile in Buenos Aires, where he lived until 1976. When a military coup in Argentina ushered in the **Guerra Sucia** (Dirty War), the Paraguayan exile moved to France and became a professor of literature at the University of Toulouse. In 1982 Roa attempted to return to Paraguay but was expelled for life by Gen. Alfredo Stroessner's government. The following year Roa was granted Spanish citizenship, and, when Stroessner fell, he returned to Paraguay. In 1989 Roa Bastos was awarded the **Premio Miguel de Cervantes**,

Augusto Roa Bastos

the most coveted distinction available to a Latin American writer apart from the Nobel Prize.

Roa Bastos's first collection of short stories, *El trueno entre las hojas* (1953; Thunder Among the Leaves), is dedicated to Miguel Angel Asturias, the Guatemalan writer who tried to bridge the gap between the Mayan world of his nation's past and present and the ladino world, the world of the mestizo and the white man where Spanish is spoken and the indigenous heritage ignored (see **Peoples and Races**). This cross-cultural project also characterizes Roa's stories, which are located in the gap between native and foreign races, Guaraní and Spanish, the rural countryside and the "civilized" city. The stories, however, only occasionally transcend the author's limited point of view as

an outsider, though they forcefully denounce the failings of Paraguayan history and the injustice and oppression that shape social and economic relations.

In later collections Roa experiments with more-complex narrative structures and abandons the simplistic representation of moral and cultural conflicts. *El trueno entre las hojas* was followed by *El baldío* (1966; The Wasteland), *Madera quemada* (1967; Burnt Wood), and *Moriencia* (1969; Slaughter). All these books combine old and new stories and include chapters from the author's novels.

Roa Bastos's first novel, *Hijo de hombre* (1960; translated as *Son of Man*), won an important prize in Buenos Aires the year before its publication. It is not so much a conventional novel as a series of semi-autonomous and interrelated chapters that tell the story of Cristóbal Jara (a Christ figure) and Miguel Vera, the narrator of five of the nine chapters and a veteran of the Chaco War. History blends with myth and with the themes of social justice, redemption, and sacrifice.

In 1974 Roa published the novel that established his international reputation, *Yo el Supremo* (translated as *I, the Supreme*), one of three major novels that appeared in the 1970s dealing with the theme of dictatorship in Latin American history. Roa's version of the **dictatorship novel** is based on the man who dominated the first decades of Paraguayan history and who continues to be a controversial figure, José Gaspar Rodríguez de Francia. Dr. Francia, as he was known, declared himself dictator for life in 1816 and shut Paraguay off from international commerce and diplomacy in an effort to make the nation self-sufficient and to avoid the political strife that characterized Latin America in the first half of the nineteenth century. He antagonized and terrorized the Creole class and the church and kept a large army recruited from among his faithful Indian supporters. Yet Francia was no petty tyrant but an intellectual fully conversant with the French Enlightenment and deserving of a chapter in Thomas Carlyle's *On Heroes, Hero-Worship, and the Heroic in History* (1849). Roa Bastos's novel, however, is not historical in any conventional sense. Historical verisimilitude is not strictly adhered to, and the very notion of narrative is secondary to other concerns. It is difficult, for example, to identify a main narrator. We have, on the one hand, Dr. Francia playing his role as dictator literally by dictating the text to his secretary Patiño, who transcribes it and alters it at will, a process meant to underscore the point that history is difficult to record and even more difficult to represent in terms of the truth. There are also several other "voices" in the novel (belonging often to recognizable historical characters) that put forth their own claims to truth.

Finally, there is a compiler who filters the vast archival material pertaining to Dr. Francia and Paraguayan history in what at times is a peculiarly idiosyncratic way. Again, historical verisimilitude is only one strand of the text, much of which is constituted by free linkages between episodes and between history, myth, and literature, made possible by textual affinities of one kind or another. In fact, it could be plausibly stated that *Yo el Supremo* is not a historical novel at all but a "text" in the poststructuralist sense. Regardless of how one defines Roa's book, *Yo el Supremo* is one of the landmarks of modern Latin American literature.

  After the supreme effort of composing his major novel Roa Bastos did not publish another one until 1992. *Vigilia del Almirante* (The Admiral's Nightwatch) was timed to coincide with the fifth centenary of the discovery of America. The admiral in question is none other than Columbus, and the novel is a "feigned history" (in the author's words) of the mariner's life and discoveries, emphasizing the obscure figure of the Unknown Pilot, the shipwreck who presumably told Columbus about the New World as he expired in the arms of the future Admiral of the Ocean Sea. *Vigilia del Almirante,* however, is not an entirely new novel but a reworking of notes and sketches that the author had prepared more than forty years earlier but had left behind in his rush to find safe haven as a political exile in Buenos Aires in 1947. In the years intervening between the dictator and the Columbus novels Roa was not inactive. He was busy writing a companion piece to *Yo el Supremo,* which he is reported to have destroyed in manuscript form. Yet this novel was reborn with the title *El fiscal* (The Prosecutor) and published in 1993.

REFERENCES:

Rubén Bareiro Saguier, *Augusto Roa Bastos* (Montevideo: Trilce, 1989);

David William Foster, *Augusto Roa Bastos* (Boston: Twayne, 1978).

             — R.G.M.

JOSÉ ENRIQUE RODÓ

Uruguayan José Enrique Rodó (1871–1917) is the author of *Ariel* (1900), one of the most influential essays in Latin American cultural history. Written against the background of the Spanish-American War (1898), in which the United States acquired the last Spanish possessions in the New World (Cuba and Puerto Rico), it argues for the consolidation of a Latin American identity grounded on a common history and ethnic tradition and warns against excessive admiration for the "Colossus of the North." Rodó places spiritual and

José Enrique Rodó

aesthetic values — represented by Ariel, the spirit of the air — over the materialist values of the new age, represented by Caliban, a hideous earthbound creature. Rodó's antithesis, reminiscent of Shakespeare's *The Tempest,* led many people to read *Ariel* as an invective against the United States and a vindication of the spiritual superiority of Latin American culture. In fact, Rodó's assessment of United States culture is quite balanced and is best summarized by his own phrase "I admire them [Americans] but love them not." One may infer that Rodó's repudiation of materialism was indirectly aimed at the immigrant masses that had settled on the shores of the Río de la Plata by the end of the nineteenth century. The elegant and refined style of *Ariel,* a prime example of Modernista prose (see **Modernismo**), embodies the aesthetic values defended by Rodó against the onslaught of materialism.

REFERENCE:

Gordon Brotherston, ed., *Ariel* (Cambridge: Cambridge University Press, 1967).

             — R.G.M.

Marta Rodríguez and Jorge Silva

MARTA RODRÍGUEZ

Marta Rodríguez (circa 1940–   ), whose first name is sometimes given in its anglicized form, *Martha,* is a Colombian director who worked with **Jorge Silva**. She studied applied cinema at the Musée de l'Homme in Paris and anthropology at the Universidad Nacional in Bogotá. While in Colombia she organized a seminar on the use of cinema for social research. In 1966 she began working with Jorge Silva on the film *Chircales* (The Brickmakers), which she was able to use to complete her degree. This documentary was completed in 1972, although an early version had been exhibited at the Muestra de Mérida (Merida Film Festival) in 1968. Before completing *Chircales* Silva and Rodríguez were hired to film a documentary on the genocide of Indians of the Guahiba tribe in the Planas region.

REFERENCES:

Julianne Burton, ed., *Cinema and Social Change in Latin America: Conversations with Latin American Filmmakers* (Austin: University of Texas Press, 1986);

Hernando Martínez Pardo, *Historia del cine colombiano* (Bogotá: América Latina, 1978), pp. 303–308.

— S.M.H.

MELITÓN RODRÍGUEZ

The Colombian photographer Melitón Rodríguez Márquez (1875–1942), active in Medellín from 1892 to 1938, was one of the first exponents of photography in Spanish America to present realistic views of his own culture, in clear contrast to the exotic images of the continent that were generally preferred in Europe and the United States. During his adolescence Rodríguez studied drawing with a local artist, and he was later an apprentice in Medellín in the commercial studio of the photographer Enrique Latorre. In 1892, when he was only sixteen years old, he opened his own studio, called Rodríguez and Jaramillo, together with a partner who provided the capital. In the mid 1890s Rodríguez opened the larger and more sophisticated Foto Rodríguez studio, at first in partnership with his brother. In 1938 he was replaced as head of the studio by three of his nine sons. For all his success as a photographer, Rodríguez had been unable to overcome the studio's constant financial difficulties.

Rodríguez worked with a wide variety of subjects. He produced portraits of prominent people in Medellín — including government officials, bullfighters, and soccer players — and of people of more modest means — for example, *Los zapateros* (Cobblers), which in 1895 won him a prize from the New York magazine *Light and Shadow; Mendigos* (1895; Beggars); and *Equipo de fútbol* (1927; Soccer Team). He also portrayed the poor, which was then unusual in Colombian photography. Regardless of the theme, Rodríguez always presented his subjects in a simple, dignified manner that minimized the anecdotal. In photographs of people at work and in numerous exterior views of Medellín, Rodríguez composed his images carefully, while at the same time capturing the action at a significant moment: students in the middle of an anatomy lesson, farmers picking coffee in the field, a circus performer on the tightrope, or cattle resting in the middle of a street in Medellín. He also traveled by mule to remote regions in his attempt to document the Colombia of his time.

REFERENCES:

Felipe Escobar, *Melitón Rodríguez: Fotografías* (Bogotá: El Ancora Ediciones, 1985);

Taller La Huella, *Crónica de la fotografía en Colombia: 1841–1948* (Bogotá: Carlos Valencia Editores, 1983).

— F.B.N.

GONZALO ROJAS

Chilean poet Gonzalo Rojas (1917–) was influenced early in his poetic career by Symbolist poets such as Arthur Rimbaud and the Comte de Lautréamont (Isidore-Lucien Ducasse), and especially by fellow Spanish Americans **Vicente Huidobro, Pablo Neruda,** and **César Vallejo.** His father, a coal miner, was a cousin of **Gabriela Mistral.** In 1938 Rojas moved to Santiago and for a brief period joined the Surrealist group **Mandrágora,** which he left in order to head north to the Chilean desert and teach reading and writing to miners. In the 1950s Rojas was living in the southern city of Concepción, where he taught at the local university and organized gatherings of Chilean and foreign writers, beginning in January 1958. In 1971 Rojas became cultural attaché in Peking. He was in Cuba when a military coup overthrew President **Salvador Allende** in 1973, preventing the poet from returning to Chile. In exile he taught at several universities in Venezuela and in the United States, and in 1981 he was able to return to his native country.

Rojas's poetic enterprise differs in execution but not in intent from that of the great visionary poets of the French and Latin American tradition going back to Charles Baudelaire in the middle of the nineteenth century and beyond him to German and English Romantics like Friedrich Hölderlin and William Blake. Modern poets often view existence as an enigma or riddle, the key to which is poetic language understood

as a secret mirror of the cosmos. Hermetic analogies and correspondences between words and other words and between words and things (the sensual world becoming a kind of ciphered text) hold the promise of a total vision that might explain the great human enigmas. In these visionary systems fragmented perceptions are unified by poetic devices that associate sounds and concepts. The female body is an important trope that allows the (male) poet to decode the mysteries of life and death.

Rojas himself has highlighted the centrality of the "Enigma" in his poetic quest and the importance of both rhythm and Eros as means to approach and solve the mystery of being. He has also stated that poetry always reveals itself to him in the context of the sacred (Rudolph Otto's *Das Heilige* [1917] has helped to shape the Chilean poet's weltanschauung). Rojas's poetry has a mischievous and uninhibited tone (inherited from Huidobro and other avant-garde poets) that differentiates it from that of predecessors like Rubén Darío and contemporaries like Octavio Paz. His poems are likely to be playful reflections on a serious theme (woman, time, death, history, poetry) orchestrated to a convulsive or swaying rhythm.

In November 1992 Rojas was awarded the National Prize for Literature in Chile, and in Spain the first Reina Sofía Prize for poetry.

Some of Gonzalo Rojas's works are *La miseria del hombre* (1948; The Misery of Man), *Contra la muerte* (1964; Against Death), *Oscuro* (1977; Obscure), *Del relámpago* (1981; expanded, 1984; Of Lightning), *Críptico y otros poemas* (1984; Cryptic and Other Poems), and *El alumbrado* (1986; The Seer). Two anthologies of Rojas's poetry have recently been published: *Las hermosas: poesías de amor* (1991; The Beautiful: Love Poems) and *Cinco visiones: selección de poemas* (1992; Five Visions: Selection of Poems). Rojas's poetry has been published in Chile, Venezuela, Mexico, and Spain. An English-language collection of his work has been published as *Schizotext and Other Poems* (1988).

REFERENCES:

Enrique Giordano, ed., *Poesía y poética de Gonzalo Rojas* (Santiago: Maitén, 1987);

Hilda R. May, *La poesía de Gonzalo Rojas* (Madrid: Hiperión, 1991).

— R.G.M.

ROMANCE

Ballads of the kind the Spanish call "romances" arrived in the Americas with the first conquistadors. Ro-

Raúl Ruiz at the Cannes Film Festival for a showing of his 1992 movie *Dark at Noon* (AP/Wide World)

mances are long poems, often set to music, that tell historical tales of legendary events and heroes. Their normal format, once set to music, is four-line stanzas with eight-syllable lines. Romances became the earliest examples of European secular music in the Americas, and their influence stimulated the explosion of popular song that continues to the present in Latin America. Improvisation of verses became an important ingredient in folk and popular songs inspired by the romance.

REFERENCE:

Gerard Béhague, "Latin American Folk Music," in *Folk and Traditional Music of the Western Continents,* by Bruno Nettl, third edition, revised and edited by Valerie Woodring Goertzen (Englewood Cliffs, N.J.: Prentice-Hall, 1990).

—R.L.S.

JORGE RUIZ

Jorge Ruiz (circa 1923–) was the most important filmmaker of the 1950s in Bolivia. His ethnographic film, *Vuelve Sebastiana* (1953; Sebastiana, Come

Home), documents the Chipaya Indians from Santa Ana de Chipaya (a people who are dying out or being acculturated) by following the biography of a twelve-year-old girl, Sebastiana Kespi. Sebastiana has been taken to an Aymara town that has assimilated many Western values, but she is rescued by her grandfather, who leads her back to the village where she was born, communicating all his wisdom to her on the way. On reaching the village, he dies of exhaustion, but the oral tradition has ensured that Sebastiana is now the living embodiment of her culture. In its privileging of the Indian way of life, *Vuelve Sebastiana* is a clear precursor of the work of the **Ukumau** group in the 1960s. Ruiz joined the Bolivian Film Institute in 1956 and made *La vertiente* (1956; Watershed), considered the first major feature-length sound film in Bolivian history. Filmed in 35 mm with direct sound, it was very much a group project; it has a dual-level plot, combining the story of a rural community's struggle to obtain drinking water with a love story (a young schoolteacher is introduced to love by a macho alligator hunter). Later on, Ruiz shifted focus somewhat, and he began to devote more time to contract work for U.S. aid agencies in Bolivia and in other parts of Latin America.

REFERENCE:

John King, *Magical Reels: A History of Cinema in Latin America* (London: Verso, 1990).

— S.M.H.

RAÚL RUIZ

Of all the Latin American filmmakers in European exile, the Chilean Raúl Ruiz (circa 1940–) has been the most prolific, completing twenty-eight films for both television and theatrical viewing in his first decade abroad. His most important films are *Tres tristes tigres* (1968; Three Trapped Tigers), dedicated to the Chilean poet **Nicanor Parra** and which Ruiz called "a visual reflection in images of our contemporary condition," and *El realismo socialista* (1972; Socialist Realism). Both these films explore the contradictions of working-class life and have violent scenes. He later made *¿Qué hacer?* (1970; What Is To Be Done?) with Saul Landau and *La colonia penal* (1970; The Penal Colony), a free interpretation of a story by Franz Kafka that takes place on an island in the Pacific two hundred miles from the coast of Peru or Ecuador and is, according to its creator, a "metaphor of conditions in Latin America." Other important works are *Nadie dijo nada* (1971; Nobody Said Anything), made for Italian television, and *La expropiación* (1972; The Expropriation), which focuses on the story of an agronomist whose mission is to expropriate an estate and who is killed by the local peasants as a result. *Les trois Couronnes du marin* (1984; *The Three Crowns of the Sailor*) is considered by some critics to be his masterpiece. Produced in partnership with French television (Antenne 2), the movie begins with a narrator's account of how a young theology student murders a teacher in a Warsaw theology school. In a dance hall the theology student meets a sailor, who tells his story for three Danish crowns. The narration shifts from the third to the first person, and another story begins, this time in Valparaíso, Chile: a sailor on a ship docked in the harbor and manned by other sailors, who are dead, must find someone to take his place before dawn. Much of the film is concerned with the realm of the uncanny and with constructing new patterns linking seemingly unconnected events (in Europe and South America). The film is populated by characters who are wanderers, social and cultural outcasts who roam through taverns and seaports exchanging stories for money and for lodging. The film reaches its climax in a gratuitous and violent murder.

Ruiz has been honored by retrospectives at the British Film Institute (1981), Madrid's Cinemateca and Action République in Paris (both 1983), and the Toronto Festival of Festivals (1985). His wife, **Valeria Sarmiento,** has collaborated with him on some features and is a director in her own right.

REFERENCES:

Julianne Burton, ed., *Cinema and Social Change in Latin America: Conversations with Latin American Filmmakers* (Austin: University of Texas Press, 1986);

Michael Chanan, ed., *Chilean Cinema* (London: BFI, 1976);

Zuzana M. Pick, *The New Latin American Cinema* (Austin: University of Texas Press, 1993).

— S.M.H.

S

ERNESTO SÁBATO

A major Argentinean novelist, philosophical essayist, and intellectual, Ernesto Sábato (1911–) was born in the small town of Rojas where his Italian immigrant parents owned a flour mill. He was sent to the city of La Plata to finish high school. At the Colegio Nacional he excelled in mathematics and had two prominent intellectuals as teachers: the Dominican Pedro Henríquez Ureña and the Argentinean **Ezequiel Martínez Estrada.** In 1937 he received a doctorate in physics from the National University of La Plata, and he taught the subject there and in Buenos Aires until 1945. At that time Sábato decided that his complex personality was incompatible with the study of science and he turned full-time to writing. In 1948 he published his first and successful short novel *El túnel* (translated as *The Tunnel*), followed by two nonfictional works: a collection of essays in which the author examines his own spiritual crisis in the context of the modern world and a book of fragments on art, sex, and language. In 1961 Sábato published another remarkable novel, *Sobre héroes y tumbas* (translated as *On Heroes and Tombs*), which, like *El túnel* and Fyodor Dostoyevsky's *Crime and Punishment* (1866), hinges on murder. Sábato's last novel to date is the apocalyptic *Abaddón el exterminador* (1974; translated as *The Angel of Darkness*). His reflections on fiction and on the writer's métier were published as *El escritor y sus fantasmas* (1963; The Writer and His Demons).

Sábato's many books made him a nationally prominent intellectual by the time of the military takeover in 1976, which signaled the beginning or the systematization of the **Guerra Sucia** (Dirty War.) His public stance on behalf of human rights and against the torturing of political prisoners made him and his family the targets of terrorist threats even before Gen. Jorge Videla came to power. When the cycle of military gov-

Ernesto Sábato, circa 1985

ernments came to an end in 1983, President Raúl Alfonsín asked Sábato to head the investigation into the crimes committed by the armed forces in the previous years. Within nine months the commission headed by Sábato brought out a report, *Nunca Más* (1985; translated as *Never Again*), that held the military forces responsible for thousands of "disappearances" of presumed political enemies. The chief military officers involved in the Dirty War were prosecuted, found guilty, and incarcerated for a period of time. Though Alfonsín's successor ultimately extended a blanket pardon to the officers convicted or suspected of human rights abuses, Sábato had performed a service of the highest importance to the nation and had demonstrated that not all moral integrity had been shattered by Argentina's radical institutional crisis.

Sábato's novels are the products of a tormented sensibility. Their overarching theme is the exploration of what André Malraux called the "human condition," an exploration undertaken on the edge of madness and fueled by emotional chaos. Sábato's writing thus joins existentialist topics to the discoveries of Surrealism, a movement in which the Argentinean novelist (then a scientist working in the Joliot-Curie lab in Paris) participated in the late 1930s. The most notorious Surrealist motif in Sábato's novels is the recurring obsession with blindness that appears in concentrated form in the "Report on the Blind," the uncanny third part of *Sobre héroes y tumbas,* one of the most acclaimed pieces of writing in contemporary fiction.

El túnel is a retrospective narration of a murder told by the murderer himself, a painter of volatile sensibility who is driven to kill the one woman who could understand him. Castel, the painter, meets María Iribarne when he shows his paintings. She is transfixed by a particular image of maternity in one of them. He desperately looks for her and later hounds her, wanting to know what she saw in the painting; she warns him that she will be bad for him. His jealousy increases when he finds out she is married to a blind man whom she deceives, perhaps with a cousin of hers. Castel follows her to a country estate and kills her. The painter tells his lurid tale to achieve catharsis but also to cast a line toward the reading public still in search of meaningful communication.

Sobre héroes y tumbas is a far more complex but equally sordid novel that counterpoints the vicissitudes of several characters in the present with an episode from nineteenth-century Argentinean history. The key character is a woman similar in some respects to María Iribarne, Alejandra, the epileptic scion of a patrician family who has an incestuous relationship with her father, Fernando Vidal, and a traumatic love affair with the idealist loner Martín. Martín's solitude is amplified by the existential anguish of the older Bruno, a family friend who hopelessly desires Alejandra's mother. In the third part of the novel Fernando Vidal descends into the sewers of the city in pursuit of the Sect of the Blind and emerges to write his "Report on the Blind," a group characterized as the epitome of evil. The fourth and final part of the novel culminates with a fire set by Alejandra in which both she and her father are

consumed and purified. Thus, the troubled Argentinean past is exorcised, with the immolation of a family whose roots reach deeply into a history of violence and factionalism. The novel is set in the last two years of the Peronist regime (1953–1955), and the fall of **Juan Domingo Perón** is viewed as the return of the strife that has characterized Argentinean history. Martín's removal to the south (the direction opposite General Lavalle's march reiterated in the novel) seems to indicate hope for national regeneration. The search for an authentic national identity coexists in the novel with the search for the meaning of human existence.

Abaddón el exterminador is a less impressive work dealing with historical evil. Its protagonist is Sábato himself (minus the accent mark); Bruno of the previous novel reappears as the author's alter ego. Formally, *Abaddón el exterminador* is not a conventional novel but a discontinuous collage of fragments, a mélange of heterogeneous genres (essays, memoirs, and sociological disquisitions) that progresses by means of dialogues. The novel ends with Sábato's death preceded by his sudden blindness and transformation into a bat. Significantly, Ernesto Sábato has not written another novel since his "death" in this one.

Together with many other honors received in his lifetime Ernesto Sábato was awarded the **Premio Miguel de Cervantes de Literatura** in 1984.

REFERENCES:

Salvador Bacarisse, *Contemporary Latin American Fiction* (Edinburgh: Scottish Academic Press, 1980);

J. Predmore, *Un estudio crítico de las novelas de Ernesto Sábato* (Madrid: Porrúa, 1981).

— R.G.M.

José Sabogal

Peruvian José Sabogal (1888–1956) was a leading Indigenist artist. Sabogal, who had Indian ancestors, was from Cajamarca, an area that during his childhood still retained many native traditions. He traveled to Europe in 1909, where he admired the art of the Spaniard Ignacio Zuloaga, and from 1912 to 1918 he studied at the Academia de Bellas Artes in Buenos Aires. Sabogal began painting local landscapes and genre scenes after a visit to Cuzco in 1913 and had his first exhibition in Lima in 1917, which was well received. During the early 1920s he also went to Mexico, where he learned about Muralism and was influenced by the cultural nationalism of this movement.

Upon his return to Lima, Sabogal actively disseminated the idea that the role of art in Peru should be the representation of native traditions and autochthonous themes, thus becoming a visual counterpart to the leading Peruvian Indigenist writer **José Mariátegui.** Soon Sabogal became one of the main spokespersons of **Indigenism:** his appointments as professor and later as director (1932–1943) of the new Escuela de Bellas Artes allowed him to dominate the Peruvian art scene for a long time. In most of his paintings, always depicting local Peruvian themes, such as *La santusa* (The Saintly Woman) and *Paisaje* (1932; Landscape), Sabogal uses a descriptive style enlivened by thick textures and expressive brush strokes. During the 1940s his work was influenced by his studies of native arts and crafts, and it encouraged others to appreciate Peruvian artisans. Among his followers were Camilo Blas, Enrique Camino Brent, and **Julia Codesido.**

REFERENCE:

Gilbert Chase, *Contemporary Art in Latin America* (New York: Free Press, 1970), pp. 99–101.

— F.B.N.

Juan José Saer

An outstanding Argentinean novelist of the post-**Cortázar** generation whose reputation has been growing steadily, Juan José Saer (1937–) was born in the province of Santa Fe but has lived in France since 1968, which accounts for the perceptible influence of French fiction and literary theory in his work. Saer's influences, however, also include **Macedonio Fernández, Roberto Arlt,** and the major authors of international modernism. Saer's most notable novels are *Nadie nada nunca* (1980; translated as *Nobody Nothing Never*), an ironic critique of the Marquis de Sade's erotic postulates; *El entenado* (1983; translated as *The Witness*); *La ocasión* (1987; The Occasion), winner of the Premio Nadal in Spain; and *Lo imborrable* (1993; The Indelible), a stylistic tour de force dealing with the main conflicts of contemporary Argentinean culture.

REFERENCE:

Guillermo Saavedra, *La curiosidad impertinente* (Rosario, Argentina: Beatriz Viterbo Editora, 1993).

— R.G.M.

Bernardo Salcedo

One of the first Colombian artists to work with **Pop Art and Assemblages** and with **Conceptual Art,** Bernardo Salcedo (1939–) studied architecture at the Universidad Nacional de Colombia in his native Bogotá. During the 1960s and 1970s Salcedo worked with col-

Idea de mi abuelo (1981; My Grandfather's Idea), by Bernardo Salcedo (Collection of Dr. Hernando Santos Castillo, Bogotá)

lages of pasted advertising photographs and boxlike constructions which included industrial objects such as small fragments of machinery, dolls' body parts, and household objects. These assemblages were evenly painted with solid colors, at first in bold reds and yellows, later in white. Salcedo's art has become increasingly conceptual in nature. In 1970 he produced a work based on Colombia's national seal, featuring images of the emblem with several of its parts erased. In his series *Señales Particulares* (1980s; Personal Signs) he uses framed photographs with everyday objects covering part of the image. The titles of these pieces reveal not only the relationship between image and object but also his interest in language and word games. For instance, his *Idea de mi abuelo* (1981; My Grandfather's Idea) features an old photograph of a man with the screw thread of the light bulb covering his face, playing on a common expression in Spanish that equates having an idea with turning on a light bulb inside one's head. Similarly, his assemblage *Objeto para elevar la mirada* (1981–1982; Object to Elevate the Gaze) features a tall, thin tripod that supports a pair of binoculars. In the mid 1980s Salcedo produced a series of art objects entitled *Cajas del Agua* (Boxes of Water), which includes wooden boxes containing saw blades and sculptures combining blades and panes of glass.

REFERENCE:

Eduardo Serrano, *Bernardo Salcedo* (New York: Center for Inter-American Relations, 1984).

— F.B.N.

ROGELIO SALMONA

One of the most important Colombian architects, Rogelio Salmona (circa 1927–) was born in Paris. His family arrived in Colombia in 1931. After secondary schooling at the Liceo Francés, he studied at the Facultad de Arquitectura of the Universidad Nacional de Bogotá. As a student he met noted French architect Le Corbusier, serving as his interpreter when he visited the school in 1948. Soon afterward, and due to the climate of political instability and violence, Salmona left the school and went to France, where he worked for Le Corbusier until the early 1950s. In Europe, Salmona traveled extensively and took classes in art history with Pierre Francastel, who helped him come to terms with his Colombian heritage. He returned to Bogotá in 1958 and began teaching at the Universidad de los Andes while he finished his degree in architecture.

During the early 1960s Salmona worked in collaboration with architects such as Arturo Robledo, Fernando Martínez Sanabria, and Guillermo Bermúdez on projects such as the residential apartment building in the new El Polo neighborhood (1960–1963), a controversial break with rational architecture. This rejection became even more pronounced in Salmona's later designs, such as the multifamily complex for the Fundación Cristiana de San Pablo para la Vivienda (1963–1966; Christian Foundation of San Pablo Housing Project), which forced him to accept the technological realities of Colombia and adopt the structural use of brick. A culminating point in this process was Salmona's Torres del Parque (1968–1973; Park Towers), three high-rise buildings designed as middle-income family housing. In this project Salmona brilliantly adapted rational architecture to the specific climatic and urban needs of Bogotá: the stepped circular motion and brick surfaces of the towers blended well with the surrounding mountains and the adjacent urban context; a bullring was included, also built in brick, as well as a park. This project also shows Salmona's interest in circular spaces, overlapping volumes, and open communal areas with free circulation.

During the 1970s the integration of buildings and communal space became one of the main concerns in Salmona's work, evidenced in his participation in the design of social housing developments financed by the Instituto de Crédito Territorial (1962–1982). Although his designs for one of them (Rafael Nuñez) were never adopted, the other (Timiza) demonstrated that it was possible to create a richer urban context even on a large scale. The reaction against rationalism became almost complete during the 1980s through the fuller use of local materials and careful historical contextualization, reaching a culminating point in another of Salmona's projects, the Casa de Huéspedes Ilustres (1980–1981; Inn for Distinguished Guests) in Cartagena. The inn was built next to the Fuerte de Manzanillo, a fort restored by Germán Tellez which became the inn's dining room. Salmona designed this building to blend with the Manzanillo fort: he used stone surfaces and severe volumes reminiscent of military architecture. He also evoked the zigzag streets of Cartagena through a sequence of corridors and patios, where he created dramatic plays of light and shadow as well as subtle contrasts between brick accents and limestone walls. Other important designs by Salmona include the Museo de Arte Moderno in Bogotá (1977–1988) and the Museo de la Cultura Quimbaya at Armenia (1983–1984).

REFERENCE:

Germán Tellez, *Rogelio Salmona: Arquitectura y poética del lugar,* Colección Somosur, volume 9 (Bogotá: Escala, 1991).

— F.B.N.

JORGE SANJINÉS

After studying philosophy and filmmaking in Chile in the late 1950s, Bolivian movie director Jorge Sanjinés (circa 1940–) returned to his native Bolivia and teamed up with scriptwriter Oscar Soria to found various institutions in the early 1960s — a film society, a movie magazine, and a short-lived film school — that were designed to provide greater public awareness of the local possibilities of the medium. The group was commissioned to make several other promotional shorts before undertaking its first independent film, a ten-minute black-and-white montage called *Revolución* (1964; Revolution), which won the Joris Ivens Prize at the Leipzig Festival. Finished shortly before the 1964 military coup, this short uses images and music to present a powerful vision of underdevelopment and class struggle in the context of the 1952 nationalist insurrection. Ironically, the new military régime of Gen. René Barrientos Ortuño (1964–1969) gave Sanjinés the opportunity to become the technical director of the Bolivian Film Institute and to make his first feature film.

Sanjinés began working with "natural" rather than professional actors during the production of the medium-length *¡Aysa!* (1965; Landslide!), shot in a mining region, and in the feature-length *Ukumau* (1969; That's the Way It Is), shot among Aymara-speaking peasants. *Ukumau* was the first feature film spoken in Aymara, Bolivia's principal Indian language. Despite the favorable reception accorded to *Ukumau* in Europe, where it was awarded the critics' prize for young directors at the Cannes Film Festival, the publicity surrounding the film's content and message prompted the Barrientos government to demand Sanjinés's resignation. The Bolivian Film Institute was not only closed down but permanently dissolved as a result.

Sanjinés persevered, however, and he, Soria, and Rada created a production company, the **Ukumau Group. Antonio Eguino** joined them for the production of perhaps Sanjinés's most celebrated work, *Yawar Malku* (1969; Blood of the Condor), a feature film, this time spoken in Quechua and based on the practice of involuntary sterilization of Bolivian indigenous women by members of the United States Peace Corps stationed in rural communities there. The film gave rise to a national furor of epic proportions and led to the closure of the Peace Corps offices in Bolivia. *El coraje del pueblo* (1971; also released as *The Courage of the People* and *The Night of San Juan*), based on the massacre of Bolivian miners by the armed forces during a strike, is the first example of the kind of on-site reconstruction of historical events in collaboration with actual participants that characterizes Sanjinés's mature work.

Despite the dislocation and hardships of political exile (Sanjinés was compelled to live outside Bolivia between 1971 and 1979), he maintained his collaborative engagement with the "popular memory" of the Andean peasantry. *Los caminos de la muerte* (Roads to Death), begun by the Ukumau Group in 1970, was left unfinished, and most of its footage was ruined in a strange accident at a German processing laboratory. *El enemigo principal* (1973; The Principal Enemy) was shot in Peru, *Fuera de aquí* (1976; Get Out of Here) in Ecuador, and *¡Basta ya!* (1979; That's Enough!) in Colombia and Venezuela. *Banderas del amanecer* (1984; Banners of Dawn), a feature-length documentary, chronicles political events in Bolivia in 1983. *La nación clandestina* (1989; The Secret Nation) tells the story of a man who has been dismissed from his Indian village

and seeks to atone for his corrupt past by dancing to death in a sacred ritual, an homage to the last Aymara great dancing lord.

REFERENCES:

Julianne Burton, ed., *Cinema and Social Change in Latin America: Conversations with Latin American Filmmakers* (Austin: University of Texas Press, 1986);

Jorge A. Schnitman, *Film Industries in Latin America* (Norwood, N.J.: ABLEX, 1984).

— S.M.H.

DOMINGO SANTA CRUZ

One of the most influential figures in the development of music in Chile during the twentieth century, Domingo Santa Cruz (1899–1987) both taught himself as a youth and had private teachers. Later, as a student at the University of Chile, he was active in musical groups and was instrumental in forming and conducting the Bach Society, an organization that later occupied an influential position in Chile's musical life.

Following his graduation in law, Santa Cruz became active in the Chilean diplomatic corps, continuing to study theory and composition under outstanding Spanish teachers while posted in Madrid (1921–1924). Upon his return to Chile, he began to dedicate his energies to reviving a national musical ambience that had become relatively inactive; his success was spectacular. As a professor at the National Conservatory (from 1928) he contributed to a total reform of fine arts education, leading to a reorganization of the conservatory. Eventually his leadership as dean of the Faculty of Fine Arts at the conservatory and then as dean of the Faculty of Musical Arts and Sciences at the university resulted in the formation of the Instituto de Extensión Musical, an umbrella organization that fostered the Institute of Folkloric Research, Institute of Musical Research, festivals of Chilean music, the Chilean Symphony Orchestra, the Chilean Ballet, chamber music organizations, a music journal (*Revista Musical Chilena*), and a system of prizes for outstanding works. His cumulative successes as a university professor, composer, musicologist, arts administrator, and leader of educational and artistic reform have been unequaled in Chilean music history.

As a composer, Santa Cruz demonstrated the influences of impressionism, atonality, and neoclassicism in his early works, which consist primarily of songs, piano works, and a string quartet. Later works of the 1940s and 1950s continued his interest in chamber music (songs, string quartets, various chamber ensembles), choral music, and symphonic works. He received several composition prizes for his music and was honored with special commissions for concerts at the Inter American Music Festivals sponsored by the **Organization of American States.**

REFERENCES:

Gerard Béhague, *Latin American Music: An Introduction* (Englewood Cliffs, N.J.: Prentice-Hall, 1979);

Composers of the Americas, volume 1 (Washington, D.C.: Pan American Union, General Secretariat, Organization of American States, 1955).

— R.L.S.

ANDRÉS DE SANTA MARÍA

Although the Colombian Impressionist painter Andrés de Santa María (1860–1945) spent most of his life in Europe, he made important contributions to the art of his country. He studied at the Ecole des Beaux-Arts in Paris when **Impressionism** was becoming an important style and adopted the looseness of forms and light effects characteristic of this movement. One of his early Impressionist paintings, *Lavanderas del Sena* (1887; Washerwomen on the Seine), won an honorable mention at the Salon des Artistes Français. After his return to Bogotá in 1893, Santa María worked with Colombian themes: his painting *Las segadoras* (1893; The Gleaners), inspired by Jean François Millet's work of the same title, features Colombian women set in their native land.

In Bogotá, Santa María taught at the Academia de Bellas Artes, introducing the use of nude models and plein air painting. In 1904, after he became director of the academia, he expanded the scope of this institution by founding the Escuela Profesional de Artes Decorativas e Industriales and organizing an art exhibition which included his own works, thus introducing Impressionism to the Colombian public. Until then, his art had been virtually unknown in Colombia, partly because art critics were more concerned with political disputes than with learning about new styles. The same year, Santa María's style shifted toward **Postimpressionism** as he used thicker brush strokes and stronger touches of color, in paintings such as *En la Playa de Macuto: María Mancini a Caballo* (1907; On Macuto Beach: María Mancini on Horseback). As a result of political pressures, Santa María returned to Europe in 1911 and settled in Brussels, where he continued painting and exhibiting successfully. Although he never returned to Colombia, in 1926 he produced a triptych for the capitol building in Bogóta. The work, which depicts Simón Bolívar's Boyacá Campaign, became highly controversial because of its expressionistic style. Santa María had two important retrospective ex-

Isabel Sarli in July 1955, after winning the Miss Argentina contest (Hulton Deutsch Collection Limited)

hibitions in Bogotá in 1931 and 1971 (posthumous) and one at the Museum of Fine Arts in Brussels in 1936.

REFERENCE:

Eduardo Serrano, *Cien años de arte colombiano: 1886–1986* (Bogotá: Museo de Arte Moderno de Bogotá, 1985).

— F.B.N.

ISABEL SARLI

Known affectionately to Argentineans as "La Coca," Isabel Sarli (circa 1930–) is sometimes called Miss Argentina as well because she represented her country in the 1955 Miss Universe contest. She became notorious after a nude appearance in the film *El trueno de las hojas* (1956; Thunder of the Leaves). She was discovered and managed by Armando Bo, a longtime campaigner against censorship but one not always taken seriously by the intellectuals of his time. Bo had produced films for luminaries such as **Torre Nilsson,** winning some recognition in the process, but after discovering Sarli, devoted himself to promoting her. Her acting talents were limited, but her erotic powers considerable. Despite efforts to have her make B movies in Hollywood for the Hispanic market, she remained at home to make outrageous films in which she overacted and appeared somewhat overweight for the erotic stereotype. In the 1990s she became the subject of books and retrospectives, suggesting that her exertions have won her some recognition, albeit somewhat tongue in cheek.

REFERENCE:

Diego Galán, "El huracán Sarli," *El País,* 4 August 1994.

— P.S.

VALERIA SARMIENTO

Chilean director Valeria Sarmiento (circa 1940–) belongs to a generation of women who began making films in the early 1970s during **Salvador Allende**'s government but were forced to leave after **Augusto Pinochet**'s coup. Her first film, *Un sueño como de colores* (1973; Color-tinted Dreams), is based on the everyday life of strippers in a popular cabaret in Santiago. After moving to Paris in 1974 she worked as an editor on the films of her husband, **Raúl Ruiz.** Her documentary, *People from Everywhere, People from Nowhere* (1979), focuses on the lives of immigrants in the suburbs of Paris and was moderately successful. Her real break came with *El hombre, cuando es hombre* (Man, When He is A Man), shot in Costa Rica and produced in Europe in 1982. The movie offers a personal view of gender relations in Latin America and is based on interviews with males of all ages, alternating with scenes of folk dances, mariachi bands, coming-out parties, and weddings. Subsequent features Sarmiento has made are *Notre mariage* (1984; Our Marriage) and *Amelia López O'Neill* (1990).

REFERENCE:

Zuzana M. Pick, *The New Latin American Cinema* (Austin: University of Texas Press, 1993).

— S.M.H.

LALO SCHIFFRIN

Argentinean pianist, composer, and conductor Lalo Schiffrin (1935–) was born in Buenos Aires and established a reputation in the United States as a composer of film and television music. Recipient of four Grammy awards and many Oscar nominations, Schiffrin has composed music for more than one hun-

dred films and television series, including *Mannix, Starsky and Hutch, Mission Impossible,* and *Petrocelli.*

Having achieved success with film and commercial music, Schiffrin returned to his early interest in classical music, especially as a conductor but also as a composer. The classical environment was a familiar one. In his youth he had studied piano with Enrique Barenboim (the father of **Daniel Barenboim**) and **Juan Carlos Paz.** Schiffrin's own father was a violinist in the **Colón Theater** Orchestra of Buenos Aires.

Schiffrin has conducted the Israel Philharmonic, the Paris Symphonia, the Los Angeles Philharmonic, and the symphony orchestras of Atlanta, Indianapolis, and Houston. Among his recorded works are an oratorio, *The Rise and Fall of the Third Reich* (1967); Guitar Concerto (1984); and *Songs of the Aztecs* for soloists and orchestra (1988).

REFERENCE:

Vicente Gesualdo, *La música en la Argentina* (Buenos Aires: Editorial Stella, 1988).

— R.L.S.

KARIN SCHMIDT

As is seen in so much of the contemporary history of dance in South America, German-born choreographer Karin Schmidt, active artistically in Bolivia in 1985–1992, exemplifies the cross-fertilization between such diverse sources as indigenous music, North American and European dance theories and techniques, South American nature, and contemporary sociopolitical issues.

A program of her work presented in Brooklyn, New York, in 1987 serves as illustration. *It's About Love,* a series of trios, duets, and solos, explored political and social controversies of Latin America as well as capturing images of its natural beauty. *María Pilar* conveyed the desperation of women who return home to discover a loved one has disappeared. *Requiem* is the dance of a woman imagining life free of the struggle for survival. *The New Way* presented a transcendent vision of peace and liberty as expressed through the flight of a flock of doves. *Signs of Distress* offered a nocturnal suite, an abstract dance without other significance.

Reflecting the fluidity of inter-American dance exchange, Schmidt has performed her solo repertory in Peru, Brazil, and Ecuador. A program of works presented in Bolivia in 1988 by Schmidt's company, Draga Danza, pushed beyond the normally conservative Bolivian norms by sharing the artistic programming with the Experimental Orchestra of Native Instru-

Manuel Scorza with Agapito Robles, delegate from Yanacocha, the setting for the first of the five novels in Scorza's *La guerra silenciosa* (1970–1979; The Silent War)

ments and the Percussion Ensemble of the Municipal Theater.

— N.D.B. & J.M.H.

MANUEL SCORZA

Neoindigenist Peruvian writer Manuel Scorza (1928–1983) is the author of *La guerra silenciosa* (1970–1979; The Silent War), a series of five novels dealing with the armed struggle in the central Andes between the Indian communities, on the one hand, and the landowners and United States companies such as the Cerro de Pasco Corporation, on the other. As secretary general of the Communal Movement Scorza witnessed the events he chronicles, which took place between 1960 and 1963. The massacre of *comuneros* described in the second novel occurred in March 1962, when the police killed twenty-seven of the villagers, who had taken over some disputed lands three months earlier. Scorza's rendition of the "silent war" is not a testimonial account but a mythical narrative that strives to

portray the Andean world and the political struggle against the outsiders from an indigenous perspective. The titles of the five novels are: *Redoble por Rancas* (1970; translated as *Drums for Rancas*), *Garabombo el invisible* (1972; Garabombo the Invisible), *El jinete insomne* (1977; The Sleepless Rider), *Cantar de Agapito Robles* (1977; Song of Agapito Robles), and *La tumba del relámpago* (1979; The Grave of Lightning). Scorza died in a plane crash in Madrid.

REFERENCE:

Anna-Marie Aldaz, *The Past of the Future: The Novelistic Cycle of Manuel Scorza* (New York: Lang, 1990).

— R.G.M.

SENDERO LUMINOSO

Sendero Luminoso, known in English as Shining Path, is a Maoist guerrilla movement that broke with other left-wing groups, such as Tupac Amaru, in the 1970s on the grounds that they were not radical enough. Prominent in the Andean region of Peru dur-

A child carrying bricks in *Chircales* (1972; The Brickmakers),
a documentary directed by Jorge Silva and Marta Rodríguez

ing the 1980s, Sendero Luminoso terrorism and guerrilla warfare are estimated by official government sources to have been responsible for hundreds of deaths each year since 1980. Sendero has done much to destabilize life in Peru, including the lives of those whose interests it ostensibly supports. Largely ignored by the outside world, at least until the late 1980s, Sendero Luminoso continues to be a significant and disruptive political force in Peru. A view of its activities is given in **Mario Vargas Llosa**'s novel *Lituma en los Andes* (1993; Lituma in the Andes). Sendero Luminoso is also the subject of *La boca del lobo* (1988; The Mouth of the Wolf), a motion picture directed by **Francisco Lombardi.**

REFERENCE:

David Scott Palmer, ed., *The Shining Path of Peru* (New York: St. Martin's Press, 1992).

— P.S.

SICU

The sicu is a form of panpipe, a musical instrument consisting of several cane tubes or reeds of different lengths tied together. The length of the tube determines its pitch; hence the tubes are arranged in a graduated scalar order with longer tubes (lower pitches) on one end progressing to shorter tubes (higher pitches) on the other end. The tops of the tubes are open, and the breath is blown across their apertures to produce the sound. The bottoms of the tubes are closed. The tuning of each tube is determined by its length and other factors, but fine tuning can be accomplished after assembly by inserting a small pea or stone in the tube to raise the pitch slightly. The panpipe of Peru has a notchless aperture, but some panpipes feature an oblique cut at the top where the breath crosses the tube.

The panpipe is found in many varieties in many parts of the world, including most parts of South America, and is known by a variety of names. In the Andean region it is most often called *siku, sicu, zampoña,* or *antara.* The name *zampoña* was used by Spaniards because similar instruments are so named in Spain. An interesting variant on the instrument is the altiplano bipolar siku. In the bipolar siku, the scale is divided between two instruments, requiring two players. One player plays the "ira" half and one player plays the "arca" half. These are Aymara and Quechua terms that refer to the two different halves of panpipes that play in cooperation. Each instrument plays every other note of the scale. In order to realize a complete melody, the two players must cooperate and achieve a musical dialogue. There is a significant symbolism in this approach: *ira* means male, that which leads; *arca* means female, that which follows. The visual representation of this relationship is to be seen in the thin cloth or string that typically connects the two halves.

REFERENCES:

Gerard Béhague, "Latin American Folk Music," in *Folk and Traditional Music of the Western Continents,* third edition, by Bruno Nettl, revised and edited by Valerie Woodring Goertzen (Englewood Cliffs, N.J.: Prentice-Hall, 1990);

Américo Valencia Chacón, *El siku o zampoña — The Altiplano Bipolar Siku: Study and Projection of Peruvian Panpipe Orchestras* (Lima: Centro de Investigación y Desarrollo de la Música Peruana, 1989).

—R.L.S.

JORGE SILVA

Originally a still photographer, Colombian Jorge Silva (circa 1940–) has been directing politically committed documentaries in Colombia since the late 1960s. An early version of his first film, made in collaboration with **Marta Rodríguez,** *Chircales* (The Brickmakers), had its debut at the Second Meeting of Latin American Filmmakers in Mérida, Venezuela, in 1968. Completed in 1972, the movie is based on the lives of brickmaking families living in the

southern suburbs of Bogotá, and it demonstrates the level of exploitation of the working class in graphic terms. The second documentary, again directed in collaboration with Marta Rodríguez, *Plantas: testimonio de un etnocidio* (Plantas: Testimony about an Ethnocide), was released in 1973. Part 1 of *Campesinos* (Peasants) won awards at several European documentary festivals in 1975 and 1976. Each of these films deals with a different sector of Colombia's lower classes — unskilled urban workers on the margins of the national economy, the indigenous population completely outside it, and agricultural workers, respectively — and demonstrates both social concern and analytical precision. Another documentary, *Nuestra voz de tierra, memoria, y futuro* (Our Voice of Earth, Memory and Future), was completed in 1981.

REFERENCE:

Julianne Burton, ed., *Cinema and Social Change in Latin America: Conversations with Latin American Filmmakers* (Austin: University of Texas Press, 1986).

—S.M.H.

SIMPLEMENTE MARÍA

A Peruvian **telenovela** (soap opera) about the upward mobility of the poor, *Simplemente María* was one of the most popular of such shows in the 1960s. María, a young, illiterate girl born to Indian parents in a small rural town, moves to Lima and finds employment first as a maid, then as a seamstress. In the meantime she falls in love with a young upper-middle-class student who deceives her, making her pregnant and then leaving her. Becoming a mother gives her an incentive to make a new life for herself and her child. The soap opera focuses on the difficulties of María's everyday life. She accepts her destiny, which is to suffer because she has sinned, but her perseverance in the face of oppression yields economic as well as spiritual rewards. *Simplemente María* was the longest-running Latin American soap opera, with more than four hundred episodes. So many new episodes were added that, as time went on, María became a great-grandmother, a fact which was not immediately apparent since she seemed to possess the secret of eternal youth. (Her role was still played by the beautiful Peruvian actress Sally Kabalach, who was only thirty toward the end of the show's run.) In Peru during the late 1960s and early 1970s a highly popular **fotonovela** (photonovel) was created to accompany the soap opera.

Antonio Skármeta

REFERENCES:

Azriel Bibliowicz, "Be Happy Because Your Father Isn't Your Father: An Analysis of Colombian *Telenovelas,*" *Journal of Popular Culture,* 14 (Winter 1980): 476–485;

William Rowe and Vivian Schelling, *Memory and Modernity: Popular Culture in Latin America* (London: Verso, 1991).

— S.M.H.

ANTONIO SKÁRMETA

Contemporary Chilean novelist and filmmaker Antonio Skármeta (1940–), born in Antofagasta, published three books of short stories before Chilean president **Salvador Allende** was violently overthrown by a military coup in September 1973: *El entusiasmo* (1967; Verve); *Desnudo en el tejado* (1969; Naked on the Roof); and *Tiro libre* (1973; Free Kick). These minimalist stories are written in an informal language patterned after that of American authors such as Norman Mailer and Jack Kerouac, and they deal with a youthful protagonist coming to terms with himself in the world. *Desnudo en el tejado* won the **Casa de las Américas Prize** in 1969.

With the fall of Allende, Skármeta was forced to leave Chile. He eventually settled in West Germany where he lived until 1989, when he returned to his native country. In Berlin, Skármeta wrote scripts for European radio and film and won several awards for his work in the media, the most important of which was the **Biarritz** prize for the film *Burning Patience,* which he wrote and directed. Skármeta also wrote his four novels in exile: *Soñé que la nieve ardía* (1975; translated as *I Dreamt the Snow Was Burning*); *La insurrección* (1982; translated as *The Insurrection*); *Ardiente paciencia* (1985; translated as *Burning Patience*); and *Match Ball* (1989). While the first three may be read as political novels, the writing never comes close to the tone of diatribe nor is the narrator's language overtly ideological. Skármeta, though younger, belongs to the generation of Latin American novelists (like Carlos Fuentes and **Julio Cortázar**) who were profoundly influenced by the poetic discoveries of the modernista and avant-garde poets; he is a firm believer in the autonomy and specificity of literary writing. *Ardiente paciencia* takes its title from a line by Symbolist poet Arthur Rimbaud, quoted by **Pablo Neruda** in his Nobel Prize acceptance speech. The protagonists of the novel, in fact, are Neruda himself and a youth to whom the poet teaches metaphors so he can seduce the girl of his dreams. The novel as well as Neruda's life both end with the military takeover. *La insurrección* is about the Sandinista defeat of dictator Anastasio Somoza in Nicaragua in 1979 and is no less "poetic" than other works by Skármeta. *Match Ball,* a postmodern reworking of Vladimir Nabokov's *Lolita,* also has features of traditional romance but is more obsessively erotic than any of the author's previous novels.

Skármeta's aesthetic creed is "Infra-Realism," an attempt to provide relief from the grandiosity of the modern Latin American novel. Infra-Realism focuses on the everyday and not on myth, allegory, or hermetic symbolic systems, all traits of the **Boom** novel. Skármeta is one of the leading novelists of the **Post-Boom** generation.

In 1992 Skármeta became a media celebrity in Chile when he began to write and host *El Show de los Libros* (The Book Show), a weekly television program that enjoyed unprecedented accolades from the critics and favorable ratings from the public.

REFERENCE:

Raúl Silva Cáceres, *Del cuerpo a las palabras: La narrativa de Antonio Skármeta* (Madrid: LAR, 1983).

— R.G.M.

Social Realism in Art

Social realism does not refer to any prescribed style but is often used to describe the work of writers, artists, and filmmakers who seek to document social and political realities and advocate change. This term is of particular importance for Latin American art, where it refers to the work of artists during the early part of the century who used figurative modes and dealt with social issues.

Although the view of art as a means of expressing social and political ideas had been present in Latin American art since the nineteenth century, this tendency became stronger with the impulse of Mexican Muralism. The influence of Muralism reached the Andean regions first, where the link between realism and social change was established during the 1920s by **Indigenism.** Many Indigenist artists such as **Camilo Egas, Eduardo Kingman, José Sabogal,** and **Julia Codesido,** who attempted to revalue the native cultures of their countries in visual terms, found in Mexican Muralism a school of art that had successfully redefined its national culture in inclusive terms, celebrating not only the urban worker but also the native races and their indigenous traditions.

When the influence of Muralism reached Brazil and the Southern Cone during the early 1930s, the economy of these countries was being adversely affected by the Great Depression. The rise in unemployment and social unrest in Chile resulted in a more democratic government, but in Argentina and Brazil it marked a lasting move away from democracy. These circumstances, and in particular the plight of the poor and the struggle of destitute workers, are reflected in the art of Argentineans Lino Eneas Spilimbergo, Juan Carlos Castagnino, and **Antonio Berni.**

In Argentina social issues had been of paramount importance in the work of the Artistas del Pueblo, associated with the **Boedo** group during the 1920s. When David Alfaro Siqueiros visited Argentina in 1933, he collaborated with Spilimbergo, Castagnino, and Berni on a mural for a private residence, but they failed to start a mural movement in Buenos Aires, mostly because of the lack of a mural tradition in this area and the conservative tendency of the government, which did not make public walls available to artists. Siqueiros also visited Chile in 1941, where he painted several murals in Chillán, but his influence there did not come to fruition until the 1960s, when an important popular mural movement emerged in Chillán.

REFERENCES:

Dawn Ades, *Art in Latin America: The Modern Era, 1820–1980* (New Haven & London: Yale University Press, 1989);

Gilbert Chase, *Contemporary Art in Latin America* (New York: Free Press, 1970).

— F.B.N.

Fernando Solanas

Argentinean movie director Fernando Ezequiel Solanas (circa 1940–) established his career in 1968, when he and Octavio Getino directed the documentary *La hora de los hornos* (1966–1969; The Hour of the Furnaces), which was much applauded at the First Encounter of Latin American Documentary Film, held in Mérida, Venezuela, in 1968. It received its world premiere at the International Festival of New Cinema in Pesaro, Italy, later in the same year, after which Solanas was carried out onto the streets on the shoulders of the crowd in a spontaneous demonstration of support. (See **Cinema in Argentina** and **New Latin American Cinema.**)

Solanas's career as a film director was interrupted by the **Guerra Sucia** (Dirty War), which forced him into exile. Solanas's probing analysis of the state of exile took many years to find funding. It was eventually released in 1985 as *Tangos, el exilio de Gardel*

Movie poster for *Sur* (1988; Southside), directed by Fernando Solanas

(Tangos, the Exile of Gardel). This film concentrates on a group of exiled artists and intellectuals in Paris and explores the ways in which they are distanced from, yet still preserve, their national identity. The troupe seeks to create a *tanguedia* (a **tango** tragicomedy) based on their own exile and also on tango, the quintessential popular song and dance form in Argentina, and one that in itself contains both comedy and tragedy. The film becomes an example of the type of artistic work that the characters are attempting to create. Solanas's next film, *Sur* (1988; Southside), is a sequel to *Tangos, el exilio de Gardel* and deals with the painful return to democracy in Argentina. He employs a similar format of people sitting around a "table of dreams," swapping memories of the past to offset the pain of the present, but *Sur* is more adept at combining the realistic and the surrealistic.

Solanas has not gone without his political enemies. When he criticized President Carlos Saúl Menem in 1991, a hit squad wounded him in the leg.

REFERENCE:

David William Foster, *Contemporary Argentine Cinema* (Columbia & London: University of Missouri Press, 1992).
— S.M.H.

JAVIER SOLOGUREN

A Peruvian poet and mentor to younger poets whose work was published by his Ediciones de la Rama Florida, Javier Sologuren (1921–   ) taught literature at the Universidad Agraria in Lima until his retirement in 1983. He also directed various literary journals and found time to travel widely. His work has been translated into several languages.

Despite the formal evolution of his poetry — which ranges over forms as varied as the sonnet, prose poems, haikus, and "décimas" (traditional poems composed of ten-line rhymed octosyllables) — Sologuren remains a confessional and existential poet. His books include *Vida continua* (1966; Ongoing Life), *Las uvas del racimo* (1975; The Grapes in the Bunch), *Jaikús escritos en un amanecer de otoño* (1981; Haikus Written during an Autumn Dawn), *Folios del enamorado y la muerte* (1980; Pages of the Lover and Death), and *Un trino en la ventana vacía* (1992; A Warble in the Empty Window). Sologuren was awarded the National Prize for Poetry in 1960.

REFERENCES:

Miguel Angel Zapata, "Continuidad de la voz en Javier Sologuren," *Inti,* 26–27 (Fall/Spring 1987–1988): 337–354;

Miguel Cabrera, "Milenaria luz: La metáfora polisémica en la poesía de Javier Sologuren," *Cuadernos Hispanoamericanos*, 444 (June 1987): 65–76.

— R.G.M.

OSVALDO SORIANO

Argentinean novelist Osvaldo Soriano (1943–) made the transition from journalism to literature in 1973 with the publication of *Triste, solitario y final* (Sad, Solitary, and Final), a novel inspired by Hollywood and by the hard-boiled detective fiction of Raymond Chandler. The protagonist is an Argentinean writer in Los Angeles researching a novel on Laurel and Hardy. Some of the characters he meets are actors Jane Fonda, Dick Van Dyke, Charlie Chaplin, and John Wayne, as well as Chandler's fictional detective Philip Marlowe, who is posing as a friend of Stan Laurel in his later years.

In 1976, as Argentina fell into the hands of the generals and was about to enter the main phase of the **Guerra Sucia** (Dirty War), Soriano left for Brussels and later settled in Paris where he lived for many years. His next two novels bear testimony to the Argentinean crisis. *No habrá más penas ni olvido* (1980; translated as *A Funny Dirty Little War*) takes its title from one of **Carlos Gardel**'s best-known tangos, "Mi Buenos Aires querido" (My Dear Buenos Aires). Set in a provincial town between 1973 and 1976, the years between the second government of **Juan Domingo Perón** and the military takeover, the novel describes a farcical but bloody war between rival factions of the Peronist movement.

Cuarteles de invierno (1982; translated as *Winter Quarters*) is a brilliant exposé of a country occupied by its own military forces. A tango singer and an aging boxer from Buenos Aires are hired by the authorities of Puerto Obligado, a town not far from the capital, to perform in a local festival. The two imported stars soon run afoul of the local authorities and eventually realize that they have only one another to depend on. The tango singer's contract is cancelled before the performance, and he becomes the boxer's manager in order to protect himself against the armed thugs chasing him. He has found out that the boxer's rival is a young army sergeant from Puerto Obligado: the spectacle has been set up to glorify the town and the army. The fight goes badly for the hired boxer, who is left near death by his rival's blows and by negligent medical care. The tango singer singlehandedly and at his own peril retrieves his dying friend from the hospital and takes him on a train bound for Buenos Aires. The novel excels in its description of the asphyxiating atmosphere of a nation under a repressive and murderous military regime but also dwells on the positive value of altruism under duress.

Soriano has published several other novels, including *Una sombra ya pronto serás* (1990; translated as *Shadows*).

REFERENCES:

Elvio E. Gandolfo, "Osvaldo Soriano: Cómo contar la historia," in *Los héroes difíciles: La literatura policial en la Argentina y en Italia*, edited by Giuseppe Petronio, Jorge B. Rivera, and Luigi Volta (Buenos Aires: Corregidor, 1991);

Marta Giacomino, "Espacios de soledad: Entrevista con Osvaldo Soriano," *Quimera* (May 1989): 45–51.

— R.G.M.

HELVIO SOTO

Chilean movie and television director Helvio Soto (circa 1940–) played a significant role in the regeneration of the Chilean movie industry in the 1960s. Two of the movies he directed during that period were controversial: *Erase un niño, un guerrillero y un caballo* (1967; There Once was a Child, a Guerrilla, and a Horse) and *Caliche sangriento* (1969; Blood Stained Mineral), about the War of the Pacific (1879–1883) between Chile and Peru. Both were banned by the Chilean Censorship Board because of their ideological content. Soto was later made director of the government television channel during **Salvador Allende**'s presidency (1970–1973). Never shy of controversy, Soto directed *Metamorfosis del jefe de la policía política* (1973; Metamorphosis of the Political Police Chief), a documentary about the divisions and tensions within Allende's Popular Unity Party. This film, which focuses in particular on the death of a worker in a shantytown in Santiago, caused embarrassment to the Left.

REFERENCE:

Michael Chanan, ed., *Chilean Cinema* (London: BFI, 1976).

— S.M.H.

JESÚS RAFAEL SOTO

Venezuelan Jesús Rafael Soto (1923–) is internationally recognized as one of the principal practitioners of **Kinetic Art.** Soto studied at the Escuela de Artes Plásticas y Aplicadas in Caracas, where he met **Alejandro Otero** and **Carlos Cruz-Diez.** After graduating in 1947, he was appointed director of the Escuela de Artes Plásticas in Maracaibo. In 1950 he left for Paris and participated in the Salon des Réalités Nouvelles,

Jesús Rafael Soto holding his *Espiral* (1955; Spiral)

which specialized in **Geometric Abstraction.** Soto's paintings from the early 1950s reveal his admiration for Piet Mondrian's sense of geometry as well as Yaacov Agam and Jean Tinguely's integration of movement into their art. In *Repetición y progresión* (1951; Repetition and Progression) Soto generated effects of optical motion through the repetition of geometric abstract elements, which links his work with Op Art. In the mid 1950s he superimposed transparent Plexiglas panels containing patterns of dots. Later he did the same with spiral lines, as in *Espiral con rojo* (1955; Spiral with Red), which produces a sense of vibrations and moiré effects as the spectator moves around the work. In 1958 Soto began his *Vibración* (Vibration) sculptures, which generate dynamic optical effects with painted and metallic squares placed at a short distance from a background crossed with thin parallel lines.

During the 1960s Soto went beyond optical motion to produce kinetic sculptures capable of real movement. In *Cinco varillas grandes* (1964; Five Large Rods), Soto suspended rods with wires in front of a backboard crossed with thin parallel lines. The rods, which move with the air displaced by passing spectators, interact with the background to produce moiré effects. Soto also worked on large-scale kinetic projects integrated with architecture. For his 1969 retrospective at the Musée d'Art Moderne de la Ville de Paris, Soto produced his first *Penetrable,* a kinetic environment of hanging plastic tubes. His objective was for the viewers to interact physically with the work and set the suspended tubing in motion, thus creating patterns of optical vibrations. In recent pieces Soto has continued to work with real motion, as in *Esfera virtual amarilla* (1983; Yellow Virtual Sphere), made up of yellow rods suspended from nylon threads and moving with the circulating air. In 1973 Soto helped establish the Museo de Arte Moderno Jesús Soto in his native Ciudad Bolívar.

REFERENCE:

Aracy Amaral, "Abstract Constructivist Trends in Argentina, Brazil, Venezuela, and Colombia," in *Latin American Artists of the Twentieth Century,* edited by Waldo Rasmussen, Fatima Bercht, and Elizabeth Ferrer (New York: Museum of Modern Art, 1993), pp. 86–99.

— F.B.N.

Ana María Stekelman

Argentinean choreographer Ana María Stekelman, a graduate of the National Dance School of Argentina, went on to study with Renate Schottelius and Paulina Ossona in Buenos Aires, at the Martha Graham School in New York, and at the Connecticut College School of Dance. She was a soloist with Oscar Araiz's ballet and the Grupo de Acción Instrumental. She was director of the **Ballet Contemporáneo del Teatro San Martín,** as well as the Taller (Workshop) in Contemporary Dance (1977–1981 and 1987–1989). She has choreographed *Memories* (Schumann) and *Dancing in the Darkness* (bolero music sung by Elvira Ríos), but she is particularly known for her work with **tango,** which is characterized by an idiosyncratic symbiosis of the voluptuousness of the music with the surprising dynamics of contemporary dance. In this vein she has created *Jasmines, Images of Tango and Folk,* and *Tango Kinesis.* She has created works for companies in the United States and Europe as well as for Argentinean ballet star Julio Bocca, for the Seville Expo of 1992, and for **Ballet del Sur** in Argentina.

—N.D.B. & J.M.H.

Grete Stern

Grete Stern (1904–   ) was one of the first modern photographers to work in Argentina. She studied art in her native Germany and worked as a graphic designer during the 1920s. After seeing photographs by Edward Weston and Paul Outerbridge in 1927, she switched to photography and apprenticed in Berlin with Walter Peterhans, who taught her to define her own vision. In 1929, when Peterhans became the director of the Bauhaus department of photography, he sold his equipment to Stern, who opened the commercial studio Ringl and Pit with Ellen Auerbach, a fellow student. Their work was recognized in articles in the magazines *Gebrauchsgraphik* in Berlin and *Cahiers d'Art* in Paris. In 1930 Stern took another course with Peterhans at the Bauhaus, where she met the Argentinean photographer Horacio Coppola, a fellow student who became her husband. In 1933 Stern, Coppola, and Auerbach left Germany for England because of the spread of Nazism. In London Stern and Auerbach continued working together as Ringl and Pit, and Stern concentrated on portraits of prominent intellectuals such as Bertolt Brecht (1933).

In 1936 Stern and her husband left for Buenos Aires, where they opened a commercial studio called Grete and Horacio Coppola. That year **Victoria Ocampo** and her magazine Sur sponsored an exhibition of their work, now considered the first of modern photography in Argentina. Stern included her portraits, whose rich range of gray tones, obtained through soft lighting, was perceived as innovative and different from the portrait styles common in Buenos Aires. Their studio became popular among intellectuals and artists who were portrayed by Stern: **Emilio Petorutti,** Lino Eneas Spilimbergo, **Jorge Luis Borges, Ernesto Sábato,** and María Elena Walsh. Soon Stern also became interested in the city's neighborhoods and began a long series of photographs of streets and old houses, later published in her books *Buenos Aires* (1953) and *Los patios* (1967).

Amor, featuring a turtle-headed man, is an example of the kind of surrealist photomontage Stern produced during the 1940s for the magazine *Idilio,* to illustrate dreams submitted by readers. Her best-known photomontage, however, shows the word *Madí* floating in front of the Buenos Aires obelisk. It was produced for the avant-garde group **Madí,** which she joined briefly. In 1946 she hosted the group's exhibition at her private residence. Her interest in art is also seen in her images of art objects. In 1946 Stern and Coppola photographed the collection of Andean pottery at the Museo de Historia Nacional in la Plata, and in 1956 she was appointed head of photography at the Museo Nacional de Bellas Artes.

Stern's work changed directions in 1959 when she taught at the Universidad Nacional del Nordeste in the city of Resistencia. She became interested in the Toba Indians who lived nearby and began to photograph them, a project later continued with the help of a state grant which allowed her to travel through the provinces of Chaco, Salta, and Formosa to photograph members of the Toba, Mataco, Pilagá, and Moscoví tribes. Her objective was not anthropological but simply to bring these often marginalized groups to the attention of the rest of the population. She exhibited the resulting photographs and published them as *Los aborígenes del Gran Chaco Argentino* (1971), a book that contributed to interest in the indigenous arts and crafts of northeastern Argentina.

REFERENCE:

Jorge Ben Gullco, "Stern," in *Fotógrafos argentinos del siglo XX* (Buenos Aires: Centro Editor de América Latina, 1982).

—F.B.N.

Alfonsina Storni

Argentinean poet Alfonsina Storni (1892–1938) was born in "Italian" Switzerland to parents who had pre-

Alfonsina Storni

viously immigrated to Argentina and were on a short trip back home. After the family's return to Argentina, Storni earned a living as a schoolteacher in the provincial city of Rosario and became a single mother, a status that did not endear her to society matrons. At twenty she settled in Buenos Aires, worked in a factory, and became a poet as well as a spokeswoman for workers and women's rights. When in 1938 she found out she had breast cancer, she drowned herself at the beach resort of Mar del Plata. On the whole, Storni's poetry is formally unremarkable, with the exception of her last book, *Mascarilla y trébol* (1938; Mask and Clover), which is experimental and hermetic. However, Storni's distinctive poetic note is rebellion against women's roles in patriarchal society and the espousal of free love.

REFERENCE:

Sonia Jones, *Alfonsina Storni* (Boston: Twayne, 1979).

— R.G.M.

SUR

An influential Argentinean magazine published regularly between 1931 and 1970, *Sur* was launched by **Victoria Ocampo** and directed by José Bianco after 1938. From the moment of its inception *Sur* was the primary bridge between European and Argentinean letters. The initial *Sur* group included **Jorge Luis Borges, Silvina Ocampo, Eduardo Mallea,** and **Oliverio Girondo.** The scope of the magazine lay somewhere between the eclecticism of the nineteenth-century review and the partisan selectiveness of the "little magazines" of the avant-garde years. Always above the political fray, *Sur* was a staunch defender of high cultural values, particularly against the inroads of nationalism, fascism, and communism. Its unstated mission, grounded in the tradition of nineteenth-century Argentinean liberalism, was the preservation of "civilized" values in the face of social and political change. Many of the essays published in *Sur* were commentaries on current events but written from a cultural perspective

The *Sur* group in 1931: (standing) Eduardo Bullrich, Jorge Luis Borges, Francisco Romero, Eduardo Mallea, Enrique Bullrich, Victoria Ocampo, and Ramón Gómez de la Serna; (seated) Pedro Henriquez Ureña, Norah Borges, María Rosa Oliver, Nenina Padilla, and Guillermo de Torre; (kneeling) Oliverio Girondo and Ernest Ansermet

that neutralized or masked their ideological leanings. The work of many important European and United States authors (André Malraux, Aldous Huxley, James Joyce, and Langston Hughes) first appeared in Spanish translation in *Sur*. The magazine published mostly stories and essays but did not neglect poetry or reviews of books and cultural events. *Sur* was not concerned with Latin America beyond the cultural borders of Buenos Aires but was widely read throughout the continent.

The triumph of the Cuban revolution led to the resignation of editor in chief José Bianco in 1961 over a dispute with owner Victoria Ocampo regarding the importance that the magazine should attribute to Castro's victory. Bianco's departure meant that *Sur* would ignore the revolution at a time when most Latin American intellectuals (including the novelists who were soon to be baptized with the sobriquet of the **"Boom"**) were strongly drawn to it. The journal thus began to lose its relevance, even in Argentina, where the political situation was radicalizing many students and intellectuals and the rhetoric of "Third Worldism" had overtaken the liberal conception of literature and culture. Changes abroad

(like the decline in importance of French "universalist" intellectuals who had been crucial to the magazine's success in the early years) also hastened the demise of *Sur*, along with the magazine's inability to keep in the forefront of literary experimentation. Ocampo ceased regular publication on the eve of the **Guerra Sucia** (Dirty War) decade.

REFERENCE:

John King, *'Sur': A Study of the Argentine Literary Journal and Its Role in the Development of a Culture* (Cambridge: Cambridge University Press, 1986).

— R.G.M.

SURREALISM IN ART

Surrealism did not develop in the art of Argentina, Brazil, Chile, Cuba, and Mexico as a unified or cohesive movement but rather as a series of isolated groups and artists who either used dreamlike images in their work with the purpose of constructing invented realities or followed the more characteristically Surrealist exploration of the unconscious through dream imagery and automatist techniques. Chronologically Surrealism first appeared in South America in Argentina in the form of the small magazine *Qué,* published by the Surrealist poet **Aldo Pellegrini** in 1926, but was overshadowed by the activities of the **Florida** and **Boedo** groups, which were on the whole uninterested in Surrealism. During the 1930s **Raquel Forner** and **Xul Solar** worked with ideas related to Surrealism, and **Antonio Berni,** who had met the Surrealists in Paris during the 1920s and exhibited his Surrealist paintings in Buenos Aires in 1933, went through a brief Surrealist period early in his career. Among the artists who considered themselves Surrealists were **Juan Batlle Planas,** who exhibited his well-known series of *Radiografías paranoicas* (Paranoid X Rays) in 1937; the members of the Grupo Orión, such as Luis Barragán, Vicente Forte, Leopoldo Presas, and Orlando Pierri, all of whom mounted an important group exhibition in 1939; and later, Miguel Caride, Leonor Fini, Noé Nojechowicz, and Roberto Aizenberg.

In Brazil Surrealist tendencies appear in Tarsila do Amaral's Anthropophagist paintings of 1928–1929 and in the early paintings of Cándido Portinari, who, like Berni, later turned to **Social Realism.** The interest in Surrealism in Chile began with the magazine *Mandrágora* (1938–1943), which organized an exhibition in 1941. Although there were several Chilean artists who worked in Surrealist modes at different times in their careers, such as **Nemesio Antúnez,** Rodolfo Opazo, Juan Gómez Quirós, Guillermo Núñez, and Ricardo Yrrarázaval, the most important of them was **Roberto Matta.** He lived most of his life in Paris and New York and became, like the Cuban Wifredo Lam, one of the main forces in the second generation of Surrealists. Matta was instrumental in the introduction of Surrealism in the United States and influential among the first generation of abstract expressionists. In 1938 André Breton, the leader of the Surrealist movement, visited Mexico, where a great number of artists, such as Frida Kahlo, Rufino Tamayo, Alice Rahon, Remedios Varo, and Leonora Carrington, were interested in Surrealism.

REFERENCES:

Dawn Ades, *Art in Latin America: The Modern Era, 1820–1980* (New Haven & London: Yale University Press, 1989);

Dore Ashton, "Surrealism and Latin America," in *Latin American Artists of the Twentieth Century,* edited by Waldo Rasmussen, Fatima Bercht, and Elizabeth Ferrer (New York: Museum of Modern Art, 1993), pp. 106–115.

— F.B.N.

SYMPHONY ORCHESTRAS

The early missionaries in South America planted the seeds of today's numerous symphony orchestras by establishing European-style instrumental ensembles for use in worship services, civic celebrations, entertainments, and festivals. Instruments and music were brought from Europe originally, but soon thereafter indigenous and Creole artisans began to produce copies and imitations of both.

Religious plays (*autos* in Spanish) containing interludes of music, dancing, and songs were performed with instrumental ensembles throughout the colonial period in the New World. The earliest surviving New World opera, *La púrpura de la rosa* (The Purple of the Rose), by Tomás de Torrejón y Velasco, produced in Lima in 1701, was preceded by spectacles of instrumental and vocal music in the viceregal theater. The **zarzuela,** Italian opera, and other theatrical events continued to nurture a variety of instrumental and orchestral music following the wars of liberation in the nineteenth century, but struggling economies and other social forces prevented an orderly, continuous development.

Orchestral concerts in South America might well have continued as isolated, irregular events had it not been for the nationalistic fervor that spread among the new republics in the late nineteenth and early twentieth centuries and the subsequent First International Conference of American States (1889–1890) that established the International Union of American Republics (later known as the Pan-American Union), which in 1948 became in turn the **Organization of American States** (OAS). Music as a means of reinforcing national pride and identity became an effective political and social implement in the emerging republics. The Pan-American Union and the OAS proposed to encourage social, economic, and cultural development in the Americas through improved communications and mutual support. The effect of these developments can be seen in the institutionalization of national symphony orchestras in the early decades of the twentieth century.

The foundation of the Orquesta del **Teatro Colón** in Buenos Aires was among the earliest in 1908, but it was followed in the 1920s and 1930s by symphony orchestras in Chile, Bolivia, Ecuador, Uruguay, Venezuela, Colombia, Peru, and Paraguay. Although economic and political misfortunes have occasionally disrupted the continuity of some national ensembles, the concept of permanent national orchestras now appears to be assured in all of the Latin American republics.

In addition to the national symphony orchestras in each of the South American republics, there are numerous other symphony and chamber orchestras associated with conservatories, universities, private foundations, and municipalities.

REFERENCES:

Gerard Béhague, *Music in Latin America: An Introduction* (Englewood Cliffs, N.J.: Prentice-Hall, 1979);

Gilbert Chase, *A Guide of the Music of Latin America* (Washington, D.C.: Pan American Union / Library of Congress, 1962).

— R.L.S.

FERNANDO DE SZYSZLO

Born in 1925, Fernando de Szyszlo is one of the most important Peruvian artists. He studied art in his native Lima and also worked in Paris and Florence during the late 1940s. In Europe he came in contact with French and Spanish Informalism and turned to **Informal Abstraction.** Soon after he returned to Lima, he exhibited his abstract paintings (1951), provoking a hostile reaction from critics and supporters of **Indigenism,** who labeled his work immoral and un-Peruvian. By following the example of **Joaquín Torres-García** and Rufino Tamayo, who had successfully combined modern style and American content, de Szyszlo found a way of overcoming the cultural identity crisis caused by Informal Abstraction, a style regarded by many as a tool of North American imperialism. He visited pre-Hispanic sites and admired native Peruvian poetry, arts, and crafts, which inspired not only his choice of colors and textures but also the themes and tone of his art. In his series *Apu Inca Atawallpaman,* based on a Quechua elegy recounting the murder of the last Inca ruler by the Spaniards, de Szyszlo transforms the free treatment of color and texture of Informal Abstraction into an evocative homage to his Peruvian heritage. During the 1950s he actively promoted the cause of Informal Abstraction through a series of lectures, international exhibitions, and shows of his own art. By the end of the decade, he was living in the United States, where he worked for the Visual Arts Division of the Pan American Union in Washington, D.C., and later lectured at Cornell and Yale. In the 1970s he settled in Lima, where he still works. In recent decades he has introduced semiabstract figures into his art, figures that suggest three-dimensional space and evoke ceremonial rituals.

REFERENCE:

Alice Thorson, "Conversation with a Peruvian Master: Fernando de Szyszlo," *Latin American Art,* 2 (Winter 1990): 23–27.

— F.B.N.

T

ENRIQUE TÁBARA

The Ecuadoran painter Enrique Tábara (1930–)
was one of the first artists in Ecuador to work with
Informal Abstraction. He studied at the Escuela de
Bellas Artes in Guayaquil and was also a student of
Hans Michaelson from Germany and Lloyd Wulf
from the United States, both contemporary artists
who arrived in Ecuador during the 1940s. Tábara
began exhibiting his abstract paintings in 1954.
Shortly afterward he traveled to Barcelona, where he
became interested in Spanish Informalism, especially
for its emphasis on textured surfaces. Tábara explored a more textural approach to painting, which
encouraged other Ecuadoran artists, such as Aníbal
Villacis and **Estuardo Maldonado,** to experiment
with different surfaces in their paintings. Like the
Peruvian **Fernando de Szyszlo,** Tábara balanced his
interest in color and texture with subtle subjective
references to pre-Columbian forms. During the
1960s Tábara traveled throughout Europe and the
United States and later settled in his native Guayaquil. In 1967 he cofounded the Grupo VAN (for
vanguard), which opposed institutionalized **Indigenism** and organized the Anti-Biennial Grupo VAN in
1968 as a protest exhibition against the First Quito
Biennial, sponsored by indigenist artists.

REFERENCES:

Félix Angel, "The Latin American Presence: Part II: The Abstract Spirit," in *The Latin American Spirit: Art and Artists
in the United States, 1920–70* (New York: Bronx Museum of
the Arts/Abrams, 1988), pp. 239–265;

Jacqueline Barnitz, *Abstract Currents in Ecuadorian Art* (New
York: Center for Inter-American Relations, 1977).

—F.B.N.

Formas entre horizontales (1977; Forms between Horizon-
tals), by Enrique Tábara (from Jacqueline Barnitz, *Abstract
Currents in Ecuadorian Art*, 1977)

TALLER DE DANZA DE CARACAS

The Taller (Workshop) de Danza de Caracas, founded
in 1974 and directed by José Ledezma, has trained
virtually an entire generation of young Venezuelan
dancers and choreographers. Ledezma was trained in
the dance technique of Merce Cunningham, a U.S.
choreographer who developed his technique based on
his early years with the Martha Graham Dance Company and on principles of chance as developed with
composer John Cage. Over the years Ledezma has de-

The opening of the eleventh exhibit of the Taller Torres-García, 12 May 1943. Joaquín Torres-García is standing fifth from the right in the front row.

veloped his own code or style of dance, combining the Cunningham technique and method with his own ideas about movement. The primary aim of the Taller de Danza de Caracas is to create dance without affectation.

— N.D.B. & J.M.H.

TALLER TORRES-GARCÍA

The Taller Torres-García was founded in Montevideo in 1943 by **Joaquín Torres-García,** who had returned to his native Uruguay in 1934 to find a conservative society whose artists were working in outdated styles. He realized that his **Constructive Art,** a synthesis of elements of the autochthonous arts of the continent and different aspects of European modernism, could both revitalize art in Uruguay and at the same time define a new art that would be unique to the Americas. Supported by a group of artists and intellectuals who shared his ideas, Torres-García founded an art center which in 1935 took the name Asociación de Arte Constructivo (AAC). Its participants, including Rosa Acle, Amalia Nieto, Héctor Ragni, and Torres-García's sons **Augusto Torres** and **Horacio Torres,** exhibited their artworks together, organized and attended Torres-García's classes and lectures on art, and published

Círculo y Cuadrado (Circle and Square), the second series of a magazine published in Paris in 1930 by the Cercle et Carré group, which Torres-García had helped to found. In 1935 Torres-García also published his book *Estructura* (Structure), introducing the Uruguayan public to his theory of Constructive Art.

The rejection of his avant-garde project by both public and critics eventually caused the demise of the AAC in 1940. However, a younger generation of artists became interested in Torres-García's ideas and encouraged him to found a new art school, the Taller Torres-García. Many of its participants, including **Julio Alpuy,** Elsa Andrada, José Gurvich, **Gonzalo Fonseca,** Francisco Matto, and Manuel Pailós, as well as Augusto and Horacio Torres, acquired most of their artistic training at the taller and firmly adhered to its utopian principles. They worked collectively in a Constructive style and used all kinds of materials and techniques, ranging from sculpture and ceramics to furniture design and painting, producing a series of twenty-seven Constructive murals in the Pabellón Martirené of the Saint Bois Hospital, the most significant modern mural project in Latin America outside Mexico. Most of these murals were later removed from the Saint Bois and subsequently destroyed in a fire at the Museum of Modern Art in Rio de Janeiro. The members of the taller also exhibited as a group and published the periodical *Removedor*. Their participation in the taller continued until the mid 1950s, when most of them dispersed to pursue individual projects. Although the taller closed in 1962, partly because its Constructive style had become overly academic, its theoretical and artistic activities had an enormous influence on later generations of Uruguayan and Latin American artists.

REFERENCE:

Mari Carmen Ramírez, ed., *The Taller Torres-García: The School of the South and Its Legacy* (Austin: University of Texas Press, 1992).

—F.B.N.

TANGO

The tango of Argentina and Uruguay is typical of the infectious nature of Latin American music and of its ability to attract audiences throughout the world. Its musical features include fused elements of the Andalusian tango, the Argentinean **milonga,** the Cuban habanera (of which it has been called a degenerate form), and the contradanza, which, along with the milonga and the habanera — incorporate African rhythmic influences.

The tango originated as a dance in the dockside brothels of Buenos Aires, where sailors from around the world seeking women, alcohol, music, and entertainment constituted the ambience in which prostitution flourished. Seldom appreciated in the development of the tango, however, is that it was also a relic of the European, largely Italian, immigrant experience in its instrumentation as well as the mood of sadness or nostalgia; one of the tango's most celebrated lyricists, Santos Discépolo, described it as "a sad thought that is danced." The tango has passed through various stages of development and popularity since its earliest appearance in Argentina in the late nineteenth century. Associated with the urban underclass, it was at first treated with contempt by Argentina's high society.

Early emphasis was on the dance, with the accompaniment of a conjunto típico (typical ensemble) consisting of harp, flute, and violin. Eventually the harp was replaced by the guitar. The addition of the **bandoneón,** a concertina-type instrument of the accordion family, gave the tango its most typical sonority. The incorporation of the piano, additional violins, and the tango canción (tango song, which featured a vocalist) was significant in the evolution from conjuntos to sextets. Among the ensemble leaders responsible for these changes were Roberto Firpo, Vicente Greco, Os-

valdo Fresedo, Tano Genaro Espósito, Augusto P. Berto, Juan Carlos Cobián, and Francisco Canaro.

As in the **gaucho** dances, the unsophisticated early practitioners of tango were neither interested in nor adept at devising complicated steps. Early tango, developed in the 1920s, consisted simply of walking. In the 1940s, the apogee for the popularity of tango in Argentina, the first spins and turns were added to these simple walking steps. An early practitioner of tango named Petróleo (Petroleum) recounted how he and a fellow tango aficionado, Cacho Lavandina, were employed as construction workers in a suburb of Buenos Aires. Lavandina, taking a break from work and practicing tango, was drinking and, in a moment of inspiration, grasped a rope hanging from the ceiling to begin experimenting with turns; hence the complicated turning of tango as we know it.

The primacy of dance as a function of the early tango was matched in song following the interpretation of "Mi noche triste" by **Carlos Gardel** in 1917. Poetic descriptions of love gone awry and daring insinuations of failed private intimacies served as a catharsis for real and imagined pain. The newly accentuated role of the vocalist attracted the interest of talented lyricists, whose bittersweet portrayal of the anguish of life and love, expressed in an improvised urban jargon, developed the early literary character of the tango. Pascual Contursi, Celedonio Flórez, José González Castillo, and Enrique Diseo were among the first wave of lyricists to capture the significance of the tango in words.

The music of the early tango ensembles and orchestras, now referred to as the Old Guard, began to give way to a new wave in the 1920s. The Guardia Nueva (New Guard) projected a more sophisticated approach to the tango, milonga, and other popular genres. An expanded harmonic vocabulary, the use of violin countermelodies to the main theme, and more solo use of the piano and the bandoneón were characteristic of the evolved tango. A short list of the many composers of the New Guard includes Gardel, Enrique Delfino, Juan de Dios Filiberto, Julio De Caro, Osvaldo Fresedo, Francisco Lomuto, and Enrique Santos Discépolo.

Women also played an important role in the early development of the tango. Among the early singers were Pepita Avellaneda, Linda Thelma (who took the tango to the Moulin Rouge in Paris), and Lola Candales from Uruguay. Among the New Guard singers were Azucena Maizani, Rosita Quiroga, Mercedes Simone, **Libertad Lamarque** ("Queen of the Tango"), and Amanda Ledesma, who figured prominently in tango films. Among women singers of the late twentieth century are Susana Rinaldi (celebrated as the most popular interpreter of the tangos of Enrique Santos

Discépolo) and Amelita Baltar (best known for her performances of "Balada para un loco" [Ballad for a Crazy Man] by **Astor Piazzola**).

By the 1940s the tango was in artistic decline and approaching obsolescence. Among the composers in the vanguard who did develop a style of tango more relevant to the times were Domingo Federico and Aníbal Troilo. Troilo's former florid, virtuoso style of playing the bandoneón was abandoned in favor of a more brusque, aggressive, and urban style supporting the vocalist.

During the early twentieth century the refined tango achieved immense popularity in Europe and the Americas. Vernon and Irene Castle introduced the stylized dance version to the United States, creating a dance craze that swept the country in spite of the objections of some that it was a serious threat to the nation's morality.

Later in the century the contemporary dancer Milena Plebs, who had been introduced to tango as a form of entertainment during the 1980s, brought tango shows to the concert stage. **Ana María Stekelman,** choreographer and former artistic director of the Ballet Contemporáneo del **Teatro San Martín** in Buenos Aires, studied tango with the same dance teacher, Miguel Angel Zotto. She choreographed and commissioned choreography that modernized tango, placing it in a theatrical or dramatic context, complete with both homo- and heterosexual innuendos.

By the early 1990s approximately one hundred tango clubs existed in Buenos Aires, a far smaller number than there are discotheques, but a far greater number than there were in the late 1980s. Celebrated equally as dance and as romantic song, over the years the tango has periodically returned in waves of popularity to Latin America, Europe, and the United States. Its continuing popularity is ensured by new recordings, touring tango groups, avant-garde groups in Paris, and specialized studies in universities and conservatories.

REFERENCES:

Rodolfo Arizaga, *Enciclopedia de la música argentina* (Buenos Aires: Fondo Nacional de las Artes, 1971);

Jorge Cardoso, *Musical Rhythms and Forms of South America,* translated by Pilar Alvarez (San Francisco: Guitar Solo Publications, 1986);

Vicente Gesualdo, *La música en la argentina* (Buenos Aires: Editorial Stella, 1988);

Peter Manuel, *Popular Musics of the Non-Western World* (Oxford: Oxford University Press, 1988);

Jaime Rico Salazar, *Carlos Gardel: Su vida y sus canciones* (Bogotá: Centro Editorial de Estudios Musicales, 1991).

—R.L.S. & J.M.H.

TANGO GUITARISTS

The earliest **tangos** were played by tercetos (trios) consisting of violin, flute, and guitar. The guitar had been an essential instrument for the **payadors** and the performance of the **milonga,** which preceded the development of the tango. Eventually the flute was replaced by the **bandoneón,** but the guitar remained an essential instrument, especially for the accompaniment of performances of vocal solos and duos. Such was the case during the early career of **Carlos Gardel,** who provided his own guitar accompaniment for folkloric songs. When Gardel joined forces with José Razzano, a talented payador, it became obvious that Razzano's guitar technique was much superior, and so Gardel focused his attention on the vocal interpretation.

Gardel's successes attracted the finest guitarists available; six of them formed the nucleus of his accompanists. José Razzano had become a popular singer-guitarist in the bars and clubs of Buenos Aires by 1911. A friendly competition developed between Razzano and Gardel, who sang in different clubs, until they began to visit and perform with each other. In 1913 they began to work together professionally as a duo. Beginning in 1917 they made primitive recordings on the Nacional-Odeón label. They were accompanied by the composer-guitarist José Ricardo, who recorded some seventy-one titles with the Gardel-Razzano duo. He was their only guitarist until 1921 and continued to accompany them sporadically until 1929.

Guillermo Desiderio Barbieri, a distinguished singer, guitarist, and composer, made his first recording with the Gardel-Razzano duo in 1921 and replaced Ricardo after his retirement in 1929. José María Aguilar joined the ensemble in 1928 for a tour of Europe. He had accompanied several of the popular women singers of the time, including Azucena Maizani and **Libertad Lamarque.** He left the Gardel-Razzano ensemble in 1931 but maintained a working relationship with Gardel; Aguilar survived the plane crash that killed Gardel. Angel Domingo Riverol was another guitarist who had joined the ensemble in 1930, having also accompanied Libertad Lamarque and others; he, however, perished with Gardel in the Medellín tragedy.

Domingo Julio Vivas, a prolific composer of tangos, accompanied Gardel on guitar and bandoneón from 1931 to 1933, an important period of recordings. A composer-guitarist who was prominent in Gardel's French-made films was Giracui Potterossi. Potterossi accompanied Gardel to New York and made a total of sixty recordings with him.

The Teatro Colón in Buenos Aires, Argentina

REFERENCES:

Rodolfo Arizaga, *Enciclopedia de la música argentina* (Buenos Aires: Fondo Nacional de las Artes, 1971);

Pedro Malavet Vega, *Cincuenta años no es nada* (San Juan, Puerto Rico: Editora Corripio, 1986).

— R.L.S.

TEATRO COLÓN

The Teatro Colón in Buenos Aires, Argentina, is one of the world's best-known theaters, known as much for its ornateness (French renaissance style) and impressive size and acoustics as for the scope of orchestral, chamber, operatic, ballet, and other performances it has presented since it opened in 1908 with a performance of *Aida*. Best known as an opera house, the Teatro Colón has hosted many of the stars of the twentieth century. It has also been the chosen place to premiere some works that have become part of the standard repertoire, such as Manuel de Falla's "Noches en los jardines de España" (Nights in the Gardens of Spain). Similarly, it has been the showplace of famous touring ballet companies, such as the Ballets Russes.

The theater has four resident artistic bodies: its own ballet corps, orchestra, and chorus, and the Buenos Aires Philharmonic Orchestra. It also has a library, a museum, and a ballet school. Annually there are about two hundred evening performances. The resi-

dent ballet company, the Ballet Estable del Teatro Colón, whose dancers are government employees, is based in the rotunda, a large circular room below the stage. In 1938 the Teatro Colón became the home of the school attached to the Municipal Ballet of Buenos Aires, a school and company directed by choreographer Margaret Wallman, who was named permanent director the same year. Under Wallman's directorship from 1938 to 1950, the company grew to number one hundred dancers, and the repertory grew from eight to more than fifty ballets, both traditional and modern. Argentinean composers were commissioned to write scores for ballets. Guest choreographers invited by Wallman included Leonide Massine, David Lichine, George Balanchine, and Bronislava Nijinska. The Taller Coreográfico, or Choreography Workshop, is another activity of the Teatro Colón. The Colón Theater Foundation, established in 1978, collaborates with the ballet company and with the Instituto Superior de Arte (also affiliated with the Teatro Colón) in giving grants to dance students and in organizing dance classes.

— N.D.B. & J.M.H.

EL TECHO DE LA BALLENA

The Venezuelan avant-garde group El Techo de la Ballena (The Roof of the Whale) began in 1961 with the publication of a manifesto stating their purpose as the attempt to revitalize the "placid mood of what passes for national culture." A third manifesto (1964) declares the group's affinities with Surrealism, Dadaism, the Beat Generation, and Marxism. (The point has been made that the group's militance is the artistic correlate of the armed insurrection waged in Caracas in the 1960s by Cuban-inspired guerrillas.) What sets this Venezuelan group apart from other analogous groups in Latin America in the same period is the important role played by the plastic arts in the elaboration of a general aesthetic program. The public events sponsored by the group tended to be art exhibits.

The group's name was deliberately ambiguous, though references to the biblical story of Jonah and the whale and to Herman Melville's Captain Ahab recur in the group's manifestos. (No explicit mention is made of the fact that **Jorge Luis Borges** uses "roof of the whale," meaning the sea, in one of his essays as an example of the *kenningar,* the metaphorical circumlocutions typical of Old Norse poetry.) Some of the group's members were poets Caupolicán Ovalles, Edmundo Aray, Juan Calzadilla, Francisco Pérez Perdomo, and Efraín Hurtado; prose writers **Salvador Garmendia** and Adriano González León; and painters Carlos Contramaestre, J. M. Cruxent, and **Jacobo Borges.** The tenuous coherence of the group ended in 1968.

— R.G.M.

TELENOVELAS

Telenovelas (soap operas) are watched by millions of viewers in every country and city of Latin America, where they are the paradigm of contemporary, urban popular culture. Several features characterize a Spanish American telenovela: first, a simple, black-and-white, sociopolitical message (for example, landowners are evil, and peasants are good, as in the Colombian soap opera *Manuela,* set during the Wars of Independence); second, a setting in a neutral, middle-class home that could be anywhere in Latin America (the action often takes place indoors); third, a fundamental discovery scene in which the main character finds out that his or her father is really someone else and that the protagonist's real family is noble or upper class. Such a scene occurs, for example, in *Esmeralda, La mentira* (Esmeralda, the Lie), *Renzo el Gitano* (Renzo the Gypsy), *Laura, volverás a mis brazos* (Laura, You'll Come Back to Me), *La ciudad grita* (The City Screams), and *Natacha,* as well as in the two best-known early soap operas, *El derecho de nacer* (The Right to Be Born) from Mexico and *Simplemente María* (Simply Maria) from Peru (both broadcast in the 1960s).

Mexico has been one of the most prolific exporters of telenovelas to other Spanish American countries as well as to Spain. The Mexican telenovela formula — melodrama, family crises, crime, love, sex, marital infidelity — has dominated the Spanish-speaking media market and has been successfully imitated by the Argentinean telenovela industry, which now ranks third, behind Brazil and Mexico, in the production and export of soap operas. An Argentinean soap of the late 1980s and early 1990s, *Amo y señor* (Master and Husband), for example, centers on the traumatic and illicit love affairs of several couples and the problems created by infidelity. Set in neutral middle-class urban surroundings (recognizably Buenos Aires), *Amo y señor* is love-centered, at times bordering on the maudlin, from a man's viewpoint. Another Argentinean soap opera, *Dulce visión* (Sweet Vision), which follows a similar plot formula, is more female-centered and involves tragic love affairs, financial scandals, dramas arranged around the need to keep information from certain people, and melodrama (in one episode, for example, a girl finds out who her parents were, quite by accident, from a stranger).

In Colombia telenovelas are monopolized by the three main television companies, known as the "pool," namely, Punch, R.T.I., and Caracol. In a study conducted in 1980, only one of the six telenovelas on the air was not produced by the pool. Soap operas are aired in Colombia at the beginning of the two slots when commercial television begins, 11:00 A.M. and 4:00 P.M.; according to the pool, telenovelas turn on television sets.

The telenovela is an example of urban popular culture that is not politically oppositional. Its typical protagonist — who is born into one social class, is raised in another, and returns to his or her original class — legitimizes myths of the dominant social class; that is, the telenovela accepts rather than questions social practice.

REFERENCES:

Azriel Bibliowicz, "Be Happy Because Your Father Isn't Your Father. An Analysis of Colombian *Telenovelas,*" *Journal of Popular Culture,* 14 (Winter 1980): 476–485;

William Rowe and Vivian Schelling, *Memory and Modernity: Popular Culture in Latin America* (London: Verso, 1991);

Joseph Straubhaar, "Television," in *Handbook of Latin American Popular Culture,* edited by Harold E. Hinds Jr. and Charles M. Tatum (Westport, Conn.: Greenwood Press, 1985), pp. 111–134.

— S.M.H.

TESTIMONIAL NARRATIVE

Testimonio, or testimony (the word in Spanish suggests the act of testifying or giving witness in a legal or religious sense), refers to a type of writing denouncing social or political injustice, and it has acquired increasing prominence in the second half of the century. Testimonial narrative was formally recognized as a genre in 1970, when the **Casa de las Américas,** the main cultural institution of revolutionary Cuba, established a separate category for testimonio in its annual contest. The rules for entries specified that testimonial narrative should document some aspect of Latin American or Caribbean reality from a direct source and should demonstrate literary excellence. The genre is formally characterized by the use of a first-person narrator (whose access to the reader is usually mediated by a transcriptor) and by the recounting of a significant life experience.

Although drawing on personal experience, testimonio differs from lives narrated in autobiographies, autobiographical novels, or bildungsromans (novels of education). Its time span follows a different convention (that of bearing witness to the events recounted), and the speaker's subjectivity is constituted or interpreted collectively. "Authors" of narrative testimonials are generally speakers inhabiting the margins of mainstream society or disempowered by traditional literary forms: ethnic minorities, revolutionaries, or schizophrenics. Although many antecedents of the genre may be found in Latin American culture (including **Ernesto "Che" Guevara**'s account of the Cuban guerrilla war, *Reminiscences of the Cuban Revolutionary War,* 1959), the first major work of testimonial narrative is Miguel Barnet's *Biografía de un cimarrón* (1967; translated as *Autobiography of a Runaway Slave*), which transcribes several interviews between a Cuban ethnographer and a former Cuban slave who lived to see Fidel Castro's revolution. Other well-known examples of the genre are Omar Cabezas's *La montaña es algo más que una inmensa estepa verde* (1985; translated as *Fire from the Mountain*) and Elena Poniatowska's *Hasta no verte Jesús mío* (1969; translated as *Until I See You My Jesus*).

Texts written by women and providing a gender-inflected view of political injustice and racial violence include Domitila Barrios de Chungara's *"Si me permiten hablar . . .": Testimonio de Domitila, una mujer de las minas de Bolivia* (1977; translated as *Let Me Speak! Testimony of Domitila, A Woman of the Bolivian Mines*) and Elizabeth Burgos's *Me llamo Rigoberta Menchú* (1983; translated as *I, Rigoberta Menchú*). The **Guerra Sucia** (Dirty War) in Argentina and the oppressive regime of Gen. **Augusto Pinochet** in Chile also provided the impetus for many such narratives: Alejandro Witker's *Prisión en Chile* (1975; Prison in Chile), Rodrigo Rojas's *Jamás de rodillas* (1974; Never on My Knees), Rolando Carrasco's *Prigué* (1977; translated as *Chile's Prisoners of War*), Aníbal Quijada

Cerda's *Cerco de púas* (1977; Barbed Wire), and Manuel Cabieses's *Chile: 11808 horas en campos de concentración* (1975; *Chile: 11808 Hours in Concentration Camps*). An exception to the leftist bent of testimonial narrative is Armando Valladares's *Contra toda esperanza* (1985; translated as *Against All Hope*), an account of the author's experience in a Cuban prison.

A distinction is sometimes made between testimonial and documentary narrative; documentary narrative, like testimonio, is based on empirical historical and political events, but unlike testimonio, documentary involves a conscious artistic re-creation of the events concerned. Colombian novelist **Gabriel García Márquez**'s narrative based on a real shipwreck is typical; its extraordinarily long title is *Relato de un náufrago que estuvo diez días a la deriva en una balsa sin comer ni beber, que fue proclamado héroe de la patria, besado por las reinas de la belleza y hecho rico por la publicidad, y luego aborrecido por el gobierno y olvidado para siempre* (1970; translated as *The Story of a Shipwrecked Sailor, Who Drifted on a Life Raft for Ten Days without Food or Water, Was Proclaimed a National Hero, Kissed by Beauty Queens, Made Rich through Publicity, and Then Spurned by the Government and Forgotten for All Time*). Other examples are Argentinean novelist and movie director Rodolfo Walsh's *Operación masacre* (1957; translated as *Operation Massacre*); Elena Poniatowska's *La noche de Tlatelolco* (1971; translated as *The Night of Tlatelolco*), which documents the massacre of students in Mexico City on 2 October 1968 as a result of a political demonstration; and Chilean Hernán Valdés's *Tejas Verdes: Diario de un campo de concentración* (1974; translated as *Tejas Verdes: Diary of a Concentration Camp*), an artistic re-creation of the author's experience of incarceration.

REFERENCES:

John Beverley, "The Margin at the Center: On Testimonio," in *Against Literature* (Minneapolis: University of Minnesota Press, 1993), pp. 69–86;

René Jara and Hernán Vidal, eds., *Testimonio y literatura* (Minneapolis: Institute for the Study of Ideologies & Literature, 1986);

Charles Tatum, "Paraliterature," in *Handbook of Latin American Literature,* edited by David William Foster (New York & London: Garland, 1992), pp. 687–728.

— S.M.H., R.G.M. & P.S.

THEATER

The theater in Spanish America has not reached the same levels of development as **poetry** and **fiction.** Only

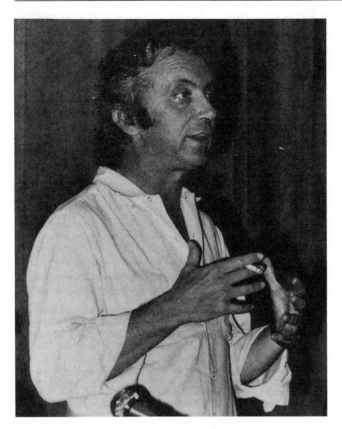

Argentinean playwright Osvaldo Dragún, who in 1981 helped to found the Teatro Abierto (Open Theater), a group that worked to revitalize the national theater of his native country

the largest capital cities (Buenos Aires and Mexico City first, Santiago and Caracas in more recent decades) have been able to support a theater establishment, but even here the predominance of commercial theater (feeding on the production of foreign plays) has tended to suppress the evolution of a properly national and artistic theater. Actors are often amateurs, and many plays never reach the stage. Frequently playwrights themselves are "amateurs," that is, novelists or poets who make successful incursions into the theater. Most of the novelists associated with the "Boom" (**Gabriel García Márquez, Mario Vargas Llosa,** Carlos Fuentes, **José Donoso,** and **Manuel Puig**) have written plays and have seen their plays produced, sometimes outside their own countries.

The most successful Latin American play of recent times, *La muerte y la doncella* (1992; translated as *Death and the Maiden*), was written by **Ariel Dorfman,** a Chilean essayist, poet, and novelist. University troupes — such as the Teatro Experimental de la Universidad de Chile (dating from 1940) — have been instrumental in stimulating and preserving a tradition of

avant-garde theater in some South American countries, while outfits such as the Teatro Popular, founded by Leónidas Barletta in Buenos Aires in the early 1930s, have made a difference in the formation of at least a semblance of a national tradition. In the Southern Cone the military dictatorships of the 1970s had a major and contradictory effect on the theater. On the one hand, actors and playwrights were persecuted and often detained; but on the other hand, theater auditoriums became gathering places for the populace at a time when public meetings and "culture" as a whole were looked upon with hostility by the henchmen of the various military regimes.

Still, it would be wrong to neglect theater in an overall assessment of Latin American literary culture, particularly in the years after 1945, when European avant-garde tendencies were felt in the South American continent and in Mexico. Individual accomplishments have compensated for the structural deficiencies of the theatrical institution. Some of the major Spanish American playwrights of the twentieth century are **Osvaldo Dragún, Griselda Gambaro, Egon Wolff, Jorge Díaz,** Enrique Buenaventura, Carlos Solórzano, and Isaac Chocrón. Older figures include Rodolfo Usigli, Celestino Gorostiza, and René Marqués. (See **Poetry** and **Fiction**.)

REFERENCES:

Marina Gálvez Acero, *El teatro hispanoamericano* (Madrid: Taurus, 1988);

Frank Dauster, *Historia del teatro hispanoamericano* (Mexico City: Ediciones de Andrea, 1973);

George W. Woodyard, *Dramatists in Revolt: The New Latin American Theater* (Austin: University of Texas Press, 1975).
                          — R.G.M.

TIPLE

The tiple is a **chordophone,** the most typical Creole instrument of Colombia. The main body of the tiple is in the form of the figure eight, resembling a small guitar. It has four courses of three strings each, tuned the same as the upper four strings of the guitar. The strings of the first course are tuned in unison; in the other courses the outer strings are tuned to an octave above the middle one to add to the sonority.

The tiple is especially adept at providing harmonic accompaniment, but it may also fulfill melodic roles. Pairs of tiples are often cast in ensemble with guitar and **bandola** for Creole genres such as the **bambuco** (both vocal and instrumental forms), the sanjuanito, and the pasillo (a Creole imitation of the European waltz).

REFERENCE:

Octavio Marulanda, *El folclor de Colombia: Práctica de la identidad cultural* (Bogotá: Artestudio Editores, 1984).

— R.L.S.

LEOPOLDO TORRE NILSSON

Leopoldo Torre Nilsson (circa 1930–   ) was one of the first major movie directors of Argentina. In 1955 he made his first major film, *Graciela,* a type of feminine bildungsroman that explores the corruption of adolescence by the adult world. It concentrates on the story of a young girl who attends a university in Buenos Aires and meets unusual individuals in her lodgings. Much of her awakening to the adult world centers on her gradual awareness of her own sexuality.

By the late 1950s Torre Nilsson's work demonstrated artistic maturity. *La casa del ángel* (1957; The House of the Angel) was included in the newly established London Film Festival and in the Cannes Film Festival, where it received unqualified praise. In this film Torre Nilsson explored the contradictions and decline of Argentinean upper-class and genteel bourgeois society; other themes include the clash between the protagonist and his environment, the relationship between childhood and adulthood, and the lack of communication between individuals.

La caída (1959; The Fall) was also an international success. Similar in setting to *Graciela,* the movie focuses on Albertina, scion of a conservative family, who goes to study in Buenos Aires and rents a room in a house dominated by four ill-behaved little children. Again the film emphasizes the lack of communication between individuals. Torre Nilsson tended to work with the same team of scriptwriter, technicians, and a few favorite actors: Elsa Daniel, Lautaro Murúa, Leonardo Favio, Graciela Borges, and the avant-garde musician **Juan Carlos Paz.** Though he was already well known by the 1960s, Torre Nilsson's later cinematic projects were plagued with financial difficulties.

REFERENCE:

John King, *Magical Reels: A History of Cinema in Latin America* (London: Verso, 1990).

— S.M.H.

AUGUSTO TORRES

A son of **Joaquín Torres-García** and a member of the **Taller Torres-García** (TTG), Uruguayan artist Augusto Torres (1913–   ) was born in Barcelona. After his family settled in Paris in 1926, he studied with the Cubists Julio González and Amadée Ozenfant and worked for the Musée du Trocadéro (now Musée de l'Homme), where he learned about tribal and pre-Columbian art. Augusto studied art with his father when the Torres-García family lived in Madrid in 1933; when they settled in Uruguay in 1934 he joined the Asociación de Arte Constructivo (1935–1940). By then his works combined translucent geometric shapes with an expressive treatment of the surface: in *Dibujo* (1937; Drawing) he includes subtle references to non-Western art, while in his painting *Naturaleza muerta en blanco y negro* (1937; Still Life in White and Black) he reveals his preference for still life.

During the 1940s Torres was a teacher of drawing and painting at the TTG, and as a member he participated in the mural decoration of the Saint Bois Hospital and produced numerous works in the **Constructive Art** style of the taller, such as the painting *Construcción en cinco colores* (1945; Construction in Five Colors). After his father's death in 1949, Torres returned to Europe; in the early 1960s he received a scholarship from the New School for Social Research and moved to New York. He returned to Uruguay in 1962 and since 1973 has alternated between homes in Montevideo and Barcelona. Since the 1960s Torres has concentrated on still life, subtly retaining from his earlier constructive period the orthogonal compositional structures and the transformation of recognizable objects into geometrized symbols, which prevents his figuration from becoming overly realistic.

REFERENCE:

Mari Carmen Ramírez, ed., *The Taller Torres-García: The School of the South and Its Legacy* (Austin: University of Texas Press, 1992).

— F.B.N.

HORACIO TORRES

Uruguayan artist Horacio Torres (1924–1976) was one of **Joaquín Torres-García**'s sons and a member of the **Taller Torres-García.** He was born in Livorno, Italy, and lived in Europe until his family settled in Montevideo in 1934, where, in spite of his youth, he studied art with his father and joined the Asociación de Arte Constructivo (1935–1940). He was also a member of the taller from its beginnings and participated in all its activities, including the 1944 mural decoration of the Saint Bois Hospital. After his father's death in 1949, he continued working at the taller, except from 1955 to 1957, when he traveled throughout Europe. Until the 1960s Torres worked in the taller's style of **Constructive Art,** applying it to a variety of media, including painting, cast cement, and cut brick reliefs, pottery, and wrought iron.

A Constructivist mural painted by Augusto Torres in the dining room of the Medical Association of Montevideo, Uruguay, 1953–1954

After Torres settled in New York in 1969, his art started to change. He abandoned Constructive Art and began to paint large canvases focusing on realistic depictions of female nudes, such as *Fragmento de desnudo sobre paños verdes* (1972; Fragment of Nude on Green Drapery). He adopted a traditional old-masters style, which he used with flair and elegance, retaining from his earlier constructive manner only the tendency to see his subject abstractly, in spite of his realism, by focusing on patterns of forms and colors rather than on the personality of the model.

REFERENCE:
Mari Carmen Ramírez, ed., *The Taller Torres-García: The School of the South and Its Legacy* (Austin: University of Texas Press, 1992).

— F.B.N.

Joaquín Torres-García

Joaquín Torres-García (1874–1949) had a leading role in avant-garde trends in Europe and in Latin America, where he introduced his **Constructive Art**, a monumen-

tal synthesis of Cubism, neoplasticism, **Surrealism,** and pre-Columbian art forms. Born in Montevideo, Torres-García studied art in Barcelona and later executed important commissions there, such as the design for the stained-glass windows of Antoni Gaudí's Sagrada Familia and the mural decoration of the Saló de Sant Jordi in Barcelona's Palace of the Generalitat (regional government). During World War I Torres-García met several avant-garde artists seeking refuge in Barcelona, such as the Uruguayan **Rafael Barradas,** whose **Vibrationist** style influenced Torres-García's art until the early 1920s. After a short period in New York, Torres-García returned to Europe and finally settled in Paris in 1927, where he developed Constructive Art and helped to found the Cercle et Carré, a short-lived group of avant-garde artists, including Piet Mondrian and Michel Seuphor, who worked in geometric styles and actively opposed the spread of Surrealism. Due to the worsening political and economic situation in Europe, in 1934 Torres-García returned to Montevideo, where he extensively exhibited his work and lectured about the latest avant-garde developments in Europe, still unknown in Uruguay. With the objective of introducing Constructive Art into Uruguay and developing

Joaquín Torres-García in his studio

it into an art form unique to the Americas, he formed the Asociación de Arte Constructivo and later the **Taller Torres-García,** which had an enormous influence in Uruguay and throughout Latin America.

Torres-García's version of European Constructivism, which he called Constructive Art or Constructive Universalism, effectively synthesized innovative aspects of different avant-garde movements. In paintings such as *Composición constructiva* (1943; Constructive Composition) he combines the simplification of forms characteristic of Cubism, the use of symbolic archetypes of Surrealism, and the compositional orthogonal grid preferred by neoplasticists such as Piet Mondrian. Torres-García also included in this work and in many others — such as his painting on hide, *Indoamérica* (1938; Indo-America), or his granite sculpture *Monumento cosmico* (1938; Cosmic Monument) — archetypes found in the arts of the pre-Inca cultures and Amerindian peoples such as the Hopi, in order to transform his modernist project into an art rooted in the Americas.

REFERENCES:

Valerie Fletcher, ed., *Crosscurrents of Modernism: Four Latin American Pioneers: Diego Rivera, Joaquín Torres-García, Wifredo Lam, Matta* (Washington, D.C.: Hirshhorn Museum & Sculpture Garden, 1992);

Mari Carmen Ramírez, ed., *The Taller Torres-García: The School of the South and Its Legacy* (Austin: University of Texas Press, 1992).

— F.B.N.

MARTA TRABA

Art critic and novelist Marta Traba (1930–1983), born in Buenos Aires and killed in a plane crash near Madrid, lived most of her life away from Argentina, especially in Colombia, where she founded the Museum of Modern Art. She was a frequent lecturer at United States universities and had settled in Paris shortly before her death. Traba's best-known work as a creative writer is the novel *Conversación al sur* (1981; translated as *Mothers and Shadows*), a dialogue between

Marta Traba (photograph by Orlando García Valverde)

two women — an older actress without political convictions and a younger activist who has been tortured — in which the political tragedy of the Southern Cone in the 1970s is re-created in its full horror. The story skips from Montevideo to Buenos Aires to Santiago, cities under military occupation in which friends and relatives of the principal interlocutors undergo prison, torture, and deportation when they are not "disappeared." The oral tone and political emphasis of the novel are superficially reminiscent of **testimonial narrative.** Traba also published *Las ceremonias del verano* (1966; Summer Rites), winner of the **Casa de las Américas** Prize; *Los laberintos insolados* (1967; The Dazed Labyrinths); and *Homérica Latina* (1979). Two posthumous publications are *En cualquier lugar* (1984; In Any Place) and *De la mañana a la noche: Cuentos norteamericanos* (1986; From Morning to Night: North American Stories).

REFERENCE:
Evelyn Picón Garfield, "Marta Traba," in her *Women's Voices from Latin America: Interviews with Six Contemporary Authors* (Detroit: Wayne State University Press, 1985).
— R.G.M.

TRISTE

As its name indicates, the triste is a sad song of Andean antiquity, whose text often relates a painful experience of love. Tristes originating in indigenous areas emphasize the haunting qualities of the pentatonic scale. As the triste's popularity spread to include Creole populations and urban areas, European major and minor scales were mixed with the pentatonic.

The sentimental character of the verse of the triste contrasts with the more lively rhythmic movement of the refrain, which is sometimes played on **quena** flutes rather than sung. Instruments typically accompanying the triste in addition to the quena are the **charango** and the **bombo.**

REFERENCES:
Isabel Aretz, *El folklore musical argentino* (Buenos Aires: Ricordi Americana S.A.E.C., 1952);
Rodolfo Arizaga, *Enciclopedia de la música argentina* (Buenos Aires: Fondo Nacional de las Artes, 1971).
— R.L.S.

TZANTICOS

Tzanticos are a group of 1960s Ecuadoran poets known for their social poetry and for their militant stance on behalf of Indian rights. *Tzantico* (meaning "headshrinker") comes from the Shuar language of a large Amazonian nation formerly known as *jíbaros,* a derogatory term meaning "savages." The Tzanticos poets published in the review *Pucuna* (blowgun), founded in 1962. Euler Granda, the author of *La voz desbordada* (1962; The Overflowing Voice) and *El lado flaco* (1968; The Weak Side), is the best-known Tzantico poet. **Aldo Pellegrini**'s *Antología de la poesía viva latinoamericana* (1966; Anthology of the Living Poetry of Latin America) contains a representative sample of Tzantico poetry.

REFERENCES:
Eduardo Escobar, *Manifiestos nadaístas* (Bogotá: Arango Editores, 1992);
Angel Rama, *Antología de 'El Techo de la Ballena'* (Caracas: Fundarte, 1987).
— R.G.M.

U

UKUMAU

The Ukumau group was a collaborative movie production venture based in Bolivia and led by director **Jorge Sanjinés;** the production group was called Ukumau Films, and the principal cinematographer was **Antonio Eguino.** Sanjinés and his collaborators produced several features in the late 1960s and early 1970s, the best known of which is *Yawar Malku* (1969; Blood of the Condor). It deals, in semidocumentary fashion, with an alleged campaign carried out by members of the U.S. Peace Corps against the native Indians and urges the preservation of the Indian heritage and cultural identity. Their next feature, *El coraje del pueblo* (1971; *The Courage of the People,* also released as *The Night of San Juan*), used survivors and witnesses to reconstruct a massacre of striking workers by the army. Soon after its release, in another shift of the government toward reaction and repression, filmmaking in Bolivia was severely limited, and Sanjinés fled into exile in Chile. Eguino, one of the founding members of the Ukumau group, decided to stay in Bolivia and make films that could be tolerated by the Bolivian censorship board.

REFERENCES:

Julianne Burton, *Cinema and Social Change in Latin America: Conversations with Film-makers* (Austin: University of Texas Press, 1986);

Jorge A. Schnitman, *Film Industries in Latin America* (Norwood, N.J.: ABLEX, 1984).

— S.M.H.

A scene from *Yawar Malku* (1969; Blood of the Condor), produced by the Ukumau group of Bolivia

UGO ULIVE

Ugo Ulive (circa 1935–), the Uruguayan movie director, began his career working in theater and went into documentaries in the mid 1950s. He made a fifty-minute fictional film, *Un vintén p'al Judas* (1959; A Dime for the Judas), which tells of a failed **tango** singer who swindles his friend on Christmas Eve. Ulive next filmed *Como el Uruguay no hay* (1960; There's Nowhere like Uruguay), an attack on the stagnation of the two main political parties (the Blancos and the Colorados) and on the growing economic and social crisis in Uruguay. Impressed by his work, the Cuban Film Insti-

275

tute invited Ulive to work in Cuba. On his return to Uruguay in 1963 he teamed up with **Mario Handler,** and together they produced a documentary on the upcoming elections in Uruguay, *Elecciones* (1966; Elections). It was screened at the *Marcha* festival in 1967 but, given its antigovernment stance, was banned later in the same year. Nevertheless, the film did receive an important commercial release thanks to the enterprise of independent producer and exhibitor **Walter Achugar.**

REFERENCE:

John King, *Magical Reels: A History of Cinema in Latin America* (London: Verso, 1990).

— S.M.H.

ULTRAÍSMO

An avant-garde poetic movement, Ultraísmo was born in Spain in 1918 and transplanted to Argentina by **Jorge Luis Borges** in March 1921, when he returned from Europe. Borges had associated in Madrid with the Spanish Ultraists and was a great admirer of Rafael Cansinos Asséns, the movement's "godfather." In Spain, Ultraísmo had been a vaguely defined project to go beyond the horizons of traditional aesthetics, but in Argentina the movement acquired a programmatic character with the publication of a manifesto (written by Borges) in December 1921 in *Nosotros,* the most widely read magazine in Buenos Aires. In September 1922 the same magazine published an anthology of Ultraist poets, thus endorsing and consolidating the movement. In his manifesto Borges explained Ultraísmo as the reduction of lyric poetry to its essential element, metaphor; the elimination of transitions and useless adjectives; the abolition of ornamental rhetoric, confessional postures, and contrived ambiguity; and the synthesis of two or more images into one. Simultaneously with the publication of the manifesto, Borges and his collaborators devised a "mural review" called *Prisma* (Prism) and plastered the walls of Buenos Aires with it, thus making up in showiness for the poster's lack of theoretical precision. The signatories of the inaugural issue of *Prisma* included Guillermo Juan, Guillermo de Torre, and Eduardo González Lanuza, whose book *Prismas* (1924) would be identified by Borges as the "archetypal" Ultraist work. (Borges's own poetry of the 1920s, however, diverges from the Ultraist creed in significant respects; his true Ultraist poems belong to an earlier period and were published by various Spanish journals). Two other publications are associated with Ultrism: *Proa* (1922–1923; 1924–1926) and *Martín Fierro* (1924–1927).

Guillermo Uribe-Holguín

REFERENCE:

Gloria Videla, *El ultraísmo* (Madrid: Gredos, 1971).

— R.G.M.

GUILLERMO URIBE-HOLGUÍN

The most influential Colombian composer of his generation, Guillermo Uribe-Holguín (1880–1971) was exposed early in his career to music in New York and Mexico City. To survive in New York he worked making popular music transcriptions (waltzes, marches, and other dances); he even tried to make a transcription of Richard Wagner's Overture to Tannhauser for banjo, an instrument that he had never seen or heard. In 1907 he began studies at the famous Schola Cantorum in Paris with the renowned composer-teacher Vincent d'Indy and also studied violin in Brussels. Although d'Indy was not an advocate of impressionism, Uribe-Holguín was thoroughly exposed to its influence in Paris, an influence that eventually revealed itself in his works. Following his return to Colombia, he became director of the Conservatorio Nacional (1910), a position he held for twenty-five years. In that role and as an active conductor-composer, he exerted considerable influence on generations of Colombian composers. After 1943 he retired from public activities in order to concentrate on composition.

He was a prolific composer with a favorable disposition toward his own musical culture. The titles of many of his works reveal the nationalistic flavor of his music: *Bochica* (symphonic poem), *Sinfonietta campesina* (country symphonietta; for small orchestra and piano), *Conquistadores* (symphonic poem), *300 trozos en el sentimiento popular* (300 pieces in popular sentiment for piano). He also composed eleven symphonies whose contents, if not titles, reflect his cultural identity.

REFERENCES:

Gerard Béhague, *Latin American Music: An Introduction* (Englewood Cliffs, N.J.: Prentice-Hall, 1979);

Composers of the Americas, volume 1 (Washington, D.C.: Pan American Union, General Secretariat, Organization of American States, 1995).

— R.L.S.

Mario Urteaga

Mario Urteaga (1875–1957) was a Peruvian painter from Cajamarca, an area rich in native traditions, which were often the themes of his paintings. Because of his choice of subject matter, art historians connect his work with **Indigenism,** but he was not an active member of this group. Urteaga spent all his life in a small town, which he left only once to go to Lima. He lived on a small farm and worked as a schoolteacher, becoming interested in painting when he was already in his thirties. As a self-taught artist, he has often been compared to Pancho Fierro, a Peruvian painter of the nineteenth century.

Urteaga's work is too sophisticated to be considered primitive, but his lack of formal training sometimes betrays a certain arbitrariness in the perspective of his paintings and the simplification of his figures. On the other hand, in many of his works in the 1930s, including *El entierro* (The Burial), *Regreso de los campesinos* (The Return of the Peasants), and *Los novios* (The Betrothed), he was successful in conveying a lyrical and spontaneous mood while at the same time keenly recording the minute details of everyday events and traditions of his hometown. His representations are more dignified than charming and reflect a view of rural Peruvian life that avoids picturesque stereotypes. Urteaga's art became known and appreciated by a broader public when, with the support of the Indigenist

Arturo Uslar Pietri

painter Camilo Blas, he exhibited his works in Lima in 1935.

REFERENCE:

Teodoro Núñez Ureta, *Pintura contemporánea: Primera parte, 1820–1920* (Lima: Banco de Crédito del Perú, 1975).

— F.B.N.

Arturo Uslar Pietri

The doyen of modern Venezuelan letters, Arturo Uslar Pietri (1906–) established his literary reputation in Venezuela and elsewhere with the novel *Las lanzas coloradas* (1930; translated as *The Red Lances*). In the late 1920s Uslar Pietri began publishing stories with the express purpose of revitalizing Venezuelan fiction by freeing it from the shackles of **Costumbrismo** and **Criollismo.** He distinguished himself in the genre of the historical novel with *Las lanzas coloradas,* a work about the wars for Venezuelan independence in the early nineteenth century. In his second novel, *El camino de El Dorado* (1947; The Road to Eldorado), Uslar goes further back in time to the days of the Spanish conquest and narrates the life of the rebel conquistador Lope de Aguirre. In 1954 Uslar was awarded the National Prize for Literature, but in the following decade of the Latin American **Boom,** Uslar could only manage a failed trilogy of novels about the Venezuela of the 1930s and 1940s, of which only two volumes were published. In 1976 he published a fictional biography of the Venezuelan dictator Juan Vicente Gómez with the title *Oficio de difuntos* (1976; Mass for the Dead), which fell short of the mark set by other **dictatorship novels** published in the mid 1970s. His last two novels also belong to the historical genre: *La isla de Róbinson* (1981; Robinson's Island), an interesting account of Simón Bolívar's mentor Simón Rodríguez, and *La visita en el tiempo* (1990; A Visit in Time), based on the life of Don Juan de Austria, the hero of the battle of Lepanto (1571). In 1991 Uslar Pietri was awarded the **Premio Rómulo Gallegos de Novela** for *La visita en el tiempo.*

Uslar Pietri's cultural importance cannot be measured only in terms of novels and stories. Since 1948, when Uslar started a newspaper column in Caracas, his large journalistic output has reached beyond the borders of Venezuela, as have his historical and political essays, forty of which were collected as *Cuarenta ensayos* in 1990. Uslar's educational activities are not negligible either. In 1953 the novelist began a weekly cultural program, which ran for three decades on Venezuelan television. Earlier he had distinguished himself as a university professor both in Venezuela and at Columbia University in New York City, where he spent a few years in political exile. His *Breve historia de la novela hispanoamericana* (1954; Brief History of the Spanish American Novel) was the end product of the Columbia years. Uslar's involvement in politics dates from 1939 and lasted until 1973, when the aging writer formally announced his retirement. At that time he had been a senator since 1958. For over a decade Uslar Pietri was also editor of *El Nacional,* one of the two main Caracas newspapers. In 1975 he became Venezuelan ambassador to UNESCO and temporarily moved to Paris to carry out his duties. In 1979 Uslar Pietri returned to Venezuela, where he continues to play a high-profile role in public service. In 1990 he was awarded an important prize in Spain — the Príncipe de Asturias de las Letras — in recognition of his contributions to the enrichment of the Spanish language and to the common cultural heritage of Hispanic countries.

REFERENCES:

Teresita J. Parra, *Visión histórica en la obra de Arturo Uslar Pietri* (Madrid: Pliegos, 1993);

Alfredo Peña, *Conversaciones con Uslar Pietri* (Caracas: Editorial Ateneo, 1978).

— R.G.M.

V

EDGAR VALCÁRCEL

Teodoro Valcárcel's son, Edgar Valcárcel (1932–), is one of Peru's distinguished contemporary pianist-composers. Born in Puno like his father, Edgar pursued early musical studies in Peru (Catholic University and the National Conservatory of Peru) and later in Buenos Aires at the Torcuato di Tella Institute. Studies in the United States took him to Hunter College of New York and the Columbia-Princeton Center for Electronic Music. His avant-garde interests have included twelve-tone composition and mixed-media works. His works have been performed in Brazil, Venezuela, Germany, Mexico, Cuba, and the United States, where he has been an active participant in concerts and festivals sponsored by the **Organization of American States.** He was named Professor Honoris Causa at Puno University. He also received the National Award for Composition in Lima and the Inocente Carreño Composition Award in Caracas.

REFERENCE:

Gerard Béhague, *Music in Latin America: An Introduction* (Englewood Cliffs, N.J.: Prentice-Hall, 1979).

— R.L.S.

TEODORO VALCÁRCEL

One of the most important and prolific nationalist composers, Teodoro Valcárcel (1902–1942) was a native of Puno, on the shore of Lake Titicaca in the high Andes of southern Peru. His early studies were in Arequipa and were followed by travel to Italy. He returned to Peru at the outbreak of World War I.

Influenced by Claude Debussy for a time, he later became interested in his own Indian musical heritage, composing piano and orchestral works reflecting a

Teodoro Valcárcel

strong influence from indigenous folk music: *Suray-Surita,* a ballet; *En las ruinas del templo del Sol* (In the

Luisa Valenzuela in the late 1980s

Ruins of the Temple of Sun), a tone poem; and *Suite incaica* (Inca Suite), which premiered at the Barcelona Festival of Ibero-American Music in 1929. Subsequent concerts in Seville and Paris brought him critical and popular acclaim. Later works include *Cantos de alma vernacular* (Vernacular Songs of the Soul) and *Cuatro canciones incaicas* (Four Inca Songs), in which a Quechua text is employed.

REFERENCE:

Gerard Béhague, *Music in Latin America: An Introduction* (Englewood Cliffs, N.J.: Prentice-Hall, 1979).

— R.L.S.

LUISA VALENZUELA

Argentinean writer Luisa Valenzuela (1938–) was writer in residence at Columbia University in 1978 and at New York University in 1985, where she also was a faculty member in the Creative Writing Division for several years. Valenzuela's fiction is characterized by formal experimentation, the use of motifs drawn from Freudian and Lacanian psychoanalysis, and a preoccupation with the relation between politics and fiction stemming from the Argentinean historical crisis of the 1970s, the **Guerra Sucia** (Dirty War). All these traits come together in Valenzuela's most impressive novel, *Cola de lagartija* (1983; translated as *The Lizard's Tail*), which focuses on the shadowy figure of José López Rega, minister of social welfare in the second government of **Juan Domingo Perón** and founder of the right-wing group Triple A — Alianza Anticomunista Argentina (Argentinean Anticommunist Alliance) — a terrorist organization responsible for the assassination of hundreds of Argentineans identified as leftist sympathizers. After Perón's death in 1974 López Rega left for Spain and went into hiding but was brought back to Argentina in 1986 to be tried. Valenzuela's interest in López Rega derives not only from the latter's lust for power but also from his penchant for the occult. López Rega, known as "the Sorcerer," apparently wrote about esoteric practices such as Brazilian candomblé and macumba, believed in the transmigration of souls, and tried on various occasions to transfer **Eva Perón**'s soul to the living body of General Perón's second wife, María Estela "Isabelita" Martínez de Perón. Reportedly, he held a strange power over the general and also over Isabelita, who was president of Argentina between 1974 and 1976.

Cola de lagartija is a hallucinatory and macabre novel which Valenzuela wrote in an attempt to understand how a sophisticated nation could succumb to the spell of a sorcerer. The protagonist — called "the Sorcerer" — rules the Kingdom of the Black Lagoon somewhere in the jungle marshlands and must nourish his power through countless sacrificial victims. He is endowed with three testicles, the third one a kind of embryonic cyst from which his heir will arise. His power is such that the novel's author-narrator — called "Luisa Valenzuela" — begins to lose her grip on the narrative as the Sorcerer's "novel" is superimposed on her own. As otherworldly as this novel seems — indeed, it could be argued that the Sorcerer's kingdom is a symbolic representation of the unconscious — it is built with the elements of contemporary Argentinean history. The remoteness of the Kingdom of the Black Lagoon, where decisions are made affecting others in distant locations, reflects the secrecy that shrouds the workings of repressive regimes. The elaborate rituals performed at the Sorcerer's behest are but an exaggeration of López Rega's esoteric leanings and utter lack of scruples in condemning ("sacrificing") presumed enemies. Indeed, it is harder to believe in López Rega as a historical character than to give credit to Valenzuela's fictional double. The emphasis in the novel on dismemberment, mutilation, body deformities, and other forms of corporal defacement reflects the widespread practice of physical torture under the Argentinean military junta.

Other notable works by Luisa Valenzuela are *Aquí pasan cosas raras* (1975; translated as *Strange Things Happen Here*) and *Cambio de armas* (1982; translated as *Other Weapons*), both collections of stories dealing with themes related to the Argentinean political situation in the 1970s. The first, written upon the author's return to Buenos Aires after a prolonged sojourn abroad, captures the atmosphere of fear and suspicion hovering over the city at a moment of violent political crisis. City and country remain unidentified, thus ensuring imaginative freedom and reflecting the uncanny transformation of a familiar landscape into a hostile environment. *Cambio de armas* is a collection of five stories in which female protagonists struggle against institutionalized violence. Male characters appear in a variety of roles, all of them determined by the context of political violence: men are romantic objects, objects of erotic fantasy, helpers such as those in fairy tales who advance the hero or heroine's quest, and torturers enthralled by their victims (who, in turn, are held in thrall by the victimizers). "I'm Your Horse in the Night" is a compelling piece about the visitation of a lover in the middle of the night. The female narrator learns in the morning that her lover — a guerrilla fighter — has been killed some time ago and begins to doubt the reality of the visit but not of the dream of erotic love. The title is taken from Afro-Brazilian folklore and alludes to the belief that spirits can return and ride a receptive medium like a horse in the night. The title story deals with a woman devoid of memory and locked up by a military torturer who visits her regularly while his two henchmen wait outside the door and peek through the peephole. Voyeurism and sadomasochism, however, are merely the background for the victim's slowly dawning awareness of herself and reconstitution of her identity, underscored in the story's climax by what appears to be her revenge against her victimizer.

In 1990 Valenzuela published *Novela negra con argentinos* (1990; Detective Novel with Argentineans) and *Realidad nacional desde la cama* (translated as *Bedside Manners*).

REFERENCE:

Sharon Magnarelli, *Reflections/Refractions: Reading Luisa Valenzuela* (New York: Lang, 1988).

— R.G.M.

CÉSAR VALLEJO

César Vallejo (1892–1938) is today one of the three or four most widely studied Latin American poets of the twentieth century. In his lifetime, however, he was a relatively obscure Peruvian émigré whose one successful publishing venture was an account of his travels through and reflections on revolutionary Russia. The reason one of the great poets in the Spanish language was recognized only posthumously is primarily that early in his career Vallejo developed an unusual and forceful poetic idiom that flew in the face of convention and was regarded as nearly illegible. The critical establishment, to be sure, was befuddled by *Trilce* (1922), Vallejo's second book and one of the most personal and compelling poetic works of any age. (The title is an untranslatable neologism.) Even within the avant-garde climate of the period the book seemed

Cesar Vallejo in France, 1929

of 2,000 copies. In 1939 Vallejo's widow brought out in Paris a limited edition of *Poemas humanos* (translated as *Human Poems*), comprising ninety-four poems written at different times in the previous fifteen years but gathered and fully revised by the author in a final burst of creativity only months before his death. (This edition did not arrive in Lima until 1950.) Also in the last months of his life, Vallejo wrote the fifteen poems on the Spanish Civil War. They were included in *España, aparta de mí este cáliz* (1939; translated as *Spain, Let this Cup Pass from Me*), published by frontline Republican soldiers. Until about 1975 this edition of 1,100 copies was believed wholly lost with the fall of the Spanish Republic in 1939, but a few copies surfaced later.

Even in his native Peru, Vallejo was known only by a small circle of intellectuals and poets until the Argentinean publisher Losada republished Vallejo's first two books in 1961; readers throughout Latin America then had a chance to make the poet's acquaintance. Since then several editions of Vallejo's complete poetry have been published, and academic studies mount yearly.

Vallejo stands out for both the content and the form of his poetry. The central theme through all his work is communion, on which Vallejo grounded his faith as a man and as a poet. Several of the early poems and some of the poems in *Trilce* are about the breakup of the family, the earliest community experienced by the poet and one securely grounded in the traditional Christian view of the world. In *Los heraldos negros,* however, the poet's faith in the Christian logos crumbles, and the world becomes an absurd game of chance. In one of the poems Vallejo uses the Nietzschean image of the gods playing dice with the cosmos. In the last poem he repeats, "I was born a day when God was sick." By the time the book was published Vallejo had lost both his closest brother and his mother and had settled in Lima, far from his native Andean village of Santiago de Chuco.

Vallejo's absurdist view of existence becomes the poetic principle of *Trilce*: "Absurdity, only you are pure," exclaims the poet in the seventy-third poem of the collection. Indeed, the book breaks with traditional poetic discourse and makes this break an important theme that resounds throughout the work. Several of the poems are self-conscious reflections on the poetic enterprise that the book haltingly carries forward. Poetic creation is viewed in terms of uncertainty, paradox, and contradiction. Archaisms and neologisms, together with unusual words probably lifted from technical or scientific manuals, entwine themselves around plain speech and deform it. Orthography, typography, and syntactic order are undermined. One poem speaks

hermetic. It disappointed those who had lauded Vallejo's earlier effort, *Los heraldos negros* (1918; translated as *The Black Heralds*), poems that for the most part were derived from the late modernista tradition (see **Modernismo**) or that were written in a new plain style that augured well for the young poet.

Both these books were published in Peru in small editions of no more than 200 copies and were the only poetic works published by Vallejo in his lifetime. There was a second, Spanish edition of *Trilce* in 1930 of the act of creation as a laborious process of fecal discharge; another celebrates the destruction of classical harmony and symmetry and adopts the Venus de Milo (not armless but one-armed to emphasize asymmetry) as its aesthetic emblem. Vallejo, however, never experiments with language for the sake of form alone; the hermetic nature of *Trilce* and of the later *Poemas humanos* is a function of existential anguish. The poet's incarceration in 1920 for a felony he did not commit (a recurrent motif in *Trilce*) was one experience that determined Vallejo's existential outlook.

In 1923 Vallejo left for Europe, never to return to his native country. He lived mostly in Paris and Madrid (where he joined the Spanish Communist Party), in ill health and poverty, surviving by means of odd jobs and the charity of friends. *Poemas humanos* is an anguished and moving record of the author's existence on the edge of the abyss and is at the same time a desperate cry for human decency and solidarity in the face of social injustice and death. A biblical tone of wrath coexists with self-deprecation; the personal blends with the political, plain speech with hermetic images. Though the poet's existential and poetic contradictions are never resolved, there are signs pointing in the direction of a newfound sense of communion with the working class. This integration into the human community is the innermost theme of *España, aparta de mí este cáliz,* which on the surface is an apotheosis of the Spanish people as they are locked in mortal combat with the fascist enemy. In the glorious suffering of the common man and woman and in their readiness to accept death, Vallejo finds a sacrificial meaning akin to the lost symbols of his childhood. The Void is filled, the spirit renewed, and the Book of Nature (whose pages were explicitly illegible in one of the *Poemas humanos*) again makes sense.

REFERENCES:

Jean Franco, *César Vallejo: The Dialectics of Poetry and Silence* (New York: Cambridge University Press, 1976);

Julio Ortega, *César Vallejo* (Madrid: Taurus, 1975).

— R.G.M.

VALS

The European waltz was widely disseminated throughout Latin America (becoming known as the vals), and in some measure its Viennese character has been preserved. More commonly, however, the waltz assumed various local characteristics and reflected nationalistic musical values. The Venezuelan vals, for example, adopted characteristics of the **joropo,** such as a 3/2 hemiola accompanying figure, syncopation, and other rhythmic devices. The Peruvian vals contains alternations of 6/8 and 3/4 meter, also incorporates syncopation, and is principally a vocal form. The Paraguayan waltz, however, more closely resembles its Viennese antecedents. In Colombia the European waltz became the *pasillo* (waltz in the style of the nation), while the slower *valse* is sung by one or two voices.

REFERENCES:

Elliot Paul Frank, "The Venezuelan Waltzes of Antonio Lauro," thesis, Florida State University, 1994;

Octavio Marulanda, *El folclor de Colombia: Práctica de la identidad cultural* (Bogotá: Artestudio Editores, 1984).

— R.L.S.

BLANCA VARELA

Peruvian poet Blanca Varela (1926–) was the most important member of the "Generation of 1950" together with **Javier Sologuren.** Varela's first book, *Ese puerto existe* (1959; That Port Exists), was published with a prologue by Mexican poet and future Nobel Prize winner Octavio Paz. Later Varela published *Luz del día* (1963; Daylight), *Valses y otras falsas confesiones* (1972; Waltzes and Other False Confessions), and *Canto villano* (1978; Rustic Song), the title under which Varela's complete poetry was published in Mexico (1986).

REFERENCE:

Ana M. Gazzolo, "Blanca Varela y la batalla poética," *Cuadernos Hispanoamericanos,* 466 (April 1989): 129–138.

— R.G.M.

MARIO VARGAS LLOSA

One of the most significant contemporary novelists in Latin America and a controversial public figure, especially after his failed bid to become president of Peru in 1990, Mario Vargas Llosa (1936–) was born in the southern Peruvian city of Arequipa but spent his childhood in Cochabamba, Bolivia, resettling in Peru, in the coastal city of Piura, after Christmas 1945. In his autobiography Vargas Llosa writes that the two determining experiences of his early years were learning to read at an early age and meeting his father in Piura for the first time. He had grown up with the conviction that his father was dead, when the truth — known to the family at large — was that his father had abandoned Vargas Llosa's mother ten years earlier and had never bothered to stay in touch. Soon after this improbable family reunion Vargas Llosa was transplanted again, this time to the capital city of Lima.

Mario Vargas Llosa

By the time he was twenty Vargas Llosa had already written several of the stories later published as *Los jefes* (1959). English translations of these stories were published with the English version of Vargas Llosa's short novel *Los cachorros* (1967) in *The Cubs and Other Stories* (1979). *Los jefes* is a dual exploration of narrative point of view and of adolescent machismo, of the violence implicit in the social relations and values of young males in a country like Peru.

Vargas Llosa's first novel, *La ciudad y los perros* (1963; translated as *The Time of the Hero*), which changed the course of Latin American fiction, was first recognized in Europe at a time when no Latin American novelists rivaled their European counterparts. *La ciudad y los perros,* awarded the prestigious **Premio Biblioteca Breve de Novela** in Barcelona, "officially" launched the **Boom** of Latin American fiction. The literal translation of the novel's title is "The City and the Cadets." *La ciudad y los perros* is a virtuoso performance in a realist key. Refining the techniques of the conventional nineteenth-century realist novel, Vargas

Llosa's first large-scale narrative effort brings to mind both Henry James's experiments with point of view and the ambitious scope and structural deliberateness of Gustave Flaubert's novels. *La ciudad y los perros* is set in the Leoncio Prado, a military school in Lima that Vargas Llosa attended between 1950 and 1952. The school serves as a microcosm of Peruvian society, since young men from all over the country and from various social classes and ethnic groups congregate within its walls. Vargas Llosa once again explores the psychology of adolescent manhood, this time in an environment dominated by a military code of honor. The novel was read in Peru as a powerful indictment of the military institution, and authorities of the Leoncio Prado publicly burned as many copies of the book as could be found. In 1967, when he received the **Premio Rómulo Gallegos de Novela** for his second novel, *La casa verde* (1966; translated as *The Green House*), Vargas Llosa delivered a now-famous speech asserting his conviction that "literature is fire" and that novelists and poets are dissidents from social and political orthodoxies.

La casa verde, the second of his three monumental novels published in the 1960s, is an ambitious exploration of Peru that takes in parts of the country only alluded to in *La ciudad y los perros,* the Amazonian jungles and the deserts of northern Peru, where Vargas Llosa spent his teens. *La casa verde* is a description of Peruvian reality on several simultaneous levels or, as Vargas Llosa himself has stated, a synthesis of several experiences he had at different times and in different places, all of which illuminate an aspect of himself and his country. La casa verde is the name of a brothel in Piura, but metaphorically the title alludes to the jungle. *Conversación en La Catedral* (1969; translated as *Conversation in The Cathedral*) focuses on the dictatorship of Gen. Manuel Odría (1948–1956), who toppled the government of José Luis Bustamante, a relative of Vargas Llosa. (See **Dictatorship Novel**.) Odría's dictatorship was not violent by Latin American standards, but it was corrupt, and corruption is the organizing motif of Vargas Llosa's vast historical mural. The novel is broadly political, like his two previous efforts, but is characterized by a subjective or personal viewpoint, from which the historical protagonists, sometimes thinly disguised under fictitious names, are seen in their human dimension, determined by everyday activities. *Conversación en La Catedral* (the "cathedral" to which the title refers is a bar where, as in Albert Camus's *The Fall,* the narrator and an interlocutor engage in a protracted conversation) recalls Flaubert's *Education Sentimentale* in that it purports to be the novel of a whole generation corrupted by the political environment at the very moment when it was coming of age.

In *La casa verde* and *Conversación en La Catedral* Vargas Llosa develops truly virtuoso techniques of textual composition to tell stories that range over time and space and involve multiple characters and perspectives as well as different degrees of interiority and exteriority. These novels are extraordinary examples of the "total novel," the cornerstone of Vargas Llosa's theory of fiction. For the Peruvian writer there is no higher narrative achievement than novels that substitute for the real world; novels, that is, that are so vast and all-embracing that they yank the reader out of the old reality and provide access to a new one. The function of this self-sufficient and internally coherent new reality is to supply whatever is missing from our daily lives but is nevertheless present in our imaginations and desires. In 1971 Vargas Llosa published a massive study of **Gabriel García Márquez,** inspired above all by the absorbing scope of the Colombian novelist's world. Vargas Llosa consolidated his reputation as a leading world novelist with works such as *Pantaleón y las visitadoras* (1973; translated as *Sergeant*

Pantoja and the Special Service), *La tía Julia y el escribidor* (1977; translated as *Aunt Julia and the Scriptwriter*), *La guerra del fin del mundo* (1981; translated as *The War of the End of the World*), *Historia de Mayta* (1984; translated as *The Real Life of Alejandro Mayta*), *El hablador* (1987; translated as *The Storyteller*), and *Lituma en los Andes* (1993; Sergeant Lituma in the Andes).

La tía Julia y el escribidor is a popular and critically acclaimed incursion into the genre of comic fiction and mass culture as well as an unusual love story between the narrator and his elder aunt. (The real-life Julia has written her own version of the affair.) Both *Pantaleón y las visitadoras* and *La tía Julia y el escribidor* are striking for their humor; previously, Vargas Llosa had declared himself totally impervious to humor. (See **Movies from Books.**)

La guerra del fin del mundo is an astounding epic rendition of the events that took place in the Brazilian backlands in the closing years of the twentieth century, when successive waves of Brazilian soldiers went into the hinterland to put down a rebellion headed by a religious fanatic who had mobilized the impoverished and credulous masses against republican institutions and their progressive ideology. The novel was inspired by Euclides Da Cunha's classic study of the rebellion, *Os Sertãos* (1902; translated as *Rebellion in the Backlands*). Vargas Llosa's narrative is less experimental and more straightforward than in his previous novels but equally if not more ambitious and at times as action-packed as this week's best-seller.

Historia de Mayta is a controversial bit of legerdemain involving the earliest guerrilla uprising in the Peruvian Andes (at the time of the **Cuban Revolution**) and the investigation into its causes and protagonists carried out (in real life and in fiction) by someone much like Mario Vargas Llosa. The novel has the same labyrinthine ambiguity as some of the fiction by **Jorge Luis Borges,** but it has bothered left-leaning critics who see it as an underhanded critique of the Peruvian Left. (It should be remembered that Vargas Llosa was a Marxist in the 1960s, a social democrat in the 1970s, and a neoconservative in the 1980s and 1990s.) Finally, *El hablador* is an ingenious and instructive counterpoint between an archaic storyteller in the tropical forests of the Amazon and his modern counterpart in "civilized" society. Part of the novel's extraordinary interest lies in Vargas Llosa's retelling (or invention) of Amazonian myths in a language as poetic and fresh as any in modern fiction.

Vargas Llosa has also written several plays, a study of Flaubert titled *La orgía perpetua: Flaubert y "Madame Bovary"* (1975; translated as *The Perpetual Orgy: Flaubert and "Madame Bovary"*), a book of critical essays on various world authors and novels titled *La verdad de las mentiras* (1990; *The Truth of Lies*), dozens of literary and political articles collected in three volumes as *Contra viento y marea* (1986–1990; Against Wind and Tide), and his autobiography, *El pez en el agua* (1993; translated as *A Fish in the Water*), in which the experiences of youth are interspersed with an account of his unsuccessful campaign for the Peruvian presidency. *Lituma en los Andes* is an incursion into political terrorism and Andean demonology.

REFERENCES:

Dick Gerdes, *Mario Vargas Llosa* (Boston: Twayne, 1985);

José Miguel Oviedo, *Mario Vargas Llosa: La invención de una realidad,* third edition (Barcelona: Seix Barral, 1982);

Raymond L. Williams, *Mario Vargas Llosa* (New York: Ungar, 1986).

— R.G.M.

ANGELINA VÁSQUEZ

Chilean director Angelina Vásquez (circa 1938–) was part of the film team **Equipo Tercer Año,** which in 1973 began filming *La batalla de Chile* (1975–1979; The Battle of Chile), directed by **Patricio Guzmán.** When **Augusto Pinochet** came to power in September of that year, Vásquez was forced to leave the country. In her later work, exile became a major theme. *Dos años en Finlandia* (1975; Two Years in Finland) is a portrait of the Chilean community there, and *Presencia lejana* (1982; Distant Presence) traces the lives of Finnish twins who immigrated to Argentina. One returned to Finland, the other stayed in Argentina, where she "disappeared" in 1977. In her feature film *Gracias a la vida* (1980; Thanks to Life) — alluding to the song of that title by the Chilean poet and popular singer **Violeta Parra** — a woman who is carrying the baby of her torturer meets her husband and children in Helsinki. The pain but also the optimism of such experiences are portrayed with great skill.

REFERENCE:

John King, *Magical Reels: A History of Cinema in Latin America* (London: Verso, 1990).

— S.M.H.

JORGE DE LA VEGA

The Argentinean Jorge de la Vega (1930–1971) excelled not only as a graphic artist, draftsman, and painter but also as a singer and songwriter. From 1948 to 1952 he studied architecture at the Universidad de Buenos Aires. A self-taught artist, de la Vega explored

Historia de los vampiros (1963; Story of the Vampires), by Jorge de la Vega (Museum of Art, Rhode Island School of Design, Providence, Nancy Sayles Day Collection of Latin American Art)

both realism and **Geometric Abstraction** before joining the **Otra Figuración** group in the early 1960s. In his painting-collage *El espejo al final de la escalera* (1963; The Mirror at the End of the Stairs) de la Vega daringly combines wrinkled pieces of canvas, buttons, and bits of jewelry to form the monstrous figure of a cat, boldly outlined with dripping black brush strokes on a flat white background. In his *Conflicto anamórfico* (1965; Anamorphic Conflict) series de la Vega also worked with anamorphic images, which he produced by rubbing one of his collages onto another canvas, a technique known as frottage; the fabric was stretched to achieve an anamorphic effect.

In 1965 de la Vega received a Fulbright Scholarship to teach at Cornell University, where he produced several satiric images of the consumer society of the United States, such as the three-canvas work *Vida cotidiana* (1965; Everyday Life), featuring smiling female and male nudes, their mingled body parts confused in a fluid mass. After he returned to Buenos Aires in 1967, de la Vega produced only a few black-and-white works. The drawings and prints of the series *Rompecabezas* (1967; Puzzle), ex-

Kiosko de Canaletas (1918; Canaletas Newsstand), by Rafael Pérez Barradas (Collection of Mr. Eduardo F. Costantini and Mrs. María Teresa de Costantini, Buenos Aires)

hibited at the Instituto Di Tella, depict an irreverent, playfully erotic image of society. Toward the end of his life de la Vega worked mainly on his singing and songwriting career, expressing his humorous view of the world through music.

REFERENCE:

Mercedes Casanegra, *Jorge de la Vega* (Buenos Aires: S. A. Alba, 1990).

— F.B.N.

VIBRACIONISMO

Vibracionismo (Vibrationism) was an avant-garde style defined in Barcelona during the mid 1910s by the Uruguayan artist **Rafael Pérez Barradas** and later adopted by his countryman **Joaquín Torres-García.** At that time Barcelona had an active avant-garde because many modern artists, including Albert Gleizes and Francis Picabia, had sought refuge there from World War I. In 1913 Barradas had become interested in Futurism while

in Italy, where he met Filippo Marinetti, the leader of the futurist movement. During the war Barradas settled in Barcelona and met Torres-García, who had lived there since the 1890s. Torres-García believed that art should not imitate but rather express through geometry the deeper nature of reality and the world around him. For this reason he was attracted to the synthesis achieved by Barradas's Vibracionismo, which combined the geometric simplification of Cubism with Futurism's emphasis on the dynamism of the modern metropolis.

Barradas and Torres-García liberated art from its traditional function as representation in order to celebrate and participate in the "vibrancy" of the modern world. For instance, in *Kiosko de Canaletas* (1918; Canaletas Newsstand) Barradas adopted the Futurists' dynamic juxtaposition of geometric fragments, numbers, and letters to suggest the high-pitched activity of a busy street. For his part, Torres-García, in works such as *Calle de Barcelona* (1917; A Barcelona Street) and *Paisaje de Nueva York* (1920; New York Landscape), balanced the simultaneous presentation of images, which was characteristic of Futurism, with the sense of orthogonal structure found in Cubism, giving his work a more stable effect.

Both Barradas and Torres-García continued working in this mode until the mid 1920s. Vibracionismo had little effect on the Latin American avant-gardes of the 1920s, because Barradas died soon after his return to Montevideo in 1928, and Torres-García stayed in Europe until 1934. The only influence exerted by Vibracionismo was at best indirect. Among the **Ultraists** Barradas met in Madrid was **Norah Borges,** who returned to work in Buenos Aires in 1921, and the few Spanish Ultraist magazines featuring Barradas's work that reached Mexico may perhaps have influenced the work of the Stridentists.

REFERENCE:

Robert Lubar, Juan Manuel Bonet, and Guillermo de Osma, *Barradas/Torres-García* (Madrid: Galería Guillermo de Osma, 1991).

— F.B.N.

Vicaría de la Solidaridad

The Vicaría de la Solidaridad (Vicariate of Solidarity) is a human rights organization set up by the Catholic Church in Chile following the military coup against Marxist president **Salvador Allende** in 1973. The Vicaría provided both legal counsel for the victims of military repression who were not already executed, "disappeared," or exiled and assistance to families of such victims. It also provided cover for lawyers and others working to document the human rights abuses perpetrated by the military authorities. Its vaults contain thousands of documented cases that may one day be brought to trial. The Vicaría was awarded the Carter-Ménil Human Rights Prize in 1987 at the Carter Presidential Center in Atlanta, Georgia.

REFERENCE:

Cynthia G. Brown, *The Vicaría de la Solidaridad in Chile* (New York: Americas Watch Committee, 1987).

— R.G.M.

Vidala and Vidalita

Popular song genres sung by **payadors,** with the second voice singing in parallel thirds, the vidala and the vidalita are both strophically arranged songs with texts in quatrains and refrains. Unlike the vidalita, which proceeds in a ternary meter, the vidala has a binary metrical organization. There are other differences as well: the poetic text of the vidala has eight to ten syllables per line; the vidalita six. The refrain and texts are variable in the vidala but invariable in the vidalita.

These genres are especially popular in secular festivals and carnivals of the Andean region of northwestern Argentina but have also been romanticized through their nationalistic association with **gaucho** songs of the pampas. Typical accompaniments consist of a drum (**bombo**) and a guitar, which is normally played in rapid arpeggios or by strumming the strings with the fingers in the **flamenco** style (*rasgueado*). The diatonic harp (without pedals) may occasionally be substituted for the guitar.

REFERENCES:

Isabel Aretz, *El folklore musical argentino* (Buenos Aires: Ricordi Americana SAEC, 1952);

Rodolfo Arizaga, *Enciclopedia de la música argentina* (Buenos Aires: Fondo Nacional de las Artes, 1971).

— R.L.S.

Viernes

Viernes (Friday) was a journal founded by a group of young poets in Venezuela in 1939, four years after the death of Juan Vicente Gómez, the general who had ruled the country since 1908. Intent on breaking out of the cultural isolation imposed by Gómez's long dictatorship, the Viernes group was founded by Angel Miguel Queremel. Its most prominent poet was Vicente Gerbasi, author of *Los espacios cálidos* (1952; The Warm Spaces). The journal ceased publication in 1941.

— R.G.M.

Nelson Villagra

Because of his exceptional range, Chilean Nelson Villagra (circa 1940–) has established himself as a leading Latin American actor. His most notable roles include the leads in *El chacal de Nahueltoro* (1968; The Jackal of Nahueltoro), directed by **Miguel Littín;** *Tres tristes tigres* (1968; Three Trapped Tigers), directed by **Raúl Ruiz**; *La tierra prometida* (1973; The Promised Land), directed by Miguel Littín; *Cantata de Chile* (1975), directed by Humberto Solás; *La última cena* (1977; The Last Supper), directed by Tomás Gutiérrez Alea; *El recurso del método* (1978; Reasons of State/Viva el Presidente), directed by Littín; and *La viuda de Montiel* (1979; Montiel's Widow), directed by Littín.

REFERENCE:

Julianne Burton, ed., *Cinema and Social Change in Latin America: Conversations with Latin American Filmmakers* (Austin: University of Texas Press, 1986).

— S.M.H.

Nelson Villagra in *Cantata de Chile* (1975; Cantata of Chile)

VILLANCICO

Although the song form has its origins in Spain, many villancicos have been produced in Latin America. Most of the Latin American villancicos are of a religious nature and dedicated to saints, angels, souls, and Jesus. A large number of the religious villancicos are specifically for the Christmas season. Most of the melodies are conjunct; that is, they avoid large, awkward skips, and their melodic motion resembles that of chant. Narrow vocal ranges and syllabic settings of texts are also common. The rhythm of the villancico is also less syncopated than that of the lively **aguinaldo.**

REFERENCES:

Isabel Aretz, *El folklore musical argentino* (Buenos Aires: Ricordi Americana SAEC, 1952);

Gerard Béhague, "Latin American Folk Music," in *Folk and Traditional Music of the Western Continents,* by Bruno Nettl, third edition, revised and edited by Valerie Woodring Goertzen (Englewood Cliffs, N.J.: Prentice-Hall, 1990).

—R.L.S.

CARLOS RAÚL VILLANUEVA

Leading Venezuelan architect Carlos Raúl Villanueva (1900–1974) was born in London and educated in France. He studied architecture at the Ecole des Beaux-Arts in Paris and in 1928 settled in Caracas. He participated in the architecture programs of the

Ministerio de Obras Públicas (Ministry of Public Works) and organized the Consejo de Protección de Monumentos Históricos (Council for the Protection of Historic Monuments). His early projects were eclectic: the Plaza de Toros (1931; Bull Ring) in Maracay combined traditional design with modern construction methods; the Museo de Bellas Artes (1935; Fine Arts Museum) in Caracas was designed in a neoclassical style; and the Escuela Gran Colombia (1939; Gran Colombia School) was built along functional lines. Villanueva also participated in efforts to urbanize and modernize Caracas, a symbol of the prosperity brought by the oil boom. Many slums that had sprung up around the city during the early part of the century were eradicated and replaced by modern housing. Villanueva's first large public project was the low-cost housing development called El Silencio (1941; Silence), built on land left after clearing away a shantytown. His design featured apartment buildings placed around an oblong plaza with fountains. He included functional features, such as balconies, cross ventilation, and protection from the tropical sun. In the lower part of the buildings opening onto the plaza, Villanueva placed colonial colonnades that harmonize with the surrounding context.

In 1944 Villanueva began to design his most ambitious and internationally celebrated project, the Ciudad Universitaria (University Campus) of the Universidad Central de Caracas. Villanueva's flexible plan grouped buildings around different activity zones. In

Carlos Raúl Villanueva, 1948 (photograph by Alfredo Boulton)

the center he placed a covered plaza, decorated with many works of art. The plaza functions as a social center and is connected to the rest of the buildings by walkways covered by concrete canopies of different shapes, which provide protection from the tropical sun and give the campus continuity. The Olympic Stadium (1950–1951) also shows a daring use of reinforced concrete for the cantilevered roof, which seemingly floats over the grandstand, although it is in fact suspended from soaring ribs. The Aula Magna, with a capacity for 2,600 people, was finished in 1952: it is a remarkable feat of engineering, carried out in conjunction with the well-known Danish firm of Christian and Nielsen. The ceiling is suspended by steel beams from an exterior planar slab of poured concrete. The interior plaster ceiling and side walls are animated by dramatic acoustical clouds designed by Alexander Calder. For the Ciudad Universitaria, Villanueva paid close attention to integrating art with architecture: he personally selected works by internationally famous artists such as Jean Arp, Anton Pevsner, and Victor Vasarely, works that were placed side by side with the art of Venezuelans such as **Alejandro Otero** and **Jesús Rafael Soto.**

REFERENCE:

Gilbert Chase, *Contemporary Art in Latin America: Painting, Graphic Art, Sculpture, Architecture* (New York: Free Press, 1970).

— F.B.N.

VIÑA DEL MAR FESTIVAL

As a result of the first meeting of the Viña del Mar Film Festival held in Chile in 1967, the term **New Latin American Cinema** was formalized. For the first time film directors from all parts of the subcontinent met, exchanged ideas, and set up an agenda for future cooperation under the leadership of Aldo Francia, a Chilean doctor-cum-cineast. This festival promoted extensive exchanges between filmmakers from Argentina, Brazil, Bolivia, Cuba, Chile, Uruguay, and Venezuela; the main focus of the debate was sociocultural and political rather than cinematic. As the Cuban delegate at the time suggested, the Viña del Mar Festival was significant because "we stopped being independent or marginal filmmakers, promising filmmakers, or amateurs experimenting and searching, in order to discover what we were without yet knowing: a new cinema, a *movement.*" The meeting set out an ambitious set of resolutions concerning future collaborative work, much of which did not materialize, but it did allow for personal contacts to develop and numerous films to be screened. Its significance lies in that it was the first step toward the elusive goal of Pan-American solidarity. A follow-up film festival, concentrating on the Latin American documentary, was held in Mérida, Venezuela, one year later, in 1968. The next year, as a direct result of the festival, the Universidad de los Andes in Venezuela founded a documentary film center, which went on to produce newsreels, documentaries, and feature films. Another film festival was held in 1969 in Viña del Mar, to pursue some of the material treated in previous gatherings. Other initiatives have carried on the work of the Viña del Mar Festival. The Cinémathèque of the Third World (1969) in Montevideo, Uruguay — together with the periodical **Marcha** — initiated the distribution and exhibition of films and a film festival. The Committee of Latin American Filmmakers (founded in 1974), subsequently expanded and reorganized as the **Nueva Fundación de Cíne Latinamericano** in 1985, and the International Festival of the **New Latin American Cinema** in Havana (1979–) have helped support the work of promising film directors and helped disseminate new ideas and strategies.

REFERENCES:

John King, *Magical Reels: A History of Cinema in Latin America* (London: Verso, 1990);

Zuzana M. Pick, *The New Latin American Cinema. A Continental Project* (Austin: University of Texas Press, 1993).

— S.M.H.

DAVID VIÑAS

Argentinean novelist David Viñas (1929–) is associated with the "generación de los parricidas" (parricidal generation), which flourished during the years following the first government of **Juan Domingo Perón.** Viñas, a Marxist whose ideological commitment has always been overt in his works, has uncompromisingly criticized bourgeois values. By the author's own admission, his novels have dealt with significant sociopolitical issues and events in his country's modern history; for example, *Cayó sobre su rostro* (1955; He Fell on His Face) deals with a rural despot, and *Los dueños de la tierra* (1958; The Owners of the Land) centers on the suppression of a farmworkers' protest. Although there is some development in technique between these novels and those written up to the late 1970s, it is only with *Cuerpo a cuerpo* (1979; Body to Body) that Viñas reaches beyond a monolithic view of events and, with a noticeably more ambitious and frag-

mentary technique, produces a work that has been called an Argentinean novel to compare with **Mario Vargas Llosa**'s *Conversación en La Catedral* (1969; translated as *Conversation in The Cathedral*). Viñas has also been important for what he represents in the recent history of Argentina: a dissident who had to flee to exile in Mexico, a man some of whose friends were "disappeared," and a Jew. (During the 1980s the role of the Jews in Argentinean cultural history was the focus of much attention.) After returning to his country, Viñas became chair of Spanish American literature at the Universidad de Buenos Aires, unsuccessfully sought political office, and continued to be prominent as a social critic and a promoter of cultural activities.

REFERENCES:

H. M. Rasi, "David Viñas, novelista y crítico comprometido," *Revista Iberoamericana,* 95 (1976): 259–265;

David Viñas, *Literatura argentina y realidad política* (Buenos Aires: Siglo Viente, 1971).

— P.S.

JORGE VINATEA REINOSO

The Peruvian painter Jorge Vinatea Reinoso (1900–1931) was one of the most interesting independent **Indigenists.** He came from a poor family in Arequipa, Peru. Like his contemporary **Julia Codesido,** he was a member of the first generation of Peruvian students to attend the Escuela Nacional de Bellas Artes during the early 1920s. He studied with the director of the school, the **Impressionist** painter Daniel Hernández, and with the Spanish sculptor Manuel Piqueras Cotolí. Vinatea Reinoso financed his studies by drawing caricatures satirizing political and social themes for magazines such as *Mundial* and *Variedades*. In 1923, after his graduation, he became professor of drawing and painting at the Escuela Nacional.

Vinatea Reinoso's works often have a spontaneous, sketchy quality, probably resulting from his years as a magazine illustrator. Paintings such as *Balseros del Titicaca* (1929; Titicaca Rafters) are dynamic compositions that seem to capture life in motion by combining thick, expressive brush strokes with a decorative treatment of the surface. In the case of *Balseros del Titicaca* the motion is activated by the multiple vertical and horizontal lines of the mastlike structures and reed rafts. Vinatea Reinoso died of tuberculosis at the age of thirty-one.

REFERENCE:

Teodoro Núñez Ureta, *Pintura contemporánea: Segunda parte* (Lima: Banco de Crédito del Perú, 1976).

— F.B.N.

La Violencia

The decade of virtual civil war in Colombia that took the lives of two hundred thousand liberal and conservative partisans and combined political conflict with criminal banditry and personal feuds came to be known as La Violencia (1948–1958). It began with the "Bogotazo," the riots in the capital city of Bogotá following the assassination of liberal leader Jorge Eliécer Gaitán, and came to an end when the government lifted the state of siege and the two main political parties agreed to alternate the presidency between them. "La Violencia " is an important theme in contemporary Colombian literature, giving rise to a host of accounts denouncing the atrocities committed by one or the other band. The subject is treated in novels such as *La mala hora* (1962; translated as *In Evil Hour*), by **Gabriel García Márquez;** *Estaba la pájara pinta sentada en el verde limón* (1984; The Speckled Bird Was Sitting in the Lemon Tree), by **Albalucía Angel;** *El día señalado* (1964; The Appointed Day), by Manuel Mejía Vallejo; and *La calle 10* (1960; Tenth Street), by Manuel Zapata Olivella.

REFERENCES:

Manuel Antonio Arango, *Gabriel García Márquez y la novela de la violencia en Colombia* (Mexico: FCE, 1985);

Jonathan Tittler, *Violencia y literatura en Colombia* (Madrid: Orígenes, 1989).

— R.G.M.

EMILIO ADOLFO WESTPHALEN

Together with Xavier Abril and **César Moro**, the poet Emilio Adolfo Westphalen (1911–) was one of the leaders of the Surrealist movement in Peru. He played an important role in Peruvian letters as founder and director of the reviews *Amaru* and *Las Moradas* (1947–1949). The author of two brief collections of poetry, *Las ínsulas extrañas* (1933; The Strange Islands) and *Abolición de la muerte* (1935; Death's Abolition), he is at once seductive and philosophical, dealing with grand themes such as love and death. His poetry from the 1930s to the 1980s is collected in *Belleza de una espada clavada en la lengua* (1986; The Beauty of a Sword Piercing a Tongue).

REFERENCE:

Alberto Escobar, *El imaginario nacional: Moro, Westphalen, Arguedas: una formación literaria* (Lima: Instituto de Estudios Peruanos, 1989).

—R.G.M. & P.S.

ALBERTO WILLIAMS

Argentinean composer, pianist, and educator, Alberto Williams (1862–1952) is considered the "father" of Argentinean music. Through his piano music he initiated the nationalistic movement that predominated in Argentina during the early decades of the twentieth century.

Born of a British father and an Argentinean mother of Basque descent, Williams was educated in Europe, where he studied with César Franck in the Paris Conservatoire. Williams returned to Argentina in 1889 and began to learn the music and dances of his people. His first compositions following his return resembled the musical postcards of nineteenth-century Romanticism: *El rancho abandonado* (The Abandoned Ranch) and *Aires de la pampa* (Airs from the Pampa), a collection of fifty works. In these and ensuing works the music of the **gauchos** and **payadors** (**vidalitas,** zambas, gatos, cielitos, and **milongas**) were sources of influence and inspiration. Although he is known for the nationalistic element in his music, he never abandoned the traditional European means of musical communication, subjecting the improvisational nature of Argentinean folk and popular music to the discipline of careful craftsmanship.

Active as a concert pianist, he also organized numerous concerts in which the works of other composers were introduced to the public. He conducted various symphony orchestras, founded the Buenos Aires Conservatory of Music, and directed it for nearly fifty years. Later renamed the Conservatorio Williams, the conservatory is the oldest active musical institution in Argentina and has been the training ground for many of the nation's outstanding composers and performers. A prolific composer (more than 110 opus numbers), Williams was also the author of two texts on music theory.

Alberto Williams

REFERENCES:

Rodolfo Arizaga and Pompeyo Camps, *Historia de la música en la Argentina* (Buenos Aires: Ricordi Americana S.A.E.C., 1990);

Gerard Béhague, *Music in Latin America: An Introduction* (Englewood Cliffs, N.J.: Prentice-Hall, 1979);

Vicente Gesualdo, *La música en la Argentina* (Buenos Aires: Editorial Stella, 1988).

—R.L.S.

AMANCIO WILLIAMS

Amancio Williams (1913–) is a leading Argentinean architect. Son of the composer **Alberto Williams,** he studied at the Facultad de Arquitectura in the Universidad de Buenos Aires (1939–1941). At the invitation of the French Ministry of Reconstruction he presented his ideas about housing at the International Architectural Exhibition, ideas that were highly praised by renowned French architect Le Corbusier. In 1959 a Williams project for an entertainment complex won the Gold Medal at the Brussels International Exhibition. Later, Ludwig Mies van der Rohe, who admired his work, asked Williams to succeed him as director of the School of Architecture of the Illinois Institute of Technology, but Williams declined, preferring to remain in Argentina.

Much of Williams's creative potential has not been realized because he has concentrated on a few complex and time-consuming projects and at the same time has spent much energy writing about the theoretical side of urban development and the treatment of three-dimensional space. Furthermore, Williams's early designs were produced during the 1940s and 1950s, which was not a propitious time for innovative architectural and urban projects. For instance, his unrealized design for a concert hall (the Sala de Conciertos y Espectáculos), on which he worked for ten years (1943–1953), was supposed to look like a hollow, spinning top with a series of secondary spaces organized in a ring around it. The whole complex was planned to be high above the ground so that a park could be developed underneath.

Williams's internationally acclaimed design for the Casa del Puente (Bridge House) was an independent project commissioned by his father and built in Mar del Plata between 1943 and 1945. The two-story house rests partially on a concrete bridge whose graceful curve is symmetrical with the streambed over which it extends. Williams believed that architects should use rather than destroy nature, and by using the bridge he allowed nature to continue under the house, thus effectively integrating the building into the surrounding landscape. Williams defined the house as a unified three-dimensional structure rather than as a collection of separate parts, but he also took extreme care with small details, ranging from the use of bare textured concrete to the wood paneling of the house's interior.

Williams has also worked on another extremely well-documented project: the first city in Antarctica, with the plans to be donated to Argentina and Chile for their joint realization, as a way of fostering friendship between two nations.

REFERENCE:

Gilbert Chase, *Contemporary Art in Latin America: Painting, Graphic Art, Sculpture, Architecture* (New York: Free Press, 1970).

— F.B.N.

EGON WOLFF

The preeminent Chilean playwright, Egon Wolff (1926–) achieved distinction in the 1950s at a time when Chilean literature as a whole was moving away from rural and proletarian themes in the direction of urban, middle-class concerns. Wolff's chief theatrical metaphor is that of the "invaded bourgeoisie," which he developed in two particularly striking plays, *Los invasores* (1963; The Invaders) and *Flores de papel* (1970; translated as *Paper Flowers*). The first depicts the repressed guilt and unconscious fears of a successful industrialist who has murdered his partner and avoided punishment. One night he hears a prowler in the house, the first of many shadowy and puzzling invaders (slum dwellers, beggars asking for money, figures who seem to pass through the walls) who disturb the industrialist and cause him to confess his crime out loud. His wife awakens him, and the protagonist and spectators alike

realize that the strange sequence of events has been a nightmare. The play's climax occurs when a prowler does break into the house as the industrialist — now fully awake — watches in horror.

Flores de papel is no less uncanny but, in the style of Wolff's plays in general, never strays far from the conventions of psychological and social realism. A vagrant helps a middle-class woman who lives alone by carrying her groceries. Once in the house the vagrant refuses payment but asks for a cup of tea. Night falls, and he still does not leave. He sleeps with the woman and soon takes over her apartment, which he ends up trashing. Then they both move to a shantytown to take up residence.

Both of these plays dramatize the bad conscience of the well-to-do and the class conflicts that defined Chilean society in the years prior to the Marxist government of President **Salvador Allende.** A later play by Wolff — *José* (1980) — stages the social contradictions of Chile after the military coup of 1973, which implanted a neoliberal economic model that created a new class of financiers and speculators. The eponymous character is a Chilean idealist returning to the country after a prolonged stay in the United States. In the new Chile José fails to find the cultural antidote to the crass materialism of North American life. On the contrary, he discovers that the success ethic that drives North American culture has been imported into Chile and has settled in the nooks and crannies of family life. In 1985 Wolff published *Háblame de Laura* (1985; Tell Me about Laura).

REFERENCE:

Margaret Sayres Peden, "The Theater of Egon Wolff," in *Dramatists in Revolt*, edited by Leon Lyday and George Woodyard (Austin: University of Texas Press, 1976).

— R.G.M.

WORLD DANCE ALLIANCE

The World Dance Alliance has a division known as the Americas Center, which is one of three organizations created to serve the needs of dance in specifically defined geographical areas. The first organizational meeting for the Americas Center was held in New York City in 1993. Delegates from Canada, Venezuela, Colombia, Costa Rica, Cuba, the Dominican Republic, Mexico, Argentina, Chile, Paraguay, Peru, Brazil, and the United States attended the meeting. Participants represented the interests of twenty-five major companies and more than twenty-four universities as well as service and government organizations. The World Dance Alliance provides a forum for communication among the various dance communities of the Americas. Meetings, workshops, panels, festival programs, a calendar of events, and a directory all focus on promoting dance and solving some of the problems in the various dance professions at the Pan-American level. Committees formed to address these issues include Health and the Dance Community; Education; Exchange of Scholars, Companies, and Individual Artists; Scholarship and Research; Preservation and Documentation of the Repertoire; and Children.

—N.D.B. & J.M.H.

X-Y-Z

XUL SOLAR

Xul Solar (1887–1963), whose real name was Oscar Agustín Alejandro Schulz Solari, was a leading figure in the introduction of modern art in Argentina. He spent his formative years traveling through Europe, where he came into contact with several avant-garde movements. In small iridescent watercolors, such as *Troncos* (1914; Trunks) and *Pareja* (1923; Couple), he reformulated the formal and conceptual innovations of these European trends into a personal synthesis that combined the bright colors of Futurism, the geometrized forms of Russian Constructivism, and the whimsical flair of Paul Klee. Although Xul Solar considered his art mainly as a record of his spiritual experiences with occult mysticism and Asian religions, he also expressed his Latin American roots in paintings such as *Nana-Watzin* (1923).

In 1924 Xul Solar returned to Buenos Aires and joined the **Florida** movement. Although his fellow vanguardists, especially **Jorge Luis Borges,** admired his work, established critics were mystified by the esoteric images of shamans and dragons found in watercolors such as *Mundo* (1925; World). Xul Solar's role in the Florida movement was gradually eclipsed by his own reluctance to sell his paintings and **Emilio Pettoruti**'s self-serving account of the history of this group.

During the following decades Xul Solar's art was influenced by the visionary experiences he described in his series of essays *San Signos* (Holy Signs), written in *neocriollo,* one of his invented languages. These visions of other dimensions, depicted in *Paisaje celestial (banderas)* (1933; Celestial Landscape [Flags]) and *Valle hondo* (1944; Deep Valley), feature snakelike beings and cosmic travelers ascending pathways framed by translucent architecture or descending through dark canyons symbolic of the hardships involved in spiritual transcendence. He also drafted astrological charts and architectural designs, modified the piano keyboard, invented a chess game with astrologically defined pieces, and created several new plastic languages, in which forms and colors have both linguistic and aesthetic value. Only after his death did his unique contribution to modern art begin to be recognized.

REFERENCES:

Daniel E. Nelson, "Xul Solar: World-Maker," in *Latin American Artists of the Twentieth Century,* edited by Waldo Rasmussen, Fatima Bercht, and Elizabeth Ferrer (New York: Museum of Modern Art, 1993), pp. 46–51;

Osvaldo Svanascini, *Xul Solar* (Buenos Aires: Ediciones Culturales Argentinas, 1962).

— F.B.N.

YARAVÍ

The musical form known as the yaraví has strong ties to Bolivia, Peru, Ecuador, and Argentina. The verse expresses a mournful, plaintive cry. The refrain, as in the **triste,** features a more lively tempo than does the verse; it is often not sung, but played on **quena** flute. The yaraví and the triste are typically accompanied by **charango** and **bombo.**

Mundo (1925; World), by Xul Solar (Rachel Adler Gallery, New York)

REFERENCE:

Isabel Aretz, *El folklore musical argentino* (Buenos Aires: Ricordi Americana S.A.E.C., 1952).

— R.L.S.

ZAPATEO

A well-known characteristic of Spanish flamenco dancing, zapateo consists of rhythmic and noisy footwork involving drumming on the floor with the shoe (*zapato* in Spanish). Sometimes another derivative, *zapateado,* is used in the same sense (though, strictly speaking, it refers to a particular Spanish dance). When similar percussive effects are achieved specifically with the heel (*tacón*), the term *taconeo* is used.

— P.S.

ZARZUELA

The most typical genre of the Spanish light musical theater, the zarzuela features music intermingled with spoken dialogue. In that regard it resembles the Italian opera buffa, the French opéra comique, and the English ballad opera, all of which contrast with opera genres which are sung throughout.

The long and varied history of the zarzuela began in the early seventeenth century in Spain. Some experts claim the first libretto was *La selva sin amor* (1629; The Forest without Love), by Lope de Vega Carpio; others credit an earlier libretto to Pedro Calderón de la Barca. The earliest known composer of zarzuelas was Juan Hidalgo. By the latter part of the seventeenth century, zarzuelas were being produced primarily for aristocratic colonists in the New World. In the eighteenth century zarzuelas and other lighter forms of musical theater began to be produced in public theaters. In the nineteenth century more-refined tastes ensured the preeminent position of Italian opera in Latin America, and interest in the zarzuela diminished. Toward the end of the nineteenth century, however, the composition and performance of zarzuelas enjoyed a popular revival but with considerable influence from the Italian opera, with full arias and recitatives. While performances have continued to attract audiences, composition of the genre has not been of primary interest to contemporary composers, resulting in a type of musical theater characterized more by nostalgia than by relevance to the modern world.

Scene from an Argentinean zarzuela

REFERENCES:

Rodolfo Arizaga and Pompeyo Camps, *Historia de la música en la Argentina* (Buenos Aires: Ricordi Americana S.A.E.C., 1990);

Gerard Béhague, *Music in Latin America: An Introduction* (Englewood Cliffs, N.J.: Prentice-Hall, 1979).

—R.L.S.

RAÚL ZURITA

Contemporary Chilean poet Raúl Zurita (1951–) achieved a substantial reputation on the strength of two books, *Purgatorio* (1979; translated in part as "Purgatory") and *Anteparaíso* (1982; translated as *Anteparadise*). The highly experimental form and thematic urgency of these books places them at the cutting edge of Chilean poetry. They represent the emergence of a neo-avant-garde writing that breaks with the great poetic models of the past and responds in new ways to social crisis. The political context of Zurita's poetry was the military dictatorship of **Augusto Pinochet.** Zurita's experiment is singular in its ability to mobilize through the power of the poetic word the positive social forces repressed by dictatorship. Zurita accomplishes this charismatic act by immersing himself in the communal language of Christian sacrifice and redemption and by dissolving or disfiguring his social identity in a collective ritual of regeneration. When composing *Purgatorio* the poet deliberately scorched his cheek with a hot iron, as if transferring to his own flesh the suffering of the Chilean people. The transfiguring effect of suffering also has religious connotations that turn the wound into a stigma and the poet into a latter-day messiah. *Purgatorio* brings together a bewildering array of signifying materials, from a picture of the author to an encephalogram and a psychiatrist's letter certifying the subject's insanity. The underlying radical distrust of language promotes a search for plenitude outside words and simultaneously alienates the poetic speaker.

The transition between *Purgatorio* and *Anteparaíso* shows the evolution of Zurita's poetics from one of individual alienation (reflecting the early years of the military regime and the privatization of culture and social life) to one of communal hope and celebration (corresponding to the strengthening of the cultural bases of the opposition). In 1981 Zurita and others founded an art collective whose task was to take culture out of the closet and into the streets. The text of *Anteparaíso* is accompanied by photos of one of the more spectacular of such public events, the reproduction in the skies over New York City of some of the lines from the poem accomplished with bursts of white smoke emitted by a hired airplane. Another dramatic event staged by Zurita was a second attempt at self-mutilation. As **Diamela Eltit** attests in the book's epi-logue, the poet threw pure ammonia on his eyes in order to go blind. In the poem the archetype of the blind seer merges with the figure of the prophet leading his people into the Promised Land.

The linguistic texture of *Anteparaíso* owes much to the Bible, but Zurita's vision is specifically indebted to the social doctrine of the Catholic Church, the implementation of whose tenets (respect for human rights, protection for the poor, moral censure of capitalist accumulation) could only irk the military authorities (see **Vicaría de la Solidaridad**). Zurita embraces the proposition that poetry can operate beyond its immediate frame of reference and offer a divided society some hope for reconciliation.

REFERENCE:

Rodrigo Cánovas, *Lihn, Zurita, Ictus, Radrigán: Literatura chilena y experiencia autoritaria* (Santiago: FLACSO, 1986).
— R.G.M.

CONTRIBUTORS

N.D.B. ....Ninotchka D. Bennahum

J.M.H. ....Jan Michael Hanvik

S.M.H. ....Stephen M. Hart

R.G.M. ....Ricardo Gutiérrez Mouat

F.B.N. ....Florencia Bazzano Nelson

M.E.S. ....Maureen E. Shea

R.L.S. ....Robert L. Smith

P.S. ....Peter Standish

INDEX OF PHOTOGRAPHS

DICTIONARY OF

TWENTIETH CENTURY CULTURE

Hispanic Culture
of South America

I N D E X

A

F

G

N

Q

R

ISBN 0-8103-8483-3
90000

9 780810 384835